THEY WORE THE DARK BLUE

A Complete Record of Dundee F.C.

in League and Cup

By
NORRIE PRICE

Published by NORRIE PRICE

AUTHOR'S NOTE

Like many others, I am proud to be a Dundee supporter and long for the days when the Dark Blues are again a force in the land. This book is intended as the companion volume to my earlier publication, "Up Wi' The Bonnets - The Centenary History of Dundee F.C." and should provide supporters with an invaluable statistical record of days gone by. Again, much of the information came from my own records but, starting in 1986, long hours of painstaking research were spent at various locations in Dundee, Aberdeen and Glasgow in order that I might compile such a detailed record.

Glancing through the finished article, countless happy memories of trips to Dens and other grounds spring to mind. Sadly, I have lost touch with many of my former matchday companions over the past thirty-two years, people like Richard Stiven, Doug Scott, Stuart and Neil Ritchie, Scott Norrie, Donnie McGuigan, Doug Lowe and Farquhar McLean. Now, however, this book and all it's associated memories, means that out of sight no longer means out of mind.

ACKNOWLEDGMENTS

I would like to express my gratitude to all who assisted in any way to the making of this publication. I am particularly grateful to Alford-based David Young for his encouragement and technical advice, and to Scotscan (Aberdeen) - especially master scanner, Mike Cheyne, and Martins the Printers for the quality of their work.

Thanks are also due to Bobby Cox for agreeing to write the foreword. Bobby was Dundee skipper through the glory years of the early 1960's and was an excellent ambassador for the club. He spent 13 years at Dens and only the legendary Doug Cowie and giant goalkeeper Bill Marsh made more appearances for the Dark Blues. As budding Grove Primary School defenders, myself and classmate Stuart Ritchie took upon ourselves the mantle of Alex. Hamilton and Bobby Cox, Dundee's famous full-back pairing of that era. "Stu" was the team's right-back, so he was "Hammy", while I wore the number three jersey and did the sliding tackles as "Coxer"!

I would again like to convey my thanks to D.C. Thomson (Dundee) for allowing me to reproduce so many of their splendid photographs and I would particularly like to thank Doug Spence and his Photofile Library staff - Ann, Joyce, Gwen, Linda, Gaynor and the others for their friendliness, assistance and infinite patience in the face of my endless requests.

Other individuals and bodies who provided information, advice, photos or other memorabilia - often at short notice - were former players Doug Cowie, George Hill and Jocky Scott, Bill Longair and David Thomson (descendants of the great players of those names), Ron Hill, Alex. Benvie, Stephen Borland - from his Broughty Ferry treasure trove, John Brown and Tom Duthie (Evening Telegraph), Alan Wilson (Dundee Courier), Doug Cowie Junr., Alastair Gibb, Ken Gibb, Jim Hendry, Jim Hill, Bob Hynd, Steve Martin, Garry McDonald, Peter Rundo, Jack Murray, Fraser Elder, Doug Lowe (The Herald), Cyril Rice (Daily Record), David Thomson, David Walker and Richard Pidgeon (The Sunday Post and Weekly News, Glasgow), the Scottish League (Anton Fagan), the Scottish Football Association, Dundee's Wellgate Library (Local History Section), Aberdeen's Central and Woodside Libraries and the Mitchell Library (Glasgow).

I would also belatedly like to record my appreciation of the assistance so willingly given by Harry Jenkins, Stuart Matheson, Ray Whyte and Pete, Duncan and Vivienne Shepherd in offloading innumerable bundles of "Up Wi The Bonnets". Grant Anderson, Gordon Dow, Jim Gordon, Jim and Linda Hendry and Steve Martin were a great help with the distribution, while Bill Leckie of the much lamented "Scottish Football Today" and Alan Saunders of Grampian Television gave the book a right good airing. Finally, I must thank my girlfriend Lorraine for her constant encouragement during this marathon project.

First published in October 1995

© Norrie Price 1995.   ISBN 0 9521426 2 7

Scanning by Scotscan, Aberdeen 01224-585808
Printed by Martins The Printers, Seaview Works, Spital, Berwick Upon Tweed (01289-306006)
Cover design, layout, publication and distribution by N. Price. 01224-639967/818697.

CONTENTS

Season by Season Facts and Figures   Page   6   -   213

Friendlies, Benefit Games and other Matches   Page 214   -   221

Dewar Shield, Summer Cup and New York
             Tournament League Tables   Page 222   -   223

The Story of Season 1993-94   Page 224   -   228

The Story of Season 1994-95   Page 229   -   236

Happy days - manager Bob Shankly and the Dundee team take the applause as they wave from the balcony of the City Chambers after winning the League Championship in 1962.

DC Thomson

Miserable conditions - Dundee's Gordon Wallace and Ally Hunter (Celtic) make a splash going for the ball at a waterlogged Hampden Park in the 1973 League Cup Final. Team-mate John Duncan and Celtic's Danny McGrain look on but Wallace had the final say when he later scored the only goal of the game.

DC Thomson

Foreword

By Bobby Cox

It gives me great pleasure to write the foreword to Norrie's book "They Wore The Dark Blue". I spent 13 enjoyable years as a player with Dundee Football Club, my home town team and my only senior club.

I grew up a Dundee supporter and was delighted when manager Willie Thornton asked me to sign for the Dark Blues in early 1956. That was not long after the break-up of George Anderson's great team and it was my privilege to come under the wing of top professionals like Doug Cowie, Albert Henderson and Bill Brown, whose experience was of great benefit to myself.

My early years at Dens coincided with an emphasis on youth development and, although there were some early problems, the improvement was evident when Dundee twice finished fourth in seasons 1958-59 and 1959-60. By then, the legendary Bob Shankly was at the helm and things really began to happen. A few changes were made and although there was disappointment the following season, Dundee went on to win the First Division Championship for the first time in their history in 1961-62.

As club captain, there was no prouder person that sunny day at Muirton and, although there was no further tangible success, the following two seasons proved the quality of that Dundee team. On our first continental foray, we reached the European Cup semi-final and in 1964 we went down to Rangers in a thrilling Scottish Cup final. Bobby Ancell then took over and I was again fortunate to be part of the squad which reached the League Cup final and the Fairs Cup semi-final in season 1967-68. However, injuries had taken their toll and in April 1969, I hung up my boots at the age of 34. I did some scouting while continuing to follow the club's fortunes and for the past seven years have also assisted in the Executive Club at Dens on match days.

During my time with Dundee, I was lucky enough to make numerous trips abroad. There were three visits to the United States and Canada, tours of Iceland and Eire, competitive matches in France, West Germany, Portugal, Belgium, Italy, Spain and Holland as well as numerous games South of the Border. Thus, I have many fond memories of Dundee F.C. down the years and I am delighted that Norrie has produced such a detailed record. I am sure his book will provide all true Dark Blues - and you can certainly count me in that category - with many hours of interesting reading and I wish every success to the author, Dundee Football Club and all their loyal supporters in the coming months.

Yours in Sport,

Season 1893-94

Date			Opponents		Score	Crowd	Scorers
Aug	12th	L	Rangers	h	3-3	5,000	Gilligan, Keillor, Dundas
	19th	L	Celtic	h	1-4	8,000	Longair
	26th	L	Renton	a	3-2		Dundas; Reid 2.
Sep	9th	L	Leith	a	5-3	4,000	Dundas 2; Keillor; Reid; Gilligan
	16th	L	Dumbarton	a	1-1		Dundas
	23rd	L	St Mirren	h	0-3	3,000	-
	23rd	SC1	Strathmore*	a	2-4		McInroy; Wilson
	30th	L	St Bernard's	h	1-3	2,000	Gilligan
Oct	7th	F	Dundee Harp	h	2-1	4,000	Keillor; Gilligan
	14th	L	Third Lanark	a	3-4	3,000	Gilligan; Ritchie 2
	21st	L	Hearts	h	2-5	5,000	George; Petrie
	28th	F	Johnstone Wands.	a	2-1	2,000	Dundas; Gilligan
Nov	4th	L	Celtic	a	1-3		McInroy
	11th	L	Leith	h	4-3	5,000	McInroy; Craig, Dundas 2
	25th	F	Strathmore	h	7-1	2,500	Dundas 4; Gilligan; Reid; Keillor
Dec	9th	L	Dumbarton	h	4-0	5,000	Thomson; Dundas 2; Keillor
	16th	L	Hearts	a	0-3		-
	23rd	FCS^	Arbroath	h	7-3	3,500	Keillor 2; Dundas 2; Gilligan 2; Thomson
Jan	1st	F	Newton Heath	h**	2-1	6,000	Dundas; Thomson
	20th	FCF	Dundee Harp	n^^	4-0	10,000	Dundas 2; Keillor; Thomson
	27th	L	St Bernards	a	5-3		Ritchie 2; Dundas; Keillor 2
Feb	10th	L	Renton	h	8-1	4,000	Dundas; Keillor 3; McInroy; Matthew; Gilligan; Thomson
	17th	L	St Mirren	a	3-10		McInroy; Matthew; Brown
	24th	L	Third Lanark	h	1-1	3,000	Dundas
Mar	10th	L	Rangers	a	2-7	3,000	Gilligan; Keillor
	31st	F	Dundonians	h	6-0	3,000	Gilligan; C. Craig; D. Craig 2; Dundas; Thomson
Apr	7th	F	Newcastle United	h	8-2	5,000	Thomson; Dundas 3; McInroy; Longair 2; Gilligan
	9th	F	Sunderland	h	1-2	8,000	Dundas
	14th	F	Aberdeen X1	a	3-1	2,000	Dundas 2; McInroy
	21st	F	Stoke City	h	2-2	7,000	Dundas; C.Craig
	28th	F	Hibernian	a	1-6	3,000	Gilligan

George Campbell - an ex-Aston Villa full-back

* Scottish Cup tie v Strathmore played on same afternoon as League game v St Mirren. ** Now Manchester United.
^ Beat Kirriemuir in Forfarshire Cup 2nd round - details unknown. ^^ Played at Carolina Port, which became Dundee's home ground on March 17th. Until then, Dundee had played at West Craigie Park, with Strathmore at Carolina Port.

Appearances

	League		Scottish Cup		Total	
Sandy Keillor	18	(9)	0		18	(9)
Jimmy Dundas	17	(12)	0		17	(12)
Bill Ferrier	17		0		17	
Sandy Gilligan	17	(6)	0		17	(6)
Bill Longair	17	(1)	0		17	(1)
Bill Thomson	17	(2)	0		17	(2)
James Brown	13	(1)	0		13	(1)
Dave Craig	13	(1)	0		13	(1)
Bob Petrie	13	(1)	0		13	(1)
Davie McInroy	9	(4)	1	(1)	10	(5)
Bill McKie	10		0		10	
Billy Matthew	8	(2)	1		9	(2)
Francis Barrett	6		0		6	
George Reid	6	(3)	0		6	(3)
George Campbell	5		0		5	
Davie Dow	2		1		3	
Alan McNaughton	2		1		3	
George Ramsay	2		1		3	
John Ritchie	2	(4)	1		3	(4)
Jimmy Craik	1		1		2	
Bill Graham	1		1		2	
Frank George	1	(1)	0		1	(1)
Willie Gibson	0		1		1	
Joe Fleming	0		1		1	
Willie Martin	0		1		1	
Bert Wilson	1		0	(1)	1	

Scottish League Division One

		Home			Away			Goals		
	P	W	D	L	W	D	L	F A		PTS
Celtic	18	7	1	1	7	0	2	53-32		29
Hearts	18	4	2	3	7	2	0	46-32		26
St Bernards	18	5	1	3	6	0	3	53-39		23
Rangers	18	6	0	3	2	4	3	44-30		20
Dumbarton	18	4	3	2	3	2	4	32-35		19
St Mirren	18	4	1	4	3	2	4	49-47		17
Third Lanark	18	4	1	4	3	2	4	38-44		17
Dundee	**18**	**3**	**2**	**4**	**3**	**1**	**5**	**47-59**		**15**
Leith Athletic	18	3	2	4	1	0	8	36-46		10
Renton	18	1	1	7	0	1	8	23-57		4

No automatic promotion or relegation. Bottom 3 teams up for re-election along with new applicants. Clyde and Dundee obtained 14 votes each and Leith got 8 to pip Cowlairs 4, Renton 3 and Hibs 1, for the Division One places.

The Record		
League	-	Eighth Place, Division One
Scottish Cup	-	First round
Forfarshire Cup	-	Winners
Top Scorer	-	Jimmy Dundas (12 goals)
Av. Home Gate	-	4,300
Players used	-	19
Sent off	-	None

Dundee F.C. Line-Ups 1893-94

		1	2	3	4	5	6	7	8	9	10	11
Aug	12th	McKie	Ferrier	Brown	Craig	Longair	Petrie	Thomson	Craik	Dundas	Gilligan	Keillor
	19th	McKie	Ferrier	Brown	Craig	Longair	Petrie	Thomson	Graham	Dundas	Gilligan	Keillor
	26th	McKie	Ferrier	Brown	Craig	Longair	Petrie	Thomson	Reid	Dundas	Gilligan	Keillor
Sep	9th	McKie	Ferrier	Brown	Craig	Longair	McNaughton	Thomson	Reid	Dundas	Gilligan	Keillor
	16th	McKie	Ferrier	Brown	Craig	Longair	Petrie	Thomson	Reid	Dundas	Gilligan	Keillor
	23rd	McKie	Ferrier	Brown	Craig	Longair	Petrie	Thomson	Reid	Dundas	Gilligan	Keillor
	23rd	Gibson	Dow	Ramsay	Fleming	Matthew	McNaughton	Wilson	Graham	McInroy	Craik	Martin
	30th	McKie	Ferrier	Brown	Craig	Longair	Petrie	Thomson	Reid	Dundas	Gilligan	Keillor
Oct	14th	McKie	Dow	Brown	Matthew	Longair	Petrie	Thomson	Dundas	Ritchie	Gilligan	Keillor
	21st	Ramsay	Dow	Ferrier	Matthew	Longair	Petrie	Reid	George	Ritchie	Gilligan	Keillor
Nov	4th	McKie	Brown	Campbell	Craig	Ferrier	Matthew	Thomson	McInroy	Dundas	Gilligan	Keillor
	11th	McKie	Ferrier	Campbell	Craig	Longair	Petrie	Thomson	McInroy	Dundas	Gilligan	Keillor
Dec	9th	Ramsay	Ferrier	Campbell	Craig	Longair	Petrie	Thomson	McInroy	Dundas	Gilligan	Keillor
	16th	Barrett	Ferrier	Campbell	Craig	Longair	Petrie	Thomson	McInroy	Dundas	Gilligan	Keillor
Jan	27th	Barrett	Ferrier	Brown	McNaughton	Longair	Matthew	Thomson	McInroy	Dundas	Ritchie	Keillor
Feb	10th	Barrett	Ferrier	Brown	Matthew	Longair	Petrie	Thomson	McInroy	Dundas	Gilligan	Keillor
	17th	Barrett	Ferrier	Brown	Matthew	Longair	Petrie	Thomson	McInroy	Dundas	Gilligan	Keillor
	24th	Barrett	Ferrier	Brown	Craig	Longair	Matthew	Thomson	McInroy	Dundas	Gilligan	Keillor
Mar	10th	Barrett	Ferrier	Campbell	Craig	Longair	Matthew	Thomson	McInroy	Dundas	Gilligan	Keillor

Dundee F.C. Season 1893-94. This was the line-up for the opening League game against Rangers at West Craigie Park. (BACK, left to right) Adam Marshall (trainer), Mr Sandy Spalding, Willie Thomson, Mr David McEwan, Mr Tom Shaw, James Brown, Bill Ferrier, Mr James McIntosh, Bill McKie, Mr J Black (referee), Dave Craig, Sandy Keillor, Mr James Petrie (President). MIDDLE - Bill Longair, Bob Petrie. FRONT - John Craik, Jimmy Dundas and Sandy Gilligan.

Alastair Gibb

They Wore The Dark Blue

Season 1894-95

Date			Opponents		Score	Crowd	Scorers
Aug	4th	F	Orion	a	4-2	4,000	Gilligan 4
	11th	L	Celtic	h	1-1	9,000	Dickson
	18th	L	Clyde	h	4-1	5,000	Gilligan 2; Sawyers; Dundas
Sep	1st	L	Rangers	a	0-1	3,500	-
	8th	L	Dumbarton	h	3-0	5,000	Sawyers; Gilligan; Fleming
	15th	L	St Mirren	a	1-5		Sawyers
	29th	L	St Bernards	h	2-2	5,000	Thomson 2
Oct	13th	L	Dumbarton	a	4-2	700	Thomson; Sawyers; Fleming 2
	20th	L	Leith Athletic	a	2-3	1,500	Sawyers; McInroy
Nov	3rd	L	Third Lanark	h	1-2	2,000	Richardson
	24th	SC1	Orion	a	5-1	3,000	Fleming; Thomson; Maxwell 3
Dec	1st	L	Leith Athletic	h	4-1	3,000	Richardson; Keillor 2; Buttar
	8th	L	St Bernards	a	0-2	1,000	-
	15th	SC2	St Mirren	h	2-0	3,000	Maxwell; Gilligan
	27th	L	Hearts	h	0-2	4,000	-
	31st	F	Arbroath	a	2-2		Richardson; McInroy
Jan	1st	F	Wanderers	h	7-1	1,000	McInroy 2; Richardson 2; Dundas
	2nd	F	Sheffield United	h	0-2	4,000	-
	5th	F	Lochee United	h	2-0	1,500	Sawyers; Maxwell
	19th	SC3	Celtic	h	1-0	12,000	Sawyers
	26th	L	Rangers	h	2-1	6,000	Sawyers; Gilligan
Feb	16th	SCS	Renton	h	1-1	6,000	Own goal
	23rd	SCS	Renton	a*	3-3	20,000	Maxwell; Gilligan; McInroy
Mar	2nd	FCS	Montrose	h	3-1	2,000	McInroy 2; Fleming
	9th	SCS	Renton	n^	0-3	29,000	-
	16th	L	St Mirren	h	0-1	3,000	-
	23rd	FCF	Lochee United	n^^	1-0		Fleming
	30th	L	Hearts	a	0-4	4,000	-
Apr	8th	F	Sunderland	h	0-2	3,000	-
	20th	F	Blackburn	h	1-3	7,000	Richardson
	27th	L	Third Lanark	a	3-1	2,000	Gilligan; Richardson; Lonie
May	4th	L	Celtic	a	1-2	6,000	Lonie
	18th	L	Clyde	a	0-2		-

* At Hampden   ^ At Parkhead   ^^ At Gayfield

Frank Barrett - Scots international keeper.

Appearances

	League		Scottish Cup		Total	
Francis Barrett	18		6		24	
Johnny Darroch	18		6		24	
Sandy Keillor	18	(2)	6		24	(2)
Bill Longair	17		6		23	
Jimmy Dundas	16	(1)	6		22	(1)
Bill Thomson	16	(3)	5	(1)	21	(4)
Bill Sawyers	14	(6)	5	(1)	19	(7)
Joe Fleming	14	(3)	3	(1)	17	(4)
Sandy Gilligan	12	(5)	5	(2)	17	(7)
George Campbell	12		3		15	
Jack Richardson	11	(3)	0		11	(3)
Davie McInroy	5	(1)	6	(1)	11	(2)
Bill Ferrier	5		3		8	
Jim Buttar	6	(1)	0		6	(1)
Jim Dickson	5	(1)	0		5	(1)
Willie Maxwell	0		5	(5)	5	(5)
Sandy Drummond	3		0		3	
Willie Lonie	3	(2)	0		3	(2)
Alan Logan	2		0		2	
George Philip	2		0		2	
Harry Erentz	1		0		1	
Bert Shepherd	1		0		1	

Scottish League Division One

		Home			Away			Goals		
	P	W	D	L	W	D	L	F A		PTS
Hearts	18	7	1	1	8	0	1	50-18		31
Celtic	18	6	2	1	5	2	2	50-29		26
Rangers	18	6	1	2	4	1	4	41-26		22
Third Lanark	18	6	0	3	4	1	4	51-39		21
St Mirren	18	6	0	3	3	1	5	34-34		19
St Bernards	18	4	0	5	4	1	4	37-40		17
Clyde	18	5	0	4	3	0	6	38-47		16
Dundee	**18**	**4**	**2**	**3**	**2**	**7**	**2**	**28-33**		**14**
Leith Athletic	18	3	1	5	0	0	9	32-64		7
Dumbarton	18	3	0	6	0	1	8	27-58		7

The bottom three clubs applied for re-election with Hibs and Motherwell of Division Two applying for election. After voting, Dundee and Dumbarton were re-elected with Hibs replacing Leith Athletic.

The Record	
League	- Eighth Place, Division One
Scottish Cup	- Semi-final
Forfarshire Cup	- Winners
Top Scorer	- Sandy Gilligan, Bill Sawyers (both 7 goals)
Av. Home Gate	- 4,500
Players used	- 22
Sent off	- None

Dundee F.C. Line-Ups 1894-95

		1	2	3	4	5	6	7	8	9	10	11
Aug	11th	Barrett	Darroch	Campbell	Buttar	Longair	Keillor	Thomson	Fleming	Sawyers	Gilligan	Dickson
	18th	Barrett	Darroch	Campbell	Dundas	Longair	Keillor	Thomson	Fleming	Sawyers	Gilligan	Dickson
Sep	1st	Barrett	Darroch	Campbell	Dundas	Longair	Keillor	Thomson	Fleming	Sawyers	Gilligan	Dickson
	8th	Barrett	Darroch	Campbell	Dundas	Longair	Keillor	Thomson	Fleming	Sawyers	Gilligan	Dickson
	15th	Barrett	Darroch	Campbell	Dundas	Longair	Keillor	Thomson	Fleming	Sawyers	Gilligan	Dickson
	29th	Barrett	Darroch	Campbell	Dundas	Longair	Keillor	Thomson	McInroy	Sawyers	Buttar	Fleming
Oct	13th	Barrett	Darroch	Campbell	Dundas	Longair	Keillor	Thomson	Richardson	Sawyers	McInroy	Fleming
	20th	Barrett	Darroch	Campbell	Dundas	Longair	Keillor	Thomson	Richardson	Sawyers	McInroy	Fleming
Nov	3rd	Barrett	Darroch	Ferrier	Dundas	Philip	Keillor	Thomson	Richardson	Sawyers	Gilligan	Fleming
	24th	Barrett	Darroch	Campbell	Dundas	Longair	Ferrier	Thomson	McInroy	Maxwell	Fleming	Keillor
Dec	1st	Barrett	Darroch	Campbell	Dundas	Longair	Ferrier	Thomson	Richardson	Buttar	Fleming	Keillor
	8th	Barrett	Darroch	Campbell	Dundas	Longair	Ferrier	Thomson	Richardson	Buttar	Fleming	Keillor
	15th	Barrett	Darroch	Ferrier	Dundas	Longair	Keillor	Thomson	McInroy	Maxwell	Sawyers	Gilligan
	27th	Barrett	Darroch	Ferrier	Dundas	Longair	Keillor	Thomson	Richardson	Buttar	Sawyers	Gilligan
Jan	19th	Barrett	Darroch	Campbell	Dundas	Longair	Keillor	Thomson	McInroy	Maxwell	Sawyers	Gilligan
	26th	Barrett	Darroch	Ferrier	Dundas	Longair	Keillor	Thomson	Richardson	Fleming	Sawyers	Gilligan
Feb	16th	Barrett	Darroch	Ferrier	Dundas	Longair	Keillor	Thomson	McInroy	Fleming	Sawyers	Gilligan
	23rd	Barrett	Darroch	Erentz	Dundas	Longair	Keillor	Thomson	McInroy	Maxwell	Sawyers	Gilligan
Mar	9th	Barrett	Darroch	Campbell	Dundas	Longair	Keillor	McInroy	Fleming	Maxwell	Sawyers	Gilligan
	16th	Barrett	Darroch	Campbell	Philip	Longair	Keillor	McInroy	Fleming	Dundas	Gilligan	Shepherd
	30th	Barrett	Darroch	Campbell	Dundas	Longair	Keillor	McInroy	Richardson	Logan	Sawyers	Fleming
Apr	27th	Barrett	Drummond	Darroch	Dundas	Longair	Keillor	Thomson	Richardson	Lonie	Sawyers	Gilligan
May	4th	Barrett	Drummond	Darroch	Dundas	Longair	Keillor	Thomson	Richardson	Lonie	Sawyers	Gilligan
	18th	Barrett	Drummond	Darroch	Dundas	Longair	Keillor	Thomson	Richardson	Logan	Lonie	Gilligan

An artist's impression of some of the early Dundee greats. (TOP, left to right), Johnny Darroch, Sandy Keillor, Adam Marshall (trainer), Bill Longair and Jimmy Dundas. David Thomson

Season 1895-96

Date			Opponents		Score	Crowd	Scorers
Aug	10th	L	Celtic	h	1-2	10,000	McDonald
	17th	L	St Bernards	a	2-4	2,500	Dundas; Lonie
	24th	L	Dumbarton	h	4-1	2,000	Gilligan 2; Dundas 2 (1 pen)
	31st	L	Hibernian	h	2-2	6,000	Keillor; own goal
Sep	7th	L	Clyde	a	1-0	-	McDonald
	14th	L	Third Lanark	a	4-3	-	Hendry; Lonie 3
	21st	L	St Mirren	h	1-1	6,000	Richardson
	28th	L	St Mirren	a	1-3	-	Sawyers
Oct	5th	L	St Bernards	h	4-1	6,000	Vail; Dundas (pen); McDonald; Sawyers
	12th	L	Hearts	h	5-0	7,500	McDonald 2; Thomson; Vail; Sawyers
	26th	L	Celtic	a	0-11	10,000	-
Nov	2nd	L	Hearts	a	0-2	7,000	-
	9th	FC1	Lochee United	a	1-1	3,000	Gilligan
	23rd	L	Third Lanark	h	2-0	2,000	Longair; McDonald
	23rd	FC1R	Lochee United	h*	2-1	2,000	Richardson; Gilligan
	30th	L	Rangers	h	1-3	3,000	Vail
Dec	7th	L	Dumbarton	a	2-1	500	Vail; Thomson
	14th	L	Clyde	h	1-2	2,000	Gilligan
	21st	FCS	Wanderers	h	5-0		McDonald 4; Gilligan
Jan	4th	F	Corinthians	h	0-1	4,000	-
	11th	SC1	Morton	a	3-2	3,000	Keillor 2; Thomson
	18th	L	Hibernian	a	1-3	4,000	Own goal
	25th	SC2	Third Lanark	a	1-4	5,000	Gilligan
Feb	1st	FCF	Arbroath	n*	0-2		-
	28th	L	Rangers	a	1-3	3,000	Keillor
Apr	4th	F	Corinthians	a	1-3	60,000	Keillor
	11th	F	Sheffield United	a	0-4	1,000	-
	25th	F	Burnley	h	2-1	5,000	Smith; Williamson

* At East Dock Street

Bill Longair - captain and influential Dundee defender.

Appearances

	League		Scottish Cup		Total	
Johnny Darroch	18		2		20	
Jimmy Dundas	18	(4)	2		20	(4)
Bill Thomson	18	(2)	2	(1)	20	(3)
Francis Barrett	17		2		19	
Charlie Burgess	17		1		18	
Bill Hendry**	16	(1)	2		18	(1)
Sandy Keillor	16	(2)	2	(2)	18	(4)
Bill Longair	16	(1)	2		18	(1)
Sandy Gilligan	12	(3)	2	(1)	14	(4)
Dave McDonald	12	(6)	2		14	(6)
Bill Sawyers	9	(3)	0		9	(3)
Harry Vail	9	(4)	0		9	(4)
Willie Lonie	7	(4)	0		7	(4)
Jack Richardson	3	(1)	2		5	(1)
Charlie Craig	1		1		2	
Tom Ford	2		0		2	
Alex Black	1		0		1	
Bill Coventry	1		0		1	
Frank Ferrier	1		0		1	
John Low	1		0		1	
George Philip	1		0		1	
George Reid	1		0		1	
Bill Toman	1		0		1	

** Joined New Brighton at the end of that season. Died in 1901.

Scottish League Division One

		Home			Away			Goals		
	P	W	D	L	W	D	L	F	A	PTS
Celtic	18	8	0	1	7	0	2	64-25		30
Rangers	18	5	2	2	6	2	1	57-39		26
Hibernian	18	6	1	2	5	1	3	58-39		24
Hearts	18	7	0	2	4	0	5	68-36		22
Dundee	**18**	**4**	**2**	**3**	**3**	**0**	**6**	**33-42**		**16**
Third Lanark	18	3	1	5	4	0	5	47-51		15
St Bernards	18	5	0	4	2	1	6	36-53		15
St Mirren	18	3	1	5	2	2	5	31-51		13
Clyde	18	2	1	6	2	2	5	39-59		11
Dumbarton	18	3	0	6	1	0	8	36-74		8

Bottom three clubs applied for re-election with Abercorn, Leith Athletic and Renton of Division Two applying for election. Clyde and St Mirren were re-elected with Abercorn replacing Dumbarton.

The Record		
League	-	Fifth Place, Division One
Scottish Cup	-	Second round
Forfarshire Cup	-	Runners-up
Top Scorer	-	Dave McDonald (6 goals)
Av. Home Gate	-	5,000
Players used	-	23
Sent off	-	None

Dundee F.C. Line-Ups 1895-96

		1	2	3	4	5	6	7	8	9	10	11
Aug	10th	Barrett	Darroch	Burgess	Dundas	Hendry	Richardson	Thomson	McDonald	Lonie	Ford	Gilligan
	17th	Barrett	Darroch	Burgess	Dundas	Hendry	Longair	Thomson	Gilligan	Lonie	Ford	McDonald
	24th	Barrett	Darroch	Burgess	Dundas	Longair	Philip	Thomson	Gilligan	Hendry	McDonald	Keillor
	31st	Barrett	Darroch	Burgess	Dundas	Longair	Low	Thomson	Gilligan	Lonie	Keillor	McDonald
Sep	7th	Barrett	Darroch	Burgess	Dundas	Longair	Hendry	Thomson	Gilligan	Lonie	McDonald	Keillor
	14th	Barrett	Darroch	Burgess	Dundas	Longair	Hendry	Thomson	Gilligan	Lonie	Richardson	Keillor
	21st	Barrett	Darroch	Burgess	Dundas	Longair	Hendry	Thomson	Gilligan	Lonie	Richardson	Keillor
	28th	Barrett	Darroch	Burgess	Dundas	Longair	Hendry	Thomson	Gilligan	Lonie	Sawyers	Keillor
Oct	5th	Barrett	Darroch	Burgess	Dundas	Longair	Hendry	Thomson	Sawyers	Vail	McDonald	Keillor
	12th	Barrett	Darroch	Burgess	Dundas	Longair	Hendry	Thomson	Sawyers	Vail	McDonald	Keillor
	26th	Barrett	Darroch	Burgess	Dundas	Longair	Ferrier	Thomson	Sawyers	Vail	McDonald	Keillor
Nov	2nd	Barrett	Darroch	Burgess	Dundas	Hendry	Reid	Thomson	Sawyers	Vail	Keillor	McDonald
	23rd	Barrett	Darroch	Burgess	Dundas	Longair	Hendry	Thomson	Sawyers	Vail	McDonald	Keillor
	30th	Barrett	Darroch	Burgess	Dundas	Longair	Hendry	Thomson	Sawyers	Vail	McDonald	Keillor
Dec	7th	Barrett	Darroch	Burgess	Dundas	Longair	Hendry	Thomson	Gilligan	Vail	Sawyers	Keillor
	14th	Barrett	Darroch	Burgess	Dundas	Longair	Hendry	Thomson	Gilligan	Vail	Sawyers	Keillor
Jan	11th	Barrett	Darroch	Burgess	Dundas	Longair	Hendry	Thomson	Gilligan	McDonald	Richardson	Keillor
	18th	Barrett	Darroch	Craig C	Dundas	Longair	Hendry	Thomson	Gilligan	Vail	McDonald	Keillor
	25th	Barrett	Darroch	Craig C	Dundas	Longair	Hendry	Thomson	Gilligan	Richardson	McDonald	Keillor
Feb	28th	Coventry	Darroch	Burgess	Dundas	Longair	Hendry	Thomson	Gilligan	Toman	Black	Keillor

Dundee F.C. Season 1895-96. (BACK ROW, left to right) Mr J. McIntosh, Mr T. Shaw, Mr W.T. Kennedy, Johnny Darroch, Fred Barrett, Charlie Burgess, Mr W. Saunders, Mr J. Black (referee). FRONT - Mr J. McMahon, Willie Thomson, Sandy Gilligan, Bill Hendry, Bill Longair, George Phillip, Alex. Black, Sandy Keillor and Adam Marshall (trainer).

DC Thomson

Season 1896-97

Date			Opponents		Score	Crowd	Scorers
Aug	15th	L	Hearts	h	0-5	8,000	-
	22nd	L	Hibernian	h	3-0	6,000	Clark 3
	29th	L	Rangers	a	1-3	13,000	Smith
Sep	5th	L	St Mirren	a	1-4	4,000	Willocks
	12th	L	Third Lanark	h	2-0	3,500	Clark; Willocks
	19th	L	Hearts	a	2-2	6,000	McArthur; Smith
	26th	L	St Bernards	h	4-1	5,000	Devlin 2; Kelso (pen); McArthur
Oct	3rd	L	Celtic	h*	2-2	17,000	Robertson; Willocks
	10th	L	Third Lanark	a	1-3	1,500	Smith
	12th	F	Sunderland	h	1-1	7,000	Smith
	17th	L	Abercorn	h	3-0	3,500	Willocks; Smith; McArthur
	24th	L	Clyde	a	2-0	2,500	Willocks; Clark
	31st	L	Hibernian	a	1-3	-	Clark
Nov	7th	L	Clyde	h	1-0	4,000	Willocks
	14th	L	St Bernards	a	1-2	-	McArthur
	14th	FC1	Lochee United	h	3-1	1,500	Willocks 2; Allan
	28th	L	Rangers	h	3-2	8,000	Devlin 2; Clark
Dec	12th	L	St Mirren	h	3-2	5,000	Clark; own goal; Smith
	12th	FCS	Forfar Athletic	a	0-6	2,000	-
Jan	9th	SC1	Inverness Caley	h	7-1	-	Willocks 3; Smith; Devlin 2; Dundas
	16th	L	Abercorn	a	7-1	2,000	Devlin 2; Willocks 2; Smith 2; Allan
	30th	SC2	Kings Park	h	5-0	2,000	Allan 3; Devlin; Willocks
Feb	13th	SC3	Rangers	h**	0-4	15,000	-
	20th	L	Celtic	a	1-0	8,000	Clark
Apr	19th	F	Preston N'th End	a	0-0	3,000	-
	21st	F	Nottingham Forest	a^	1-2		Smith

* £303-3-0d excluding stand; ** £3030-0-0d total;
^ Played at Crystal Palace, the winners collecting a prize of £11

Bob Kelso - top class defender from Everton.

Appearances

	League		S/Cup		Total	
Joe Devlin	18	(6)	3	(3)	21	(9)
Jack Hillman	18		3		21	
Stuart Hall	17		3		20	
Sandy Keillor	17		3		20	
Jim Smith	17	(7)	3	(1)	20	(8)
Dave Willocks	17	(9)	3	(3)	20	(12)
Joe Clark	16	(8)	3	(1)	19	(9)
Bob Kelso	16	(1)	3		19	(1)
Charlie Burgess	14		3		17	
Bill McArthur	11	(4)	1		12	(4)
Jimmy Dundas	9		2	(1)	11	(1)
Dicky Allan	8	(1)	3	(3)	11	(4)
Jim Hamilton	8		0		8	
Tom Stormont	6		0		6	
Alex. Robertson	4	(1)	0		4	(1)
Alex. Epsie	2		0		2	

Scottish League Division One

	P	Home			Away			Goals		PTS
		W	D	L	W	D	L	F	A	
Hearts	18	7	2	0	6	0	3	47-22		28
Hibernian	18	9	0	0	3	2	4	50-20		26
Rangers	18	9	0	0	2	3	4	64-30		25
Celtic	18	6	2	1	4	2	3	42-18		24
Dundee	**18**	**7**	**1**	**1**	**3**	**1**	**5**	**38-30**		**22**
St Mirren	18	7	1	1	2	0	7	38-29		19
St Bernards	18	4	0	5	3	0	6	32-40		14
Third Lanark	18	3	1	5	2	0	7	29-46		11
Clyde	18	3	0	6	1	0	8	27-65		8
Abercorn	18	1	1	7	0	0	9	21-88		3

Bottom three clubs applied for re-election with Partick Thistle, Leith Athletic and Kilmarnock of Division Two applying for election. Thirds and Clyde were re-elected with Partick replacing Abercorn.

The Record		
Scottish League	-	**Fifth place, Division One**
Scottish Cup	-	**Third round**
Forfarshire Cup	-	**Semi-final**
Top Scorer	-	**Dave Willocks (12)**
Av. Home Gate	-	**6,700**
Players used	-	**16**
Sent off	-	**One**

Dundee F.C. Line-Ups 1896-97

		1	2	3	4	5	6	7	8	9	10	11
Aug	15th	Hillman	Kelso	Hamilton	Stormont	Hall	Keillor	Allan	Willocks	Devlin	Robertson	Smith
	22nd	Hillman	Kelso	Burgess	Stormont	Hall	Keillor	Allan	Clark	Devlin	Willocks	Smith
	29th	Hillman	Hamilton	Burgess	Stormont	Hall	Keillor	Allan	Clark	Devlin	Willocks	Smith
Sep	5th	Hillman	Hamilton	Burgess	Stormont	Hall	Keillor	Allan	McArthur	Devlin	Willocks	Smith
	12th	Hillman	Kelso	Burgess	Hall	Epsie	Keillor	Clark	Devlin	McArthur	Willocks	Smith
	19th	Hillman	Kelso	Burgess	Hall	Epsie	Keillor	Clark	Devlin	McArthur	Willocks	Smith
	26th	Hillman	Kelso	Burgess	Hall	Stormont	Keillor	Clark	Devlin	McArthur	Willocks	Smith
Oct	3rd	Hillman	Kelso	Burgess	Hall	Dundas	Keillor	Clark	Devlin	Robertson	Willocks	Smith
	10th	Hillman	Kelso	Burgess	Hall	Dundas	Stormont	Clark	Devlin	Robertson	Willocks	Smith
	17th	Hillman	Kelso	Burgess*	Hall	Dundas	Keillor	Clark	Devlin	McArthur	Willocks	Smith
	24th	Hillman	Kelso	Hamilton	Stormont	Dundas	Keillor	Clark	Devlin	McArthur	Willocks	Smith
	31st	Hillman	Kelso	Hamilton	Hall	Dundas	Stormont	Clark	Devlin	McArthur	Willocks	Keillor
Nov	7th	Hillman	Kelso	Burgess	Hall	Dundas	Keillor	Clark	Devlin	McArthur	Willocks	Smith
	14th	Hillman	Kelso	Burgess	Hall	Dundas	Keillor	Clark	Devlin	Robertson	McArthur	Smith
	28th	Hillman	Kelso	Burgess	Hall	Dundas	Keillor	Allan	Clark	Devlin	Willocks	Smith
Dec	12th	Hillman	Kelso	Hamilton	Hall	Dundas	Keillor	Allan	Clark	Devlin	Willocks	Smith
Jan	9th	Hillman	Kelso	Burgess	Hall	Dundas	Keillor	Allan	Clark	Devlin	Willocks	Smith
	16th	Hillman	Kelso	Burgess	Hall	McArthur	Keillor	Allan	Clark	Devlin	Willocks	Smith
	30th	Hillman	Kelso	Burgess	Hall	McArthur	Keillor	Allan	Clark	Devlin	Willocks	Smith
Feb	13th	Hillman	Kelso	Burgess	Hall	Dundas	Keillor	Allan	Clark	Dundas	Willocks	Smith
	20th	Hillman	Kelso	Burgess	Hall	McArthur	Keillor	Allan	Clark	Devlin	Willocks	Smith

Look here - the referee has a word of advice for Dundee F.C. stalwart Jimmy Dundas during a break in play.

David Thomson

They Wore The Dark Blue

Season 1897-98

Date			Opponents		Score	Crowd	Scorers
Sep	4th	L	Clyde	h	6-0	3,000	McVean 3; Blyth; Devlin; Keillor
	11th	L	St Bernards	h	0-0	7,500	-
	25th	L	Partick Thistle	a	1-3	2,500	Willocks
Oct	2nd	L	Third Lanark	h	4-2	6,000	Willocks; Devlin; McVean 2
	9th	L	St Mirren	a	1-2	5,000	Devlin
	16th	L	Hearts	h	1-6	4,000	Malloch
	16th	FC1	Arbroath	a	0-1	4,000	-
	23rd	L	Partick Thistle	h	5-0	4,000	Keillor; Willocks 2; McVean; Devlin
	30th	L	Hearts	a	0-2	7,000	-
Nov	6th	L	Celtic	h	1-2	11,000	Blyth (pen)
	13th	L	Hibernian	a	0-2		-
	20th	L	St Mirren	h	0-0	3,800	-
	27th	L	Clyde	a	5-1		Willocks 2; own goal; Malloch; Keillor
Dec	4th	L	Hibernian	h	1-1	4,000	Pollock
	11th	L	St Bernards	a	1-4		McArthur
	25th	L	Rangers	a	0-5	6,000	-
Jan	3rd	F	Arbroath	a	3-3	2,000	McVean; Keillor 2
	5th	F	Forfar Athletic	a	1-2	1,500	Willocks
	8th	SC1	Partick Thistle	h	2-1	3,000	Malloch; Willocks
	15th	L	Celtic	a	1-2	6,000	Battles
	22nd	SC2	St Mirren	h	2-0	5,000	Kelso (pen); McArthur
	29th	L	Third Lanark	a	0-3	6,000	-
Feb	5th	SC3	Hearts	h	3-0	8,000	Willocks; McArthur; Malloch
	12th	L	Rangers	h	2-1	10,000	Battles; McVean
	19th	SCS	Kilmarnock	a*	2-3	11,000	McVean; Malloch
Apr	30th	F	Wanderers	h	6-1	2,000	Ferguson; McInroy; McArthur 2;

* Cash v Kilmarnock in the Cup semi-final was £223-0-0d

Appearances

	League		Scottish Cup		Total	
Jack Hillman	18		4		22	
Dave Willocks*	18	(6)	4	(2)	22	(8)
Bob Kelso	18		3	(1)	21	(1)
Malcolm McVean	16	(7)	4	(1)	20	(8)
Barney Battles	15	(2)	4		19	(2)
Bill McArthur*	14	(1)	4	(2)	18	(3)
Sandy Keillor	16	(3)	1		17	(3)
Charlie Burgess	12		4		16	
John Malloch*	12	(2)	4	(3)	16	(5)
Joe Clark*	11		4		15	
Bill Longair	10		4		14	
Bob Blyth	9	(2)	0		9	(2)
Joe Devlin	8	(4)	0		8	(4)
Sam Gilligan	2		4		6	
Jake Pollock	6	(1)	0		6	(1)
John Madden	4		0		4	
Joe Fleming	3		0		3	
Bill Fullerton	2		0		2	
Jim Hannah	2		0		2	
George Ferguson	1		0		1	
Bob McCulloch	1		0		1	

* After an acrimonious end of the season dispute, they joined ex Dundee captain Bill Hendry at
..New Brighton. Longair joined Broughton United while Kelso also moved South.

Scottish League Division One

		Home			Away			Goals		
	P	W	D	L	W	L	D	F	A	PTS
Celtic	18	8	1	0	7	2	0	56-13		33
Rangers	18	7	1	1	6	2	1	71-15		29
Hibernian	18	6	1	2	4	1	4	47-29		22
Hearts	18	5	2	2	3	2	4	54-33		20
Third Lanark	18	5	0	4	3	2	4	37-38		18
St Mirren	18	5	1	3	3	1	5	30-36		18
Dundee	**18**	**4**	**3**	**2**	**1**	**0**	**8**	**29-36**		**13**
Partick Thistle	18	5	1	3	1	0	8	34-65		13
St Bernards	18	4	0	5	0	1	8	35-67		9
Clyde	18	1	2	6	0	1	8	21-83		5

Bottom three clubs applied for re-election with Kilmarnock, Leith Athletic and Port
Glasgow of Division Two applying for election. Partick Thistle, St Bernards and Clyde
were all re-elected.

The Record		
League	-	Seventh Place, Division One
Scottish Cup	-	Semi-final
Forfarshire Cup	-	First round
Top Scorer	-	Dave Willocks,
		Malcolm McVean (both 8 goals)
Av. Home Gate	-	5,900
Players used	-	21
Sent off	-	None

They Wore The Dark Blue

Dundee F.C. Line-Ups 1897-98

		1	2	3	4	5	6	7	8	9	10	11
Sept	4th	Hillman	Kelso	Battles	Blyth	McArthur	Keillor	McVean	Clark	Devlin	Willocks	Hannah
	11th	Hillman	Kelso	Battles	Blyth	McArthur	Keillor	McVean	Clark	Devlin	Willocks	Ferguson
	25th	Hillman	Kelso	Battles	Blyth	McArthur	Keillor	McVean	Clark	Devlin	Willocks	Hannah
Oct	2nd	Hillman	Kelso	Battles	Blyth	McArthur	Keillor	McVean	Devlin	Madden	Willocks	Malloch
	9th	Hillman	Kelso	Battles	Blyth	McArthur	Keillor	McVean	Devlin	Madden	Willocks	Malloch
	16th	Hillman	Kelso	Battles	Blyth	McArthur	Keillor	McVean	Clark	Devlin	Willocks	Malloch
	23rd	Hillman	Kelso	Burgess	Blyth	Longair	Battles	McVean	Devlin	Willocks	Malloch	Keillor
	30th	Hillman	Kelso	Burgess	Blyth	Devlin	Battles	McVean	Clark	Willocks	McArthur	Keillor
Nov	6th	Hillman	Kelso	Burgess	Blyth	Longair	Battles	McVean	Madden	Willocks	Malloch	Keillor
	13th	Hillman	Kelso	Burgess	McArthur	Longair	Keillor	McVean	Fleming	Pollock	Willocks	Fullerton
	20th	Hillman	Keillor	Burgess	McArthur	Longair	Keillor	McVean	Clark	Pollock	Willocks	Fullerton
	27th	Hillman	Kelso	Burgess	Battles	Longair	Keillor	Clark	Fleming	Pollock	Willocks	Malloch
Dec	4th	Hillman	Kelso	Burgess	Battles	Longair	Keillor	Fleming	McVean	Pollock	Willocks	Malloch
	11th	Hillman	Kelso	Burgess	Battles	Longair	Keillor	Madden	McArthur	Pollock	Willocks	Malloch
	25th	Hillman	Kelso	Burgess	Battles	McArthur	Keillor	McVean	Clark	Pollock	Willocks	Malloch
Jan	8th	Hillman	Kelso	Burgess	Battles	Longair	Keillor	McVean	Clark	McArthur	Willocks	Malloch
	15th	Hillman	Kelso	Burgess	Battles	Longair	Gilligan	McVean	Clark	McArthur	Willocks	Malloch
	22nd	Hillman	Kelso	Burgess	Battles	Longair	Gilligan	McVean	Clark	McArthur	Willocks	Malloch
	29th	Hillman	Gilligan	Burgess	McCulloch	Longair	Keillor	McVean	Clark	McArthur	Willocks	Malloch
Feb	5th	Hillman	Kelso	Burgess	Gilligan	Longair	Battles	McVean	Clark	McArthur	Willocks	Malloch
	12th	Hillman	Kelso	Burgess	Battles	Longair	Gilligan	McVean	Clark	McArthur	Willocks	Malloch
	19th	Hillman	Kelso	Burgess	Battles	Longair	Gilligan	McVean	Clark	McArthur	Willocks	Malloch

An artist's impression of the hectic scenes outside the Carolina Port turnstiles as enthusiastic fans gather for the Scottish Cup quarter-final tie against Hearts.

David Thomson

They Wore The Dark Blue

Season 1898-99

Date			Opponents		Score	Crowd	Scorers
Aug	15th	F	Lochee United	a	2-2		McColl (pen); W. McDonald
	27th	F	Wanderers	h	3-6	2,000	McLay; W. McDonald; Keillor
Sep	3rd	L	St Bernards	h	1-1	2,500	McNicoll o.g.
	10th	L	Clyde	a	0-1		-
	17th	L	Hibernian	h	2-4	5,000	McLay; Symers
	24th	L	Third Lanark	a	1-3		W. McDonald
Oct	1st	L	Partick Thistle	h	5-1	2,500	McLay; Methven 2; Bunce; Gerrard
	8th	L	Rangers	h	1-2	7,500	W. McDonald
	10th	B	Celtic	h	0-2	5,000	-
			(Sandy Keillor Benefit £143)				
	15th	L	Hibernian	a	0-5		-
	15th	FC1	Wanderers	h	1-7	2,500	Maurice
	22nd	L	Third Lanark	h	1-3	3,000	Gardner o.g.
	29th	L	St Mirren	a	1-5	2,500	J. Turner
Nov	5th	L	St Mirren	h	1-7	3,000	T. McDonald
	12th	L	Clyde	h	1-3	2,000	J. Turner
	19th	L	Celtic	h	1-4	5,000	Craig
	26th	L	Hearts	a	3-6	1,500	W. McDonald; Craig 2
Dec	3rd	L	Hearts	h	2-5	2,000	Leckie; W. Turner
	17th	L	Rangers	a	0-7	3,000	-
	24th	L	St Bernards	a	2-2		Stewart; Methven
	31st	L	Partick Thistle	a	0-2		-
Jan	2nd	F	Wanderers	h	5-0	4,000	Methven; McNiff 3; Stewart
	3rd	F	Aberdeen	a*	2-2	3,000	Stewart; McNiff
	7th	L	Celtic	a	1-4		Craig
	14th	SC1	Ayr Parkhouse	a	1-3	2,500	Brown

* The first meeting between the clubs, played at Central Park, Kittibrewster.
Cash for game v. Clyde (a) £119-1-6d and v. Partick (h) £77

Tom Stewart - Dundee goalkeeping stalwart.

Appearances

	League		Scottish Cup		Total	
Sandy Keillor	17		1		18	
Stuart Methven	14	(3)	1		15	(3)
Tom Stewart	14		1		15	
Bill Davidson	14		0		14	
Willie McDonald	14	(3)	0		14	(3)
Jim Gerrard	9	(1)	1		10	(1)
Tom Leckie	10	(1)	0		10	(1)
Dave T. McDonald	9	(1)	0		9	(1)
James McLay	9	(2)	0		9	(2)
James Ireland	7		1		8	
Charlie Craig	7	(4)	0		7	(4)
Wm John Lyon	7		0		7	
Jimmy Skene	6		1		7	
John Bett	5		1		6	
Willie McColl	5		1		6	
Allan Scott	6		0		6	
Jim Turner	6	(2)	0		6	(2)
Frank Ferrier	4		1		5	
Harry Stewart	4	(1)	1		5	(1)
John Bunce	4	(1)	0		4	(1)
George Philip	3		0		3	
Billy Ritchie (gk)	3		0		3	
Stuart Symers	3	(1)	0		3	(1)
George Whyte	3		0		3	
Alex Brown	1		1	(1)	2	(1)
Ed Lister	2		0		2	
John Ritchie (cf)	2		0		2	
Alex. Black	1		0		1	
John Dawson	1		0		1	
Jimmy Jeffray	1		0		1	
Davie McInroy	1		0		1	
Ward Miller	1		0		1	

Scottish League Division One

	P	Home			Away			Goals		
		W	D	L	W	D	L	F	A	PTS
Rangers	18	9	0	0	9	0	0	79-18		36
Hearts	18	7	1	1	5	1	3	56-30		26
Celtic	18	7	0	2	4	2	3	41-33		24
Hibernian	18	5	2	2	5	1	3	42-33		23
St Mirren	18	5	2	2	3	2	4	46-32		20
Third Lanark	18	4	2	3	3	1	5	33-38		17
St Bernards	18	2	2	5	2	2	5	30-37		12
Clyde	18	2	3	4	2	1	6	23-48		12
Partick Thistle	18	1	0	8	1	2	6	19-58		6
Dundee	**18**	**1**	**1**	**7**	**0**	**1**	**8**	**23-65**		**4**

Bottom three clubs applied for re-election with Kilmarnock, Leith Athletic and Port Glasgow of Division Two applying for election. Clyde and Dundee were re-elected with Kilmarnock replacing Partick Thistle.

The Record		
Scottish League	-	Tenth Place, Division One
Scottish Cup	-	First Round
Forfarshire Cup	-	First Round
Top Scorer	-	Charlie Craig (4 goals)
Av. Home Gate	-	3,600
Players used	-	37
Sent off	-	None

Appearances (Ctd)

	League		Scottish Cup	Total	
Jake Pollock	1		0	1	
Rod Roberts	1		0	1	
Alex. Robertson	1		0	1	
Jim Thomson	1		0	1	
Billy Turner	1	(1)	0	1	(1)

Dundee F.C. Line-Ups 1898-99

		1	2	3	4	5	6	7	8	9	10	11
Sep	3rd	Stewart T	Davidson	Philip	Ireland	Leckie	Keillor	Pollock	Bett	Methven	McDonald W	McLay
	10th	Stewart T	Davidson	Skene	Leckie	Whyte	Keillor	Robertson	Bett	Methven	McDonald W	McLay
	17th	Stewart T	Davidson	Skene	Leckie	Whyte	Keillor	Symers	Bett	Methven	McDonald W	McLay
	24th	Stewart T	Davidson	Skene	Leckie	Whyte	Keillor	Black	Bett	Methven	McDonald W	McLay
Oct	1st	Stewart T	Davidson	Skene	Leckie	Philip	Keillor	Bunce	Methven	Gerrard	McDonald W	McLay
	8th	Stewart T	Davidson	Skene	Leckie	Gerrard	Keillor	Bunce	McDonald T	Methven	McDonald W	McLay
	15th	Stewart T	Davidson	Skene	Leckie	Gerrard	Keillor	Bunce	McDonald T	Methven	McDonald W	McInroy
	22nd	Stewart T	Davidson	Philip	Lyon	Leckie	Keillor	Bunce	McDonald T	Methven	McDonald W	McLay
	29th	Roberts	Davidson	Craig	Lyon	Leckie	Keillor	Turner	McDonald T	Gerrard	McDonald W	McLay
Nov	5th	Stewart T	Davidson	Craig	Lyon	Ireland	Keillor	Turner	McDonald T	Methven	McDonald W	McLay
	12th	Stewart T	Davidson	Craig	Lyon	Gerrard	Keillor	Turner	McDonald T	Methven	McDonald W	McColl
	19th	Ritchie	Davidson	Scott	Lyon	Jeffray	Keillor	Turner	McDonald T	Lester	McDonald W	Craig
	26th	Ritchie	Davidson	Scott	Lyon	Ireland	Keillor	Turner	McDonald T	Lester	McDonald W	Craig
Dec	3rd	Stewart T	Davidson	Scott	Lyon	Leckie	Keillor	Turner J	Turner W	McDonald T	McDonald W	Craig
	17th	Stewart T	Miller	Scott	Ferrier	Ireland	Keillor	Methven	Dawson	Gerrard	McColl	Stewart H
	24th	Stewart T	Ireland	Ferrier	Bett	Gerrard	Keillor	Symers	Methven	Ritchie	McColl	Stewart H
	31st	Stewart T	Ferrier	Scott	Ireland	Gerrard	Keillor	Symers	Methven	Ritchie	McColl	Stewart H
Jan	7th	Ritchie	Thomson	Scott	Ireland	Gerrard	Ferrier	Craig	Methven	Brown	McColl	Stewart H
	14th	Stewart T	Ireland	Skene	Ferrier	Gerrard	Keillor	Bett	Methven	Brown	McColl	Stewart H

"Plum" Longair - the big defender twice joined English clubs only to return to his beloved Dundee. A great favourite with the fans, thousands lined the streets for his funeral in 1926.   W. Longair

Season 1899-1900

Date			Opponents		Score	Crowd	Cash	Scorers
Sep	2nd	L	Clyde	h	3-1	9,000		McDonald; Low; Stewart
	9th	L	St Mirren	a	0-4			-
	16th	L	Hibernian	h	2-2	6,000		Longair; Steven
	23rd	L	St Bernards	h	3-0	5,000		Keillor; Low; McDermott
Oct	7th	L	St Bernard	a	0-2		£188	-
	14th	L	St Mirren	h	5-2	7,000	£186	Robertson 2; Low; McDermott 2 (1 pen)
	21st	L	Kilmarnock	a	1-2	3,000		McDermott
	28th	L	Third Lanark	h	0-0	4,000		-
Nov	4th	L	Rangers	a	0-6	6,000		-
	11th	L	Hearts	a	1-4	2,000		Anderson
	11th	FC1	Arbroath	a	1-2	4,000		McDonald W.
	18th	L	Hibernian	a	3-3	2,000		Robertson; 2; McDiarmid
	25th	L	Celtic	h	1-2	10,000	£252	Robertson
Dec	2nd	L	Clyde	a	7-0			Johnstone; Low; McDiarmid 3; Robertson; Steven
	16th	L	Hearts	h	1-1	7,000		Steven
	23rd	L	Celtic	a	1-1			Robertson
	30th	L	Third Lanark	a	3-3			Robertson 2; McDiarmid
Jan	6th	L	Kilmarnock	h	3-3	5,000		McDermott; McDiarmid 2
	13th	SC1	Douglas Wand.	h	8-0	3,000		McDiarmid 2; Low 2; Keillor; Robertson 2; McDermott
	20th	L	Rangers	h	2-3	12,000	£306	McDiarmid; McDermott
	27th	SC2	Clyde	h	3-3	5,000		McDiarmid; Robertson 2
Feb	17th	SC2	Clyde	a	3-0	5,000		McDermott 2; McDiarmid
	24th	SC3	Queens Park	a	0-1	8,000		-
Mar	3rd	F	Everton	h	0-2	5,000	-	
Apr	21st	F	Sunderland	h	1-1	5,000		McDermott
	25th	CSS*	Wanderers	h	3-3			Robertson 2; Steven
May	7th	CSSR	Wanderers	a	1-0			McDermott
	12th	CSF	Arbroath	h	2-1			Stewart; McDiarmid

* CS = Dundee Charity Shield

CS = Dundee and District Charity Shield

Sandy Keillor - a Dundee hero in the early days.

Appearances

	League		Scottish Cup		Total	
Bill Longair	18	(1)	4		22	(1)
Tommy McDermott	18	(7)	4	(3)	22	(10)
David Steven	18	(3)	4		22	(3)
Willie Baird	17		4		21	
Tommy Low	17	(4)	4	(2)	21	(6)
Jimmy Sharp	17		4		21	
Tom Stewart	16		4		20	
Sandy Keillor	15	(1)	4	(1)	19	(2)
Alex. Robertson	15	(9)	4	(4)	19	(13)
Willie Johnstone	15	(1)	3		18	(1)
Fred McDiarmid	12	(7)	4	(4)	16	(11)
John Watson	6		0		6	
Harry Stewart	5	(1)	0		5	(1)
George Anderson	2	(1)	0		2	(1)
Bill Douglas	2		0		2	
John Halkett	1		1		2	
Dave T. McDonald	2	(1)	0		2	(1)
Bob Crook	1		0		1	
George Philip	1		0		1	

Scottish League Division One

			Home			Away			Goals		
	P	W	D	L	W	D	L	F	A	PTS	
Rangers	18	8	2	0	7	1	1	69-27		32	
Celtic	18	6	2	1	3	5	1	46-27		25	
Hibernian	18	5	3	1	4	3	2	43-24		24	
Hearts	18	7	1	1	8	3	2	41-24		23	
Kilmarnock	18	4	3	2	2	3	4	30-37		18	
Dundee	**18**	**3**	**4**	**2**	**1**	**3**	**5**	**36-39**		**15**	
Third Lanark	18	5	2	2	0	3	6	31-38		15	
St Mirren	18	3	4	2	0	2	7	30-46		12	
St Bernards	18	3	3	3	1	1	7	29-47		12	
Clyde	18	2	0	7	0	0	9	24-70		4	

Bottom three clubs applied for re-election with Partick Thistle, Morton and Port Glasgow of Division Two applying for election. St Mirren were re-elected with Partick Thistle and Morton replacing St Bernards and Clyde.

The Record		
League	-	Sixth Place, Division One
Scottish Cup	-	Third Round
Forfarshire Cup	-	First Round
Charity Shield	-	Winners
Top Scorer	-	Alex. Robertson (13 goals)
Av. Home Gate	-	7,100
Players used	-	19
Sent off	-	None

Dundee F.C. Line-Ups 1899-1900

		1	2	3	4	5	6	7	8	9	10	11
Sep	2nd	Stewart T	Watson	Sharp	Keillor	Baird	Longair	Low	Steven	McDonald	McDermott	Stewart H
	9th	Stewart T	Watson	Sharp	Johnstone	Baird	Longair	Low	Steven	McDonald	McDermott	Stewart H
	16th	Stewart T	Watson	Sharp	Johnstone	Baird	Longair	Low	Steven	Robertson	McDermott	Halkett
	23rd	Stewart T	Watson	Sharp	Johnstone	Longair	Keillor	Low	Steven	Robertson	McDermott	Stewart H
Oct	7th	Stewart T	Watson	Sharp	Baird	Longair	Keillor	Low	Steven	Robertson	McDermott	Stewart H
	14th	Douglas	Baird	Sharp	Johnstone	Longair	Keillor	Low	Steven	Robertson	McDermott	McDiarmid
	21st	Douglas	Baird	Sharp	Johnstone	Longair	Keillor	Low	Steven	Robertson	McDermott	McDiarmid
	28th	Stewart T	Baird	Sharp	Johnstone	Longair	Keillor	Low	Steven	Robertson	McDermott	McDiarmid
Nov	4th	Stewart T	Baird	Watson	Johnstone	Longair	Crook	Low	Steven	Robertson	McDermott	McDiarmid
	11th	Stewart T	Baird	Sharp	Johnstone	Longair	Keillor	Low	Steven	Robertson	McDermott	Anderson
	18th	Stewart T	Baird	Sharp	Johnstone	Longair	Keillor	Low	Steven	Robertson	McDermott	McDiarmid
	25th	Stewart T	Baird	Sharp	Johnstone	Longair	Keillor	Low	Steven	Robertson	McDermott	McDiarmid
Dec	2nd	Stewart T	Baird	Sharp	Johnstone	Longair	Keillor	Low	Steven	Robertson	McDermott	McDiarmid
	16th	Stewart T	Baird	Sharp	Johnstone	Longair	Keillor	Low	Steven	Anderson	McDermott	McDiarmid
	23rd	Stewart T	Baird	Sharp	Johnstone	Longair	Keillor	Low	Steven	Robertson	McDermott	McDiarmid
	30th	Stewart T	Baird	Sharp	Johnstone	Longair	Keillor	McDiarmid	Steven	Robertson	McDermott	Stewart H
Jan	6th	Stewart T	Baird	Sharp	Johnstone	Longair	Keillor	Low	Steven	Robertson	McDermott	McDiarmid
	13th	Stewart T	Baird	Sharp	Halkett	Longair	Keillor	Low	Steven	Robertson	McDermott	McDiarmid
	20th	Stewart T	Philip	Sharp	Baird	Longair	Keillor	Low	Steven	Robertson	McDermott	McDiarmid
	27th	Stewart T	Baird	Sharp	Johnstone	Longair	Keillor	Low	Steven	Robertson	McDermott	McDiarmid
Feb	17th	Stewart T	Baird	Sharp	Johnstone	Longair	Keillor	Low	Steven	Robertson	McDermott	McDiarmid
	24th	Stewart T	Baird	Sharp	Johnstone	Longair	Keillor	Low	Steven	Robertson	McDermott	McDiarmid

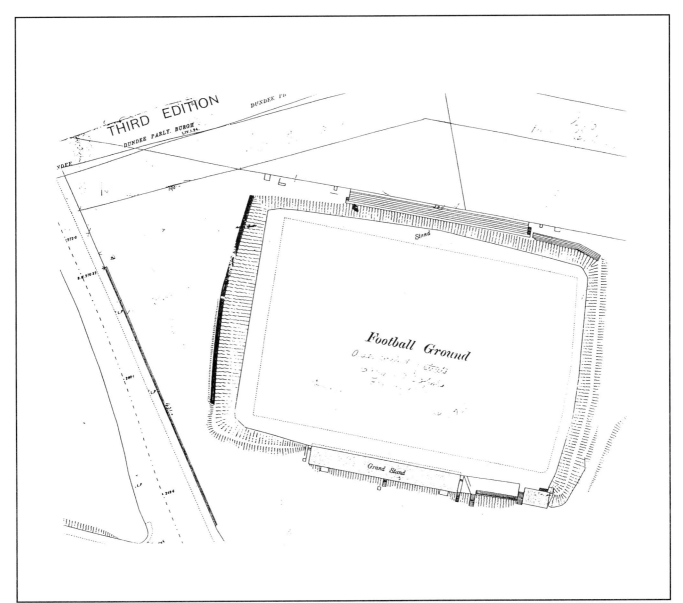

August 1899 saw Dundee F.C. move from Carolina Port to Dens Park. This plan shows the layout of the new ground which is considerably smaller than the present Dens Park Stadium. Provost Road is to the West with Sandeman Street to the North.

Bob Hynd

They Wore The Dark Blue

Season 1900-01

Date			Opponents		Score	Crowd	Cash	Scorers
Aug	25th	L	Kilmarnock	a	0-2			-
Sep	1st	L	Queens Park	h	4-0	11,000	£310	Mackay 2; Steven; Russell o.g.
	8th	L	Hearts	a	4-0	6,500	£150	McGeoch; Steven 2; Mackay
	15th	L	Kilmarnock	h	3-0	10,000		McDermott (pen); Steven 2
	29th	L	Hearts	h	1-2	6,000		Sharp
Oct	6th	L	Third Lanark	a	1-2			Steven
	13th	L	Morton	h	5-2	8,000	£179	McGeoch 2; A. Robertson 2; Steven
	20th	L	Rangers	a	2-4			McDiarmid; McDonald
	27th	L	Hibernian	a	1-2			McDiarmid
Nov	3rd	L	St Mirren	h	1-1	5,000		McDiarmid
	10th	L	Celtic	h	1-1	14,000	£333	A. Robertson
	17th	L	Partick Thistle	a	1-1			McDermott
	24th	L	Third Lanark	h	0-0	7,000		
Dec	1st	L	Hibernian	h	1-3	5,000		Boyd
	15th	L	Rangers	h	1-5	10,000	£278	Mackay
	22nd	L	Celtic	a	2-1	3,000		Steven; A. Robertson
	29th	L	Partick Thistle	h	4-0	6,000	£120	A. Robertson 2; Mackay; McDermott (pen)
Jan	5th	L	Queens Park	a	0-1			-
	12th	SC1	Arthurlie	h	3-1	5,000		McDermott; Longair; McDonald
	19th	L	Morton	a	1-5			A. Robertson
Feb	9th	SC2	Clyde	a	5-3	6,000		McDiarmid 2; Mackay 2; A. Robertson
	16th	SC3	Celtic	h	0-1	17,000	£472	-
	23rd	FCS	Arbroath	a	4-3	3,500		McDiarmid 2; J. Halkett; Steven
Mar	9th	FCF	Wanderers	h	1-0	4,000		J. Halkett
	23rd	DSS	Dunblane	a	4-0			Boyd; McDiarmid; McGeoch; Gowans
	30th	L	St Mirren	a	3-3			McDermott; Mackay; J. Robertson
Apr	13th	DSF	East Stirling	h	6-1	5,000		McDiarmid; Halkett 2; McDermott; Steven; McGeoch;

Appearances

	League		Scottish Cup		Total	
Sandy Keillor	20		3		23	
Bill Longair	20		3	(1)	23	(1)
Jimmy Sharp	20	(1)	3		23	(1)
Tom Stewart	20		3		23	
Fred McDiarmid	19	(3)	3	(2)	22	(5)
Tommy McDermott	18	(4)	3	(1)	21	(5)
Willie Baird	18		1		19	
David Steven	17	(8)	0		17	(8)
Hugh Goldie	15		2		17	
Archie McGeoch	14	(3)	0		14	(3)
Alex. Robertson	11	(7)	2	(1)	13	(8)
David Mackay	9	(6)	3	(2)	12	(8)
Willie Johnstone	6		3		9	
Dave T. McDonald	5	(1)	3	(1)	8	(1)
Bob Boyd	5	(1)	1		6	(1)
Jim Robertson	1	(1)	0		1	(1)
Eddie Tarbat	1		0		1	
Archie Taylor	1		0		1	

Scottish League Division One

		Home			Away			Goals		
	P	W	D	L	W	D	L	F	A	PTS
Rangers	20	10	0	0	7	1	2	60-25		35
Celtic	20	7	1	2	6	2	2	49-28		29
Hibernian	20	6	3	1	3	4	3	29-22		25
Morton	20	6	1	3	3	2	5	40-40		21
Kilmarnock	20	6	2	2	1	2	7	35-47		18
Third Lanark	20	5	4	1	1	2	7	20-29		18
Dundee	**20**	**4**	**3**	**3**	**2**	**2**	**6**	**36-35**		**17**
Queens Park	20	4	3	3	3	0	7	33-37		17
St Mirren	20	5	1	4	0	5	5	33-43		16
Hearts	20	1	3	6	4	1	5	22-30		14
Partick Thistle	20	2	1	7	2	1	7	28-49		10

League reverts to 10 teams. Bottom three clubs applied for re-election with St Bernards, Airdrie and Abercorn of Division Two applying for election. St Mirren and Hearts were re-elected .

The Record		
League	-	Seventh Place, Division One
Scottish Cup	-	Third round
Forfarshire Cup	-	Winners
Dewar Shield	-	Winners
Top Scorer	-	David Steven, David Mackay, Alex. Robertson (all 8 goals)
Av. Home Gate	-	8,000
Players used	-	18
Sent off	-	None

Dundee F.C. Line-Ups 1900-01

		1	2	3	4	5	6	7	8	9	10	11
Aug	25th	Stewart	Baird	Sharp	Goldie	Longair	Keillor	McDiarmid	Steven	McGeoch	McDermott	McDonald
Sep	1st	Stewart	Baird	Sharp	Goldie	Longair	Keillor	Mackay	Steven	McGeoch	McDermott	McDiarmid
	8th	Stewart	Baird	Sharp	Goldie	Longair	Keillor	Mackay	Steven	McGeoch	McDermott	McDiarmid
	15th	Stewart	Baird	Sharp	Goldie	Longair	Keillor	Mackay	Steven	McGeoch	McDermott	McDiarmid
	29th	Stewart	Baird	Sharp	Goldie	Longair	Keillor	Mackay	Steven	McGeoch	McDermott	McDiarmid
Oct	6th	Stewart	Baird	Sharp	Goldie	Longair	Keillor	Steven	McDonald	McGeoch	McDermott	McDiarmid
	13th	Stewart	Baird	Sharp	Goldie	Longair	Keillor	McDiarmid	Steven	McGeoch	McDonald	Robertson
	20th	Stewart	Baird	Sharp	Goldie	Longair	Keillor	McDiarmid	Steven	McDermott	McDonald	Robertson
	27th	Stewart	Baird	Sharp	Johnstone	Longair	Keillor	McDiarmid	Steven	McGeoch	McDermott	Robertson
Nov	3rd	Stewart	Baird	Sharp	Goldie	Longair	Keillor	McDiarmid	Steven	McGeoch	McDermott	Robertson
	10th	Stewart	Baird	Sharp	Goldie	Longair	Keillor	McDiarmid	Steven	McGeoch	McDermott	Robertson
	17th	Stewart	Baird	Sharp	Goldie	Longair	Keillor	McDiarmid	Steven	McGeoch	McDermott	Robertson
	24th	Stewart	Baird	Sharp	Goldie	Longair	Keillor	McDiarmid	Steven	McGeoch	McDermott	Robertson
Dec	1st	Stewart	Baird	Sharp	Goldie	Longair	Keillor	McDiarmid	Robertson	McGeoch	McDermott	Boyd
	15th	Stewart	Baird	Sharp	Goldie	Longair	Keillor	McDiarmid	Steven	Mackay	McDermott	Boyd
	22nd	Stewart	Baird	Sharp	Johnstone	Longair	Keillor	Robertson	Steven	Mackay	McDermott	Boyd
	29th	Stewart	Baird	Sharp	Johnstone	Longair	Keillor	Robertson	Steven	Mackay	McDermott	Boyd
Jan	5th	Stewart	Baird	Sharp	Johnstone	Longair	Keillor	McDiarmid	McGeoch	Mackay	McDermott	Boyd
	12th	Stewart	Baird	Sharp	Johnstone	Longair	Keillor	McDiarmid	McDonald	Mackay	McDermott	Boyd
	19th	Stewart	Taylor	Sharp	Johnstone	Longair	Keillor	Tarbat	Steven	Robertson	McDermott	McDiarmid
Feb	9th	Stewart	Goldie	Sharp	Johnstone	Longair	Keillor	McDiarmid	Mackay	McDonald	McDermott	Robertson
	16th	Stewart	Goldie	Sharp	Johnstone	Longair	Keillor	McDiarmid	Mackay	McDonald	McDermott	Robertson
Mar	30th	Stewart	Goldie	Sharp	Johnstone	Longair	Keillor	Robertson J	McDermott	Mackay	McDonald	McDiarmid

Dundee F.C. Season 1900-01. (BACK ROW, left to right), R. Marshall (trainer), Willie Baird, John Watson, Tom Stewart, Harry Stewart, Jimmy Sharp. MIDDLE - Sandy Keillor, Bill Longair, Jim McAuley. FRONT - Tommy Low, David Steven, Alex. Robertson, Tommy McDermott and Fred McDiarmid. DC Thomson

Season 1901-02

Date			Opponents		Score	Crowd	Cash	Scorers
Aug	17th	L	Celtic	a	1-1	-	-	Mackay
	24th	L	Kilmarnock	h	0-0	8,000	-	-
	31st	L	Rangers	h	0-3	12,000	£330	-
Sep	7th	L	Morton	a	4-1		-	Atherton; Turnbull 2; McDiarmid
	14th	L	St Mirren	h	1-2	7,000	£185	Atherton
	21st	L	Hibernian	h	1-0	5,000	-	Barron
Oct	5th	L	Queens Park	a	0-1		-	-
	12th	L	Hearts	a	0-4		-	-
	19th	L	Third Lanark	h	1-1	6,000	-	Steven
	26th	L	St Mirren	a	0-3		-	-
Nov	2nd	L	Morton	h	0-0	6,000	-	-
	9th	L	Kilmarnock	a	0-4		-	-
	16th	L	Celtic	h	2-3	8,000	£225	Cowie; Mackay
	30th	L	Hibernian	a	0-5		-	-
Dec	7th	L	Hearts	h	2-0	7,000	£147	Robertson; Mackay
	14th	F	Derby County	h	1-2	4,000	-	Lloyd
	28th	L	Third Lanark	a	0-0		-	-
Jan	11th	SC1	Ayr United	a	0-0	3,000	-	-
	18th	SC1R	Ayr United	h	2-0	11,088	£243	Mackay 2
	18th	FC1	Forfar Athletic	a	0-1		-	-
	25th	SC2	Kilmarnock	a	0-2	6,000	-	-
Mar	1st	L	Queens Park	h	2-0	3,000	-	Turnbull; Lloyd
	29th	L	Rangers	a*	1-3		-	Turnbull
Apr	26th	F	North'n LeagueX1	h	0-1	2,000	-	-

*Earlier game on Nov 23rd, 1901 was abandoned due to fog with Rangers leading 2-1

Fred McDiarmid - grand winger for Dundee.

Appearances

	League		Scottish Cup		Total	
Peter Robertson	18	(1)	3		21	(1)
Jimmy Sharp	18		3		21	
Arthur Howes	17		3		20	
Bill Longair	16		3		19	
Fred McDiarmid	16	(1)	1		17	(1)
Hugh Goldie	14		2		16	
David Mackay	13	(3)	3	(2)	16	(5)
Jimmy Turnbull	13	(4)	3		16	(4)
Willie Johnstone	12		0		12	
Tom Atherton	8	(2)	2		10	(2)
Tommy McDermott	10		0		10	
Dave Storrier	7		3		10	
Sandy MacFarlane	6		3		9	
Frank Lloyd	5	(1)	3		8	(1)
David Steven	7	(1)	0		7	(1)
John Halkett	6		0		6	
John Barron	3	(1)	0		3	(1)
Geordie Henderson	3		0		3	
Sandy Keillor	2		0		2	
Dave Cowie	1	(1)	0		1	(1)
Alick Halkett	1		0		1	
Jimmy Jeffray	1		0		1	
Archie McGeoch	1		0		1	
Tom Stewart	1		0		1	

Scottish League Division One

		Home			Away			Goals		
	P	W	D	L	W	D	L	F	A	PTS
Rangers	18	6	1	2	7	1	1	43-29		28
Celtic	18	5	2	2	6	2	1	38-28		26
Hearts	18	6	2	1	4	0	5	32-21		22
Third Lanark	18	3	3	3	4	2	3	30-26		19
St Mirren	18	3	3	3	5	0	4	29-28		19
Hibernian	18	3	1	5	3	3	3	36-23		16
Kilmarnock	18	4	2	3	1	4	4	22-27		16
Queens Park	18	5	1	3	0	3	6	21-32		14
Dundee	**18**	**3**	**3**	**3**	**1**	**2**	**6**	**15-21**		**13**
Morton	18	0	2	7	1	3	5	20-41		7

No relegation, League increased to 12 teams with Port Glasgow and Partick Thistle elected to Division One.

The Record		
League	-	Ninth Place, Division One
Scottish Cup	-	Second round
Forfarshire Cup	-	First round
Top Scorer	-	David Mackay (5 goals)
Av. Home Gate	-	6,900
Players used	-	24
Sent off	-	None

Dundee F.C. Line-Ups 1901-02

		1	2	3	4	5	6	7	8	9	10	11
Aug	17th	Howes	Goldie	Sharp	Johnstone	Longair	Robertson	McDiarmid	Mackay	Turnbull	McDermott	Halkett J
	24th	Howes	Goldie	Sharp	Johnstone	Longair	Robertson	McDiarmid	Mackay	Turnbull	McDermott	Halkett J
	31st	Howes	Goldie	Sharp	Johnstone	Longair	Robertson	Atherton	McDiarmid	Turnbull	McDermott	Halkett J
Sep	7th	Howes	Goldie	Sharp	Johnstone	Longair	Robertson	McDiarmid	Atherton	Turnbull	McDermott	Halkett J
	14th	Howes	Goldie	Sharp	Johnstone	Longair	Robertson	McDiarmid	McDermott	Barron	Mackay	Halkett J
	21st	Howes	Goldie	Sharp	Halkett A	Longair	Robertson	McDiarmid	Steven	Turnbull	McDermott	McDiarmid
Oct	5th	Howes	Goldie	Sharp	Johnstone	Longair	Robertson	Mackay	Barron	Turnbull	McDermott	McDiarmid
	12th	Howes	Goldie	Sharp	Jeffray	Longair	Robertson	Barron	Mackay	Turnbull	McDermott	McDiarmid
	19th	Howes	Goldie	Sharp	Johnstone	Goldie	Robertson	Atherton	Steven	Turnbull	McDermott	McDiarmid
	26th	Howes	Goldie	Sharp	Johnstone	Longair	Robertson	Atherton	Steven	Turnbull	McDermott	McDiarmid
Nov	2nd	Howes	Goldie	Sharp	Johnstone	Robertson	Keillor	Atherton	Steven	Turnbull	Mackay	McDiarmid
	9th	Howes	Storrier	Sharp	Goldie	Robertson	Johnstone	Keillor	Steven	McGeoch	Mackay	McDiarmid
	16th	Howes	Storrier	Sharp	Goldie	Longair	Robertson	McDiarmid	Steven	MacFarlane	Mackay	Cowie
	30th	Stewart	Storrier	Sharp	Goldie	Longair	Robertson	Lloyd	Steven	Mackay	MacFarlane	McDiarmid
Dec	7th	Howes	Storrier	Sharp	Johnstone	Longair	Robertson	Lloyd	Steven	Mackay	MacFarlane	Atherton
	28th	Howes	Storrier	Sharp	Johnstone	Longair	Robertson	Lloyd	Turnbull	Mackay	MacFarlane	Atherton
Jan	11th	Howes	Storrier	Sharp	Goldie	Longair	Robertson	Lloyd	Turnbull	Mackay	MacFarlane	Atherton
	18th	Howes	Storrier	Sharp	Goldie	Longair	Robertson	Lloyd	Turnbull	Mackay	MacFarlane	Atherton
	25th	Howes	Storrier	Sharp	Henderson	Longair	Robertson	Lloyd	Turnbull	Mackay	MacFarlane	McDiarmid
Mar	1st	Howes	Storrier	Sharp	Henderson	Longair	Robertson	Lloyd	Turnbull	Mackay	MacFarlane	McDiarmid
	29th	Howes	Storrier	Sharp	Henderson	Longair	Robertson	Lloyd	MacFarlane	Turnbull	Mackay	McDiarmid

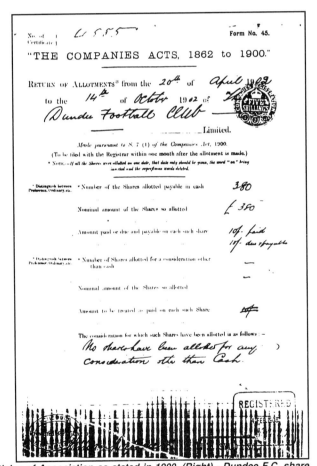

Historical documents (Left) - the first page of Dundee F.C's Articles of Association as stated in 1900. (Right) - Dundee F.C. share certificate for 380 shares at a cost of £380, a considerable amount for 1902 and probably held by one of the Dens directors.

They Wore The Dark Blue

Season 1902-03

Date			Opponents		Score	Crowd	Cash	Scorers
Aug	16th	L	Queens Park	h	2-0	8,000	£207	White; Bell
	23rd	L	Hearts	a	2-0	-		MacFarlane; Turnbull
	30th	L	Kilmarnock	h	2-0	10,000	£250	Turnbull; Bell
Sep	6th	L	Partick Thistle	a	2-0		-	MacFarlane; Bell
	13th	L	Port Glasgow	h	2-1	8,000	-	MacFarlane; Bell
	20th	L	St Mirren	h	2-1	13,000	-	McDiarmid; Bell
	27th	L	Hibernian	a	0-1	18,000	-	-
Oct	4th	L	Third Lanark	h	0-0	14,000	£345	-
	11th	L	St Mirren	a	0-1	11,500	£248	-
	18th	L	Hearts	h	0-1	12,800	£302	-
	25th	L	Hibernian	h	0-3	15,000	£373	-
Nov	1st	L	Port Glasgow	a	0-0		-	-
	15th	L	Morton	h	3-0	12,000	-	Bell; Gilligan; White
	22nd	L	Morton	a	2-0		-	McDiarmid; T. Robertson
	29th	L	Celtic	a	2-2		-	MacFarlane; White
Dec	6th	L	Rangers	h	3-1	12,000	£332	McDiarmid; White 2
	13th	L	Kilmarnock	a	2-0	3,000	£ 69	Gilligan; White
	20th	L	Queens Park	a	0-0	10,000	£215	-
	27th	L	Partick Thistle	h	3-0	6,000	£175	Dickson 3
Jan	17th	L	Rangers	a	1-1	10,000	-	Dickson
	24th	SC1	Barholm Rovers	h	Walkover		-	
	24th	FC1	Forfar Athletic	a	2-2			Gilligan; Turnbull
	31st	SC2	Nithsdale Wand	h	7-0	5,000	-	Dickson 3; White 3; T. Robertson
Feb	3rd	SC3	Hibernian	a	0-0	15,000	-	-
	7th	FC1R	Forfar Athletic	h	3-0			Kerr; Gilligan; McNiff
	14th	SC3R	Hibernian	h	0-0	24,000	£666	-
	21st	SC3R	Hibernian	Ibrox	1-0	36,000	£1,010	Bell
	28th	SCS	Hearts	h	0-0	22,000	£603	-
Mar	7th	SCSR	Hearts	a	0-1	32,000	£650	-
	7th	FCS	Wanderers	h	6-0			Dickson 3; Kerr 2; Gibson
	21st	L	Celtic	h	2-0*	9,000	-	Sharp (pen); MacFarlane
Apr	4th	L	Third Lanark	a	1-0		-	Gilligan
	4th	FCF	Montrose	a	2-1	2,000		Kerr; Turnbull
	18th	DSS	St Johnstone	h	3-0	5,000		Dickson 2 (1 pen); Kerr
May	2nd	DSF	Victoria United	a	2-1	3,000		Dickson; Kerr

Johnny Darroch - Dens defensive stalwart.

* Previously played on November 8th but abandoned after 85 minutes with Dundee leading 1-0.
Celtic, challenging strongly for the title at that time, appealed against the failing light.

Appearances

	League		Scottish Cup		Total	
Johnny Darroch	22		6		28	
Sandy MacFarlane	22	(5)	6		28	(5)
Billy Muir	22		6		28	
Jimmy Sharp	22	(1)	6		28	(1)
Alan Bell	21	(6)	6	(1)	27	(7)
Fred McDiarmid	22	(3)	4		26	(3)
Peter Robertson	20		6		26	
Willie White	20	(6)	6	(3)	26	(9)
Dicky Boyle	16		5		21	
Tommy Robertson	13	(1)	6	(1)	19	(2)
George Henderson	12		0		12	
Jimmy Turnbull	12	(2)	0		12	(2)
Sam Gilligan	8	(3)	1		9	(3)
Jimmy Dickson	3	(4)	5	(3)	8	(7)
Dave "Chappie" Gowans	4		0		4	
Alick Halkett	2		2		4	
Jimmy Jeffray	0		1		1	
Joe Kerr	0		1		1	

Scottish League Division One

		Home			Away			Goals		
	P	W	D	L	W	D	L	F A		PTS
Hibernian	22	8	3	0	8	2	1	48-18		37
Dundee	**22**	**8**	**1**	**2**	**5**	**4**	**2**	**31-12**		**31**
Rangers	22	7	3	1	5	2	4	56-30		29
Hearts	22	6	2	3	5	4	2	46-27		28
Celtic	22	4	6	1	4	4	3	36-30		26
St Mirren	22	4	4	3	3	4	4	39-40		22
Third Lanark	22	6	2	3	2	3	6	34-27		21
Partick Thistle	22	4	4	3	2	3	6	34-50		19
Kilmarnock	22	3	3	5	3	1	7	24-43		16
Queens Park	22	4	3	4	1	2	8	33-48		15
Port Glasgow	22	3	3	5	0	2	9	26-49		11
Morton	22	2	1	8	0	4	7	22-55		9

No relegation, League increased to 14 teams with Airdrie and Motherwell promoted.

The Record		
League	-	Runners-up, Division One
Scottish Cup	-	Semi-final
Forfarshire Cup	-	Winners
Dewar Shield	-	Winners
Top Scorer	-	Willie White (9 goals)
Av. Home Gate	-	10,900
Players used	-	18
Sent off	-	None

Dundee F.C. Line-Ups 1902-03

		1	2	3	4	5	6	7	8	9	10	11
Aug	16th	Muir	Darroch	Sharp	Henderson	Boyle	Robertson P	Bell	MacFarlane	Turnbull	White	McDiarmid
	23rd	Muir	Darroch	Sharp	Henderson	Boyle	Robertson P	Bell	MacFarlane	Turnbull	White	McDiarmid
	30th	Muir	Darroch	Sharp	Henderson	Gowans	Robertson P	Bell	MacFarlane	Turnbull	White	McDiarmid
Sep	6th	Muir	Darroch	Sharp	Henderson	Gowans	Robertson P	Bell	White	Turnbull	MacFarlane	McDiarmid
	13th	Muir	Darroch	Sharp	Henderson	Boyle	Robertson P	Bell	White	Turnbull	MacFarlane	McDiarmid
	20th	Muir	Darroch	Sharp	Henderson	Robertson P	Gowans	Bell	White	Turnbull	MacFarlane	McDiarmid
	27th	Muir	Darroch	Sharp	Henderson	Robertson P	Gowans	Bell	White	Turnbull	MacFarlane	McDiarmid
Oct	4th	Muir	Darroch	Sharp	Henderson	Robertson P	Boyle	Bell	White	Turnbull	MacFarlane	McDiarmid
	11th	Muir	Darroch	Sharp	Henderson	Robertson P	Boyle	Robertson T	White	Turnbull	MacFarlane	McDiarmid
	18th	Muir	Darroch	Sharp	Henderson	Robertson P	McDiarmid	Robertson T	White	MacFarlane	Bell	Turnbull
	25th	Muir	Darroch	Sharp	Henderson	Robertson P	Boyle	Bell	Dickson	Turnbull	MacFarlane	McDiarmid
Nov	1st	Muir	Darroch	Sharp	Henderson	Robertson P	McDiarmid	Bell	White	Turnbull	MacFarlane	Robertson T
	15th	Muir	Darroch	Sharp	Boyle	Robertson P	McDiarmid	Bell	White	Gilligan	MacFarlane	Robertson T
	22nd	Muir	Darroch	Sharp	Boyle	Robertson P	McDiarmid	Bell	White	Gilligan	MacFarlane	Robertson T
	29th	Muir	Darroch	Sharp	Boyle	Robertson P	McDiarmid	Bell	White	Gilligan	MacFarlane	Robertson T
Dec	6th	Muir	Darroch	Sharp	Boyle	Halkett	McDiarmid	Bell	White	Gilligan	MacFarlane	Robertson T
	13th	Muir	Darroch	Sharp	Boyle	Robertson P	McDiarmid	Bell	White	Gilligan	MacFarlane	Robertson T
	20th	Muir	Darroch	Sharp	Boyle	Robertson P	McDiarmid	Bell	White	Gilligan	MacFarlane	Robertson T
	27th	Muir	Darroch	Sharp	Boyle	Robertson P	McDiarmid	Bell	White	Dickson	MacFarlane	Robertson T
Jan	17th	Muir	Darroch	Sharp	Boyle	Robertson P	McDiarmid	Bell	White	Dickson	MacFarlane	Robertson T
	24th	WALKOVER										
	31st	Muir	Darroch	Sharp	Boyle	Robertson P	McDiarmid	Bell	White	Dickson	MacFarlane	Robertson T
Feb	3rd	Muir	Darroch	Sharp	Boyle	Robertson P	McDiarmid	Bell	White	Dickson	MacFarlane	Robertson T
	14th	Muir	Darroch	Sharp	Halkett	Robertson P	Boyle	Bell	White	Dickson	MacFarlane	Robertson T
	21st	Muir	Darroch	Sharp	Halkett	Robertson P	Jeffray	Bell	White	Dickson	MacFarlane	Robertson T
	28th	Muir	Darroch	Sharp	Boyle	Robertson P	McDiarmid	Bell	White	Dickson	MacFarlane	Robertson T
Mar	7th	Muir	Darroch	Sharp	Boyle	Robertson P	McDiarmid	Bell	White	Gilligan	MacFarlane	Robertson T
	21st	Muir	Darroch	Sharp	Halkett	Boyle	McDiarmid	Bell	Kerr	Gilligan	MacFarlane	Robertson T
Apr	4th	Muir	Darroch	Sharp	Boyle	Robertson P	McDiarmid	Bell	White	Gilligan	MacFarlane	Robertson T

High drama - the Scottish Cup matched Dundee with high-flying Hibernian. It took three games - watched by a bumper 75,000 before a spectacular Johnny Bell goal decided the tie in the Dark Blues favour.

DC Thomson

They Wore The Dark Blue

Season 1903-04

Date			Opponents		Score	Crowd	Cash	Scorers
Aug	15th	L	Morton	h	6-0	10,200	£234	Wilson 2; MacFarlane (pen); Lennie; Bell; Dickson
	22nd	L	Queens Park	h	3-0	10,640	£241	McFarlane; 2; Lennie
	29th	L	Hearts	a	2-4	10,000	£348	Wilson; Bell
Sep	5th	L	Kilmarnock	h	4-0	8,740	£194	Lennie; Wilson; Dickson; Sharp (pen)
	12th	L	Port Glasgow	h	3-1	8,800	£200	Wilson 2; Lennie
	19th	L	Motherwell	a	3-1	-		Lennie; Dickson 2
	26th	L	St Mirren	a	0-2	8,000	£127	-
Oct	3rd	L	Third Lanark	h	0-1	11,480	£273	-
	10th	L	Celtic	a	2-4		£188	Horne; MacFarlane
	17th	L	Hearts	h	2-1	11,720	£275	Morgan; Wilson
	24th	L	St Mirren	h	1-1	9,560	£223	Dickson
	31st	L	Rangers	a	1-6	10,300	£251	Lennie
Nov	7th	L	Kilmarnock	a	1-0	-		Dickson
	14th	L	Airdrie	h	4-3	7,500	£157	Wilson; Sharp 2; Dickson
	21st	L	Rangers	h	3-1	14,400	£344	Boyle; Dickson; Robertson
	28th	L	Hibernian	a	1-0	1,500	£ 41	Dickson
Dec	5th	L	Motherwell	h	7-1	6,260	£133	Horne; Dickson 3; Bell; MacFarlane ; Morgan
	12th	L	Hibernian	h	1-2	10,000	£220	Morgan
	19th	L	Airdrie	a	1-2	-		Dickson
Jan	2nd	L	Morton	a	1-1	3,000	£ 81	McDiarmid
	9th	L	Queens Park	a	1-2	6,500	£150	Dickson
	16th	L	Partick Thistle	h	3-0	7,500	£155	Morgan; MacFarlane; Lennie
	16th	FC1	Forfar Athletic	a	0-0	2,000		-
	23rd	SC1	Queens Park	h	3-0	15,000	£364	Bell; Jeffrey; Morgan
	30th	L	Celtic	h	2-1	17,700	£420	MacFarlane; Boyle
Feb	6th	L	Partick Thistle	a	1-6	-		MacFarlane
	6th	FC1R	Forfar Athletic	h	8-1	3,000		Kerr 6; Halkett 2
	13th	SC2	Abercorn	h	4-0	5,000	-	Morgan 2; Boyle; Lennie
	20th	SC3	Celtic	a	1-1	19,000	£433	McAuley
	27th	SC3R	Celtic	h	0-0	21,000	£556	-
Mar	5th	SC3R	Celtic	a	0-5	39,000	£912	-
	12th	FCS	Wanderers	h	0-0	4,000		-
	19th	FCSR	Wanderers	a	1-3	3,000		Kerr
	26th	L	Port Glasgow	a	0-1	-		-
Apr	23rd	L	Third Lanark	a	1-4	7,000	£160	Cowie

Willie Lennie - winger joined Aberdeen after row at Dens.

Appearances

	League		Scottish Cup		Total	
Dicky Boyle	26	(2)	5	(1)	31	(3)
Fred McDiarmid	26	(1)	5		31	(1)
Sandy MacFarlane	26	(8)	5		31	(8)
Jimmy Jeffray	25		5	(1)	30	(1)
Billy Muir	23		5		28	
Alan Bell	21	(3)	5	(1)	26	(4)
Hugh Morgan	18	(4)	5	(3)	23	(7)
Willie Lennie	16	(7)	5	(1)	21	(8)
Jimmy Sharp	16	(3)	5		21	(3)
Jimmy Dickson	20	(14)	0		20	(14)
Alick Halkett	13		3		16	
Peter Robertson	13	(1)	0		13	(1)
David Wilson	13	(8)	0		13	(8)
Andy Horne	11	(2)	0		11	(2)
Johnny Darroch	8		2		10	
Willie McAuley	2		5	(1)	7	(1)
David Foster	3		0		3	
John Chaplin	2		0		2	
Arthur Brand	1		0		1	
Dave Cowie	1	(1)	0		1	(1)
Sam Gilligan	1		0		1	
Charlie Morris	1		0		1	

Scottish League Division One

		Home			Away			Goals		
	P	W	D	L	W	D	L	F	A	PTS
Third Lanark	26	10	2	1	10	1	2	61-26		43
Hearts	26	13	0	0	5	3	5	63-35		39
Celtic	26	11	1	1	7	1	5	69-28		38
Rangers	26	10	3	0	6	3	4	80-33		38
Dundee	**26**	**10**	**1**	**2**	**3**	**1**	**9**	**55-46**		**28**
St Mirren	26	10	1	2	1	4	8	45-38		27
Partick Thistle	26	7	4	2	3	3	7	43-40		27
Queens Park	26	4	7	2	2	2	9	28-47		21
Port Glasgow	26	6	3	4	2	1	10	33-49		20
Hibernian	26	5	3	5	2	2	9	31-42		19
Morton	26	5	1	7	2	3	8	31-51		18
Airdrie	26	5	1	7	2	3	8	32-62		18
Motherwell	26	5	1	7	1	2	10	26-61		15
Kilmarnock	26	3	3	7	1	2	12	27-66		13

The bottom 3 clubs applied for re-election with Hamilton, Clyde and Ayr of Division 2 applying for election. Airdrie, Motherwell and Kilmarnock were all re-elected.

The Record		
League	-	Fifth Place, Division One
Scottish Cup	-	Third round
Forfarshire Cup	-	Semi-final
Top Scorer	-	Jimmy Dickson (14 goals)
Av. Home Gate	-	10,350
Players used	-	22
Sent off	-	None

Dundee F.C. Line-Ups 1903-04

		1	2	3	4	5	6	7	8	9	10	11
Aug	15th	Muir	Darroch	Jeffray	Halkett	Boyle	McDiarmid	Bell	Dickson	Wilson	MacFarlane	Lennie
	22nd	Muir	Darroch	Jeffray	Halkett	Boyle	McDiarmid	Bell	Dickson	Wilson	MacFarlane	Lennie
	29th	Muir	Jeffray	Sharp	Halkett	Boyle	McDiarmid	Bell	Gilligan	Wilson	MacFarlane	Lennie
Sep	5th	Muir	Sharp	Jeffray	Halkett	Boyle	McDiarmid	Bell	Dickson	Wilson	MacFarlane	Lennie
	12th	Muir	Sharp	Jeffray	Halkett	Boyle	McDiarmid	Bell	Dickson	Wilson	MacFarlane	Lennie
	19th	Muir	Robertson	Jeffray	Halkett	Boyle	McDiarmid	Bell	Dickson	Wilson	MacFarlane	Lennie
	26th	Muir	Robertson	Jeffray	Boyle	Morris	McDiarmid	Bell	Dickson	Wilson	MacFarlane	Lennie
Oct	3rd	Muir	Chaplin J	Jeffray	Boyle	Robertson	McDiarmid	Bell	Dickson	Wilson	Morgan	MacFarlane
	10th	Muir	Boyle	Jeffray	Halkett	Robertson	McDiarmid	Bell	Morgan	Dickson	Horne	MacFarlane
	17th	Muir	Boyle	Jeffray	Halkett	Robertson	McDiarmid	Dickson	Morgan	Wilson	MacFarlane	Lennie
	24th	Muir	Bell	Jeffray	Halkett	Robertson	McDiarmid	Dickson	Morgan	Wilson	MacFarlane	Lennie
	31st	Muir	Boyle	Jeffray	Halkett	Robertson	McDiarmid	Dickson	Morgan	Wilson	MacFarlane	Lennie
Nov	7th	Muir	Sharp	Jeffray	Boyle	Robertson	McDiarmid	Dickson	Morgan	Wilson	MacFarlane	Lennie
	14th	Muir	Sharp	Jeffray	Boyle	Robertson	McDiarmid	Dickson	Morgan	Wilson	MacFarlane	Horne
	21st	Muir	Sharp	Jeffray	Boyle	Robertson	McDiarmid	Bell	Morgan	Dickson	MacFarlane	Horne
	28th	Foster	Sharp	Jeffray	Boyle	Robertson	McDiarmid	Bell	Morgan	Dickson	MacFarlane	Horne
Dec	5th	Muir	Sharp	Jeffray	Boyle	Robertson	McDiarmid	Bell	Morgan	Dickson	MacFarlane	Horne
	12th	Muir	Sharp	Jeffray	Boyle	Robertson	McDiarmid	Bell	Morgan	Dickson	MacFarlane	Horne
	19th	Muir	Sharp	Jeffray	Halkett	McDiarmid	Boyle	Bell	Morgan	Dickson	MacFarlane	Horne
Jan	2nd	Muir	Darroch	Jeffray	Halkett	Boyle	McDiarmid	Bell	MacFarlane	Dickson	Horne	Lennie
	9th	Muir	Darroch	Sharp	Halkett	Boyle	McDiarmid	Bell	Morgan	Dickson	MacFarlane	Lennie
	16th	Foster	Darroch	Sharp	Boyle	Jeffray	McDiarmid	Bell	Morgan	MacFarlane	Horne	Lennie
	23rd	Muir	Darroch	Sharp	Boyle	Jeffray	McDiarmid	Bell	Morgan	McAuley	MacFarlane	Lennie
	30th	Muir	Darroch	Sharp	Boyle	Jeffray	McDiarmid	Bell	Morgan	McAuley	MacFarlane	Lennie
Feb	6th	Foster	Darroch	Sharp	Boyle	Jeffray	McDiarmid	Bell	Morgan	McAuley	MacFarlane	Horne
	13th	Muir	Darroch	Sharp	Boyle	Jeffray	McDiarmid	Bell	Morgan	McAuley	MacFarlane	Lennie
	20th	Muir	Sharp	Jeffray	Halkett	Boyle	McDiarmid	Bell	Morgan	McAuley	MacFarlane	Lennie
	27th	Muir	Sharp	Jeffray	Halkett	Boyle	McDiarmid	Bell	Morgan	McAuley	MacFarlane	Lennie
Mar	5th	Muir	Sharp	Jeffray	Halkett	Boyle	McDiarmid	Bell	Morgan	McAuley	MacFarlane	Lennie
	26th	Muir	Darroch	Sharp	Boyle	Jeffray	McDiarmid	Bell	Morgan	Brand	MacFarlane	Horne
Apr	23rd	Muir	Chaplin J	Sharp	Boyle	Jeffray	McDiarmid	Bell	Morgan	Cowie	MacFarlane	Lennie

Up go the heads - Dundee are under pressure as Partick Thistle mount another attack at Firhill. The Dark Blues struggled to a 6-1 defeat, their biggest reverse of the season.   DC Thomson

They Wore The Dark Blue

Season 1904-05

Date			Opponents		Score	Crowd	Cash	Scorers
Aug	20th	L	St Mirren	h	2-0	7,500	£186	McAteer 2 (1 pen)
	27th	L	Queens Park	a	1-0	9,000	£200	MacFarlane
Sep	3rd	L	Airdrie	h	0-1	7,000	£163	-
	10th	L	Rangers	h	0-3	14,760	£341	-
	17th	L	Hibernian	a	1-1	7,000	-	Bell
	24th	L	Kilmarnock	h	3-0	7,000	£154	Brand; MacFarlane 2
Oct	1st	L	Motherwell	a	2-0	4,500	£112	McAteer; Cowie
	8th	L	St Mirren	a	1-1	-	-	Cowie
	15th	L	Morton	h	6-1	6,400	£137	Brown 3; Boyle; Cowie 2
	22nd	L	Partick Thistle	h	0-1	6,800	£157	-
	29th	L	Rangers	a	1-2	13,000	£279	MacFarlane
Nov	5th	L	Airdrie	a	0-2	5,500	£130	-
	12th	L	Hearts	h	2-0	7,300	£160	Wilson; Bell
	19th	L	Celtic	a	0-3	8,000	£178	-
Dec	3rd	L	Hibernian	h	4-1	-	£125	Cowie 2; Wilson; Findlay
	10th	L	Third Lanark	h	0-0	6,000	£123	-
	17th	L	Morton	a	1-5	2,000	£ 50	Brand
	26th	L	Third Lanark	a	2-2	3,000	-	Cowie 2
	31st	L	Port Glasgow	h	4-0	3,100	-	Cowie; MacFarlane 2; Brown
Jan	7th	L	Motherwell	h	0-0	5,000	£100	-
	14th	L	Celtic	h	2-1	13,000	-	Brown; Wilson
	21st	L	Partick Thistle	a	1-2	-	-	Brown
	21st	FC1	Wanderers	h	3-1	2,200	£54	Kerr 2; McHardy
	28th	SC1	Hearts	h	1-3	14,000	£360	MacFarlane
Feb	4th	FCS*	Forfar Athletic	a	4-2			McNaught; Kerr 2; McHardy
	11th	L	Kilmarnock	a	1-2	-	-	Jeffray
	25th	L	Hearts	a	1-3	-	-	Brand
Mar	25th	L	Port Glasgow	a	0-1	-	-	-
Apr	1st	L	Queens Park	h	3-0	3,500	£ 85	Bell; Brown; Cowie
	8th	DSS	Aberdeen	h	2-1	5,000		McHardy; Kerr
	21st	F	Middlesbrough	a	0-1	3,000	-	-
	22nd	F	New Brompton	a	3-1			MacFarlane 2; Brown
	22nd	DSF	Alloa Athletic	h	4-0	3,000		Burnett 2; Findlay 2
	24th	F	Woolwich Arsenal	a	0-3*	5,000	-	-
	25th	F	Bradford	a	3-3	5,000	-	Cowie 2; McFarlane

John Chaplin - part of 1910 Scottish Cup side

* Jeffray sent off for kicking Bellamy, later to join Dundee ** Arbroath unable to play final and trophy awarded to Dundee.

Appearances

	League	Scottish Cup	Total
Dicky Boyle	26 (1)	1	27 (1)
John Chaplin	25	1	26
Alan Bell	24 (3)	1	25 (3)
Sandy MacFarlane	24 (6)	1 (1)	25 (7)
Billy Muir	24	1	25
Dave Cowie	23 (10)	1	24 (10)
Jimmy Jeffray	22 (1)	1	23 (1)
Tom McAteer	22 (3)	1	23 (3)
Fred McDiarmid	19	0	19
Tom Brown	13 (7)	0	13 (7)
Arthur Brand	12 (3)	1	13 (3)
David Wilson*	10 (3)	0	10 (3)
John McKenzie	9	0	9
Jim Burnett	8	0	8
Bob Findlay	7 (1)	1	8 (1)
Hugh McNaught	7	1	8
Billy Thomson	5	0	5
John McHardy	3	0	3
Matthew Riley	2	0	2
Johnny Darroch	1	0	1

* Later that term the ex-Raith Rovers player joined Hearts before moving to Leeds United. However, on October 27th, 1906, while playing for the Elland Road club, Wilson collapsed after heading the ball and died of heart failure.

Scottish League Division One

		Home			Away			Goals		
	P	W	D	L	W	D	L	F A		PTS
Celtic	26	8	4	1	10	1	2	68-31		41
Rangers	26	10	1	2	9	2	2	83-28		41
Third Lanark	26	11	1	1	3	6	4	60-28		35
Airdrie	26	6	4	3	5	1	7	38-45		27
Hibernian	26	7	5	1	2	3	8	39-39		26
Partick Thistle	26	8	0	5	4	2	7	36-56		26
Dundee	**26**	**8**	**2**	**3**	**2**	**3**	**8**	**38-32**		**25**
Hearts	26	10	0	3	1	3	9	43-44		25
Kilmarnock	26	8	2	3	1	3	9	29-45		23
St Mirren	26	4	4	5	5	0	8	33-36		22
Port Glasgow	26	6	3	4	2	2	9	30-48		21
Queens Park	26	5	3	5	1	5	7	28-45		20
Morton	26	6	3	4	1	1	11	27-50		18
Motherwell	26	4	1	8	2	1	10	28-53		14

No relegation, League increased to 16 clubs. Falkirk (2nd) and Aberdeen (7th) from Division Two are elected.

The Record		
League	-	Seventh Place, Division One
Scottish Cup	-	First round
Forfarshire Cup	-	Winners**
Dewar Shield	-	Winners
Top Scorer	-	Dave Cowie (10 goals)
Av. Home Gate	-	7,300
Players used	-	20
Sent off	-	None

Dundee F.C. Line-Ups 1904-05

		1	2	3	4	5	6	7	8	9	10	11
Aug	20th	Muir	Chaplin J	Jeffray	Boyle	McAteer	McDiarmid	Bell	Brand	Burnett	MacFarlane	Thomson
	27th	Muir	Chaplin J	Jeffray	Boyle	McAteer	McDiarmid	Bell	Brand	McHardy	MacFarlane	Thomson
Sep	3rd	Muir	Chaplin J	Jeffray	Boyle	McAteer	McDiarmid	Bell	Brand	Wilson	MacFarlane	Thomson
	10th	Muir	Darroch	Chaplin J	Boyle	Jeffray	McDiarmid	Bell	Brand	McAteer	MacFarlane	Cowie
	17th	Muir	Chaplin J	Jeffray	Boyle	McAteer	McDiarmid	Bell	Brand	Brown	MacFarlane	Cowie
	24th	Muir	Chaplin J	Jeffray	Boyle	McAteer	McDiarmid	McHardy	Brand	Brown	MacFarlane	Cowie
Oct	1st	Muir	Chaplin J	Jeffray	Boyle	McAteer	McDiarmid	McHardy	Brand	Brown	MacFarlane	Cowie
	8th	Muir	Chaplin J	McKenzie	Boyle	McAteer	McDiarmid	Bell	Brand	Brown	MacFarlane	Cowie
	15th	Muir	Chaplin J	McKenzie	Boyle	McAteer	McDiarmid	Bell	Brand	Brown	MacFarlane	Cowie
	22nd	Muir	Chaplin J	Jeffray	Boyle	McAteer	McDiarmid	Bell	Brand	Brown	MacFarlane	Cowie
	29th	Muir	Chaplin J	McKenzie	Boyle	Jeffray	McDiarmid	Bell	MacFarlane	Brown	Thomson	Cowie
Nov	5th	Muir	Chaplin J	McKenzie	Boyle	Jeffray	McDiarmid	Bell	MacFarlane	Burnett	Thomson	Cowie
	12th	Muir	Chaplin J	McKenzie	Boyle	McAteer	McDiarmid	Bell	Wilson	Burnett	MacFarlane	Cowie
	19th	Muir	Chaplin J	McKenzie	Boyle	McAteer	McDiarmid	Bell	Wilson	Burnett	MacFarlane	Cowie
Dec	3rd	Muir	Chaplin J	McKenzie	Boyle	McAteer	Jeffray	Bell	Wilson	Cowie	MacFarlane	Findlay
	10th	Muir	Chaplin J	McKenzie	Boyle	McAteer	Jeffray	Bell	Wilson	Cowie	MacFarlane	Findlay
	17th	Muir	Chaplin J	McKenzie	Boyle	McAteer	Jeffray	Bell	Wilson	Cowie	MacFarlane	Brand
	26th	Riley	Chaplin J	McNaught	Boyle	McAteer	Jeffray	Bell	Wilson	Cowie	MacFarlane	Findlay
	31st	Muir	Chaplin J	McNaught	Boyle	McAteer	Jeffray	Bell	Brown	Cowie	MacFarlane	Findlay
Jan	7th	Muir	Chaplin J	McNaught	Boyle	McAteer	Jeffray	Bell	Wilson	Cowie	MacFarlane	Findlay
	14th	Muir	McNaught	Jeffray	Boyle	McAteer	McDiarmid	Bell	Brand	Wilson	Cowie	Findlay
	21st	Muir	Chaplin J	McNaught	Boyle	McAteer	Jeffray	Bell	Brand	Wilson	Cowie	Findlay
	28th	Muir	Chaplin J	McNaught	Boyle	McAteer	Jeffray	Bell	Brand	Cowie	MacFarlane	Findlay
Feb	11th	Muir	Chaplin J	McNaught	Boyle	Jeffray	McDiarmid	Bell	Brand	Burnett	MacFarlane	Cowie
	25th	Riley	Chaplin J	McNaught	Boyle	Jeffray	McDiarmid	Bell	MacFarlane	Burnett	Cowie	Brand
Mar	25th	Muir	Chaplin J	Jeffray	Boyle	McAteer	McDiarmid	Bell	MacFarlane	Brown	Burnett	Cowie
Apr	1st	Muir	Chaplin J	Jeffray	Boyle	McAteer	McDiarmid	Bell	MacFarlane	Brown	Burnett	Cowie

North East derby - Dundee beat Aberdeen 2-1 in the Dewar Shield semi-final at Dens.
Aberdeen were formed in 1903 after Orion and Victoria United amalgamated.

They Wore The Dark Blue

Season 1905-06

Date			Opponents		Score	Crowd	Cash	Scorers
Aug	19th	L	St Mirren	h	1-2	9,500	£214	Fraser (pen)
	26th	L	Hibernian	a	1-2	5,000	£104	Bell
	30th	B	Rangers	h	1-4	4,000		McLuckie
			(Fred McDiarmid Benefit)					
Sep	2nd	L	Morton	h	3-1	6,300	£127	Dainty (pen); McLuckie; MacFarlane
	9th	L	Partick Thistle	h	1-1	6,000	£136	McLuckie
	16th	L	Motherwell	a	1-4	-	-	Webb
	23rd	L	Queens Park	h	1-0	7,280	£159	Dainty (pen)
	30th	L	Port Glasgow	a	1-1	3,800	£ 70	Bell
Oct	7th	L	Kilmarnock	h	2-1	4,800	£100	McDiarmid; Webb
	9th	F	Newcastle United	h	1-1	6,000	£133	McLuckie
	14th	L	Rangers	a	1-1		£271	MacFarlane
	21st	L	Hearts	h	1-1	14,000	£341	Nimmo
	28th	L	Celtic	a	1-3		£213	Webb
Nov	4th	L	Third Lanark	h	2-0	8,000	£152	McLuckie; Fraser
	11th	L	Falkirk	a	0-2	-	£ 89	
	18th	L	Aberdeen	h	6-0	13,000	£279	McLuckie 3; Henderson; MacFarlane 2
	25th	L	Airdrie	h	2-1	-	-	MacFarlane; Dainty
Dec	2nd	L	St Mirren	a	1-1	-	-	MacFarlane
	9th	L	Falkirk	h	3-0	8,300	£178	MacFarlane; Webb 2
	16th	L	Kilmarnock	a	2-2	-	-	Fraser 2
	23rd	L	Hibernian	h	1-1	8,600	£199	MacFarlane
	25th	L	Third Lanark	a	2-1	2,500	£ 74	Webb; McLuckie
	30th	L	Port Glasgow	h	1-1	5,800	£129	Webb
Jan	1st	F	Derby County	h	1-1	10,000	£196	Webb
	6th	L	Aberdeen	a	2-1	4,000		Dainty; Bell
	13th	L	Hearts	a	0-4	-	-	-
	20th	L	Motherwell	h	2-0	6,800	£124	Dainty (pen); McLuckie
	27th	SC1	Celtic	h	1-2	26,000	£670	Fraser
Feb	3rd	L	Celtic	h	1-0	10,800	£189	McLuckie
	3rd	FCS	Arbroath	a	0-2	1,500		-
	17th	L	Rangers	h	1-1	10,000	£208	McLuckie
	24th	L	Morton	a	0-0	-	-	-
Mar	3rd	L	Partick Thistle	a	0-1	-	-	-
	10th	L	Airdrie	h	0-0	5,000	£106	-
	31st	L	Queens Park	a	0-0	-	£ 95	-

The Record		
League	-	Seventh Place, Division One
Scottish Cup	-	First round
Forfarshire Cup	-	Semi-final
Top Scorer	-	Jimmy McLuckie (10 goals)
Av. Home Gate	-	6,600
Players used	-	18
Sent off	-	One

Appearances

	League		Scottish Cup		Total	
Herbert Dainty	30	(5)	1		31	(5)
Billy Muir	30		1		31	
Fred McDiarmid	29	(1)	1		30	(1)
Jack Fraser	28	(4)	1	(1)	29	(5)
Jimmy McLuckie	28	(10)	1		29	(10)
Charlie Webb	28	(7)	1		29	(7)
Jimmy Jeffray	26		1		27	
George Henderson	25	(1)	1		26	(1)
Sandy MacFarlane	24	(8)	1		25	(8)
John McKenzie	24		1		25	
Alan Bell	22	(3)	0		22	(3)
Dave Cowie	10		0		10	
Johnny Darroch	8		0		8	
Alex Mitchell	5		1		6	
Dicky Boyle	5		0		5	
Tom McAteer	4		0		4	
Allan Nimmo	3	(1)	0		3	(1)
James Lyon	1		0		1	

Scottish League Division One

		Home			Away			Goals		
	P	W	D	L	W	D	L	F	A	PTS
Celtic	30	13	0	2	11	1	3	76-19		49
Hearts	30	12	3	0	6	4	5	64-27		43
Airdrie	30	8	4	3	7	4	4	53-31		38
Rangers	30	9	2	4	6	5	4	58-48		37
Partick Thistle	30	9	3	3	6	3	6	44-40		36
Third Lanark	30	10	0	5	6	2	7	62-38		34
Dundee	**30**	**8**	**6**	**1**	**3**	**6**	**6**	**40-33**		**34**
St Mirren	30	10	2	3	3	3	9	41-37		31
Morton	30	5	5	5	5	1	9	35-54		26
Motherwell	30	7	4	4	2	4	9	50-64		26
Hibernian	30	7	1	7	3	4	8	35-40		25
Aberdeen	30	7	4	4	1	4	10	36-48		24
Falkirk	30	7	5	3	2	0	13	52-68		23
Kilmarnock	30	8	3	4	0	1	14	46-68		20
Port Glasgow	30	4	3	8	2	5	8	38-68		20
Queens Park	30	4	3	8	1	1	13	41-88		14

No relegation, League increased to 18 clubs with Clyde (2nd) and Hamilton (4th) elected from Division Two.

Dundee F.C. Line-Ups 1905-06

		1	2	3	4	5	6	7	8	9	10	11
Aug	19th	Muir	McAteer	McKenzie	Henderson	Dainty	McDiarmid	Bell	MacFarlane	McLuckie	Fraser	Cowie
	26th	Muir	Darroch	McKenzie	Boyle	Dainty	McDiarmid	Bell	Cowie	McLuckie	MacFarlane	Fraser
Sep	2nd	Muir	Darroch	McKenzie	Boyle	Dainty	McDiarmid	Webb	Fraser	McLuckie	MacFarlane	Cowie
	9th	Muir	Darroch	McKenzie	Boyle	Dainty	McDiarmid	Webb	MacFarlane	McLuckie	Fraser	Cowie
	16th	Muir	Darroch	Jeffray	McAteer	Dainty	Henderson	Webb	MacFarlane	McLuckie	Cowie	Fraser
	23rd	Muir	Darroch	Jeffray	Henderson	Dainty	McDiarmid	Bell	Webb	Cowie	McLuckie	Fraser
	30th	Muir	Darroch	Jeffray	Henderson	Dainty	McDiarmid	Bell	Webb	Cowie*	McLuckie	Fraser
Oct	7th	Muir	Darroch	Jeffray	Henderson	Dainty	McDiarmid	Bell	Webb	Cowie	McLuckie	Fraser
	14th	Muir	Darroch	Jeffray	Henderson	Dainty	McDiarmid	Bell	MacFarlane	Webb	McLuckie	Fraser
	21st	Muir	McKenzie	Jeffray	Henderson	Dainty	McDiarmid	Bell	Nimmo	Webb	McLuckie	Fraser
	28th	Muir	McKenzie	Jeffray	Henderson	Dainty	McDiarmid	Bell	Nimmo	Webb	MacFarlane	Fraser
Nov	4th	Muir	McKenzie	Jeffray	Henderson	Dainty	McDiarmid	Bell	MacFarlane	Webb	McLuckie	Fraser
	11th	Muir	McKenzie	Jeffray	Henderson	Dainty	McDiarmid	Bell	MacFarlane	Webb	McLuckie	Fraser
	18th	Muir	McKenzie	Jeffray	Henderson	Dainty	McDiarmid	Bell	MacFarlane	Webb	McLuckie	Fraser
	25th	Muir	McKenzie	Jeffray	Henderson	Dainty	McDiarmid	Bell	MacFarlane	Webb	McLuckie	Fraser
Dec	2nd	Muir	McKenzie	Jeffray	Henderson	Dainty	McDiarmid	Bell	MacFarlane	Webb	McLuckie	Fraser
	9th	Muir	McKenzie	Jeffray	Henderson	Dainty	McDiarmid	Bell	MacFarlane	Webb	McLuckie	Fraser
	16th	Muir	McKenzie	Jeffray	McAteer	Dainty	McDiarmid	Bell	MacFarlane	Webb	McLuckie	Fraser
	23rd	Muir	McKenzie	Jeffray	McAteer	Dainty	McDiarmid	Bell	MacFarlane	Webb	McLuckie	Fraser
	25th	Muir	McKenzie	Jeffray	Henderson	Dainty	McDiarmid	Bell	MacFarlane	Webb	McLuckie	Fraser
	30th	Muir	McKenzie	Jeffray	Henderson	Dainty	McDiarmid	Bell	MacFarlane	Webb	Cowie	Fraser
Jan	6th	Muir	McKenzie	Jeffray	Henderson	Dainty	Boyle	Bell	MacFarlane	Webb	McLuckie	McDiarmid
	13th	Muir	McKenzie	Jeffray	Henderson	Dainty	Boyle	Bell	MacFarlane	Webb	McLuckie	McDiarmid
	20th	Muir	McKenzie	Jeffray	Henderson	Dainty	McDiarmid	Mitchell	MacFarlane	Webb	McLuckie	Fraser
	27th	Muir	McKenzie	Jeffray	Henderson	Dainty	McDiarmid	Mitchell	MacFarlane	Webb	McLuckie	Fraser
Feb	3rd	Muir	McKenzie	Jeffray	Henderson	Dainty	McDiarmid	Mitchell	MacFarlane	Webb	McLuckie	Fraser
	17th	Muir	McKenzie	Jeffray	Henderson	Dainty	McDiarmid	Bell	MacFarlane	Webb	McLuckie	Fraser
	24th	Muir	McKenzie	Jeffray	Henderson	Dainty	McDiarmid	Mitchell	MacFarlane	Webb	McLuckie	Fraser
Mar	3rd	Muir	McKenzie	Jeffray	Henderson	Dainty	McDiarmid	Mitchell	Cowie	Webb	McLuckie	Fraser
	10th	Muir	McKenzie	Jeffray	Henderson	Dainty	McDiarmid	Mitchell	MacFarlane	Webb	McLuckie	Fraser
	31st	Muir	Lyon	Jeffray	Henderson	Dainty	McDiarmid	Bell	Webb	McLuckie	Nimmo	Fraser

Dundee F.C. Season 1905-06. BACK - William Wallace (manager), unknown, Alan Bell, Billy Muir, unknown, John Darroch, unknown, Jack Fraser, Bill Longair (trainer). FRONT - both unknown, Sandy MacFarlane, Herbert Dainty, Fred McDiarmid, unknown, Geordie Henderson.

They Wore The Dark Blue

Season 1906-07

Date			Opponents		Score	Crowd	Cash	Scorers
Aug	18th	L	Port Glasgow	h	0-1	8,600	£190	
	25th	L	Hamilton	a	3-1	6,000	£148	MacFarlane; Cox; Dainty
Sep	1st	L	Falkirk	h	3-2	7,000	£158	Cox 2; Dainty (pen)
	8th	L	Hearts	a	0-0	-		
	22nd	L	Rangers	h	2-0	14,600	£337	Cox; Russell
	24th	L	Clyde	a	1-1	4,000	£ 96	Dainty
	29th	L	Hibernian	a	4-0	6,000	£137	Cox 2; Fraser; MacFarlane
Oct	6th	L	Morton	h	1-0	7,400	£161	Dainty (pen)
	13th	L	Motherwell	a	3-0			Webb; Russell; Fraser
	20th	L	Celtic	h	0-0	27,000	£725	-
	27th	L	Partick Thistle	a	0-0	4,000	£100	-
Nov	3rd	L	Kilmarnock	h	4-2	8,100	£172	Dainty; MacFarlane; Jeffray; Cox
	10th	L	Aberdeen	h	0-0	10,200	£230	-
	17th	L	St Mirren	a	1-1			Russell
	24th	L	Airdrie	a	2-1	6,300	£135	Cox; MacFarlane
Dec	1st	L	Port Glasgow	a	1-1			Fraser
	8th	L	Aberdeen	a	3-0	9,500	£214	Webb 2; Cox
	15th	L	Partick Thistle	h	5-0	7,800	£172	MacFarlane; Dainty; McDermott; Fraser; Cox
	22nd	L	Morton	a	2-1	4,006	£100	Webb; McDermott
	25th	L	Third Lanark	a	0-2	5,500	£135	
	29th	L	St Mirren	h	2-1	4,400	£ 88	Cox; McDermott
Jan	1st	L	Clyde	h	0-1	8,380	£185	
	12th	L	Queens Park	a	2-1	6,000	£145	Mitchell; McDermott
	19th	L	Motherwell	h	1-0	7,500	£163	MacFarlane
Feb	9th	SC1	Partick Thistle	a	2-2	13,160	£301	Webb; Cox
	16th	SC1R	Partick Thistle	h	5-1	18,080	£421	McDermott 3; Cox 2
	23rd	SC2	Renton	a	0-1	6,500	£153	-
	23rd	FC1	Montrose	a	0-0			-
Mar	2nd	L	Third Lanark	h	2-1	5,500	£119	McDermott; Fraser
	9th	L	Kilmarnock	a	3-1	-		Fraser; McDermott; Cox
	9th	FC1R	Montrose	h	3-0			McDonald 2; Thomson
	16th	L	Hamilton	h	1-0	5,000	£ 92	Cox
	23rd	L	Celtic	a	0-0	35,000	£803	-
	23rd	FCS	Lochee United	h	5-1	2,500		Carmichael 2; Nimmo; Thomson 2 (1 pen)
	30th	L	Airdrie	h	1-1	6,600	£141	Jeffray
Apr	1st	L	Rangers	a	2-2	12,000		Cox 2
	6th	L	Falkirk	a	2-4	4,500	£105	McDermott; Cox
	6th	FCF	Arbroath	h	0-1	2,000		-
	8th	L	Hearts	h	2-0	5,800	£120	Cox 2
	13th	L	Queens Park	h	0-0	6,500	£140	-
	20th	L	Hibernian	h	0-0	5,100	£105	-

Sandy MacFarlane - quality forward from Newcastle.

The Record

League	-	Second Place, Division One
Scottish Cup	-	Second round
Forfarshire Cup	-	Runners-up
Top Scorer	-	Billy Cox (21 goals)
Av. Home Gate	-	8,600
Players used	-	19
Sent off	-	One

Appearances

	League		Scottish Cup		Total	
Herbert Dainty	34	(6)	3		37	(6)
Sandy MacFarlane	34	(6)	3		37	(6)
John McKenzie	34		3		37	
Billy Muir	32		3		35	
Billy Cox	31	(18)	3	(3)	34	(21)
Jack Fraser	30	(6)	3		33	(6)
Jimmy Jeffray	31	(2)	1		32	(2)
Bert Lee	28		3		31	
Charlie Webb	26	(4)	3	(1)	29	(5)
Tommy McDermott	20	(7)	3	(3)	23	(10)
George Henderson	20		0		20	
Stuart McDonald	13		3		16	
Albert Oswald	13		2		15	
John Russell	9	(3)	0		9	(3)
Alex Mitchell	8	(1)	0		8	(1)
Davie Glen	4		0		4	
Bob Crumley	2		0		2	
Alex. Fairweather	2		0		2	
Allan Nimmo	2		0		2	
James Reid	1		0		1	

Scottish League Division One

		Home			Away			Goals		
	P	W	D	L	W	D	L	F	A	PTS
Celtic	34	13	4	0	10	5	2	80-30		55
Dundee	**34**	**10**	**5**	**2**	**8**	**7**	**2**	**53-26**		**48**
Rangers	34	9	5	3	10	2	5	69-33		45
Airdrie	34	12	1	4	6	5	6	59-44		42
Falkirk	34	12	4	1	5	3	9	73-58		41
Third Lanark	34	8	5	4	7	4	6	57-48		39
St Mirren	34	6	8	3	6	5	6	50-44		37
Clyde	34	9	3	5	6	3	8	47-52		36
Hearts	34	7	7	3	4	6	7	46-43		35
Motherwell	34	8	3	6	4	6	7	45-48		33
Aberdeen	34	7	6	4	3	4	10	48-54		30
Hibernian	34	7	5	5	3	5	9	40-49		30
Morton	34	9	4	4	2	2	13	41-50		28
Partick Thistle	34	7	3	7	2	5	10	40-60		26
Queens Park	34	7	1	9	2	5	10	51-66		24
Hamilton	34	5	1	11	3	4	10	40-64		21
Kilmarnock	34	7	3	7	1	2	14	40-72		21
Port Glasgow	34	4	6	7	3	1	13	30-67		21

The bottom three clubs were re-elected ahead of St Bernards, Vale of Leven and Arthurlie from Division Two.

Dundee F.C. Line-Ups 1906-07

		1	2	3	4	5	6	7	8	9	10	11
Aug	18th	Muir	McKenzie	Jeffray	Lee	Dainty	Henderson	Oswald	Webb	Cox	MacFarlane	Fraser
	25th	Muir	McKenzie	Jeffray	Lee	Dainty	Henderson	Webb	Nimmo	Cox	MacFarlane	Fraser
Sep	1st	Muir	McKenzie	Jeffray	Lee	Dainty	Henderson	Webb	Fairweather	Cox	MacFarlane	Fraser
	8th	Muir	McKenzie	Jeffray	Lee	Dainty	Henderson	Webb	Fairweather	Cox	MacFarlane	Fraser
	22nd	Muir	McKenzie	Jeffray	Lee	Dainty	Henderson	Webb	Russell	Cox	MacFarlane	Fraser
	24th	Muir	McKenzie	Jeffray	Lee	Dainty	Henderson	Webb	Russell	Cox	MacFarlane	Fraser
	29th	Muir	McKenzie	Oswald	Lee	Dainty	Jeffray	Webb	Russell	Cox	MacFarlane	Fraser
Oct	6th	Muir	McKenzie	Oswald	Lee	Dainty	Jeffray	Webb	Nimmo	Cox	MacFarlane	Fraser
	13th	Muir	McKenzie	Jeffray	Lee	Dainty	Henderson	Webb	Russell	Cox	MacFarlane	Fraser
	20th	Muir	McKenzie	Jeffray	Lee	Dainty	Henderson	Webb	Russell	Cox	MacFarlane	Fraser
	27th	Muir	McKenzie	Jeffray	Lee	Dainty	Henderson	Webb	Cox	Oswald	MacFarlane	Russell
Nov	3rd	Muir	McKenzie	Jeffray	Lee	Dainty	Henderson	Webb	Russell	Cox	MacFarlane	Mitchell
	10th	Muir	McKenzie	Jeffray	Lee	Dainty	Henderson	Webb	Russell	Cox	MacFarlane	Mitchell
	17th	Muir	McKenzie	Jeffray	Lee	Dainty	Henderson*	Webb	Russell	Cox	MacFarlane	Fraser
	24th	Muir	McKenzie	Jeffray	Lee	Dainty	Henderson	Webb	McDermott	Cox	MacFarlane	Fraser
Dec	1st	Muir	McKenzie	Jeffray	Lee	Dainty	Henderson	Webb	McDermott	Cox	MacFarlane	Fraser
	8th	Muir	McKenzie	Jeffray	Lee	Dainty	Henderson	Webb	McDermott	Cox	MacFarlane	Fraser
	15th	Muir	McKenzie	Jeffray	Lee	Dainty	McDonald	Webb	McDermott	Cox	MacFarlane	Fraser
	22nd	Muir	McKenzie	Jeffray	Lee	Dainty	McDonald	Webb	McDermott	Cox	MacFarlane	Fraser
	25th	Muir	McKenzie	Jeffray	Lee	Dainty	McDonald	Mitchell	McDermott	Webb	MacFarlane	Fraser
	29th	Muir	McKenzie	Oswald	Lee	Dainty	McDonald	Mitchell	McDermott	Cox	MacFarlane	Fraser
Jan	12th	Muir	McKenzie	Oswald	Lee	Ramsay	McDonald	Mitchell	McDermott	Cox	MacFarlane	Fraser
	19th	Muir	McKenzie	Oswald	Lee	Dainty	Henderson	Mitchell	McDermott	Cox	MacFarlane	Fraser
Feb	9th	Muir	McKenzie	Oswald	Lee	Dainty	McDonald	Webb	McDermott	Cox	MacFarlane	Fraser
	16th	Muir	McKenzie	Oswald	Lee	Dainty	McDonald	Webb	McDermott	Cox	MacFarlane	Fraser
	23rd	Muir	McKenzie	Jeffray	Lee	Dainty	McDonald	Webb	McDermott	Cox	MacFarlane	Fraser
Mar	2nd	Crumley	McKenzie	Jeffray	Lee	Dainty	McDonald	Reid	McDermott	Cox	MacFarlane	Fraser
	9th	Muir	McKenzie	Oswald	Lee	Dainty	Henderson	Webb	McDermott	Cox	MacFarlane	Fraser
	16th	Crumley	McKenzie	Jeffray	Lee	Dainty	Henderson	Webb	McDermott	Cox	MacFarlane	Mitchell
	23rd	Muir	McKenzie	Oswald	Lee	Dainty	Jeffray	Glen	McDermott	Cox	MacFarlane	Fraser
	30th	Muir	McKenzie	Oswald	Henderson	Dainty	Jeffray	McDonald	McDermott	Cox	MacFarlane	Fraser
Apr	1st	Muir	McKenzie	Jeffray	Henderson	Dainty	McDonald	Webb	McDermott	Cox	MacFarlane	Fraser
	6th	Muir	McKenzie	Jeffray	Henderson	Dainty	McDonald	MacFarlane	McDermott	Glen	Cox	Fraser
	8th	Muir	McKenzie	Oswald	McDonald	Dainty	Jeffray	Webb	McDermott	Cox	MacFarlane	Fraser
	13th	Muir	McKenzie	Oswald	McDonald	Dainty	Jeffray	Webb	McDermott	Glen	MacFarlane	Fraser
	20th	Muir	McKenzie	Oswald	McDonald	Dainty	Jeffray	Webb	McDermott	Glen	MacFarlane	Fraser

A kick in time - Dundee's Scottish international keeper Billy Muir boots the ball clear of the onrushing Partick Thistle forwards in the league match at Dens.   DC Thomson

They Wore The Dark Blue

Season 1907-08

Date		Opponents		Score	Crowd	Cash	Scorers
Aug	17th L	Falkirk	a	2-1	-	£145	McDermott; Hunter
	24th L	Partick Thistle	h	1-0	10,000	£242	Dean (pen)
	31st L	Celtic	a	2-3	27,000	£733	MacFarlane; Dean (pen)
Sep	7th L	Airdrie	h	3-1	10,280	£240	Webb 3
	14th L	Hearts	a	0-1	18,000	£436	
	21st L	Aberdeen	h	1-0	10,000	£217	Dean (pen)
	24th L	Morton	h	5-2	8,280	£210	Webb; McDermott 2; Dean (pen); MacFarlane
Oct	5th L	Motherwell	a	1-0	6,000	£166	Fraser
	12th L	Clyde	h	6-1	8,000		Hunter 3; Webb; Neal; Dainty
	19th L	Queens Park	h	5-0	7,000	£183	Hunter 3; Webb; Dainty
	26th L	St Mirren	h	6-0	17,000	£378	McDermott 4; Hunter; Jeffray
Nov	2nd L	Hibernian	a	1-0	10,000	£249	Hunter
	9th L	Third Lanark	h	1-0	9,800	£226	Dainty
	16th L	Port Glasgow	a	5-0	1,200	£37	MacFarlane 3; Hunter 2
	23rd L	Kilmarnock	h	4-0	9,000	£209	MacFarlane; Dainty; McDermott; Hunter
	30th L	Hamilton	h	3-0	8,000	£198	MacFarlane 2; McDermott
Dec	7th L	Aberdeen	a	1-1	17,000	£410	Hunter
	14th L	Morton	a	2-2	4,500	£111	Dainty; Lee
	21st L	Rangers	h	1-2	15,000	£335	Hunter
	25th L	Third Lanark	a	1-1	8,000	£197	Dean (pen)
	28th L	Clyde	a	3-2	-		Dainty; Lee; Hunter
Jan	1st L	Port Glasgow	h	3-1	10,000	£190	Currie; Neal; Dainty
	2nd L	Hibernian	h	0-1	11,000	£242	-
	4th L	Hearts	h	0-0	9,000	£232	-
	11th L	Airdrie	a	2-0	-		Dean; Webb
	18th L	Partick Thistle	a	3-0	-		Dainty (pen); Hunter; MacFarlane
	25th SC1	Airdrie	a	1-0	9,000	£276	Neal
Feb	1st L	Motherwell	h	0-0	8,000	£196	-
	8th SC2	Aberdeen	a	0-0	15,000		-
	8th FC1	Wanderers	h	4-1			Currie; Hall 2; Jackson
	15th SC2R	Aberdeen	h	2-2	24,000	£594	Hall 2
	22nd SC2R	Aberdeen	lbr	1-3	19,525		Hall
	29th L	Falkirk	h	2-2	8,000		Langlands; Dean
Mar	7th L	Hamilton	a	1-2	5,500	£140	Hunter
	14th L	Queens Park	a	3-1	13,000	£328	Dean 2 (1 pen); Langlands
	14th FCS	Montrose	h	1-1			Currie
	21st L	Kilmarnock	a	1-1	5,500	£139	Fraser
	21st FCSR	Montrose	a	0-0			-
	28th L	Celtic	h	2-0	16,000	£385	Dean (pen); Hunter
	28th FCSR	Montrose	a	3-5 aet*			Jackson; Hall 2
Apr	20th L	Rangers	a	0-2	-		-
	28th L	St Mirren	a	0-0	-		-

*After extra-time, 3-3 after 90 minutes

Herbert Dainty - centre-half with the scoring touch.

The Record	
League	- Fourth Place, Division One
Scottish Cup	- Second round
Forfarshire Cup	- Semi-final
Top Scorer	- John Hunter (18 goals)
Av. Home Gate	- 10,250
Players used	- 19
Sent off	- None

Appearances

	League		Scottish Cup		Total	
Bob Crumley	34		4		38	
Herbert Dainty	33	(8)	4		37	(8)
Jack Fraser	33	(2)	4		37	(2)
Sandy MacFarlane	33	(9)	4		37	(9)
George Chaplin	32		4		36	
John McKenzie	31		4		35	
John Hunter	30	(18)	4		34	(18)
Bert Lee	28	(2)	4		32	(2)
Jimmy Jeffray	25	(1)	4		29	(1)
Charlie Webb	21	(7)	3		24	(7)
Alfred Dean	18	(10)	1		19	(10)
Bert Neal	17	(2)	2	(1)	19	(3)
Tommy McDermott	17	(9)	0		17	(9)
James Jackson	7		0		7	
George Langlands	7	(2)	0		7	(2)
Sandy Hall	3		2	(3)	5	(3)
Archie Harper	3		0		3	
Pat Currie	1	(1)	0		1	(1)
Jimmy Lawson	1		0		1	

Scottish League Division One

		Home			Away			Goals		
	P	W	D	L	W	D	L	F	A	PTS
Celtic	34	15	2	0	9	5	3	86-27		55
Falkirk	34	13	2	2	9	5	3	103-42		51
Rangers	34	10	5	2	11	3	3	74-40		50
Dundee	**34**	**12**	**3**	**2**	**8**	**5**	**4**	**71-28**		**48**
Hibernian	34	10	1	6	7	7	3	55-45		42
Airdrie	34	10	3	4	8	2	7	58-41		41
St Mirren	34	6	6	5	7	4	6	50-59		36
Aberdeen	34	9	5	3	3	4	10	45-44		35
Third Lanark	34	8	3	6	5	4	8	45-50		33
Motherwell	34	8	2	7	4	5	8	61-53		31
Hamilton	34	7	6	4	3	2	12	55-65		28
Hearts	34	9	1	7	2	5	10	50-62		28
Morton	34	5	6	6	4	3	10	43-66		27
Partick Thistle	34	3	7	7	5	2	10	38-61		25
Kilmarnock	34	5	7	5	1	6	10	38-61		25
Queens Park*	34	5	5	7	2	3	12	54-84		22
Clyde*	34	4	4	9	1	4	12	36-75		18
Port Glasgow*	34	3	4	10	2	3	12	39-98		17

* Re-elected ahead of Abercorn, Raith Rovers and Vale of Leven from Division 2.

Dundee F.C. Line-Ups 1907-08

		1	2	3	4	5	6	7	8	9	10	11
Aug	17th	Crumley	McKenzie	Chaplin	Lee	Dainty	Jeffray	Dean	McDermott	Hunter	MacFarlane	Fraser
	24th	Crumley	McKenzie	Chaplin	Lee	Dainty	Jeffray	Dean	McDermott	Hunter	MacFarlane	Fraser
	31st	Crumley	McKenzie	Chaplin	Lee	Dainty	Jeffray	Dean	McDermott	Hunter	MacFarlane	Fraser
Sep	7th	Crumley	McKenzie	Chaplin	Lee	Dainty	Jeffray	Dean	Hunter	Webb	MacFarlane	Fraser
	14th	Crumley	McKenzie	Chaplin	Lee	Dainty	Jeffray	Dean	Hunter	Webb	MacFarlane	Fraser
	21st	Crumley	McKenzie	Chaplin	Lee	Dainty	Jeffray	Dean	Hunter	Webb	MacFarlane	Fraser
	24th	Crumley	McKenzie	Chaplin	Lee	Dainty	Jeffray	Dean	McDermott	Webb	MacFarlane	Fraser
Oct	5th	Crumley	McKenzie	Chaplin	Lee	Dainty	Jeffray	Dean	McDermott	Webb	MacFarlane	Fraser
	12th	Crumley	McKenzie	Chaplin	Neal	Dainty	Jeffray	Webb	McDermott	Hunter	MacFarlane	Fraser
	19th	Crumley	McKenzie	Chaplin	Neal	Dainty	Jeffray	Webb	McDermott	Hunter	MacFarlane	Jackson
	26th	Crumley	McKenzie	Chaplin	Neal	Dainty	Jeffray	Webb	McDermott	Hunter	MacFarlane	Fraser
Nov	2nd	Crumley	McKenzie	Chaplin	Neal	Dainty	Jeffray	Webb	McDermott	Hunter	MacFarlane	Fraser
	9th	Crumley	McKenzie	Chaplin	Neal	Dainty	Jeffray	Webb	McDermott	Hunter	MacFarlane	Fraser
	16th	Crumley	McKenzie	Chaplin	Neal	Dainty	Jeffray	Webb	McDermott	Hunter	MacFarlane	Fraser
	23rd	Crumley	McKenzie	Chaplin	Lee	Dainty	Neal	Webb	McDermott	Hunter	MacFarlane	Fraser
	30th	Crumley	McKenzie	Chaplin	Lee	Dainty	Jeffray	Webb	McDermott	Hunter	MacFarlane	Fraser
Dec	7th	Crumley	McKenzie	Chaplin	Lee	Dainty	Jeffray	Webb	McDermott	Hunter	MacFarlane	Fraser
	14th	Crumley	McKenzie	Chaplin	Lee	Dainty	Jeffray	Webb	McDermott	Hunter	MacFarlane	Fraser
	21st	Crumley	McKenzie	Chaplin	Lee	Dainty	Jeffray	Webb	McDermott	Hunter	MacFarlane	Fraser
	25th	Crumley	McKenzie	Chaplin	Lee	Dainty	Jeffray	Dean	MacFarlane	Hunter	Fraser	Jackson
	28th	Crumley	McKenzie	Chaplin	Lee	Dainty	Jeffray	Dean	MacFarlane	Hunter	Fraser	Jackson
Jan	1st	Crumley	McKenzie	Harper	Neal	Dainty	Lee	Dean	MacFarlane	Currie	Fraser	Jackson
	2nd	Crumley	McKenzie	Chaplin	Neal	Lee	Jeffray	Webb	MacFarlane	Hunter	Fraser	Jackson
	4th	Crumley	McKenzie	Chaplin	Lee	Dainty	Jeffray	Webb	MacFarlane	Hunter	Fraser	Jackson
	11th	Crumley	McKenzie	Chaplin	Lee	Dainty	Jeffray	Dean	Hunter	Webb	MacFarlane	Fraser
	18th	Crumley	McKenzie	Chaplin	Lee	Dainty	Neal	Webb	McDermott	Hunter	MacFarlane	Fraser
	25th	Crumley	McKenzie	Chaplin	Lee	Dainty	Jeffray	Webb	Neal	Hunter	MacFarlane	Fraser
Feb	1st	Crumley	McKenzie	Chaplin	Lee	Dainty	Jeffray	Jackson	Hunter	Webb	MacFarlane	Fraser
	8th	Crumley	McKenzie	Chaplin	Lee	Dainty	Jeffray	Webb	Neal	Hunter	MacFarlane	Fraser
	15th	Crumley	McKenzie	Chaplin	Lee	Dainty	Jeffray	Webb	Hunter	Hall	MacFarlane	Fraser
	19th	Crumley	McKenzie	Chaplin	Lee	Dainty	Jeffray	Dean	Hunter	Hall	MacFarlane	Fraser
	29th	Crumley	McKenzie	Chaplin	Lee	Dainty	Neal	Dean	Hunter	Langlands	MacFarlane	Fraser
Mar	7th	Crumley	Harper	Jeffray	Lee	Dainty	Neal	Dean	Langlands	Hunter	Hall	Fraser
	14th	Crumley	McKenzie	Chaplin	Lee	Dainty	Neal	Dean	Langlands	Hall	MacFarlane	Fraser
	21st	Crumley	McKenzie	Chaplin	Lee	Dainty	Neal	Dean	Langlands	Hunter	MacFarlane	Fraser
	28th	Crumley	Harper	Chaplin	Lee	Dainty	Neal	Dean	Langlands	Hunter	MacFarlane	Fraser
Apr	20th	Crumley	McKenzie	Chaplin	Lee	Dainty	Neal	Dean	Langlands	Hunter	MacFarlane	Fraser
	28th	Crumley	Lawson	Chaplin	Lee	Dainty	Neal	Hall	Langlands	Hunter	MacFarlane	Fraser

The Scotland team which beat Wales 2-1 at Dens Park in 1908. (BACK), Mr Liddell (SFA President), Mr Mason, (Burslem, referee), Bill Longair (trainer). MIDDLE - Walker (Hearts), McNair (Celtic), Gault (Rangers), G. Chaplin and MacFarlane (both Dundee), Mr McDowall (SFA secretary). FRONT - Lennie (Aberdeen), Agnew (Kilmarnock), Thomson (Hearts), Rennie (Hibs) and Speirs (Rangers). DC Thomson

They Wore The Dark Blue

Season 1908-09

Date			Opponents		Score	Crowd	Cash	Scorers
Aug	15th	L	Hearts	h	2-1	12,000	£297	Hunter; Langlands
	22nd	L	Airdrie	a	5-2	-	-	Fraser 3; Hunter; Langlands
	29th	L	Celtic	h	2-1	21,000	£525	Hunter; Bellamy
Sep	5th	L	Partick Thistle	a	1-1	3,000	£111	Lee
	12th	L	Falkirk	h	1-1	11,000	£290	Hunter
	19th	L	Morton	a	0-0	5,000	£131	-
	26th	L	Queens Park	h	7-1	7,000	£175	Hunter 3; MacFarlane 3; Bellamy
	28th	L	Rangers	a	0-2	34,000	£792	-
Oct	3rd	L	Hamilton	a	1-0	5,000	£134	Lee
	10th	L	Celtic	a	0-2	14,000	£437	-
	17th	L	Hibernian	h	3-0	9,000	£226	Hunter; MacFarlane; Fraser
	24th	L	Aberdeen	a	1-1	12,500	£345	Langlands
	31st	L	Motherwell	h	3-1	7,000	£185	Bellamy; Hunter 2
Nov	7th	L	Port Glasgow	a	3-2	2,000		Bellamy; Langlands; Hunter
	14th	L	Kilmarnock	h	5-0	7,000	£180	MacFarlane; Bellamy 2 (1 pen); Hunter; Fraser
	21st	L	Falkirk	a	3-3	7,000	£180	Langlands; Bellamy; Hunter
	28th	L	Airdrie	h	1-0	7,000		Hunter
Dec	12th	L	Aberdeen	h	2-2	14,000	£333	Dainty (pen); Hunter
	19th	L	St Mirren	h	4-1	9,000	£194	Hunter; Langlands; Dainty; MacFarlane
	25th	L	Third Lanark	a	1-2	7,000	£176	Hunter
	26th	L	Kilmarnock	a	0-2			-
Jan	1st	L	Port Glasgow	h	1-0	7,000	£181	Hunter
	2nd	L	Motherwell	a	4-1	6,000	£146	Hunter 2; Lee; MacFarlane
	9th	L	Rangers	h	4-0	16,000	£401	Hunter 3; MacFarlane
	16th	L	Partick Thistle	h	3-2	6,000	£136	McCann; Hunter 2
	23rd	SC1	Ayr Parkhouse	h	9-0	12,000	£220	Hunter 3; Bellamy 3 (2 pen); MacFarlane; Dainty; Langlands
	30th	L	Clyde	h	1-0	14,000	£304	Bellamy
Feb	6th	SC2	Rangers	h	0-0	28,000	£778**	-
	13th	SC2R	Rangers	a	0-1	54,500	£1,621	-
	13th	FC1	Arbroath	a	3-1	2,000		Hall; Cooper; Kemp
	20th	L	Hibernian	a	1-0	-		Bellamy
	27th	L	Morton	h	1-2	6,000	£142	Fraser
	27th	FCS	Forfar Athletic	a	0-0			-
Mar	6th	L	Clyde	a	2-0	3,000	£113	Bellamy; Hunter
	6th	FCSR	Forfar Athletic	h	4-1	3,000		Hall 4
	13th	L	St Mirren	a	2-1	7,000	£179	Dainty; MacFarlane
	20th	L	Hearts	a	0-1		£302	-
	20th	FCF	Brechin City	h	2-0	3,000		Kemp 2
	27th	L	Third Lanark	h	1-0	6,000	£143	Lee
	27th	DSS	Aberdeen	a	0-0*	4,000		-
Apr	3rd	L	Hamilton	h	3-0	5,000	£102	Hunter; Langlands; Mair
	24th	L	Queens Park	a	2-0	6,000	£145	Bellamy; Langlands

* Dundee refused to play extra-time as stipulated and subsequently scratched after being unable to fit in replay.
** Official attendance, estimated crowd was actually 31,000

Jack Fraser - appearance for Scotland while at Dens.

The Record		
League	-	Runners-up, Division One
Scottish Cup	-	Second round
Forfarshire Cup	-	Winners
Dewar Shield	-	Semi-final
Top Scorer	-	John Hunter (32 goals)
Av. Home Gate	-	9,650
Players used	-	19
Sent off	-	One

Appearances

	League		Scottish Cup		Total	
Bob Crumley	33		3		36	
Bert Lee	33	(4)	3		36	(4)
Sandy MacFarlane	33	(9)	3	(1)	36	(10)
Jack Fraser	32	(4)	3		35	(4)
John Hunter	32	(29)	3	(3)	35	(32)
Jimmy Bellamy	31	(11)	3	(3)	34	(14)
Herbert Dainty	30	(3)	3	(1)	33	
Bert Neal	30		3		33	
George Langlands	29	(8)	3	(1)	32	(9)
John Chaplin	26		3		29	
Jimmy Lawson	25		0		25	
Davie Mair	16	(1)	3		19	(1)
Davie McCann	7	(1)	0		7	(1)
George Chaplin	6		0		6	
Albert Oswald	4		0		4	
Sandy Hall	3		0		3	
Willie Cooper	2		0		2	
Fred Kemp	1		0		1	
George Phillip	1		0		1	

Scottish League Division One

		Home			Away			Goals		
	P	W	D	L	W	D	L	F A		PTS
Celtic	34	11	3	3	12	2	3	71-21		51
Dundee	34	14	2	1	8	4	5	**70-32**		**50**
Clyde	34	12	2	3	9	4	4	61-37		48
Rangers	34	10	5	2	9	2	5	91-38		45
Airdrie	34	8	5	4	8	4	5	67-46		41
Hibernian	34	12	3	2	4	4	9	40-32		39
St Mirren	34	11	2	4	4	4	9	53-45		36
Aberdeen	34	11	2	4	4	4	9	61-53		36
Falkirk	34	10	4	3	3	3	11	58-56		33
Kilmarnock	34	11	2	4	2	5	10	47-61		33
Third Lanark	34	9	4	4	2	6	9	56-49		32
Hearts	34	8	5	4	4	2	10	54-49		32
Port Glasgow	34	6	5	6	4	3	10	39-52		28
Motherwell	34	8	3	6	3	3	11	47-73		28
Queens Park	34	2	6	9	4	7	6	42-65		25
Hamilton*	34	4	7	6	2	5	10	42-72		24
Morton*	34	5	6	6	3	1	13	39-90		23
Partick Thistle*	34	2	1	14	0	3	14	38-102		8

* Re-elected ahead of Abercorn, Raith Rovers and Vale of Leven from Division Two

Dundee F.C. Line-Ups 1908-09

		1	2	3	4	5	6	7	8	9	10	11
Aug	15th	Crumley	Lawson	Chaplin G	Lee	Dainty	Neal	Bellamy	MacFarlane	Hunter	Langlands	Fraser
	22nd	Crumley	Lawson	Chaplin G	Neal	Dainty	Mair	Bellamy	Langlands	Hunter	MacFarlane	Fraser
	29th	Crumley	Lawson	Chaplin G	Lee	Dainty	Neal	Bellamy	Langlands	Hunter	MacFarlane	Fraser
Sep	5th	Crumley	Lawson	Chaplin G	Lee	Dainty	Neal	Bellamy	Langlands	Hunter	MacFarlane	Fraser
	12th	Crumley	Lawson	Oswald	Lee	Dainty	Neal	Bellamy	Langlands	Hunter	MacFarlane	Fraser
	19th	Crumley	Lawson	Chaplin G	Neal	Lee	Mair	Hall	Hunter	Bellamy	MacFarlane	Fraser
	26th	Crumley	Lawson	Chaplin G	Lee	Dainty	Neal	Bellamy	Langlands	Hunter	MacFarlane	Cooper
	28th	Crumley	Lawson	Chaplin J	Lee	Dainty	Neal	Bellamy	Langlands	Hunter	MacFarlane	Cooper
Oct	3rd	Crumley	Lawson	Chaplin J	Lee	Dainty	Neal	Bellamy	Langlands	Hunter	MacFarlane	Fraser
	10th	Philip	Lawson	Chaplin J	Lee	Dainty	Neal	Hall	Langlands	Hunter	Fraser	McCann
	17th	Crumley	Lawson	Chaplin J	Neal	Lee	Mair	Bellamy	Langlands	Hunter	MacFarlane	Fraser
	24th	Crumley	Lawson	Chaplin J	Lee	Dainty	Neal	Bellamy	Langlands	Hunter	MacFarlane	Fraser
	31st	Crumley	Lawson	Chaplin J	Lee	Dainty	Neal	Bellamy	Langlands	Hunter	MacFarlane	Fraser
Nov	7th	Crumley	Lawson	Chaplin J	Lee	Dainty	Neal	Bellamy	Langlands	Hunter	MacFarlane	Fraser
	14th	Crumley	Lawson	Chaplin J	Lee	Dainty	Neal	Bellamy	Langlands	Hunter	MacFarlane	Fraser
	21st	Crumley	Lawson	Chaplin J	Lee	Dainty	Neal	Bellamy	Langlands	Hunter	MacFarlane	Fraser
	28th	Crumley	Lawson	Chaplin J	Lee	Dainty	Neal	Bellamy	Langlands	Hunter	MacFarlane	Fraser
Dec	5th	Crumley	Lawson	Chaplin J	Lee	Dainty	Neal	Bellamy	Langlands	Hunter	MacFarlane	Fraser
	12th	Crumley	Lawson*	Chaplin J	Lee	Dainty	Neal	Bellamy	Langlands	Hunter	MacFarlane	Fraser
	19th	Crumley	Lawson	Chaplin J	Lee	Dainty	Neal	Bellamy	Langlands	Hunter	MacFarlane	Fraser
	25th	Crumley	Oswald	Chaplin J	Lee	Dainty	Neal	Bellamy	Langlands	Hunter	MacFarlane	Fraser
	26th	Crumley	Oswald	Chaplin J	Lee	Dainty	Neal	Bellamy	Langlands	Hunter	MacFarlane	Fraser
Jan	1st	Crumley	Neal	Chaplin J	Lee	Dainty	Mair	Bellamy	McCann	Hunter	MacFarlane	Fraser
	2nd	Crumley	Neal	Chaplin J	Lee	Dainty	Mair	Bellamy	McCann	Hunter	MacFarlane	Fraser
	9th	Crumley	Neal	Chaplin J	Lee	Dainty	Mair	Bellamy	McCann	Hunter	MacFarlane	Fraser
	16th	Crumley	Neal	Oswald	Lee	Dainty	Mair	Bellamy	McCann	Hunter	MacFarlane	Fraser
	23rd	Crumley	Neal	Chaplin J	Lee	Dainty	Mair	Bellamy	Langlands	Hunter	MacFarlane	Fraser
	30th	Crumley	Neal	Chaplin J	Lee	Dainty	Mair	Bellamy	Langlands	Hunter	MacFarlane	Fraser
Feb	6th	Crumley	Neal	Chaplin J	Lee	Dainty	Mair	Bellamy	Langlands	Hunter	MacFarlane	Fraser
	13th	Crumley	Neal	Chaplin J	Lee	Dainty	Mair	Bellamy	Langlands	Hunter	MacFarlane	Fraser
	20th	Crumley	Neal	Chaplin J	Lee	Dainty	Mair	Bellamy	Langlands	Hunter	MacFarlane	Fraser
	27th	Crumley	Lawson	Chaplin J	Lee	Dainty	Mair	McCann	Kemp	Langlands	MacFarlane	Fraser
Mar	6th	Crumley	Lawson	Chaplin J	Lee	Dainty	Mair	Bellamy	Langlands	Hunter	MacFarlane	Fraser
	13th	Crumley	Lawson	Chaplin J	Lee	Dainty	Mair	Bellamy	Langlands	Hunter	MacFarlane	Fraser
	20th	Crumley	Lawson	Chaplin J	Lee	Dainty	Mair	Hall	McCann	Langlands	MacFarlane	Fraser
	27th	Crumley	Neal	Chaplin J	Lee	Dainty	Mair	Bellamy	Langlands	Hunter	MacFarlane	Fraser
Apr	3rd	Crumley	Lawson	Chaplin J	Neal	Lee	Mair	Bellamy	Langlands	Hunter	MacFarlane	Fraser
	24th	Crumley	Lawson	Chaplin J	Neal	Lee	Mair	Bellamy	Langlands	Hunter	MacFarlane	Fraser

New crowd record - after crushing Ayr Parkhouse 9-0 in the first round, Dundee met Rangers before a new record crowd of 28,000 at Dens. This was 4,000 higher than the previous best of 24,000 against Hibs in 1903 and Aberdeen in 1908. DC Thomson

Season 1909-10

Date		Opponents		Score	Crowd	Scorers
Aug	21st	L	Motherwell	h	2-0	10,000	Menzies; Bellamy (pen)
	28th	L	Morton	a	0-1		-
Sep	4th	L	Rangers	h	4-2	17,000	Langlands; McCann 2; Fraser
	18th	L	St Mirren	h	2-1	12,000	Langlands; MacFarlane
	27th	L	Rangers	a	1-2	35,000	Lee
Oct	2nd	L	Celtic	a	0-1		
	16th	L	Kilmarnock	h	2-2	10,000	Lee; Bellamy
	23rd	L	St Mirren	a	2-3		Bellamy 2
	30th	L	Third Lanark	h	2-0	9,000	Hunter; MacFarlane
Nov	6th	L	Hibernian	a	0-0		
	13th	L	Hearts	h	4-1	12,000	Hunter; Langlands; Fraser; Bellamy
	20th	L	Port Glasgow	h	4-0	8,000	Hall 2; Bellamy; MacFarlane
	27th	L	Queens Park	a	0-3	8,000	-
Dec	4th	L	Clyde	h	1-1	7,000	McCann
	11th	L	Falkirk	a	1-6		Lee
	18th	L	Airdrie	h	3-0	6,000	Bellamy 2; Fraser
	25th	L	Third Lanark	a	2-0		Dainty; Hunter
Jan	1st	L	Aberdeen	h	0-0	12,000	-
	3rd	L	Hearts	a	0-1		-
	8th	L	Hamilton	a	3-3		Hall; Bellamy 2
	15th	L	Falkirk	h	1-0	18,000	Hall
	22nd	SC1	Beith	a*	1-1	9,000	G. Comrie
	29th	SC1R	Beith	h	1-0	6,000	Langlands
Feb	5th	SC2	Falkirk	h	3-0	20,000	Hall; Bellamy; Hunter
	12th	L	Morton	h	2-1	8,000	Hunter; Bellamy
	19th	FC1	Dundee Hibs	a	2-1	6,000	Hall 2
	26th	SC3	Motherwell	a	3-1	15,000	Hall 3
Mar	5th	L	Hamilton	h	2-1	8,000	Hall; Langlands
	5th	FCS	Arbroath	a	0-3	2,000	-
	12th	SCS	Hibernian	a	0-0	17,000	-
	19th	SCSR	Hibernian	h	0-0	23,000	-
	23rd	SCSR	Hibernian	Park.	1-0	20,000	Hunter
	26th	L	Port Glasgow	a	3-0	8,000	Bellamy; McCann; Langlands
	28th	L	Partick Thistle	a	0-1	12,000	-
Apr	2nd	L	Queens Park	h	3-0	6,000	Hunter 2; Richmond o.g.
	6th	L	Partick Thistle	h	1-1	3,000	Hall
	9th	SCF	Clyde	Ibrox	2-2	60,000	Hunter; Langlands
	13th	L	Hibernian	h	4-2	6,000	Hall 2; Dinnie 2
	16th	SCFR	Clyde	Ibrox	0-0	20,000	-
	19th	L	Airdrie	a	0-3		-
	20th	SCFR	Clyde	Ibrox	2-1	24,000	Bellamy; Hunter
	23rd	L	Aberdeen	a	1-3	8,000	Fraser
	25th	L	Motherwell	a	1-1		Bellamy
	26th	L	Kilmarnock	a	1-2		Langlands
	27th	L	Clyde	a	0-2		-
	30th	L	Celtic	h	0-0	10,000	

* Beith conceded ground rights, and played at Dens. Cup Cash v. Hibs (Parkhead) £660; v. Clyde (1st replay) £762-17/- (2nd replay) £796-19/-

John Hunter - got winning goal in Scottish Cup Final

The Record		
League	-	Sixth Place, Division One
Scottish Cup	-	Winners
Forfarshire Cup	-	Semi-final
Top Scorer	-	Jimmy Bellamy (15 goals)
Av. Home Gate	-	10,000
Players used	-	30
Sent off	-	Two

Appearances

	League		Scottish Cup		Total	
Bob Crumley	31		10		41	
Jack Fraser	29	(4)	10		39	(4)
Herbert Dainty	28	(1)	10		38	(1)
Jimmy Bellamy	27	(13)	10	(2)	37	(15)
Bert Lee	27	(3)	10		37	(3)
John Hunter	26	(6)	10	(4)	36	(10)
John Chaplin	26		9		35	
George Langlands	25	(6)	8	(2)	33	(8)
George Comrie	22		10	(1)	32	(1)
Sandy MacFarlane	20	(3)	7		27	(3)
Sandy Hall	20	(8)	5	(4)	25	(12)
Jimmy Lawson	21		4		25	
Bert Neal	10		6		16	
Davie Mair	14		0		14	
Bob McEwan	10		1		11	
Davie McCann	10	(4)	0		10	(4)
John Graydon	8		0		8	
Charlie Dinnie	6	(2)	0		6	(2)
John Comrie	5		0		5	
Davie Gowans	3		0		3	
George Phillip (gk)	3		0		3	
James Jackson	2		0		2	
Alex Menzies	2	(2)	0		2	
Jim Munro	2		0		2	
Frank Allan	1		0		1	
Tom Dorward	1		0		1	

Scottish League Division One

	P	Home			Away			Goals		PTS
		W	D	L	W	D	L	F A		
Celtic	34	13	4	0	11	2	4	63-22		54
Falkirk	34	14	3	0	8	8	4	71-28		52
Rangers	34	14	2	1	6	4	7	70-35		46
Aberdeen	34	10	4	3	6	4	7	44-29		40
Clyde	34	10	4	3	4	5	8	47-40		37
Dundee	**34**	**12**	**5**	**0**	**2**	**7**	**12**	**69-44**		**36**
Third Lanark	34	10	2	5	3	6	8	62-44		34
Hibernian	34	10	4	3	4	2	11	33-40		34
Airdrie	34	7	5	5	5	4	8	47-57		33
Motherwell	34	8	5	4	4	3	10	59-60		32
Kilmarnock	34	10	3	4	2	5	10	53-59		32
Hearts	34	9	3	5	4	3	10	53-40		31
St Mirren	34	11	0	6	2	5	10	48-58		31
Queens Park	34	8	5	4	4	1	12	50-74		30
Hamilton	34	9	4	4	2	2	13	50-67		28
Partick Thistle	34	6	6	5	2	4	11	45-59		26
Morton	34	9	1	7	2	2	13	38-60		25
Port Glasgow*	34	2	3	12	1	2	14	25-93		11

* Relegated after losing out to Raith Rovers in election vote.

Appearances (Ctd.)

	League	S/Cup	Total
Jim Lang	1	0	1
James Lyon	1	0	1
George Richardson	1	0	1
George Steven	1	0	1

Dundee FC Line-Ups 1909-10

		1	2	3	4	5	6	7	8	9	10	11
Aug	21st	Crumley	Lawson	Chaplin J	Lee	Dainty	Neal	Bellamy	Langlands	Menzies	MacFarlane	Fraser
	28th	Crumley	Lawson	Chaplin J	Lee	Dainty	Neal	Langlands	MacFarlane	Hall	Menzies	Fraser
Sep	4th	Crumley	Lawson	Chaplin J	Lee	Dainty	Mair	Bellamy	McCann	Langlands	McFarlane	Fraser
	18th	Crumley	Lawson	Chaplin J	Lee	Dainty	Mair	Bellamy	McCann	Langlands	MacFarlane	Fraser
	27th	Crumley	Lawson	Chaplin J	Lee	Dainty	Mair	Bellamy	McCann	Langlands	MacFarlane	Fraser
Oct	2nd	Crumley	Neal	Chaplin J	Lee	Dainty	Neal	Bellamy	McCann	Langlands	MacFarlane	Fraser
	16th	Crumley	Lawson	Chaplin J	Lee	Dainty	Mair	Bellamy	Langlands	Hunter	Steven	Fraser
	23rd	Crumley	Dainty	Chaplin J	Lee	Comrie	Mair	Bellamy	Langlands	Hunter	MacFarlane	Fraser
	30th	Crumley	Lawson	Chaplin J	Lee	Dainty	Comrie	Bellamy	Langlands	Hunter	MacFarlane	Fraser
Nov	6th	Crumley	Lawson	Chaplin J	Lee	Dainty	Comrie	Bellamy	Langlands	Hunter	MacFarlane	Fraser
	13th	Crumley	Lawson	Chaplin J	Lee	Dainty	Comrie	Bellamy	Langlands	Hunter	MacFarlane	Fraser
	20th	Crumley	Lawson	Chaplin J	Lee	Dainty	Comrie	Bellamy	Langlands	Hall	MacFarlane	Fraser
	27th	Crumley	Lawson	Chaplin J	Neal	Dainty	Comrie	Bellamy	Langlands	Hall	MacFarlane	Fraser
Dec	4th	Crumley	Lawson	Chaplin J	Lee	Dainty	Comrie	Bellamy	Langlands	Hall	McCann	Fraser
	11th	Crumley	Lawson	Chaplin J	Lee	Dainty	Comrie	Bellamy	Langlands	Hall	McCann	Fraser
	18th	Crumley	Chaplin J	McEwan	Lee	Comrie	Mair	Bellamy	Langlands	Hall	Graydon	Fraser
	25th	Crumley	Chaplin J	McEwan	Lee	Dainty	Comrie	Hall	Langlands	Hunter	MacFarlane	Fraser
Jan	1st	Crumley	Chaplin J	McEwan	Lee	Dainty	Comrie	Bellamy	Langlands	Hunter	MacFarlane	Fraser
	3rd	Crumley	Chaplin J	McEwan	Lee	Dainty	Comrie	Bellamy	Langlands	Hunter	MacFarlane	Fraser
	8th	Crumley	Neal	Chaplin	Lee	Dainty	Comrie	Bellamy	Huntere	Hall	MacFarlane	Fraser
	15th	Crumley	Neal	Chaplin	Lee	Dainty	Comrie	Bellamy	Hunter	Hall	MacFarlane	Fraser
	22nd	Crumley	Neal	Chaplin J	Lee	Dainty	Comrie	Bellamy	Hunter	Hall	MacFarlane	Fraser
	29th	Crumley	Neal	Chaplin J	Lee	Dainty	Comrie	Bellamy	Langlands	Hunter	MacFarlane	Fraser
Feb	5th	Crumley	Neal	Chaplin J	Lee	Dainty	Comrie	Bellamy	Hunter	Hall	MacFarlane	Fraser
	12th	Crumley	Neal	Chaplin J	Lee	Dainty	Comrie	Bellamy	Hunter	Hall	Mair	Fraser
	26th	Crumley	Neal	Chaplin J	Lee	Dainty	Comrie	Bellamy	Hunter	Hall	Langlands*	Fraser
Mar	5th	Crumley	Lawson	Chaplin J	Lee	Dainty	Comrie	Bellamy	Hunter	Hall	Langlands	Fraser
	12th	Crumley	Lawson	Chaplin J	Lee	Dainty	Comrie	Bellamy	Hunter	Hall	Langlands	Fraser
	19th	Crumley	Lawson	Chaplin J	Lee	Dainty	Comrie	Bellamy	Hunter	Hall	Langlands	Fraser
	23rd	Crumley	Lawson	Chaplin J	Lee	Dainty	Comrie	Bellamy	Langlands	Hunter	MacFarlane	Fraser
	26th	Crumley	Lawson	Chaplin J	Lee	Comrie	Mair	Bellamy	Newman*	Langlands	MacFarlane	McCann
	28th	Crumley	Lawson	Chaplin J	Lee	Dainty	Mair	Hall	Langlands	Hunter	MacFarlane	Fraser
Apr	2nd	Crumley	Allan	Chaplin J	Neal	Dainty	Mair	Bellamy	Langlands	Hunter	MacFarlane	Fraser
	6th	Phillip	Neal	McEwan	Gowans	Comrie J	Comrie G	McCann	Dinnie	Hall	Graydon	Jackson
	9th	Crumley	Lawson	Chaplin J	Lee	Dainty	Comrie G	Bellamy	Langlands	Hunter	MacFarlane	Fraser
	13th	Phillip	Lawson	McEwan	Gowans	Comrie J	Comrie G	McCann	Dinnie	Hall	Graydon	Jackson
	16th	Crumley	Neal	Chaplin J	Lee	Dainty	Comrie G	Bellamy	Langlands	Hunter	MacFarlane	Fraser
	19th	Phillip	Lawson	Dorward	Gowans	Comrie J	Mair	Richardson	Dinnie	Hall	Graydon	Munro
	20th	Crumley	Neal	McEwan	Lee	Dainty	Comrie	Bellamy	Langlands	Hunter	MacFarlane	Fraser
	23rd	Crumley	Neal	McEwan	Lee	Dainty	Comrie	Bellamy	Richardson	Hunter	Langlands	Munro
	25th	Crumley	Lawson	Langlands	Lee	Dainty	Mair	Bellamy	Hunter	Hall	Graydon	Fraser
	26th	Crumley	Lyon	McEwan	Dinnie	Comrie J	Mair	Hall	Graydon	Langlands	Bellamy	Fraser
	27th	Crumley	Lawson	McEwan	Comrie J	Dainty	Comrie G	Hall	Langlands	Hunter	Dinnie	Fraser
	30th	Crumley	Lawson	McEwan	Lee	Dainty	Comrie G	Bellamy	Graydon	Hall	McCann	Fraser

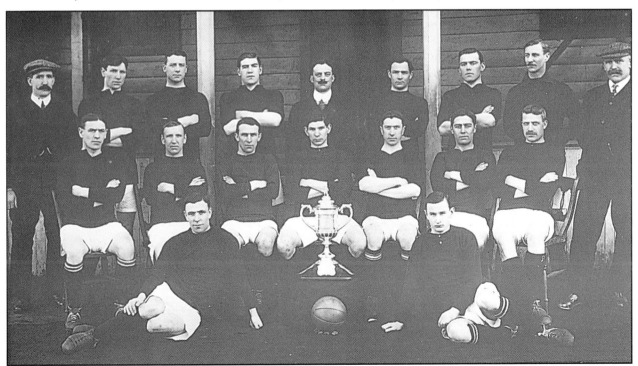

Dundee F.C.'s 1909-10 Scottish Cup winning squad. (BACK, left to right) Jimmy Dundas (trainer), Bert Neal, Bob McEwan, George Comrie, William Wallace (manager), Herbert Dainty, John Chaplin, Bob Crumley, Bill Longair (trainer). MIDDLE - Sandy Hall, John Hunter, George Langlands, Bert Lee, Sandy MacFarlane, Jimmy Lawson, Jack Fraser. FRONT - Jimmy Bellamy and Davie McCann.

Season 1910-11

Date			Opponents		Score	Crowd	Scorers
Aug	20th	L	Motherwell	a	0-3	9,000	-
	27th	L	Hibernian	h	1-1	10,000	Hamilton
Sep	3rd	L	Rangers	a	2-1	30,000	Lindley 2
	17th	L	Celtic	a	1-2	25,000	Lindley
	24th	L	Queens Park	h	5-0	8,000	Lindley; Hamilton; MacFarlane 2; Mair
	26th	L	Clyde	a	1-1	-	Hamilton
Oct	1st	L	Falkirk	a	1-0	11,000	Hamilton
	8th	L	Kilmarnock	h	2-1	6,000	Hamilton; Lee
	15th	L	Airdrie	a	1-3	7,000	Dainty
	22nd	L	Third Lanark	h	2-1	8,000	MacFarlane; Bellamy
	29th	L	Hearts	a	3-2	-	Hamilton 2; Lindley
Nov	5th	L	Partick Thistle	h	2-1	9,000	McLachlan; Mair
	12th	L	Aberdeen	h	2-0	12,000	Hamilton; MacFarlane
	19th	L	Morton	a	1-1	7,000	McLachlan
	26th	L	Celtic	h	1-0	20,000	McLachlan
Dec	3rd	L	Kilmarnock	a	0-2	9,000	-
	10th	L	Hearts	h	4-1	6,000	Bellamy 2; Hamilton 2
	17th	L	Clyde	h	1-0	10,000	Bellamy
	24th	L	Aberdeen	a	0-0	18,000	
	26th	L	Third Lanark	a	0-2	7,000	-
	31st	L	Hamilton	h	2-0	5,000	Mair; Hamilton
Jan	2nd	L	Falkirk	h	1-1	13,000	Comrie
	7th	L	Raith Rovers	a	1-2	6,000	Hamilton
	14th	L	St Mirren	h	5-1	7,000	Fraser 2; Langlands; Bellamy; Graydon
	21st	L	Raith Rovers	h	3-1	4,000	Fraser; Walker; Hamilton
	21st	FC1	Forfar Athletic	a	2-3		McEwan; McLachlan
	28th	SC1	Hibernian	h	2-1	22,000	MacFarlane; Hamilton
Feb	4th	L	Partick Thistle	a	2-3	6,000	Fraser; Bellamy
	11th	SC2	Partick Thistle	a	3-0	28,000	Comrie; Langlands; Hamilton
	18th	L	Hibernian	a	1-4	3,000	Langlands
	25th	SC3	Rangers	h	2-1	30,000	Hamilton; Lee
Mar	11th	SCS	Hamilton	a	2-3	15,000	Bellamy 2 (1 pen)
	25th	L	St Mirren	a	0-1	1,000	-
Apr	1st	L	Queens Park	a	2-1	7,000	Comrie; McLachlan
	8th	L	Rangers	h	0-2	12,000	-
	10th	L	Airdrie	h	1-0	7,000	Hamilton
	15th	L	Motherwell	h	3-1	8,000	Bellamy; Hamilton 2
	19th	L	Hamilton	a	2-2		Neal; Hamilton
	29th	L	Morton	h	1-2	6,000	Lindsay

Cup Cash v. Partick Thistle £700, Rangers £850, Hamilton £367

Bob Crumley - local keeper who came good at Dens.

Appearances

	League		S/Cup		Total	
Herbert Dainty	32	(1)	4		36	(1)
Jimmy Bellamy	31	(7)	4	(2)	35	(9)
Bob Crumley	31		4		35	
RC Hamilton	31	(17)	4	(3)	35	(20)
Sandy MacFarlane	30	(5)	4	(1)	34	(6)
Bert Neal	30	(1)	4		34	(1)
George Comrie	26	(2)	4	(1)	30	(3)
Bert Lee	22	(1)	4	(1)	26	(2)
Jack Fraser	18	(4)	3		21	(4)
George Langlands	16	(2)	3	(1)	19	(3)
Jimmy Lawson	19		0		19	
Davie Mair	19	(3)	0		19	(3)
John McLachlan	16	(3)	0		16	(3)
Tom Lindley	13	(5)	1		14	(5)
Archie Lindsay	9	(1)	4		13	(1)
John Chaplin	9		0		9	
Billy Dickson	4		0		4	
Andy Walker	3	(1)	1		4	(1)
John Graydon	2	(1)	0		2	(1)
John Hunter	2		0		2	
Jim Law	2		0		2	
Bob McEwan	2		0		2	
Bill Phillip (gk)	2		0		2	
John Comrie	1		0		1	
David Martin	1		0		1	
George Philip	1		0		1	
John Lyall	1		0		1	
Bill Wylie	1		0		1	

Scottish League Division One

		Home			Away			Goals		
	P	W	D	L	W	D	L	F	A	PTS
Rangers	34	12	2	3	11	4	2	90-34		52
Aberdeen	34	12	5	0	7	5	5	53-28		48
Falkirk	34	12	4	1	5	6	6	65-42		44
Partick Thistle	34	13	4	0	4	4	9	50-41		42
Celtic	34	11	4	2	4	7	6	48-18		41
Dundee	**34**	**13**	**2**	**2**	**5**	**3**	**9**	**54-42**		**41**
Clyde	34	8	6	3	6	5	6	45-36		39
Third Lanark	34	8	5	4	8	2	7	59-53		39
Hibernian	34	11	2	4	4	4	9	44-48		36
Kilmarnock	34	9	3	5	3	7	7	42-45		34
Airdrie	34	9	4	4	3	5	9	49-53		33
St Mirren	34	11	2	4	1	5	11	46-57		31
Morton	34	4	8	5	5	3	9	49-51		29
Hearts	34	7	6	4	1	2	14	42-59		24
Raith Rovers	34	6	6	5	1	4	12	36-55		24
Hamilton*	34	7	3	7	1	2	14	31-60		21
Motherwell*	34	6	3	8	2	1	14	34-56		14
Queens Park*	34	5	2	10	0	2	15	28-80		14

* Re-elected ahead of Dumbarton, Ayr and Albion Rovers from Division Two.

The Record		
League	-	Sixth Place, Division One
Scottish Cup	-	Semi-final
Forfarshire Cup	-	First round
Top Scorer	-	Bob Hamilton (20 goals)
Av. Home Gate	-	8,300
Players used	-	28
Sent off	-	None

Dundee F.C. Line-Ups 1910-11

		1	2	3	4	5	6	7	8	9	10	11
Aug	20th	Crumley	Chaplin J	McEwan	Neal	Dainty	Comrie G	Bellamy	Langlands	Hunter	MacFarlane	Fraser
	27th	Crumley	Neal	Chaplin J	Lee	Dainty	Comrie G	Bellamy	McLachlan	Hamilton	Hunter	Fraser
Sep	3rd	Crumley	Neal	Chaplin J	Lee	Dainty	Mair	Bellamy	McLachlan	Hamilton	MacFarlane	Lindley
	17th	Crumley	Neal	Chaplin J	Lee	Dainty	Mair	Bellamy	Langlands	Hamilton	MacFarlane	Lindley
	24th	Crumley	Neal	Lawson	Lee	Dainty	Mair	Bellamy	Langlands	Hamilton	MacFarlane	Lindley
	26th	Crumley	Neal	Lawson	Lee	Dainty	Mair	Dickson	Langlands	Hamilton	MacFarlane	Lindley
Oct	1st	Crumley	Neal	Chaplin J	Lee	Dainty	Mair	Dickson	Langlands	Hamilton	MacFarlane	Lindley
	8th	Crumley	Neal	Chaplin J	Lee	Dainty	Mair	Bellamy	Dickson	Hamilton	Fraser	Lindley
	15th	Crumley	Neal	Chaplin J	Lee	Dainty	Mair	Bellamy	Langlands	Hamilton	MacFarlane	Fraser
	22nd	Crumley	Neal	Chaplin J	Comrie G	Dainty	Mair	Bellamy	McLachlan	Hamilton	MacFarlane	Fraser
	29th	Crumley	Neal	McEwan	Comrie G	Dainty	Mair	Bellamy	McLachlan	Hamilton	MacFarlane	Lindley
Nov	5th	Crumley	Neal	Chaplin J	Comrie	Dainty	Mair	Bellamy	McLachlan	Hamilton	MacFarlane	Lindley
	12th	Crumley	Neal	Lawson	Comrie G	Dainty	Mair	Bellamy	McLachlan	Hamilton	MacFarlane	Lindley
	19th	Crumley	Neal	Lawson	Comrie G	Dainty	Mair	Bellamy	McLachlan	Hamilton	MacFarlane	Lindley
	26th	Crumley	Neal	Lawson	Comrie G	Dainty	Mair	Bellamy	McLachlan	Hamilton	MacFarlane	Lindley
Dec	3rd	Crumley	Neal	Lawson	Comrie G	Dainty	Mair	Bellamy	McLachlan	Hamilton	MacFarlane	Lindley
	10th	Crumley	Neal	Lawson	Comrie G	Dainty	Lee	Bellamy	McLachlan	Hamilton	MacFarlane	Fraser
	17th	Crumley	Neal	Lawson	Comrie G	Dainty	Lee	Bellamy	McLachlan	Hamilton	MacFarlane	Fraser
	24th	Crumley	Neal	Lawson	Comrie G	Dainty	Mair	Bellamy	Langlands	Hamilton	MacFarlane	Lindley
	26th	Crumley	Neal	Lawson	Lee	Comrie G	Mair	Bellamy	Langlands	Hamilton	MacFarlane	Fraser
	30th	Crumley	Lee	Neal	Comrie G	Dainty	Mair	Bellamy	Langlands	Hamilton	MacFarlane	Fraser
Jan	2nd	Crumley	Neal	Lawson	Comrie G	Dainty	Mair	Bellamy	Langlands	Hamilton	MacFarlane	Dickson
	7th	Crumley	Neal	Lawson	Comrie G	Dainty	Mair	Bellamy	Langlands	Hamilton	MacFarlane	Fraser
	14th	Crumley	Neal	Lawson	Comrie G	Dainty	Lee	Bellamy	Langlands	Walker	Graydon	Fraser
	21st	Crumley	Neal	Lawson	Comrie G	Dainty	Lee	Bellamy	Langlands	Walker	Hamilton	Fraser
	28th	Crumley	Neal	Lindsay	Comrie G	Dainty	Lee	Bellamy	Hamilton	Walker	MacFarlane	Lindley
Feb	4th	Crumley	Neal	Lindsay	Comrie G	Dainty	Lee	Bellamy	Hamilton	Walker	MacFarlane	Fraser
	11th	Crumley	Neal	Lindsay	Comrie G	Dainty	Lee	Bellamy	Langlands	Hamilton	MacFarlane	Fraser
	18th	Crumley	Lawson	Lindsay	Comrie J	Comrie G	Lee	Bellamy	Langlands	Hamilton	MacFarlane	Fraser
	25th	Crumley	Neal	Lindsay	Comrie G	Dainty	Lee	Bellamy	Langlands	Hamilton	MacFarlane	Fraser
Mar	11th	Crumley	Neal	Lindsay	Comrie G	Dainty	Lee	Bellamy	Langlands	Hamilton	MacFarlane	Fraser
	25th	Crumley	Neal	Lindsay	Comrie	Dainty	Lee	MacFarlane	Langlands	Martin	McLachlan	Fraser
Apr	1st	Phillip	Neal	Lindsay	Comrie G	Dainty	Lee	Bellamy	McLachlan	Hamilton	MacFarlane	Fraser
	8th	Phillip	Neal	Lindsay	Comrie G	Dainty	Lee	Bellamy	McLachlan	Hamilton	MacFarlane	Fraser
	10th	Crumley	Lawson	Lindsay	Philip	Dainty	Comrie G	Bellamy	Langlands	Hamilton	MacFarlane	Law
	15th	Crumley	Lawson	Lindsay	Comrie G	Dainty	Lee	Bellamy	McLachlan	Hamilton	MacFarlane	Law
	19th	Crumley	Lawson	Lindsay	Neal	Dainty	Lee	Bellamy	McLachlan	Hamilton	MacFarlane	Graydon
	29th	Lyall	Lawson	Lindsay	Comrie G	Dainty	Lee	Bellamy	Wylie	Hamilton	MacFarlane	Fraser

To the rescue - Dundee right-back Bert Neal clears off the line after keeper Bob Crumley is beaten by a shot.   DC Thomson

They Wore The Dark Blue

Season 1911-12

Date			Opponents		Score	Crowd	Scorers
Aug	19th	L	Motherwell	h	3-1	10,000	MacFarlane 2; Bellamy
	26th	L	Hibernian	a	1-2	11,000	Girdwood o.g.
Sep	2nd	L	Rangers	a	1-2	30,000	Hamilton
	16th	L	Celtic	h	3-1	20,000	Bellamy 2; MacFarlane
	23rd	L	Queens Park	h	4-0	5,000	MacFarlane; Martin 2; Bellamy (pen)
	30th	L	Airdrie	h	1-1	3,000	McLachlan
Oct	7th	L	Hearts	h	1-1	7,000	Hamilton
	14th	L	Raith Rovers	a	1-1	7,000	Hamilton
	21st	L	Morton	h	0-3	5,000	-
	28th	L	Hearts	a	4-1	10,000	Hamilton 2; Langlands; Bellamy (pen)
Nov	4th	L	Hibernian	h	3-2	6,000	Hamilton 2; Comrie
	11th	L	Airdrie	a	0-0		-
	18th	L	St Mirren	h	4-0	5,000	Fraser; Langlands; Hamilton; Bellamy
	25th	L	Kilmarnock	a	0-1	4,000	-
Dec	2nd	L	Clyde	h	2-0	5,000	Fraser; Bellamy
	9th	L	Falkirk	h	1-1	6,000	McLachlan
	16th	L	Aberdeen	a	1-2	10,000	Comrie
	23rd	L	Hamilton	h	2-0	4,000	Langlands; Martin
	25th	L	Third Lanark	a	0-1	10,000	-
	30th	L	Clyde	a	0-3	8,000	-
Jan	1st	L	Falkirk	a	0-0	10,000	-
	6th	L	Motherwell	a	0-0	6,000	-
	13th	L	Aberdeen	h	4-0	12,000	Langlands; Bellamy 2; Wylie
	20th	L	Queens Park	a	0-1	8,000	-
	27th	SC1	Partick Thistle	a	2-2	15,000	Neal; McLachlan
Feb	3rd	SC1	Partick Thistle	h	3-0	18,000	Hamilton; Wylie; McLachlan
	10th	L	Raith Rovers	h	2-2	5,000	Bellamy; Comrie
	17th	L	Partick Thistle	a	0-2	12,000	-
	17th	FC1	Forfar Athletic	a	1-0	2,000	Martin
	24th	SC2	Hearts	a	0-1	30,000	-
Mar	2nd	L	Celtic	a	0-2	6,000	-
	9th	L	Partick Thistle	h	0-2	4,000	-
	16th	L	Rangers	h	2-1	8,000	Bellamy; Wylie
	23rd	L	Kilmarnock	h	5-2	4,000	McLachlan (pen); Hamilton 3; Langlands
	30th	L	Third Lanark	h	3-1	5,000	Wylie; Bellamy; Langlands
Apr	6th	L	St Mirren	a	1-1	4,000	MacFarlane
	6th	FCS	Dundee Hibs*	h	2-2	3,500	Graydon; McKnight
	20th	L	Hamilton	a	1-0	3,000	Hamilton
	20th	FCF	Brechin City	h	2-0	3,000	Martin; Phillip
	27th	L	Morton	a	2-4	4,000	Hamilton 2

Cup Cash v. Partick Thistle (a) £450; Hearts £896 * No replay, Dundee reach final on toss of coin

R.C. Hamilton - ex-Ranger was again top scorer.

The Record

League	-	Eighth Place, Division One
Scottish Cup		Second round
Forfarshire Cup		Winners
Top Scorer		RC Hamilton (15 goals)
Av. Home Gate		6,700
Players used		22
Sent off		None

Appearances

	League	S/Cup	Total
John Lyall	34	3	37
Bert Neal	33	3 (1)	36 (1)
Jimmy Bellamy	30 (12)	3	33 (12)
R.C. Hamilton	30 (14)	3 (1)	33 (15)
Andy Aitken	29	3	32
George Comrie	28 (3)	3	31 (3)
George Langlands	28 (6)	3	31 (6)
John McLachlan	27 (3)	3 (2)	30 (5)
Jimmy Lawson	22	3	25
John Ferguson	21	3	24
Archie Lindsay	23	0	23
Sandy MacFarlane	21 (5)	0	21 (5)
Jack Fraser	18 (2)	0	18 (2)
Bill Wylie	11 (3)	3 (1)	14 (4)
David Martin	7 (3)	0	7 (3)
George Philip	5	0	5
Davie Mair	2	0	2
Jim Duncan	1	0	1
John Graydon	1	0	1
Joe Johnstone	1	0	1
Bob McKnight	1	0	1
Andy Walker	1	0	1

Scottish League Division One

		Home			Away			Goals		
	P	W	D	L	W	D	L	F A	PTS
Rangers	34	16	0	1	8	3	6	86-34	51
Celtic	34	14	3	0	3	8	6	58-33	45
Clyde	34	10	1	6	9	3	5	56-32	42
Hearts	34	11	2	4	5	6	6	54-40	40
Partick Thistle	34	7	8	2	9	0	8	47-40	40
Morton	34	10	3	4	4	6	7	44-44	37
Falkirk	34	10	3	4	5	3	9	46-43	36
Dundee	**34**	**11**	**4**	**2**	**2**	**5**	**10**	**52-41**	**35**
Aberdeen	34	9	4	4	5	3	9	44-44	35
Airdrie	34	8	5	4	4	3	10	40-41	32
Third Lanark	34	10	1	6	2	6	9	40-57	31
Hamilton	34	7	5	5	4	3	10	32-44	30
Hibernian	34	10	3	4	2	2	13	44-47	29
Motherwell	34	7	2	8	4	3	10	34-44	27
Raith Rovers	34	6	6	5	3	3	11	39-59	27
Kilmarnock*	34	7	3	7	4	1	12	38-60	26
Queens Park*	34	6	6	5	2	3	12	29-53	25
St Mirren*	34	5	6	6	2	4	11	32-59	24

* Re-elected ahead of Ayr United, Abercorn and Dumbarton from Division Two.

Dundee F.C. Line-Ups 1911-1912

		1	2	3	4	5	6	7	8	9	10	11
Aug	19th	Lyall	Lawson	Lindsay	Comrie G	Neal	Mair	Bellamy	McLachlan	Hamilton	MacFarlane	Fraser
	26th	Lyall	Aitken	Lindsay	Comrie	Neal	Mair	Bellamy	Langlands	Hamilton	MacFarlane	Fraser
Sep	2nd	Lyall	Ferguson	Lindsay	Comrie	Neal	Aitken	Bellamy	McLachlan	Hamilton	Graydon	Fraser
	16th	Lyall	Ferguson	Lindsay	Comrie	Neal	Aitken	Hamilton	McLachlan	Martin	MacFarlane	Bellamy
	23rd	Lyall	Ferguson	Lindsay	Comrie	Neal	Aitken	Bellamy	Langlands	Martin	MacFarlane	Hamilton
	30th	Lyall	Ferguson	Lindsay	Comrie	Neal	Aitken	Bellamy	McLachlan	Martin	MacFarlane	Hamilton
Oct	7th	Lyall	Ferguson	Lindsay	Comrie	Neal	Fraser	Aitken	McLachlan	Martin	MacFarlane	Hamilton
	14th	Lyall	Ferguson	Lindsay	Comrie	Neal	Aitken	Bellamy	McLachlan	Hamilton	MacFarlane	Fraser
	21st	Lyall	Ferguson	Lindsay	Aitken	Neal	Comrie	Bellamy	Langlands	McLachlan	MacFarlane	Fraser
	28th	Lyall	Ferguson	Lindsay	Aitken	Neal	Comrie	Bellamy	McLachlan	Hamilton	Langlands	Fraser
Nov	4th	Lyall	Lawson	Lindsay	Aitken	Neal	Comrie	Bellamy	McLachlan	Hamilton	Langlands	Fraser
	11th	Lyall	Lawson	Lindsay	Neal	Aitken	Comrie	Duncan	McLachlan	Hamilton	Langlands	Fraser
	18th	Lyall	Lawson	Lindsay	Neal	Aitken	Comrie	Bellamy	Langlands	Hamilton	MacFarlane	Fraser
	25th	Lyall	Lawson	Lindsay	Neal	Aitken	Comrie	Bellamy	Langlands	Hamilton	MacFarlane	Fraser
Dec	2nd	Lyall	Lawson	Lindsay	Neal	Philip	Comrie	Bellamy	Langlands	Hamilton	MacFarlane	Fraser
	9th	Lyall	Lawson	Lindsay	Philip	Neal	Comrie	Bellamy	Langlands	Hamilton	McLachlan	Fraser
	16th	Lyall	Lawson	Lindsay	Neal	Aitken	Comrie	Bellamy	McLachlan	Hamilton	Langlands	Fraser
	23rd	Lyall	Lawson	Ferguson	Neal	Aitken	Comrie	Bellamy	McLachlan	Martin	Langlands	MacFarlane
	25th	Lyall	Lawson	Ferguson	Neal	Aitken	Comrie	Bellamy	McLachlan	Martin	Langlands	MacFarlane
	30th	Lyall	Lawson	Lindsay	Neal	Aitken	Comrie	Bellamy	Wylie	Hamilton	Langlands	MacFarlane
Jan	1st	Lyall	Lawson	Ferguson	Neal	Aitken	Comrie	Hamilton	McLachlan	Walker	Langlands	Wylie
	6th	Lyall	Lawson	Ferguson	Neal	Aitken	Comrie	Hamilton	McLachlan	Martin	Langlands	Wylie
	13th	Lyall	Lawson	Ferguson	Aitken	Neal	Comrie	Bellamy	McLachlan	Hamilton	Langlands	Wylie
	20th	Lyall	Lawson	Ferguson	Aitken	Neal	Comrie	Bellamy	McLachlan	Hamilton	Langlands	Wylie
	27th	Lyall	Lawson	Ferguson	Neal	Aitken	Comrie	Bellamy	McLachlan	Hamilton	Langlands	Wylie
Feb	3rd	Lyall	Lawson	Ferguson	Neal	Aitken	Comrie	Bellamy	McLachlan	Hamilton	Langlands	Wylie
	10th	Lyall	Neal	Ferguson	MacFarlane	Aitken	Comrie	Bellamy	McLachlan	Hamilton	Langlands	Wylie
	17th	Lyall	Ferguson	Lindsay	Neal	Aitken	Comrie	Bellamy	McLachlan	Hamilton	Langlands	Wylie
	24th	Lyall	Lawson	Ferguson	Neal	Aitken	Comrie	Bellamy	McLachlan	Hamilton	Langlands	Wylie
Mar	2nd	Lyall	Lawson	Ferguson	Neal	Aitken	Comrie	Bellamy	McLachlan	Hamilton	Langlands	Wylie
	9th	Lyall	Lawson	Johnstone	Neal	Aitken	Comrie	Bellamy	McLachlan	Langlands	MacFarlane	Fraser
	16th	Lyall	Lawson	Ferguson	Philip	Neal	MacFarlane	Bellamy	McLachlan	Hamilton	Langlands	Wylie
	23rd	Lyall	Lindsay	Ferguson	Philip	Neal	MacFarlane	Bellamy	McLachlan	Hamilton	Langlands	Wylie
	30th	Lyall	Lawson	Ferguson	Neal	Aitken	MacFarlane	Bellamy	McLachlan	Hamilton	Langlands	Wylie
Apr	6th	Lyall	Lawson	Lindsay	Neal	Aitken	MacFarlane	Bellamy	McLachlan	Hamilton	Langlands	Fraser
	20th	Lyall	Lawson	Lindsay	Neal	Aitken	Ferguson	Bellamy	McLachlan	Hamilton	Langlands	Fraser
	27th	Lyall	Lawson	Lindsay	Philip	Aitken	MacFarlane	Bellamy	Langlands	Hamilton	McKnight	Wylie

Oh Geordie - Dundee inside-left Geordie Langlands bursts through the Partick Thistle defence at Firhill but although his shot beat the home keeper, the ball bounced harmlessly past the far post. DC Thomson

Season 1912-13

Date		Opponents		Score	Crowd	Scorers
Aug	17th	L	Motherwell	a	0-0	8,000	-
	24th	L	Aberdeen	h	1-3	16,000	Neal
	31st	L	Rangers	a	3-3	35,000	B. Hamilton; Neal; Steven
Sep	7th	L	Clyde	h	1-3	12,000	Wylie
	21st	L	Celtic	h	3-1	20,000	D. Hamilton; Steven 2
	28th	L	Queens Park	h	1-0	7,000	B. Hamilton
Oct	5th	L	Kilmarnock	a	0-2	4,000	-
	12th	L	Falkirk	h	2-2	6,000	Johnstone; Steven
	19th	L	Partick Thistle	a	0-2	10,000	-
	26th	L	Third Lanark	h	1-0	6,000	Walker
Nov	2nd	L	Airdrie	a	1-1	5,000	Walker
	9th	L	Raith Rovers	h	1-0	3,000	Walker
	16th	L	Morton	h	0-1	6,000	-
	23rd	L	Hamilton	a	0-1	4,000	-
	30th	L	Hibernian	h	2-2	6,000	Philip; Walker (pen)
Dec	7th	L	St Mirren	a	0-2	5,000	-
	14th	L	Hearts	h	3-0	6,000	Own goal; Walker; Wylie
	21st	L	Celtic	a	0-2	8,000	-
	25th	L	Third Lanark	a	1-4	8,000	MacFarlane
	28th	L	Partick Thistle	h	1-0	4,000	MacFarlane
Jan	1st	L	Aberdeen	a	0-1	-	-
	4th	L	Falkirk	a	0-2	6,000	-
	11th	L	Airdrie	h	1-1	2,500	MacFarlane
	18th	L	Queens Park	a	3-1	6,000	Philip; Walker; Steven
	18th	FC1	Arbroath	h	2-2		Langlands; Sotherwaite
	25th	L	Hibernian	a	0-4	9,000	-
Feb	1st	L	Kilmarnock	h	0-0	6,000	-
	1st	FC1R	Arbroath	a	2-0		McBride; Ford o.g.
	8th	SC2	Thornhill	h	5-0	10,000	B. Hamilton 2; Wylie; Langlands; Montgomery
	15th	L	Raith Rovers	a	0-0	6,000	-
	15th	FCS	Wanderers	h	6-1		Brown 3; Fraser; Ross; McIntosh
	22nd	SC3	Partick Thistle	a	1-0	18,000	B. Hamilton
Mar	1st	L	Motherwell	h	0-0	5,000	-
	8th	SC4	Clyde	h	1-1	25,000	Wylie
	15th	SC4	Clyde	a	0-0	27,000	-
	19th	SC4	Clyde	Ham	1-2	16,000	B. Hamilton
	22nd	L	Hearts	a	3-4	12,000	Ross; B. Hamilton 2
	29th	L	Morton	a	1-1	5,000	Steven
Apr	5th	L	Hamilton	h	2-1	4,000	MacFarlane; Wylie
	7th	L	St Mirren	h	0-0	2,500	-
	12th	L	Clyde	a	2-2	2,000	Walker; Wylie
	12th	FCF	Montrose	h	1-1		Steven
	19th	L	Rangers	h	0-0	12,000	-
	26th	FCFR	Montrose	h	7-0	3,000	Steven 2; Walker (pen); Brown 2; Ross 2

Cup Cash v. Partick Thistle £460; v. Clyde (h) £710, (a) £850, (Hampden) £315

John Lyall - Dundonian played for Scotland.

The Record

League	-	14th Place, Division One
Scottish Cup	-	Fourth round
Forfarshire Cup	-	Winners
Top Scorer	-	Bob Hamilton (8 goals)
Av. Home gate	-	7,300
Players used	-	27
Sent off	-	None

Appearances

	League	S/Cup	Total
Bill Wylie	32 (4)	5 (2)	37 (6)
R.C. Hamilton	28 (4)	5 (4)	33 (8)
George Philip	28 (2)	5	33 (2)
John Lyall	26	5	31
Alec Aitken	25	5	30
Jimmy Lawson	29	1	30
Joe Johnstone	23 (1)	4	27 (1)
Tom Tait	22	5	27
Sandy MacFarlane	20 (4)	3	23 (4)
Andy Walker	19 (7)	1	20 (7)
Bert Neal	18 (2)	0	18 (2)
David Ross	17	0	17
George Steven	17 (6)	0	17 (6)
Dave Hamilton	14 (1)	0	14 (1)
George Langlands	8	5 (1)	13 (1)
Bert McIntosh	9	0	9
Dave Balfour	8	0	8
Tom Kelso	4	4	8
Bill Read	5	3	8
Bill Montgomery	4	4 (1)	8 (1)
Frank Young	8	0	8
Bob McKnight	3	0	3
Jim Sotherwaite	3	0	3
Andy Fraser	1	0	1
Jim Melville	1	0	1
Pat McBride	1	0	1
Jim Strachan	1	0	1

Scottish League Division One

		Home			Away			Goals		
	P	W	D	L	W	D	L	F	A	PTS
Rangers	34	13	2	2	11	3	3	76-41		53
Celtic	34	13	2	2	9	3	5	53-28		49
Hearts	34	10	4	3	7	3	7	71-43		41
Airdrie	34	10	4	3	5	7	5	64-46		41
Falkirk	34	9	4	4	5	8	4	56-38		40
Motherwell	34	7	5	5	5	8	4	47-39		37
Aberdeen	34	9	4	4	5	5	7	47-40		37
Hibernian	34	9	3	5	7	2	8	63-55		37
Clyde	34	6	8	3	7	1	9	41-44		35
Hamilton	34	9	4	4	3	4	10	44-47		32
Kilmarnock	34	8	4	5	2	7	8	37-54		31
St Mirren	34	9	4	4	1	6	10	50-60		30
Morton	34	8	3	6	3	4	10	50-59		29
Dundee	**34**	**7**	**7**	**3**	**1**	**6**	**10**	**33-46**		**29**
Third Lanark	34	4	7	6	4	5	8	31-41		28
Raith Rovers	34	5	7	5	3	3	11	46-60		26
Partick Thistle	34	9	3	5	1	1	15	40-55		24
Queens Park	34	4	3	10	1	0	16	34-87		13

* No relegation, League increased to 20 teams with election of Ayr United (1st) and Dumbarton (6th) from Division Two.

Dundee F.C. Line-Ups 1912-13

		1	2	3	4	5	6	7	8	9	10	11
Aug	17th	Lyall	Young	Lawson	Tait	Neal	MacFarlane	Hamilton R	Langlands	Walker	Sotherwaite	Hamilton D
	24th	Lyall	Young	Lawson	Tait	Neal	MacFarlane	Wylie	Hamilton R	Walker	Langlands	Hamilton D
	31st	Lyall	Young	Lawson	Philip	Neal	MacFarlane	Wylie	Langlands	Hamilton R	Steven	Hamilton D
Sep	7th	Lyall	Young	Lawson	Philip	Neal	MacFarlane	Wylie	Ross	Hamilton R	Steven	Hamilton D
	21st	Lyall	Young	Lawson	Philip	Neal	Johnstone	Wylie	Ross	Hamilton R	Steven	Hamilton D
	28th	Balfour	Young	Lawson	Philip	Neal	Johnstone	Wylie	Ross	Hamilton R	Steven	Hamilton D
Oct	5th	Balfour	Young	Lawson	Philip	Neal	Johnstone	Wylie	Ross	Hamilton R	Steven	Hamilton D
	12th	Balfour	Lawson	Aitken	Philip	Strachan	Johnstone	Wylie	Ross	Hamilton R	Steven	Wylie
	19th	Lyall	Lawson	Aitken	Philip	Neal	Johnstone	McBride	Langlands	Hamilton R	Steven	Wylie
	26th	Lyall	Lawson	Aitken	Tait	Philip	Johnstone	Hamilton R	Ross	Walker	McKnight	Wylie
Nov	2nd	Lyall	Lawson	Aitken	Tait	Philip	Johnstone	Wylie	Ross	Walker	McKnight	Steven
	9th	Lyall	Lawson	Aitken	Tait	Philip	Johnstone	Wylie	Ross	Walker	Hamilton R	Steven
	16th	Lyall	Lawson	Aitken	Tait	Philip	Johnstone	Hamilton R	Ross	Walker	McKnight	Wylie
	23rd	Lyall	Lawson	Aitken	Neal	Philip	Johnstone	Hamilton R	Ross	Walker	Sotherwaite	Steven
	30th	Balfour	Lawson	Aitken	Tait	Philip	Johnstone	Wylie	Ross	Walker	Steven	Hamilton D
Dec	7th	Balfour	Lawson	Aitken	Tait	Philip	Johnstone	Wylie	Ross	Walker	MacFarlane	Hamilton D
	14th	Lyall	Lawson	Aitken	Tait	Philip	Johnstone	Wylie	Ross	Walker	MacFarlane	Hamilton D
	21st	Lyall	Lawson	Aitken	Tait	Philip	Johnstone	Wylie	Ross	Walker	MacFarlane	Hamilton D
	25th	Lyall	Lawson	Aitken	Tait	McIntosh	Neal	Wylie	Walker	Hamilton R	MacFarlane	Hamilton D
	28th	Lyall	Young	Aitken	McIntosh	Neal	Johnstone	Wylie	Walker	Hamilton R	MacFarlane	Steven
Jan	1st	Lyall	Lawson	Aitken	Neal	McIntosh	Johnstone	Wylie	Walker	Hamilton R	MacFarlane	Steven
	4th	Lyall	Lawson	Aitken	Tait	McIntosh	Johnstone	Wylie	Ross	Hamilton R	MacFarlane	Hamilton D
	11th	Balfour	Johnstone	Aitken	Tait	Philip	McIntosh	Walker	MacFarlane	Hamilton R	Steven	Wylie
	18th	Balfour	Johnstone	Aitken	Tait	Philip	McIntosh	Hamilton R	MacFarlane	Walker	Steven	Wylie
	25th	Balfour	Johnstone	Aitken	Tait	Philip	McIntosh	Hamilton R	MacFarlane	Fraser A	Steven	Wylie
Feb	1st	Lyall	Lawson	Aitken	Tait	Philip	Johnstone	Hamilton R	Sotherwaite	Walker	MacFarlane	Wylie
	8th	Lyall	Lawson	Aitken	Tait	Philip	Johnstone	Hamilton	Montgomery	Walker	Langlands	Wylie
	15th	Lyall	Lawson	Aitken	Tait	Philip	Johnstone	Hamilton R	Montgomery	Walker	MacFarlane	Wylie
	22nd	Lyall	Kelso	Aitken	Tait	Philip	Johnstone	Montgomery	MacFarlane	Hamilton R	Langlands	Wylie
Mar	1st	Lyall	Kelso	Aitken	Tait	Philip	Johnstone	Lawson	MacFarlane	Hamilton R	Langlands	Wylie
	8th	Lyall	Kelso	Aitken	Tait	Philip	MacFarlane	Read	Montgomery	Hamilton R	Langlands	Wylie
	15th	Lyall	Kelso	Aitken	Tait	Philip	Johnstone	Read	MacFarlane	Hamilton R	Langlands	Wylie
	19th	Lyall	Kelso	Aitken	Tait	Philip	Johnstone	Read	MacFarlane	Hamilton R	Langlands	Wylie
	22nd	Lyall	Kelso	Lawson	Tait	Neal	McIntosh	Read	Ross	Hamilton R	Langlands	Wylie
	29th	Lyall	Kelso	Lawson	Tait	Philip	Neal	Steven	Ross	Hamilton R	Montgomery	Wylie
Apr	5th	Lyall	Kelso	Aitken	Tait	Philip	Neal	Read	MacFarlane	Hamilton R	Montgomery	Wylie
	7th	Lyall	Lawson	Aitken	McIntosh	Philip	Neal	Read	MacFarlane	Hamilton R	Montgomery	Wylie
	12th	Lyall	Lawson	Aitken	Tait	Philip	Neal	Read	MacFarlane	Walker	Langlands	Wylie
	19th	Lyall	Lawson	Aitken	McIntosh	Philip	Neal	Read	Melville	Hamilton R	Langlands	Wylie

Close call - Dundee centre-forward Andy Walker (left) challenges Thornhill keeper Johnstone for the loose ball with visiting left-back Dunlop looking on. The Dark Blues cruised to a comfortable 5-0 victory in the Scottish Cup tie at Dens. DC Thomson

They Wore The Dark Blue

Season 1913-14

Date			Opponents		Score	Crowd	Scorers
Aug	16th	L	St Mirren	h	1-0	16,000	Montgomery
	23rd	L	Clyde	a	1-2		Hogg
	30th	L	Ayr United	h	2-0	6,000	Hogg; Skene
Sep	6th	L	Motherwell	a	1-0	10,000	Skene
	13th	L	Airdrie	h	2-0	4,000	Steven; Montgomery
	20th	L	Rangers	a	1-0	15,000	Kelso
	27th	L	Queens Park	h	5-2	12,000	Skene 2; Hogg 2; Kelso
Oct	4th	L	Hibernian	a	1-4	9,000	Hogg
	6th	L	Falkirk	h	4-1	7,000	Read; Kelso (pen); Hogg; Barbour
	11th	L	Hamilton	h	1-0	12,000	Hogg
	18th	L	Celtic	a	0-1	25,000	-
	25th	L	Raith Rovers	h	2-1	12,000	Kelso (pen); Hogg
Nov	1st	L	Partick Thistle	a	1-2	16,000	Barbour
	8th	L	Falkirk	a	0-4	4,000	-
	15th	L	Morton	h	1-2	10,000	Hamilton
	22nd	L	Hearts	h	2-2	16,000	Hogg; Hamilton
	29th	L	Kilmarnock	a	0-0	5,000	-
Dec	6th	L	Dumbarton	h	5-1	8,000	Skene 2; Wall; Steven; Montgomery
	13th	L	Airdrie	a	0-3	5,000	-
	20th	L	Rangers	h	0-2	18,000	-
	25th	L	Third Lanark	a	1-2	10,000	Adams
	27th	L	Raith Rovers	a	1-4	2,000	Skene
Jan	1st	L	Aberdeen	h	0-1	10,000	-
	3rd	L	Hibernian	h	2-2	12,000	Steven; Kelso
	10th	L	Morton	a	0-3	6,000	-
	17th	L	Celtic	h	0-1	20,000	-
	24th	L	Hearts	a	0-3	12,000	-
	31st	L	Partick Thistle	h	4-1	8,000	Philip 3; McCulloch
Feb	7th	SC2	St Mirren	a	1-2	16,000	Philip
	7th	FC1	Arbroath	h	0-1	3,000	-
	14th	L	Ayr United	a	3-1	6,000	Philip 2; Wylie
	21st	L	Hamilton	a	1-1	5,000	Neish
	28th	L	St Mirren	a	3-0	7,000	Philip 3
Mar	4th	L	Clyde	h	2-0	10,000	Philip; Hogg
	7th	L	Dumbarton	a	3-2	4,000	Steven; Montgomery; Philip
	28th	L	Aberdeen	a	2-2	10,000	Philip; Hogg
Apr	4th	L	Motherwell	h	2-1	7,000	Hogg; McCulloch
	11th	L	Kilmarnock	h	3-1	8,000	Hogg; Philip 2
	18th	L	Queens Park	a	4-0	7,000	Hogg 3; Philip
	29th	L	Third Lanark	h	3-1	5,000	Hogg; Brown 2

Billy Hogg - a class act on the right wing.

The Record		
League	-	Seventh Place, Division One
Scottish Cup	-	Second round
Forfarshire Cup	-	First round
Top Scorer	-	Billy Hogg (17 goals)
Av. Home Gate	-	10,600
Players used	-	26
Sent off	-	Two

Appearances

	League	S/Cup	Total
Bert McIntosh	37	1	38
George Philip	37 (14)	1 (1)	38 (15)
Billy Hogg	34 (17)	1 (0)	35 (17)
Tom Kelso	33 (5)	1	34 (5)
Bill Montgomery	28 (4)	1	29 (4)
Alec Aitken	27	1	28
George Steven	28 (4)	0	28 (4)
Dave "Roy" McDonald	23	1	24
John Lyall	22	0	22
Napper Thomson	19	1	20
Bill Wylie	19 (1)	0	19 (1)
John Barbour	17 (2)	1	18 (2)
Dave Balfour	16	1	17
Len Wall	17 (1)	0	17 (1)
Tom McCulloch	11 (2)	1	12 (2)
Clyde Skene	12 (7)	0	12 (7)
Harry Adams	8 (1)	0	8 (1)
Bill Read	7 (1)	0	7 (1)
George Smith	7	0	7
Jimmy Lawson	7	0	7
Bob RC Hamilton	4 (2)	0	4 (2)
Joe Johnstone	3	0	3
Tommy Neish	2 (1)	0	2 (1)
Davie Brown	1 (2)	0	1 (2)
Bob Husson	1	0	1
Jim Melville	1	0	1

Scottish League Division One

		Home			Away			Goals		
	P	W	D	L	W	D	L	F A		PTS
Celtic	38	15	3	1	15	2	2	81-14		65
Rangers	38	14	3	2	13	2	4	79-31		59
Hearts	38	17	1	1	6	7	6	70-29		54
Morton	38	16	0	3	10	2	7	76-51		54
Falkirk	38	14	4	1	6	5	8	69-51		49
Airdrie	38	10	7	2	8	5	6	72-43		48
Dundee	**38**	**13**	**2**	**4**	**6**	**3**	**10**	**64-53**		**43**
Third Lanark	38	10	4	5	3	6	10	42-51		36
Clyde	38	8	5	6	3	6	10	44-44		33
Ayr United	38	8	3	8	5	4	10	56-72		33
Raith Rovers	38	9	4	6	4	2	13	56-57		32
Kilmarnock	38	8	3	8	3	6	10	40-68		31
Hibernian	38	6	2	11	6	4	9	58-67		30
Aberdeen	38	5	8	6	5	2	12	38-55		30
Partick Thistle	38	9	4	6	1	5	13	37-51		29
Queens Park	38	7	6	6	3	3	13	52-84		29
Hamilton	38	8	4	7	3	2	14	49-66		28
Motherwell	38	9	2	8	2	4	13	46-65		28
Dumbarton	38	7	4	8	3	3	13	45-87		27
St Mirren	38	6	5	8	2	1	16	38-73		22

Although organized football would continue, there would be no promotion or relegation at the end of this season due to the outbreak of the Great War.

Dundee F.C. Line-Ups 1913-14

		1	2	3	4	5	6	7	8	9	10	11
Aug	16th	Lyall	Lawson	Aitken	McIntosh	Philip	Johnstone	Hogg	Barbour	Montgomery	Melville	Wylie
	23rd	Lyall	Kelso	Lawson	McIntosh	Philip	Johnstone	Hogg	Barbour	Adams	Montgomery	Wylie
	30th	Lyall	Kelso	Aitken	McIntosh	Philip	Thomson	Hogg	Barbour	Skene	Montgomery	Wylie
Sep	6th	Lyall	Kelso	Aitken	McIntosh	Philip	Thomson	Hogg	Read	Skene	Montgomery	Wylie
	13th	Lyall	Kelso	Aitken	McDonald	Philip	Johnstone	Hogg	Steven	Skene	Montgomery	Wylie
	20th	Lyall	Kelso	Aitken	McIntosh	Philip	McDonald	Hogg	Steven	Skene	Montgomery	Wylie
	27th	Lyall	Kelso	Aitken	McIntosh	Philip	McDonald	Hogg	Steven	Skene	Montgomery	Wylie
Oct	4th	Lyall	Kelso	Aitken	McIntosh	Philip	McDonald	Hogg	Steven	Skene	Montgomery	Barbour
	6th	Lyall	Kelso	Aitken	McIntosh	Philip	McDonald	Hogg	Steven	Read	Montgomery	Barbour
	11th	Lyall	Lawson	Aitken	McIntosh	Philip	McDonald	Read	Montgomery	Hogg	Barbour	Neish
	18th	Lyall	Kelso	Aitken	McIntosh	Philip	McDonald	Read	Steven	Hogg	Barbour	Wylie
	25th	Lyall	Kelso	Aitken	McIntosh	Philip	McDonald	Read	Steven	Hogg	Barbour	Wylie
Nov	1st	Lyall	Kelso	Aitken	McIntosh	Philip	McDonald	Hogg	Steven	Skene	Barbour	Smith
	8th	Balfour	Kelso	Aitken	McIntosh	Philip	McDonald	Hogg	Steven	Skene	Barbour	Smith
	15th	Lyall	Kelso	Aitken	McIntosh	Philip	Thomson	Hogg	Montgomery	Hamilton	Barbour	Steven
	22nd	Lyall	Kelso	Aitken	McIntosh	Philip	Thomson	Hogg	Steven	Hamilton	Montgomery	Wylie
	29th	Lyall	Kelso	Aitken	McIntosh	Philip	Thomson	Hogg	Steven	Hamilton	Montgomery	Wylie
Dec	6th	Lyall	Kelso	Aitken	McIntosh	Philip	Wall	Hogg	Steven	Skene	Montgomery	Wylie
	13th	Lyall	Kelso	Aitken*	McIntosh	Philip	Wall	Hogg	Steven	Hamilton	Montgomery	Wylie
	20th	Lyall	Kelso	Thomson	McIntosh	Philip	Wall	Hogg	Steven	Skene	Barbour	Wylie
	25th	Lyall	Kelso	Thomson	McIntosh	Philip	Wall	Read	Adams	Hogg	Steven	Wylie
	27th	Lyall	Kelso	Thomson	McIntosh	Philip	Wall	Hogg	Adams	Skene	Barbour	Smith
Jan	1st	Lyall	Kelso	Thomson	McIntosh	Philip	Wall	Hogg	Adams	Skene	Smith	Barbour
	3rd	Balfour	Kelso	Thomson	McIntosh	Philip	Wall	Read	Steven	Adams	Smith	Wylie
	10th	Balfour	Kelso	Thomson	McIntosh	Philip	McDonald	Wylie	McCulloch	Adams	Wall	Smith
	17th	Balfour	Kelso	Aitken	McIntosh	Philip	McDonald	Wylie	Steven	Adams	Montgomery	Smith
	24th	Balfour	Kelso	Aitken	McIntosh	Philip	Thomson	Wylie	Steven	Adams	Montgomery	Barbour
	31st	Balfour	Kelso	Aitken	McIntosh	McDonald	Thomson	Hogg	McCulloch	Philip	Montgomery	Barbour
Feb	7th	Balfour	Kelso	Aitken	McIntosh*	McDonald	Thomson	Hogg	McCulloch	Philip	Montgomery	Barbour
	14th	Balfour	Kelso	Aitken	McIntosh	McDonald	Thomson	Hogg	McCulloch	Philip	Montgomery	Wylie
	21st	Balfour	Kelso	Aitken	McIntosh	McDonald	Wall	Hogg	Steven	Philip	Montgomery	Neish
	28th	Balfour	Husson	Aitken	McIntosh	McDonald	Wall	Hogg	McCulloch	Philip	Montgomery	Steven
Mar	4th	Balfour	Kelso	Aitken	McIntosh	McDonald	Wall	Hogg	McCulloch	Philip	Montgomery	Steven
	7th	Balfour	Kelso	Aitken	McIntosh	McDonald	Wall	Hogg	McCulloch	Philip	Montgomery	Wall
	28th	Balfour	Kelso	Thomson	McIntosh	McDonald	Wall	Hogg	McCulloch	Philip	Montgomery	Steven
Apr	4th	Balfour	Kelso	Thomson	McIntosh	McDonald	Wall	Hogg	McCulloch	Philip	Montgomery	Steven
	11th	Balfour	Kelso	Thomson	McIntosh	McDonald	Wall	Hogg	McCulloch	Philip	Montgomery	Steven
	18th	Balfour	Thomson	Aitken	McIntosh	McDonald	Wall	Hogg	McCulloch	Philip	Montgomery	Steven
	29th	Balfour	Thomson	Aitken	McIntosh	McDonald	Wall	Hogg	McCulloch	Brown	Montgomery	Steven

Heads or tails - Dundee skipper George Philip and St Mirren captain Burden toss a coin for choice of ends in the Scottish Cup tie at Paisley. Philip made a sensational switch from centre-half to centre-forward, netting 15 goals in 14 games. DC Thomson

Season 1914-15

Date			Opponents		Score	Crowd	Scorers
Aug	15th	L	Aberdeen	h	1-3	8,000	Steven
	22nd	L	Partick Thistle	a	1-4		McIntosh
	29th	L	Hamilton	h	1-0	6,000	Brown
Sep	5th	L	St Mirren	a	1-0		Brown
	12th	L	Rangers	h	1-1	12,000	Steven
	19th	L	Dumbarton	a	1-1		Steven
	26th	L	Celtic	h	1-3	12,000	McCulloch
Oct	3rd	L	Celtic	a	0-6	7,000	-
	5th	L	Dumbarton	h	0-0	5,000	-
	10th	L	Falkirk	a	1-0		Steven
	17th	L	Hearts	h	1-2	10,000	Hog
	24th	L	Airdrie	a	4-3		McCann; J. McDonald; Hutcheson; Stirling
	31st	L	Kilmarnock	a	0-1	3,000	-
Nov	7th	L	Morton	a	0-2		-
	14th	L	Motherwell	h	1-0	2,000	McCann
	21st	L	Hibernian	a	0-2		-
	28th	L	Raith Rovers	a	1-1		Brown
Dec	5th	L	Third Lanark	h	0-0	1,500	-
	12th	L	Ayr United	h	2-3	2,000	Adams; Cargill
	19th	L	Hamilton	a	0-2		-
	25th	L	Third Lanark	a	0-7	2,000	-
	26th	L	Hibernian	h	2-4	3,500	Brown; Steven
Jan	1st	L	Aberdeen	a	1-2	6,000	Fisher
	2nd	L	Queens Park	a	3-0		Brown; Steven 2
	9th	L	Falkirk	h	1-0	5,000	Brown
	16th	L	Hearts	a	2-3	10,000	Brown 2
	23rd	L	Morton	h	1-1	7,000	Brown
	30th	L	Motherwell	a	1-1		Brown
Feb	6th	L	Partick Thistle	h	1-2	1,000	Brown
	13th	L	Clyde	a	1-1	3,000	Fisher
	20th	L	St Mirren	h	2-1	6,000	McIntosh; Brown
	27th	L	Airdrie	h	2-0	6,000	Brown 2
Mar	6th	L	Rangers	a	0-2	6,000	-
	6th	FCS	Dundee Hibs	a	1-3	5,000	Adams
	20th	L	Kilmarnock	a	2-3		Brown 2
Apr	3rd	L	Queens Park	h	2-0	5,000	Brown 2
	10th	L	Ayr United	a	0-0		-
	12th	L	Clyde	h	3-0	3,000	Brown; Hutcheson; McIntosh
	17th	L	Raith Rovers	h	2-0	4,000	Hogg; Steven

Bert McIntosh - the big left-half played in every game.

The Record		
League	-	15th Place, Division One
Scottish Cup	-	Suspended until end of war
Forfarshire Cup	-	Semi-final
Top Scorer	-	Davie Brown (19 goals)
Av. Home Gate	-	5,400
Players used	-	23
Sent off	-	None

Appearances

	League	Total
Bert McIntosh	38 (3)	38 (3)
Dave Hutcheson	37 (2)	37 (2)
Napper Thomson	33	33
George Steven	32 (8)	32 (8)
Dave "Roy" McDonald	30	30
Davie Brown	28 (19)	28 (19)
Tom McCulloch	30 (1)	30 (1)
Billy Hogg	28 (2)	28 (2)
Alec Aitken	25	25
Bill Masterton	24	24
David Cargill	16 (1)	16 (1)
Paddy Burns	16	16
Billy Fisher	16 (2)	16 (2)
Dave Balfour	14	14
John McDonald	13 (1)	13 (1)
John Stirling	12 (1)	12 (1)
Bill Montgomery	9	9
George Smith	5	5
Harry Adams	4 (1)	4 (1)
Dave McCann	4 (2)	4 (2)
Walter Miller	2	2
William Anderson	1	1
Bill Milne	1	1

Scottish League Division One

		Home			Away			Goals		
	P	W	D	L	W	D	L	F	A	PTS
Celtic	38	18	1	0	12	4	3	91-25		65
Hearts	38	17	1	1	10	6	3	83-32		61
Rangers	38	11	1	7	12	3	4	74-47		50
Morton	38	13	4	2	5	8	6	74-48		48
Ayr United	38	13	3	3	7	5	7	55-40		48
Falkirk	38	10	5	5	6	2	11	48-58		39
Hamilton	38	9	5	5	7	1	11	60-55		38
Partick Thistle	38	10	3	6	5	5	9	56-58		38
St Mirren	38	9	4	6	5	4	10	56-65		36
Airdrie	38	9	4	6	5	3	11	54-60		35
Hibernian	38	9	5	5	3	6	10	59-66		35
Kilmarnock	38	12	2	5	3	2	14	55-59		34
Dumbarton	38	9	3	7	4	5	10	51-66		34
Aberdeen	38	7	7	5	4	4	11	39-52		33
Dundee	**38**	**8**	**4**	**7**	**4**	**5**	**10**	**43-61**		**33**
Third Lanark	38	7	8	4	3	4	12	51-57		32
Clyde	38	8	4	7	4	2	13	44-59		30
Motherwell	38	7	5	7	3	5	11	49-66		30
Raith Rovers	38	5	8	6	4	2	13	53-68		28
Queens Park	38	3	2	14	1	3	15	27-90		13

Since 1913-14 there had been no promotion or relegation and at the end of 1914-15, it was decided to scrap Division Two until the end of the Great War.

Dundee F.C. Line-Ups 1914-15

		1	2	3	4	5	6	7	8	9	10	11
Aug	15th	Balfour	Thomson	Aitken	McIntosh	McDonald D	Hutcheson	Hogg	McCulloch	Milne	Montgomery	Steven
	22nd	Balfour	Thomson	Aitken	McIntosh	McDonald D	Hutcheson	Hogg	McCulloch	Brown	Montgomery	Steven
	29th	Balfour	Thomson	Burns	McIntosh	McDonald D	Stirling	Hogg	McCulloch	Brown	Steven	McDonald J
Sep	5th	Balfour	Thomson	Aitken	McIntosh	McDonald D	Hutcheson	Hogg	Steven	Brown	Montgomery	McDonald J
	12th	Balfour	Thomson	Burns	McIntosh	McDonald D	Hutcheson	Hogg	McCulloch	Brown	Montgomery	Steven
	19th	Balfour	Thomson	Burns	McIntosh	McDonald D	Hutcheson	Hogg	Steven	Brown	Montgomery	McCulloch
	26th	Balfour	Thomson	Burns	McIntosh	McDonald D	Hutcheson	Hogg	Steven	Brown	McCulloch	McDonald J
Oct	3rd	Balfour	Thomson	Aitken	McIntosh	McDonald D	Hutcheson	Hogg	Steven	Miller	Montgomery	McDonald J
	5th	Masterton	Thomson	Burns	McIntosh	McDonald D	Hutcheson	Hogg	McCulloch	Miller	Montgomery	McDonald J
	10th	Masterton	Aitken	Burns	McIntosh	McDonald D	Hutcheson	Hogg	McCulloch	Brown	Steven	McDonald J
	17th	Masterton	Aitken	Burns	McIntosh	McDonald D	Hutcheson	Hogg	McCulloch	Brown	Steven	McDonald J
	24th	Masterton	Aitken	Burns	McIntosh	Stirling	Hutcheson	Hogg	McCulloch	McCann	Steven	McDonald J
	31st	Masterton	Aitken	Burns	McIntosh	McDonald D	Hutcheson	Hogg	McCulloch	McCann	Steven	McDonald J
Nov	7th	Masterton	Thomson	Burns	McIntosh	McDonald D	Hutcheson	Hogg	McCulloch	McCann	Steven	McDonald J
	14th	Masterton	Thomson	Burns	McIntosh	Stirling	Hutcheson	Hogg	McCulloch	McCann	Steven	McDonald J
	21st	Masterton	Thomson	Burns	McIntosh	Stirling	Hutcheson	Hogg	McCulloch	McDonald D	Steven	McDonald J
	28th	Masterton	McDonald D	Burns	McIntosh	Stirling	Hutcheson	Hogg	McCulloch	Brown	Steven	Cargill
Dec	5th	Masterton	Thomson	Burns	McIntosh	Stirling	Hutcheson	Hogg	Adams	McDonald D	McCulloch	Cargill
	12th	Masterton	Thomson	Burns	McIntosh	Stirling	Hutcheson	Hogg	Adams	Brown	McCulloch	Cargill
	19th	Masterton	Thomson	Aitken	McIntosh	McDonald D	Hutcheson	Hogg	Adams	Brown	Montgomery	Cargill
	25th	Masterton	Thomson	Burns	McIntosh	McDonald D	Hutcheson	Fisher	Adams	Hogg	Montgomery	McDonald J
	26th	Balfour	Anderson	Thomson	McIntosh	Stirling	Hutcheson	Fisher	McCulloch	Brown	Steven	Cargill
Jan	1st	Masterton	Thomson	Aitken	McIntosh	Stirling	Hutcheson	Fisher	McCulloch	Brown	Steven	Cargill
	2nd	Masterton	Thomson	Aitken	McIntosh	Stirling	Hutcheson	Fisher	Smith	Brown	Steven	Cargill
	9th	Masterton	Thomson	Aitken	McIntosh	Stirling	Hutcheson	Fisher	Steven	Brown	Smith	Cargill
	16th	Masterton	Thomson	Aitken	McIntosh	McDonald D	Hutcheson	Fisher	Steven	Brown	Smith	Cargill
	23rd	Masterton	Thomson	Aitken	McIntosh	McDonald D	Hutcheson	Fisher	Steven	Brown	Smith	Cargill
	30th	Masterton	Thomson	Aitken	McIntosh	McDonald D	Hutcheson	Fisher	Steven	Brown	McCulloch	Cargill
Feb	6th	Masterton	Thomson	Aitken	McIntosh	Stirling	Hutcheson	Fisher	Steven	Brown	McCulloch	Cargill
	13th	Masterton	Thomson	Aitken	McIntosh	McDonald D	Hutcheson	Fisher	Steven	Brown	McCulloch	Cargill
	20th	Masterton	Thomson	Aitken	Mcintosh	McDonald D	Hutcheson	Fisher	Steven	Brown	McCulloch	Cargill
	27th	Masterton	Thomson	Aitken	McIntosh	McDonald D	Hutcheson	Hogg	Steven	Brown	McCulloch	Cargill
Mar	6th	Masterton	Thomson	Aitken	McIntosh	McDonald D	Hutcheson	Hogg	McCulloch	Brown	Smith	Cargill
	20th	Balfour	Thomson	Aitken	McIntosh	McDonald D	Hutcheson	Fisher	Steven	Brown	McCulloch	Hogg
Apr	3rd	Balfour	Thomson	Aitken	McIntosh	McDonald D	Hutcheson	Fisher	Steven	Brown	McCulloch	Hogg
	10th	Balfour	Thomson	Aitken	McIntosh	McDonald D	Hutcheson	Fisher	Steven	Brown	McCulloch	Hogg
	12th	Balfour	Thomson	Aitken	McIntosh	McDonald D	Hutcheson	Fisher	Steven	Brown	McCulloch	Hogg
	17th	Balfour	Thomson	Aitken	McIntosh	McDonald D	Hutcheson	Fisher	Steven	Brown	McCulloch	Hogg

Last line of defence - Dens Park defensive stalwarts, right-back David "Napper" Thomson, goalkeeper Billy Masterton and left-back Alec Aitken give a show of solidarity in front of the stand. DC Thomson

49

Season 1915-16

Date			Opponents		Score	Crowd	Scorers
Aug	21st	L	Ayr United	h	2-0	5,000	Brown; Troup
	28th	L	Morton	a	1-3	6,000	Brown
Sep	4th	L	Motherwell	h	1-3	5,000	Fisher
	11th	L	Airdrie	a	2-1		Troup; Stirling
	18th	L	Celtic	h	0-2	12,000	-
	25th	L	Queens Park	h	7-1	7,000	Brown 5; Troup 2
Oct	2nd	L	Dunfermline	a	1-1	3,000	Fisher
	9th	L	St Mirren	h	1-0	4,000	Troup
	16th	L	Clyde	a	0-2		-
	23rd	L	Third Lanark	h	1-0	5,000	Brown
	30th	L	Falkirk	a	0-2		-
Nov	6th	L	Hearts	h	1-0	5,000	Brown
	13th	L	Kilmarnock	a	0-2		-
	20th	L	Aberdeen	a	0-2	6,000	-
	27th	L	Hamilton	h	3-1	3,000	McCulloch; Brown; McIntosh
Dec	4th	L	Partick Thistle	a	0-2	3,000	-
	11th	L	Motherwell	a	0-3		-
	18th	L	Raith Rovers	h	3-0	6,000	Stirling; McCulloch 2
	25th	L	Hibernian	a	2-0		Brown 2
Jan	1st	L	Aberdeen	h	1-1	10,000	Brown
	3rd	L	Airdrie	h	4-0	8,000	Brown 3; own goal
	8th	L	Third Lanark	a	1-2		Fisher
	15th	L	Rangers	h	2-0	11,000	Brown 2
	22nd	L	St Mirren	a	2-1		McDonald; McCulloch
	29th	L	Clyde	h	1-0	6,000	Brown
Feb	5th	L	Hamilton	a	4-4	4,000	McCulloch; McDonald (pen); Brown; Steven
	12th	L	Hibernian	h	2-1	6,000	Duffus; Brown
	19th	L	Partick Thistle	h	3-0	7,000	Troup; McIntosh; Steven
	28th	L	Celtic	a	0-3		-
Mar	4th	L	Falkirk	h	3-3	5,000	McDonald 2 (2 pens); Steven
	11th	L	Ayr United	a	2-1	3,000	Brown 2
	18th	L	Dunfermline	h	0-1	4,000	-
Apr	1st	L	Raith Rovers	a	2-0	4,000	McCulloch; Duffus
	8th	L	Kilmarnock	h	2-0	3,500	Brown 2
	10th	L	Rangers	a	2-3	5,000	Brown 2
	15th	L	Queens Park	a	0-2	5,000	-
	22nd	L	Morton	h	0-1	3,000	-
	30th	L	Hearts	a	0-1		-

Davie Brown - top scorer for three successive seasons.

The Record		
League	-	Eighth Place, Division One
Scottish Cup	-	Suspended until end of war
Forfarshire Cup	-	Suspended until end of war
Top Scorer	-	Davie Brown (27 goals)
Av. Home Gate	-	6,200
Players used	-	18
Sent off	-	None

Appearances

	League	Total
Davie Brown	38 (27)	38 (27)
George Steven	38 (3)	38 (3)
Dave "Roy" McDonald	37 (4)	37 (4)
Tom McCulloch	33 (6)	33 (6)
Ernie Ferguson	31	31
Alec Troup	30 (6)	30 (6)
Paddy Burns	29	29
Billy Fisher	29 (3)	29 (3)
Bert McIntosh	27 (2)	27 (2)
Bobby Duffus	25 (2)	25 (2)
Joe Fraser	20	20
John Stirling	20 (2)	20 (2)
Dave Balfour	18	18
Alec Aitken	16	16
Napper Thomson	14	14
Sid Lamb	11	11
Bob Husson	1	1
Joe Johnstone	1	1

Scottish League Division One

		Home			Away			Goals		
	P	W	D	L	W	D	L	F A		PTS
Celtic	38	15	3	1	17	0	2	116-23		67
Rangers	38	15	2	2	10	4	5	87-39		56
Morton*	37	15	0	3	7	7	5	86-35		51
Ayr United	38	12	4	3	8	4	7	72-45		48
Partick Thistle	38	13	2	4	6	6	7	65-41		46
Hearts*	38	12	1	6	8	5	5	66-45		46
Hamilton	38	13	2	4	6	1	12	68-76		41
Dundee	**38**	**13**	**2**	**4**	**5**	**2**	**12**	**56-49**		**40**
Dumbarton	38	9	6	4	4	5	10	54-64		37
Kilmarnock	38	9	5	5	3	6	10	46-49		35
Aberdeen	38	8	8	3	3	4	12	51-64		34
Falkirk	38	8	6	5	4	3	12	45-61		33
St Mirren	38	11	1	7	2	3	14	50-67		30
Motherwell	38	5	7	7	6	1	12	55-82		30
Airdrie	38	8	6	5	3	2	14	44-74		30
Third Lanark	38	6	5	8	3	6	10	40-56		29
Clyde	38	7	2	10	4	5	10	49-71		29
Queens Park	38	7	5	7	4	1	14	53-100		28
Hibernian	38	7	2	10	2	5	12	44-71		25
Raith Rovers	38	8	3	8	1	2	16	30-65		23

* Morton v Hearts postponed but was never played.

Dundee F.C. Line-Ups 1915-16

		1	2	3	4	5	6	7	8	9	10	11
Aug	21st	Balfour	Ferguson	Aitken	McIntosh	McDonald	Stirling	Fisher	McCulloch	Brown	Troup	Steven
	28th	Balfour	Ferguson	Aitken	McIntosh	McDonald	Stirling	Fisher	McCulloch	Brown	Troup	Steven
Sep	4th	Brown	Aitken	Burns	McIntosh	McDonald	Duffus	Fisher	Steven	Brown	Troup	McCulloch
	11th	Balfour	Aitken	Burns	McIntosh	McDonald	Stirling	Fisher	Steven	Brown	Troup	McCulloch
	18th	Balfour	Aitken	Burns	McIntosh	McDonald	Stirling	Fisher	Steven	Brown	Troup	McCulloch
	25th	Balfour	Aitken	Burns	McIntosh	McDonald	Stirling	Fisher	Steven	Brown	Troup	McCulloch
Oct	2nd	Balfour	Aitken	Burns	McIntosh	McDonald	Stirling	Fisher	McCulloch	Brown	Troup	Steven
	9th	Balfour	Ferguson	Aitken	McIntosh	McDonald	Stirling	Fisher	Steven	Brown	Troup	Lamb
	16th	Balfour	Ferguson	Aitken	McIntosh	McDonald	Stirling	Fisher	Steven	Brown	Troup	Lamb
	23rd	Brown	Ferguson	Aitken	McIntosh	McDonald	Stirling	Fisher	Steven	Brown	Troup	Lamb
	30th	Balfour	Ferguson	Aitken	McIntosh	McDonald	Duffus	Fisher	Steven	Brown	Troup	McCulloch
Nov	6th	Balfour	Ferguson	Aitken	McIntosh	McDonald	Duffus	Fisher	McCulloch	Brown	Troup	Steven
	13th	Balfour	Ferguson	Aitken	Duffus	McDonald	Stirling	Fisher	McCulloch	Brown	Troup	Steven
	20th	Balfour	Fisher	Burns	McIntosh	McDonald	Duffus	Fisher	McCulloch	Brown	Troup	Steven
	27th	Balfour	Aitken	Burns	McIntosh	McDonald	Duffus	Fisher	McCulloch	Brown	Troup	Steven
Dec	4th	Balfour	Aitken	Burns	Ferguson	McDonald	Stirling	Thomson	McCulloch	Brown	Troup	Steven
	11th	Balfour	Aitken	Burns	Johnstone	McDonald	Duffus	Ferguson	McCulloch	Brown	Steven	Lamb
	18th	Balfour	Ferguson	Burns	McIntosh	Duffus	Stirling	Thomson	McCulloch	Brown	Steven	Lamb
	25th	Fraser	Ferguson	Burns	McIntosh	McDonald	Duffus	Fisher	McCulloch	Brown	Steven	Lamb
Jan	1st	Fraser	Ferguson	Burns	McIntosh	McDonald	Duffus	Fisher	McCulloch	Brown	Steven	Lamb
	3rd	Fraser	Ferguson	Burns	Thomson	McDonald	Duffus	Fisher	McCulloch	Brown	Steven	Lamb
	8th	Fraser	Ferguson	Burns	McIntosh	McDonald	Duffus	Fisher	McCulloch	Brown	Steven	Lamb
	15th	Fraser	Ferguson	Burns	McIntosh	McDonald	Duffus	Fisher	Thomson	Brown	Steven	Troup
	22nd	Fraser	Ferguson	Burns	Thomson	McDonald	Duffus	Fisher	McCulloch	Brown	Steven	Troup
	29th	Fraser	Ferguson	Burns	McIntosh	McDonald	Stirling	Fisher	McCulloch	Brown	Steven	Troup
Feb	5th	Fraser	Ferguson	Burns	Thomson	McDonald	Duffus	Fisher	McCulloch	Brown	Steven	Troup
	12th	Fraser	Ferguson	Burns	McIntosh	McDonald	Duffus	Fisher	McCulloch	Brown	Steven	Troup
	19th	Fraser	Ferguson	Burns	McIntosh	McDonald	Duffus	Fisher	McCulloch	Brown	Steven	Troup
	28th	Fraser	Ferguson	Burns	McIntosh	McDonald	Duffus	Fisher	McCulloch	Brown	Steven	Troup
Mar	4th	Fraser	Ferguson	Burns	Thomson	McDonald	Duffus	McIntosh	McCulloch	Brown	Steven	Troup
	11th	Fraser	Ferguson	Burns	Stirling	McDonald	Duffus	Fisher	Thomson	Brown	Steven	Troup
	18th	Fraser	Thomson	Burns	Stirling	McDonald	Duffus	Fisher	McCulloch	Brown	Steven	Troup
Apr	1st	Fraser	Ferguson	Burns	Stirling	McDonald	Duffus	Thomson	McCulloch	Brown	Steven	Troup
	8th	Fraser	Ferguson	Burns	Stirling	McDonald	Duffus	Husson	McCulloch	Brown	Steven	Troup
	10th	Fraser	Ferguson	Burns	Stirling	McDonald	Duffus	Thomson	McCulloch	Brown	Steven	Troup
	15th	Fraser	Ferguson	Burns	McIntosh	McDonald	Duffus	Thomson	McCulloch	Brown	Steven	Troup
	22nd	Fraser	Ferguson	Burns	McIntosh	McDonald	Stirling	Thomson	McCulloch	Brown	Steven	Lamb
	30th	Fraser	Ferguson	Thomson	McIntosh	McDonald	Stirling	Fisher	McCulloch	Brown	Steven	Lamb

Dundee F.C. around 1914 or 1915. (BACK, left to right). William Wallace (manager), Dave Hutcheson, Bert McIntosh, Dave Balfour, unknown, Ernie Ferguson. FRONT - Billy Hogg, Alec Aitken, David "Napper" Thomson, George Philip, unknown, unknown and Bill Longair (trainer).

DC Thomson

Season 1916-17

Date		Opponents		Score	Crowd	Scorers
Aug 19th	L	Rangers	a	0-3	10,000	-
26th	L	Clyde	h	0-1	7,000	-
Sep 2nd	L	Motherwell	a	2-4		Brown; McCulloch
9th	L	Aberdeen	h	1-1	8,000	Steven
16th	L	Hibernian	a	2-1		Herron; Troup
23rd	L	Airdrie	h	2-2	5,000	McDonald; Brown
30th	L	Queens Park	a	2-2	4,000	Brown 2
Oct 7th	L	Falkirk	h	1-2	6,000	Steven
14th	L	Morton	a	0-1	3,000	-
21st	L	Hamilton	h	3-1	7,000	Brown 2; McCulloch
28th	L	Kilmarnock	a	0-3	3,000	-
Nov 4th	L	Celtic	h	1-2	14,000	Brown
11th	L	Dumbarton	a	3-4	2,000	Brown 2; Troup
18th	L	St Mirren	h	0-2	1,200	-
25th	L	Partick Thistle	a	0-3		-
Dec 2nd	L	Third Lanark	h	0-2	3,000	-
9th	L	Raith Rovers	h	6-2	2,000	Brown 6
16th	L	Hearts	a	0-1		-
23rd	L	Airdrie	a	3-2		Brown 2; Steven
30th	L	Kilmarnock	h	0-2	4,000	-
Jan 1st	L	Aberdeen	a	1-5	4,000	Brown
2nd	L	Hibernian	h	3-1	4,000	McCulloch 2; Steven
6th	L	Falkirk	a	0-2	3,000	-
20th	L	Ayr United	h	2-1	4,000	Stirling; Brown
27th	L	Hearts	h	2-3	4,000	F. Murray; McCulloch
Feb 3rd	L	Ayr United	a	2-1	3,000	Fisher; Brown
10th	L	Partick Thistle	h	5-1	5,000	Thomson 2; Brown; Stirling; F. Murray
17th	L	Celtic	a	0-2	10,000	-
24th	L	Morton	h	3-1	4,000	Brown 2; Steven
Mar 3rd	L	Raith Rovers	a	2-3	3,000	McCulloch; Steven
10th	L	St Mirren	a	0-2	5,000	-
17th	L	Dumbarton	h	4-1	5,000	Brown 3; Fisher
24th	L	Clyde	a	0-2	3,000	-
31st	L	Queens Park	h	2-1	4,000	Thomson; Brown
Apr 7th	L	Hamilton	a	4-2	5,000	Heron; Brown 3
14th	L	Motherwell	h	0-2	4,000	-
21st	L	Third Lanark	a	0-0	5,000	-
28th	L	Rangers	h	2-1	7,500	Brown; Fisher

Alec Troup - brilliant attacker earned 4 full Scotland caps.

The Record		
Scottish Cup	-	Suspended until end of war
Forfarshire Cup	-	Suspended until end of war
League	-	16th Place, Division One
Top Scorer	-	Davie Brown (31 goals)
Av. Home Gate	-	5,200
Players used	-	26
Sent off	-	None

Appearances

	League		Total	
Bob Bower	37		37	
Davie Brown	36	(31)	36	(31)
Tom McCulloch	31	(6)	31	(6)
John Stirling	31	(2)	31	(2)
Napper Thomson	29	(3)	29	(3)
Bert McIntosh	27		27	
Bobby Duffus	26		26	
Jim Herron	26	(2)	26	(2)
George Steven	26	(6)	26	(6)
Paddy Burns	23		23	
Frank Murray	21	(2)	21	(2)
Billy Fisher	16	(3)	16	(3)
Ernie Ferguson	15		15	
Dave "Roy" McDonald	14	(1)	14	(1)
Alec Troup**	11	(2)	11	(2)
Alec Aitken	10		10	
John Baxter	10		10	
John Moyes	5		5	
George Murray	5		5	
Dave Erskine	4		4	
Dave Pearson	4		4	
David Cargill	3		3	
Bob Roberts	3		3	
Ralph Rogerson	2		2	
Jack Simpson	1		1	
Tommy Taylor	1		1	
"Newman"	1		1	

Scottish League Division One

		Home			Away			Goals		
	P	W	D	L	W	D	L	F	A	PTS
Celtic	38	13	5	1	14	5	0	79-17		64
Morton	38	16	1	2	8	5	6	72-39		54
Rangers	38	16	1	2	8	4	7	68-32		53
Airdrie	38	16	1	2	5	7	7	71-38		50
Third Lanark	38	11	7	1	8	4	7	53-37		49
Kilmarnock	38	12	2	5	6	5	8	69-46		43
St Mirren	38	8	7	4	7	3	9	49-43		40
Motherwell	38	9	4	6	7	2	10	57-59		38
Partick Thistle	38	9	5	5	5	2	12	44-43		35
Dumbarton	38	8	6	5	4	5	10	79-73		35
Hamilton	38	11	3	5	2	6	11	53-73		35
Falkirk	38	7	5	7	5	5	9	58-57		34
Clyde	38	6	7	6	4	7	8	41-52		34
Hearts	38	9	1	9	5	3	11	44-59		32
Ayr United	38	6	6	7	6	1	12	47-59		31
Dundee*	**38**	**9**	**2**	**8**	**4**	**2**	**13**	**58-71**		**30**
Hibernian	38	6	6	7	4	4	11	57-62		30
Queens Park	38	7	4	8	4	3	12	56-81		29
Raith Rovers	38	6	2	11	2	5	12	42-91		23
Aberdeen	38	6	4	9	1	3	15	36-68		21

* At the end of this season, Dundee, along with other North East clubs Raith Rovers and Aberdeen, were asked to drop out of the Scottish League until the end of the war. This was to reduce travelling costs for other clubs, most of whom played in Central or the West of Scotland. ** Limited availability due to military duties.

Dundee F.C. Line-Ups 1916-17

		1	2	3	4	5	6	7	8	9	10	11
Aug	19th	Bower	Aitken	Burns	Stirling	McDonald	Duffus	Fisher	Moyes	Brown	McCulloch	Steven
	26th	Bower	Aitken	Burns	Stirling	McDonald	Duffus	Fisher	McCulloch	Brown	Steven	Erskine
Sep	2nd	Bower	Ferguson	Burns	Stirling	Murray	Duffus	Herron	McCulloch	Brown	Troup	Steven
	9th	Bower	Ferguson	Burns	Stirling	Murray	Duffus	Herron	McCulloch	Brown	Steven	Troup
	16th	Bower	Ferguson	Burns	Stirling	McDonald	Duffus	Herron	McCulloch	Brown	Steven	Troup
	23rd	Bower	Ferguson	Burns	Stirling	McDonald	Duffus	Herron	Moyes	Brown	Steven	Troup
	30th	Bower	Thomson	Aitken	Stirling	McDonald	Duffus	Herron	McCulloch	Brown	Steven	Fisher
Oct	7th	Bower	Thomson	Aitken	Stirling	McDonald	Duffus	Herron	McCulloch	Brown	Steven	Fisher
	14th	Bower	Ferguson	Thomson	Stirling	McDonald	Duffus	Herron	McCulloch	Brown	Steven	Troup
	21st	Bower	Ferguson	Thomson	McIntosh	McDonald	Duffus	Herron	McCulloch	Brown	Steven	Troup
	28th	Bower	Thomson	Aitken	McIntosh	McDonald	Duffus	Herron	McCulloch	Brown	Steven	Moyes
Nov	4th	Bower	Ferguson	Thomson	McIntosh	McDonald	Duffus	Herron	McCulloch	Brown	Steven	Troup
	11th	Bower	Ferguson	Thomson	McIntosh	McDonald	Roberts	Fisher	Moyes	Brown	Pearson	Troup
	18th	Bower	Burns	Thomson	McIntosh	McDonald	Roberts	Fisher	Moyes	Brown	Pearson	McCulloch
	25th	Bower	Thomson	Aitken	Stirling	McDonald	Roberts	Herron	McCulloch	Brown	Murray	Troup
Dec	2nd	Bower	Thomson	Aitken	McIntosh	McDonald	Stirling	Herron	McCulloch	Brown	Murray	Duffus
	9th	Bower	Thomson	Aitken	McIntosh	Duffus	Stirling	Heron	Murray F	Brown	Steven	McCulloch
	16th	Bower	Thomson	Aitken	McIntosh	Duffus	Stirling	Heron	Murray F	Brown	Steven	Troup
	23rd	Bower	Thomson	Aitken	Stirling	McIntosh	Duffus	Murray G	Murray F	Brown	Steven	McCulloch
	30th	Bower	Thomson	Burns	Stirling	McIntosh	Duffus	Herron	Murray F	Pearson	McCulloch	Steven
Jan	1st	Bower	Thomson	Burns	Stirling	McIntosh	Duffus	Fisher	Murray F	Brown	McCulloch	Steven
	2nd	Bower	Thomson	Burns	Murray G	Stirling	Duffus	Herron	Murray F	Brown	McCulloch	Steven
	6th	Bower	Thomson	Burns	Stirling	McIntosh	Duffus	Herron	Murray F	Brown	McCulloch	Steven
	20th	Bower	Baxter	Burns	McIntosh	Thomson	Stirling	Herron	Murray F	Brown	McCulloch	Steven
	27th	Bower	Baxter	Burns	McIntosh	Thomson	Stirling	Herron	Murray F	Brown	McCulloch	Steven
Feb	3rd	Newman	Baxter	Ferguson	McIntosh	Thomson	Stirling	Fisher	Murray F	Brown	McCulloch	Troup
	10th	Bower	Baxter	Burns	McIntosh	Thomson	Stirling	Fisher	Murray F	Brown	McCulloch	Cargill
	17th	Bower	Baxter	Ferguson	McIntosh	Thomson	Duffus	Herron	Murray F	Brown	McCulloch	Cargill
	24th	Bower	Baxter	Ferguson	McIntosh	Thomson	Stirling	Herron	Fisher	Brown	McCulloch	Steven
Mar	3rd	Bower	Baxter	Burns	McIntosh	Thomson	Stirling	Herron	Murray F	Brown	McCulloch	Steven
	10th	Bower	Ferguson	Burns	McIntosh	Duffus	Stirling	Herron	Fisher	Brown	Pearson	Cargill
	17th	Bower	Baxter	Burns	McIntosh	Duffus	Stirling	Fisher	Murray F	Brown	Steven	Thomson
	24th	Bower	Ferguson	Burns	McIntosh	Duffus	Stirling	Fisher	Taylor	Murray	Rogerson	Simpson
	31st	Bower	Ferguson	Burns	McIntosh	Thomson	Stirling	Herron	Murray F	Brown	McCulloch	Steven
Apr	7th	Bower	Baxter	Burns	McIntosh	Thomson	Stirling	Herron	Rogerson	Brown	McCulloch	Erskine
	14th	Bower	Baxter	Burns	McIntosh	Thomson	Stirling	Herron	Murray F	Brown	Steven	Erskine
	21st	Bower	Ferguson	Burns	McIntosh	Duffus	Stirling	Fisher	Murray F	Brown	McCulloch	Erskine
	28th	Bower	Thomson	Burns	Murray G	McIntosh	Duffus	Herron	Murray F	Brown	McCulloch	Fisher

Under pressure - Dundee keeper Dave Balfour has to step lively to block this scoring attempt by Hearts at Tynecastle in 1914. The Dark Blues Scottish international full-back Tom Kelso stands guard on the line.

DC Thomson

Season 1917-18

Date			Opponents		Score	Crowd	Scorers
Aug	18th	EL	Dundee Hibs	h	5-1	4,000	Taylor 2; Lamb; F Murray; Heron
Sep	1st	EL	Cowdenbeath	h	3-4	3,000	Heron; F Murray; Taylor
	8th	EL	Raith Rovers	a	0-0		-
	15th	EL	Dundee Hibs	a	2-0	6,000	Nairn; Lamb
	22nd	EL	Dunfermline	h	2-1	3,000	Moyes; Taylor
	29th	EL	Cowdenbeath	a	0-5		-
Oct	13th	EL	Armadale	a	0-9		-
	20th	EL	East Fife	h	5-1		Taylor 2; F Murray; McCann; Lamb
	27th	EL	Dunfermline	a	2-1		Moyes; Taylor
Nov	3rd	EL	Raith Rovers	h	4-0		Taylor; Murray; Moyes; Lamb
	10th	LC	Dundee Hibs	a	1-1		Taylor
	17th	EL	East Fife	a	2-5		Taylor; Heron
	24th	LC	Dundee Hibs	a	2-1 (3-2)		Murray; Duffus
Dec	1st	EL	Armadale	h	2-0		Moyes; Taylor
	8th	EL	Cowdenbeath	a	3-0		Lamb; Taylor; Kelly
	15th	EL	Raith Rovers	h	2-5	3,000	Taylor; Murray
	29th	LC	Dunfermline	h	11-2		Taylor 2; Lamb; McCann 3; Murray 2; Heron 3
Jan	1st	EL	Armadale	h	4-0	2,500	Taylor 2; Philip; Duffus
	5th	EL	Armadale	a	1-1		F Murray
	26th	EL	Dundee Hibs	h	1-2		Lamb
Feb	2nd	EL	Raith Rovers	a	2-1		Taylor 2
	16th	EL	East Fife	h	4-1		Heron; Moyes 2; Taylor
	23rd	EL	Dundee Hibs	a	2-1		Heron; Taylor
Mar	9th	EL	East Fife	a	1-1		Murray
	16th	EL	Dunfermline	h	8-1		Murray; Lamb 4; Taylor 3
	23rd	EL	Dunfermline	a	2-0		Nairn; Taylor
	30th	PC	Armadale	h	3-0		Taylor; Heron; Moyes
Apr	6th	EL	Cowdenbeath	h	2-0		Taylor 2
	13th	PC	East Fife	h	1-1		Murray
	20th	PCF	Dundee Hibs	h	2-0		Moyes; Nairn
	27th	EC	Dundee Hibs	h	2-2		Murray 2

George Philip - Sunderland star made a guest appearance.

EL = Eastern League, PC = Penman Cup, LC = Loftus Cup, EC = Eastern Cup (East Fife scratched to Dundee in semi-final)

Appearances

	League		LC		PC		EC		Total	
Paddy Burns	24		3		3		1		31	
Bill Nairn	24	(2)	3		3	(1)	1		31	(3)
John Stirling	24		3		3		1		31	
Tommy Taylor	24	(24)	3	(3)	3	(1)	1		31	(28)
Bob Husson	24		2		3		1		30	
Frank Murray	22	(8)	3	(3)	3	(1)	1	(2)	29	(14)
Jim Heron	21	(5)	3	(3)	2	(1)	1		27	(9)
John Moyes	18	(6)	3		3	(2)	1		25	(8)
George Anderson**	17		3		3		1		24	
Bobby Duffus	17	(1)	3	(1)	3		1		24	(2)
Sid Lamb	18	(10)	3	(1)	2		1		24	(11)
Dave McCann	12	(1)	0	(3)	1		0		13	(4)
Bob Bower	7		0		0		0		7	
George Murray	7		0		0		0		7	
Isaac Reid	2		0		1		0		3	
George Goldie	1		0		0		0		1	
Dave "Roy" McDonald	0		1		0		0		1	
Bob Kelly	1	(1)	0		0		0		1	
George Philip	1	(1)	0		0		0		1	(1)
James Strachan	1		0		0		0		1	

Eastern Division

	P	W	D	L	F	A	PTS
Dundee*	**24**	**15**	**6**	**3**	**59-40**		**33**
Cowdenbeath	24	15	6	3	49-18		33
Raith Rovers	22	11	6	5	40-24		27
Armadale	20	7	8	5	36-33		19
Dundee Hibs	23	7	11	5	30-45		19
Dunfermline	24	6	15	3	37-61		15
East Fife	21	5	13	4	18-48		12

The Record		
League	-	Champions, Eastern Division
Scottish Cup	-	Suspended until end of war
Forfarshire Cup	-	Suspended until end of war
Penman Cup	-	Winners
Loftus Cup	-	Winners
Top Scorer	-	Tommy Taylor (28 goals)
Av. Home Gate	-	Unknown
Players used	-	18
Sent off	-	None

* After this season Dundee F.C. went into abeyance and did not play again until season 1919-20. ** A guest player from Aberdeen F.C.,who later became Dundee's director-manager in 1944.

Dundee FC Line-Ups 1917-18

Date		1	2	3	4	5	6	7	8	9	10	11
Aug	18th	Bower	Husson	Burns	Nairn	Murray G	Stirling	Heron	Moyes	Taylor	Murray F	Lamb
Sep	1st	Bower	Husson	Burns	Nairn	Murray G	Stirling	Heron	Moyes	Taylor	Murray F	Lamb
	8th	Bower	Husson	Burns	Nairn	Murray G	Stirling	Heron	Moyes	Taylor	Murray F	Lamb
	15th	Bower	Husson	Burns	Nairn	Murray G	Stirling	McCann	Moyes	Taylor	Murray F	Lamb
	22nd	Bower	Husson	Burns	Nairn	Murray G	Stirling	Heron	Moyes	Taylor	Murray F	McCann
	29th	Bower	Husson	Burns	Nairn	Murray G	Stirling	Heron	Moyes	Taylor	Murray F	Lamb
Oct	20th	Anderson	Husson	Burns	Nairn	Stirling	Duffus	Heron	McCann	Taylor	Murray F	Lamb
	27th	Anderson	Husson	Burns	Nairn	Stirling	Duffus	Heron	McCann	Taylor	Murray F	Lamb
Nov	3rd	Anderson	Husson	Burns	Nairn	Stirling	Duffus	Reid	Moyes	Taylor	Murray F	Lamb
	10th	Anderson	Husson	Burns	Nairn	Stirling	Duffus	Heron	Moyes	Taylor	Murray F	Lamb
	17th	Anderson	Husson	Burns	Nairn	Stirling	Duffus	Heron	Moyes	Taylor	Murray F	Lamb
	24th	Anderson	McDonald	Burns	Nairn	Stirling	Duffus	Heron	Moyes	Taylor	Murray F	Lamb
Dec	1st	Anderson	Husson	Burns	Nairn	Stirling	Duffus	Heron	Moyes	Taylor	Murray F	Lamb
	8th	Anderson	Husson	Burns	Nairn	Stirling	Duffus	Heron	Moyes	Taylor	Kelly	McCann
	15th	Anderson	Husson	Burns	Nairn	Stirling	Duffus	Heron	Moyes	Taylor	Murray F	McCann
	29th	Anderson	Husson	Burns	Nairn	Stirling	Duffus	Heron	McCann	Taylor	Murray F	Lamb
Jan	1st	Anderson	Husson	Burns	Nairn	Stirling	Duffus	Heron	McCann	Taylor	Philip	Lamb
	5th	Anderson	Husson	Burns	Nairn	Stirling	Duffus	Reid	Strachan	Taylor	Murray F	Lamb
	26th	Anderson	Husson	Burns	Nairn	Stirling	Duffus	Heron	McCann	Taylor	Murray F	Lamb
Feb	2nd	Anderson	Husson	Goldie	Nairn	Stirling	Duffus	Heron	Moyes	Taylor	Murray F	McCann
	16th	Anderson	Husson	Burns	Nairn	Stirling	Duffus	Heron	Moyes	Taylor	Murray F	McCann
	23rd	Anderson	Husson	Burns	Nairn	Stirling	Duffus	Heron	Moyes	Taylor	Murray F	Lamb
Mar	9th	Anderson	Husson	Burns	Nairn	Stirling	Duffus	Heron	Moyes	Taylor	Murray F	Lamb
	16th	Anderson	Husson	Burns	Nairn	Stirling	Duffus	Heron	Moyes	Taylor	Murray F	Lamb
	23rd	Anderson	Husson	Burns	Nairn	Stirling	Duffus	Heron	Moyes	Taylor	Murray F	McCann
	30th	Anderson	Husson	Burns	Nairn	Stirling	Duffus	Heron	Moyes	Taylor	Murray F	McCann
Apr	6th	Anderson	Husson	Burns	Nairn	Stirling	Duffus	Heron	Moyes	Taylor	Murray F	Lamb
	13th	Anderson	Husson	Burns	Nairn	Stirling	Duffus	Heron	Moyes	Taylor	Murray F	Lamb
	20th	Anderson	Husson	Burns	Nairn	Stirling	Duffus	Reid	Moyes	Taylor	Murray F	Lamb
	27th	Anderson	Husson	Burns	Nairn	Stirling	Duffus	Heron	Moyes	Taylor	Murray F	Lamb

Close call at Dens - Dunfermline live dangerously as a Dundee forward crashes the ball off the crossbar in a lightning raid.

Season 1919-20

Date			Opponents		Score	Crowd	Scorers
Aug	16th	L	Motherwell	a	1-3		D. Brown
	23rd	L	Third Lanark	h	3-1	20,000	D. McDonald; Buchan; Thomson (pen)
	30th	L	Partick Thistle	a	0-1		-
Sep	3rd	L	Airdrie	a	2-1		D. Brown 2
	6th	L	St Mirren	h	1-2	13,000	D. Brown
	13th	L	Falkirk	a	1-2		D. Brown
	20th	L	Hearts	h	1-0	16,000	D. Brown
	22nd	L	Aberdeen	a	0-2	12,000	-
Oct	4th	L	Airdrie	h	1-1	14,000	Troup
	6th	L	Motherwell	h	3-0	14,000	D. Brown 2; Slade
	11th	L	Dumbarton	a	3-0		D. Brown 2; McLaughlan
	18th	L	Hamilton	a	1-0		D. Brown
	25th	L	Rangers	h	0-2	28,000	-
Nov	1st	L	Clydebank	a	3-3		Slade 2; Bell
	8th	L	Clyde	h	3-0	12,000	Bell 2; Troup
	15th	L	Raith Rovers	a	3-1		Rawlings; Bell 2
	22nd	L	Albion Rovers	h	3-2	15,000	D. McDonald; Bell 2
	29th	L	Ayr United	h	7-1	14,000	Bell 3; Slade 2; Nicoll; McLaughlan
Dec	6th	L	Morton	a	0-0		
	13th	L	Raith Rovers	h	5-4	12,000	Bell 2; Slade 2; McLaughlan
	20th	L	Queens Park	a	2-3	20,000	Bell; Slade
	25th	L	Third Lanark	a	0-2	16,000	-
	27th	L	Hibernian	h	3-1	14,000	Bell 2; Slade
Jan	1st	L	Aberdeen	h	1-3	20,000	Troup
	3rd	L	Albion Rovers	a	2-1		Bell; McLaughlan
	10th	L	Kilmarnock	h	3-2	10,000	Bell; 2 o.g.'s
	17th	L	Clyde	a	2-3		Bell 2
	24th	SC1	Airdrie	h	1-0	25,000	Slade
	31st	L	Celtic	h	2-1	20,000	Bell; McLaughlan
Feb	7th	SC2	Celtic	h	1-3	34,000	McLaughlan
	14th	L	Hearts	a	1-2	20,000	Slade
	21st	L	Falkirk	h	1-0	10,000	Troup
	28th	L	St Mirren	a	3-1		Bell 3
Mar	13th	L	Kilmarnock	a	2-4		Jackson; Slade
	20th	L	Dumbarton	h	3-1	10,000	Bell; Cowan; Rawlings
	20th	FCS	Arbroath	a	2-1	3,000	Connelly; Nairn
	27th	L	Queens Park	h	1-1	14,000	Bell
Apr	3rd	L	Hamilton	h	2-1	12,000	Downie 2
	10th	L	Ayr United	a	3-5		Bell 2; Downie
	12th	L	Clydebank	h	1-0	15,000	Nicoll
	17th	L	Partick Thistle	h	2-1	18,000	Rawlings; D. McDonald
	21st	L	Morton	h	2-0	16,000	Bell; D. McDonald
	24th	L	Rangers	a	1-6		Slade
	24th	FCF	Dundee Hibs	h	0-1	12,000	-
	26th	L	Celtic	a	1-1		Slade
May	1st	FCF*	Dundee Hibs	h	0-1	12,000	-
	11th	L	Hibernian	a	0-0	7,000	

* Replayed after Dundee appeal against ineligible player

Johnny Bell - the Lochee lad was Dundee's top scorer.

The Record

League	-	Fourth Place, Division One
Scottish Cup	-	Second round
Forfarshire Cup	-	Runners up
Top Scorer	-	Johnny Bell (28 goals)
Av. Home Gate	-	15,100
Players used	-	29
Sent off	-	One

Appearances

	League		Scottish Cup		Total	
Davie Raitt	41		2		43	
Napper Thomson	40	(1)	2		42	(1)
Alec Troup	40	(4)	2		42	(4)
Bert McIntosh	39		2		41	
Dyken Nicoll	33	(2)	2		35	(2)
James Watson	30		2		32	
Donald Slade	29	(13)	2	(1)	31	(14)
Johnny Bell	28	(28)	2		30	(28)
Archie Rawlings	27	(3)	2		29	(3)
Davie Hutcheson	22		1		23	
Dave McDonald	23	(4)	0		23	(4)
John Jackson	20	(1)	2		22	(1)
Jim McLaughlan	18	(5)	1	(1)	19	(6)
Davie Brown	13	(11)	0		13	(11)
Dave "Roy" McDonald	8		0		8	
Tom Capper	7		0		7	
George Henderson	7		0		7	
Willie Brown	6		0		6	
Colin Buchan	6	(1)	0		6	(1)
Willie Cowan	5	(1)	0		5	(1)
John Vallis	5		0		5	
Jim Downie	3	(3)	0		3	(3)
Bill Nairn	3		0		3	
Jim Orr	3		0		3	
Tom Fleming	2		0		2	
Peter Connelly	1		0		1	

Scottish League Division One

		Home			Away			Goals		
	P	W	D	L	W	D	L	F A		PTS
Rangers	42	18	2	1	13	7	1	105-25		71
Celtic	42	15	6	0	14	4	3	89-31		68
Motherwell	42	15	6	0	8	5	8	74-53		57
Dundee	**42**	**16**	**2**	**3**	**6**	**4**	**11**	**79-65**		**50**
Clydebank	42	10	6	5	10	2	9	78-55		48
Morton	42	10	6	5	6	7	8	71-48		45
Airdrie	42	11	6	4	6	4	11	57-43		44
Third Lanark	42	11	4	6	5	7	9	56-62		43
Kilmarnock	42	14	0	7	6	3	12	59-74		43
Ayr United	42	11	7	3	4	3	14	72-69		40
Dumbarton	42	7	9	5	6	4	11	57-65		39
Queens Park	42	11	5	5	3	9	13	67-54		38
Partick Thistle	42	12	5	4	1	7	13	51-62		38
St Mirren	42	9	3	9	6	5	10	63-81		38
Clyde	42	11	4	6	3	5	13	64-71		37
Hearts	42	8	5	8	6	4	11	57-72		37
Aberdeen	42	8	7	6	3	6	12	46-64		35
Hibernian	42	10	3	8	3	4	14	60-79		33
Raith Rovers	42	10	3	8	1	3	13	61-83		32
Falkirk	42	10	6	5	0	5	16	45-74		31
Hamilton	42	10	5	6	1	2	18	56-86		29
Albion Rovers	42	7	4	10	3	4	14	43-77		28

Appearances (Ctd)

	League	Scottish Cup	Total
Ernie Ferguson	1	0	1
John Patterson	1	0	1
George Stuart	1	0	1

Dundee F.C. Line-Ups 1919-20

		1	2	3	4	5	6	7	8	9	10	11
Aug	16th	Capper	Raitt	Thomson	McIntosh	Nicoll	Hutcheson	McDonald D	Buchan	Brown D	Brown W	Troup
	23rd	Capper	Raitt	Thomson	McIntosh	Nicoll	Hutcheson	McDonald D	Buchan	Brown D	Brown W	Troup
	30th	Capper	Raitt	Thomson	McIntosh	Nicoll	Hutcheson	Orr	Buchan	Brown D	Brown W	Troup
Sep	3rd	Capper	Raitt	Thomson	McIntosh	Nicoll	McDonald R	Henderson	Brown W	Brown D	Buchan	Troup
	6th	Capper	Raitt	Thomson	McIntosh	Nicoll	McDonald R	Henderson	Brown W	Brown D	Buchan	Troup
	13th	Capper	Raitt	McDonald R	McIntosh	Nicoll	Stuart	Henderson	McDonald D	Brown D	Brown W	Troup
	20th	Watson	Raitt	McDonald R	McIntosh	Nicoll	Thomson	Henderson	McDonald D	Brown D	Patterson	Troup
	22nd	Watson	Raitt	Fleming	McIntosh	Nicoll	McDonald R	Henderson	McDonald D	Brown D	Thomson	Troup
Oct	4th	Watson	Raitt	Thomson	McIntosh	Nicoll	Hutcheson	McDonald D	McLaughlan	Brown D	Slade	Troup
	6th	Watson	Raitt	Thomson	McIntosh	Nicoll	Hutcheson	McDonald D	McLaughlan	Brown D	Slade	Troup
	11th	Watson	Raitt	Thomson	McIntosh	Nicoll	Hutcheson	McDonald D	McLaughlan	Brown D	Slade	Troup
	18th	Watson	Raitt	Thomson	McIntosh	Nicoll	Hutcheson	McDonald D	McLaughlan	Brown D	Slade	Troup
	25th	Watson	Raitt	Fleming	Thomson	Nicoll	Hutcheson	Henderson	McLaughlan	Brown D	Slade	Troup
Nov	1st	Watson	Raitt	Thomson	McIntosh	Nicoll	Hutcheson	Henderson	McLaughlan	Bell	Slade	Troup
	8th	Watson	Raitt	Thomson	McIntosh	Nicoll	Hutcheson	Rawlings	McLaughlan	Bell	Slade	Troup
	15th	Watson	Raitt	Thomson	McIntosh	Nicoll	Hutcheson	Rawlings	McLaughlan	Bell	Slade	Troup
	22nd	Watson	Raitt	Thomson	McIntosh	Nicoll	Hutcheson	Rawlings	McDonald D	Bell	Slade	Troup
	29th	Watson	Raitt	Thomson	McIntosh	Nicoll	Hutcheson	Rawlings	McLaughlan	Bell	Slade	Troup
Dec	6th	Watson	Raitt	Thomson	McIntosh	Nicoll	Hutcheson	Rawlings	McLaughlan	Bell	Slade	Troup
	13th	Capper	Raitt	Thomson	Nairn	McIntosh	Hutcheson	Rawlings	McLaughlan	Bell	Slade	Troup
	20th	Watson	Raitt	Thomson	McIntosh	Hutcheson	Nairn	Rawlings	McLaughlan	Bel	Slade	Troup
	25th	Watson	Raitt	Thomson	McIntosh	Hutcheson	Jackson*	Rawlings	McLaughlan	Bell	Slade	Troup
	27th	Watson	Raitt	Thomson	McIntosh	Hutcheson	Nairn	Rawlings	McLaughlan	Bell	Slade	McDonald D
Jan	1st	Watson	Raitt	Thomson	McIntosh	Hutcheson	Jackson	Rawlings	McLaughlan	Bell	Slade	Troup
	3rd	Watson	Raitt	Thomson	McIntosh	Hutcheson	Jackson	Rawlings	McLaughlan	Bell	Slade	Troup
	10th	Watson	Raitt	Thomson	McIntosh	Hutcheson	Jackson	Rawlings	Slade	Bell	Orr	Troup
	17th	Watson	Raitt	Thomson	Hutcheson	Nicoll	Jackson	McDonald D	McLaughlan	Bell	Orr	Troup
	24th	Watson	Raitt	Thomson	McIntosh	Nicol	Hutcheson	Rawlings	Jackson	Bell	Slade	Troup
	31st	Watson	Raitt	Thomson	McIntosh	Nicoll	Jackson	Rawlings	McLaughlan	Bell	Slade	Troup
Feb	7th	Watson	Raitt	Thomson	McIntosh	Nicoll	Jackson	Rawlings	McLaughlan	Bell	Slade	Troup
	14th	Watson	Raitt	Thomson	McIntosh	Nicoll	Jackson	Rawlings	McDonald D	Bell	Slade	Troup
	21st	Watson	Raitt	Thomson	McIntosh	Nicoll	Jackson	Rawlings	McDonald D	Bell	Slade	Troup
	28th	Watson	Raitt	Thomson	McDonald R	Nicoll	Jackson	Rawlings	McDonald D	Bell	Slade	Troup
Mar	13th	Watson	Raitt	Thomson	McIntosh	Nicoll	Jackson	Rawlings	Cowan	Bell	Slade	Troup
	20th	Watson	Raitt	Thomson	McIntosh	Nicoll	Jackson	Rawlings	Cowan	Bell	Slade	Troup
	27th	Watson	Raitt	Thomson	McIntosh	McDonald R	Jackson	Rawlings	Cowan	Bell	McDonald D	Troup
Apr	3rd	Vallis	Raitt	Thomson	McIntosh	Nicoll	Jackson	Rawlings	Downie	Bell	McDonald D	Troup
	10th	Vallis	Raitt	Thomson	Connelly	McIntosh	Jackson	Rawlings	Cowan	Bell	Downie	McDonald D
	12th	Vallis	Raitt	Thomson	McIntosh	Nicoll	Jackson	Rawlings	McDonald D	Bell	Cowan	Troup
	17th	Vallis	Raitt	Thomson	McIntosh	Nicoll	Jackson	Rawlings	McDonald D	Bell	Slade	Troup
	21st	Vallis	Ferguson	Thomson	McIntosh	Nicoll	Jackson	Rawlings	McDonald D	Bell	Slade	Troup
	24th	Vallis	Raitt	McDonald R	McIntosh	Nicoll	Jackson	Rawlings	McDonald D	Bell	Slade	Troup
	26th	Watson	Raitt	Thomson	McIntosh	Nicoll	Jackson	Rawlings	Downie	Bell	Slade	Troup
May	11th	Watson	Raitt	Thomson	McIntosh	Nicoll	Jackson	Rawlings	McDonald D	Buchan	Slade	Thomson

Dundee F.C. Season 1919-20. (BACK, left to right) Davie Raitt, David "Napper" Thomson, Jim Watson, Dave Hutcheson, Dyken Nicoll, Bert McIntosh, Jim Downie, Jim Orr, Ernie Ferguson, Bill Longair (trainer). FRONT - Archie Rawlings, Jim McLaughlan, Johnny Bell, Donald Slade, Alec Troup and Colin Buchan.

DC Thomson

Season 1920-21

Date			Opponents		Score	Crowd	Scorers
Aug	16th	L	Falkirk	a	2-2	7,000	Bell 2
	21st	L	Aberdeen	h	1-1	18,000	Bell
	25th	L	Third Lanark	a	1-0	15,000	Troup
	28th	L	Dumbarton	a	1-1		Bell
Sep	4th	L	Falkirk	h	2-0	18,000	Irving; Troup
	8th	L	Hamilton	a	0-1		-
	11th	L	St Mirren	a	1-0		Bell
	18th	L	Third Lanark	h	2-1	17,000	Johnstone; Bell
	25th	L	Queens Park	h	1-1	19,000	Bell
Oct	2nd	L	Raith Rovers	a	2-1		Bell; McLean
	4th	L	Hearts	h	3-0	14,000	Bell 2; Honeyman
	9th	L	Motherwell	a	2-1		Bell; Hogg
	16th	L	Celtic	h	1-2	25,000	Bell
	23rd	L	Hearts	a	1-3		Bell
	30th	L	Kilmarnock	h	3-1	16,000	Bell; Troup; Cowan
Nov	6th	L	Rangers	a	0-5		-
	13th	L	Airdrie	h	0-1	14,000	-
	20th	L	Hibernian	a	0-2		-
	27th	L	Clyde	h	2-1	12,000	McLean; Thomson (pen)
Dec	4th	L	Ayr United	a	1-1		Troup
	11th	L	Albion Rovers	h	3-0	14,000	McLean 2; Thomson (pen)
	18th	L	Partick Thistle	a	1-2		McLean
	25th	L	Hamilton	h	4-0	11,000	Bell 2; McDonald; McLean
	25th	FC1	Forfar Athletic	a	1-0	2,000	Cowan
Jan	1st	L	Aberdeen	a	0-0	20,000	-
	3rd	L	Hibernian	h	1-1	20,000	Nicoll
	8th	L	Morton	h	0-0	15,000	-
	15th	L	Queens Park	a	0-0		
	22nd	SC1	Inverness Caley	h	8-1	18,000	T. Jackson; Philip 3; Troup; Nicoll; Thomson; McLean
	29th	L	Dumbarton	h	2-1	15,000	Bell; Thomson (pen)
Feb	5th	SC2	Stenhousemuir	h	1-0	16,000	Bell
	9th	L	Clydebank	a	1-0		T. Jackson
	12th	L	Rangers	h	1-2	28,000	T. Jackson
	19th	SC3	Aberdeen	h	0-0	27,000	-
	22nd	SC3R	Aberdeen	a	1-1	20,000	Hutton o.g.
	26th	L	Raith Rovers	h	0-0	15,000	-
	29th	SC3R	Aberdeen	lbr	2-0	15,000	Philip; Troup
Mar	5th	SC4	Albion Rovers	h	0-2	13,000	-
	9th	L	Celtic	a	0-2		-
	12th	L	Partick Thistle	h	1-0	4,000	Bell
	12th	FCS	Brechin City	a	2-2	1,500	T. Jackson; Honeyman
	19th	L	Kilmarnock	a	0-5		-
	19th	FCSR	Brechin City	h	1-0	4,000	T. Jackson
	26th	L	Ayr United	h	2-0	9,000	Troup; Bell
Apr	2nd	L	Albion Rovers	a	3-2		McLean; Bell; Troup
	4th	L	Morton	a	0-1		-
	9th	L	Motherwell	h	2-1	12,000	Cowan; Bell
	11th	L	Clydebank	h	2-0	12,000	Bell; Kilpatrick
	16th	L	Airdrie	a	1-1		Bell
	16th	FCF	Arbroath	h	2-2	9,000	Bannister (pen); Connelly
	23rd	L	St Mirren	h	2-0	11,000	Bell 2
	27th	FCFR	Arbroath	a	0-3	2,000	-
	30th	L	Clyde	a	2-5		J. Jackson; Thomson (pen)

Cup Cash v. Stenhousemuir £700, v. Aberdeen (a) £1,056, v. Albion Rovers (h) £625.

Alec Troup and Davie McDonald - the Dens wing men caused havoc in opposing defences.

The Record

League	-	Fourth Place, Division One
Scottish Cup	-	Quarter-final
Forfarshire Cup	-	Runners-up
Top Scorer	-	Johnny Bell (26 goals)
Av. Home Gate	-	15,200
Players used	-	22
Sent off	-	None

Appearances

	League		Scottish Cup		Total	
Tom Gibbon	41		6		47	
Alec Troup	39	(6)	6 (2)		45	(8)
John Jackson	37	(1)	6		43	(1)
Davie Raitt	38		5		43	
Napper Thomson	35	(4)	6 (1)		41	(5)
Johnny Bell	36	(25)	4 (1)		40	(26)
Sam Irving	35	(1)	5		40	(1)
Willie McLean	30	(6)	6 (1)		37	(7)
Dyken Nicol	30	(1)	3		32	(1)
George Philip	25		3 (4)		28	(4)
Tom Kilpatrick	22	(1)	5		27	(1)
Willie Cowan	17	(2)	3		20	(2)
Dave Hutcheson	16		3		19	
John Honeyman	12	(1)	1		13	(1)
Dave McDonald	13	(1)	0		13	(1)
Tom Fleming	10		1		11	
Joe Johnstone	6	(1)	1		7	(1)
Isaac Reid	6		0		6	
Donald Slade	6		0		6	
Tom Jackson	3	(2)	2 (1)		5	(3)
John Davidson	2		0		2	
Billy Hogg	2		0		2	

Scottish League Division One

		Home			Away			Goals		
	P	W	D	L	W	D	L	F	A	PTS
Rangers	42	19	1	1	16	5	0	91-24		76
Celtic	42	16	3	2	14	3	4	86-35		60
Hearts	42	15	2	4	5	8	0	74-49		50
Dundee	42	13	5	3	6	6	9	54-48		49
Motherwell	42	11	5	5	8	5	8	75-48		48
Partick Thistle	42	10	9	2	7	3	11	53-39		46
Clyde	42	16	3	2	5	0	16	63-62		45
Third Lanark	42	10	3	8	9	3	9	74-61		44
Morton	42	10	8	3	5	6	10	66-58		44
Airdrie	42	9	5	7	8	4	9	71-64		43
Aberdeen	42	9	7	5	5	7	9	53-54		42
Kilmarnock	42	13	2	6	4	6	11	62-68		42
Hibernian	42	9	5	7	7	4	10	58-57		41
Ayr United	42	10	8	3	4	4	13	62-69		40
Hamilton	42	9	8	4	5	4	12	44-57		40
Raith Rovers	42	14	0	7	2	5	14	64-58		37
Albion Rovers	42	6	5	10	5	7	9	57-68		34
Falkirk	42	7	6	8	4	6	11	54-72		34
Queens Park	42	6	8	7	5	3	13	45-80		33
Clydebank	42	6	6	9	1	8	12	47-72		28
Dumbarton	42	9	1	11	1	3	17	41-89		24
St Mirren	42	5	2	14	2	2	17	43-92		18

Dundee F.C. Line-Ups 1920-21

		1	2	3	4	5	6	7	8	9	10	11
Aug	16th	Gibbon	Raitt	Thomson	Irving	Nicoll	Jackson	McDonald	Philip	Bell	Slade	Troup
	21st	Gibbon	Raitt	Thomson	Irving	Nicoll	Jackson	McDonald	Philip	Bell	Slade	Troup
	25th	Gibbon	Raitt	Thomson	Irving	Nicoll	Jackson	McDonald	Philip	Bell	Slade	Troup
	28th	Gibbon	Raitt	Thomson	Irving	Nicoll	Jackson	McDonald	Philip	Bell	Slade	Troup
Sep	4th	Gibbon	Raitt	Thomson	Irving	Nicoll	Jackson	McDonald	Philip	Bell	Slade	Troup
	8th	Gibbon	Fleming	Raitt	Irving	Nicoll	Jackson	McDonald	Philip	Bell	Slade	Troup
	11th	Gibbon	Raitt	Thomson	Irving	Nicoll	Jackson	Davidson	Johnstone	Bell	Philip	Troup
	18th	Gibbon	Raitt	Thomson	Irving	Nicoll	Jackson	Davidson	Johnstone	Bell	Philip	Troup
	25th	Gibbon	Raitt	Thomson	Irving	Nicoll	Jackson	Honeyman	McLean	Bell	Philip	Troup
Oct	2nd	Gibbon	Raitt	Thomson	Irving	Nicoll	Philip	Cowan	McLean	Bell	Honeyman	Troup
	4th	Gibbon	Raitt	Thomson	Irving	Nicoll	Philip	Cowan	McLean	Bell	Honeyman	Troup
	9th	Gibbon	Raitt	Thomson	Irving	Nicol	Philip	Hogg	McLean	Bell	Honeyman	Troup
	16th	Gibbon	Raitt	Thomson	Irving	Nicoll	Philip	Hogg	McLean	Bell	Honeyman	Troup
	23rd	Gibbon	Raitt	Thomson	Irving	Nicoll	Philip	Reid	McLean	Bell	Jackson	Troup
	30th	Gibbon	Raitt	Thomson	Irving	Nicoll	Jackson	Reid	Cowan	Bell	McLean	Troup
Nov	6th	Gibbon	Raitt	Thomson	Irving	Nicoll	Jackson	Reid	Cowan	Bell	McLean	Troup
	13th	Gibbon	Fleming	Raitt	Irving	Nicoll	Jackson	Kilpatrick	Philip	Bell	McLean	Troup
	20th	Gibbon	Fleming	Raitt	Hutcheson	Nicoll	Jackson	Kilpatrick	Irving	Bell	McLean	Troup
	27th	Gibbon	Raitt	Thomson	Hutcheson	Nicoll	Jackson	Kilpatrick	McLean	Philip	McDonald	Troup
Dec	4th	Gibbon	Raitt	Thomson	Hutcheson	Nicoll	Jackson	Kilpatrick	McLean	Philip	McDonald	Troup
	11th	Gibbon	Raitt	Thomson	Hutcheson	Nicoll	Jackson	Kilpatrick	McLean	Philip	McDonald	Troup
	18th	Gibbon	Raitt	Thomson	Hutcheson	Nicoll	Jackson	Honeyman	McLean	Philip	McDonald	Troup
	25th	Gibbon	Raitt	Thomson	Irving	Nicoll	Jackson	Honeyman	McLean	Bell	McDonald	Troup
Jan	1st	Gibbon	Raitt	Thomson	Irving	Nicoll	Jackson	Honeyman	McLean	Bell	McDonald	Troup
	3rd	Gibbon	Raitt	Thomson	Irving	Nicoll	Jackson	Kilpatrick	McLean	Bell	McDonald	Troup
	8th	Gibbon	Raitt	Thomson	Johnstone	Nicoll	Jackson	Kilpatrick	McLean	Bell	Honeyman	Troup
	15th	Gibbon	Raitt	Thomson	Johnstone	Nicoll	Jackson	Bell	McLean	Philip	Honeyman	Troup
	22nd	Gibbon	Raitt	Thomson	Johnstone	Nicoll	Jackson	Bell	McLean	Philip	Jackson T	Troup
	29th	Gibbon	Raitt	Thomson	Irving	Nicoll	Jackson	Kilpatrick	McLean	Bell	Jackson T	Troup
Feb	5th	Gibbon	Raitt	Thomson	Irving	Nicoll	Jackson	Kilpatrick	McLean	Bell	Jackson T	Troup
	9th	Gibbon	Raitt	Fleming	Irving	Hutcheson	Jackson	Kilpatrick	Cowan	Jackson T	Philip	Reid
	12th	Gibbon	Raitt	Fleming	Irving	Hutcheson	Jackson	Kilpatrick	Cowan	Jackson T	McLean	Reid
	19th	Gibbon	Raitt	Thomson	Irving	Nicoll	Jackson	Kilpatrick	Cowan	Bell	McLean	Troup
	22nd	Gibbon	Fleming	Thomson	Irving	Hutcheson	Jackson	Kilpatrick	McLean	Bell	Cowan	Troup
	26th	Gibbon	Fleming	Thomson	Irving	Hutcheson	Jackson	Kilpatrick	McLean	Bell	Cowan	Reid
	29th	Gibbon	Raitt	Thomson	Irving	Hutcheson	Jackson	Kilpatrick	McLean	Philip	Cowan	Troup
Mar	5th	Gibbon	Raitt	Thomson	Irving	Hutcheson	Jackson	Kilpatrick	McLean	Philip	Honeyman	Troup
	9th	Gibbon	Raitt	Fleming	Irving	Hutcheson	Johnstone	Kilpatrick	Cowan	Bell	Philip	Troup
	12th	Gibbon	Hutcheson	Fleming	Irving	McLean	Jackson	Kilpatrick	Cowan	Bell	Philip	Troup
	19th	Gibbon	Fleming	Thomson	Irving	Hutcheson	Jackson	Kilpatrick	Cowan	Bell	McLean	Troup
	26th	Gibbon	Raitt	Thomson	Irving	Hutcheson	Jackson	Kilpatrick	Cowan	Bell	McLean	Troup
Apr	2nd	Gibbon	Raitt	Thomson	Irving	Hutcheson	Jackson	Kilpatrick	Honeyman	Bell	McLean	Troup
	4th	Gibbon	Raitt	Thomson	Irving	Hutcheson	Jackson	Kilpatrick	Cowan	Bell	McLean	Troup
	9th	Gibbon	Raitt	Thomson	Irving	Hutcheson	Jackson	Kilpatrick	Cowan	Bell	McLean	Troup
	11th	Gibbon	Raitt	Thomson	Irving	Hutcheson	Jackson	Honeyman	Cowan	Bell	Kilpatrick	Troup
	16th	Gibbon	Fleming	Thomson	Johnstone	Philip	Jackson	Kilpatrick	Cowan	Bell	McLean	Troup
	23rd	Gibbon	Raitt	Thomson	Irving	Philip	Jackson	Kilpatrick	Cowan	Bell	McLean	Troup
	30th	Gibbon	Raitt	Thomson	Irving	Hutcheson	Johnstone	Kilpatrick	Cowan	Bell	McLean	Troup

Some Dundee F.C. stars of the early 1920's - George Philip, John Jackson, Johnny Bell, David Thomson, Davie Raitt and Alec Troup.

Season 1921-22

Date			Opponents		Score	Crowd	Scorers
Aug	17th	L	Airdrie	h	1-1	15,000	McLean
	20th	L	Falkirk	a	0-1	7,000	-
	27th	L	Third Lanark	h	2-0	17,000	Cowan; Bell
Sep	3rd	L	Aberdeen	a	2-1		Bird; Nicoll
	10th	L	Morton	a	1-2	9,000	Bird
	17th	L	Ayr United	h	1-0	20,000	McLean
	21st	L	Motherwell	a	1-2		Halliday
	24th	L	Queens Park	h	3-1	15,000	Bird 2; Troup
Oct	1st	L	Airdrie	a	2-0		Halliday; Troup
	3rd	L	Motherwell	h	1-1	16,000	Halliday
	3rd	FC1	Forfar Athletic	a	1-1	3,000	Cumming
	8th	L	Celtic	h	0-0	26,000	-
	15th	L	Hearts	a	0-0		-
	22nd	L	Kilmarnock	h	5-0	12,000	Bird; Halliday 2; McLean; Troup
	29th	L	Clydebank	a	3-0		Halliday; Bird; Johnstone
Nov	5th	L	Rangers	h	0-0	30,000	-
	12th	L	Hibernian	a	1-1		Halliday
	19th	L	Albion Rovers	h	2-0	10,000	Halliday; Bird
	26th	L	St Mirren	a	1-2	15,000	Bell
Dec	3rd	L	Clyde	h	2-1	17,000	McLean; Bird
	10th	L	Raith Rovers	a	0-0		-
	17th	L	Dumbarton	a	0-2		-
	24th	L	Hamilton	h	2-0	10,000	Bell; McLean
	26th	L	Rangers	a	1-2	12,000	Troup
	31st	L	Clyde	a	1-3		Bird
Jan	2nd	L	Aberdeen	h	1-0	25,000	Bird
	3rd	L	Hibernian	h	0-0	15,000	-
	7th	L	Partick Thistle	a	1-4		McLean
	14th	L	Morton	h	2-1	14,000	Halliday 2
	21st	L	Queens Park	a	3-0		Halliday
	28th	SC1	Stenhousemuir	a	2-0	7,000	Halliday; McDonald
Feb	4th	L	St Mirren	h	2-2	10,000	Halliday 2
	11th	SC2	Royal Albert	a	1-0	7,000	Halliday
	15th	L	Kilmarnock	a	3-5		Bird 2; Ross
	18th	L	Dumbarton	h	2-0	11,000	Halliday; Ross
	25th	SC3	Aberdeen	a	0-3	26,577	-
Mar	1st	L	Partick Thistle	h	0-0	10,000	-
	4th	L	Albion Rovers	a	0-1		-
	11th	L	Third Lanark	a	0-1		-
	18th	L	Hearts	h	2-0	14,000	Halliday 2
	23rd	FC1R	Forfar Athletic	h	0-2	5,000	-
	25th	L	Hamilton	a	2-1		Halliday; McLean
Apr	8th	L	Celtic	a	0-4		-
	15th	L	Falkirk	h	3-0	11,000	Halliday 3
	19th	L	Raith Rovers	h	1-0	12,000	Cowan
	22nd	L	Clydebank	h	1-1	10,000	Cowan
	29th	L	Ayr United	a	2-0		Halliday; Bird

Cup Cash v. Royal Albert £190

Willie Fotheringham - the big keeper was an ever-present.

The Record		
League	-	Fourth Place, Division One
Scottish Cup	-	Third round
Forfarshire Cup	-	First round
Top Scorer	-	Davie Halliday (25 goals)
Av. Home Gate	-	15,300
Players used	-	23
Sent off	-	None

Appearances

	League	Scottish Cup	Total	
Willie Fotheringham	42	3	45	
Dyken Nicoll	39 (1)	2	41	(1)
Davie Raitt	37	3	40	
Alec Troup	38 (3)	2	40	(3)
Walter Bird	35 (14)	3	38	(14)
Willie McLean	31 (7)	1	32	(7)
Napper Thomson	29	3	32	
Davie Halliday	28 (23)	3 (2)	31	(25)
Jock Ross	23 (2)	3	26	(2)
Sam Irving	24	0	24	
John Jackson	20	3	23	
Willie Cowan	16 (3)	2	18	(3)
Johnny Bell	17 (3)	0	17	(3)
Andy Herd	15	2	17	
Bob Willis	15	0	15	
George Aimer	13	0	13	
George Thompson	12	1	13	
Tom Kilpatrick	11	0	11	
Hugh Lorimer	8	0	8	
Dave McDonald	4 (1)	1	5	(1)
Joe Johnstone	4 (1)	0	4	(1)
Tom Fleming	2	0	2	
Dave Cumming	1	0	1	

Scottish League Division One

		Home			Away			Goals		
	P	W	D	L	W	D	L	F	A	PTS
Celtic	42	19	2	0	8	11	2	83-20		67
Rangers	42	15	4	2	13	6	2	83-26		66
Raith Rovers	42	12	7	2	7	6	8	66-43		51
Dundee	42	13	8	0	6	3	12	**57-40**		**49**
Falkirk	42	13	6	2	3	11	7	48-38		49
Partick Thistle	42	12	6	3	8	2	11	57-43		48
Hibernian	42	11	7	3	5	7	9	55-44		46
St Mirren	42	11	6	4	6	6	9	68-61		46
Third Lanark	42	10	7	4	7	5	9	58-52		46
Clyde	42	12	7	2	4	5	12	60-51		44
Albion Rovers	42	11	4	6	18	6	6	55-51		44
Morton	42	14	5	2	17	2	5	58-57		42
Motherwell	42	15	3	3	1	4	16	63-58		39
Ayr United	42	11	6	4	2	6	13	55-63		38
Aberdeen	42	10	5	6	3	4	14	48-54		35
Airdrie	42	10	4	7	2	7	12	46-56		35
Kilmarnock	42	12	6	3	1	3	17	56-83		35
Hamilton	42	7	8	6	2	8	11	51-62		34
Hearts	42	9	6	6	2	4	15	50-60		32
Dumbarton	42	9	4	8	1	6	14	46-81		30
Queens Park	42	5	5	11	4	5	12	38-82		28
Clydebank	42	5	6	10	1	2	18	34-103		20

Dundee F.C. Line-Ups 1921-22

		1	2	3	4	5	6	7	8	9	10	11
Aug	17th	Fotheringham	Raitt	Thomson	Irving	Nicoll	Jackson	Kilpatrick	Bird	Bell	McLean	Troup
	20th	Fotheringham	Raitt	Thomson	Irving	Thompson	Nicoll	Kilpatrick	Bird	Bell	Halliday	Troup
	27th	Fotheringham	Raitt	Thomson	Irving	Thompson	Nicoll	Kilpatrick	Cowan	Bell	Bird	Troup
Sep	3rd	Fotheringham	Raitt	Thomson	Irving	Thompson	Nicoll	Kilpatrick	McLean	Bell	Bird	Troup
	10th	Fotheringham	Raitt	Thomson	Irving	Thompson	Nicoll	Ross	McLean	Bell	Bird	Halliday
	17th	Fotheringham	Raitt	Thomson	Irving	Thompson	Nicoll	Ross	McLean	Bell	Bird	Troup
	21st	Fotheringham	Raitt	Thomson	Irving	Thompson	Nicoll	Ross	Cowan	Halliday	Bird	Troup
	24th	Fotheringham	Raitt	Thomson	Irving	Nicoll	Jackson	Ross	Cowan	Halliday	Bird	Troup
Oct	1st	Fotheringham	Fleming	Thomson	Irving	Nicoll	Jackson	Ross	Cowan	Halliday	Bird	Troup
	3rd	Fotheringham	Fleming	Thomson	Irving	Nicoll	Jackson	Ross	Cowan	Halliday	Bird	Troup
	8th	Fotheringham	Raitt	Thomson	Willis	Nicoll	Irving	Kilpatrick	McLean	Halliday	Bird	Troup
	15th	Fotheringham	Raitt	Thomson	Willis	Nicoll	Johnstone	Kilpatrick	McLean	Halliday	Bird	Troup
	22nd	Fotheringham	Raitt	Thomson	Willis	Nicoll	Irving	Ross	McLean	Halliday	Bird	Troup
	29th	Fotheringham	Raitt	Thomson	Johnstone	Nicoll	Irving	Kilpatrick	McLean	Halliday	Bird	Troup
Nov	5th	Fotheringham	Raitt	Thomson	Willis	Nicoll	Irving	Kilpatrick	McLean	Halliday	Bird	Troup
	12th	Fotheringham	Raitt	Thomson	Willis	Nicoll	Irving	Kilpatrick	McLean	Halliday	Bird	Troup
	19th	Fotheringham	Raitt	Thomson	Willis	Nicoll	Irving	Kilpatrick	McLean	Halliday	Bird	Troup
	26th	Fotheringham	Raitt	Thomson	Willis	Nicoll	Irving	Kilpatrick	McLean	Bell	Bird	Troup
Dec	3rd	Fotheringham	Raitt	Thomson	Willis	Nicoll	Johnstone	Lorimer	McLean	Bell	Bird	Troup
	10th	Fotheringham	Raitt	Thomson	Irving	Nicoll	Thompson	Lorimer	McLean	Bell	Bird	Troup
	17th	Fotheringham	Raitt	Thomson	Irving	Nicoll	Johnstone	Lorimer	McLean	Bell	Bird	Troup
	24th	Fotheringham	Raitt	Thomson	Irving	Nicoll	Willis	Lorimer	McLean	Bell	Bird	Troup
	26th	Fotheringham	Raitt	Thomson	Willis	Nicoll	Hird	Lorimer	McLean	Bell	Bird	Troup
	31st	Fotheringham	Raitt	Thomson	Willis	Nicoll	Hird	Lorimer	McLean	Bell	Bird	Troup
Jan	2nd	Fotheringham	Raitt	Thomson	Willis	Nicoll	Jackson	Cumming	McLean	Bell	Bird	Troup
	3rd	Fotheringham	Raitt	Aimer	Herd	Nicoll	Jackson	Lorimer	McLean	Bell	Bird	Troup
	7th	Fotheringham	Raitt	Thomson	Herd	Nicoll	Jackson	Lorimer	McLean	Bell	Bird	Troup
	14th	Fotheringham	Raitt	Aimer	Herd	Thompson	Jackson	Ross	McLean	Halliday	Bird	Troup
	21st	Fotheringham	Raitt	Aimer	Herd	Thompson	Jackson	Ross	McLean	Halliday	Bird	McDonald
	28th	Fotheringham	Raitt	Thomson	Herd	Thompson	Jackson	Ross	McLean	Halliday	Bird	McDonald
Feb	4th	Fotheringham	Raitt	Aimer	Herd	Nicoll	Jackson	Ross	McLean	Halliday	Bird	McDonald
	11th	Fotheringham	Raitt	Thomson	Herd	Nicoll	Jackson	Ross	Cowan	Halliday	Bird	Troup
	15th	Fotheringham	Raitt	Thomson	Herd	Thompson	Willis	Ross	Cowan	Halliday	Bird	Troup
	18th	Fotheringham	Raitt	Thomson	Herd	Nicoll	Jackson	Ross	Cowan	Halliday	Bird	Troup
	25th	Fotheringham	Raitt	Thomson	Thompson	Nicoll	Jackson	Ross	Cowan	Halliday	Bird	Troup
Mar	1st	Fotheringham	Hird	Aimer	Willis	Nicoll	Jackson	Ross	Cowan	Halliday	McDonald	Troup
	4th	Fotheringham	Hird	Aimer	Willis	Nicoll	Jackson	Ross	Cowan	Bell	Halliday	McDonald
	11th	Fotheringham	Hird	Aimer	Nicol	Thompson	Jackson	Ross	Bird	Halliday	Cowan	Troup
	18th	Fotheringham	Raitt	Aimer	Herd	Nicoll	Jackson	Ross	McLean	Halliday	Bird	Troup
	25th	Fotheringham	Raitt	Aimer	Herd	Nicoll	Jackson	Ross	McLean	Halliday	Cowan	Troup
Apr	8th	Fotheringham	Raitt	Aimer	Herd	Nicoll	Jackson	Ross	McLean	Halliday	Cowan	Troup
	15th	Fotheringham	Raitt	Aimer	Irving	Nicoll	Jackson	Ross	McLean	Halliday	Cowan	Troup
	19th	Fotheringham	Raitt	Aimer	Irving	Nicoll	Jackson	Ross	McLean	Halliday	Cowan	Troup
	22nd	Fotheringham	Raitt	Aimer	Irving	Nicoll	Jackson	Ross	McLean	Halliday	Cowan	Troup
	29th	Fotheringham	Raitt	Thomson	Irving	McLean	Nicoll	Ross	Cowan	Halliday	Bird	Troup

Dens Park on August 27th, 1921. Willie Fotheringham collects the ball with right-back Davie Raitt blocking the progress of Third Lanark's Reid. In the background, the new North stand nears completion. It towers over the old structure which was removed soon afterwards.

They Wore The Dark Blue

Season 1922-23

Date			Opponents		Score	Crowd	Scorers
Aug	19th	L	Aberdeen	h	1-1	18,000	D. McLean
	26th	L	Hearts	a	1-2	26,000	D. McLean
	29th	L	Clyde	a	3-4	10,000	D. McLean 3
Sep	2nd	L	Kilmarnock	h	2-0	15,000	D. McLean 2
	9th	L	Motherwell	a	4-3		Bell; Cowan; D McLean; Troup
	16th	L	Partick Thistle	h	1-0	17,000	D. McLean
	23rd	L	Celtic	h	0-1	25,000	-
	30th	L	Albion Rovers	a	0-0		-
Oct	2nd	L	Third Lanark	h	2-0	18,000	Cowan 2
	7th	L	Ayr United	h	1-0	15,000	D. McLean
	14th	L	Alloa	a	3-1	5,000	D. McLean 2; Halliday
	21st	L	Hamilton	h	3-0	17,000	Cowan; D. McLean; Halliday
	28th	L	Raith Rovers	a	3-0		Cowan; D. McLean 2
Nov	4th	L	Airdrie	h	1-0	20,000	D. McLean
	11th	L	Hibernian	a	3-3		D. McLean; Halliday 2
	18th	L	St Mirren	h	2-0	15,000	D. McLean 2
	25th	L	Morton	a	3-2		D. McLean 2; Halliday
Dec	2nd	L	Raith Rovers	h	0-4	18,000	-
	9th	L	Rangers	a	1-4		Knox
	16th	L	Alloa	h	2-1	14,000	D. McLean; Troup
	23rd	L	Falkirk	a	0-1		-
	25th	L	Third Lanark	a	0-2		-
	30th	L	Albion Rovers	h	4-0	8,000	W. McLean; McDonald 2; Halliday
Jan	1st	L	Aberdeen	a	0-0	25,000	-
	2nd	L	Hibernian	h	1-0	20,000	McDonald
	6th	L	Kilmarnock	a	0-2		-
	13th	SC1	Vale of Atholl	h	6-0	12,000	Cowan 2 (1 pen); Halliday 3; Troup
	20th	L	Hearts	h	0-0	12,000	-
	27th	SC2	St Bernards	h	0-0	17,000	-
	31st	SC2R	St Bernards	a	3-2	13,000	Halliday; D. McLean; Knox
Feb	3rd	L	Partick Thistle	a	0-2		-
	6th	L	St Mirren	a	0-4	2,000	-
	10th	SC3	Hamilton	h	0-0	11,000	-
	14th	SC3R	Hamilton	a	1-0	15,000	Knox
	17th	L	Airdrie	a	1-1		W. McLean
	24th	SC4	Third Lanark	a	1-1	38,000	Halliday
	28th	SC4R	Third Lanark	h	0-0	17,000	-
Mar	3rd	L	Ayr United	a	0-1		-
	5th	SC4R	Third Lanark	Ibrox	0-1	31,215	-
	10th	L	Morton	h	0-1	14,000	-
	17th	L	Celtic	a	1-2		Gibson
	24th	L	Rangers	h	1-2	20,000	Halliday
	28th	FCS	Montrose	h	6-0	4,000	Halliday 4; Letham 2
	31st	L	Hamilton	a	0-0		-
Apr	7th	L	Clyde	h	1-0	10,000	Thomson (pen)
	9th	L	Falkirk	h	3-0	10,000	Bird; Halliday 2
	14th	L	Motherwell	h	3-1	10,000	Cowan; Halliday; Thomson (pen)

Cup Cash v. St Bernards (h) £800, v. Hamilton (h) £400, v. Third Lanark (a) £1,400.

Sam Irving - polished Irish international wing-half.

The Record

League	-	Seventh Place, Division One
Scottish Cup	-	Quarter-final
Forfarshire Cup	-	Winners (Final, August 1923)
Top Scorer	-	Davie McLean (23 goals)
Av. Home Gate	-	15,600
Players used	-	25
Sent off	-	None

Appearances

	League		Scottish Cup		Total	
Willie Fotheringham	38		8		46	
Sam Irving	29		8		37	
Napper Thomson	30	(2)	7		37	(2)
Willie Cowan	30	(6)	6	(2)	36	(8)
Jock Ross	27		8		35	
Davie Halliday	26	(10)	8	(5)	34	(15)
Davie McLean	25	(22)	7	(1)	32	(23)
Willie Knox	23	(1)	8	(2)	31	(3)
Willie Rankine	27		4		31	
Jock McDonald	25	(3)	3		28	(3)
Dyken Nicoll	16		5		21	
Crawford Letham	19		2		21	
George Aimer	16		1		17	
Alec Troup	16	(2)	1	(1)	17	(3)
Walter Bird	12	(1)	4		16	(1)
Willie McLean	10	(2)	3		13	(2)
George Greenshields	11		0		11	
Neil Turner	8		1		9	
Ralph Rogerson	5		2		7	
Johnny Bell	6	(1)	0		6	(1)
Hugh Coyle	4		1		5	
Peter Dyer	2		0		2	
George Gibson	2	(1)	0		2	(1)
Bob Maiden	2		0		2	
Bob Willis	2		0		2	

Scottish League Division One

		Home			Away			Goals		
	P	W	D	L	W	D	L	F	A	PTS
Rangers	38	15	4	0	8	5	6	67-29		55
Airdrie	38	14	4	1	6	6	7	58-38		50
Celtic	38	10	5	4	9	3	7	52-39		46
Falkirk	38	9	10	0	5	7	7	44-32		45
Aberdeen	38	10	6	3	5	6	8	46-34		42
St Mirren	38	11	6	2	4	6	9	54-44		42
Dundee	**38**	**13**	**2**	**4**	**4**	**5**	**10**	**51-45**		**41**
Hibernian	38	14	2	3	3	5	11	45-40		41
Raith Rovers	38	9	8	2	4	5	10	31-53		39
Ayr United	38	11	6	2	2	6	11	43-74		38
Partick Thistle	38	11	4	4	3	5	11	51-48		37
Hearts	38	6	10	3	5	5	9	51-50		37
Motherwell	38	10	6	3	3	4	12	59-60		36
Morton	38	9	3	7	3	8	8	44-47		35
Kilmarnock	38	11	1	7	3	6	10	57-66		35
Clyde	38	10	4	5	2	5	12	36-44		33
Third Lanark	38	8	5	6	3	3	13	40-59		30
Hamilton	38	8	6	5	3	1	15	43-59		29
Albion Rovers	38	7	3	9	1	7	11	38-64		26
Alloa	38	3	7	9	3	4	12	27-52		23

Dundee F.C. Line-Ups 1922-23

		1	2	3	4	5	6	7	8	9	10	11
Aug	19th	Fotheringham	Thomson	Aimer	Irving	McLean W	Greenshields	Turner	Cowan	McLean D	McDonald	Troup
	26th	Fotheringham	Maiden	Thomson	Irving	Nicoll	Greenshields	Turner	McLean W	McLean D	Cowan	Troup
	29th	Fotheringham	Maiden	Thomson	Irving	Nicoll	Greenshields	Turner	McLean W	McLean D	Cowan	Troup
Sep	2nd	Fotheringham	Nicoll	Thomson	Irving	Rankine	Greenshields	Ross	Bird	McLean D	McDonald	Troup
	9th	Fotheringham	Aimer	Thomson	Letham	Rankine	Greenshields	Bell	Cowan	McLean D	McDonald	Troup
	16th	Fotheringham	Aimer	Thomson	Letham	Rankine	Greenshields	Bell	Cowan	McLean D	McDonald	Troup
	23rd	Fotheringham	Aimer	Thomson	Letham	Rankine	Greenshields	Bell	Cowan	McLean D	Bird	Troup
	30th	Fotheringham	Aimer	Thomson	Nicoll	Rankine	Greenshields	Ross	McLean D	Halliday	Cowan	Troup
Oct	2nd	Fotheringham	Irving	Thomson	Nicoll	Rankine	Greenshields	Bell	McLean D	Halliday	Cowan	Troup
	7th	Fotheringham	Irving	Troup	Nicoll	Rankine	Greenshields	Bell	Cowan	McLean D	McDonald	Troup
	14th	Fotheringham	Irving	Thomson	Ross	Rankine	Letham	Turner	Cowan	McLean D	McDonald	Halliday
	21st	Fotheringham	Irving	Thomson	Ross	Rankine	Letham	Turner	Cowan	McLean D	McDonald	Halliday
	28th	Fotheringham	Irving	Thomson	Ross	Rankine	Letham	Turner	Cowan	McLean D	McDonald	Halliday
Nov	4th	Fotheringham	Irving	Thomson	Ross	Rankine	Letham	Turner	Cowan	McLean D	McDonald	Halliday
	11th	Fotheringham	Irving	Thomson	Ross	Rankine	Letham	Knox	Cowan	McLean D	McDonald	Halliday
	18th	Fotheringham	Irving	Thomson	Ross	Rankine	Irving	Knox	Cowan	McLean D	McDonald	Halliday
	25th	Fotheringham	Irving	Thomson	Ross	Rankine	Letham	Knox	Cowan	McLean D	McDonald	Halliday
Dec	2nd	Fotheringham	Irving	Thomson	Ross	Rankine	Letham	Knox	Cowan	McLean D	McDonald	Halliday
	9th	Fotheringham	Aimer	Thomson	Ross	Rankine	Greenshields	Knox	Bird	McLean D	Cowan	Halliday
	16th	Fotheringham	Aimer	Thomson	Ross	Rankine	Nicoll	Knox	Bird	McLean D	Cowan	Troup
	23rd	Fotheringham	Aimer	Thomson	Ross	Nicoll	Irving	Knox	Bird	McLean D	Cowan	Troup
	25th	Fotheringham	Willis	Aimer	Ross	Nicol	Irving	Knox	Bird	Halliday	Cowan	Troup
	30th	Fotheringham	Willis	Aimer	Ross	Nicoll	Irving	Knox	McLean W	Halliday	McDonald	Troup
Jan	1st	Fotheringham	Ross	Aimer	Irving	Nicoll	Letham	Knox	McLean W	Halliday	Cowan	McDonald
	2nd	Fotheringham	Ross	Aimer	Irving	Nicoll	Letham	Knox	McLean W	Halliday	McDonald	Troup
	6th	Fotheringham	Rogerson	Aimer	Ross	Nicoll	Irving	Knox	Cowan	Halliday	McLean W	McDonald
	13th	Fotheringham	Rogerson	Aimer	Ross	Irving	Letham	Knox	Cowan	Halliday	McDonald	Troup
	20th	Fotheringham	Rogerson	Thomson	Ross	Rankine	Irving	Knox	Cowan	McLean D	McDonald	Troup
	27th	Fotheringham	Rogerson	Thomson	Ross	Rankine	Irving	Knox	Cowan	McLean D	McDonald	Halliday
	31st	Fotheringham	Ross	Thomson	Irving	Rankine	Coyle	Knox	Cowan	McLean D	McLean W	Halliday
Feb	3rd	Fotheringham	Rogerson	Aimer	Irving	Rankine	Coyle	Knox	Cowan	Halliday	McLean W	Bell
	6th	Fotheringham	Rogerson	Aimer	Nicoll	Rankine	Irving	Turner	McLean	Dyer	Letham	Halliday
	10th	Fotheringham	Ross	Thomson	Nicoll	Rankine	Irving	Knox	Cowan	McLean D	McLean W	Halliday
	14th	Fotheringham	Ross	Thomson	Coyle	Nicoll	Irving	Knox	McLean W	McLean D	Bird	Halliday
	17th	Fotheringham	Ross	Thomson	Coyle	Nicoll	Irving	Knox	McLean W	McLean D	Bird	Halliday
	24th	Fotheringham	Ross	Thomson	Coyle	Nicoll	Irving	Knox	Cowan	McLean D	Bird	Halliday
	28th	Fotheringham	Ross	Thomson	Nicoll	Rankine	Irving	Knox	Cowan	McLean D	Bird	Halliday
Mar	3rd	Fotheringham	Ross	Rogerson	Coyle	Rankine	Letham	Knox	McLean W	McLean D	Gibson	Halliday
	5th	Fotheringham	Rogerson	Thomson	Irving	Nicoll	Letham	Knox	Bird	McLean D	McDonald	Halliday
	10th	Fotheringham	Aimer	Thomson	Irving	Nicoll	Coyle	Knox	Bird	Dyer	McDonald	Turner
	17th	Fotheringham	Ross	Thomson	Coyle	Rankine	Irving	Knox	Bird	Halliday	Gibson	Halliday
	24th	Fotheringham	Ross	Thomson	Coyle	Rankine	Irving	Knox	Cowan	Halliday	Bird	McDonald
	31st	Fotheringham	Ross	Thomson	Coyle	Rankine	Irving	Knox	Cowan	Halliday	Letham	McDonald
Apr	7th	Fotheringham	Ross	Thomson	Coyle	Rankine	Irving	Knox	Cowan	Halliday	Letham	McDonald
	9th	Fotheringham	Ross	Thomson	Coyle	Rankine	Irving	Knox	Bird	Halliday	Cowan	McDonald
	14th	Fotheringham	Ross	Thomson	Coyle	Rankine	Letham	Knox	Bird	Halliday	Cowan	McDonald

A group of Dundee F.C. stalwarts in front of the old wooden South stand, which burnt down in December 1921. Willie Fotheringham, Jock Ross, Davie Halliday, George Thompson, Bob Willis and Walter Bird. DC Thomson

They Wore The Dark Blue

Season 1923-24

Date			Opponents		Score	Crowd	Scorers
Aug	15th	FCF*	Forfar Athletic	h	2-0		Halliday; Gordon
	18th	L	Raith Rovers	a	0-3		-
	25th	L	Hearts	h	5-1	13,000	Knox 2; Bird 2; McLean
Sep	1st	L	Aberdeen	a	0-0		-
	8th	L	Third Lanark	h	1-0	12,000	D. McDonald
	15th	L	St Mirren	a	2-2		D. McDonald; Halliday
	22nd	L	Queens Park	h	3-0	14,000	Halliday 3
	29th	L	Kilmarnock	a	3-1		J. McDonald; McLean; Halliday
Oct	1st	FC1	Dundee Hibs	h	0-1	10,000	-
	6th	L	Rangers	h	1-4	27,000	Halliday
	13th	L	Motherwell	a	2-4		Halliday; J. McDonald
	20th	L	Airdrie	h	3-1	16,000	Halliday 2; J. McDonald
	27th	L	Hibernian	h	7-2	12,000	J. McDonald; Halliday 4; Duncan; McLean
Nov	3rd	L	Morton	a	1-2		Halliday
	10th	L	Clydebank	h	4-1	12,000	Halliday 3; Irving
	17th	L	Celtic	a	0-0		-
	24th	L	Hamilton	a	0-0		-
Dec	1st	L	Falkirk	h	4-2	12,000	McLean 2; Halliday; Duncan
	8th	L	Partick Thistle	h	0-0	12,000	-
	15th	L	Ayr United	a	0-2		-
	22nd	L	Celtic	h	2-1	15,000	Halliday; McLean
	29th	L	Hearts	a	0-1		-
Jan	1st	L	Aberdeen	h	1-1	20,000	McLean
	2nd	L	Falkirk	a	1-4		Halliday
	5th	L	Raith Rovers	h	1-1	11,000	Duncan
	12th	L	Rangers	a	1-1	17,000	Halliday
	19th	L	Kilmarnock	h	4-2	8,000	Halliday 3; McLean
	26th	SC1	Dykehead	h	2-0	12,000	McLean; Halliday
Feb	2nd	L	Clyde	a	2-0		Halliday 2
	9th	SC2	Raith Rovers	h	0-0	27,000	-
	13th	SC2R	Raith Rovers	a	0-1	11,000	-
	16th	L	Hibernian	a	0-2		-
	20th	L	Ayr United	h	2-1	10,000	Duncan; Halliday
	23rd	L	Third Lanark	a	5-3		Halliday 4; McGrory
	27th	L	Airdrie	a	2-4	4,000	Halliday 2
Mar	1st	L	Morton	h	1-1	6,000	Duncan
	8th	L	Motherwell	h	4-1	18,000	McLean 2; Halliday 2
	15th	L	Hamilton	h	1-1	10,000	McLean
	22nd	L	Partick Thistle	a	2-5		McLean; Halliday
	29th	L	St Mirren	h	1-1	4,000	Halliday
Apr	5th	L	Clyde	h	3-1	7,000	Duncan 2; Halliday
	12th	L	Queens Park	a	1-1	13,000	McGrory
	19th	L	Clydebank	a	0-0		-

Davie Halliday - his record of 38 League goals remains.

The Record		
League	-	Fifth Place, Division One
Scottish Cup	-	Second round
Forfarshire Cup	-	First Round
Top Scorer	-	Davie Halliday (39 goals)
Av. Home Gate	-	12,600
Players used	-	23
Sent off	-	None

* 1922-23 Forfarshire Cup Final; Cup Cash v. Raith Rovers (a) £530

Appearances

	League	Scottish Cup	Total
Davie Halliday	36 (38)	3 (1)	39 (39)
Willie Fotheringham	35	3	38
Jock McDonald	36 (4)	2	38 (4)
Hugh Coyle	33	3	36
Davie McLean	33 (12)	3 (1)	36 (13)
Willie Rankine	33	3	36
Charlie Duncan	30 (7)	3	33 (7)
Jock Ross	29	3	32
Napper Thomson	28	3	31
Finlay Brown	27	3	30
Willie Knox	24 (2)	2	26 (2)
Jock Gilmour	16	0	16
Sam Irving	12 (1)	0	12 (1)
Tom McGrory	12 (2)	0	12 (2)
Crawford Letham	10	0	10
Walter Bird	8 (2)	0	8 (2)
Dave McDonald	6 (2)	2	8 (2)
Harry McGregor	3	0	3
Jim O'Neill	3	0	3
Francis Gordon	1	0	1
Andy Herd	1	0	1
Alec Ross	1	0	1
Jimmy Walker	1	0	1

Scottish League Division One

		Home			Away			Goals		
	P	W	D	L	W	D	L	F A	PTS	
Rangers	38	14	4	1	11	5	3	72-22	59	
Airdrie	38	13	6	0	7	4	8	72-46	50	
Celtic	38	11	5	3	6	7	6	56-33	46	
Raith Rovers	38	13	3	3	5	4	10	56-38	43	
Dundee	**38**	**12**	**6**	**1**	**3**	**7**	**9**	**70-57**	**43**	
St Mirren	38	10	5	4	5	7	7	53-45	42	
Hibernian	38	12	3	4	3	8	8	66-52	41	
Partick Thistle	38	9	4	6	6	5	8	58-55	39	
Hearts	38	12	4	3	2	6	11	61-50	38	
Motherwell	38	11	4	4	4	3	12	58-63	37	
Morton	38	12	3	4	4	2	13	48-54	37	
Hamilton	38	11	2	6	4	4	11	52-57	36	
Aberdeen	38	11	5	3	2	5	12	37-41	36	
Ayr United	38	11	7	1	1	3	15	38-60	34	
Falkirk	38	10	4	5	3	2	14	46-53	32	
Kilmarnock	38	9	4	6	3	4	12	48-65	32	
Queens Park	38	7	7	5	4	2	13	43-60	31	
Third Lanark	38	9	3	7	2	5	12	54-78	30	
Clyde	38	8	6	5	2	3	14	40-70	29	
Clydebank	38	8	3	8	2	2	15	42-71	25	

Dundee F.C. Line-Ups 1923-24

		1	2	3	4	5	6	7	8	9	10	11
Aug	18th	Fotheringham	Ross J	Thomson	Bird	Rankine	Coyle	Knox	Gordon	Halliday	McDonald J	Walker
	25th	Fotheringham	Brown	Thomson	Ross J	Rankine	Coyle	Knox	Bird	McLean	McDonald J	Halliday
Sep	1st	Fotheringham	Ross J	Thomson	Ross J	Rankine	Coyle	Knox	Bird	McLean	McDonald J	Halliday
	8th	Fotheringham	Brown	Gilmour	Ross J	Rankine	Coyle	Knox	Bird	Halliday	McDonald D	McDonald J
	15th	Fotheringham	Brown	Gilmour	Ross J	Rankine	Coyle	Knox	Bird	Halliday	McDonald D	McDonald J
	22nd	Fotheringham	Brown	Thomson	Ross J	Rankine	Coyle	Knox	Bird	Halliday	McDonald D	McDonald J
	29th	Fotheringham	Brown	Thomson	Ross J	Irving	Coyle	Knox	Bird	McLean	McDonald J	Halliday
Oct	6th	Fotheringham	Brown	Thomson	Ross J	Irving	Coyle	Knox	Duncan	McLean	McDonald J	Halliday
	13th	Fotheringham	Brown	Gilmour	Ross J	Rankine	Irving	Knox	McLean	Halliday	Duncan	McDonald J
	20th	Fotheringham	Brown	Gilmour	Ross J	Rankine	Coyle	Knox	McLean	Halliday	Duncan	McDonald J
	27th	Fotheringham	Brown	Gilmour	Irving	Rankine	Coyle	Knox	McLean	Halliday	Duncan	McDonald J
Nov	3rd	Fotheringham	Brown	Gilmour	Irving	Rankine	Coyle	Knox	McLean	Halliday	Duncan	McDonald J
	10th	Fotheringham	Brown	Gilmour	Ross J	Rankine	Irving	Knox	McLean	Halliday	Duncan	McDonald J
	17th	Fotheringham	Brown	Gilmour	Ross J	Rankine	Coyle	Knox	McLean	Halliday	Duncan	McDonald J
	24th	Fotheringham	Brown	Gilmour	Ross J	Rankine	Coyle	Knox	McLean	Halliday	Duncan	McDonald J
Dec	1st	Fotheringham	Brown	Gilmour	Ross J	Rankine	Coyle	Knox	McLean	Halliday	Duncan	McDonald J
	8th	Fotheringham	Thomson	Gilmour	Ross J	Rankine	Coyle	Knox	McLean	Halliday	Duncan	McDonald J
	15th	Fotheringham	Thomson	Gilmour	Ross J	Rankine	Coyle	Knox	McLean	Halliday	Duncan	McDonald J
	22nd	Fotheringham	Thomson	Gilmour	Letham	Ross J	Coyle	Knox	McLean	Halliday	Duncan	McDonald J
	29th	Fotheringham	Thomson	Gilmour	Letham	Ross J	Coyle	Knox	McLean	Halliday	Duncan	McDonald J
Jan	1st	Fotheringham	Thomson	Gilmour	Letham	Ross J	Coyle	Bird	McLean	Halliday	Duncan	McDonald J
	2nd	Fotheringham	Brown	Thomson	Ross J	Rankine	Coyle	Knox	McLean	Halliday	Duncan	McDonald J
	5th	Fotheringham	Brown	Thomson	Ross J	Rankine	Coyle	Knox	McLean	Halliday	Duncan	McDonald J
	12th	Fotheringham	Brown	Thomson	Ross J	Rankine	Coyle	O'Neill	McLean	Halliday	Duncan	McDonald J
	19th	Fotheringham	Brown	Thomson	Ross J	Rankine	Coyle	O'Neill	McLean	Halliday	Duncan	McDonald J
	26th	Fotheringham	Brown	Thomson	Ross J	Rankine	Coyle	McDonald D	McLean	Halliday	Duncan	McDonald J
Feb	2nd	Fotheringham	Brown	Thomson	Ross J	Rankine	Coyle	Knox	McLean	Halliday	Duncan	McDonald J
	9th	Fotheringham	Brown	Thomson	Ross J	Rankine	Coyle	Knox	McLean	Halliday	Duncan	McDonald J
	13th	Fotheringham	Brown	Thomson	Ross J	Rankine	Coyle	Knox	McLean	Halliday	Duncan	McDonald D
	16th	Fotheringham	Brown	Thomson	Letham	Rankine	Coyle	McDonald D	O'Neill	Duncan	McGrory	McDonald J
	20th	Fotheringham	Brown	Thomson	Letham	Rankine	Coyle	Duncan	McLean	Halliday	McGrory	McDonald J
	27th	Fotheringham	Brown	Thomson	Irving	Rankine	Coyle	Duncan	McLean	Halliday	McGrory	McDonald J
Mar	1st	Fotheringham	Brown	Thomson	Letham	Rankine	Hird	Duncan	McLean	Halliday	McGrory	McDonald J
	8th	Fotheringham	Brown	Thomson	Irving	Rankine	Coyle	Duncan	McLean	Halliday	McGrory	McDonald J
	15th	Fotheringham	Thomson	Gilmour	Letham	Rankine	Coyle	Duncan	McLean	Ross A	McGrory	McDonald J
	22nd	McGregor	Brown	Thomson	Ross J	Rankine	Irving	Duncan	McLean	Halliday	McGrory	McDonald J
	29th	McGregor	Ross J	Thomson	Irving	Rankine	Letham	Duncan	McLean	Halliday	McGrory	McDonald J
Apr	5th	McGregor	Ross J	Thomson	Coyle	Rankine	Letham	Duncan	McLean	Halliday	McGrory	McDonald J
	12th	Fotheringham	Ross J	Thomson	Coyle	Rankine	Letham	Duncan	McLean	Halliday	McGrory	McDonald J
	19th	Fotheringham	Ross J	Thomson	Irving	Rankine	Coyle	Knox	McLean	Halliday	McGrory	McDonald

Dundee F.C. Season 1923-24. (BACK, left to right) David "Napper" Thomson, Willie Rankine, Davie Halliday, Jock Britton, Henry Nicholson, Colin McNab. FRONT - Sam Irving, Davie McLean, Jock Ross, Charlie Duncan and Jock McDonald.

DC Thomson

65

Season 1924-25

Date		Opponents		Score	Crowd	Scorers
Aug	16th	L	Celtic	h	0-0	22,000	-
	23rd	L	Partick Thistle	a	1-1		Halliday
	30th	L	Hearts	h	6-0	17,000	Halliday 4; McLean 2
Sep	6th	L	St Mirren	a	1-2		Halliday
	13th	L	Kilmarnock	h	3-1	12,000	Halliday; Nicholson 2
	17th	FC1	Brechin City	h	3-0		Duncan; A. Ross 2
	20th	L	Motherwell	a	1-4		Thomson (pen)
	27th	L	Queens Park	h	2-4	11,000	Halliday 2
Oct	4th	L	St Johnstone	a	2-1	13,000	Duncan 2
	11th	L	Morton	h	0-0	13,000	-
	18th	L	Aberdeen	a	0-0	18,000	-
	25th	L	Hibernian	a	2-4		McDonald; Halliday
Nov	1st	L	Third Lanark	h	1-2	9,000	Duncan
	8th	L	Ayr United	a	0-1		-
	15th	L	Cowdenbeath	h	1-1	15,000	Duncan
	22nd	L	Hamilton	a	1-4		Irving
	29th	L	Raith Rovers	h	2-0	13,000	Halliday; McDonald
Dec	6th	L	Rangers	h	0-0	20,000	-
	13th	L	Falkirk	a	2-1		Halliday; McLean
	20th	L	Airdrie	h	3-2	18,000	Duncan; Thomson (pen); Brown
	25th	L	Third Lanark	a	0-3		-
	27th	L	Morton	a	1-1		Hunter
Jan	1st	L	Aberdeen	h	2-0	8,000	Halliday; Duncan
	3rd	L	Partick Thistle	h	0-2	10,000	-
	5th	L	Raith Rovers	a	3-4		McDonald; McLean; Duncan
	10th	L	Kilmarnock	a	1-4	5,000	Hunter
	17th	L	Falkirk	h	1-0	10,000	Halliday
	24th	SC1	Johnstone	h	5-0	6,200	Halliday 3; McLean; J. Rankine
	31st	L	Cowdenbeath	a	0-2		-
Feb	7th	SC2	Lochgelly Utd.	h	2-1	6,000	Duncan; W. Rankine
	10th	L	Rangers	a	0-2		-
	14th	L	Hamilton	h	2-0	3,000	Duncan; Halliday
	21st	SC3	Airdrie	h	3-1	22,373	McLean; Duncan; Halliday
	25th	L	Ayr United	h	1-0	7,000	Halliday
	28th	L	Celtic	a	0-4		-
Mar	7th	SC4	Broxburn	h	1-0	15,541	Halliday
	10th	L	Queens Park	a	1-0	4,000	Gilmour
	14th	L	Motherwell	h	1-0	9,000	Rankin
	21st	SCS	Hamilton	h	1-1	21,814	Duncan
	24th	SCSR	Hamilton	E.Rd	2-0	14,000	McLean; J. Rankine
	28th	L	St Johnstone	h	2-0	10,000	Halliday; Duncan
Apr	4th	L	Hibernian	h	3-0	12,000	McLean; Halliday 2
	11th	SCF	Celtic	Hamp	1-2	75,137	McLean
	15th	L	St Mirren	h	0-2	2,500	-
	18th	L	Hearts	a	0-1		-
	22nd	L	Airdrie	a	1-1		W. Rankine
	29th	FCS	Forfar Athletic	h	4-3	600	McLean 2; J. Rankin; Gilmour

Cup Cash v. Johnstone £260, v. Lochgelly Utd £225, v. Airdrie £901, v. Broxburn £616,
v. Hamilton (h) £1,184, v. Hamilton (Easter Road) £697-15-10d

Jock Ross - gritty skipper led Dundee to Cup Final.

The Record		
League	-	Eighth Place, Division One
Scottish Cup	-	Runners-up
Forfarshire Cup	-	Winners (Final Aug. 19th)
Top Scorer	-	Davie Halliday (24 goals)
Av. Home Gate	-	11,600
Players used	-	24
Sent off	-	One

Appearances

	League		Scottish Cup		Total	
Jock Britton	37		7		44	
Davie Halliday	36	(19)	7	(5)	43	(24)
Napper Thomson	36	(2)	6		42	(2)
Davie McLean	33	(5)	7	(4)	40	(9)
Willie Rankine	32	(1)	7	(1)	39	(2)
Jock Ross	32		4		36	
Sam Irving	28	(1)	7		35	(1)
Charlie Duncan	27	(9)	6	(3)	33	(12)
Jock McDonald	29	(3)	3		32	(3)
Colin McNab	21		4		25	
Finlay Brown	18	(1)	3		21	(1)
Jock Gilmour	13	(1)	7		20	(1)
Jimmy Hunter	18	(2)	1		19	(2)
John Rankine	11	(1)	7	(2)	18	(3)
Willie Knox	16		1		17	
Henry Nicholson	10	(2)	0		10	(2)
Hugh Coyle	4		0		4	
Crawford Letham	4		0		4	
George Gibson	3		0		3	
Dave Robb	3		0		3	
Norman Wilson	3		0		3	
John Barclay	2		0		2	
Bill Marsh	1		0		1	
Jock Thomson	1		0		1	

Scottish League Division One

	P	Home W	D	L	Away W	D	L	Goals F	A	PTS
Rangers	38	16	3	0	9	7	3	76-26		60
Airdrie	38	15	4	0	10	3	6	85-31		57
Hibernian	38	16	1	2	6	7	6	78-43		52
Celtic	38	13	3	3	5	5	9	77-44		44
Cowdenbeath	38	13	3	3	3	7	9	76-65		42
St Mirren	38	12	2	5	6	2	11	65-63		40
Partick Thistle	38	8	6	5	6	4	9	60-61		38
Dundee	**38**	**11**	**4**	**4**	**3**	**4**	**12**	**47-54**		**36**
Raith Rovers	38	11	4	4	3	4	12	53-61		36
Hearts	38	10	6	3	2	5	12	64-68		35
St Johnstone	38	8	7	4	4	4	11	57-72		35
Kilmarnock	38	10	4	5	2	5	12	53-64		33
Hamilton	38	10	2	7	5	1	13	50-63		33
Morton	38	8	7	4	4	2	13	46-69		33
Abercorn	38	7	4	8	4	6	9	46-56		32
Falkirk	38	10	4	5	2	4	13	44-54		32
Queens Park	38	9	4	6	3	4	12	50-71		32
Motherwell	38	9	5	5	1	5	13	54-63		30
Ayr United	38	7	6	6	4	2	13	53-65		30
Third Lanark	38	5	5	9	6	3	10	53-84		30

Dundee F.C. Line-Ups 1924-25

		1	2	3	4	5	6	7	8	9	10	11
Aug	16th	Britton	Brown	Thomson D	Ross	Rankine W	Letham	Nicolson	McLean	Halliday	Duncan	McDonald
	23rd	Britton	Ross	Thomson D	Robb	Rankine	Letham	Nicholson	McLean	Halliday	Hunter	McDonald
	30th	Britton	Ross	Thomson D	Robb	Rankine	Letham	Nicholson	McLean	Halliday	Hunter	McDonald
Sep	6th	Britton	Ross	Thomson D	Letham	Rankine	Robb	Nicholson	McLean	Halliday	Hunter	McDonald
	13th	Britton	Ross	Thomson D	Irving	Rankine	Coyle	Nicholson	McLean	Halliday	Hunter	McDonald
	20th	Britton	Brown	Thomson D	Irving	Rankine	Coyle	Nicholson	Duncan	Halliday	Hunter	McDonald
	27th	Britton	Thomson D	Gilmour	Wilson	Rankine	Irving	Nicholson	McLean	Halliday	Hunter	McDonald
Oct	4th	Britton	Ross*	Thomson D	Wilson	Rankine	Irving	Nicholson	McLean	Duncan	Gibson	McDonald
	11th	Britton	Ross	Thomson D	Wilson	Rankine	Irving	Nicholson	McLean	Halliday	Gibson	McDonald
	18th	Britton	Brown	Thomson D	Irving	McNab	Coyle	Knox	McLean	Duncan	Hunter	McDonald
	25th	Britton	Brown	Thomson D	Coyle	McNab	Irving	Duncan	McLean	Halliday	Hunter	McDonald
Nov	1st	Britton	Ross	Thomson D	Thomson J	McNab	Irving	Duncan	McLean	Halliday	Hunter	Barclay
	8th	Britton	Brown	Gilmour	Ross	McNab	Irving	Duncan	McLean	Halliday	Gibson	Barclay
	15th	Britton	Brown	Thomson D	Ross	McNab	Irving	Knox	Hunter	Halliday	Duncan	McDonald
	22nd	Britton	Brown	Thomson D	Ross	McNab	Irving	Knox	Hunter	Halliday	Duncan	McDonald
	29th	Britton	Brown	Thomson D	Ross	Rankine	Irving	Knox	McLean	Halliday	Duncan	McDonald
Dec	6th	Britton	Brown	Thomson D	Ross	Rankine	Irving	Knox	McLean	Halliday	Duncan	McDonald
	13th	Britton	Brown	Thomson D	Ross	Rankine	Irving	Knox	McLean	Halliday	Duncan	McDonald
	20th	Britton	Brown	Thomson D	Ross	Rankine	Irving	Knox	McLean	Halliday	Duncan	McDonald
	25th	Britton	Ross	Thomson D	Irving	Rankine	McNab	Nicholson	McLean	Halliday	Duncan	McDonald
	27th	Britton	Thomson D	Gilmour	Ross	Rankine	McNab	Duncan	McLean	Halliday	Hunter	McDonald
Jan	1st	Britton	Gilmour	Thomson D	Irving	Rankine	McNab	Knox	McLean	Halliday	Duncan	McDonald
	3rd	Britton	Gilmour	Thomson D	Ross	Rankine	McNab	Knox	McLean	Halliday	Duncan	McDonald
	5th	Britton	Gilmour	Thomson D	Ross	Rankine	McNab	Duncan	McLean	Halliday	Hunter	McDonald
	10th	Brown	Ross	Thomson D	Irving	Rankine	McNab	Knox	McLean	Halliday	Hunter	McDonald
	17th	Brown	Ross	Thomson D	Irving	Rankine	McNab	Knox	Hunter	Halliday	Rankine J	McDonald
	24th	Brown	Ross	Gilmour	Irving	Rankine W	McNab	Knox	McLean	Halliday	Rankine J	McDonald
	31st	Brown	Ross	Gilmour	Irving	Rankine	McNab	Knox	McLean	Halliday	Rankine J	McDonald
Feb	7th	Britton	Gilmour	Thomson D	Irving	Rankine W	McNab	Rankine J	McLean	Duncan	Hunter	Halliday
	10th	Britton	Ross	Thomson	Irving	Rankine W	McNab	Knox	McLean	Halliday	Duncan	McDonald
	14th	Britton	Ross	Thomson D	Irving	Rankine	McNab	Duncan	McLean	Halliday	Rankine J	McDonald
	21st	Britton	Thomson D	Gilmour	Ross	Rankine	Irving	Duncan	McLean	Halliday	Rankine J	McDonald
	25th	Britton	Thomson D	Gilmour	Ross	Rankine	Irving	Duncan	McLean	Halliday	Rankine J	McDonald
	28th	Britton	Thomson D	Gilmour	Ross	Rankine	McNab	Knox	Duncan	Halliday	Rankine J	McDonald
Mar	7th	Britton	Thomson D	Gilmour	Ross	Rankine	Irving	Duncan	McLean	Halliday	Rankine J	McDonald
	10th	Britton	Brown	Thomson D	Ross	Rankine	Irving	Duncan	McLean	Halliday	Rankine J	Gilmour
	14th	Britton	Brown	Thomson D	Ross	Rankine	Irving	Duncan	McLean	Halliday	Rankine J	Gilmour
	21st	Brown	Britton	Thomson D	McNab	Rankine	Irving	Duncan	McLean	Halliday	Rankine J	Gilmour
	24th	Britton	Brown	Thomson D	McNab	Rankine	Irving	Duncan	McLean	Halliday	Rankine J	Gilmour
	28th	Britton	Brown	Thomson D	McNab	Rankine	Irving	Duncan	McLean	Halliday	Hunter	Gilmour
Apr	4th	Britton	Brown	Thomson D	Ross	Rankin	Irving	Duncan	McLean	Halliday	Rankin J	McDonald
	11th	Britton	Brown	Thomson D	Ross	Rankine	Irving	Duncan	McLean	Halliday	Rankin J	Gilmour
	15th	Marsh	Brown	Thomson D	Ross	Rankine	McNab	Knox	McLean	Halliday	Rankin J	Hunter
	18th	Britton	Brown	Thomson D	Ross	Rankine	McNab	Knox	McLean	Halliday	Rankine J	Hunter
	22nd	Britton	Brown	Thomson D	McNab	Rankine	Irving	Ross	McLean	Duncan	Rankine J	Halliday

Preview of the Dundee v. Celtic Scottish Cup Final at Hampden Park in 1925.　DC Thomson

They Wore The Dark Blue

Season 1925-26

Date				Opponents		Score	Crowd	Scorers
Aug	15th	L	Morton	h	3-0	16,000	A. Ross; Irving; Duncan
	19th	FCF*	Arbroath	h	1-0	6,000	Duncan
	22nd	L	St Johnstone	h	0-1	15,000	-
	29th	L	St Mirren	a	2-2		Anderson 2
Sep	5th	L	Hibernian	a	1-2		McLean
	12th	L	Hamilton	h	2-2	12,000	McLean; Hunter
	19th	L	Cowdenbeath	a	0-5		-
	26th	L	Clydebank	h	3-1	12,000	Campbell; Cook; A. Ross
Oct	3rd	L	Hearts	h	1-0	10,000	D. Thomson (pen)
	5th	L	Motherwell	h	1-2	11,000	Campbell
	10th	L	Raith Rovers	a	0-1		-
	17th	L	Aberdeen	h	3-2	12,000	Finlay 2; Nicholson
	24th	L	Rangers	a	2-1		A. Ross; Nicholson
	31st	L	Celtic	a	0-0		-
Nov	7th	L	Partick Thistle	h	3-1	11,000	A. Ross 3
	14th	L	Airdrie	a	1-4		A. Ross
	21st	L	Dundee United	h	0-0	18,000	-
	28th	L	Morton	a	0-3		-
Dec	5th	L	Queens Park	a	3-1		Barclay 2; McLean
	12th	L	Kilmarnock	h	1-0	8,000	Cook
	19th	L	St Johnstone	a	0-0		-
	26th	L	Hibernian	h	1-4	8,000	Barclay
Jan	1st	L	Aberdeen	a	1-2		Finlay
	2nd	L	Raith Rovers	h	1-1	12,000	Campbell
	4th	L	Dundee United	a	1-0	20,000	McLean
	9th	L	St Mirren	h	1-1	11,000	D. Thomson (pen)
	16th	L	Kilmarnock	a	2-5		A. Ross 2
	20th	SC1	Inverness Caley	h	2-0	3,300	Campbell 2
	30th	L	Clydebank	a	2-1		Irving; Campbell
Feb	6th	SC2	Aberdeen	a	0-0	12,251	-
	10th	SC2	Aberdeen	h	0-3	9,681	-
	13th	L	Hamilton	a	0-0		-
	17th	L	Falkirk	h	1-0	3,000	Cook
	23rd	L	Partick Thistle	a	1-0		Campbell
	27th	L	Rangers	h	1-5	15,000	Meagher
Mar	6th	L	Falkirk	a	0-1		-
	17th	L	Celtic	h	1-2	12,000	McNulty
	20th	L	Motherwell	a	0-2		-
	27th	L	Hearts	a	2-2		Campbell 2
Apr	3rd	L	Airdrie	h	0-1	8,000	-
	10th	L	Queens Park	h	2-1	6,000	Campbell; Meagher
	17th	FCS	Forfar Athletic	a	0-0		-
	24th	L	Cowdenbeath	h	4-3	6,000	Campbell; Meagher 2; J. Thomson

Napper Thomson - top class full-back for the Dark Blues.

The Record		
League	-	10th Place, Division One
Scottish Cup	-	Second round
Forfarshire Cup	-	Winners (final on 18-08-26)
Top Scorer	-	Andy Campbell (11 goals)
Av. Home Gate	-	10,900
Players used	-	24
Sent off	-	One

* 1924-25 Competition. Cup Cash v. Inverness Caley £126, Aberdeen (a) £793, v. Aberdeen (h) £677

Appearances

	League	Scottish Cup	Total
Willie Cook	36 (3)	2	38 (3)
Colin McNab	33	3	36
Willie Rankine	33	3	36
Finlay Brown	32	3	35
Napper Thomson	32 (2)	3	35 (2)
Jock Britton	31	3	34
Sam Irving	31 (2)	3	34 (2)
Andy Finlay	24 (3)	2	26 (3)
Andy Campbell	21 (9)	3 (2)	24 (11)
Davie McLean	23 (4)	1	24 (4)
Alec Ross	18 (9)	1	19 (9)
Jock Ross	16	0	16
Henry Nicholson	12 (2)	0	12 (2)
Charlie Duncan	11 (1)	0	11 (1)
Jock Gilmour	11	0	11
Jimmy Hunter	11 (1)	0	11 (1)
Bernie McNulty	8 (1)	3	11 (1)
John Barclay	9 (3)	1	10 (3)
Jim Meagher	10 (4)	0	10 (4)
Bill Marsh	7	0	7
Dave Robb	4	0	4
John Anderson	3 (2)	0	2 (2)
John Rankine	2	0	2
Jock Thomson	2 (1)	0	2 (1)

Scottish League Division One

		Home			Away			Goals		
	P	W	D	L	W	D	L	F A		PTS
Celtic	38	15	4	0	10	4	5	97-40		58
Airdrie	38	13	3	2	10	1	8	95-54		50
Hearts	38	14	2	3	7	6	6	87-56		50
St Mirren	38	12	4	3	8	3	8	62-52		47
Motherwell	38	15	1	3	4	7	8	67-46		46
Rangers	38	12	1	6	7	5	7	79-55		44
Cowdenbeath	38	14	3	2	4	3	12	87-68		42
Falkirk	38	8	10	1	6	4	9	61-57		42
Kilmarnock	38	11	4	4	6	3	10	79-77		41
Dundee	**38**	**9**	**4**	**6**	**5**	**5**	**9**	**47-59**		**37**
Aberdeen	38	10	4	5	3	6	10	49-54		36
Hamilton	38	10	5	4	3	4	12	68-79		35
Queens Park	38	10	1	8	5	3	11	70-81		34
Partick Thistle	38	8	6	5	2	7	10	64-73		33
Morton	38	9	5	5	3	2	14	57-84		31
Hibernian	38	8	3	8	4	3	12	72-77		30
Dundee United	38	7	4	8	4	2	13	52-74		28
St Johnstone	38	5	8	6	4	2	13	43-78		28
Raith Rovers	38	9	2	8	2	2	15	46-81		26
Clydebank	38	7	3	9	0	5	14	55-92		22

Dundee F.C. Line-Ups 1925-26

		1	2	3	4	5	6	7	8	9	10	11
Aug	15th	Britton	Brown	Thomson D	Ross J	Rankine W	Irving	Duncan	McLean	Ross A	Rankine J	Cook
	22nd	Britton	Thomson D	Gilmour	Ross J	Rankine W	Irving	Duncan	McLean	Ross A	Rankine J	Cook
	29th	Britton	Brown	Thomson D	McNab	Rankine W	Irving	Duncan	McLean	Anderson	Finlay	Cook
Sep	5th	Britton	Brown	Thomson D	McNab	Rankine W	Irving	Duncan	McLean	Anderson	Finlay	Cook
	12th	Britton	Brown	Thomson D	McNab	Rankine W	Irving	Duncan	Hunter	McLean	Finlay	Cook
	19th	Britton	Brown	Thomson D	Ross J	Rankine W	McNab	Cook	Duncan	Campbell	Finlay	Barclay
	26th	Britton	Brown	Thomson D	McNab	Rankine W	Irving	Duncan	Ross A	Campbell	Finlay	Cook
Oct	3rd	Britton	Brown	Thomson D	McNab	Rankine W	Irving	Ross A	Hunter	Campbell	Finlay	Cook
	5th	Britton	Brown	Thomson D	McNab	Rankine W	Irving	Ross A	Hunter	Campbell	Duncan	Cook
	10th	Britton	Brown	Thomson D	McNab	Rankine W	Irving	Duncan	Ross A	Gilmour	Finlay	Cook
	17th	Britton	Thomson D	Gilmour	McNab	Rankine W	Irving	Nicholson	McLean	Ross A	Finlay	Cook
	24th	Britton	Brown	Thomson D	McNab	Rankine W	Irving	Nicholson	McLean	Ross A	Finlay	Cook
	31st	Britton	Brown	Thomson D	Ross J	Rankine W	Irving	Nicholson	McLean	Ross A	Hunter	Cook
Nov	7th	Britton	Brown	Thomson D	Ross J	Rankine W	Irving	Nicholson	McLean	Ross A	Finlay	Cook
	14th	Britton	Brown	Thomson D	McNab	Rankine W	Irving	Duncan	McLean	Ross A	Finlay	Cook
	21st	Britton	Brown	Thomson D	McNab	Rankine W	Irving	Duncan	McLean	Ross A	Finlay	Cook
	28th	Britton	Brown	Thomson D	McNab	Rankine W	Irving	McNulty	McLean	Ross s A	Finlay	Cook
Dec	5th	Britton	Brown	Thomson D	McNab	Rankine W	Irving	McNulty	McLean	Ross A	Finlay	Barclay
	12th	Britton	Brown	Thomson D	McNab	Rankine W	Irving	Cook	McLean	Ross A	Finlay	Barclay
	19th	Briton	Brown	Thomson D	McNab	Rankine W	Irving	Cook	Nicholson	Ross A	Finlay	Barclay
	26th	Britton	Brown	Thomson D	McNab	Rankine W	Irving	Cook	Nicholson	Ross A	Finlay	Barclay
Jan	1st	Britton	Brown	Thomson D	Ross J	Rankine W	Irving	Cook	McLean	Campbell	Finlay	Barclay
	2nd	Britton	Brown	Thomson D	McNab	Rankine W	Irving	McNulty	McLean	Campbell	Finlay	Cook
	4th	Britton	Brown	Thomson D	McNab	Rankine W	Robb	Cook*	McLean	Campbell	Finlay	Gilmour
	9th	Britton	Brown	Thomson D	McNab	Rankine W	Robb	McNulty	McLean	Campbell	Anderson	Cook
	16th	Britton	Brown	Ross J	McNab	Rankine W	Irving	McNulty	Ross A	Campbell	Gilmour	Barclay
	20th	Britton	Brown	Thomson D	McNab	Rankine W	Irving	McNulty	McLean	Campbell	Ross A	Barclay
	30th	Britton	Brown	Thomson D	McNab	Rankine W	Irving	McNulty	McLean	Campbell	Finlay	Cook
Feb	6th	Britton	Brown	Thomson D	McNab	Rankine W	Irving	McNulty	McLean	Campbell	Finlay	Cook
	10th	Britton	Brown	Thomson D	McNab	Rankine W	Irving	McNulty	McLean	Campbell	Finlay	Cook
	13th	Britton	Brown	Thomson D	McNab	Rankine W	Robb	Nicholson	Meagher	Campbell	Finlay	Cook
	17th	Marsh	Brown	Thomson D	McNab	Rankine W	Irving	Ross J	Hunter	Campbell	Finlay	Cook
	23rd	Britton	Brown	Gilmour	McNab	Ross J	Irving	Cook	Hunter	Campbell	Meagher	Barclay
	27th	Britton	Thomson D	Gilmour	McNab	Ross J	Robb	Cook	McLean	Campbell	Meagher	Barclay
Mar	6th	Britton	Ross J	Thomson D	McNab	Rankine W	Irving	Nicholson	Hunter	Campbell	Meagher	Cook
	17th	Marsh	Ross J	Thomson D	McNab	Rankine	Irving	McNulty	Hunter	Campbell	Meagher	Cook
	20th	Marsh	Ross J	Gilmour	McNab	Rankine W	Irving	Nicholson	Hunter	Campbell	Meagher	Cook
	27th	Marsh	Brown	Gilmour	Ross J	McNab	Irving	Nicholson	Hunter	Campbell	Meagher	Cook
Apr	4th	Marsh	Brown	Gilmour	McNab	Ross J	Irving	Nicholson	McLean	Campbell	Meagher	Cook
	10th	Marsh	Brown	Gilmour	McNab	Ross J	Thomson J	Nicholson	Finlay	Campbell	Meagher	Cook
	24th	Marsh	Brown	Thomson D	McNab	Rankine W	Thomson J	McNulty	Hunter	Campbell	Meagher	Cook

Dundee F.C. Season 1925-26 (BACK, left to right) John Vickers (trainer), Henry Nicholson, Jock Ross, Jock Britton, David "Napper" Thomson, Davie McLean. FRONT - Alec Ross, Sam Irving, Finlay Brown, Willie Rankine, Jimmy Hunter and Willie Cook. DC Thomson

They Wore The Dark Blue

Season 1926-27

Date		Opponents		Score	Crowd	Scorers
Aug	14th L	Hearts	h	4-1	15,000	W. Rankine; Irving; Townrow; McGinn
	16th FCSR*	Forfar Athletic	h	2-1	4,000	Townrow; Campbell
	18th FCF*	Arbroath	Tann.	4-2		McGinn 2; Campbell; Rankine
	21st L	St Johnstone	a	1-0		Campbell
	28th L	Dundee United	h	5-0	20,000	Campbell 4; Meagher
Sep	4th L	Partick Thistle	a	3-3		Campbell 2; Townrow
	8th DSS	Falkirk	h	0-1	3,000	-
	11th L	Airdrie	h	1-0	14,000	Townrow
	18th L	Motherwell	a	5-2		Campbell; D. Thomson; Cook 3
	25th L	Dunfermline	h	1-1	14,000	Meagher
Oct	2nd L	Celtic	a	0-0		-
	9th L	St Mirren	h	2-1	11,000	Campbell; Cook
	16th L	Cowdenbeath	h	1-2	13,000	Meagher
	23rd L	Falkirk	a	1-3		Cassidy
	30th L	Aberdeen	a	1-2		Campbell
Nov	6th L	Hibernian	h	3-0	8,000	Campbell 3
	13th L	Kilmarnock	a	2-3		McGinn; Cook
	20th L	Hamilton	a	4-1		Cook; Campbell 2; Hunter
	27th L	Morton	h	6-1	6,000	Campbell 4; Hunter; Cook
Dec	4th L	Clyde	a	2-2		Cassidy; Hunter
	11th L	Rangers	h	1-1	20,000	Hunter
	25th L	Hearts	a	0-0		-
Jan	1st L	Aberdeen	h	1-1	18,000	McNab
	3rd L	Dundee United	a	0-1	25,000	-
	8th L	Partick Thistle	h	4-2	12,000	Campbell 2; Cook; Jackson o.g.
	15th L	Airdrie	a	1-3		Campbell
	22nd SC1	Motherwell	h	3-0	22,098	Campbell 2; Cook
	29th L	Motherwell	h	3-1	10,000	Campbell 3
Feb	5th SC2	Kilmarnock	a	1-1	14,000	Townrow
	9th SC2	Kilmarnock	h	5-1	13,000	Campbell 2; Cassidy; Cook
	12th L	Celtic	h	1-2	18,000	Cook
	19th SC3	Celtic	h	2-4	34,477	Campbell; Cook
	22nd L	St Mirren	a	2-2		Ramage 2
	26th L	Cowdenbeath	a	1-0		Meagher
Mar	12th L	St Johnstone	h	4-1	12,000	Agar; Campbell; McNab; Kirkwood o.g.
	16th L	Falkirk	h	2-3	7,000	Cassidy; Cook
	19th L	Hibernian	a	1-0		Campbell
	26th L	Kilmarnock	h	1-2	6,000	Gilmour (pen)
Apr	2nd L	Hamilton	h	1-0	4,000	Cassidy
	9th L	Morton	a	1-3		Gilmour (pen)
	11th FC1**	Dundee United	h	7-2		Ramage 4; Cook 2; McNab
	16th L	Clyde	h	1-2	4,000	Ramage
	18th L	Queens Park	a	4-1		Campbell 2; McNab; Townrow
	23rd L	Rangers	a	0-0		-
	30th L	Queens Park	h	3-0	3,000	Ramage; Brown; Townrow

Cup Cash v. Motherwell £890, v. Kilmarnock (h) £550, v. Celtic £1,512 (excluding stand).

* 1925-26 Forfarshire Cup ** 1926-27 Forfarshire Cup not completed.

Andy Campbell - Dundee's top scorer with 35 goals

The Record		
League	-	Fifth Place, Division One
Scottish Cup	-	Third round
Forfarshire Cup	-	Semi-final**
Dewar Shield	-	Semi-Final
Top Scorer	-	Andy Campbell (35 goals)
Av. Home Gate	-	11,300
Players used	-	22
Sent off	-	None

Appearances

	League		Scottish Cup		Total	
Finlay Brown	38	(1)	4		42	(1)
Bill Marsh	38		4		42	
Willie Cook	33	(11)	4	(3)	37	(14)
Andy Campbell	32	(30)	4	(5)	36	(35)
Hugh McGinn	30	(2)	4		34	(2)
Willie Rankine	30	(1)	4		34	(1)
Joe Cassidy	27	(4)	4	(1)	31	(5)
Napper Thomson	25	(1)	4		29	(1)
Colin McNab	24	(3)	4		28	(3)
Frank Townrow	23	(5)	4	(1)	27	(6)
Jock Thomson	23		1		24	
Jimmy Hunter	18	(4)	0		18	(4)
Jock Gilmour	17	(2)	0		17	(2)
Jock Ross	15		2		17	
Jim Meagher	15	(5)	0		15	(5)
John Crawford	13		0		13	
Andy Ramage	7	(4)	0		7	(4)
Bobby Farrell	4		0		4	
Alfred Agar	3	(1)	0		3	(1)
John Devine	1		0		1	
Tom Flanagan	1		0		1	
Sam Irving	1	(1)	0		1	(1)

Scottish League Division One

		Home			Away			Goals		
	P	W	D	L	W	D	L	F	A	PTS
Rangers	38	15	2	2	8	8	3	85-41		56
Motherwell	38	13	2	4	10	3	6	81-52		51
Celtic	38	14	2	3	7	5	7	101-55		49
Airdrie	38	13	5	1	5	4	10	97-64		45
Dundee	**38**	**11**	**3**	**5**	**6**	**6**	**7**	**77-51**		**43**
Falkirk	38	11	7	1	5	3	11	77-60		42
Cowdenbeath	38	12	3	4	6	3	10	74-60		42
Aberdeen	38	11	6	2	2	8	9	73-72		40
Hibernian	38	11	5	3	5	2	12	62-71		39
St Mirren	38	13	1	5	3	4	12	78-76		37
Partick Thistle	38	10	3	6	5	3	11	89-74		36
Queens Park	38	11	2	6	4	4	11	74-74		36
Hearts	38	7	7	5	5	4	10	65-64		35
St Johnstone	38	8	7	4	5	2	12	55-69		35
Hamilton	38	7	5	7	6	4	9	60-82		35
Kilmarnock	38	8	5	6	4	3	12	54-71		32
Clyde	38	7	7	5	3	2	14	54-85		29
Dunfermline	38	7	3	9	3	5	11	53-85		28
Morton	38	11	0	8	1	4	14	56-101		28
Dundee United	38	6	5	8	1	3	15	56-101		22

They Wore The Dark Blue

Dundee F.C. Line-Ups 1926-27

		1	2	3	4	5	6	7	8	9	10	11
Aug	14th	Marsh	Brown	Thomson D	Thomson J	Rankine	Irving	McGinn	Townrow	Campbell	Meagher	Cook
	21st	Marsh	Brown	Thomson D	Ross J	Rankine	Thomson J	McGinn	Townrow	Campbell	Meagher	Cook
	28th	Marsh	Brown	Thomson D	Ross J	Rankine	Thomson J	McGinn	Townrow	Campbell	Meagher	Cook
Sep	4th	Marsh	Brown	Thomson D	Ross J	Rankine	Thomson J	McGinn	Townrow	Campbell	Meagher	Cook
	11th	Marsh	Brown	Thomson D	Ross J	Rankin	Thomson J	McGinn	Townrow	Campbell	Meagher	Cook
	18th	Marsh	Brown	Thomson D	Ross J	Rankine	Thomson J	McGinn	Townrow	Campbell	Cassidy	Cook
	25th	Marsh	Brown	Thomson	Ross	Rankine	Thomson	McGinn	Meagher	Campbell	Cassidy	Ramage
Oct	2nd	Marsh	Brown	Thomson	Ross	Rankine	Thomson	McGinn	Meagher	Campbell	Cassidy	Cook
	9th	Marsh	Brown	Gilmour	Ross	Rankine	Thomson	McGinn	Meagher	Campbell	Cassidy	Cook
	16th	Marsh	Brown	Gilmour	Ross	Rankine	Thomson	McGinn	Meagher	Campbell	Cassidy	Cook
	23rd	Marsh	Brown	Thomson	Ross	Rankine	Thomson	McGinn	Hunter	Campbell	Cassidy	Cook
	30th	Marsh	Brown	Thomson	Ross	Rankine	Thomson	McGinn	Hunter	Campbell	Cassidy	Cook
Nov	6th	Marsh	Brown	Thomson	Ross	Rankine	Thomson	McGinn	Hunter	Campbell	Cassidy	Cook
	13th	Marsh	Brown	Gilmour	Ross	Rankine	Thomson J	McGinn	Hunter	Campbell	Meagher	Cook
	20th	Marsh	Brown	Thomson D	McNab	Rankine	Thomson J	McGinn	Hunter	Campbell	Cassidy	Cook
	27th	Marsh	Brown	Thomson D	McNab	Rankine	Thomson J	McGinn	Hunter	Campbell	Cassidy	Cook
Dec	4th	Marsh	Brown	Thomson D	McNab	Rankine	Thomson	McGinn	Hunter	Campbell	Cassidy	Cook
	11th	Marsh	Brown	Thomson	McNab	Rankine	Thomson J	McGinn	Hunter	Campbell	Cassidy	Cook
	25th	Marsh	Brown	Thomson	McNab	Rankine	Thomson J	McGinn	Hunter	Campbell	Cassidy	Cook
Jan	1st	Marsh	Brown	Thomson	McNab	Rankine	Thomson	McGinn	Hunter	Campbell	Cassidy	Cook
	3rd	Marsh	Brown	Gilmour	McNab	Rankine	Thomson	McGinn	Hunter	Campbell	Cassidy	Cook
	8th	Marsh	Brown	Gilmour	McNab	Rankine	Thomson	McGinn	Townrow	Campbell	Cassidy	Cook
	15th	Marsh	Brown	Thomson	McNab	Rankine	Thomson	Meagher	Townrow	Campbell	Cassidy	Cook
	22nd	Marsh	Brown	Thomson	McNab	Rankine	Thomson	McGinn	Townrow	Campbell	Cassidy	Cook
	29th	Marsh	Brown	Thomson	McNab	Rankine	Meagher	McGinn	Townrow	Campbell	Cassidy	Cook
Feb	5th	Marsh	Brown	Thomson	McNab	Rankine	Ross J	McGinn	Townrow	Campbell	Cassidy	Cook
	9th	Marsh	Brown	Thomson	McNab	Rankine	Gilmour	McGinn	Townrow	Campbell	Cassidy	Cook
	12th	Marsh	Brown	Thomson	McNab	Townrow	Gilmour	McGinn	Hunter	Campbell	Cassidy	Cook
	16th	Marsh	Brown	Gilmour	McNab	Ross J	Crawford	McGinn	Townrow	Campbell	Meagher	Cook
	19th	Marsh	Brown	Thomson	McNab	Rankine	Ross	McGinn	Townrow	Campbell	Cassidy	Cook
	22nd	Marsh	Brown	Gilmour	McNab	Townrow	Crawford	McGinn	Hunter	Ramage	Meagher	Cook
	26th	Marsh	Brown	Gilmour	McNab	Townrow	Crawford	McGinn	Hunter	Ramage	Meagher	Cook
Mar	12th	Marsh	Brown	Thomson	McNab	Townrow	Crawford	Agar	Hunter	Campbell	Cassidy	Cook
	16th	Marsh	Brown	Thomson	McNab	Townrow	Crawford	Agar	Hunter	Campbell	Cassidy	Cook
	19th	Marsh	Brown	Gilmour	McNab	Rankine	Crawford	Agar	Townrow	Campbell	Cassidy	Cook
	26th	Marsh	Brown	Gilmour	McNab	Rankine	Crawford	McGinn	Townrow	Campbell	Cassidy	Cook
Apr	2nd	Marsh	Brown	Gilmour	McNab	Rankine	Crawford	McGinn	Townrow	Ramage	Cassidy	Cook
	9th	Marsh	Brown	Gilmour	McNab	Ross	Crawford	McGinn	Townrow	Ramage	Hunter	Cook
	16th	Marsh	Brown	Devine	McNab	Rankine	Crawford	Farrell	Townrow	Ramage	Cassidy	Gilmour
	18th	Marsh	Brown	Thomson	McNab	Rankine	Crawford	Farrell	Townrow	Campbell	Cassidy	Gilmour
	23rd	Marsh	Brown	Thomson	McNab	Rankine	Crawford	Farrell	Townrow	Campbell	Cassidy	Gilmour
	30th	Marsh	Brown	Thomson	McNab	Townrow	Crawford	Farrell	Hunter	Ramage	Flanagan	Gilmour

Dundee F.C. Season 1926-27 (BACK, left to right) Johnny Brown (trainer), Finlay Brown, Joe Cassidy, Willie Rankine, Bill Marsh, Jock Ross, David "Napper" Thomson, Bill Longair (trainer). FRONT - Hugh McGinn, Frank Townrow, Andy Campbell, Jock Thomson, Jim Meagher and Willie Cook.

Stephen Borland

Season 1927-28

Date			Opponents		Score	Crowd	Scorers
Aug	13th	L	Cowdenbeath	a	0-1		-
	17th	DSS	Falkirk	h	0-1	4,000	-
	20th	L	Motherwell	h	0-3	12,000	-
	27th	L	St Mirren	a	0-0		-
Sep	3rd	L	Partick Thistle	h	4-2	10,000	Hunter; O'Hare; Campbell; Cook
	10th	L	Bo'ness	a	0-2	5,000	-
	17th	L	St Johnstone	h	1-2	12,000	Pirie
	24th	L	Airdrie	a	1-1	5,000	O'Hare
Oct	1st	L	Celtic	h	1-4	18,000	Gilmour (pen)
	3rd	FC1*	Dundee United	a	4-3	5,000	Hunter; O'Hare 2; McNab
	8th	L	Hearts	a	0-1		-
	15th	L	Aberdeen	h	3-2	12,000	Smith 2; Godfrey
	22nd	L	Falkirk	h	1-0	3,000	Smith
	29th	L	Dunfermline	a	1-3		Smith
Nov	5th	L	Hibernian	a	0-4		-
	12th	L	Kilmarnock	h	7-0	5,000	O'Hare; Smith 3; Cassidy 2; Brown
	19th	L	Hamilton	h	3-1	5,000	O'Hare; Smith; Cook
	26th	L	Raith Rovers	a	1-1		O'Hare
Dec	3rd	L	Clyde	h	4-3	5,000	McNab; Smith; Cassidy; Cook
	10th	L	Rangers	a	1-5		O'Hare
	17th	L	Queens Park	h	1-3	7,000	O'Hare
	24th	L	Cowdenbeath	h	3-1	5,000	Smith; O'Hare; Gilmour (pen)
	31st	L	Partick Thistle	a	2-2		Smith; Thomson
Jan	2nd	L	Aberdeen	a	1-3		Smith
	3rd	L	Bo'ness	h	3-2	4,000	O'Hare 2; Gilmour (pen)
	7th	L	St Mirren	h	2-1	5,000	O'Hare; McNab
	14th	L	St Johnstone	a	1-5		Smith
	21st	SC1	Stranraer	a	4-2	2,000	Townrow; McGarry; Cook; Hunter
	28th	L	Hearts	h	2-7	6,000	O'Hare; Smith
Feb	4th	SC2	Dundee United	a	3-3	20,000	Lawley; Whitlow 2
	8th	SC2	Dundee United	h	1-0	12,389	O'Hare
	11th	L	Airdrie	h	3-0	4,000	O'Hare 2; Smith
	14th	L	Celtic	a	1-3		Smith
	18th	SC3	Dunfermline	h	1-2	11,808	Whitlow
	22nd	L	Dunfermline	h	3-2	2,000	Craddock 2; Smith
	25th	L	Falkirk	a	1-5		McNab
Mar	7th	L	Motherwell	a	2-2		Cassidy; Smith
	10th	L	Hibernian	h	4-1	4,000	Townrow 2; Smith 2
	17th	L	Kilmarnock	a	2-1		Lawley; Smith
	24th	L	Hamilton	a	3-3		Smith; Townrow; Cassidy
	31st	L	Raith Rovers	h	1-2	7,000	Smith
Apr	7th	L	Clyde	a	0-0		-
	18th	L	Rangers	h	0-1	10,000	-
	21st	L	Queens Park	a	2-1		Smith; Cook

Bill Marsh - the big keeper made 417 appearances.

Cup Cash v. Dundee Utd (a) £900, v. Dundee Utd (h) £500, v. Dunfermline £464;
* 1927-28 Forfarshire Cup not completed.

The Record

League	-	14th Place, Division One
Scottish Cup	-	Third round
Forfarshire Cup	-	Semi-final*
Dewar Shield	-	Semi-final
Top Scorer	-	Gus Smith (24 goals)
Av. Home Gate	-	7,200
Players used	-	25
Sent off	-	None

Appearances

	League	Scottish Cup	Total
Jock Thomson	38 (1)	4	42 (1)
Bill Marsh	35	4	39
Jock Gilmour	34 (3)	4	38 (3)
Colin McNab	34 (3)	0	38 (3)
Willie Cook	30 (4)	3 (1)	33 (5)
Willie O'Hare	29 (14)	4 (1)	33 (15)
Finlay Brown	30 (1)	1	31 (1)
Gus Smith	29 (24)	1	30 (24)
Frank Townrow	26 (3)	4 (1)	30 (4)
Joe Cassidy	24 (5)	2	26 (5)
Jock Ross	20	4	24
Ed Godfrey	21 (1)	2	23 (1)
John Crawford	18	2	20
George Lawley	12 (1)	3 (1)	15 (2)
Bobby Farrell	12	0	12
Jimmy Hunter	6 (1)	1 (1)	7 (2)
Andy Campbell	5 (1)	0	5 (1)
Fred Whitlow	2	3 (3)	5 (3)
Claude Craddock	2 (2)	1	3 (2)
Jim Meagher	3	0	3
Peter Robertson	3	0	3
Jim Pirie	2 (1)	0	2 (1)
Ed McGarry	1	1 (1)	2 (1)
Bob Kearney	1	0	1
Billy McNeill	1	0	1

Scottish League Division One

	P	Home W	D	L	Away W	D	L	Goals F A	PTS
Rangers	38	17	1	1	9	7	3	109-36	60
Celtic	38	14	3	2	9	6	4	93-39	55
Motherwell	38	12	4	3	11	5	3	92-46	55
Hearts	38	10	5	4	10	2	7	89-50	47
St Mirren	38	11	6	2	7	2	10	77-76	44
Partick Thistle	38	10	5	4	8	2	9	85-67	43
Abercorn	38	15	1	3	4	4	11	71-61	43
Kilmarnock	38	10	5	4	5	5	9	68-78	40
Cowdenbeath	38	8	4	7	8	3	8	66-68	39
Falkirk	38	12	1	6	4	4	11	76-69	37
St Johnstone	38	9	4	6	5	4	10	66-67	36
Hibernian	38	11	6	2	2	3	14	73-75	35
Airdrie	38	8	3	8	4	8	7	56-69	35
Dundee	**38**	**12**	**0**	**7**	**2**	**7**	**10**	**65-80**	**35**
Clyde	38	7	6	6	3	5	11	46-72	31
Queens Park	38	10	4	5	2	2	15	69-80	30
Raith Rovers	38	7	5	7	4	2	13	60-89	29
Hamilton	38	9	4	6	2	2	15	67-86	28
Bo'ness United	38	6	8	5	3	0	16	48-86	26
Dunfermline	38	4	1	14	0	3	16	41-126	12

Dundee F.C. Line-Ups 1927-28

		1	2	3	4	5	6	7	8	9	10	11
Aug	13th	Marsh	Brown	Gilmour	McNab	Thomson	Crawford	McNeill	Townrow	Campbell	Cassidy	Cook
	20th	Marsh	Brown	Gilmour	McNab	Thomson	Crawford	Farrell	Townrow	Campbell	O'Hare	Cook
	27th	Marsh	Brown	Gilmour	McNab	Townrow	Thomson	Farrell	O'Hare	Campbell	Hunter	Cook
Sep	3rd	Marsh	Brown	Gilmour	McNab	Townrow	Thomson	Farrell	O'Hare	Campbell	Hunter	Cook
	10th	Marsh	Brown	Gilmour	McNab	Townrow	Thomson	Farrell	O'Hare	Campbell	Hunter	Cook
	17th	Marsh	Brown	Gilmour	McNab	Thomson	Crawford	Farrell	O'Hare	Pirie	Cassidy	Cook
	24th	Marsh	Brown	Gilmour	McNab	Thomson	Crawford	Godfrey	O'Hare	Pirie	Cassidy	Cook
Oct	1st	Marsh	Brown	Gilmour	McNab	Thomson	Crawford	Godfrey	Townrow	O'Hare	Cassidy	Cook
	8th	Marsh	Brown	Gilmour	McNab	Thomson	Crawford	Godfrey	Hunter	Smith	O'Hare	Cook
	15th	Marsh	Brown	Gilmour	McNab	Thomson	Crawford	Godfrey	Townrow	Smith	O'Hare	Cook
	22nd	Marsh	Brown	Gilmour	McNab	Thomson	Crawford	Godfrey	O'Hare	Smith	Meagher	Cook
	29th	Marsh	Brown	Gilmour	McNab	Thomson	Crawford	Godfrey	O'Hare	Smith	Meagher	Cook
Nov	5th	Marsh	Brown	Gilmour	McNab	Thomson	Crawford	Godfrey	O'Hare	Smith	Meagher	Cook
	12th	Marsh	Brown	Gilmour	McNab	Thomson	Crawford	Godfrey	O'Hare	Smith	Cassidy	Cook
	19th	Marsh	Brown	Gilmour	McNab	Thomson	Crawford	Godfrey	O'Hare	Smith	Cassidy	Cook
	26th	Marsh	Brown	Ross	McNab	Thomson	Crawford	Godfrey	O'Hare	Smith	Cassidy	Cook
Dec	3rd	Marsh	Brown	Ross	McNab	Thomson	Crawford	Godfrey	O'Hare	Smith	Cassidy	Cook
	10th	Marsh	Brown	Ross	McNab	Townrow	Thomson	Godfrey	O'Hare	Smith	Cassidy	Cook
	17th	Marsh	Brown	Ross	McNab	Townrow	Thomson	Godfrey	Hunter	O'Hare	Cassidy	Cook
	24th	Marsh	Brown	Gilmour	McNab	Thomson	Crawford	Godfrey	O'Hare	Smith	Cassidy	Cook
	31st	Marsh	Brown	Gilmour	McNab	Thomson	Crawford	Godfrey	O'Hare	Smith	Cassidy	Cook
Jan	2nd	Marsh	Ross	Gilmour	McNab	Thomson	Townrow	Godfrey	O'Hare	Smith	Cassidy	Cook
	3rd	Marsh	Ross	Gilmour	McNab	Thomson	Townrow	Godfrey	O'Hare	Smith	Cassidy	Farrell
	7th	Marsh	Ross	Gilmour	McNab	Thomson	Townrow	Godfrey	O'Hare	Smith	Cassidy	Farrell
	14th	Marsh	Ross	Gilmour	Kearney	Thomson	Townrow	Godfrey	O'Hare	Smith	Cassidy	Farrell
	21st	Marsh	Ross	Gilmour	Townrow	McCarthy	Thomson	Godfrey	O'Hare	Smith	Hunter	Cook
	28th	Marsh	Brown	Gilmour	Townrow	McCarthy	Thomson	Godfrey	O'Hare	Smith	Hunter	Cook
Feb	2nd	Marsh	Brown	Gilmour	Ross	Thomson	Townrow	Lawley	O'Hare	Whitlow	Cassidy	Cook
	8th	Marsh	Ross	Gilmour	Thomson	Townrow	Crawford	Lawley	O'Hare	Whitlow	Cassidy	Cook
	11th	Marsh	Ross	Gilmour	Thomson	Townrow	Crawford	Lawley	O'Hare	Whitlow	Smith	Cook
	14th	Marsh	Ross	Gilmour	Thomson	Townrow	Crawford	Godfrey	O'Hare	Smith	Whitlow	Lawley
	18th	Marsh	Ross	Craddock	Thomson	Townrow	Crawford	Godfrey	O'Hare	Craddock	Whitlow	Lawley
	22nd	Marsh	Ross	Gilmour	McNab	Townrow	Thomson	Lawley	O'Hare	Smith	Craddock	Cook
	25th	Marsh	Ross	Gilmour	McNab	Townrow	Thomson	Lawley	O'Hare	Smith	Cassidy	Cook
Mar	7th	Marsh	Brown	Gilmour	McNab	Ross	Thomson	Lawley	Townrow	Smith	Cassidy	Cook
	10th	Marsh	Brown	Gilmour	McNab	Ross	Thomson	Lawley	Townrow	Smith	Cassidy	Cook
	17th	Robertson	Brown	Gilmour	McNab	Ross	Thomson	Lawley	Townrow	Smith	Cassidy	Farrell
	24th	Robertson	Brown	Gilmour	McNab	Ross	Thomson	Lawley	Townrow	Smith	Cassidy	Farrell
	31st	Robertson	Brown	Gilmour	McNab	Ross	Thomson	Lawley	Townrow	Smith	Cassidy	Farrell
Apr	7th	Marsh	Brown	Gilmour	McNab	Ross	Thomson	Lawley	Townrow	Smith	Cassidy	Farrell
	18th	Marsh	Brown	Gilmour	McNab	Ross	Thomson	Lawley	Townrow	Smith	Cassidy	Cook
	21st	Marsh	Brown	Gilmour	McNab	Ross	Thomson	Lawley	Craddock	Smith	Townrow	Cook

Dundee F.C. Season 1927-28. (BACK, left to right) Jock Gilmour, Frank Townrow, Finlay Brown, Jock Thomson, Bill Marsh, Jim Meagher, Joe Cassidy, Johnny Brown (trainer). FRONT - Hugh McGinn, Colin McNab, Willie Cook, Willie Rankine, Jock Ross, Willie O'Hare, Gus Smith and Jimmy Hunter.

DC Thomson

Season 1928-29

Date		Opponents		Score	Crowd	Scorers
Aug 11th	L	Celtic	h	0-1	19,000	-
18th	L	Partick Thistle	a	2-4		Campbell; Townrow
25th	L	St Mirren	h	2-3	10,000	Craddock; Gilmour (pen)
29th	FC1	Montrose	h	7-0		Smith 6; Crawford
Sep 1st	L	Kilmarnock	a	1-3		Campbell
8th	L	Rangers	h	2-3	16,000	O'Hare; Cook
15th	L	Hamilton	h	0-1	9,000	-
22nd	L	Falkirk	a	3-1		Smith 2; Craddock
29th	L	Hearts	h	5-3	14,000	Smith; Cook; Thomson; Gilmour 2
Oct 6th	L	Raith Rovers	a	3-0		Smith 2; McNab
13th	L	Third Lanark	h	2-2	12,000	McNab; Craddock
20th	L	St Johnstone	a	2-2		Smith 2
27th	L	Ayr United	h	2-3	9,000	Townrow; Smith
Nov 3rd	L	Airdrie	a	1-1		Townrow
10th	L	Clyde	a	1-2		Townrow
17th	L	Aberdeen	h	1-1	12,000	Craddock
24th	L	Cowdenbeath	a	2-4		Townrow; Smith
Dec 1st	L	Queens Park	a	4-2		O'Hare 3; Cook
8th	L	Motherwell	h	3-0	7,000	Smith 2; O'Hare
15th	L	Hibernian	a	0-2		-
22nd	L	Partick Thistle	h	0-0	8,000	-
25th	L	Third Lanark	a	2-1		Barrett; Lawley
29th	L	Celtic	a	1-2		Smith
Jan 1st	L	St Johnstone	h	0-2	10,000	-
2nd	L	Ayr United	a	3-0		Thomson; Lawley; Craddock
12th	L	Kilmarnock	h	1-3	8,000	Townrow
19th	SC1	King's Park	h	1-1	2,000	Smith
23rd	SC1R	King's Park	a	5-1	3,500	Crickett o.g.; Smith 2; O'Hare; Gilmour (pen)
26th	L	Hibernian	h	1-0	7,000	Townrow
Feb 2nd	SC2	Brechin City	h	6-1	4,000	McNab; Campbell; Craddock; Townrow 2; Lawley
9th	L	Falkirk	h	1-2	3,000	Thomson
16th	SC3	Dundee United	h	1-1	23,000	Lawley
20th	SC3R	Dundee United	a	0-1	14,000	-
23rd	L	Raith Rovers	h	0-3	2,000	-
Mar 6th	L	Hearts	a	1-1	6,000	Campbell
9th	L	Airdrie	h	2-2	4,000	Campbell; Barrett
16th	L	Clyde	h	1-2	4,000	Gibb
23rd	L	Aberdeen	a	0-4	12,000	-
30th	L	Cowdenbeath	h	4-0	5,000	Gibb; Robertson; McNab; Townrow
Apr 6th	L	Queens Park	h	0-0	6,000	-
12th	L	Hamilton	a	3-3	3,000	Campbell 2; Gibb
20th	L	Motherwell	a	1-1	2,000	Townrow
22nd	L	St Mirren	a	2-2		O'Hare
25th	FCS	Forfar Athletic	a	2-3	1,500	Robertson; Smith
29th	L	Rangers	a	0-3		-

Cup Cash v. Kings Park (h) £70; v. Kings Park (a) £300; v. Dundee Utd (h) £879, v. Dundee Utd (a) £519.

Willie Cook - touchline terror for the Dark Blues.

The Record

League	-	18th Place, Division One
Scottish Cup	-	Third round
Forfarshire Cup	-	Semi-final
Top Scorer	-	Gus Smith (15 goals)
Av. Home Gate	-	8,700
Players used	-	23
Sent off	-	Two

Appearances

	League		Scottish Cup		Total	
Jock Gilmour	35	(3)	5	(1)	40	(4)
Jock Thomson	35	(3)	5		40	(3)
Colin McNab	34	(3)	5	(1)	39	(4)
Bill Marsh	33		5		38	
Jim Paton	32		5		37	
Frank Townrow	31	(9)	5	(2)	36	(11)
Finlay Brown	29		5		34	
George Lawley	22	(2)	5	(2)	27	(4)
Willie O'Hare	21	(7)	3	(1)	24	(8)
Gus Smith	19	(12)	3	(3)	22	(15)
Claude Craddock	18	(5)	3	(1)	21	(6)
Peter Barrett	15		4		19	
Willie Cook	18	(3)	0		18	(3)
Jock Ross	17		0		17	
Andy Campbell	15	(6)	1	(1)	16	(7)
Jimmy Robertson	10	(1)	0		10	(1)
Henry Nicholson	9		0		9	
Willie Gibb	8	(3)	0		8	(3)
Archie Campbell	4		1		5	
Peter Robertson	5		0		5	
John Crawford	3		0		3	
Tom Lynch	3		0		3	
Tom McCarthy	1		0		1	

Scottish League Division One

	P	Home			Away			Goals		PTS
		W	D	L	W	D	L	F	A	
Rangers	38	14	5	0	16	2	1	107-32		67
Celtic	38	13	2	4	9	5	5	67-44		51
Motherwell	38	12	4	3	8	6	5	85-66		50
Hearts	38	13	4	2	6	5	8	91-57		47
Queens Park	38	13	1	5	5	6	8	100-69		43
Partick Thistle	38	12	3	4	5	4	10	91-72		41
Aberdeen	38	14	3	2	2	5	12	81-68		40
St Mirren	38	9	3	7	7	5	7	78-75		40
St Johnstone	38	11	4	4	3	6	10	57-70		38
Kilmarnock	38	9	4	6	5	4	10	79-74		36
Falkirk	38	11	5	3	3	3	13	68-86		36
Hamilton	38	9	6	4	4	3	12	58-83		35
Cowdenbeath	38	10	3	6	4	2	13	55-69		33
Hibernian	38	9	5	5	4	1	14	54-62		32
Airdrie	38	10	4	2	2	3	14	53-65		31
Ayr United	38	5	3	8	4	4	11	65-84		31
Clyde	38	9	4	6	3	2	14	47-71		30
Dundee	**38**	**4**	**5**	**10**	**5**	**6**	**8**	**59-69**		**29**
Third Lanark	38	8	3	8	2	3	14	71-102		26
Raith Rovers	38	7	5	7	2	1	16	52-105		24

Dundee F.C. Line-Ups 1928-29

		1	2	3	4	5	6	7	8	9	10	11
Aug	11th	Robertson P	Brown	Gilmour	McNab	Ross	Thomson	Barrett	O'Hare	Campbell	Craddock	Robertson J
	18th	Robertson P	Brown	Gilmour	McNab	Ross	Thomson	Barrett	Townrow	Campbell	Craddock	Cook
	25th	Robertson P	Brown	Gilmour	McNab	Ross	Thomson	Barrett	Townrow	Campbell	Craddock	Cook
Sep	1st	Robertson P	Brown	Gilmour	McNab	Ross	Thomson	Barrett	O'Hare	Campbell	Craddock	Cook
	8th	Robertson P	Paton	Gilmour	McNab*	Thomson	Ross J	Barret	O'Hare	Smith	Robertson J	Cook
	15th	Marsh	Paton	Gilmour	McNab	Thomson	Campbell Ar	Lawley	O'Hare	Campbell	Robertson	Cook
	22nd	Marsh	Paton	Brown	McNab	Gilmour	Thomson	Lawley	Townrow	Smith	Craddock	Cook
	29th	Marsh	Paton	Brown	McNab	Gilmour	Thomson	Lawley	Townrow	Smith	Craddock	Cook
Oct	6th	Marsh	Paton	Brown	McNab	Gilmour	Thomson	Lawley	Townrow	Smith	Craddock	Cook
	13th	Marsh	Paton	Brown	McNab	Gilmour	Thomson	Barrett	Townrow	Smith	Craddock	Cook
	20th	Marsh	Paton	Brown	McNab	Gilmour	Thomson	Lynch	Townrow	Smith	Craddock	Cook
	27th	Marsh	Paton	Brown	McNab	Gilmour	Thomson	Lynch	Townrow	Smith	Robertson	Cook
Nov	3rd	Marsh	Ross	Paton	McNab	Gilmour	Thomson	Lawley	Townrow	Smith	Craddock	Cook
	10th	Marsh	Ross	Paton	McNab	Gilmour	Campbell Ar	Lawley	Townrow	Smith	Craddock	Cook
	17th	Marsh	Ross	Paton	McNab	Gilmour	Campbell Ar	Lawley	Townrow	Smith	Craddock	Cook
	24th	Marsh	Ross	Paton	McNab	Gilmour	Campbell Ar	Lawley	Townrow	Smith	Craddock	Cook
Dec	1st	Marsh	Brown	Paton	McNab	Gilmour	Thomson	Lawley	Townrow	O'Hare	Craddock	Cook
	8th	Marsh	Brown	Paton	McNab	Gilmour	Thomson	Lawley	Townrow	Smith	O'Hare	Cook
	15th	Marsh	Brown	Paton	McNab	Gilmour	Thomson	Lawley	Townrow	Smith	O'Hare	Cook
	22nd	Marsh	Brown	Paton	McNab	Gilmour	Thomson	Lawley	Townrow	Smith	O'Hare	Lynch
	25th	Marsh	Brown	Paton	McNab	Gilmour*	Thomson	Lawley	Townrow	Smith	O'Hare	Barrett
	29th	Marsh	Brown	Paton	McNab	Gilmour	Thomson	Lawley	Townrow	Smith	O'Hare	Barrett
Jan	1st	Marsh	Brown	Paton	McNab	Gilmour	Thomson	Lawley	Townrow	Smith	O'Hare	Barrett
	2nd	Marsh	Brown	Paton	Ross	Gilmour	Thomson	Lawley	Townrow	O'Hare	Craddock	Smith
	12th	Marsh	Brown	Paton	McNab	Ross	Thomson	Lawley	Townrow	O'Hare	Robertson	Smith
	19th	Marsh	Brown	Paton	McNab	Gilmour	Thomson	Lawley	Townrow	O'Hare	Campbell Ar	Smith
	23rd	Marsh	Brown	Paton	McNab	Gilmour	Thomson	Lawley	Townrow	Smith	O'Hare	Barrett
	26th	Marsh	Brown	Paton	McNab	Gilmour	Thomson	Lawley	Townrow	O'Hare	Craddock	Barrett
Feb	2nd	Marsh	Brown	Paton	McNab	Gilmour	Thomson	Lawley	Townrow	Campbell	Craddock	Barrett
	9th	Marsh	Brown	Paton	McNab	Gilmour	Thomson	Lawley	O'Hare	Campbell	Robertson	Barrett
	16th	Marsh	Brown	Paton	McNab	Gilmour	Thomson	Lawley	Townrow	Smith	Craddock	Barrett
	20th	Marsh	Brown	Paton	McNab	Gilmour	Thomson	Lawley	Townrow	O'Hare	Craddock	Barrett
	23rd	Marsh	Brown	Paton	McNab	Gilmour	Thomson	Lawley	O'Hare	Campbell	Craddock	Barrett
Mar	6th	Marsh	Ross	Paton	McNab	Gilmour	Thomson	Barrett	Townrow	Campbell	O'Hare	Crawford
	9th	Marsh	Ross	Paton	McNab	Thomson	Crawford	Barrett	Townrow	Campbell	O'Hare	Nicholson
	16th	Marsh	Ross	Paton	McNab	Gilmour	Thomson	Barrett	Townrow	Gibb	Craddock	Nicholson
	23rd	Marsh	Brown	Paton	McNab	Thomson	Crawford	Lawley	Campbell	Gibb	O'Hare	Nicholson
	30th	Marsh	Brown	Paton	McNab	Gilmour	Thomson	Gibb	Townrow	Campbell	Robertson	Nicholson
Apr	6th	Marsh	Brown	Paton	McNab	Gilmour	Thomson	Gibb	Townrow	Campbell	Robertson	Nicholson
	12th	Marsh	Brown	Paton	McNab	Gilmour	Thomson	Gibb	Townrow	Campbell	Robertson	Nicholson
	20th	Marsh	Brown	Paton	Ross	Gilmour	Thomson	Townrow	Campbell	Gibb	Robertson	Nicholson
	22nd	Marsh	Brown	Gilmour	Ross	McCarthy	Thomson	Townrow	Campbell	Gibb	O'Hare	Nicholson
	27th	Marsh	Brown	Gilmour	Ross	McCarthy	Thomson	Lawley	Townrow	Gibb	O'Hare	Nicholson

Dundee F.C. players at training under the watchful eye of Johnny Brown. (BACK - left to right) Johnny Brown, Jock Ross, Bob Kearney, Peter Robertson, John Crawford, Jock Thomson, Billy McNeill, Willie O'Hare, Finlay Brown. Front - Colin McNab, Tom Nicol, Frank Townrow, Jock Gilmour, Bill Marsh, Joe Cassidy. Sitting - Jimmy Hunter and Bobby Farrell. DC Thomson

Season 1929-30

Date			Opponents		Score	Crowd	Scorers
Aug	10th	L	Partick Thistle	a	2-0		Townrow; O'Hare
	17th	L	Falkirk	h	0-0	10,000	-
	24th	L	Motherwell	a	0-3	5,000	-
	31st	L	Dundee United	h	1-0	16,000	Townrow
Sep	7th	L	St Mirren	a	0-3	8,000	-
	14th	L	St Johnstone	h	0-1	12,000	-
	21st	L	Celtic	a	1-1	8,000	Pryde
	28th	L	Kilmarnock	h	2-2	12,000	Thomson; Ferguson
Oct	5th	L	Queens Park	h	1-0	7,000	Ferguson
	7th	FCS	Montrose	h	3-4	3,500	Campbell; Brown; Townrow
	12th	L	Hamilton	a	0-2	6,000	-
	19th	L	Hibernian	h	4-0	5,000	McNab; McCarthy; Thomson; Robertson
	26th	L	Aberdeen	a	0-1		-
Nov	2nd	L	Clyde	h	0-1	5,000	-
	9th	L	Morton	a	1-2	5,000	Campbell
	16th	L	Airdrie	h	3-0	5,000	Campbell; O'Hare; Feeney
	23rd	L	Cowdenbeath	a	1-2	1,000	Campbell
	30th	L	Ayr United	a	2-2	3,000	Feeney; Campbell
Dec	7th	L	Rangers	a	1-4	8,000	Feeney
	14th	L	Hearts	h	3-0	8,000	McNab; Campbell; O'Hare
	21st	L	Partick Thistle	h	2-4	5,000	Campbell 2
	25th	L	St Johnstone	a	1-0	3,500	O'Hare
	28th	L	Falkirk	a	2-5	6,000	Milne 2
Jan	1st	L	Aberdeen	h	0-3	18,000	-
	2nd	L	Hibernian	a	1-0	8,000	Robb o.g.
	4th	L	Motherwell	h	0-3	9,000	-
	11th	L	Dundee United	a	1-0	17,000	Campbell
	18th	SC1	Morton	h	2-0	14,000	Campbell 2
	25th	L	St Mirren	h	1-3	8,000	Nelson
Feb	1st	SC2	St Johnstone	h	4-1	7,000	Campbell 2; Milne; O'Hare
	8th	L	Celtic	h	2-2	10,000	Campbell; Milne
	15th	SC3	Airdrie	h	0-0	20,000	-
	19th	SC3R	Airdrie	a	0-0 (aet)	8,000	-
	22nd	L	Queens Park	a	1-2	8,000	Campbell
	24th	SC3R	Airdrie	Ibrox	2-1	12,000	Robertson; O'Hare
Mar	1st	SC4	Hearts	h	2-2	31,000	Campbell; Robertson
	5th	SC4	Hearts	a	0-4	32,000	-
	8th	L	Clyde	a	1-1		Campbell
	12th	L	Hamilton	h	3-2	3,000	O'Hare; Campbell; Troup
	15th	L	Morton	h	3-2	7,000	Troup 2; Ritchie
	22nd	L	Airdrie	a	2-3		Robertson; Campbell
	29th	L	Cowdenbeath	h	3-0	5,000	Ritchie; Troup; O' Hare
Apr	5th	L	Ayr United	h	3-0	6,000	Campbell 3
	19th	L	Hearts	a	0-1	6,000	-
	21st	L	Kilmarnock	a	2-0	3,000	O'Hare; McNab
	23rd	L	Rangers	h	1-3	5,000	Troup

Cup Cash v. Hearts (h) £1,250

Jock Thomson pictured with Alec Troup on the winger's return from Everton. Soon afterwards, Thomson joined Everton.

The Record

League	-	14th Place, Division One
Scottish Cup	-	Quarter-final
Forfarshire Cup	-	Semi-final
Top Scorer	-	Andy Campbell (20 goals)
Av. Home Gate	-	8,600
Players used	-	23
Sent off	-	None

Appearances

	League		Scottish Cup		Total	
Tom McCarthy	38	(1)	7		45	(1)
Colin McNab	37	(3)	7		44	(3)
Finlay Brown	36		7		43	
Jock Gilmour	36		7		43	
Willie O'Hare	34	(8)	7	(2)	41	(10)
Jimmy Robertson	34	(2)	7	(2)	41	(4)
Andy Campbell	31	(15)	7	(5)	38	(20)
Bill Marsh	33		4		37	
Jock Thomson	26	(2)	7		33	(2)
Hugh Ferguson	17	(2)	0		17	(2)
Willie Milne	11	(3)	5	(1)	16	(4)
Tom Lynch	15		0		15	
Harry Ritchie	10	(2)	5		15	(2)
Willie Blyth	13		0		13	
John Nelson	9	(1)	2		11	(1)
Alec Troup	9	(5)	2		11	(5)
Frank Townrow	10	(2)	0		10	(2)
Tom Murray	5		3		8	
Owen Feeney	5	(3)	0		5	(3)
Jim Pryde	4	(1)	0		4	(1)
Bill Proctor	2		0		2	
Morton Dempster	1		0		1	
Davie Hopewell	1		0		1	

Scottish League Division One

	P	Home W	D	L	Away W	D	L	Goals F	A	PTS
Rangers	38	18	0	1	10	4	5	94-32		60
Motherwell	38	17	0	2	8	5	6	104-48		55
Aberdeen	38	14	5	0	9	2	8	85-61		53
Celtic	38	12	1	6	10	4	5	88-46		49
St Mirren	38	11	2	6	7	3	9	73-56		41
Partick Thistle	38	11	4	4	5	5	9	72-61		41
Falkirk	38	11	5	3	5	4	10	62-64		41
Kilmarnock	38	12	2	5	3	7	9	77-73		37
Ayr United	38	10	5	4	6	1	12	70-92		38
Hearts	38	8	6	5	6	3	10	69-69		37
Clyde	38	8	4	7	5	7	7	64-69		37
Airdrie	38	11	3	5	5	1	13	60-66		36
Hamilton	38	12	3	4	2	4	13	76-81		35
Dundee	**38**	**9**	**3**	**7**	**5**	**3**	**11**	**51-58**		**34**
Queens Park	38	9	2	8	6	2	11	67-80		34
Cowdenbeath	38	10	3	6	3	4	12	64-74		33
Hibernian	38	7	6	6	2	5	12	45-62		29
Morton	38	7	5	7	3	2	14	67-95		27
Dundee United	38	5	6	8	2	2	15	56-109		22
St Johnstone	38	5	5	9	1	2	16	28-96		19

Dundee F.C. Line-Ups 1929-30

		1	2	3	4	5	6	7	8	9	10	11
Aug	10th	Marsh	Brown	Gilmour	McNab	McCarthy	Thomson	Lynch	Townrow	Ferguson	O'Hare	Robertson
	17th	Murray	Brown	Gilmour	McNab	McCarthy	Thomson	Lynch	Townrow	Ferguson	O'Hare	Robertson
	24th	Marsh	McNab	Gilmour	Blyth	McCarthy	Thomson	Nelson	Townrow	O'Hare	Robertson	Lynch
	31st	Marsh	Brown	Gilmour	McNab	McCarthy	Thomson	Lynch	Townrow	Ferguson	O'Hare	Robertson
Sep	7th	Marsh	Brown	Gilmour	McNab	McCarthy	Thomson	Lynch	Townrow	Ferguson	O'Hare	Robertson
	14th	Marsh	Brown	Gilmour	McNab	McCarthy	Thomson	Lynch	Townrow	Ferguson	O'Hare	Robertson
	21st	Marsh	Brown	Gilmour	McNab	McCarthy	Thomson	Lynch	Campbell	Ferguson	Robertson	Pryde
	28th	Marsh	Brown	Gilmour	McNab	McCarthy	Thomson	Lynch	Campbell	Ferguson	Robertson	Pryde
Oct	5th	Marsh	Brown	Gilmour	McNab	McCarthy	Thomson	Lynch	Campbell	Ferguson	Robertson	Pryde
	12th	Marsh	Brown	Gilmour	McNab	McCarthy	Thomson	Lynch	Campbell	Ferguson	Robertson	Pryde
	19th	Marsh	Brown	Gilmour	McNab	McCarthy	Thomson	Nelson	Campbell	Ferguson	O'Hare	Robertson
	26th	Marsh	Brown	Gilmour	McNab	McCarthy	Thomson	Lynch	Campbell	Ferguson	O'Hare	Robertson
Nov	2nd	Marsh	Brown	Gilmour	Townrow	McCarthy	Thomson	Lynch	Campbell	Ferguson	O'Hare	Robertson
	9th	Marsh	Brown	Gilmour	McNab	McCarthy	Thomson	Ferguson	Campbell	Milne	Robertson	O'Hare
	16th	Marsh	Brown	Gilmour	McNab	McCarthy	Thomson	Ferguson	Campbell	Feeney	Robertson	O'Hare
	23rd	Marsh	Brown	Gilmour	McNab	McCarthy	Thomson	Ferguson	Campbell	Feeney	Robertson	O'Hare
	30th	Marsh	Brown	Gilmour	McNab	McCarthy	Thomson	Lynch	Campbell	Feeney	Robertson	O'Hare
Dec	7th	Marsh	Brown	Gilmour	McNab	McCarthy	Thomson	Ferguson	Townrow	Feeney	Campbell	O'Hare
	14th	Marsh	Brown	Gilmour	McNab	McCarthy	Thomson	Ferguson	Milne	Campbell	Robertson	O'Hare
	21st	Marsh	Brown	Gilmour	McNab	McCarthy	Thomson	Lynch	Milne	Campbell	Robertson	O'Hare
	25th	Marsh	Brown	Gilmour	McNab	McCarthy	Thomson	Lynch	Milne	Campbell	Robertson	O'Hare
	28th	Marsh	Brown	Proctor	McNab	McCarthy	Thomson	Nelson	Milne	Campbell	Robertson	O'Hare
Jan	1st	Marsh	Brown	Proctor	McNab	McCarthy	Blyth	Nelson	Milne	Campbell	Robertson	O'Hare
	2nd	Marsh	Brown	Gilmour	McNab	McCarthy	Blyth	Nelson	Townrow	Milne	Campbell	O'Hare
	4th	Marsh	Brown	Gilmour	McNab	McCarthy	Blyth	Nelson	Milne	Feeney	Campbell	O'Hare
	11th	Marsh	Brown	Gilmour	McNab	McCarthy	Thomson	Nelson	Milne	Campbell	Robertson	O'Hare
	18th	Marsh	Brown	Gilmour	McNab	McCarthy	Thomson	Nelson	Milne	Campbell	Robertson	O'Hare
	25th	Marsh	Brown	Gilmour	McNab	McCarthy	Thomson	Nelson	Milne	Campbell	Robertson	O'Hare
Feb	1st	Marsh	Brown	Gilmour	McNab	McCarthy	Thomson	Nelson	Milne	Campbell	Robertson	O'Hare
	8th	Marsh	Brown	Gilmour	McNab	McCarthy	Thomson	Nelson	Milne	Campbell	Robertson	O'Hare
	15th	Marsh	Brown	Gilmour	McNab	McCarthy	Thomson	Ritchie	Milne	Campbell	Robertson	O'Hare
	19th	Marsh	Brown	Gilmour	McNab	McCarthy	Thomson	Ritchie	Milne	Campbell	Robertson	O'Hare
	22nd	Murray	Brown	Gilmour	McNab	McCarthy	Blyth	Ritchie	Townrow	Campbell	O'Hare	Dempster
	24th	Murray	Brown	Gilmour	McNab	McCarthy	Thomson	Ritchie	Milne	Campbell	Robertson	O'Hare
Mar	1st	Murray	Brown	Gilmour	McNab	McCarthy	Thomson	Ritchie	O'Hare	Campbell	Robertson	Troup
	5th	Murray	Brown	Gilmour	McNab	McCarthy	Thomson	Ritchie	O'Hare	Campbell	Robertson	Troup
	8th	Murray	Hopewell	Gilmour	McNab	McCarthy	Thomson	Ritchie	O'Hare	Campbell	Robertson	Troup
	12th	Murray	Brown	Gilmour	McNab	McCarthy	Blyth	Ritchie	O'Hare	Campbell	Robertson	Troup
	15th	Murray	Brown	Gilmour	McNab	McCarthy	Blyth	Ritchie	O'Hare	Campbell	Robertson	Troup
	22nd	Marsh	Brown	Gilmour	McNab	McCarthy	Blyth	Ritchie	O'Hare	Campbell	Robertson	Troup
	29th	Marsh	Brown	Gilmour	McNab	McCarthy	Blyth	Ritchie	O'Hare	Campbell	Robertson	Troup
Apr	5th	Marsh	Brown	Gilmour	McNab	McCarthy	Blyth	Ritchie	O'Hare	Campbell	Robertson	Troup
	19th	Marsh	Brown	Gilmour	McNab	McCarthy	Blyth	Ritchie	O'Hare	Campbell	Robertson	Troup
	21st	Marsh	Brown	Gilmour	McNab	McCarthy	Blyth	Ritchie	O'Hare	Campbell	Robertson	Troup
	23rd	Marsh	Brown	Gilmour	McNab	McCarthy	Blyth	Ritchie	O'Hare	Campbell	Robertson	Troup

Dundee F.C. 1929-30. BACK - Jock Thomson, Bill Marsh, Tommy Murray, Jock Gilmour. MIDDLE - Finlay Brown, Willie Blyth, Colin McNab, Tom McCarthy, Johnny Brown (trainer). FRONT - John Nelson, Tom Lynch, Frank Townrow, Hugh Ferguson, Willie O' Hare, Jimmy Robertson, Jim Pryde.

Season 1930-31

Date			Opponents		Score	Crowd	Scorers
Aug	8th	L	Clyde	h	2-1	12,000	Troup; Campbell
	16th	L	East Fife	a	2-1	8,000	Campbell; Robertson
	23rd	L	Rangers	h	0-1	20,000	-
	30th	L	Morton	a	1-2		Campbell
Sep	6th	L	Hamilton	h	4-2	10,000	Ritchie; Blyth; Robertson; McNab
	13th	L	Queens Park	a	2-2	8,000	Campbell 2
	17th	FCS	Montrose	h	3-0		Campbell 3
	20th	L	Aberdeen	h	4-2	12,000	Robertson 2; Campbell; Ritchie
	27th	L	Hibernian	a	4-2	10,000	Ritchie; Robertson; Campbell
	29th	FCF	Forfar Athletic	h	1-2		Robertson
Oct	4th	L	Falkirk	h	3-1	10,000	Robertson 2; Campbell
	11th	L	Kilmarnock	a	2-1	5,000	Ritchie; Campbell
	18th	L	Cowdenbeath	h	2-0	15,000	Troup (pen); Robertson
	25th	L	St Mirren	a	1-3	7,000	Ritchie
Nov	1st	L	Motherwell	h	2-1	10,000	McCarthy; Robertson
	8th	L	Ayr United	a	6-2	3,000	Robertson 3; Troup 3
	15th	L	Airdrie	a	0-2		-
	22nd	L	Hearts	h	1-3	10,000	Ritchie
Dec	6th	L	Leith Athletic	h	6-0	7,000	Ritchie 3; Dempster 2; O'Hare
	13th	L	Partick Thistle	h	0-0	18,000	-
	20th	L	Clyde	a	2-2	3,000	Dempster; Troup (pen)
	27th	L	East Fife	h	2-0	10,000	Dempster 2
Jan	1st	L	Aberdeen	a	1-6	20,000	Campbell
	3rd	L	Rangers	a	0-3	12,000	-
	5th	L	Hibernian	h	1-0	4,000	Campbell
	10th	L	Morton	h	3-0	9,000	Troup; Ritchie; Dempster
	17th	SC1	Fraserburgh	h	10-1	5,527	Dempster 2; Ritchie 2; McNab 2; Troup; Blyth; Gavigan; Campbell
	24th	L	Hamilton	a	0-1	4,000	-
	31st	SC2	Rangers	a	2-1	17,000	Campbell; Robertson
Feb	7th	L	Falkirk	a	1-4		Campbell
	14th	SC3	Aberdeen	h	1-1	38,099	Campbell
	18th	SC3R	Aberdeen	a	0-2	28,527	-
	21st	L	Cowdenbeath	a	0-3	3,000	-
	28th	L	Queens Park	h	3-0	3,000	Robertson 2; Dempster
Mar	7th	L	Motherwell	a	0-2	5,000	-
	9th	L	St Mirren	h	2-0	4,000	Campbell 2
	18th	L	Ayr United	h	5-2	2,000	Ritchie; Balfour 4
	21st	L	Airdrie	h	0-1	3,000	-
	25th	L	Celtic	a	2-2	10,000	Troup; Balfour
	28th	L	Kilmarnock	h	0-2	3,000	-
Apr	4th	L	Hearts	a	0-2	10,000	-
	18th	L	Leith Athletic	a	1-3	5,000	Balfour
	22nd	L	Celtic	h	0-0	14,000	-
	25th	L	Partick Thistle	a	1-4		Lynch

Cup Cash v. Aberdeen (h) £1,526-14-0, v. Aberdeen (a) £1,138.

Jock Gilmour - the long-serving left-back played for Scotland v. Wales in 1931.

The Record		
League	-	Eighth Place, Division One
Scottish Cup	-	Third round
Forfarshire Cup	-	Runners-up
Top Scorer	-	Andy Campbell (17 goals)
Av. Home Gate	-	9,100
Players used	-	20
Sent off	-	None

Appearances

	League	Scottish Cup	Total
Finlay Brown	37	4	41
Bill Marsh	36	4	40
Alec Troup	35 (8)	4 (1)	39 (9)
Tom McCarthy	33 (1)	3	36 (1)
Willie Blyth	31 (1)	4 (1)	35 (2)
Colin McNab	31 (1)	4 (2)	35 (3)
Harry Ritchie	31 (11)	4 (2)	35 (13)
Jimmy Robertson	32 (14)	3 (1)	35 (15)
Peter Gavigan	29	4 (1)	33 (1)
Jock Gilmour	29	4	33
Andy Campbell	28 (14)	4 (3)	32 (17)
Scott Symon	21	1	22
George Dempster	12 (7)	1 (2)	13 (9)
Harry Smith	7	0	7
John Whyte	7	0	7
Davie Balfour	6 (6)	0	6 (6)
Tom Lynch	4 (1)	0	4 (1)
Willie O'Hare	4 (1)	0	4 (1)
Willie Milne	3	0	3
Tom Murray	2	0	2

Scottish League Division One

		Home			Away			Goals		
	P	W	D	L	W	D	L	F	A	PTS
Rangers	38	16	2	1	11	4	5	96-29		60
Celtic	38	16	2	1	8	8	3	101-34		58
Motherwell	38	14	5	0	10	3	6	102-42		56
Partick Thistle	38	16	2	1	8	3	8	76-43		53
Hearts	38	12	3	5	7	4	8	90-63		44
Aberdeen	38	13	3	3	4	4	11	79-63		41
Cowdenbeath	38	12	3	4	5	4	10	58-65		41
Dundee	**38**	**13**	**2**	**4**	**4**	**3**	**12**	**65-63**		**39**
Airdrie	38	11	2	6	6	3	10	59-66		39
Hamilton	38	12	4	3	4	1	14	59-57		37
Kilmarnock	38	11	2	6	4	3	12	59-60		35
Clyde	38	7	3	9	8	1	10	60-87		34
Queens Park	38	9	6	4	4	1	14	71-72		33
Falkirk	38	10	1	8	4	3	12	77-87		32
St Mirren	38	8	5	6	3	3	13	49-72		30
Morton	38	8	3	8	3	4	12	58-83		29
Leith Athletic	38	5	6	8	3	5	11	51-85		27
Ayr United	38	8	5	6	0	6	13	53-92		27
Hibernian	38	8	4	7	1	3	15	49-81		25
East Fife	38	7	4	8	1	0	15	45-113		20

Dundee F.C. Line-Ups 1930-31

		1	2	3	4	5	6	7	8	9	10	11
Aug	9th	Marsh	Brown	Gilmour	Whyte	McCarthy	Blyth	Ritchie	Milne	Campbell	Robertson	Troup
	16th	Marsh	Brown	Gilmour	Whyte	McCarthy	Blyth	Gavigan	Ritchie	Campbell	Robertson	Troup
	23rd	Marsh	Brown	Gilmour	Whyte	McCarthy	Blyth	Gavigan	Ritchie	Campbell	Robertson	Troup
	30th	Marsh	Brown	Gilmour	Whyte	McCarthy	Blyth	Gavigan	Ritchie	Campbell	Robertson	Troup
Sep	6th	Marsh	Brown	Gilmour	McNab	McCarthy	Blyth	Gavigan	Ritchie	Campbell	Robertson	Troup
	13th	Marsh	Brown	Gilmour	McNab	McCarthy	Blyth	Gavigan	Ritchie	Campbell	Robertson	Troup
	20th	Marsh	Brown	Gilmour	McNab	McCarthy	Blyth	Gavigan	Ritchie	Campbell	Robertson	Troup
	27th	Marsh	Brown	Gilmour	McNab	McCarthy	Blyth	Gavigan	Ritchie	Campbell	Robertson	Troup
Oct	4th	Marsh	Brown	Gilmour	McNab	McCarthy	Blyth	Gavigan	Ritchie	Campbell	Robertson	Troup
	11th	Marsh	Brown	Gilmour	McNab	McCarthy	Blyth	Gavigan	Ritchie	Campbell	Robertson	Troup
	18th	Marsh	Brown	Symon	McNab	McCarthy	Blyth	Gavigan	Ritchie	Campbell	Robertson	Troup
	25th	Marsh	Brown	Symon	Whyte	McCarthy	Blyth	Gavigan	Ritchie	Campbell	Robertson	Troup
Nov	1st	Marsh	Brown	Symon	McNab	McCarthy	Blyth	Gavigan	Ritchie	Campbell	Robertson	Troup
	8th	Marsh	Brown	Symon	McNab	McCarthy	Blyth	Gavigan	Ritchie	Campbell	Robertson	Troup
	15th	Marsh	Brown	Symon	McNab	McCarthy	Blyth	Gavigan	Ritchie	Campbell	Robertson	Troup
	22nd	Marsh	Brown	Gilmour	McNab	McCarthy	Blyth	Gavigan	Ritchie	Campbell	Robertson	Troup
Dec	6th	Marsh	Brown	Gilmour	McNab	McCarthy	Symon	Gavigan	Ritchie	Dempster	O'Hare	Troup
	13th	Marsh	Brown	Gilmour	McNab	McCarthy	Symon	Gavigan	Ritchie	Dempster	Robertson	Troup
	20th	Murray	Brown	Gilmour	McNab	McCarthy	Symon	Gavigan	Ritchie	Dempster	Robertson	Troup
	27th	Marsh	Brown	Gilmour	McNab	McCarthy	Blyth	Gavigan	Ritchie	Dempster	Campbell	Troup
Jan	1st	Marsh	Brown	Gilmour	McNab	McCarthy	Blyth	Gavigan	Ritchie	Dempster	Campbell	Troup
	3rd	Marsh	Brown	Gilmour	McNab	McCarthy	Symon	Gavigan	Ritchie	Dempster	Campbell	Troup
	5th	Marsh	Brown	Gilmour	McNab	McCarthy	Symon	Gavigan	Ritchie	Dempster	Campbell	Troup
	10th	Marsh	Brown	Gilmour	McNab	Symon	Blyth	Gavigan	Ritchie	Dempster	Campbell	Troup
	17th	Marsh	Brown	Gilmour	McNab	Symon	Blyth	Gavigan	Ritchie	Dempster	Campbell	Troup
	24th	Marsh	Brown	Gilmour	McNab	McCarthy	Symon	Gavigan	Ritchie	Campbell	Robertson	Troup
	31st	Marsh	Brown	Gilmour	McNab	McCarthy	Blyth	Gavigan	Ritchie	Campbell	Robertson	Troup
Feb	7th	Marsh	Brown	Gilmour	McNab	McCarthy	Milne	Gavigan	Ritchie	Campbell	Robertson	Dempster
	14th	Marsh	Brown	Gilmour	McNab	McCarthy	Blyth	Gavigan	Ritchie	Campbell	Robertson	Troup
	18th	Marsh	Brown	Gilmour	McNab	McCarthy	Blyth	Gavigan	Ritchie	Campbell	Robertson	Troup
	21st	Marsh	Brown	McCarthy	McNab	Symon	Blyth	Gavigan	Smith	Campbell	Robertson	Ritchie
	28th	Marsh	Brown	McCarthy	McNab	Symon	Blyth	Gavigan	Smith	Dempster	Robertson	Troup
Mar	7th	Marsh	Brown	Gilmour	McNab	Symon	Blyth	Gavigan	Smith	Dempster	Robertson	Troup
	9th	Marsh	Brown	Gilmour	McNab	McCarthy	Blyth	Ritchie	Milne	Campbell	Robertson	Dempster
	18th	Marsh	Brown	Gilmour	McNab	Symon	Blyth	Ritchie	Campbell	Balfour	Robertson	Troup
	21st	Murray	Brown	Gilmour	McNab	Symon	Blyth	Ritchie	Campbell	Balfour	Robertson	Troup
	25th	Marsh	Brown	McCarthy	Whyte	Symon	Blyth	Lynch	Smith	Balfour	Robertson	Troup
	28th	Marsh	Brown	McCarthy	Whyte	Symon	Blyth	Lynch	Smith	Balfour	Robertson	Troup
Apr	4th	Marsh	McCarthy	McNab	McNab	Symon	Blyth	Ritchie	Campbell	Balfour	Robertson	Troup
	18th	Marsh	Brown	Gilmour	McNab	Symon	Blyth	Lynch	O'Hare	Balfour	Robertson	Troup
	22nd	Marsh	Brown	Gilmour	McNab	McCarthy	Blyth	Gavigan	Smith	O'Hare	Robertson	Troup
	25th	Marsh	Brown	Gilmour	McNab	McCarthy	Blyth	Gavigan	Smith	O'Hare	Robertson	Troup

All set for training - BACK - Johnny Brown (trainer), Colin McNab, Lew Morgan, Tom Smith, Tom Dorward, John Cameron, Tom McCarthy. SITTING - Jock Gilmour, Harry Smith, Jimmy Guthrie, Finlay Brown. FRONT - Andy Campbell and Jimmy Robertson.

They Wore The Dark Blue

Season 1931-32

Date			Opponents		Score	Crowd	Scorers
Aug	8th	L	Rangers	a	1-4	40,000	Craigie
	12th	FC1	Arbroath	h	3-2	3,000	Craigie 3
	15th	L	Morton	h	2-1	12,000	Campbell 2
	22nd	L	Hamilton	a	2-6	6,000	Craigie 2
	26th	L	St Mirren	h	1-2	7,000	Robertson
	29th	L	Queens Park	h	4-0	9,000	Campbell 3; Troup
Sep	2nd	L	Ayr United	h	2-2	7,000	Gilmour (pen); Craigie
	5th	L	Aberdeen	a	1-1	17,000	Craigie
	12th	L	Dundee United	h	1-1	17,000	Campbell
	16th	L	Partick Thistle	a	3-1		Campbell; Balfour; Lynch
	19th	L	Leith Athletic	a	0-1	6,000	-
	26th	L	Clyde	h	1-1	7,000	Balfour
	28th	L	Third Lanark	h	6-3	7,000	Balfour 2; Campbell 2; Robertson; Lynch
Oct	3rd	L	Falkirk	a	2-5	5,000	Robertson; Balfour
	10th	L	Kilmarnock	h	1-1	8,000	Lynch
	17th	L	Celtic	h	2-0	18,000	Craigie 2
	24th	L	Hearts	a	1-3	16,000	Lynch
	31st	L	Cowdenbeath	h	0-4	6,000	-
Nov	7th	L	Airdrie	a	2-2	3,000	Robertson; Campbell
	14th	L	Motherwell	h	2-2	6,000	Campbell; Balfour
	21st	L	Third Lanark	a	1-6	7,000	Symon
	28th	L	St Mirren	a	1-6	10,000	Balfour
Dec	5th	L	Ayr United	a	0-1	3,000	-
	12th	L	Partick Thistle	h	3-1	4,000	Balfour 3
	19th	L	Rangers	h	4-2	16,000	Balfour 3; H. Smith
	26th	L	Morton	a	1-4		McNab
Jan	1st	L	Aberdeen	h	0-0	16,000	-
	2nd	L	Dundee United	a	3-0	16,000	Campbell 2; Balfour
	9th	L	Hamilton	h	0-3	4,000	-
	16th	SC1	Morton	h	4-1	9,200	Troup; McNab; Balfour; Campbell
	23rd	L	Queens Park	a	1-0	10,000	Balfour
	30th	SC2	Dunfermline	a	0-1	8,000	-
Feb	6th	L	Clyde	a	1-0	8,000	Balfour
	13th	L	Falkirk	h	2-0	1,000	Balfour; H. Smith
	20th	L	Kilmarnock	a	0-0	5,000	-
	27th	L	Celtic	a	2-0	6,000	Balfour 2
Mar	5th	L	Hearts	h	1-0	5,000	Troup
	12th	L	Cowdenbeath	a	1-2	1,500	Symon
	19th	L	Airdrie	h	4-1	5,000	McNab; Gavigan; Balfour 2
	26th	L	Motherwell	a	0-4	6,000	-
Apr	2nd	L	Leith Athletic	h	2-2	3,000	Campbell; Troup
	4th	FCS	Dundee United	h	2-3	1,500	Balfour; Milne o.g.

Scott Symon - an influential wing-half for the Dark Blues.

The Record		
League	-	11th Place, Division One
Scottish Cup	-	Second round
Forfarshire Cup	-	Semi-final
Top Scorer	-	Davie Balfour (22 goals)
Av. Home Gate	-	8,300
Players used	-	21
Sent off	-	One

Appearances

	League	Scottish Cup	Total
Andy Campbell	37 (14)	2 (1)	39 (15)
Bill Marsh	37	2	39
Alec Troup	36 (3)	2 (1)	38 (4)
Jock Gilmour	32 (1)	2	34 (1)
Colin McNab	32 (2)	2 (1)	34 (3)
Scott Symon	32 (2)	2	34 (2)
Jimmy Robertson	30 (4)	2	32 (4)
Lew Morgan	28	2	30
Davie Balfour	24 (21)	2 (1)	26 (22)
Tom McCarthy	22	2	24
Finlay Brown	21	0	21
Willie Blyth	19	0	19
Peter Gavigan	19 (1)	0	19 (1)
Harry Smith	12 (2)	2	14 (2)
Tom Lynch	13 (4)	0	13 (4)
Jim Craigie	12 (7)	0	12 (7)
Monty Munro	4	0	4
Willie Milne	3	0	3
Tom Smith	2	0	2
Alex. Lindsay	2	0	2
Archie McNiven	1	0	1

Scottish League Division One

		Home			Away			Goals		
	P	W	D	L	W	D	L	F A		PTS
Motherwell	38	18	1	0	12	5	2	119-31		66
Rangers	38	16	2	1	12	3	4	118-42		61
Celtic	38	13	2	4	7	6	6	94-50		48
Third Lanark	38	15	1	3	6	3	10	92-81		46
St Mirren	38	13	2	4	7	2	10	77-56		44
Partick Thistle	38	11	3	5	8	1	10	58-59		42
Aberdeen	38	10	6	3	6	3	10	57-49		41
Hearts	38	10	5	4	7	0	12	63-61		39
Kilmarnock	38	13	2	4	3	5	11	68-70		39
Hamilton	38	11	3	5	5	3	11	84-59		38
Dundee	**38**	**9**	**7**	**3**	**5**	**3**	**11**	**61-72**		**38**
Cowdenbeath	38	11	4	4	4	4	11	66-78		38
Clyde	38	10	5	4	3	4	12	58-70		35
Airdrie	38	10	5	4	3	1	15	74-81		32
Morton	38	10	4	5	2	3	14	78-87		31
Queens Park	38	9	2	8	4	3	12	59-79		31
Ayr United	38	9	1	9	2	6	11	70-90		29
Falkirk	38	10	3	6	1	2	16	70-76		27
Dundee United	38	4	5	10	2	2	15	40-118		19
Leith Athletic	38	6	0	13	0	4	15	46-137		16

Dundee F.C. Line-Ups 1931-32

		1	2	3	4	5	6	7	8	9	10	11
Aug	8th	Marsh	Brown	Gilmour	McNab	McCarthy	Blyth	Gavigan	Campbell	Craigie	Robertson	Troup
	15th	Marsh	Brown	Gilmour	McNab	McCarthy	Blyth	Gavigan	Campbell	Craigie	Lindsay	Troup
	22nd	Marsh	Brown	Gilmour	McNab	McCarthy	Blyth	Gavigan	Lindsay	Craigie	Robertson	Troup
	26th	Marsh	Brown	Morgan	McNab	McCarthy	Blyth	Gavigan	Campbell	Craigie	Robertson	Troup
	29th	Marsh	Brown	Gilmour	McNab	McCarthy	Blyth	Gavigan	Smith	Craigie	Campbell	Troup
Sep	2nd	Marsh	Brown	Gilmour	McNab	McCarthy	Blyth	Gavigan	Milne	Craigie	Campbell	Troup
	5th	Marsh	Brown	Morgan	McNab	Symon	Blyth	Lynch	Campbell	Craigie	Robertson	Troup
	12th	Marsh	Brown	Morgan	McNab	Symon	Blyth	Lynch	Campbell	Craigie	Robertson	Troup
	16th	Marsh	Brown	Morgan	McNab	Symon	Blyth	Lynch	Campbell	Balfour	Robertson	Troup
	19th	Marsh	Brown	Morgan	McNab	Symon	Blyth	Lynch	Campbell	Balfour	Robertson	Troup
	26th	Marsh	Brown	Morgan	McNab	Symon	Blyth	Lynch	Campbell	Balfour	Robertson	Troup
	28th	Marsh	Morgan	Gilmour	McNab	Symon	Blyth	Lynch	Campbell	Balfour	Robertson	Troup
Oct	3rd	Marsh	Morgan	Gilmour	McNab	Symon	Blyth	Lynch	Campbell	Balfour	Robertson	Troup
	10th	Marsh	Morgan	Gilmour	McNab	Symon	Blyth	Lynch	Campbell	Balfour	Robertson	Troup
	17th	Marsh	Morgan	Gilmour	McNab	Symon	Blyth	Lynch	Campbell	Craigie	Robertson	Troup
	24th	Marsh	Morgan	Gilmour	McNab	Symon	Blyth	Lynch	Campbell	Craigie	Robertson	Troup
	31st	Marsh	Morgan	Gilmour	Blyth	Symon	Smith T	Lynch	Campbell	Craigie	Robertson	Troup
Nov	7th	Marsh	Brown	Morgan	Symon	Gilmour	Smith T	Lynch	Smith H	Campbell	Robertson	Troup
	14th	Marsh	Brown	Morgan	Symon	Gilmour	Blyth	Gavigan	Smith H	Balfour	Campbell	Troup
	21st	Marsh	Brown	Morgan	Symon	Milne	Gilmour	Gavigan	Smith H	Craigie	Campbell	Munro
	28th	Marsh	Brown	Morgan	Symon	Milne	Gilmour	Gavigan	Campbell	Balfour	Robertson	Munro
Dec	5th	Marsh	Brown	Morgan	McNab	Symon	Gilmour	Gavigan	Smith H	Campbell	Robertson	Troup
	12th	Marsh	Brown	Gilmour	McNab	McCarthy	Symon	Gavigan	Smith H	Balfour	Campbell	Troup
	19th	Marsh	Brown	Gilmour	McNab	McCarthy	Symon	Gavigan	Smith H	Balfour	Campbell	Troup
	26th	McNiven	Brown	Gilmour	McNab	McCarthy	Symon	Gavigan	Smith H	Balfour	Campbell	Troup
Jan	1st	Marsh	Brown	Gilmour	McNab	McCarthy	Symon	Lynch	Robertson	Balfour	Campbell	Troup
	2nd	Marsh	Morgan	Gilmour	McNab	McCarthy	Symon	Munro	Robertson	Balfour	Campbell	Troup
	9th	Marsh	Brown	Gilmour	McNab	McCarthy	Symon	Munro	Robertson	Balfour	Campbell	Troup
	16th	Marsh	Morgan	Gilmour	McNab	McCarthy	Symon	Robertson	Smith H	Balfour	Campbell	Troup
	23rd	Marsh	Morgan	Gilmour	McNab	McCarthy	Symon	Robertson	Smith H	Balfour	Campbell	Troup
	30th	Marsh	Morgan	Gilmour	McNab	McCarthy	Symon	Robertson	Smith H	Balfour	Campbell	Troup
Feb	6th	Marsh	Morgan	Gilmour	McNab	McCarthy	Symon	Robertson	Smith H	Balfour	Campbell	Troup
	13th	Marsh	Morgan	Gilmour	McNab	McCarthy	Symon	Robertson	Smith H	Balfour	Campbell	Troup
	20th	Marsh	Morgan	Gilmour	McNab	McCarthy	Symon	Robertson	Smith H	Balfour	Campbell	Troup
	27th	Marsh	Morgan	Gilmour	McNab	McCarthy	Symon	Gavigan	Robertson	Balfour	Campbell	Troup
Mar	5th	Marsh	Morgan	Gilmour	McNab	McCarthy	Symon	Gavigan	Robertson	Balfour	Campbell	Troup
	12th	Marsh	Morgan	Gilmour	Blyth	McCarthy	Symon	Gavigan	Robertson	Balfour	Campbell	Troup
	19th	Marsh	Morgan	Gilmour	McNab*	McCarthy	Symon	Gavigan	Robertson	Balfour	Campbell	Troup
	26th	Marsh	Morgan	Gilmour	McNab	McCarthy	Symon	Gavigan	Robertson	Balfour	Campbell	Troup
Apr	2nd	Marsh	Morgan	Gilmour	McNab	McCarthy	Symon	Gavigan	Robertson	Balfour	Campbell	Troup

All smiles as this trio of Dens Park defenders take a well earned break from training. Left to right - centre-half Tom McCarthy, left-back Jock Gilmour and goalkeeper Bill Marsh.

DC Thomson

Season 1932-33

Date			Opponents		Score	Crowd	Scorers
Aug	13th	L	Hamilton	h	1-5	6,000	Balfour
	20th	L	Queens Park	a	0-2	7,000	-
	24th	L	Motherwell	h	0-3	9,000	-
	27th	L	St Johnstone	h	0-0	8,000	-
Sep	3rd	L	Clyde	a	3-0	8,000	Robertson 3
	7th	FC1	Brechin City	a	1-1	1,200	Gilmour
	10th	L	Aberdeen	h	0-2	10,000	-
	17th	L	Hearts	a	0-1		-
	21st	FC1R	Brechin City	h	2-2	1,000	Troup; Robertson
	24th	L	Falkirk	h	3-0	1,000	Robertson 2; Munro
	28th	FC2R	Brechin City	Forfar	2-0	1,400	Balfour 2
Oct	1st	L	Morton	a	4-1	3,000	Robertson 3; Campbell
	8th	L	Rangers	h	0-3	6,000	-
	15th	L	Kilmarnock	a	2-2	3,000	Munro; Miller
	22nd	L	Cowdenbeath	a	1-4		Gilmour (pen)
	29th	L	Airdrie	h	4-2	3,000	Crapnell o.g.; Balfour; McCarthy; Guthrie
Nov	5th	L	Motherwell	a	1-6		Robertson
	12th	L	Third Lanark	h	2-2	3,500	Robertson 2
	19th	L	St Mirren	h	1-1	6,000	Balfour
	26th	L	Ayr United	h	1-1	3,000	Guthrie
Dec	3rd	L	Partick Thistle	a	0-4		-
	10th	L	Celtic	a	2-3		Balfour 2
	17th	L	East Stirling	h	3-0	3,000	Balfour 2; Miller
	24th	L	Hamilton	a	2-1		Balfour 2
	26th	L	Third Lanark	a	1-1		Robertson
	31st	L	Queens Park	h	2-1	6,000	Robertson; Miller
Jan	2nd	L	Aberdeen	a	2-3	15,000	Robertson 2
	3rd	L	Hearts	h	2-2	9,000	H. Smith; Miller
	6th	L	St Johnstone	a	1-2	7,000	Robertson
	14th	L	Clyde	h	2-1	7,000	Gilmour (pen); Munro
	21st	SC1	Cowdenbeath	a	1-1	4,500	Miller
	25th	SC1	Cowdenbeath	h	3-0	8,000	Guthrie 3
	28th	L	Falkirk	a	0-0	8,000	-
Feb	2nd	SC2	Bo'ness United	h	4-0	3,000	Balfour 3; Symon
	11th	L	Morton	h	2-2	4,000	Troup; Balfour
	18th	SC3	Motherwell	a	0-5	8,000	-
	25th	L	Rangers	a	4-6		T. Smith; McNab 2; H. Smith
Mar	11th	L	Cowdenbeath	h	4-2	2,500	Robertson 2; Gilmour; Troup
	18th	L	Airdrie	a	0-3		-
	25th	L	St Mirren	a	1-2		Robertson
	29th	L	Kilmarnock	h	3-0	1,500	Blyth; Miller; Troup
Apr	1st	FCS	Arbroath	h	2-0	1,000	Blyth; Guthrie
	8th	L	Ayr United	a	0-6		-
	15th	L	Partick Thistle	h	1-0	3,000	Guthrie
	19th	FCF	Montrose	Gayfield	1-1	2,000	Guthrie
	22nd	L	Celtic	h	3-0	10,000	Robertson; Miller; H. Smith
	26th	FCFR	Montrose	Gayfield	0-1	2,500	-
	29th	L	East Stirling	a	2-3		Robertson 2

Cup Cash v. Cowdenbeath (a) £170, v. Cowdenbeath (h) £400, v. Bo'ness £150, v. Motherwell £300

Dundee's Scottish international Jimmy Robertson at training with Dens inside-forward Harry Smith.

The Record

League	-	15th Place, Division One
Scottish Cup	-	Third round
Forfarshire Cup	-	Runners-up
Top Scorer	-	Jimmy Robertson (22 goals)
Av. Home Gate	-	5,300
Players used	-	20
Sent off	-	None

Appearances

	League		Scottish Cup		Total	
Tom McCarthy	38	(1)	4		42	(1)
Lew Morgan	38		4		42	
Jock Gilmour	36	(3)	4		40	(3)
Monty Munro	30	(3)	3		33	(3)
Jimmy Robertson	31	(22)	2		33	(22)
Alec Troup	28	(3)	4		32	(3)
Andy Miller	26	(6)	4	(1)	30	(7)
Scott Symon	26		4	(1)	30	(1)
Willie Blyth	20	(1)	4		24	(1)
Bill Marsh	23		0		23	
Tom Smith	21	(1)	0		21	(1)
Jimmy Guthrie	17	(3)	3	(3)	20	(6)
Dave Edwards	15		4		19	
Colin McNab	17	(2)	1		18	(2)
Davie Balfour	12	(10)	3	(3)	15	(13)
Harry Smith	15	(3)	0		15	(3)
John Cameron	12		0		12	
Andy Campbell	9	(1)	0		9	(1)
Finlay Brown	2		0		2	
Bill Newton	2		0		2	

Scottish League Division One

		Home			Away			Goals		
	P	W	D	L	W	D	L	F	A	PTS
Rangers	38	14	5	0	12	5	2	113-43		62
Motherwell	38	15	1	3	12	4	3	114-53		59
Hearts	38	15	3	1	6	5	8	84-51		50
Celtic	38	13	3	3	7	5	7	75-44		48
St Johnstone	38	15	2	2	2	8	9	70-40		44
Aberdeen	38	13	4	2	5	2	12	85-58		42
St Mirren	38	12	3	4	6	3	10	73-60		42
Hamilton	38	11	5	3	7	1	11	90-78		42
Queens Park	38	11	5	3	6	2	11	78-79		41
Partick Thistle	38	9	3	7	8	3	8	75-55		40
Falkirk	38	9	5	5	6	1	12	70-69		36
Clyde	38	12	0	7	3	5	11	69-75		35
Third Lanark	38	12	3	4	2	4	13	70-80		35
Kilmarnock	38	8	5	6	5	4	10	72-86		35
Dundee	**38**	**9**	**6**	**4**	**3**	**3**	**13**	**60-77**		**33**
Ayr United	38	11	2	6	2	2	15	62-95		30
Cowdenbeath	38	9	3	7	1	2	16	65-111		25
Airdrie	38	9	2	8	1	1	17	55-102		23
Morton	38	4	3	12	2	6	11	49-97		21
East Stirling	38	6	3	10	1	0	18	55-115		17

Dundee F.C. Line-Ups 1932-33

		1	2	3	4	5	6	7	8	9	10	11
Aug	13th	Marsh	Morgan	Gilmour	McNab	McCarthy	Smith T	Cameron	Robertson	Balfour	Campbell	Troup
	20th	Marsh	Morgan	Gilmour	McNab	McCarthy	Smith T	Munro	Miller	Robertson	Smith H	Troup
	24th	Marsh	Morgan	Gilmour	McNab	McCarthy	Smith T	Munro	Miller	Balfour	Robertson	Troup
	27th	Marsh	Morgan	Gilmour	McNab	McCarthy	Smith T	Cameron	Miller	Robertson	Campbell	Troup
Sep	3rd	Marsh	Morgan	Gilmour	McNab	McCarthy	Smith T	Cameron	Miller	Robertson	Smith H	Munro
	10th	Marsh	Morgan	Gilmour	McNab	McCarthy	Smith T	Cameron	Miller	Robertson	Smith H	Munro
	17th	Marsh	Morgan	Gilmour	McNab	McCarthy	Smith T	Balfour	Cameron	Robertson	Campbell	Munro
	24th	Marsh	Morgan	Gilmour	McNab	McCarthy	Smith T	Munro	Cameron	Robertson	Campbell	Munro
Oct	1st	Marsh	Morgan	Gilmour	McNab	McCarthy	Smith T	Blyth	Miller	Robertson	Campbell	Munro
	8th	Marsh	Morgan	Gilmour	McNab	McCarthy	Smith T	Blyth	Miller	Robertson	Campbell	Munro
	15th	Marsh	Brown	Morgan	Symon	McCarthy	Smith T	Munro	Miller	Robertson	Campbell	Troup
	22nd	Marsh	Morgan	Gilmour	Symon	McCarthy	Smith T	Munro	Miller	Robertson	Campbell	Troup
	29th	Marsh	Morgan	Gilmour	Symon	McCarthy	Smith T	Munro	Guthrie	Balfour	Robertson	Troup
Nov	5th	Marsh	Morgan	Gilmour	Symon	McCarthy	Smith T	Munro	Guthrie	Balfour	Robertson	Troup
	12th	Edwards	Morgan	Gilmour	Symon	McCarthy	Smith T	Munro	Guthrie	Balfour	Robertson	Troup
	19th	Edwards	Morgan	Gilmour	Symon	McCarthy	Smith T	Munro	Guthrie	Balfour	Robertson	Troup
	26th	Edwards	Morgan	Gilmour	Symon	McCarthy	Smith T	Munro	Guthrie	Balfour	Campbell	Troup
Dec	3rd	Edwards	Morgan	Gilmour	McNab	McCarthy	Blyth	Munro	Guthrie	Cameron	Smith H	Troup
	10th	Edwards	Morgan	Gilmour	Symon	McCarthy	Blyth	Munro	Guthrie	Balfour	Miller	Troup
	17th	Edwards	Morgan	Gilmour	Symon	McCarthy	Blyth	Munro	Guthrie	Balfour	Miller	Troup
	24th	Edwards	Morgan	Gilmour	Symon	McCarthy	Blyth	Munro	Guthrie	Balfour	Miller	Troup
	26th	Edwards	Morgan	Gilmour	McNab	McCarthy	Blyth	Munro	Smith H	Robertson	Miller	Troup
	31st	Edwards	Morgan	Gilmour	Symon	McCarthy	Blyth	Smith H	Cameron	Robertson	Miller	Newton
Jan	2nd	Edwards	Brown	Morgan	Symon	McCarthy	Blyth	Cameron	Smith H	Robertson	Miller	Newton
	3rd	Edwards	Morgan	Gilmour	Symon	McCarthy	Blyth	McNab	Smith H	Robertson	Miller	Cameron
	7th	Edwards	Morgan	Gilmour	Symon	McCarthy	Blyth	McNab	Smith H	Robertson	Miller	Munro
	14th	Edwards	Morgan	Gilmour	Symon	McCarthy	Blyth	Munro	Guthrie	Robertson	Miller	Troup
	21st	Edwards	Morgan	Gilmour	Symon	McCarthy	Blyth	Munro	Robertson	Balfour	Miller	Troup
	25th	Edwards	Morgan	Gilmour	Symon	McCarthy	Blyth	McNab	Guthrie	Robertson	Miller	Troup
	28th	Marsh	Morgan	Gilmour	Symon	McCarthy	Blyth	Munro	Guthrie	Robertson	Miller	Troup
Feb	2nd	Edwards	Morgan	Gilmour	Symon	McCarthy	Blyth	Munro	Guthrie	Balfour	Miller	Troup
	11th	Marsh	Morgan	Gilmour	Symon	McCarthy	Blyth	Munro	Guthrie	Balfour	Miller	Troup
	18th	Edwards	Morgan	Gilmour	Symon	McCarthy	Blyth	Munro	Guthrie	Balfour	Miller	Troup
	25th	Edwards	Morgan	Gilmour	Symon	McCarthy	Smith T	Munro	Smith H	McNab	Miller	Troup
Mar	11th	Marsh	Morgan	Gilmour	Symon	McCarthy	Blyth	Munro	Smith H	Robertson	Miller	Troup
	18th	Marsh	Morgan	Gilmour	Symon	McCarthy	Smith T	Munro	Smith H	Robertson	Cameron	Troup
	25th	Marsh	Morgan	Gilmour	Symon	McCarthy	Smith T	Munro	Smith H	Robertson	Cameron	Troup
	29th	Marsh	Morgan	Gilmour	Symon	McCarthy	Blyth	Munro	Guthrie	Robertson	Miller	Troup
Apr	8th	Marsh	Morgan	Gilmour	Symon	McCarthy	Smith T	Munro	Guthrie	Robertson	Blyth	Troup
	15th	Marsh	Morgan	Gilmour	Symon	McCarthy	Blyth	McNab	Guthrie	Robertson	Miller	Troup
	22nd	Marsh	Morgan	Gilmour	Symon	McCarthy	Blyth	Smith H	Guthrie	Robertson	Miller	Troup
	29th	Edwards	Morgan	Gilmour	Symon	McCarthy	Blyth	McNab	Guthrie	Robertson	Miller	Smith H

Dundee defenders Tom McCarthy and Colin McNab can only look on as the high-flying McFadyen of Motherwell heads for goal. The Fir Park side, who were the reigning League Champions, finished runners-up in 1932-33.

They Wore The Dark Blue

Season 1933-34

Date			Opponents		Score	Crowd	Scorers
Aug	12th	L	St Johnstone	a	1-0	9,000	Lee
	19th	L	Clyde	h	1-1	10,000	Lee
	23rd	L	Motherwell	a	0-1		-
	26th	L	Falkirk	a	1-2	6,000	Lee
Sep	2nd	L	QOS	h	8-0	7,000	Blyth; Murdoch; Paterson; Morgan (pen); Mackay 3; Lee
	9th	L	Aberdeen	a	3-1	17,000	Mackay 2; Lee
	13th	L	Third Lanark	h	3-0	8,000	Robertson; Lee; Mackay
	16th	L	Queens Park	h	1-0	18,000	Murdoch
	23rd	L	Rangers	a	0-1	12,000	-
	30th	L	Hearts	h	0-1	12,000	-
Oct	7th	L	Hamilton	a	2-3		Murdoch; Paterson
	9th	FC1	Dundee United	h	3-2	1,000	Mackay 2; Robertson
	14th	L	Kilmarnock	h	0-2	12,000	-
	21st	L	Cowdenbeath	h	4-2	5,000	Murdoch; Lee 2; Mackay
	28th	L	Airdrie	a	1-2	2,500	Mackay
Nov	4th	L	Motherwell	h	2-3	20,000	Robertson 2
	11th	L	Third Lanark	a	1-4	3,500	Morgan (pen)
	18th	L	St Mirren	a	3-0	4,500	Lee; Kirby; Murdoch
	25th	L	Ayr United	a	3-3		Robertson; Kirby; Blyth
Dec	2nd	L	Partick Thistle	h	1-2	5,000	Murdoch
	9th	L	Celtic	h	3-2	12,000	Kirby; Guthrie; Lee
	16th	L	Hibernian	a	1-2	8,000	Guthrie
	23rd	L	St Johnstone	h	3-0	15,000	Mackay
	30th	L	Clyde	a	0-3		-
Jan	1st	L	Aberdeen	h	1-1	15,000	Kirby
	2nd	L	Hearts	a	1-6	15,000	Murdoch
	6th	L	Falkirk	h	1-3	5,000	Rennie
	13th	L	QOS	a	1-3	5,000	Guthrie
	20th	SC1	Kings Park	a	1-0	6,300	Rankin
	27th	L	Rangers	h	0-6	20,000	-
Feb	3rd	SC2	Aberdeen	a	0-2	26,943	-
	17th	L	Queens Park	a	4-2	3,000	Rennie 2; Rankin; Blyth
	24th	L	Hamilton	h	1-1	3,500	Rankin
Mar	3rd	L	Kilmarnock	a	3-1		Rennie; Murdoch 2
	10th	L	Cowdenbeath	a	1-1		Rennie
	17th	L	Airdrie	h	4-0	3,000	Guthrie; Murdoch; Mackay; Kirby (pen)
	24th	L	St Mirren	h	3-0	4,000	Rankin; Mackay 2
	31st	L	Ayr United	h	2-1	4,000	McCarthy; Mackay
Apr	7th	L	Partick Thistle	a	1-1	10,000	Rennie
	21st	L	Celtic	a	2-3	3,000	Rankin; Mackay
	25th	FCS	Arbroath	a	1-3	3,000	T. Smith
	28th	L	Hibernian	h	1-0	1,000	Mackay

Cup Cash v. Kings Park £227, v. Aberdeen £1,539

Lew Morgan and Danny Paterson go flat-out during sprint training at Dens.

The Record		
League	-	12th Place, Division One
Scottish Cup	-	Second round
Forfarshire Cup	-	Semi-final
Top Scorer	-	Morgan Mackay (17 goals)
Av. Home Gate	-	9,400
Players used	-	21
Sent off	-	Two

Appearances

	League	Scottish Cup	Total
Bill Marsh	37	2	39
Lew Morgan	37 (2)	2	39 (2)
Johnny Murdoch	37 (10)	2	39 (10)
Scott Symon	35	2	37
Jock Gilmour	33	2	35
Willie Blyth	31 (3)	2	33 (3)
Tom McCarthy	31 (1)	2	33 (1)
Morgan Mackay	31 (17)	2	33 (17)
Pat Lee	25 (10)	1	26 (10)
Norman Kirby	23 (5)	2	25 (5)
Jimmy Guthrie	20 (4)	1	21 (4)
Jimmy Robertson	20 (4)	0	20 (4)
Tom Smith	19	0	19
Bobby Rankin	11 (4)	2 (1)	13 (5)
Danny Paterson	11 (2)	0	11 (2)
Bobby Rennie	8 (6)	0	8 (6)
Alfred Lawson	3	0	3
Eddie McGoldrick	3	0	3
Harry Smith	2	0	2
Finlay Brown	1	0	1
Bob Peden	1	0	1

Scottish League Division One

		Home			Away			Goals		
	P	W	D	L	W	D	L	F A		PTS
Rangers	38	16	3	0	14	3	2	118-41		66
Motherwell	38	14	2	3	15	2	2	97-45		62
Celtic	38	12	5	2	6	6	7	78-53		47
Queen of the South	38	11	2	6	10	1	8	75-78		45
Aberdeen	38	12	4	3	6	4	9	90-57		44
Hearts	38	11	5	3	6	5	8	86-59		44
Kilmarnock	38	11	3	5	6	6	7	73-64		43
Ayr United	38	10	4	5	6	6	7	87-92		40
St Johnstone	38	11	3	5	6	3	10	74-53		40
Falkirk	38	12	3	4	4	3	12	73-68		38
Hamilton	38	9	5	5	6	3	10	65-79		38
Dundee	38	10	3	6	5	3	11	68-64		36
Partick Thistle	38	9	2	8	5	3	11	72-78		33
Clyde	38	8	5	6	2	6	11	56-70		31
Queens Park	38	7	3	9	6	2	11	65-85		31
Hibernian	38	8	2	9	4	1	14	51-69		27
St Mirren	38	5	4	10	4	5	10	46-75		27
Airdrie	38	7	3	9	3	3	13	59-103		26
Third Lanark	38	6	6	7	2	3	14	62-103		25
Cowdenbeath	38	4	3	12	1	2	16	58-118		15

They Wore The Dark Blue

Dundee F.C. Line-Ups 1933-34

		1	2	3	4	5	6	7	8	9	10	11
Aug	12th	Marsh	Morgan	Gilmour	Blyth	McCarthy	Smith T	Murdoch	Smith H	Robertson	Lee	Paterson
	19th	Marsh	Morgan	Gilmour	Blyth	McCarthy	Smith T	Murdoch	Guthrie	Robertson	Lee	Paterson
	23rd	Marsh	Morgan	Gilmour	Symon	McCarthy	Blyth	Murdoch	Robertson	Mackay	Lee	Paterson
	26th	Marsh	Morgan	Gilmour	Blyth	Symon	Smith T	Murdoch	Robertson	Mackay	Lee	Paterson
Sep	2nd	Marsh	Morgan	Gilmour	Blyth	Symon	Smith T	Murdoch	Robertson	Mackay	Lee	Paterson
	9th	Marsh	Morgan	Gilmour	Blyth*	Symon	Smith T	Murdoch	Robertson	Mackay	Lee	Paterson
	13th	Marsh	Morgan	Gilmour	Blyth	Symon	Smith T	Murdoch	Robertson	Mackay	Lee	Paterson
	16th	Marsh	Morgan	Gilmour	Blyth	Symon	Smith T	Murdoch	Robertson	Mackay	Lee	Paterson
	23rd	Marsh	Morgan	Gilmour	Symon	McCarthy	Smith T	Murdoch	Robertson	Mackay	Lee	Paterson
	30th	Marsh	Lawson	Gilmour	Symon	McCarthy	Smith T	Murdoch	Robertson	Mackay	Lee	Paterson
Oct	7th	Marsh	Morgan	Gilmour	Symon	McCarthy	Blyth	Murdoch	Robertson	Mackay	Lee	Paterson
	14th	Marsh	Morgan	Gilmour	Blyth	Symon	Smith T	Murdoch	Smith H	Mackay	Lee	Robertson
	21st	Marsh	Morgan	Gilmour	Blyth	Symon	Smith T	Murdoch	McGoldrick	Mackay	Lee	Robertson
	28th	Marsh	Morgan	Gilmour	Symon	McCarthy	Blyth	Murdoch	McGoldrick	Mackay	Lee	Robertson
Nov	4th	Marsh	Morgan	Gilmour	Symon	McCarthy	Blyth	Murdoch	Mackay	Robertson	Lee	Kirby
	11th	Peden	Morgan	Lawson	Symon	McCarthy	Blyth	Murdoch	Mackay	Robertson	Guthrie	Kirby
	18th	Marsh	Morgan	McCarthy	Blyth	Symon	Smith T	Murdoch	Mackay	Robertson	Lee	Kirby
	25th	Marsh	Morgan	McCarthy	Blyth	Symon	Smith T	Murdoch	Mackay	Robertson	Lee	Kirby
Dec	2nd	Marsh	Morgan	McCarthy	Blyth	Symon	Smith T	Murdoch	Mackay	Robertson	Lee	Kirby
	9th	Marsh	Morgan	Gilmour	Symon	McCarthy	Blyth	Murdoch	Guthrie	Robertson	Lee	Kirby
	16th	Marsh	Morgan	Gilmour	Symon	McCarthy	Blyth	Murdoch	Guthrie	Mackay	Lee	Kirby
	23rd	Marsh	Morgan	Gilmour	Symon	McCarthy	Blyth	Murdoch	Guthrie	Mackay	Lee	Kirby
	30th	Marsh	Morgan	Lawson	Symon	McCarthy	Gilmour	Murdoch	Guthrie	Mackay	Lee	Kirby
Jan	1st	Marsh	Morgan	Gilmour	Symon	McCarthy	Blyth	Murdoch	Guthrie	Mackay	Lee	Kirby
	2nd	Marsh	Morgan	Gilmour	Symon	McCarthy	Blyth	Murdoch	Guthrie	Mackay	Lee	Kirby
	6th	Marsh	Morgan	Gilmour	Symon	Brown	McCarthy	Murdoch	Guthrie	Rennie	Lee	Kirby
	13th	Marsh	Morgan	Gilmour	Symon	McCarthy	Blyth	Murdoch	Guthrie	Rennie	Mackay	Kirby
	20th	Marsh	Morgan	Gilmour	Symon	McCarthy	Blyth	Murdoch	Guthrie	Mackay	Rankin	Kirby
	27th	Marsh	Morgan	Gilmour	Symon	McCarthy	Blyth	Murdoch	Guthrie	Mackay	Rankin	Kirby
Feb	3rd	Marsh	Morgan	Gilmour	Symon	McCarthy	Blyth	Murdoch	Lee	Mackay	Rankin	Kirby
	17th	Marsh	Morgan	Gilmour	Symon	McCarthy	Blyth	Murdoch	Guthrie	Rennie	Rankin	Kirby
	24th	Marsh	Morgan	Gilmour	Symon	McCarthy	Blyth	Murdoch	Guthrie	Rennie	Rankin	Kirby
Mar	3rd	Marsh	Morgan	Gilmour	Symon	McCarthy	Blyth	Murdoch	Guthrie	Rennie	Rankin	Kirby
	10th	Marsh	Morgan	Gilmour	Symon	McCarthy	Blyth	Murdoch	McGoldrick	Rennie	Rankin	Kirby
	17th	Marsh	Morgan	Gilmour	Blyth*	McCarthy	Smith T	Murdoch	Guthrie	Mackay	Rankin	Kirby
	24th	Marsh	Morgan	Gilmour	Symon	McCarthy	Smith T	Murdoch	Guthrie	Mackay	Rankin	Kirby
	31st	Marsh	Morgan	Gilmour	Symon	McCarthy	Smith T	Murdoch	Guthrie	Mackay	Rankin	Kirby
Apr	7th	Marsh	Morgan	McCarthy	Mackay	Symon	Smith T	Murdoch	Guthrie	Rennie	Rankin	Kirby
	21st	Marsh	Morgan	Gilmour	Symon	McCarthy	Blyth	Murdoch	Guthrie	Mackay	Rankin	Kirby
	28th	Marsh	Morgan	Gilmour	Symon	McCarthy	Smith T	Blyth	Guthrie	Mackay	Rankin	Rennie

Dundee F.C. Season 1933-34. BACK - Johnny Brown (trainer) Tom McCarthy, Lew Morgan, Bill Marsh, Scott Symon, Tom Smith, Jimmy Guthrie. FRONT - Willie Blyth, Johnny Murdoch, Jimmy Robertson, Morgan Mackay, Jock Gilmour, Pat Lee, Danny Paterson, Harry Smith

Season 1934-35

Date			Opponents		Score	Crowd	Scorers
Aug	11th	L	Albion Rovers	h	3-2	10,000	Kirby; Coats 2
	18th	L	QOS	a	0-1	7,500	-
	22nd	L	Dunfermline	h	1-1	8,000	Kirby (pen)
	25th	L	Rangers	h	3-2	22,500	Coats 2; Mackay
Sep	1st	L	Hearts	a	1-1	15,000	Rankin
	8th	L	Aberdeen	h	0-0	18,500	
	12th	L	Airdrie	a	3-0	5,000	Coats 2; Robertson
	15th	L	Queens Park	a	0-4	8,000	-
	22nd	L	Hamilton	h	2-1	6,000	Kirby; Coats
	29th	L	Clyde	a	2-2	9,000	Coats 2
Oct	1st	L	Celtic	h	0-0	18,000	-
	6th	L	St Johnstone	h	1-2	22,000	Coats
	13th	L	Kilmarnock	a	0-2		-
	20th	L	Motherwell	a	3-5	6,000	Coats; Robertson 2
	27th	L	Falkirk	h	1-0	5,500	Rankin
Nov	3rd	L	St Mirren	a	1-0		Guthrie
	10th	L	Ayr United	h	5-4	4,000	Coats 2; Rankin; Robertson; McNaughton
	17th	L	Partick Thistle	a	4-1	9,000	McNaughton; Coats
	24th	L	Celtic	a	0-4	9,000	-
Dec	1st	L	Hibernian	h	0-2	5,000	-
	8th	L	Dunfermline	a	5-2	5,000	Robertson 2; Coats 2; Guthrie
	15th	L	Airdrie	h	2-0	3,500	Coats; McNaughton
	22nd	L	Albion Rovers	a	2-1	6,000	Coats 2
	29th	L	QOS	h	5-0	7,500	Guthrie; Coats 2; Robertson (pen); McNaughton
Jan	1st	L	Aberdeen	a	0-3		-
	2nd	L	Hearts	h	1-5	23,500	McNaughton
	5th	L	Rangers	a	1-3	18,000	Robertson
	12th	L	Queens Park	h	4-1	6,000	Guthrie; Robertson; Coats 2
	19th	L	Hamilton	a	1-1	5,000	Coats
	26th	SC1	Motherwell	h	0-1	27,000	-
Feb	2nd	L	Clyde	h	2-2	3,000	McNaughton; Robertson
	16th	L	St Johnstone	a	1-0	7,000	Coats
	23rd	L	Motherwell	h	3-1	6,000	Coats; McNaughton; Guthrie
Mar	2nd	L	Kilmarnock	h	0-2	3,500	-
	9th	L	Partick Thistle	h	2-0	3,500	Mackay; Coats
	16th	L	Falkirk	a	1-1	7,000	Mackay
	23rd	L	St Mirren	h	0-2	3,000	-
	30th	L	Ayr United	a	2-3	8,000	McNaughton; Robertson
Apr	27th	L	Hibernian	a	1-2	8,000	Coats

Cup Cash v. Motherwell £1,342-9-9d.

Tommy Robertson - the ex-Ayr player was a big hit at outside-right for Dundee.

The Record	
League	- Eighth Place, Division One
Scottish Cup	- First round
Forfarshire Cup	- Winners (played in 1935-36)
Top Scorer	- Archie Coats (30 goals)
Av. Home Gate	- 9,500
Players used	- 23
Sent off	- One

Appearances

	League	Scottish Cup	Total
Archie Coats	38 (30)	1	39 (30)
Lew Morgan	37	1	38
Jimmy Guthrie	36 (5)	1	37 (5)
Tommy Robertson	36 (11)	1	37 (11)
Scott Symon	36	1	37
Jock Gilmour	35	1	36
Bill Marsh	31	1	32
Gibby McNaughton	30 (8)	1	31 (8)
Norman Kirby	26 (3)	1	27 (3)
Willie Blyth	25	0	25
Tom Smith	22	1	23
Bobby Rankin	16 (3)	1	17 (3)
John Russell	13	0	13
Tom McCarthy	11	0	11
Albert Lamb	7	0	7
Morgan Mackay	7 (3)	0	7 (3)
William Pollock	3	0	3
Bobby Rennie	3	0	3
Dennis Quigley	2	0	2
Tom Wemyss	2	0	2
Bob Hogg	1	0	1
Eddie McGoldrick	1	0	1
Dave Russell	1	0	1

Scottish League Division One

	P	Home W	D	L	Away W	D	L	Goals F	A	PTS
Rangers	38	14	3	2	11	2	6	96	46	55
Celtic	38	15	2	2	9	2	8	92	45	52
Hearts	38	11	5	3	9	5	5	87	51	50
Hamilton	38	14	4	1	5	6	8	87	67	48
St Johnstone	38	13	4	2	5	6	8	66	46	46
Aberdeen	38	13	3	3	4	7	8	68	54	44
Motherwell	38	12	4	3	3	6	10	83	64	40
Dundee	**38**	**10**	**4**	**5**	**6**	**4**	**9**	**63**	**63**	**40**
Kilmarnock	38	10	3	6	6	3	10	76	68	38
Clyde	38	9	6	4	5	4	10	71	69	38
Hibernian	38	10	7	2	4	1	14	59	70	36
Queens Park	38	11	4	4	2	6	11	61	80	36
Partick Thistle	38	10	5	4	5	0	14	61	68	35
Airdrie	38	10	3	6	3	4	12	64	72	33
Dunfermline	38	8	4	7	5	1	13	56	96	31
Albion Rovers	38	8	4	7	2	5	12	62	77	29
Queen of the South	38	9	2	8	2	5	12	52	72	29
Ayr United	38	10	2	7	2	3	15	61	82	29
St Mirren	38	7	3	9	4	2	13	49	70	27
Falkirk	38	8	3	8	1	3	15	58	82	24

Dundee F.C. Line-Ups Ups 1934-35

		1	2	3	4	5	6	7	8	9	10	11
Aug	11th	Marsh	Morgan	Gilmour	Russell J	Symon	Smith T	Robertson T	Guthrie	Coats	Rankin	Kirby
	18th	Marsh	Morgan	Gilmour	Russell J	Symon	Smith T	Robertson T	Guthrie	Coats	Rankin	Kirby
	22nd	Marsh	Morgan	Gilmour	Russell J	Symon	Smith T	Robertson T	Guthrie	Coats	Rankin	Kirby
	25th	Marsh	Morgan	Gilmour	Symon	McCarthy	Russell J	Mackay	Guthrie	Coats	Rankin	Kirby
Sep	1st	Marsh	Morgan	Gilmour	Symon	McCarthy	Russell J	Robertson T	Guthrie	Coats	Rankin	Kirby
	8th	Marsh	Morgan	Gilmour	Symon	McCarthy	Russell J	Robertson T	Guthrie	Coats	Rankin	Kirby
	12th	Marsh	Morgan	Gilmour	Symon	McCarthy	Blyth	Robertson T	Guthrie	Coats	McNaughton	Kirby
	15th	Marsh	Morgan	Gilmour	Symon	McCarthy	Russell J	Robertson T	McGoldrick	Coats	McNaughton	Kirby
	22nd	Marsh	Morgan	Gilmour	Symon	McCarthy	Blyth	Robertson T	Guthrie	Coats	McNaughton	Kirby
	29th	Marsh	Morgan	Hogg	Symon	McCarthy	Blyth	Robertson T	Guthrie	Coats	McNaughton	Kirby
Oct	1st	Marsh	Morgan	Gilmour	Symon	McCarthy	Blyth	Robertson T	Guthrie	Coats	McNaughton	Kirby
	6th	Marsh	Morgan	Gilmour	Symon	McCarthy	Blyth	Quigley	Guthrie	Coats	McNaughton	Kirby
	13th	Marsh	Morgan	Gilmour	Blyth	McCarthy	Russell J	Quigley	Mackay	Coats	Rankin	Kirby
	20th	Marsh	Morgan	Gilmour	Blyth	McCarthy	Smith T	Robertson T	Guthrie	Coats	McNaughton	Rankin
	27th	Marsh	Morgan	Gilmour	Blyth	Symon	Smith T	Robertson T	Guthrie	Coats	McNaughton	Rankin
Nov	3rd	Lamb	Morgan	Gilmour	Blyth	Symon	Smith T	Robertson T	Guthrie	Coats	McNaughton	Rankin
	10th	Lamb	Morgan	Gilmour	Blyth	Symon	Smith T	Robertson T	Guthrie	Coats	McNaughton	Rankin
	17th	Marsh	Morgan	Gilmour	Blyth	Symon	Smith T	Robertson T	Guthrie	Coats	McNaughton	Rankin
	24th	Marsh	Morgan	Gilmour	Blyth	Symon	Smith T	Robertson T	Guthrie	Coats	McNaughton	Rankin
Dec	1st	Marsh	Morgan	Gilmour	Blyth	Symon	Smith T	Robertson T	Guthrie	Coats	McNaughton	Mackay
	8th	Marsh	Morgan	Gilmour	Blyth	Symon	Smith T	Robertson T	Guthrie	Coats	McNaughton	Rankin
	15th	Marsh	Morgan	Gilmour	Blyth	Symon	Smith T	Robertson T	Guthrie	Coats	McNaughton	Rankin
	22nd	Marsh	Morgan	Gilmour	Blyth	Symon	Smith T	Robertson T	Guthrie	Coats	McNaughton	Pollock
	29th	Lamb	Morgan	Gilmour	Blyth	Symon	Smith T	Robertson T	Guthrie	Coats	McNaughton	Kirby
Jan	1st	Lamb	Morgan	Gilmour	Blyth	Symon	Smith T	Robertson T	Guthrie	Coats	McNaughton	Pollock
	2nd	Lamb	Morgan	Gilmour	Blyth	Symon	Smith T	Robertson T	Guthrie	Coats	McNaughton	Kirby
	5th	Lamb	Morgan	Gilmour	Blyth	Symon	Smith T	Robertson T	Guthrie	Coats	McNaughton	Kirby
	12th	Lamb	Morgan	Gilmour	Blyth	Symon	Smith T	Robertson T	Guthrie	Coats	Rankin	Kirby
	19th	Marsh	Morgan	Gilmour*	Blyth	Symon	Smith T	Robertson T	Guthrie	Coats	McNaughton	Kirby
	26th	Marsh	Morgan	Gilmour	Guthrie	Symon	Smith T	Robertson T	McNaughton	Coats	Rankin	Kirby
Feb	2nd	Marsh	Morgan	Gilmour	Russell J	Symon	Smith T	Robertson T	Guthrie	Coats	McNaughton	Kirby
	16th	Marsh	Rennie	Morgan	Blyth	Symon	Russell J	Robertson T	Guthrie	Coats	McNaughton	Kirby
	23rd	Marsh	Rennie	Morgan	Blyth	Symon	Russell J	Robertson T	Guthrie	Coats	McNaughton	Kirby
Mar	2nd	Marsh	Morgan	Gilmour	Blyth	Symon	Smith T	Robertson T	Guthrie	Coats	McNaughton	Kirby
	9th	Marsh	Morgan	Gilmour	Guthrie	Symon	Russell J	Robertson T	Mackay	Coats	McNaughton	Kirby
	16th	Marsh	Morgan	Gilmour	Guthrie	Symon	Russell J	Robertson T	Mackay	Coats	McNaughton	Kirby
	23rd	Marsh	Morgan	Gilmour	Guthrie	Symon	Russell J	Robertson T	Mackay	Coats	McNaughton	Kirby
	30th	Marsh	Morgan	Gilmour	Guthrie	Symon	Wemyss	Robertson T	Mackay	Coats	McNaughton	Kirby
Apr	27th	Marsh	Rennie	Gilmour	Wemyss	Symon	Smith T	Robertson T	Guthrie	Coats	McNaughton	Pollock

No chance - Dundee's Archie Coats, hidden by two defenders, blasts a shot into the roof of the Arbroath net to give Dundee victory in the Forfarshire Cup Final replay at Tannadice in 1935.

Season 1935-36

Date			Opponents		Score	Crowd	Scorers
Aug	10th	L	Hamilton	a	2-2		Robertson; Coats
	12th	FCS*	Dundee United		2-2	11,013	Robertson; Coats
	17th	L	Queens Park	h	6-4	11,000	Robertson 2; Phillips; Coats 3
	19th	FCSR*	Dundee United	h	8-1	14,000	Coats 3; Phillips 2; Robertson 2; McNaughton
	24th	L	Rangers	a	3-4	18,000	Coats 2; McNaughton
	31st	L	Hearts	h	2-5	15,000	Munro o.g.; McNaughton
Sep	4th	FCF*	Arbroath	Tan	1-1	11,600	Kirby (pen)
	7th	L	St Johnstone	a	0-2	6,000	-
	14th	L	Clyde	h	4-3	7,000	Kirby; Phillips; Coats; Robertson
	18th	FCFR*	Arbroath	Tan	1-0	8,600	Coats
	21st	L	Aberdeen	a	1-4	18,000	Phillips
	28th	L	QOS	h	1-1	7,000	Robertson
Oct	2nd	DSS	Aberdeen	h	2-3	3,800	Robertson; Reid
	5th	L	Albion Rovers	a	1-1	4,000	McNaughton
	7th	L	Third Lanark	h	3-2	10,000	Coats 2; McNaughton
	12th	L	Kilmarnock	h	0-0	6,000	-
	19th	L	Hibernian	a	1-2	8,000	Kirby
	26th	L	Ayr United	h	6-1	6,000	Kirby; Coats 2; Phillips; McNaughton; Robertson
Nov	2nd	L	Celtic	a	2-4	11,000	Robertson; Coats
	9th	L	Dunfermline	h	2-3	7,000	Adamson; Coats
	16th	L	Partick Thistle	h	3-3	6,000	Robertson; McNaughton; Coats
	23rd	L	Arbroath	a	0-1	6,500	-
	30th	L	Motherwell	h	2-2	6,000	Guthrie; Coats
Dec	7th	L	Airdrie	h	1-0	5,000	Coats
	14th	L	Third Lanark	a	2-2	3,500	Coats 2
	21st	L	Hamilton	h	3-0	7,000	Coats; Robertson; Smith
	28th	L	Queens Park	a	2-3	6,000	Coats; Robertson
Jan	1st	L	Aberdeen	h	2-2	21,000	Coats; Phillips
	2nd	L	Hearts	a	0-3		-
	4th	L	Rangers	h	0-3	20,000	-
	11th	L	St Johnstone	h	0-2	9,000	-
	18th	L	Clyde	a	1-2	8,000	Phillips
	25th	SC1	Babcock Wilcox	h	6-0	1,073	Robertson; Guthrie; Coats; Smith; Adamson 2
Feb	1st	L	QOS	a	4-3	5,000	Coats 2; Guthrie; Robertson (pen)
	8th	SC2	Airdrie	h	2-1	13,367	Coats 2
	15th	L	Albion Rovers	h	2-0	6,000	Coats 2
	22nd	SC3	Clyde	a	1-1	20,874	Robertson
	26th	SC3	Clyde	h	0-3	12,000	-
	29th	L	Kilmarnock	a	1-4		Robertson
Mar	7th	L	Hibernian	h	2-1	6,000	Kirby; Coats
	14th	L	Ayr United	a	2-1	6,000	Robertson; Guthrie
	21st	L	Celtic	h	0-2	20,500	-
	28th	L	Dunfermline	a	2-2	4,000	Baxter 2
Apr	11th	L	Partick Thistle	a	1-1		Coats
	18th	L	Arbroath	h	3-0	10,000	Baxter 2; Coats
	22nd	FCS**	Montrose	a	0-3	1,500	-
	25th	L	Motherwell	a	0-3	1,500	-

Caption under photo: *Jimmy Guthrie - creative player at either wing-half or inside-forward.*

The Record		
League	-	12th Place, Division One
Scottish Cup	-	Third round
Forfarshire Cup	-	Semi-final
Dewar Shield	-	Semi-final
Top Scorer	-	Archie Coats (31 goals)
Av. Home Gate	-	9,800
Players used	-	24
Sent off	-	One

* 1934-35 Forfarshire Cup; ** 1935-36 Forfarshire Cup. Scottish Cup Cash v. Babcock & Wilcox £60-10-6, v. Airdrie £513, v. Clyde (a) £942.

Appearances

	League		Scottish Cup		Total	
Archie Coats	38	(28)	4	(3)	42	(31)
Jimmy Guthrie	38	(3)	4	(1)	42	(4)
Tommy Robertson	37	(13)	4	(2)	41	(15)
Tom Smith	35	(1)	4	(1)	39	(2)
Norman Kirby	36	(4)	2		38	(4)
Bill Marsh	33		4		37	
Bobby Rennie	30		4		34	
John Evans	29		4		33	
Len Richards	29		4		33	
Billy Phillips	26	(7)	4		30	(7)
Gibby McNaughton	17	(5)	0		17	(5)
John Russell	13		3		16	
Matt Innes	13		0		13	
Bobby Adamson	5	(3)	2		7	(3)
Arthur Baxter	8	(4)	0		8	(4)
Emryss Warren	7		0		7	
Jock Gilmour	6		0		6	
Johnny Lynch	5		0		5	
Tom Wemyss	4		1		5	
Lew Morgan	3		0		3	
David Linton	2		0		2	
Albert Presdee	2		0		2	
Andy Cowie	1		0		1	
Joe Lindsay	1		0		1	

Scottish League Division One

		Home			Away			Goals	
	P	W	D	L	W	D	L	F A	PTS
Celtic	38	17	1	1	15	1	3	115-33	66
Rangers	38	14	3	2	13	4	2	110-43	61
Aberdeen	38	15	3	1	11	6	2	96-50	61
Motherwell	38	12	3	4	6	9	4	77-58	48
Hearts	38	14	4	1	6	3	10	88-55	47
Hamilton	38	11	4	4	4	3	12	77-74	37
St Johnstone	38	10	4	5	5	3	11	70-81	37
Kilmarnock	38	10	4	5	4	3	12	69-64	35
Third Lanark	38	11	4	4	4	1	14	63-65	35
Partick Thistle	38	12	5	2	0	5	14	64-72	34
Arbroath	38	6	6	7	5	5	9	46-69	33
Dundee	**38**	**9**	**5**	**5**	**2**	**5**	**12**	**67-80**	**32**
Queens Park	38	8	6	5	3	4	12	58-75	32
Dunfermline	38	6	6	7	6	2	11	67-92	32
Queen of the South	38	9	6	4	2	3	14	54-72	31
Albion Rovers	38	8	2	9	5	2	12	69-92	30
Hibernian	38	7	3	9	4	4	11	56-82	29
Clyde	38	10	1	8	0	7	12	63-84	28
Airdrie	38	8	4	7	1	5	13	68-91	27
Ayr United	38	5	2	9	3	1	15	53-98	25

They Wore The Dark Blue

Dundee F.C Line-Ups 1935-36

		1	2	3	4	5	6	7	8	9	10	11
Aug	10th	Marsh	Morgan	Gilmour	Guthrie	Evans	Smith T	Robertson T	McNaughton	Coats	Phillips	Kirby
	17th	Marsh	Morgan	Gilmour	Guthrie	Wemyss	Smith T	Robertson T	McNaughton	Coats	Phillips	Kirby
	24th	Lynch	Morgan	Gilmour	Guthrie	Evans	Smith T	Robertson T	McNaughton	Coats	Phillips	Kirby
	28th	Lynch	Rennie	Richards	Guthrie	Evans	Smith T	Robertson T	McNaughton	Coats	Phillips	Kirby
	31st	Lynch	Rennie	Gilmour	Guthrie	Evans	Smith T	Robertson T	McNaughton	Coats	Phillips	Kirby
Sep	7th	Lynch	Rennie	Gilmour	Guthrie	Evans	Smith T	Robertson T	Adamson	Coats	Phillips	Kirby
	14th	Marsh	Rennie	Gilmour	Guthrie	Evans	Smith T	Robertson T	McNaughton	Coats	Phillips	Kirby
	21st	Marsh	Rennie	Richards	Guthrie	Evans	Smith T	Robertson T	McNaughton	Coats	Phillips	Kirby
	28th	Marsh	Rennie	Richards	Russell J	Evans	Smith T	Robertson T	Guthrie	Coats	Phillips	Kirby
Oct	5th	Marsh	Rennie	Richards	Guthrie	Russell J	Smith T	Robertson T	McNaughton	Coats	Phillips	Kirby
	7th	Marsh	Rennie	Richards	Guthrie	Russell J	Smith T	Robertson T	McNaughton	Coats	Phillips	Kirby
	12th	Marsh	Warren	Richards	Guthrie	Russell J	Smith T	Robertson T	McNaughton	Coats	Phillips	Kirby
	19th	Marsh	Warren	Richards	Guthrie	Presdee	Smith T	Robertson T	McNaughton	Coats	Phillips	Kirby
	26th	Marsh	Warren	Richards	Guthrie	Russell J	Smith T	Robertson T	McNaughton	Coats	Phillips	Kirby
Nov	2nd	Marsh	Warren	Richards	Guthrie	Russell J	Smith T	Robertson T	McNaughton	Coats	Adamson	Kirby
	9th	Marsh	Warren	Richards	Guthrie	Russell J	Smith T	Robertson T	McNaughton	Coats	Adamson	Kirby
	16th	Marsh	Rennie	Richards	Guthrie	Presdee	Wemyss	Robertson T	McNaughton	Coats	Phillips	Kirby
	23rd	Marsh	Rennie	Richards	Russell J	Evans	Smith T	Robertson T	Guthrie	Coats	McNaughton	Kirby
	30th	Marsh	Rennie	Richards	Innes	Evans	Smith T	Robertson T	Guthrie	Coats	Phillips	Kirby
Dec	7th	Marsh	Rennie	Richards	Innes	Evans	Smith T	Robertson T	Guthrie	Coats	Phillips	Kirby
	14th	Marsh	Rennie	Richards	Innes	Evans	Smith T	Robertson T	Guthrie	Coats	Phillips	Kirby
	21st	Marsh	Rennie	Richards	Innes	Evans	Smith T	Robertson T	Guthrie	Coats	Phillips	Kirby
	28th	Marsh	Rennie	Richards	Innes	Evans	Smith T	Robertson T	Guthrie	Coats	Phillips	Linton
Jan	1st	Marsh	Rennie	Richards	Innes	Evans	Smith T	Robertson T	Guthrie	Coats	Phillips	Kirby
	2nd	Marsh	Rennie	Richards	Innes	Evans	Smith T	Robertson T	Guthrie	Coats	McNaughton	Kirby
	4th	Marsh	Rennie	Richards	Innes	Evans	Smith T	Robertson T	Guthrie	Coats	Phillips	Kirby
	11th	Marsh	Rennie	Lindsay	Innes	Evans	Smith T	Robertson T	Guthrie	Coats	Phillips	Kirby
	18th	Lynch	Rennie	Richards	Russell J	Evans	Smith T	McNaughton	Guthrie	Coats	Phillips	Kirby
	25th	Marsh	Rennie	Richards	Russell	Evans	Smith T	Robertson T	Guthrie	Coats	Phillips	Adamson
Feb	1st	Marsh	Rennie	Richards	Russell	Evans	Smith T	Robertson T	Guthrie	Coats	Phillips	Adamson
	8th	Marsh	Rennie	Richards	Russell	Evans	Smith T	Robertson T	Guthrie	Coats	Phillips	Adamson
	15th	Marsh	Rennie	Richards	Russell	Evans	Smith T	Robertson T	Guthrie	Coats	Phillips	Kirby
	22nd	Marsh	Rennie	Richards	Russell	Evans	Smith T	Robertson T	Guthrie	Coats	Phillips	Kirby
	26th	Marsh	Rennie	Richards	Wemyss	Evans	Smith T	Robertson T	Guthrie	Coats	Phillips	Kirby
	29th	Marsh	Rennie	Richards*	Wemyss	Evans	Innes	Robertson T	Guthrie	Coats	Baxter	Kirby
Mar	7th	Marsh	Rennie	Richards	Innes	Evans	Smith T	Robertson T	Guthrie	Coats	Baxter	Kirby
	14th	Marsh	Rennie	Richards	Innes	Evans	Smith T	Robertson T	Guthrie	Coats	Baxter	Kirby
	21st	Marsh	Rennie	Richards	Innes	Evans	Smith T	Robertson T	Guthrie	Coats	Baxter	Kirby
	28th	Marsh	Rennie	Warren	Russell J	Evans	Smith T	Linton	Guthrie	Coats	Baxter	Kirby
Apr	11th	Marsh	Rennie	Richards	Russell J	Evans	Smith T	Robertson T	Guthrie	Coats	Baxter	Kirby
	18th	Marsh	Rennie	Warren	Wemyss	Evans	Smith T	Robertson T	Guthrie	Coats	Baxter	Kirby
	25th	Marsh	Rennie	Richards	Cowie	Evans	Adamson	Robertson T	Guthrie	Coats	Baxter	Kirby

Dundee F.C. Season 1935-36. (BACK, left to right) Jack Qskley (trainer), Lew Morgan, Len Richards, Bill Marsh, Jimmy Guthrie, Tom Wemyss, Tom Smith, Billy McCandless (manager). FRONT - Jock Gilmour, Tom Robertson, Gibby McNaughton, Archie Coats, Billy Phillips, Norman Kirby and John Evans.

Season 1936-37

Date			Opponents		Score	Crowd	Scorers
Aug	8th	L	Rangers	h	0-0	22,000	-
	15th	L	Kilmarnock	a	1-1		Coats
	19th	L	Rangers	a	0-3		-
	22nd	L	St Johnstone	h	3-1	16,000	Baxter 2; Phillips
	29th	L	Clyde	a	2-1	8,000	Baxter; Rennie
Sep	5th	L	Albion Rovers	h	1-0	9,000	Coats
	9th	L	Kilmarnock	h	2-2	9,000	Coats; Rennie (pen)
	12th	L	QOS	a	2-2	3,000	Coats 2; Baxter
	19th	L	Aberdeen	h	2-2	27,000	Phillips; Coats
	23rd	FC1	Dundee United	a	1-3	6,500	Phillips
	26th	L	Queens Park	a	2-0	8,000	Coats 2
Oct	3rd	L	Hamilton	h	1-2	10,000	-
	10th	L	Hearts	a	0-4	16,000	-
	17th	L	Celtic	h	0-0	24,000	-
	24th	L	Dunfermline	a	4-3	3,000	Baxter; Coats 2; Guthrie
	31st	L	Partick Thistle	a	1-1	15,000	Coats
Nov	7th	L	Arbroath	h	6-1	10,000	Phillips; Baxter; Smith; Coats 2; Fordyce o.g.
	14th	L	Motherwell	a	1-2	5,000	Phillips
	21st	L	Falkirk	a	0-5	9,000	-
	28th	L	Third Lanark	h	3-2	7,000	Kirby (pen); Coats; Baxter
Dec	5th	L	Hibernian	h	3-1	6,000	Kirby; Phillips; Coats
	12th	L	St Mirren	a	0-4	6,500	-
	19th	L	St Johnstone	a	3-3	7,000	Coats; Baxter; Kirby (pen)
	26th	L	Clyde	h	2-2	7,000	Kirby; Coats
Jan	1st	L	Aberdeen	a	1-3	28,000	Coats
	2nd	L	Hearts	h	1-0	22,000	Coats
	9th	L	Albion Rovers	a	1-1	2,500	Coats
	16th	L	QOS	h	1-3	7,000	Kirby (pen)
	23rd	L	Hamilton	a	1-5	4,000	Rintoul
	30th	SC1	East Stirling	h	4-1	5,966	Phillips 2; Baxter; Coats
Feb	6th	L	Queens Park	h	2-2	5,000	Latimer; Coats
	13th	SC2	Queens Park	h	2-0	16,000	Coats; Kirby
	20th	L	Celtic	a	2-1	8,000	Coats 2 (1 pen)
	27th	SC3	Clyde	a	0-0	20,000	-
Mar	3rd	SC3	Clyde	h	0-1	14,000	-
	6th	L	Dunfermline	h	2-2	3,000	Baxter 2
	20th	L	Arbroath	a	0-3	4,000	-
	27th	L	Motherwell	h	0-0	6,000	-
Apr	3rd	L	Falkirk	h	1-1	3,000	Coats
	10th	L	Third Lanark	a	0-4	6,000	-
	12th	L	Partick Thistle	h	2-2	3,500	Kirby (pen); Baxter
	19th	L	Hibernian	a	0-0	3,000	-
	24th	L	St Mirren	h	4-0	1,200	Guthrie; Baxter; Coats 2

David Linton - Dundee's promising young outside-left showed up well.

The Record		
League	-	Ninth Place, Division One
Scottish Cup	-	Third round
Forfarshire Cup	-	First round
Top Scorer	-	Archie Coats (27 goals)
Av. Home gate	-	10,400
Players used	-	20
Sent off	-	None

Appearances

	League	Scottish Cup	Total
Arthur Baxter	38 (12)	4 (1)	42 (13)
Archie Coats	38 (25)	4 (2)	42 (27)
Tom Smith	38	4	42
John Evans	36	4	40
John Latimer	37 (3)	3	40 (3)
Bobby Rennie	36 (2)	4	40 (2)
Billy Phillips	34 (5)	4 (2)	38 (7)
Jimmy Guthrie	32 (2)	4	36 (2)
Norman Kirby	25 (6)	4 (1)	29 (7)
Bill Marsh	26	1	27
Len Richards	22	1	23
John Reddish	14	3	17
Johnny Lynch	12	3	15
David Linton	12	0	12
Andy Cowie	6	1	7
John Laurie	4	0	4
Matt Innes	3	0	3
Willie Watson	2	0	2
Bobby Adamson	2	0	2
David Rintoul	2 (1)	0	2 (1)

Scottish League Division One

		Home			Away			Goals		
	P	W	D	L	W	D	L	F A	PTS
Rangers	38	15	3	1	11	6	2	88-32	61
Aberdeen	38	15	4	0	8	4	7	89-44	54
Celtic	38	14	3	2	8	5	6	89-58	52
Motherwell	38	14	1	4	8	6	5	96-54	51
Hearts	38	17	0	2	7	3	9	99-60	51
Third Lanark	38	12	4	3	8	2	9	79-61	46
Falkirk	38	13	1	5	6	5	8	98-66	44
Hamilton	38	12	2	5	6	3	10	91-96	41
Dundee	**38**	**7**	**10**	**2**	**5**	**5**	**9**	**58-69**	**39**
Clyde	38	10	4	5	6	2	11	59-70	38
Kilmarnock	38	10	5	4	4	4	11	60-70	37
St Johnstone	38	13	1	5	1	7	11	74-68	36
Partick Thistle	38	8	6	5	3	6	10	73-68	34
Arbroath	38	9	5	5	4	0	15	57-84	31
Queens Park	38	3	7	9	6	5	8	51-77	30
St Mirren	38	9	2	8	2	5	12	68-81	29
Hibernian	38	2	11	6	4	2	13	54-83	25
Queen of the South	38	6	4	9	2	4	13	49-95	24
Dunfermline	38	3	7	9	2	4	13	65-98	21
Albion Rovers	38	4	2	13	1	4	14	53-116	16

Dundee F.C. Line-Ups 1936-37

		1	2	3	4	5	6	7	8	9	10	11
Aug	8th	Marsh	Rennie	Richards	Innes	Evans	Smith T	Latimer	Guthrie	Coats	Baxter	Kirby
	15th	Marsh	Rennie	Richards	Innes	Evans	Smith T	Latimer	Guthrie	Coats	Baxter	Kirby
	19th	Marsh	Rennie	Richards	Guthrie	Evans	Smith T	Latimer	Phillips	Coats	Baxter	Kirby
	22nd	Marsh	Rennie	Richards	Guthrie	Evans	Smith T	Latimer	Phillips	Coats	Baxter	Kirby
	29th	Marsh	Rennie	Richards	Guthrie	Evans	Smith T	Latimer	Phillips	Coats	Baxter	Linton
Sep	5th	Marsh	Rennie	Richards	Guthrie	Evans	Smith T	Latimer	Phillips	Coats	Baxter	Linton
	9th	Marsh	Rennie	Richards	Guthrie	Evans	Smith T	Latimer	Phillips	Coats	Baxter	Linton
	12th	Marsh	Rennie	Richards	Guthrie	Evans	Smith T	Latimer	Phillips	Coats	Baxter	Linton
	19th	Marsh	Rennie	Richards	Guthrie	Evans	Smith T	Latimer	Phillips	Coats	Baxter	Linton
	26th	Marsh	Rennie	Richards	Guthrie	Evans	Smith T	Latimer	Phillips	Coats	Baxter	Linton
Oct	3rd	Marsh	Rennie	Richards	Guthrie	Evans	Smith T	Latimer	Phillips	Coats	Baxter	Linton
	10th	Marsh	Rennie	Richards	Guthrie	Evans	Smith T	Latimer	Phillips	Coats	Baxter	Kirby
	17th	Marsh	Rennie	Richards	Guthrie	Evans	Smith T	Latimer	Phillips	Coats	Baxter	Kirby
	24th	Marsh	Rennie	Richards	Guthrie	Evans	Smith T	Latimer	Phillips	Coats	Baxter	Linton
	31st	Marsh	Rennie	Richards	Guthrie	Evans	Smith T	Latimer	Phillips	Coats	Baxter	Linton
Nov	7th	Marsh	Rennie	Richards	Guthrie	Evans	Smith T	Latimer	Phillips	Coats	Baxter	Linton
	14th	Marsh	Rennie	Richards	Guthrie	Evans	Smith T	Latimer	Phillips	Coats	Baxter	Linton
	21st	Marsh	Rennie	Richards	Guthrie	Evans	Smith T	Latimer	Phillips	Coats	Baxter	Linton
	28th	Marsh	Rennie	Reddish	Guthrie	Evans	Smith T	Latimer	Phillips	Coats	Baxter	Kirby
Dec	5th	Marsh	Rennie	Reddish	Guthrie	Evans	Smith T	Latimer	Phillips	Coats	Baxter	Kirby
	12th	Marsh	Rennie	Reddish	Guthrie	Evans	Smith T	Latimer	Phillips	Coats	Baxter	Kirby
	19th	Marsh	Rennie	Reddish	Cowie	Evans	Smith T	Latimer	Phillips	Coats	Baxter	Kirby
	26th	Lynch	Rennie	Reddish	Innes	Evans	Smith T	Latimer	Phillips	Coats	Baxter	Kirby
Jan	1st	Lynch	Rennie	Reddish	Cowie	Evans	Smith T	Latimer	Phillips	Coats	Baxter	Kirby
	2nd	Lynch	Rennie	Richards	Adamson	Evans	Smith T	Latimer	Phillips	Coats	Baxter	Kirby
	9th	Lynch	Rennie	Richards	Guthrie	Evans	Smith T	Latimer	Phillips	Coats	Baxter	Kirby
	16th	Lynch	Rennie	Richards	Guthrie	Evans	Smith T	Latimer	Phillips	Coats	Baxter	Kirby
	23rd	Lynch	Cowie	Richards	Guthrie	Evans	Smith T	Latimer	Dempster	Coats	Baxter	Rintoul
	30th	Lynch	Rennie	Richards	Guthrie	Evans	Smith T	Latimer	Phillips	Coats	Baxter	Kirby
Feb	6th	Lynch	Rennie	Reddish	Guthrie	Watson	Smith T	Latimer	Phillips	Coats	Baxter	Kirby
	13th	Marsh	Rennie	Reddish	Guthrie	Evans	Smith T	Latimer	Phillips	Coats	Baxter	Kirby
	20th	Lynch	Cowie	Reddish	Laurie	Evans	Smith T	Latimer	Phillips	Coats	Baxter	Kirby
	27th	Lynch	Rennie	Reddish	Guthrie	Evans	Smith T	Cowie	Phillips	Coats	Baxter	Kirby
Mar	3rd	Lynch	Rennie	Reddish	Guthrie	Evans	Smith T	Latimer	Phillips	Coats	Baxter	Kirby
	6th	Lynch	Rennie	Reddish	Guthrie	Evans	Smith T	Latimer	Phillips	Coats	Baxter	Kirby
	20th	Lynch	Rennie	Reddish	Laurie	Evans	Smith T	Phillips	Guthrie	Coats	Baxter	Kirby
	27th	Marsh	Rennie	Reddish	Guthrie	Evans	Smith T	Latimer	Baxter	Coats	Phillips	Kirby
Apr	3rd	Marsh	Rennie	Reddish	Guthrie	Evans	Smith T	Latimer	Baxter	Coats	Phillips	Kirby
	10th	Marsh	Rennie	Reddish	Guthrie	Evans	Smith T	Latimer	Baxter	Coats	Phillips	Kirby
	12th	Marsh	Rennie	Reddish	Guthrie	Evans	Smith T	Latimer	Baxter	Coats	Phillips	Kirby
	19th	Lynch	Cowie	Rennie	Laurie	Evans	Smith T	Latimer	Baxter	Coats	Phillips	Kirby
	24th	Lynch	Cowie	Rennie	Laurie	Watson	Smith T	Latimer	Guthrie	Coats	Baxter	Kirby

Another one for Archie - Dundee centre-forward Archie Coats races through to send the ball past the Clyde keeper at Dens. The prolific centre netted 132 goals in 202 games for the Dark Blues and missed only two games in his six year spell at Dundee.

They Wore The Dark Blue

Season 1937-38

Date			Opponents		Score	Crowd	Scorers
Aug	14th	L	Arbroath	a	3-0	9,500	Baxter 2 (1 pen); Regan
	21st	L	Clyde	h	4-1	15,000	Kirby; Baxter 2; Regan
	25th	L	Arbroath	h	1-0	11,000	Kirby
	28th	L	Morton	a	2-0	8,000	Regan; Baxter
Sep	4th	L	QOS	h	4-1	15,000	Kirby; Baxter 2; Coats
	11th	L	Aberdeen	a	3-2	24,000	Coats; Baxter 2
	14th	L	Clyde	a	2-3	9,000	Coats; McMenemy
	18th	L	Queens Park	h	2-0	14,000	McMenemy; Cross o.g.
	25th	L	Hamilton	a	0-4	6,000	-
	30th	L	QOS	a	2-2	6,000	Regan; Baxter
Oct	2nd	L	Kilmarnock	h	1-2	8,000	Baxter
	4th	L	Third Lanark	h	2-1	15,000	Regan; Coats
	9th	L	Rangers	a	0-6	25,000	-
	16th	L	Hearts	h	0-2	20,000	-
	23rd	L	Partick Thistle	h	5-3	11,000	Baxter 2 (1 pen); Smith; McMenemy; Laurie
	30th	L	St Johnstone	a	2-4	7,000	Baxter
Nov	6th	L	Motherwell	h	2-2	16,000	Coats; Smith
	13th	L	Falkirk	h	1-4	10,000	Boyd
	20th	L	Third Lanark	a	3-4	6,000	Boyd; Cowie (pen); Holland
	27th	L	Hibernian	h	1-2	8,000	McMenemy
Dec	25th	L	Morton	h	2-2	4,500	Coats 2
Jan	1st	L	Aberdeen	h	0-1	22,000	-
	3rd	L	Hearts	a	1-2		McMenemy
	8th	L	Queens Park	a	1-3	6,000	Kirby
	15th	L	Hamilton	h	3-0	6,500	Kirby; McMenemy; Coats
	22nd	SC1	Albion Rovers	a	2-4	6,000	Coats; Baxter
	29th	L	Kilmarnock	a	1-3		Boyd
Feb	5th	L	Rangers	h	6-1	15,000	Baxter 3 (1 pen); Coats 2; Boyd
	12th	FCSF	Arbroath	a	2-0	3,378	McMenemy; Coats
	19th	L	Partick Thistle	a	0-1	10,000	-
	26th	L	St Johnstone	h	6-1	11,000	Coats; McMenemy 2; Baxter 2; Laurie
Mar	5th	L	St Mirren	h	0-0	8,000	-
	12th	L	Motherwell	a	1-1		Baxter
	19th	L	St Mirren	a	1-2	4,000	McMenemy
Apr	2nd	L	Hibernian	h	1-2	5,000	Laurie
	11th	L	Ayr United*	h	5-1	8,000	Coats 2; Roberts; Baxter 2
	16th	L	Celtic	h	2-3	21,000	Roberts; Cowie (pen)
	23rd	L	Falkirk	a	0-5		-
	27th	FCF	Dundee United	h	3-0	3,000	Baxter; Regan; Miller
	30th	L	Ayr United	a	0-0	9,000	-

Archie Coats and Tom Smith - both played for the Scottish League against the Irish League.

The Record		
League	-	19th Place, Division One
Scottish Cup	-	First round
Forfarshire Cup	-	Winners
Top Scorer	-	Arthur Baxter (24 goals)
Av. Home Gate	-	12,800
Players used	-	19
Sent off	-	None

* Earlier game v. Ayr United at Dens abandoned after 70 mts. due to frost. Dundee led 3-1.
Cup Cash - v. Albion Rovers £204.

Appearances

	League	Scottish Cup	Total
Archie Coats	38 (13)	1 (1)	39 (14)
Arthur Baxter	36 (23)	1 (1)	37 (24)
Andy Cowie	36 (2)	1	37 (2)
Harry McMenemy	36 (9)	1	37 (9)
John Laurie	33	0	33
Jimmy Boyd	26 (4)	1	27 (4)
Tom Smith	27 (2)	0	27 (2)
Norman Kirby	23 (5)	1	24 (5)
Len Richards	23	1	24
Johnny Lynch	22	1	23
Bobby Rennie	19	1	20
John Evans	20	0	20
Jimmy Morgan	18	1	19
Bill Marsh	16	0	16
Bobby Regan	16 (5)	0	16 (5)
Sam Roberts	12 (2)	0	12 (2)
Harry Sneddon	11	1	12
Bobby Adamson	3	0	3
Gilbert Holland	3 (1)	0	3 (1)

Scottish League Division One

		Home			Away			Goals		
	P	W	D	L	W	D	L	F A	PTS
Celtic	38	16	3	0	11	4	4	114-42	61
Hearts	38	16	2	1	10	4	5	90-70	58
Rangers	38	11	5	3	7	8	4	75-49	49
Falkirk	38	9	4	6	10	5	4	82-52	47
Motherwell	38	12	5	2	5	5	9	78-69	44
Aberdeen	38	12	3	4	3	6	10	74-59	39
Partick Thistle	38	12	2	5	3	7	9	68-70	39
St Johnstone	38	11	4	4	5	3	11	78-81	39
Third Lanark	38	7	8	4	4	5	10	68-73	35
Hibernian	38	8	8	3	3	5	11	57-65	35
Arbroath	38	8	7	4	3	6	10	58-79	35
Queens Park	38	6	8	5	5	4	10	59-74	34
Hamilton	38	9	3	7	4	4	11	81-76	33
St Mirren	38	11	2	6	3	3	13	58-66	33
Clyde	38	6	9	4	4	4	11	68-78	33
Queen of the South	38	6	4	9	5	5	7	58-71	33
Ayr United	38	6	9	4	3	6	10	66-85	33
Kilmarnock	38	9	5	5	3	4	12	65-91	33
Dundee	**38**	**10**	**3**	**6**	**3**	**3**	**13**	**70-74**	**32**
Morton	38	5	1	13	1	2	16	64-126	15

They Wore The Dark Blue

Dundee F.C. Line-Ups 1937-38

		1	2	3	4	5	6	7	8	9	10	11
Aug	14th	Marsh	Cowie	Rennie	Adamson	Evans	Smith T	Regan	Baxter	Coats	McMenemy	Kirby
	21st	Marsh	Cowie	Rennie	Adamson	Evans	Smith T	Regan	Baxter	Coats	McMenemy	Kirby
	25th	Marsh	Cowie	Rennie	Adamson	Evans	Smith T	Regan	Baxter	Coats	McMenemy	Kirby
	28th	Marsh	Cowie	Rennie	Laurie	Evans	Smith T	Regan	Baxter	Coats	McMenemy	Kirby
Sep	4th	Marsh	Cowie	Rennie	Laurie	Evans	Smith T	Regan	Baxter	Coats	McMenemy	Kirby
	11th	Marsh	Cowie	Rennie	Laurie	Evans	Smith T	Regan	Baxter	Coats	McMenemy	Kirby
	14th	Marsh	Cowie	Rennie	Laurie	Evans	Smith T	Regan	Baxter	Coats	McMenemy	Kirby
	18th	Marsh	Cowie	Rennie	Laurie	Evans	Smith T	Regan	Baxter	Coats	McMenemy	Kirby
	25th	Marsh	Cowie	Rennie	Laurie	Evans	Smith T	Regan	Baxter	Coats	McMenemy	Kirby
	30th	Marsh	Cowie	Rennie	Laurie	Evans	Smith T	Boyd	Baxter	Coats	McMenemy	Regan
Oct	2nd	Marsh	Cowie	Richards	Laurie	Evans	Smith T	Boyd	Baxter	Coats	McMenemy	Regan
	4th	Lynch	Cowie	Rennie	Laurie	Evans	Smith T	Regan	Boyd	Coats	Baxter	Kirby
	9th	Marsh	Cowie	Rennie	Laurie	Evans	Smith T	Regan	Boyd	Coats	Baxter	Kirby
	16th	Lynch	Cowie	Rennie	Laurie	Evans	Smith T	Boyd	Baxter	Coats	McMenemy	Kirby
	23rd	Marsh	Cowie	Rennie	Laurie	Evans	Smith T	Regan	Baxter	Coats	McMenemy	Kirby
	30th	Marsh	Cowie	Rennie	Laurie	Evans	Smith T	Regan	Baxter	Coats	McMenemy	Kirby
Nov	6th	Marsh	Rennie	Richards	Laurie	Evans	Smith T	Coats	Baxter	Holland	McMenemy	Kirby
	13th	Marsh	Cowie	Richards	Laurie	Morgan	Smith T	Coats	Boyd	Holland	McMenemy	Kirby
	20th	Lynch	Cowie	Richards	Laurie	Morgan	Smith T	Coats	Boyd	Holland	McMenemy	Kirby
	27th	Lynch	Cowie	Richards	Laurie	Morgan	Smith T	Boyd	Baxter	Coats	McMenemy	Kirby
Dec	25th	Lynch	Cowie	Richards	Laurie	Morgan	Smith T	Boyd	Baxter	Coats	McMenemy	Kirby
Jan	1st	Lynch	Cowie	Richards	Laurie	Evans	Smith T	Boyd	Baxter	Coats	McMenemy	Kirby
	3rd	Lynch	Cowie	Richards	Laurie	Evans	Smith T	Boyd	Baxter	Coats	McMenemy	Kirby
	8th	Lynch	Cowie	Richards	Laurie	Evans	Smith T	Boyd	Baxter	Coats	McMenemy	Kirby
	15th	Lynch	Rennie	Richards	Cowie	Morgan	Sneddon	Boyd	Baxter	Coats	McMenemy	Kirby
	22nd	Lynch	Rennie	Richards	Cowie	Morgan	Sneddon	Boyd	Baxter	Coats	McMenemy	Kirby
	29th	Lynch	Cowie	Richards	Laurie	Morgan	Sneddon	Boyd	Baxter	Coats	McMenemy	Regan
Feb	5th	Lynch	Cowie	Richards	Laurie	Morgan	Sneddon	Boyd	Baxter	Coats	McMenemy	Roberts
	19th	Lynch	Cowie	Richards	Laurie	Morgan	Sneddon	Boyd	Baxter	Coats	McMenemy	Roberts
	26th	Lynch	Cowie	Richards	Laurie	Morgan	Sneddon	Boyd	Baxter	Coats	McMenemy	Roberts
Mar	5th	Lynch	Cowie	Richards	Laurie	Morgan	Sneddon	Boyd	Baxter	Coats	McMenemy	Roberts
	12th	Lynch	Cowie	Richards	Laurie	Morgan	Sneddon	Boyd	Baxter	Coats	McMenemy	Roberts
	19th	Lynch	Cowie	Richards	Laurie	Morgan	Sneddon	Boyd	Baxter	Coats	McMenemy	Roberts
Apr	2nd	Lynch	Cowie	Richards	Laurie	Morgan	Sneddon	Boyd	Baxter	Coats	McMenemy	Roberts
	11th	Lynch	Cowie	Richards	Laurie	Morgan	Sneddon	Boyd	Baxter	Coats	McMenemy	Roberts
	16th	Lynch	Cowie	Richards	Laurie	Morgan	Sneddon	Boyd	Baxter	Coats	McMenemy	Roberts
	18th	Lynch	Cowie	Richards	Laurie	Morgan	Smith T	Boyd	Baxter	Coats	McMenemy	Roberts
	23rd	Lynch	Cowie	Richards	Laurie	Morgan	Smith T	Boyd	Baxter	Coats	McMenemy	Roberts
	30th	Lynch	Rennie	Richards	Cowie	Morgan	Smith T	Boyd	Baxter	Coats	McMenemy	Roberts

Hot shot five - the Dens Park forwards who cracked in 17 goals as the Dark Blues opened the season with five successive wins. Left to right - Bobby Regan, Arthur Baxter, Archie Coats, Harry McMenemy and Norman Kirby. DC Thomson

Season 1938-39

Date			Opponents		Score	Crowd	Scorers
Aug	13th	L	Brechin City	h	5-0	7,000	Melville; Brown o.g.; Coats 2; Cowie (pen)
	20th	L	Morton	a	1-2	6,500	Miller
	27th	L	Stenhousemuir	h	3-1	6,000	Baxter 2; Coats
Sep	3rd	L	Dunfermline	a	1-4	3,000	Smith
	10th	L	Edinburgh City	h	2-2	3,000	Coats; Sneddon
	17th	L	Dundee United	a	0-3	12,000	-
	24th	L	Forfar Athletic	h	10-2	3,500	Sneddon; Coats 3; Stewart 3; Baxter 2; Gray
Oct	1st	L	Leith Athletic	a	1-3	2,000	McGillivray
	3rd	FC1	Montrose	h	4-4	2,000	McGillivray 3; Roberts
	8th	L	East Stirling	h	5-6	4,000	Stewart; McGillivray 3; Roberts
	15th	L	East Fife	h	1-1	10,000	McGillivray
	22nd	L	Cowdenbeath	a	1-3	5,000	Coats
	29th	L	Dumbarton	a	4-4	4,000	McGillivray; Stewart; McAllister o.g.; Laurie
Nov	5th	L	Airdrie	h	1-2	6,000	Stewart
	12th	L	Kings Park	a	1-3	3,000	McGillivray
	19th	L	Alloa	a	1-2	2,500	Bulloch o.g.
	26th	L	Montrose	h	5-0	3,000	McGillivray 3 (1 pen)
Dec	3rd	L	St Bernards	h	3-0	4,000	Kirby; McGillivray; Roberts
	10th	L	Forfar Athletic	a	1-2		Coats
	17th	L	Alloa	h	1-4	2,000	McGillivray (pen)
	24th	L	Stenhousemuir	a	1-1	1,500	McGillivray
	31st	L	Morton	h	2-1	4,000	Coats 2
Jan	3rd	L	Edinburgh City	a	4-1		Laurie 3; McGillivray
	14th	L	Airdrie	a	6-3		Coats 2; McGillivray 4 (1 pen)
	28th	L	Cowdenbeath	h	5-0	4,000	McGillivray 3 (1 pen); Wilson; Coats
Feb	4th	SC2	Clyde	h	0-0	15,286	-
	8th	SC2R	Clyde	a	0-1	15,000	-
	18th	L	Kings Park	h	3-0	2,000	Coats; Melville; Wilson
	25th	L	Leith Athletic	h	7-0	2,500	McGillivray; Ramsay 2; Coats 2; Wilson; Sneddon
Mar	4th	L	East Stirling	a	5-3	1,000	Coats 3; McGillivray 2
	11th	L	East Fife	a	2-0	2,500	Sneddon; Coats
	18th	L	Dundee United	h	2-0	12,500	McGillivray; Wilson
Apr	1st	L	Dunfermline	h	7-1	3,800	Melville; Coats 3; Stewart; McGillivray 2 (1 pen)
	8th	L	St Bernards	a	1-1	2,000	Stewart
	15th	L	Dumbarton	h	1-1	1,700	Wilson
	19th	FC1R	Montrose	a	2-3	1,500	Wilson; McGillivray
	29th	L	Montrose	a	5-5	1,500	Stewart; Melville 2; Coats; McGillivray

Cup Cash v. Clyde (h) £711-1-6d

Bill Masson - brought some stability to a leaky defence.

Appearances

	League	Scottish Cup	Total
Archie Coats	34 (26)	2	36 (26)
Johnny Lynch	33	2	35
Bobby Rennie	31	2	33
Harry Sneddon	29 (4)	2	31 (4)
George Stewart	28 (9)	2	30 (9)
Charlie McGillivray	26 (29)	2	28 (29)
Norman Kirby	19 (1)	2	21 (1)
Sam Roberts	21 (2)	1	22 (2)
Willie Cook	18 (1)	2	20 (1)
John Laurie	18 (4)	2	20 (4)
Andy Cowie	17 (1)	0	17 (1)
Johnston Melville	17 (5)	0	17 (5)
Tom Smith	17 (1)	0	17 (1)
Bill Masson	13	2	15
Arthur Baxter	14 (4)	0	14 (4)
Bobby Wilson	11 (5)	1	12 (5)
Jimmy Morgan	9	0	9
John Borthwick	6	0	6
Norman Miller	4 (1)	0	4 (1)
Bob Ramsay	2 (2)	0	2 (2)
Frank Sweeney	2	0	2
Micky Clark	1	0	1
Jim Dougal	1	0	1
Frank Galloway	1	0	1
Charlie Gray	1 (1)	0	1
Ronnie McWalter	1	0	1

Scottish League Division Two

		Home			Away			Goals		
	P	W	D	L	W	D	L	F A		PTS
Cowdenbeath	34	14	3	0	14	1	2	120-45		60
Alloa	34	13	2	2	9	2	6	91-46		48
East Fife	34	12	0	5	9	6	2	119-61		48
Airdrie	34	13	0	4	8	5	4	85-57		47
Dunfermline	34	12	3	2	6	2	9	99-78		41
Dundee	**34**	**11**	**3**	**3**	**4**	**4**	**9**	**99-63**		**37**
St Bernards	34	12	1	4	3	5	9	79-79		36
Stenhousemuir	34	11	3	3	4	2	11	74-69		35
Dundee United	34	12	0	5	3	3	11	78-69		33
Brechin City	34	8	6	3	3	3	11	82-106		31
Dumbarton	34	6	6	5	3	6	8	68-76		30
Morton	34	10	4	3	1	2	14	74-88		28
Kings Park	34	8	2	7	4	0	13	87-92		26
Montrose	34	7	3	7	3	2	12	82-96		25
Forfar	34	9	3	5	2	0	15	74-138		25
Leith Athletic	34	7	3	7	3	1	13	57-83		24
East Stirling	34	5	3	9	4	1	12	89-130		22
Edinburgh City	34	4	1	12	2	3	12	58-119		16

The Record		
League	-	Sixth Place, Division Two
Scottish Cup	-	Second round
Forfarshire Cup	-	First round
Top Scorer	-	Charlie McGillivray (29 goals)
Av. Home Gate	-	4,600
Players used	-	26
Sent off	-	None

Dundee F.C. Line-Ups 1938-39

		1	2	3	4	5	6	7	8	9	10	11
Aug	13th	Lynch	Cowie	Rennie	Laurie	Morgan	Sneddon	Melville	Baxter	Coats	Smith T	Roberts
	20th	Lynch	Cowie	Rennie	Smith T	Morgan	Sneddon	Melville	Miller	Coats	Baxter	Roberts
	27th	Lynch	Cowie	Rennie	Laurie	Morgan	Sneddon	Melville	Baxter	Coats	Smith T	Roberts
Sep	3rd	Lynch	Cowie	Rennie	Laurie	Morgan	Sneddon	Melville	Baxter	Coats	Smith T	Roberts
	10th	Lynch	Cowie	Rennie	Laurie	Morgan	Smith T	Melville	Baxter	Coats	Wilson	Snedddon
	17th	Lynch	Cowie	Rennie	Laurie	Smith T	Sneddon	Coats	Stewart	Miller	Baxter	Roberts
	24th	Lynch	Rennie	Borthwick	Cowie	Smith T	Sneddon	Gray	Stewart	Coats	Baxter	Roberts
Oct	1st	Lynch	Rennie	Borthwick	Cowie	Smith T	Sneddon	McGillivray	Stewart	Coats	Baxter	Roberts
	8th	Galloway	Rennie	Borthwick	Cowie	Sneddon	Smith T	Melville	Coats	McGillivray	Stewart	Roberts
	15th	Lynch	Cowie	Borthwick	Laurie	Sneddon	Stewart	Melville	Coats	McGillivray	Baxter	Roberts
	22nd	Lynch	Cowie	Rennie	Laurie	Sneddon	Stewart	Melville	Coats	McGillivray	Baxter	Roberts
	29th	Lynch	Cowie	Rennie	Laurie	Sneddon	Smith T	Cook	Coats	McGillivray	Stewart	Roberts
Nov	5th	Lynch	Cowie	Rennie	Laurie	Junior	Sneddon	Cook	Stewart	Coats	Baxter	Roberts
	12th	Lynch	Cowie	Rennie	Laurie	Sweeney	Smith T	Cook	Coats	McGillivray	Baxter	Roberts
	19th	Lynch	Rennie	Kirby	Laurie	Cowie	Smith T	Cook	Coats	McGillivray	Stewart	Roberts
	26th	Lynch	Rennie	Kirby	Stewart	Cowie	Smith T	Cook	Coats	Miller	McGillivray	Roberts
Dec	3rd	Lynch	Rennie	Kirby	Stewart	Cowie	Smith T	Melville	Baxter	Coats	McGillivray	Roberts
	10th	Lynch	Rennie	Kirby	Stewart	Masson	Sneddon	Melville	Baxter	Coats	McGillivray	Roberts
	17th	Lynch	Kirby	Borthwick	Laurie	Masson	Smith T	Miller	Stewart	Coats	McGillivray	Roberts
	24th	Lynch	Clark	Rennie	Stewart	Masson	Sneddon	Cook	McGillivray	Coats	Smith T	Kirby
	31st	Lynch	Rennie	Kirby	Stewart	Masson	Sneddon	Laurie	Smith T	Coats	McGillivray	Cook
Jan	3rd	Lynch	Rennie	Kirby	Stewart	Masson	Sneddon	Laurie	Wilson	Coats	McGillivray	Cook
	14th	Lynch	Rennie	Kirby	Stewart	Masson	Sneddon	Laurie	Wilson	Coats	McGillivray	Cook
	28th	Lynch	Rennie	Kirby	Stewart	Masson	Sneddon	Laurie	Wilson	Coats	McGillivray	Cook
Feb	4th	Lynch	Rennie	Kirby	Stewart	Masson	Sneddon	Laurie	Wilson	Coats	McGillivray	Cook
	8th	Lynch	Rennie	Kirby	Stewart	Masson	Sneddon	Laurie	Roberts	Coats	McGillivray	Cook
	11th	Lynch	Rennie	Borthwick	Stewart	Masson	Sneddon	Roberts	Laurie	Coats	McGillivray	Cook
	18th	Lynch	McWalter^	Kirby	Stewart	Masson	Sneddon	Melville	McGillivray	Coats	Wilson	Cook
	25th	Lynch	Rennie	Kirby	Stewart	Masson	Sneddon	Ramsay^	Wilson	Coats	McGillivray	Cook
Mar	4th	Lynch	Rennie	Kirby	Stewart	Masson	Sneddon	Melville	Wilson	Coats	McGillivray	Cook
	11th	Lynch	Rennie	Kirby	Stewart	Masson	Sneddon	Melville	Wilson	Coats	McGillivray	Cook
	18th	Lynch	Rennie	Kirby	Stewart	Masson	Sneddon	Melville	Wilson	Coats	McGillivray	Cook
Apr	1st	Lynch	Rennie	Kirby	Dougal^	Morgan	Sneddon	Melville	Stewart	Coats	McGillivray	Cook
	8th	Lynch	Rennie	Kirby	Laurie	Morgan	Sneddon	Ramsay^	Stewart	Coats	McGillivray	Cook
	15th	Lynch	Rennie	Kirby	Stewart	Morgan	Sneddon	Melville	Wilson	Coats	McGillivray	Roberts
	29th	Lynch	Rennie	Kirby	Stewart	Morgan	Sneddon	Melville	Wilson	Coats	McGillivray	Roberts

^ indicates trialist.

Too late - Dundee United goalkeeper Smith dives in vain as Bobby Wilson nets Dundee's second in a 2-0 win at Dens. That brought revenge for the earlier defeat at Tannadice but was small consolation when the Dark Blues failed to get promotion. DC Thomson

95

Season 1939-40

Scottish League Division Two

Date			Opponents		Score	Crowd	Scorers
Aug	12th	L	Raith Rovers	h	5-1	11,000	McGillivray 3; Coats; Adam
	19th	L	Airdrie	a	4-2	2,000	Adam; Warnock; Coats 2
	26th	L	Dumbarton	h	3-1	12,000	Warnock; Coats; Adam
	30th	FC1	Dundee United	h	6-1	8,300	McGillivray 3 (1 pen); Coats 2; Robertson o.g.
Sep	2nd	L	Morton	a	1-1		McGillivray

On September 3rd the outbreak of World War 2 saw League football suspended, but, in October, new Eastern and Western Divisions were formed.

Scottish League Eastern Division

Date			Opponents		Score	Crowd	Scorers
Oct	7th	FCS	Forfar Athletic	a	5-2	1,200	Adam; Allan; Coats; Cook 2
	21st	L	Hibernian	h	2-1	4,500	Adam 2
	28th	L	Dunfermline	a	0-2	3,000	-
Nov	4th	L	Alloa	h	1-1	1,000	Wattie
	11th	L	Raith Rovers	a	1-2		Adam
	18th	L	Arbroath	h	9-3	3,000	Adam 3; Coats 2; Wattie 2; Easson; Cook
	25th	L	Falkirk	a	1-6	2,500	Cook
Dec	2nd	L	St Johnstone	a	2-2	2,500	Adam; Coats
	9th	L	Hearts	h	4-6	3,670	Adam (pen); Follon; Easson; Coats
	16th	L	Kings Park	h	5-0	1,700	Cook; McGillivray 2; Coats 2
	23rd	L	Stenhousemuir	a	3-0	900	McGillivray; Easson; Coats
	30th	L	Aberdeen	h	3-1	4,297	Coats 2; Adam
Jan	1st	L	Dundee United	a	1-2	5,500	McGillivray (pen)
	2nd	L	St Bernards	h	2-2	1,276	McGillivray 2 (1 pen)
	6th	L	Cowdenbeath	a	1-1		Coats
	13th	L	East Fife	h	2-0	2,500	Coats; Morgan
Feb	10th	L	Raith Rovers	h	2-3	2,500	Easson; Cook
	17th	L	Arbroath	a	1-3		McGillivray
	24th	WC1	Third Lanark	h	1-1	7,000	McGillivray (pen)
Mar	2nd	WC1R	Third Lanark	a	1-3	8,600	Adam
	9th	L	Alloa	a	2-2		Coats 2
	16th	L	Kings Park	h	3-3	1,000	Hill; Adam; McGillivray
	30th	L	Aberdeen	a	0-3	4,000	-
Apr	3rd	L	Hibernian	a	0-6		-
	6th	L	Dundee United	h	2-1	8,000	Coats; Adam
	8th	L	Dunfermline	h	2-2	2,500	Coats; McGillivray
	13th	L	St Bernards	a	0-0		-
	17th	L	Stenhousemuir	h	7-1	600	Coats 4; Cook; McGillivray; Davidson
	29th	L	East Fife	a	0-3		-
May	4th	L	St Johnstone	h	7-2	1,500	Coats 4; Adam 2; Davidson
	8th	FCF	Arbroath	h	1-1	2,000	McGillivray
	11th	L	Hearts	a	3-2	1,500	Adam; Davidson; Coats
	15th	FCFR	Arbroath	a	0-2	1,500	-
	18th	L	Falkirk	h	4-2	3,000	Adam; Coats 2; McGillivray

Appearances

	Div. 2		East Div.		War Cup		Total	
Archie Coats	4	(4)	28	(26)	2		34	(30)
Willie Cook	4		26	(5)	2		32	(5)
Johnny Lynch	4		24		2		30	
Charlie McGillivray	4	(4)	24	(11)	2	(1)	30	(16)
Hugh Adam	3	(3)	24	(15)	2	(1)	29	(19)
Jimmy Morgan	4		23	(1)	2		29	(1)
Bobby Rennie	2		22		2		26	
Norman Kirby	4		19		2		25	
Harry Sneddon	4		16		2		22	
George Stewart	4		15		2		21	
Bob Allan	2		14		0		16	
Bill Masson	0		16		0		16	
Jimmy Easson	0		15	(4)	0		15	(4)
Gerry Follon	0		9	(1)	1		10	(1)
George Hill	0		9	(1)	1		10	(1)
Bobby Ross	0		8		0		8	
Bill Peattie	0		6		0		6	
John Wattie	1		6	(3)	0		7	(3)
Jim Mathieson	0		4		0		4	
Dave Warnock	4	(2)	0		0		4	(2)
Doug Davidson	3	(3)	0		0		3	(3)
Andy Kemp	0		2		0		2	
Bert Lamb	0		1		0		1	
Ronnie McWalter	0		1		0		1	
Andrew Morgan	0		1		0		1	
Henry Morris	0		1		0		1	
John Ross	0		1		0		1	

Bobby Rennie - hard-tackling right-back, aptly nicknamed "Tiger".

Scottish League Division Two

	P	W	D	L	F A	PTS
Dundee	4	3	1	0	13-3	7
Dunfermline	4	2	2	0	10-5	6
Kings Park	4	2	2	0	11-7	6
East Fife	4	2	1	1	12-6	5
Queens Park	4	1	3	0	7-5	5
Stenhousemuir	4	2	1	1	6-5	5
Dundee United	4	2	1	1	8-7	5
Dumbarton	4	2	1	1	9-9	5
East Stirling	4	1	2	1	7-7	4
St Bernards	4	1	2	1	7-7	4
Airdrie	4	2	0	2	7-8	4
Edinburgh City	4	1	1	2	9-8	3
Montrose	4	1	1	2	7-8	3
Raith Rovers	4	1	1	2	8-12	3
Morton	4	1	1	2	4-7	3
Leith Athletic	4	1	0	3	4-7	2
Brechin City	4	0	2	2	3-8	2
Forfar Athletic	4	0	0	4	7-18	0

The Record

Scottish League Div. 2	-	First Place at Closedown
Eastern Division	-	Sixth Place
Scottish War Cup	-	First round
Forfarshire Cup	-	Runners-up
Top Scorer	-	Archie Coats (34 goals)
Av. Home Gate	-	11,500 D2; 2,860 ED
Players used	-	26
Sent off	-	None

Eastern Division

		Home			Away			Goals		
	P	W	D	L	W	D	L	F	A	PTS
Falkirk	29	12	2	1	8	3	3	106-47		45
Hearts	29	11	1	2	7	3	5	104-66		40
Dunfermline	29	12	0	3	7	2	5	80-55		40
Aberdeen	29	12	3	0	4	1	9	86-50		36
St Johnstone	29	10	3	2	3	5	6	84-69		34
Dundee	29	9	3	2	2	5	8	70-62		30
Alloa	29	7	2	6	6	2	6	56-60		30
Hibernian	29	7	1	6	5	4	6	82-65		29
Dundee United	29	9	2	3	3	0	12	68-77		26
East Fife	29	7	1	7	4	2	8	80-91		25
Raith Rovers	29	6	2	6	4	1	10	69-85		23
Kings Park	29	5	4	5	4	0	11	62-88		22
St Bernards	29	7	2	5	1	3	11	44-77		21
Stenhousemuir	29	6	2	7	1	1	12	52-98		17
Arbroath	29	5	4	6	1	1	12	44-91		17
Cowdenbeath*	29	4	1	2	3	0	5	38-44		15

* Resigned after playing half their games. In May 1940, Dundee decided to close down for the duration of the War and did not restart until 1944.

Dundee F.C. Line-Ups 1939-40

	1	2	3	4	5	6	7	8	9	10	11
Aug 12th	Lynch	Allan	Kirby	Stewart	Morgan J	Sneddon	Warnock	Adam	Coats	McGillivray	Cook
19th	Lynch	Allan	Kirby	Stewart	Morgan J	Sneddon	Warnock	Adam	Coats	McGillivray	Cook
26th	Lynch	Rennie	Kirby	Stewart	Morgan J	Sneddon	Warnock	Adam	Coats	McGillivray	Cook
Sep 2nd	Lynch	Rennie	Kirby	Stewart	Morgan J	Sneddon	Warnock	Wattie	Coats	McGillivray	Cook
Oct 21st	Lynch	Rennie	Kirby	Stewart	Masson	Sneddon	Adam	Easson	Coats	McGillivray	Cook
28th	Lynch	Rennie	Kirby	Allan	Masson	Sneddon	Adam	Easson	Coats	McGillivray	Cook
Nov 4th	Lynch	Rennie	Kirby	Allan	Morgan J	Masson	Cook	Adam	Coats	Easson	Wattie
11th	Lynch	Allan	Rennie	Easson	Morgan J	Sneddon	Cook	Adam	Coats	McGillivray	Wattie
18th	Lamb	Allan	Rennie	Stewart	Morgan J	Masson	Cook	Adam	Coats	Easson	Wattie
25th	Lynch	Allan	Rennie	Follon	Morgan J	Masson	Cook	McGillivray	Coats	Easson	Wattie
Dec 2nd	Lynch	Allan	Rennie	Stewart	Morgan J	Masson	Coats	Follon	McGillivray	Adam	Cook
9th	Lynch	Allan	Rennie	Stewart	Masson	Sneddon	Follon	Adam	Coats	Easson	Cook
16th	Lynch	Rennie	Kirby	Stewart	Masson	Sneddon	Adam	Easson	Coats	McGillivray	Cook
23rd	Lynch	Rennie	Kirby	Morgan	Masson	Sneddon	Easson	Adam	Coats	McGillivray	Cook
30th	Lynch	Allan	Rennie	Stewart	Morgan J	Sneddon	Easson	Adam	Coats	McGillivray	Cook
Jan 1st	Lynch	Allan	Rennie	Morgan	Masson	Sneddon	Follon	Adam	Coats	McGillivray	Wattie
2nd	Lynch	Allan	Rennie	Morgan	Masson	Sneddon	Easson	Adam	Coats	McGillivray	Wattie
6th	Lynch	Allan	Rennie	Morgan	Masson	Sneddon	Easson	Adam	Coats	McGillivray	Kirby
13th	Lynch	Allan	Rennie	Morgan	Masson	Sneddon	Easson	Adam	Coats	McGillivray	Cook
Feb 10th	Lynch	Allan	Rennie	Morgan	Masson	Sneddon	Easson	Ross J	Coats	McGillivray	Cook
17th	Lynch	Rennie	Kirby	Morgan	Masson	Sneddon	Adam	Stewart	Coats	McGillivray	Cook
24th	Lynch	Rennie	Kirby	Stewart	Morgan J	Sneddon	Hill	Adam	Coats	McGillivray	Cook
Mar 2nd	Lynch	Rennie	Kirby	Stewart	Morgan J	Sneddon	Follon	Adam	Coats	McGillivray	Cook
9th	Lynch	Rennie	Kirby	Stewart	Kemp	Sneddon	Follon	Adam	Coats	McGillivray	Cook
16th	Lynch	Rennie	Kirby	Stewart	Kemp	Follon	Hill	Adam	Coats	McGillivray	Cook
30th	Lynch	Allan	Kirby	Stewart	Morgan J	McGillivray	Hill	Adam	Coats	Easson	Cook
Apr 3rd	Lynch	Rennie	Kirby	Stewart	Morgan J	Ross B	Hill	Follon	Morris	McGillivray	Cook
6th	Lynch	McWalter	Kirby	Stewart	Morgan J	Ross B	Hill	Adam	Coats	McGillivray	Cook
8th	Lynch	Peattie	Kirby	Stewart	Morgan J	Ross B	Hill	Adam	Coats	McGillivray	Cook
13th	Lynch	Peattie	Kirby	Follon	Morgan J	Ross B	Hill	Adam	Coats	McGillivray	Cook
17th	Lynch	Peattie	Kirby	Stewart	Morgan J	Ross B	Hill	Davidson	Coats	McGillivray	Cook
29th	Newman	Peattie	Kirby	Stewart	Morgan J	Ross B	Hill	Morgan A	Coats	McGillivray	Cook
May 4th	Mathieson	Peattie	Kirby	Ross B	Morgan J	Sneddon	Hill	Adam	Coats	Davidson	Cook
11th	Mathieson	Peattie	Rennie	Follon	Morgan J	Sneddon	Kirby	Adam	Coats	Davidson	Cook
18th	Mathieson	Peattie	Rennie	Ross B	Morgan J	Masson	Kirby	Adam	Coats	McGillivray	Cook

Dundee's promotion hopefuls in July 1939. However, due to the Second World War it was another eight years before the Dens Parkers returned to the First Division. (BACK, left to right) George Stewart, Jimmy Morgan, Archie Coats, Bill Masson and Willie Arbuckle (trainer). FRONT - Johnny Lynch, Norman Kirby, Harry Sneddon and Charlie McGillivray. DC Thomson

Season 1944-45

Date			Opponents		Score	Crowd	Scorers
Aug	5th	L	Raith Rovers	a	4-2	5,000	Turnbull 2; Roberts; Newman
	19th	L	Aberdeen	h	2-1	13,000	Turnbull; Cox
	26th	L	Dundee United	a	2-1	15,500	Turnbull 2
Sep	2nd	L	Rangers	h	5-3	16,132	Anderson 3; Gray (pen); Roberts
	9th	L	Hearts	a	3-1	1,700	Anderson 2; Hill
	16th	L	Arbroath	a	4-1	5,500	Turnbull 3; Auld
	23rd	L	Falkirk	h	1-2	11,000	Turnbull
	30th	L	Hearts	h	6-0	11,000	Turnbull 3; Auld; McCall 2
Oct	2nd	FCS1	Dundee United	h	2-1	10,000	McCall; Turnbull (pen)
	7th	L	East Fife	a	0-1	6,000	-
	14th	L	Arbroath	h	6-2	6,100	Auld 2; Anderson 4 (1 pen)
	21st	L	Raith Rovers	h	4-6	10,042	Hill; Gray; Turnbull; Collins
	28th	L	Aberdeen	a	3-2	15,000	Anderson 3
Nov	4th	L	Dundee United	h	2-2	10,800	Ruse; Anderson
	11th	L	Dunfermline	a	4-3	5,000	McCall; Anderson; Blyth o.g.; McKenzie
	18th	L	Falkirk	a	2-1		Anderson; Turnbull
	25th	L	East Fife	h	1-1	10,300	Turnbull
Dec	2nd	L	Rangers	a	1-0		Anderson
	9th	L	Dunfermline	h	3-1	13,500	Anderson 2; Hill
	16th	NES	Raith Rovers	h	2-1	4,127	Moir; Anderson
	23rd	NES	Raith Rovers	a	2-0 (4-1)	5,000	Turnbull; Hill
	30th	NEF	Aberdeen	h	0-5	19,098	-
Jan	1st	L	Aberdeen	a	0-5	16,000	-
	2nd	L	Dundee United	h	4-1	10,000	Auld; Turnbull 2; Anderson
	6th	L	Falkirk	h	5-1	9,000	Turnbull 4; Ancell
	13th	L	Hearts	a	3-5	3,000	Ewen; Turnbull 2
Feb	10th	L	East Fife	a	4-1		Hill; Turnbull 2; Ewen
	17th	L	Rangers	a	5-2	9,000	Turnbull 2; McCall; Woodburn o.g.; Ewen
	24th	L	Hearts	h	5-1	8,000	Dunn o.g.; McCall; Turnbull 2; Hill
Mar	3rd	L	Dundee United	a	4-0	11,000	Ruse; Turnbull; Hill; Gray
	10th	L	Rangers	h	2-3	14,205	Ewen; Ancell
	17th	L	Falkirk	a	2-1		Ventre; Ruse
	24th	L	Raith Rovers	a	1-2		Ewen
	31st	L	Arbroath	h	3-2	8,300	Turnbull 2; Auld
Apr	7th	L	Aberdeen	h	1-4	13,200	Ewen
	14th	L	Dunfermline	a	0-2	1,200	-
	21st	L	East Fife	h	3-2	9,000	Turnbull 2; Smith
	28th	L	Arbroath	a	1-2	2,500	Turnbull
May	5th	L	Raith Rovers	h	4-0	8,000	Smith; Turnbull 3
	9th	FCS2	Dundee United	a	2-1 (4-2)	10,000	Anderson(pen); Turnbull
	12th	L	Dunfermline	h	1-2	7,370	Anderson
	30th	FCF	Arbroath	h	6-0	6,500	Ruse; Baxter; Ewen; Smith; Mills; Hill

Ronnie Turnbull - the Dens Park centre-forward hit 39 goals.

The Record

League (1st Series)	-	NE Division Champions
League (2nd Series)	-	Fourth Place, NE Division
NE Supp. Cup	-	Runners-up
Forfarshire Cup	-	Winners
Top Scorer	-	Ronnie Turnbull (39 goals)
Av. Home Gate	-	12,300
Players used	-	28 plus trialists
Sent off	-	None

NE = North East Supplementary Cup for top 4 teams; BP = Bonus Points for goals

Appearances

	1st Series	2nd Series	NESC	Total
Gibby McKenzie	18 (1)	18	3	39 (1)
Sammy Cox	16 (1)	16	2	34 (1)
Ronnie Turnbull	14 (15)	18 (23)	2 (1)	34 (39)
Reuben Bennett	18	12	3	33
George Hill	17 (3)	13 (3)	3 (1)	33 (7)
Tommy Gray	18 (2)	12 (1)	3	32 (3)
Ernie Ewen	8	13 (6)	3	24 (6)
Willie Anderson	16 (18)	5 (2)	2 (1)	23 (21)
Willie Westwater	7	13	3	22
Reggie Smith	5	13 (2)	3	21 (2)
Andy McCall	9 (3)	10 (2)	1	20 (5)
Bobby Ancell	16	3 (2)	0	19 (2)
Bobby Auld	9 (4)	4 (2)	0	13 (6)
Vic Ruse	5 (1)	7 (2)	0	12 (3)
Trialists (various)	5 (1)	5	2	12 (1)
Charlie Thomson	0	9	1	10
Bobby Rennie	7	2	0	9
Jimmy Andrews	0	5	0	5
Sam Roberts	4 (2)	0	0	4 (2)
Roy Henderson	0	4	0	3
Billy Moir	1	1	1	3
John Ventre	0	3 (1)	0	3 (1)
John Laurie	1	1	0	2
John Niven	0	2	0	2
Alex. Smith	1	1	0	2
John Barron	1	0	0	1
Alec Collins	1 (1)	0	0	1 (1)
Jimmy Morgan	1	0	0	1
Doug Berrie	0	1	0	1

Scottish League North East Division

First Series (August to December)

		Home			Away			Goals		
	P	W	D	L	W	D	L	F	A	PTS
Dundee	**18**	**5**	**2**	**2**	**8**	**0**	**1**	**53-30**		**28**
Aberdeen	18	8	0	1	5	1	3	65-21		27
Raith Rovers	18	6	1	2	4	1	4	42-32		22
Dunfermline	18	4	4	1	4	1	4	49-36		21
Rangers	18	5	1	3	2	1	6	32-32		16
East Fife	18	4	2	3	2	2	5	31-44		16
Arbroath	18	4	2	3	2	2	5	30-43		16
Dundee United	18	4	0	5	1	3	5	34-49		13
Hearts	18	3	1	5	2	1	6	31-49		12
Falkirk	18	1	1	7	2	2	5	16-47		9

Scottish League North East Division

Second Series (January to May)

		Home			Away			Goals			
	P	W	D	L	W	D	L	F	A	BP	PTS
Aberdeen	18	6	2	1	5	1	2	63-19		6	31
East Fife	18	6	2	1	4	1	4	39-29		4	28
Rangers	18	7	0	2	3	3	3	41-25		4	27
Dundee	**18**	**6**	**0**	**3**	**4**	**0**	**5**	**49-36**		**4**	**24**
Dunfermline	18	5	3	1	4	0	5	38-35		3	24
Dundee United	18	4	2	3	3	0	6	31-54		3	19
Arbroath	18	4	1	4	1	3	5	31-43		4	18
Raith Rovers	18	5	0	4	2	1	6	39-37		3	18
Hearts	18	5	2	2	0	2	7	48-19		4	18
Falkirk	18	3	0	6	1	1	7	32-57		2	11

Dundee F.C. Line-Ups 1944-45

		1	2	3	4	5	6	7	8	9	10	11
Aug	12th	Bennett	Ancell	McCall	Anderson	Gray	McKenzie	Newman	Ewen	Turnbull	Auld	Roberts
	19th	Bennett	Ancell	Rennie	McKenzie	Gray	Cox	Anderson	Ewen	Turnbull	Auld	Hill
	26th	Bennett	Ancell	Rennie	McKenzie	Gray	Cox	Anderson	Ewen	Turnbull	Auld	Hill
Sep	2nd	Bennett	Cox	Ancell	McKenzie	Gray	Newman	Hill	Ewen	Anderson	McCall	Roberts
	9th	Bennett	Cox	Ancell	McKenzie	Gray	Morgan	Hill	Ewen	Anderson	McCall	Roberts
	16th	Bennett	Cox	Ancell	Anderson	Gray	McKenzie	Hill	Ewen	Turnbull	McCall	Auld
	23rd	Bennett	Rennie	Ancell	McKenzie	Gray	Newman	Hill	McCall	Turnbull	Auld	Roberts
	30th	Bennett	Rennie	Ancell	McKenzie	Gray	Cox	Hill	Ruse	Turnbull	McCall	Auld
Oct	7th	Bennett	Rennie	Ancell	McKenzie	Gray	Cox	Anderson	Ruse	Turnbull	McCall	Hill
	14th	Bennett	Cox	Rennie	Laurie	Gray	McKenzie	Anderson	Ruse	Turnbull	Auld	Hill
	21st	Bennett	Cox	Rennie	McKenzie	Gray	Barron	Collins	Turnbull	Anderson	Auld	Hill
	28th	Bennett	Ancell	Westwater	McKenzie	Gray	Cox	Anderson	Ruse	Turnbull	Newman	Hill
Nov	4th	Bennett	Westwater	Ancell	McKenzie	Gray	Cox	Hill	Ruse	Anderson	Smith R	Smith A
	11th	Bennett	Ancell	Westwater	McKenzie	Gray	Cox	Turnbull	McCall	Anderson	Smith R	Hill
	18th	Bennett	Ancell	Westwater	McKenzie	Gray	Cox	Turnbull	Ewen	Anderson	Smith R	Hill
	25th	Bennett	Cox	Westwater	Anderson	Gray	McKenzie	Ancell	McCall	Turnbull	Auld	Hill
Dec	2nd	Bennett	Ancell	Westwater	McKenzie	Gray	Cox	Turnbull	Newman	Anderson	Smith R	Hill
	9th	Bennett	Ancell	Westwater	McKenzie	Gray	Cox	Moir	Ewen	Anderson	Smith R	Hill
	16th	Bennett	Newman	Westwater	McKenzie	Gray	McCall	Moir	Ewen	Anderson	Smith R	Hill
	23rd	Bennett	Newman	Westwater	McKenzie	Gray	Cox	Moir	Ewen	Turnbull	Smith R	Hill
	30th	Bennett	Thomson	Westwater	McKenzie	Gray	Cox	Anderson	Ewen	Turnbull	Smith R	Hill
Jan	1st	Henderson	Thomson	Westwater	McKenzie	Gray	Cox	Moir	Ewen	Turnbull	Smith R	Auld
	2nd	Henderson	Thomson	Westwater	McKenzie	Gray	Smith R	Anderson	Ewen	Turnbull	McCall	Auld
	6th	Henderson	Thomson	Westwater	McKenzie	Gray	Smith R	Ancell	Ewen	Turnbull	McCall	Auld
	13th	Henderson	Westwater	Laurie	McKenzie	Gray	Cox	Ruse	Ewen	Turnbull	McCall	Auld
Feb	10th	Bennett	Cox	Westwater	McKenzie	Newman	Smith R	Moir	Ewen	Turnbull	McCall	Hill
	17th	Bennett	Thomson	Westwater	McKenzie	Cox	Smith R	Ruse	Ewen	Turnbull	McCall	Hill
	24th	Bennett	Thomson	Westwater	McKenzie	Cox	Smith R	Gray	Ewen	Turnbull	McCall	Hill
Mar	3rd	Bennett	Ancell	Westwater	McKenzie	Cox	Smith R	Gray	Ruse	Turnbull	McCall	Hill
	10th	Bennett	Ancell	Westwater	McKenzie	Cox	Smith R	Gray	Ewen	Turnbull	McCall	Hill
	17th	Bennett	Rennie	Westwater	McKenzie	Gray	Cox	Ruse	Ventre	Turnbull	Smith R	Hill
	24th	Bennett	Cox	Thomson	McKenzie	Gray	Smith R	Newman	Ewen	Turnbull	Ventre	Hill
	31st	Bennett	Rennie	Cox	McKenzie	Gray	McCall	Hill	Ruse	Turnbull	Ventre	Auld
Apr	7th	Bennett	Westwater	Thomson	McKenzie	Cox	Smith R	Ruse	Ewen	Turnbull	McCall	Hill
	14th	Bennett	Cox	Westwater	Anderson	Gray	McKenzie	Hill	Ewen	Turnbull	Ruse	Andrews
	21st	Bennett	Berrie	Westwater	McKenzie	Gray	Smith R	Hill	Anderson	Turnbull	Cox	Andrews
	28th	Bennett	Cox	McCall	McKenzie	Gray	Smith A	Anderson	Newman	Turnbull	Newman	Andrews
May	5th	Niven	Thomson	Cox	McKenzie	Gray	Smith R	Newman	Ewen	Turnbull	Beaton	Andrews
	12th	Niven	Thomson	Cox	Anderson	Gray	McKenzie	Hill	Ewen	Turnbull	Beaton	Andrews

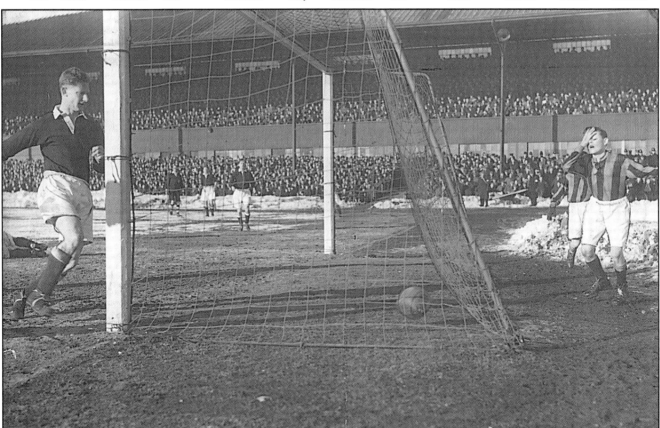

Too late Bobby - left-back Bobby Ancell can only watch as the ball bounces into the back of the Dundee net at snow-covered Dens. There is no disguising the ballboy's feelings in this picture from 1950.

DC Thomson

Season 1945-46

Date		Opponents		Score	Crowd	Scorers
Aug 11th	L	East Fife	h	2-1	8,934	Juliussen; Ewen
18th	L	Arbroath	a	4-1	4,000	Hill; Ewen; Juliussen 2
25th	L	Dumbarton	h	5-2	8,500	Ouchterlonie; Moir; Anderson 3
Sep 1st	L	Airdrie	a	3-3		Laurie; Anderson (pen); McKenzie
8th	L	Dundee United	h	1-0	12,341	Ouchterlonie
15th	L	Alloa	a	1-0		Anderson
22nd	L	Stenhousemuir	a	5-1		Hill 2; Anderson; Ouchterlonie; Rattray
29th	L	Raith Rovers	a	5-0	7,000	Juliussen; Ouchterlonie; Anderson; Hill 2
Oct 6th	L	Ayr United	h	1-4	12,333	Juliussen
13th	L	St Johnstone	h	5-1	12,679	Anderson 2; Juliussen 2; Hill
20th	L	Albion Rovers	a	2-0		Hill; Anderson
27th	L	Dunfermline	a	6-0		Ouchterlonie; Hill; Juliussen 3; Ancell
Nov 3rd	L	Cowdenbeath	h	5-0	6,214	Anderson; Smith; Juliusen 3
10th	L	Arbroath	h	8-0	9,500	Juliussen 5; Anderson; Follon; Smith
17th	L	East Fife	a	4-1	5,000	Follon; Anderson; Juliussen 2
24th	L	Dumbarton	a	1-0		Gallacher
Dec 1st	L	Airdrie	h	4-1	13,349	Hill 2; Juliussen; Ouchterlonie
8th	L	Stenhousemuir	h	6-1	5,243	Juliussen 4; Hill 2
15th	L	Alloa	h	5-1	5,000	Turnbull; Hill 4 (2 pens)
22nd	L	Raith Rovers	h	7-0	6,209	Cox; Turnbull; Gallacher 2; Juliussen 3
29th	L	Ayr United	a	1-2		Gallacher
Jan 1st	L	Dundee United	a	3-2	16,500	Juliussen; Bowman (pen); Turnbull
2nd	L	Cowdenbeath	a	2-2		Anderson; Hill
2nd	FC1	Montrose	a	3-0	2,000	Rattray 2; Andrews
5th	L	St Johnstone	a	1-4	8,000	Juliussen
12th	L	Albion Rovers	h	2-0	12,226	Juliussen; Turnbull
19th	L	Dunfermline	h	3-1	5,269	Bowman 2 (2 pens); Anderson
26th	SU1	Cowdenbeath	a	4-1		Turnbull 2; Gallacher; Ancell
Feb 2nd	SU1	Cowdenbeath	h	2-2 (6-3)	11,285	Juliussen; Anderson
9th	SU2	Alloa	h	6-2	15,472	Anderson 2; (1 pen); Juliussen 4
16th	SUS	Airdrie	h	1-1	22,370	Ouchterlonie (pen)
20th	SUSR	Airdrie	a	1-2 (2-3)	15,886	Juliussen
23rd	LC	Stirling Albion	a	0-2	6,000	-
Mar 2nd	LC	Arbroath	h	0-0	11,143	-
16th	LC	Stirling Albion	h	8-1	13,315	Cox 2; Juliussen 3; Turnbull; Ouchterlonie 2
23rd	LC	Arbroath	a	3-1	9,000	Ouchterlonie; Cox; McKenzie
Apr 6th	LCQ	Rangers	Ham	1-3	45,000	Ouchterlonie
20th	SVC1	Hibernian	a	0-3	18,500	
27th	SVC1	Hibernian	h	2-0 (2-3)	20,000	Juliussen 2
May 7th	FC1	Montrose	h	2-2 (5-2)	2,276	Juliussen 2

Reuben Bennett - the big keeper arrived from Hull City in 1944.

The Record		
League	-	'B' Division Champions*
League Cup	-	Quarter-final
Scottish Victory Cup	-	First round
Supplementary Cup	-	Semi-final
Forfarshire Cup	-	Winners (Final 16-04-47)
Top Scorer	-	Bert Juliussen (42)
Av. Home Gate	-	9,000
Players used	-	30
Sent off	-	None

Appearances

	League		L/Cup		SVC	SUC		Total	
Gibby McKenzie	26	(1)	4	(1)	2	5		37	(2)
Tommy Gray	24		5		2	5		36	
Kinnaird Ouchterlonie	24	(6)	5	(4)	1	3		33	(11)
Reuben Bennett	24		4		2	1		31	
Bobby Ancell	17	(1)	4		2	5	(1)	28	(2)
Sammy Cox	17	(1)	5	(3)	0	5		27	(4)
Bob Bowman	23	(3)	2		0	2		27	(3)
Bert Juliussen	18	(31)	3	(3)	2	(2)	4	(6)	27	(42)
Willie Anderson	19	(15)	1		0	5	(3)	25	(18)
George Hill	23	(17)	0		1	1		25	(17)
Reggie Smith	16	(2)	0		1	0		17	(2)
Tommy Gallacher	10	(4)	1		0	5	(1)	16	(5)
Ronnie Turnbull	9	(4)	4	(1)	0	3	(2)	16	(7)
Jimmy Andrews	6		4		0	0		10	
Alec McIntosh	5		4		1	5		10	
Gerry Follon	3	(2)	3		2	0		8	(2)
Peter Rattray	5	(1)	3		0	0		8	(1)
Johnny Lynch	0		1		0	4		5	
Alex Lawrie	3		0		1	0		4	
Frank Joyner	0		1		2	0		3	
Mike Clark	2		0		0	0		2	
Archie Coats	2		0		0	0		2	
Ernie Ewen	2	(2)	0		0	0		2	(2)
John Laurie	2	(1)	0		0	0		2	(1)
Billy Moir	2	(1)	0		0	0		2	(1)
Willie Westwater	2		0		0	0		2	
Alec Beaton	1		0		0	0		1	
Doug Cowie	0		1		0	0		1	
Harry Sneddon	0		0		1	0		1	
John Marshall	0		0		1	0		1	

Scottish League 'B' Division

		Home			Away			Goals		
	P	W	D	L	W	D	L	F	A	PTS
Dundee	26	12	0	1	9	2	2	92-28		44
East Fife	26	9	2	2	6	2	5	64-34		34
Ayr United	26	8	3	2	7	1	5	69-43		34
Airdrie	26	8	4	1	6	1	6	69-50		33
St Johnstone	26	6	4	3	6	2	5	66-60		30
Albion Rovers	26	9	2	2	5	0	8	45-41		30
Alloa	26	6	2	5	6	2	5	59-53		28
Dumbarton	26	8	1	4	3	3	7	59-54		26
Dunfermline	26	7	1	5	3	3	7	63-47		24
Cowdenbeath	26	6	4	3	2	1	10	43-62		21
Stenhousemuir	26	4	3	6	2	2	9	36-89		17
Dundee United	26	6	0	7	0	3	10	46-70		15
Raith Rovers	26	5	0	8	1	2	10	48-80		14
Arbroath	26	5	0	8	1	2	10	40-88		14

League Cup Section

	P	W	D	L	F	A	PTS
Dundee	4	2	1	1	11- 2		5
Stirling Albion	4	2	0	2	6-10		4
Arbroath	4	1	1	2	3- 6		3

* No promotion - Season 1945-46 regarded as unofficial since many players remained in the armed forces. SU = Supplementary Cup ('B' Division sides only); LC = League Cup; SVC = Scottish Victory Cup; FC = Forfarshire Cup.

They Wore The Dark Blue

Dundee F.C. Line-Ups 1945-46

		1	2	3	4	5	6	7	8	9	10	11
Aug	11th	Clark	Gray	Cox	McKenzie	Bowman	Smith R	Hill	Ewen	Stirling	Ouchterlonie	Juliussen
	18th	Bennett	Cox	Westwater	McKenzie	Gray	Smith R	Moir	Ewen	Juliussen	Ouchterlonie	Hill
	25th	Bennett	Cox	Lawrie	McKenzie	Gray	Smith R	Moir	Bowman	Anderson	Ouchterlonie	Hill
Sep	1st	Bennett	Bowman	Lawrie	McKenzie	Gray	Smith R	Hill	Laurie	Anderson	Ouchterlonie	Andrews
	8th	Bennett	Bowman	Ancell	McKenzie	Gray	Smith R	Hill	Laurie	Anderson	Ouchterlonie	Andrews
	15th	Bennett	Bowman	Lawrie	McKenzie	Gray	Smith R	Hill	Ouchterlonie	Anderson	Rattray	Andrews
	22nd	Bennett	Bowman	Ancell	McKenzie	Gray	Smith R	Hill	Ouchterlonie	Anderson	Rattray	Andrews
	29th	Bennett	Bowman	Ancell	McKenzie	Gray	Smith R	Anderson	Ouchterlonie	Juliussen	Rattray	Hill
Oct	6th	Clark	Westwater	Ancell	McKenzie	Gray	Cox	Anderson	Ouchterlonie	Juliussen	Rattray	Hill
	13th	Bennett	Bowman	Ancell	McKenzie	Gray	Smith R	Anderson	Rattray	Juliussen	Cox	Hill
	20th	Bennett	Bowman	Cox	McKenzie	Gray	Smith R	Anderson	Ouchterlonie	Juliussen	Coats	Hill
	27th	Bennett	Bowman	Cox	McKenzie	Gray	Smith R	Anderson	Ancell	Juliussen	Ouchterlonie	Hill
Nov	3rd	Bennett	Bowman	Cox	McKenzie	Gray	Smith R	Anderson	Follon	Juliussen	Ouchterlonie	Hill
	10th	Bennett	Cox	Ancell	McKenzie	Bowman	Smith R	Anderson	Follon	Juliussen	Ouchterlonie	Hill
	17th	Bennett	Bowman	Ancell	McKenzie	Gray	Smith R	Anderson	Follon	Juliussen	Ouchterlonie	Turnbull
	24th	Bennett	Bowman	Cox	McKenzie	Gray	Smith R	Anderson	Gallacher	Coats	Ouchterlonie	Hill
Dec	1st	Bennett	Bowman	Ancell	McKenzie	Gray	Smith R	Anderson	Gallacher	Juliussen	Ouchterlonie	Hill
	8th	Bennett	Bowman	Ancell	McKenzie	Gray	Cox	Turnbull	Gallacher	Juliussen	Ouchterlonie	Hill
	15th	Bennett	Bowman	Ancell	McKenzie	Gray	Cox	Anderson	Gallacher	Juliussen	Turnbull	Hill
	22nd	Bennett	Bowman	Ancell	McKenzie	Gray	Cox	Turnbull	Gallacher	Juliussen	Ouchterlonie	Hill
	29th	Bennett	Bowman	Ancell	McKenzie	Gray	Cox	Anderson	Gallacher	Turnbull	Ouchterlonie	Hill
Jan	1st	Bennett	McIntosh	Ancell	McKenzie	Gray	Bowman	Turnbull	Gallacher	Juliussen	Ouchterlonie	Hill
	2nd	Bennett	McIntosh	Ancell	McKenzie	Bowman	Cox	Anderson	Gallacher	Juliussen	Ouchterlonie	Hill
	5th	Bennett	Bowman	McIntosh	McKenzie	Gray	Cox	Turnbull	Beaton	Juliussen	Ouchterlonie	Hill
	12th	Bennett	McIntosh	Ancell	McKenzie	Gray	Cox	Turnbull	Gallacher	Juliussen	Ouchterlonie	Andrews
	19th	Bennett	McIntosh	Ancell	McKenzie	Gray	Bowman	Anderson	Gallacher	Turnbull	Ouchterlonie	Andrews
	26th	Bennett	McIntosh	Ancell	McKenzie	Gray	Cox	Anderson	Gallacher	Turnbull	Ouchterlonie	Hill
Feb	2nd	Lynch	McIntosh	Ancell	McKenzie	Gray	Cox	Anderson	Gallacher	Stirling	Ouchterlonie	Juliussen
	9th	Lynch	McIntosh	Ancell	McKenzie	Gray	Cox	Anderson	Gallacher	Stirling	Ouchterlonie	Juliussen
	16th	Lynch	McIntosh	Ancell	McKenzie	Gray	Cox	Anderson	Gallacher	Turnbull	Bowman	Juliussen
	20th	Lynch	McIntosh	Ancell	McKenzie	Gray	Cox	Anderson	Gallacher	Juliussen	Bowman	Turnbull
	23rd	Bennett	Gray	McIntosh	Cowie	Bowman	Cox	Anderson	Turnbull	Juliussen	Ouchterlonie	Andrews
Mar	2nd	Bennett	McIntosh	Ancell	McKenzie	Gray	Cox	Follon	Gallacher	Turnbull	Ouchterlonie	Andrews
	16th	Bennett	McIntosh	Ancell	McKenzie	Gray	Cox	Follon	Ouchterlonie	Turnbull	Rattray	Andrews
	23rd	Bennett	McIntosh	Ancell	McKenzie	Gray	Cox	Turnbull	Ouchterlonie	Juliussen	Rattray	Andrews
Apr	6th	Lynch	Cox	Ancell	McKenzie	Gray	Bowman	Follon	Ouchterlonie	Juliussen	Rattray	Joyner
	20th	Bennett	Lawrie	Ancell	McKenzie	Gray	Smith R	Stewart	Follon	Juliussen	Ouchterlonie	Joyner
	27th	Bennett	McIntosh	Ancell	McKenzie	Gray	Sneddon	Hill	Marshall	Juliussen	Follon	Joyner

The crowds queue up at Dens - with servicemen returning from the armed forces, there was a boom in post-war football attendances. In 1945-46 Dundee's largest home attendance was the 22,370 crowd for the Supplementary Cup semi-final against Airdrie. DC Thomson

Season 1946-47

Date		Opponents		Score	Crowd	Scorers
Aug 10th	L	East Fife	a	6-2	8,000	Joyner 3; Juliussen 2; Pattillo
17th	L	Airdrie	h	1-1	21,074	Pattillo
24th	L	Dundee United	a	2-1	21,000	Juliussen; Turnbull
31st	L	Arbroath	h	5-0	14,500	Pattillo; Rattray 2; Ewen; Juliussen
Sep 4th	FCS**	Arbroath	a	4-3	4,000	Rattray; Juliussen 3
7th	L	Dumbarton	a	1-2		Juliussen
11th	FCS**	Arbroath	h	3-2 (7-5)	7,000	Pattillo 2; Juliussen
14th	L	Alloa	h	6-2	14,000	Juliussen 4; Ewen; Pattillo
21st	LC	Raith Rovers	a	2-0	6,000	Pattillo 2
28th	LC	Stenhousemuir	h	4-0	13,000	Juliussen; Ewen 3
Oct 12th	LC	Raith Rovers	h	3-1	15,000	Ewen; Pattillo 2
19th	LC	Stenhousemuir	a	4-0	1,000	Ewen 2; Pattillo 2
Nov 2nd	L	Raith Rovers	a	4-1	8,000	Juliussen 2; Gunn; Pattillo
9th	L	Stenhousemuir	h	4-1	11,000	Ewen 3 (1 pen); Juliussen
16th	L	Cowdenbeath	a	8-2	6,500	Turnbull 3; Ewen 3 (1 pen); Pattillo 2
23rd	L	Dunfermline	a	5-2	6,000	Hill; Ewen 3; Turnbull
30th	L	Albion Rovers	h	6-2	16,000	Turnbull 4; McKenzie; Gunn
Dec 7th	L	St Johnstone	a	5-1	10,000	Pattillo 2; Ewen 2; Turnbull
14th	L	Ayr United	a	6-2	5,500	Hill; Turnbull 2; Gunn; McKenzie; Pattillo
21st	L	East Fife	h	2-0	17,500	Pattillo; Hill
28th	L	Airdrie	a	1-2	15,000	Smith
Jan 1st	L	Dundee United	h	2-0	24,000	Turnbull; Ewen
2nd	L	Arbroath	a	4-1		Ewen 2 (1 pen); Hill; Turnbull
4th	L	Cowdenbeath	h	6-2	12,000	Turnbull 3; Juliussen; Ewen 2
11th	L	Stenhousemuir	a	0-0		-
18th	L	St Johnstone	h	2-0	16,800	Gunn; Turnbull
25th	SC1	Celtic	h	2-1	36,000	Ewen; Turnbull
Feb 1st	L	Albion Rovers	a	2-2	4,000	Joyner; Pattillo
22nd	SC3	Albion Rovers	h	3-0	20,269	Ewen; Pattillo 2
Mar 1st	LCQ	Aberdeen	h	0-1	28,300	-
5th	LCQ	Aberdeen	a	2-3(2-4)	18,000	Juliussen 2
8th	L	Alloa	a	10-0	3,700	Gunn; Juliussen 6; Rattray; Smith; Ewen
22nd	L	Dunfermline	h	10-0	14,000	Rattray; Juliussen 7; Ewen 2 (1 pen)
29th	SCQ	Aberdeen	h	1-2*	38,000	Ewen
Apr 5th	L	Dumbarton	h	4-0	5,837	Smith; Rattray 3
16th	FCF**	Forfar Athletic	h	6-1	4,000	Juliussen 4; Pattillo; Boyd
19th	FC1	Montrose	a	6-5	1,200	Juliussen 2; Pattillo 2; Ewen
23rd	L	Raith Rovers	h	5-2	10,000	Ewen; Juliussen 3; Pattillo
May 3rd	L	Ayr United	h	6-2	4,000	Gunn; Ewen 2; Juliussen; Smith; Pattillo
14th	FCS	Arbroath	a	4-3	5,000	Ewen 3; Turnbull
17th	FCF	Dundee United	h	5-0	14,000	Juliussen 4; Pattillo

* 1-1 after 90 minutes, then sudden death. After 20 minutes extra-time, another 10 mts played then 10 minutes more with the winner scored in the 129th minute. ** Forfarshire Cup 1945-46.

Bobby Ancell - a cultured full-back who later returned as manager.

The Record

League	-	'B' Division Champions
League Cup	-	Quarter-final
Scottish Cup	-	Third round
Forfarshire Cup	-	Winners
Top Scorers	-	Bert Juliussen, Ernie Ewen (both 33 goals)
Av. Home Gate	-	13,900
Players used	-	20
Sent off	-	None

Appearances

	League	L/Cup	S/Cup	Total
Reggie Smith	26 (4)	6	3	35 (4)
Ernie Ewen	25 (24)	6 (6)	3 (3)	34 (33)
Tommy Gray	24	6	3	33
Gibby McKenzie	24 (2)	6	3	33 (2)
Bobby Ancell	24	6	2	32
Gerry Follon	23	6	3	32
Johnny Pattillo	23 (14)	6 (6)	3 (2)	32 (22)
Ally Gunn	19 (6)	6	3	28 (6)
Reuben Bennett	18	6	2	26
George Hill	18 (4)	4	0	22 (4)
Bert Juliussen	15 (30)	5 (3)	2	22 (33)
Ronnie Turnbull	15 (18)	3	2 (1)	20 (19)
Johnny Lynch	8	0	1	9
Alfie Boyd	6	0	2	8
Alec McIntosh	5	0	0	5
Peter Rattray	5 (7)	0	0	5 (7)
Frank Joyner	3 (4)	0	1	4 (4)
Doug Cowie	3	0	0	3
Kinnaird Ouchterlonie	1	0	0	1
Jimmy Andrews	1	0	0	1

Scottish League 'B' Division

		Home			Away			Goals		
	P	W	D	L	W	D	L	F	A	PTS
Dundee	26	12	1	0	9	2	2	113-30		45
Airdrie	26	10	2	1	9	2	2	78-38		42
East Fife	26	8	3	2	4	4	5	58-39		31
Albion Rovers	26	6	4	3	4	3	6	50-54		27
Alloa	26	8	3	2	3	2	8	51-57		27
Raith Rovers	26	7	3	3	3	3	7	45-52		26
Stenhousemuir	26	7	1	5	1	6	6	43-53		23
Dunfermline	26	6	2	5	4	1	8	50-72		23
St Johnstone	26	6	2	5	3	2	8	45-47		22
Dundee United	26	7	1	5	2	3	8	53-60		22
Ayr United	26	8	1	4	1	1	11	56-73		20
Arbroath	26	4	3	6	3	3	7	42-63		20
Dumbarton	26	4	4	5	3	0	10	41-54		18
Cowdenbeath	26	5	4	4	1	2	10	44-77		18

League Cup Section

	P	W	D	L	F	A	PTS
Dundee	4	4	0	0	13-1		8
Stenhousemuir	4	1	0	3	5-10		2
Raith Rovers	4	1	0	3	5-12		2

They Wore The Dark Blue

Dundee F.C. Line-Ups 1946-47

		1	2	3	4	5	6	7	8	9	10	11
Aug	10th	Bennett	McIntosh	Ancell	Follon	Cowie	Smith	Hill	Pattillo	Juliussen	Ewen	Joyner
	17th	Bennett	Gray	Ancell	McKenzie	Cowie	Smith	Hill	Pattillo	Juliussen	Ewen	Joyner
	24th	Bennett	McIntosh	Ancell	McKenzie	Gray	Smith	Gunn	Pattillo	Turnbull	Ouchterlonie	Juliussen
	31st	Bennett	McIntosh	Ancell	McKenzie	Gray	Smith	Pattillo	Ewen	Juliussen	Rattray	Andrews
Sep	7th	Bennett	McIntosh	Follon	McKenzie	Gray	Smith	Pattillo	Ewen	Juliussen	Rattray	Hill
	14th	Bennett	Follon	Ancell	McKenzie	Gray	Smith	Gunn	Pattillo	Juliussen	Ewen	Hill
	21st	Bennett	Follon	Ancell	McKenzie	Gray	Smith	Gunn	Pattillo	Juliussen	Ewen	Hill
	28th	Bennett	Follon	Ancell	McKenzie	Gray	Smith	Gunn	Pattillo	Juliussen	Ewen	Hill
Oct	12th	Bennett	Follon	Ancell	McKenzie	Gray	Smith	Gunn	Pattillo	Juliussen	Ewen	Hill
	19th	Bennett	Follon	Ancell	McKenzie	Gray	Smith	Gunn	Pattillo	Turnbull	Ewen	Hill
Nov	2nd	Bennett	Follon	Ancell	McKenzie	Gray	Smith	Gunn	Pattillo	Juliussen	Ewen	Hill
	9th	Bennett	Follon	Ancell	McKenzie	Gray	Smith	Gunn	Pattillo	Juliussen	Ewen	Hill
	16th	Bennett	Follon	Ancell	McKenzie	Gray	Smith	Gunn	Pattillo	Turnbull	Ewen	Hill
	23rd	Bennett	Follon	Ancell	McKenzie	Gray	Smith	Gunn	Pattillo	Turnbull	Ewen	Hill
	30th	Bennett	Follon	Ancell	McKenzie	Gray	Smith	Gunn	Pattillo	Turnbull	Ewen	Hill
Dec	7th	Bennett	Follon	Ancell	McKenzie	Gray	Smith	Gunn	Pattillo	Turnbull	Ewen	Hill
	14th	Bennett	Follon	Ancell	McKenzie	Gray	Smith	Gunn	Pattillo	Turnbull	Ewen	Hill
	21st	Bennett	Follon	Ancell	McKenzie	Gray	Smith	Gunn	Pattillo	Turnbull	Ewen	Hill
	28th	Bennett	Follon	Ancell	McKenzie	Gray	Smith	Gunn	Pattillo	Turnbull	Ewen	Hill
Jan	1st	Lynch	Follon	Ancell	McKenzie	Gray	Smith	Gunn	Ewen	Turnbull	Pattillo	Hill
	2nd	Lynch	Follon	Ancell	McKenzie	Gray	Smith	Hill	Ewen	Turnbull	Pattillo	Juliussen
	4th	Lynch	Follon	Ancell	McKenzie	Gray	Smith	Hill	Ewen	Turnbull	Pattillo	Juliussen
	11th	Lynch	Follon	McIntosh	McKenzie	Gray	Smith	Hill	Ewen	Turnbull	Pattillo	Juliussen
	18th	Bennett	Follon	Ancell	McKenzie	Gray	Smith	Gunn	Ewen	Turnbull	Pattillo	Hill
	25th	Bennett	Follon	Ancell	McKenzie	Gray	Smith	Gunn	Pattillo	Turnbull	Ewen	Juliussen
Feb	1st	Lynch	Follon	Ancell	McKenzie	Boyd	Smith	Gunn	Pattillo	Turnbull	Ewen	Joyner
	22nd	Bennett	Follon	Gray	McKenzie	Boyd	Smith	Gunn	Pattillo	Turnbull	Ewen	Joyner
Mar	1st	Bennett	Follon	Ancell	McKenzie	Gray	Smith	Gunn	Pattillo	Turnbull	Ewen	Juliussen
	5th	Bennett	Follon	Ancell	McKenzie	Gray	Smith	Turnbull	Ewen	Juliussen	Pattillo	Gunn
	8th	Bennett	Follon	Ancell	McKenzie	Gray	Boyd	Gunn	Ewen	Juliussen	Rattray	Smith
	22nd	Bennett	Follon	Ancell	McKenzie	Gray	Boyd	Gunn	Ewen	Juliussen	Rattray	Smith
	29th	Lynch	Follon	Ancell	McKenzie	Gray	Boyd	Gunn	Pattillo	Juliussen	Ewen	Smith
Apr	5th	Lynch	Follon	Ancell	McKenzie	Gray	Boyd	Gunn	Ewen	Turnbull	Rattray	Smith
	23rd	Lynch	Follon	Ancell	McKenzie	Gray	Boyd	Gunn	Ewen	Juliussen	Pattillo	Smith
May	3rd	Lynch	Gray	Ancell	McKenzie	Cowie	Boyd	Gunn	Ewen	Juliussen	Pattillo	Smith

The Dundee forwards who scored 20 goals - the prolific Juliussen netting 13 - in successive 10-0 wins over Alloa and Dunfermline. (left to right) - Ally Gunn, Ernie Ewen, Bert Juliussen, Peter Rattray and Reggie Smith. DC THOMSON

Season 1947-48

Date		Opponents		Score	Crowd	Scorers
Aug 9th	LC	Third Lanark	h	5-0	24,313	Ewen 3; Turnbull 2
13th	L	Morton	a	0-3	12,000	-
16th	LC	Celtic	a	1-1	35,000	Turnbull
23rd	LC	Rangers	a	0-3	25,000	-
27th	L	QOS	h	1-0	20,000	Ewen
30th	LC	Third Lanark	a	1-5	15,000	Stott
Sep 6th	LC	Celtic	h	4-1	35,000	Pattillo; Ewen 2 (1 pen); Juliussen
13th	LC	Rangers	h	1-1	39,000	Gallacher
20th	L	Aberdeen	a	2-3	20,000	Juliussen 2
27th	L	Airdrie	h	6-0	16,000	Juliussen 3; Pattillo; Turnbull; Ewen
Oct 4th	L	Clyde	a	4-1	15,000	Turnbull 3; Pattillo
6th	L	Hearts	h	2-1	26,000	Pattillo; Ewen
18th	L	Airdrie	a	0-2	8,000	-
25th	L	Queens Park	h	2-1	18,000	Pattillo; Turnbull
Nov 8th	L	St Mirren	h	6-1	19,000	Hill; Juliussen 2; Pattillo; Smith; Turnbull
15th	L	Hibernian	a	1-2	35,000	Turnbull
22nd	L	Motherwell	a	2-0	10,000	Turnbull 2
29th	L	Third Lanark	h	5-2	18,000	Hill; Ewen 2 (1 pen); Juliussen 2
Dec 6th	L	Celtic	a	1-1	25,000	Juliussen
13th	L	Partick Thistle	h	2-2	22,000	Juliussen 2
20th	L	Morton	h	0-4	19,000	-
25th	L	Rangers	h	1-3	25,000	Ewen
27th	L	QOS	a	5-2	8,000	Pattillo; Ewen
Jan 1st	L	Aberdeen	h	0-0	14,000	-
3rd	L	Rangers	a	1-2	35,000	Juliussen
10th	L	Clyde	h	7-0	20,000	Pattillo 2 (1 pen); Rattray; Smith; Gunn; Juliussen 2
17th	L	Hearts	a	1-0	25,000	Johnsen
24th	SC1	Hearts	h	2-4	31,500	Juliussen; Pattillo
Feb 14th	L	Queens Park	a	1-0	15,000	Rattray
21st	L	Falkirk	h	4-0	12,000	Pattillo 2; Rattray; Juliussen
28th	L	St Mirren	a	1-4	12,000	Pattillo
Mar 6th	L	Falkirk	a	2-3		Ewen; Juliussen
13th	L	Motherwell	h	2-0	21,000	Paton o.g.; Boyd
20th	L	Third Lanark	a	4-1	6,000	Gunn; Pattillo; Ewen 2
Apr 3rd	L	Partick Thistle	a	2-6	15,000	Gunn; Ewen
17th	L	Celtic	h	2-3	31,000	Ewen; Mackay
May 1st	L	Hibernian	h	3-1	30,000	Mackay; Ewen; Pattillo

Johnny Pattillo - his experience played a big part in Dundee's post war revival.

The Record		
League	-	Fourth Place 'A' Division
League Cup	-	Qualifying stages only
Scottish Cup	-	First round
Forfarshire Cup	-	Semi-final (20-09-48)
Top Scorer	-	Bert Juliussen (20 goals)
Av. Home Gate	-	20,700
Players used	-	25
Sent off	-	None

Appearances

	League		L/Cup		S/Cup		Total	
Alfie Boyd	30	(1)	6		1		37	(1)
Gerry Follon	28		6		1		35	
Bobby Ancell	27		6		0		33	
Johnny Pattillo	26	(13)	5	(1)	1	(1)	32	(15)
Ernie Ewen	24	(13)	6	(5)	0		30	(18)
George Hill	24	(2)	4		1		29	(2)
Bert Juliussen	20	(18)	3	(1)	1	(1)	24	(20)
Johnny Lynch	19		6		0		25	
Reggie Smith	19	(2)	3		1		23	(2)
Tommy Gallacher	19		1	(1)	1		21	(1)
Ally Gunn	16	(2)	3		1		20	(2)
Doug Cowie	15		3		0		18	
Ronnie Turnbull	11	(9)	6	(3)	0		17	(12)
Tommy Gray	11		5		0		16	
Jock Brown	10		0		1		11	
Peter Rattray	7	(3)	0		1		8	(3)
Andy Irvine	6		0		1		7	
George 'Piper' Mackay	6	(2)	0		0		6	(2)
George Stewart	5		0		0		5	
Jack Bruce	4		0		0		4	
Gibby McKenzie	1		1		0		2	
Bob Bowman	1		0		0		1	
Alec Stott	0		1	(1)	0		1	(1)
Jack Johnsen	1	(1)	0		0		1	(1)
Jimmy Steadward	1		0		0		1	

Scottish League 'A' Division

		Home			Away			Goals		
	P	W	D	L	W	D	L	F	A	PTS
Hibernian	30	13	2	0	9	2	4	86-27		48
Rangers	30	10	2	3	11	2	2	64-28		46
Partick Thistle	30	7	3	5	9	1	5	61-42		36
Dundee	**30**	**10**	**2**	**3**	**5**	**1**	**9**	**67-51**		**33**
St Mirren	30	9	2	4	4	3	8	54-58		31
Clyde	30	8	3	4	4	4	7	52-57		31
Falkirk	30	6	5	4	4	5	6	55-48		30
Motherwell	30	7	2	6	6	1	8	45-47		29
Hearts	30	7	3	5	3	5	7	37-42		28
Aberdeen	30	8	4	3	2	4	9	45-45		27
Third Lanark	30	8	1	6	2	5	8	56-73		26
Celtic	30	5	4	6	5	1	9	41-56		25
QOS	30	7	3	5	3	2	10	49-74		25
Morton	30	3	4	8	6	2	7	47-43		24
Airdrie	30	7	1	7	0	6	9	40-78		21
Queens Park	30	5	2	8	4	0	11	45-75		20

League Cup Section

	P	W	D	L	F	A	PTS
Rangers	6	4	1	1	12- 4		9
Dundee	**6**	**2**	**2**	**2**	**12-13**		**6**
Celtic	6	2	1	3	9-11		5
Third Lanark	6	2	0	4	12-17		4

Dundee F.C. Line-Ups 1947-48

		1	2	3	4	5	6	7	8	9	10	11
Aug	9th	Lynch	Follon	Ancell	McKenzie	Gray	Boyd	Gunn	Ewen	Turnbull	Smith	Hill
	13th	Lynch	Follon	Ancell	McKenzie	Gray	Boyd	Gunn	Ewen	Turnbull	Smith	Hill
	16th	Lynch	Follon	Ancell	Cowie	Gray	Boyd	Gunn	Ewen	Turnbull	Pattillo	Hill
	23rd	Lynch	Follon	Ancell	Pattillo	Gray	Boyd	Gunn	Ewen	Turnbull	Juliussen	Hill
	27th	Lynch	Follon	Ancell	Pattillo	Gray	Boyd	Gunn	Ewen	Turnbull	Juliussen	Hill
	30th	Lynch	Follon	Ancell	Pattillo	Gray	Boyd	Bowman	Ewen	Turnbull	Stott	Hill
Sep	6th	Lynch	Follon	Ancell	Cowie	Boyd	Smith	Gray	Ewen	Turnbull	Pattillo	Juliussen
	13th	Lynch	Follon	Ancell	Cowie	Boyd	Smith	Pattillo	Ewen	Turnbull	Gallacher	Juliussen
	20th	Lynch	Follon	Ancell	Cowie	Boyd	Smith	Pattillo	Ewen	Turnbull	Gallacher	Juliussen
	27th	Lynch	Follon	Ancell	Cowie	Boyd	Smith	Hill	Ewen	Turnbull	Pattillo	Juliussen
Oct	4th	Lynch	Follon	Ancell	Cowie	Boyd	Smith	Hill	Ewen	Turnbull	Pattillo	Juliussen
	6th	Lynch	Follon	Ancell	Cowie	Boyd	Smith	Hill	Ewen	Turnbull	Pattillo	Juliussen
	18th	Lynch	Follon	Ancell	Bruce	Boyd	Smith	Hill	Ewen	Turnbull	Pattillo	Juliussen
	25th	Lynch	Follon	Ancell	Bruce	Boyd	Smith	Gray	Ewen	Turnbull	Pattillo	Hill
Nov	8th	Lynch	Follon	Ancell	Bruce	Boyd	Smith	Gunn	Pattillo	Turnbull	Juliussen	Hill
	15th	Lynch	Follon	Ancell	Bruce	Boyd	Smith	Gunn	Pattillo	Turnbull	Juliussen	Hill
	22nd	Lynch	Follon	Ancell	Cowie	Boyd	Smith	Gunn	Ewen	Turnbull	Juliussen	Hill
	29th	Lynch	Follon	Ancell	Cowie	Boyd	Smith	Gunn	Ewen	Juliussen	Gallacher	Hill
Dec	6th	Lynch	Follon	Ancell	Cowie	Boyd	Gallacher	Gunn	Ewen	Juliussen	Pattillo	Hill
	13th	Lynch	Follon	Ancell	Cowie	Boyd	Smith	Gunn	Ewen	Juliussen	Pattillo	Hill
	20th	Lynch	Follon	Ancell	Cowie	Boyd	Smith	Gallacher	Ewen	Juliussen	Pattillo	Hill
	25th	Steadward	Follon	Ancell	Cowie	Boyd	Smith	Gray	Ewen	Pattillo	Gallacher	Hill
	27th	Lynch	Follon	Ancell	Smith	Boyd	Rattray	Hill	Gallacher	Pattillo	Ewen	Mackay
Jan	1st	Lynch	Follon	Ancell	Irvine	Gray	Boyd	Gunn	Gallacher	Juliussen	Smith	Hill
	3rd	Lynch	Irvine	Ancell	Gallacher	Gray	Boyd	Gunn	Pattillo	Juliussen	Smith	Hill
	10th	Brown	Follon	Irvine	Gallacher	Boyd	Smith	Gunn	Pattillo	Juliussen	Rattray	Hill
	17th	Brown	Follon	Irvine	Gallacher	Boyd	Smith	Gunn	Pattillo	Johnsen	Rattray	Hill
	24th	Brown	Follon	Irvine	Gallacher	Boyd	Smith	Gunn	Pattillo	Juliussen	Rattray	Hill
Feb	14th	Brown	Follon	Ancell	Gallacher	Boyd	Cowie	Pattillo	Ewen	Juliussen	Rattray	Hill
	21st	Brown	Follon	Ancell	Gallacher	Boyd	Cowie	Pattillo	Ewen	Juliussen	Rattray	Hill
	28th	Brown	Irvine	Ancell	Gallacher	Boyd	Cowie	Pattillo	Ewen	Juliussen	Rattray	Hill
Mar	6th	Brown	Follon	Ancell	Gallacher	Boyd	Cowie	Pattillo	Ewen	Juliussen	Rattray	Hill
	13th	Brown	Follon	Ancell	Gallacher	Gray	Cowie	Pattillo	Ewen	Stewart	Boyd	Mackay
	20th	Brown	Follon	Ancell	Gallacher	Gray	Boyd	Gunn	Pattillo	Stewart	Ewen	Mackay
Apr	3rd	Brown	Follon	Ancell	Gallacher	Gray	Boyd	Gunn	Pattillo	Stewart	Ewen	Mackay
	17th	Brown	Follon	Irvine	Gallacher	Gray	Boyd	Gunn	Pattillo	Stewart	Ewen	Mackay
May	1st	Lynch	Follon	Ancell	Gallacher	Gray	Boyd	Gunn	Pattillo	Stewart	Ewen	Mackay

Dundee FC 1947-48, (BACK, left to right) R. Bennett, A. Lawrie, R. Wilson, G. Stewart, J. Lynch, A. Smith, J. McAlpine, P. Rattray, P. Barrie. MIDDLE - W. Cameron (trainer-masseur), B. Bowman, D. Cowie, G. McKenzie, A. Irvine, B. Ancell, J. Dickson, T. Gray, J. Bruce, A. Boyd, A. McCall (trainer). FRONT - A. Stott, A. Gunn, E. Ewen, R. Turnbull, G. Anderson (manager), B. Juliussen, R. Smith, J. Pattillo and G. Hill.

Season 1948-49

Date		Opponents		Score	Crowd	Scorers
Aug 14th	L	Hearts	h	2-1	30,000	Stewart; Gunn
18th	L	Clyde	a	3-3	20,000	Ewen; Gunn; Stewart
21st	L	Aberdeen	h	3-0	30,000	Stott; Gunn; Ewen
28th	L	Rangers	a	1-1	55,000	Stott
Sep 1st	L	East Fife	h	2-5	29,500	Stott; Gunn
11th	LC	Albion Rovers	h	2-1	20,000	Pattillo 2
18th	LC	Falkirk	a	3-2	7,000	Gunn; Rattray; Stott
20th	FCS*	Arbroath	a	0-5	4,000	-
25th	LC	Motherwell	a	1-0	9,000	Stott
Oct 2nd	LC	Albion Rovers	a	3-2	10,000	Gerrie; Hill; Pattillo
9th	LC	Falkirk	h	4-2	16,000	Boyd (pen); Rattray; Fiddes o.g. Pattillo
16th	LC	Motherwell	h	0-1	23,000	
23rd	L	Celtic	a	1-0	25,000	Gerrie
30th	LCQ	Alloa	h	1-1**	13,000	Gunn
Nov 3rd	LCQR	Alloa	a	3-1	9,500	Stott; Boyd; Pattillo
6th	L	Albion Rovers	a	6-0	8,000	Gunn; Stott 4; Mackay
13th	L	QOS	h	2-1	18,000	Pattillo; Stott
20th	LCS	Rangers	Ham	1-4	50,996	Smith (pen)
27th	L	St Mirren	h	1-0	18,000	Boyd
Dec 4th	L	Hibernian	a	1-2		Malloch
11th	L	Motherwell	a	2-0	12,000	Hill; Gunn
18th	L	Third Lanark	h	1-1	16,500	Hill
25th	L	Clyde	h	3-1	19,000	Stott 2; Ewen
Jan 1st	L	Aberdeen	a	3-1	26,000	Pattillo; Stott; Follon
3rd	L	Rangers	h	3-1	39,975	Ewen; Stott 2
8th	L	Hearts	a	1-0	40,000	Stott
15th	L	Morton	h	3-1	16,000	Stott 3
22nd	SC1	St Johnstone	h	6-1	14,000	Stott 4; Pattillo 2
29th	L	East Fife	a	0-3	15,000	-
Feb 5th	SC2	St Mirren	h	0-0	34,000	-
8th	SC2R	St Mirren	a	2-1	28,000	Gunn; Stott
12th	L	Partick Thistle	a	4-4	37,000	Gunn 2; Boyd; Pattillo
19th	L	Albion Rovers	h	5-0	17,000	Pattillo 2; Andrews; Stott 2
26th	L	QOS	a	1-0	11,500	Gunn
Mar 5th	SCQ	Hearts	a	4-2	37,356	Gunn; Hill; Gerrie; Pattillo
12th	L	St Mirren	a	1-6	14,000	Gerrie
19th	L	Hibernian	h	4-3	32,500	Pattillo; Stott; Bruce; Hill
26th	SCS	Clyde	E.Rd	2-2	33,000	Gunn; Stott (pen)
Apr 2nd	L	Third Lanark	a	3-2	6,000	Stott 2; Pattillo
4th	SCSR	Clyde	Ham	1-2	50,000	Milligan o.g.
11th	L	Celtic	h	3-2	29,000	Stott; Gerrie
16th	L	Morton	a	2-2	15,000	Ewen; Stott
20th	L	Falkirk	h	3-1	21,500	Gunn; Stott 2
23rd	L	Partick Thistle	h	4-2	25,000	Stott 2; Gerrie; Pattillo
27th	L	Motherwell	h	2-1	26,000	Pattillo; Stott
30th	L	Falkirk	a	1-4	18,000	Stott

Alec Stott - the 39-goal centre-forward gives the Albion Rovers defence a hard time.

*1947-48 Forfarshire Cup; ** a.e.t. 1-1 after 90 minutes. Cup Cash v. St Johnstone £901; v. St Mirren (h) £2,350; (a) £1,879; v. Hearts £3,342; v. Clyde (Hamp. £3,600 exc. stands)

The Record

League	-	'A' Division Runners-Up
League Cup	-	Semi-final
Scottish Cup	-	Semi-final
Forfarshire Cup	-	Winners (Final on 23-08-50)
Top Scorer	-	Alec Stott (39 goals)
Av. Home Gate	-	24,500
Players used	-	24
Sent off	-	None

Appearances

	League		L/Cup		S/Cup		Total	
Tommy Gallacher	29		9		6		44	
Alf Boyd	29	(2)	9	(2)	5		43	(4)
Gerry Follon	28	(1)	9		5		42	(1)
Ally Gunn	28	(10)	9	(2)	5	(3)	42	(15)
Johnny Pattillo	25	(9)	9	(5)	6	(3)	40	(17)
Alec Stott	23	(30)	4	(3)	6	(6)	33	(39)
Doug Cowie	23		1		6		30	
Johnny Lynch	23		2		5		30	
George Hill	18	(3)	5	(1)	5	(1)	28	(5)
Andy Irvine	19		0		5		24	
Tommy Gray	11		9		1		21	
Ernie Ewen	15	(5)	1		2		18	(5)
Syd Gerrie	11	(5)	4	(1)	3	(1)	18	(7)
Bobby Ancell	7		9		0		16	
Jimmy Andrews	10	(1)	3		2		15	(1)
Reggie Smith	8		3	(1)	1		12	(1)
Jock Brown	4		7		0		11	
Peter Rattray	3		5	(2)	0		8	(2)
Reuben Bennett	3		0		1		4	
George 'Piper' Mackay	3	(1)	1		0		4	(1)
Jimmy Malloch	4	(1)	0		0		4	(1)
Jack Bruce	2	(1)	0		1		3	
Jack Court	2		0		1		3	
George Stewart	2	(2)	0		0		2	(2)

Scottish League 'A' Division

		Home			Away			Goals		
	P	W	D	L	W	D	L	F A	PTS	
Rangers	30	11	3	1	9	3	3	63-32	46	
Dundee	**30**	**13**	**1**	**1**	**7**	**4**	**4**	**71-48**	**45**	
Hibernian	30	9	3	3	8	2	5	75-52	39	
East Fife	30	9	1	5	7	2	6	64-46	35	
Falkirk	30	9	3	3	3	5	7	70-54	32	
Celtic	30	7	3	5	5	4	6	48-40	31	
Third Lanark	30	9	2	4	4	3	8	56-52	31	
Hearts	30	8	2	5	4	4	6	64-54	30	
St Mirren	30	9	3	3	4	1	10	51-47	30	
Queen of the South	30	8	3	4	3	5	7	47-53	30	
Partick Thistle	30	4	8	3	5	1	9	5063	27	
Motherwell	30	7	2	6	3	3	9	44-49	25	
Aberdeen	30	5	4	6	2	7	6	39-48	25	
Clyde	30	5	4	6	4	2	9	50-67	24	
Morton	30	4	6	5	3	2	10	39-51	22	
Albion Rovers	30	3	1	11	0	1	14	30-105	8	

League Cup Section

	P	W	D	L	F A	PTS
Dundee	6	5	0	1	13-8	10
Motherwell	6	4	0	2	11-5	8
Falkirk	6	2	0	4	8-11	4
Albion Rovers	6	1	0	5	9-17	2

Dundee F.C. Line-Ups 1948-49

		1	2	3	4	5	6	7	8	9	10	11
Aug	14th	Lynch	Follon	Ancell	Gallacher	Gray	Boyd	Gunn	Pattillo	Stewart	Ewen	Mackay
	18th	Lynch	Follon	Ancell	Gallacher	Gray	Boyd	Gunn	Pattillo	Stewart	Ewen	Andrews
	21st	Lynch	Follon	Ancell	Gallacher	Gray	Boyd	Gunn	Pattillo	Stott	Ewen	Andrews
	28th	Lynch	Follon	Ancell	Gallacher	Gray	Boyd	Gunn	Pattillo	Stott	Ewen	Andrews
Sep	1st	Lynch	Follon	Ancell	Gallacher	Gray	Boyd	Gunn	Pattillo	Stott	Ewen	Andrews
	11th	Brown	Follon	Ancell	Gallacher	Gray	Boyd	Gunn	Pattillo	Stott	Ewen	Hill
	18th	Brown	Follon	Ancell	Gallacher	Gray	Boyd	Gunn	Pattillo	Stott	Rattray	Hill
	25th	Brown	Follon	Ancell	Gallacher	Gray	Boyd	Gunn	Pattillo	Stott	Rattray	Hill
Oct	2nd	Brown	Follon	Ancell	Gallacher	Gray	Boyd	Gunn	Pattillo	Gerrie	Rattray	Hill
	9th	Lynch	Follon	Ancell	Gallacher	Gray	Boyd	Gunn	Pattillo	Gerrie	Rattray	Andrews
	16th	Lynch	Follon	Ancell	Gallacher	Gray	Boyd	Gunn	Pattillo	Gerrie	Rattray	Andrews
	23rd	Brown	Follon	Ancell	Gallacher	Gray	Boyd	Gunn	Pattillo	Gerrie	Smith	Andrews
	30th	Brown	Follon	Ancell	Gallacher	Gray	Boyd	Gunn	Pattillo	Gerrie	Smith	Andrews
Nov	2nd	Brown	Follon	Ancell	Gallacher	Gray	Boyd	Gunn	Pattillo	Stott	Smith	Hill
	6th	Lynch	Follon	Ancell	Cowie	Gray	Boyd	Gunn	Court	Stott	Smith	Mackay
	13th	Brown	Follon	Ancell	Gallacher	Gray	Boyd	Gunn	Pattillo	Stott	Smith	Mackay
	20th	Brown	Follon	Ancell	Cowie	Gray	Boyd	Gunn	Gallacher	Pattillo	Smith	Mackay
	27th	Lynch	Follon	Ancell	Gallacher	Cowie	Boyd	Gunn	Pattillo	Malloch	Smith	Hill
Dec	4th	Lynch	Follon	Ancell	Gallacher	Cowie	Boyd	Gunn	Pattillo	Malloch	Smith	Hill
	11th	Lynch	Follon	Irvine	Gallacher	Cowie	Boyd	Gunn	Rattray	Malloch	Smith	Hill
	18th	Lynch	Follon	Irvine	Gallacher	Cowie	Boyd	Gunn	Rattray	Malloch	Smith	Hill
	25th	Lynch	Follon	Irvine	Gallacher	Cowie	Boyd	Gunn	Pattillo	Stott	Ewen	Hill
Jan	1st	Lynch	Follon	Irvine	Gallacher	Cowie	Boyd	Gunn	Pattillo	Stott	Ewen	Hill
	3rd	Lynch	Follon	Irvine	Gallacher	Cowie	Boyd	Gunn	Pattillo	Stott	Ewen	Hill
	8th	Lynch	Follon	Irvine	Gallacher	Cowie	Boyd	Gunn	Pattillo	Stott	Ewen	Hill
	15th	Lynch	Follon	Irvine	Gallacher	Cowie	Boyd	Gunn	Pattillo	Stott	Ewen	Hill
	22nd	Lynch	Follon	Irvine	Gallacher	Cowie	Smith	Gunn	Pattillo	Stott	Ewen	Hill
	29th	Lynch	Follon	Irvine	Gallacher	Cowie	Smith	Gunn	Pattillo	Stott	Ewen	Hill
Feb	5th	Lynch	Follon	Irvine	Gallacher	Cowie	Boyd	Gunn	Pattillo	Stott	Ewen	Hill
	8th	Lynch	Follon	Irvine	Gallacher	Cowie	Boyd	Gunn	Pattillo	Stott	Gerrie	Andrews
	12th	Brown	Follon	Irvine	Gallacher	Cowie	Boyd	Gunn	Pattillo	Stott	Gerrie	Andrews
	19th	Bennett	Follon	Irvine	Gallacher	Cowie	Boyd	Gunn	Pattillo	Stott	Gerrie	Andrews
	26th	Bennett	Follon	Irvine	Gallacher	Cowie	Boyd	Gunn	Pattillo	Stott	Gerrie	Andrews
Mar	5th	Bennett	Follon	Irvine	Gallacher	Cowie	Boyd	Gunn	Pattillo	Stott	Gerrie	Hill
	12th	Bennett	Follon	Irvine	Gallacher	Cowie	Boyd	Gunn	Pattillo	Stott	Gerrie	Andrews
	19th	Brown	Follon	Bruce	Gallacher	Cowie	Boyd	Gunn	Pattillo	Stott	Ewen	Hill
	26th	Lynch	Follon	Irvine	Gallacher	Cowie	Boyd	Gunn	Pattillo	Stott	Gerrie	Hill
Apr	2nd	Lynch	Bruce	Gray	Gallacher	Cowie	Boyd	Hill	Pattillo	Stott	Court	Andrews
	4th	Lynch	Bruce	Gray	Gallacher	Cowie	Boyd	Hill	Pattillo	Stott	Court	Andrews
	11th	Lynch	Gray	Boyd	Gallacher	Cowie	Rattray	Gunn	Ewen	Stott	Gerrie	Hill
	16th	Lynch	Follon	Boyd	Gallacher	Gray	Cowie	Pattillo	Ewen	Stott	Gerrie	Hill
	20th	Lynch	Follon	Irvine	Gallacher	Cowie	Boyd	Gunn	Ewen	Stott	Gerrie	Hill
	23rd	Lynch	Follon	Irvine	Gallacher	Cowie	Boyd	Gunn	Pattillo	Stott	Gerrie	Hill
	27th	Lynch	Follon	Irvine	Gallacher	Cowie	Boyd	Gunn	Pattillo	Stott	Gerrie	Hill
	30th	Lynch	Follon	Irvine	Gallacher	Cowie	Boyd	Gunn	Pattillo	Stott	Gerrie	Hill

Title challenge - Ally Gunn shoots but to the relief of Partick Thistle keeper Bobby Henderson the ball hit the side net. Right - Johnny Pattillo watches as Alec Stott (out of picture) beats keeper Clark for the first of his hat-trick in Dundee's 3-1 win over Morton at Dens.

Season 1949-50

Date		Opponents		Score	Crowd	Scorers
Aug 13th	LC	Clyde	h	1-1	28,500	Ewen
17th	LC	Motherwell	a	0-2	18,000	-
20th	LC	Partick Thistle	h	5-2	25,000	Hill; Stott 3; Gerrie
27th	LC	Clyde	a	0-2	16,000	-
31st	LC	Motherwell	h	0-1	20,000	-
Sep 3rd	LC	Partick Thistle	a	2-4	40,000	Ewen; Fraser
7th	FCS*	Forfar Athletic	h	5-1	9,000	Gerrie 3 (2 pens); Fraser 2
10th	L	Stirling Albion	a	2-2	15,000	Fraser; Andrews
17th	L	QOS	h	3-0	19,000	Boyd (pen); Fraser 2
24th	L	Aberdeen	a	2-2	23,000	Fraser; Rattray
Oct 1st	L	Motherwell	h	3-1	18,000	Fraser 2; Boyd (pen)
15th	L	Clyde	h	2-3	19,000	Gunn; Boyd
22nd	L	Celtic	h	3-0	35,000	Rattray; Gerrie;Gunn
29th	L	Partick Thistle	a	3-2	20,000	Rattray 2; Andrews
Nov 5th	L	Raith Rovers	h	2-1	20,000	Gerrie 2
12th	L	QOS	a	1-1	6,000	Gunn
19th	L	Falkirk	h	2-0	13,000	Boyd (pen); Gerrie
26th	L	St Mirren	a	1-1	35,000	Gunn
Dec 3rd	L	Hibernian	h	1-2	28,000	Rattray
10th	L	East Fife	h	1-0	22,000	Gerrie
17th	L	Third Lanark	a	0-1	5,000	-
24th	L	Stirling Albion	h	4-1	13,000	Toner 2; Stewart; Gerrie
31st	L	Rangers	a	2-2	35,000	Toner; Stewart
Jan 2nd	L	Aberdeen	h	1-1	32,000	Gerrie
3rd	L	Motherwell	a	2-0	20,000	Gerrie; Hill
7th	L	Hearts	h	3-1	33,500	Gerrie 2; Gunn
14th	L	Clyde	a	0-1	11,000	-
21st	L	Celtic	a	0-2	15,000	-
28th	SC1	Hearts	a	1-1	39,568	Gerrie
Feb 4th	L	Partick Thistle	h	1-0	21,000	Cowie
6th	SC1R	Hearts	h	1-2**	29,000	Toner
25th	L	Falkirk	a	2-2	10,000	Fraser 2
Mar 4th	L	St Mirren	h	2-0	13,000	Fraser 2
11th	L	Hibernian	a	2-4	33,000	Gerrie 2
18th	L	East Fife	a	0-1	7,000	-
25th	L	Third Lanark	h	1-4	11,000	Ewen
29th	FC1	Arbroath	a	2-2	2,000	Pattillo; Beaton (pen)
Apr 5th	FC1R	Arbroath	h	3-3	3,000	Massie (pen); Fraser; Copland
8th	L	Raith Rovers	a	1-4	10,000	Boyd
12th	FC1R	Arbroath	h	2-1	4,000	Gerrie; Ewen
17th	L	Rangers	h	0-1	32,000	-
22nd	L	Hearts	a	2-6	22,000	Gerrie; Hill
May 3rd	FSF	Forfar Athletic	a	2-0	2,900	Andrews; Pattillo
13th	FCF	Brechin City	h	3-2 aet	3,500	Gerrie 2; Andrews

* 1948-49 Forfarshire Cup, Final on 23-08-50. ** aet, 1-1 after 90 mts.
Cup Cash v. Hearts (a) £2,695.

Jack Cowan - the Canadian left-back was another astute Dundee signing.

The Record		
League	-	Sixth Place, 'A' Division
League Cup	-	Qualifying Stages only
Scottish Cup	-	First round
Forfarshire Cup	-	Winners
Top Scorer	-	Jimmy Fraser (11 goals)
Av. Home Gate	-	22,000
Players used	-	25
Sent off	-	None

Appearances

	League		L/Cup		S/Cup		Total	
Alfie Boyd	29	(5)	6		2		37	(5)
Ally Gunn	27	(5)	5		2		34	(5)
Gerry Follon	24		6		2		32	
Syd Gerrie	25	(13)	4	(1)	2	(1)	31	(15)
Doug Cowie	22	(1)	6		1		29	(1)
Johnny Pattillo	21		5		2		28	
Johnny Lynch	20		4		2		26	
Jack Cowan	21		0		2		23	
Jimmy Fraser	21	(10)	2	(1)	0		23	(11)
Tommy Gallacher	16		6		1		23	
George Hill	17	(2)	5	(1)	0		22	(3)
Jimmy Andrews	15	(2)	0		2		17	(2)
Peter Rattray	15	(5)	2		0		17	(5)
Ernie Ewen	8	(1)	3	(2)	2		13	(3)
Jimmy Toner	10	(3)	0		2	(1)	12	(4)
Bill Brown	10		0		0		10	
Alan Massie	6		2		0		8	
Jimmy McIlhatton	5		2		0		7	
Bobby Ancell	6		0		0		6	
Andy Irvine	3		2		0		5	
Alec Stott	0		4	(3)	0		4	(3)
Jimmy Archibald	3		0		0		3	
George Stewart	4	(2)	0		0		4	(2)
Alec Beaton	2		0		0		2	
Jimmy Steadward	0		2		0		2	

Scottish League 'A' Division

		Home			Away			Goals		
	P	W	D	L	W	D	L	F A		PTS
Rangers	30	11	3	1	11	3	1	58-26		50
Hibernian	30	13	0	2	9	5	1	86-34		49
Hearts	30	12	1	2	8	2	5	86-40		43
East Fife	30	8	3	4	7	4	4	58-43		37
Celtic	30	11	4	0	3	3	9	51-50		35
Dundee	**30**	**10**	**1**	**4**	**2**	**6**	**7**	**49-46**		**31**
Partick Thistle	30	8	1	6	3	2	8	55-45		29
Aberdeen	30	7	2	6	4	2	9	48-56		26
Raith Rovers	30	7	4	4	2	4	9	45-54		26
Motherwell	30	6	3	6	4	2	9	53-58		25
St Mirren	30	6	4	5	2	5	8	42-49		25
Third Lanark	30	7	2	6	4	1	10	44-62		25
Clyde	30	6	3	6	4	1	10	56-73		24
Falkirk	30	3	7	5	4	3	8	48-72		24
QOS	30	5	5	5	0	1	14	33-63		16
Stirling Albion	30	4	2	9	2	1	12	38-77		15

League Cup Section

	P	W	D	L	F A	PTS
Partick Thistle	6	4	1	1	14-10	9
Motherwell	6	2	3	1	7- 6	7
Clyde	6	1	3	2	8- 9	5
Dundee	**6**	**1**	**1**	**4**	**8-12**	**3**

Dundee F.C. Line-Ups 1949-50

		1	2	3	4	5	6	7	8	9	10	11
Aug	13th	Lynch	Follon	Massie	Gallacher	Cowie	Boyd	McIlhatton	Ewen	Fraser	Gerrie	Hill
	17th	Lynch	Follon	Massie	Gallacher	Cowie	Boyd	Gunn	Pattillo	Stott	Ewen	Hill
	20th	Lynch	Follon	Irvine	Gallacher	Cowie	Boyd	Gunn	Pattillo	Stott	Gerrie	Hill
	27th	Lynch	Follon	Irvine	Gallacher	Cowie	Boyd	Gunn	Pattillo	Stott	Gerrie	Hill
	31st	Steadward	Follon	Boyd	Gallacher	Cowie	Rattray	Gunn	Pattillo	Stott	Gerrie	Hill
Sep	3rd	Steadward	Follon	Boyd	Gallacher	Cowie	Rattray	Gunn	Pattillo	Fraser	Ewen	McIlhatton
	10th	Lynch	Follon	Cowan	Gallacher	Cowie	Boyd	Gunn	Rattray	Fraser	Gerrie	Andrews
	17th	Lynch	Follon	Cowan	Gallacher	Cowie	Boyd	Gunn	Rattray	Fraser	Gerrie	Andrews
	24th	Lynch	Follon	Cowan	Gallacher	Cowie	Boyd	Gunn	Rattray	Fraser	Gerrie	Andrews
Oct	1st	Lynch	Follon	Cowan	Gallacher	Cowie	Boyd	Gunn	Rattray	Fraser	Gerrie	Andrews
	15th	Lynch	Follon	Cowan	Gallacher	Cowie	Boyd	Gunn	Rattray	Fraser	Ewen	Andrews
	22nd	Lynch	Follon	Cowan	Gallacher	Cowie	Boyd	Gunn	Rattray	Fraser	Gerrie	Andrews
	29th	Lynch	Follon	Cowan	Gallacher	Cowie	Boyd	Gunn	Rattray	Fraser	Gerrie	Andrews
Nov	5th	Lynch	Follon	Cowan	Gallacher	Boyd	Rattray	Gunn	Pattillo	Fraser	Gerrie	Andrews
	12th	Lynch	Follon	Cowan	Gallacher	Boyd	Rattray	Gunn	Pattillo	Fraser	Gerrie	Andrews
	19th	Lynch	Follon	Cowan	Gallacher	Boyd	Rattray	Gunn	Pattillo	Fraser	Gerrie	Andrews
	26th	Lynch	Follon	Cowan	Gallacher	Boyd	Rattray	Gunn	Pattillo	Fraser	Gerrie	Andrews
Dec	3rd	Lynch	Follon	Ancell	Gallacher	Boyd	Rattray	Gunn	Pattillo	Fraser	Gerrie	Hill
	10th	Lynch	Massie	Ancell	Gallacher	Pattillo	Irvine	Gunn	McIlhatton	Fraser	Gerrie	Hill
	17th	Lynch	Massie	Ancell	Follon	Boyd	Irvine	Gunn	McIlhatton	Fraser	Gerrie	Hill
	24th	Lynch	Massie	Ancell	Cowie	Pattillo	Boyd	Gunn	Toner	Stewart	Gerrie	Hill
	31st	Lynch	Massie	Ancell	Cowie	Pattillo	Boyd	Gunn	Toner	Stewart	Gerrie	Hill
Jan	2nd	Lynch	Massie	Ancell	Cowie	Pattillo	Boyd	Gunn	Toner	Stewart	Gerrie	Hill
	3rd	Lynch	Massie	Archibald	Cowie	Pattillo	Boyd	McIlhatton	Toner	Gerrie	Ewen	Hill
	7th	Lynch	Follon	Archibald	Cowie	Pattillo	Boyd	Gunn	Toner	Gerrie	Ewen	Andrews
	14th	Brown	Follon	Archibald	Cowie	Pattillo	Boyd	Hill	Toner	Gerrie	Ewen	Andrews
	21st	Lynch	Follon	Cowan	Cowie	Pattillo	Boyd	Gunn	Toner	Gerrie	Ewen	Hill
	28th	Lynch	Follon	Cowan	Cowie	Pattillo	Boyd	Gunn	Toner	Gerrie	Ewen	Andrews
Feb	4th	Brown	Follon	Cowan	Gallacher	Pattillo	Boyd	McIlhatton	Cowie	Fraser	Andrews	Hill
	6th	Lynch	Follon	Cowan	Gallacher	Pattillo	Boyd	Gunn	Toner	Gerrie	Ewen	Andrews
	25th	Brown	Follon	Cowan	Cowie	Pattillo	Boyd	Gunn	Toner	Fraser	Stewart	Hill
Mar	4th	Brown	Follon	Cowan	Cowie	Pattillo	Boyd	Gunn	Toner	Fraser	Irvine	Hill
	11th	Brown	Follon	Cowan	Cowie	Pattillo	Boyd	Gunn	Toner	Fraser	Gerrie	Hill
	18th	Brown	Follon	Cowan	Cowie	Pattillo	Boyd	Gunn	Beaton	Fraser	Gerrie	Hill
	25th	Brown	Follon	Cowan	Cowie	Pattillo	Boyd	Gunn	Beaton	Fraser	Ewen	McIlhatton
Apr	8th	Brown	Pattillo	Cowan	Rattray	Cowie	Boyd	Gunn	Fraser	Gerrie	Andrews	Hill
	17th	Brown	Follon	Cowan	Gallacher	Boyd	Rattray	Gunn	Pattillo	Gerrie	Ewen	Hill
	22nd	Brown	Follon	Cowan	Gallacher	Cowie	Boyd	Gunn	Rattray	Gerrie	Ewen	Hill

Reuben to the rescue - Dundee keeper Reuben Bennett grabs the ball from inrushing Hearts winger Bobby Flavell in the Scottish Cup quarter-final against Hearts at Tynecastle in 1949. Gerry Follon and Doug Cowie stand by.

D. Cowie Jnr.

Season 1950-51

Date		Opponents		Score	Crowd	Scorers
Aug 12th	LC	Hibernian	a	0-2	40,000	-
16th	LC	Falkirk	h	1-2	15,000	Follon
19th	LC	St Mirren	h	3-1	18,000	Gerrie; Rattray 2
23rd	FCF*	Arbroath	h	2-0	5,500	Gerrie 2
26th	LC	Hibernian	h	0-2**	25,500	-
30th	LC	Falkirk	a	2-1	9,000	Rattray; Gerrie
Sep 2nd	LC	St Mirren	a	1-3	12,000	Boyd
9th	L	Hearts	h	1-0	25,000	Gunn
16th	L	Rangers	a	0-0	35,000	-
23rd	L	Aberdeen	h	2-0	34,000	Steel; Toner
30th	L	Morton	a	3-2	15,000	Mitchell o.g.; Steel; Boyd (pen)
Oct 7th	L	Falkirk	h	2-0	24,000	Toner 2
14th	L	Clyde	a	1-2	25,000	Gunn
21st	L	Celtic	a	0-0	30,000	-
28th	L	Partick Thistle	h	3-2	25,000	Steel; Boyd; Gerrie
Nov 4th	L	Raith Rovers	a	1-0	19,000	Gerrie
11th	L	Motherwell	h	0-0	30,000	-
18th	L	Third Lanark	a	0-2	14,000	-
25th	L	St Mirren	h	5-0	20,000	Christie 2; Pattillo 2; Boyd (pen)
Dec 2nd	L	Hibernian	a	0-2	31,000	-
9th	L	East Fife	a	3-1	8,000	Williams; Hill; Pattillo
16th	L	Airdrie	h	3-0	13,000	Steel 2; Boyd (pen)
23rd	L	Hearts	a	1-1	18,000	Pattillo
30th	L	Rangers	h	2-0	37,400	Gunn; Ewen
Jan 1st	L	Aberdeen	a	0-1	30,000	-
2nd	L	Morton	h	2-1	35,000	Ziesing; Ewen
6th	L	Falkirk	a	1-2	10,000	Ziesing
20th	L	Celtic	h	3-1	28,000	Boyd 2 (1 pen); Ziesing
27th	SC1	Dundee United	h	2-2	38,000	Boyd (pen); Ewen
31st	SC1R	Dundee United	a	1-0	20,000	Steel
Feb 10th	SC2	St Johnstone	a	3-1	29,972	Boyd (pen); Christie; Ewen
17th	L	Motherwell	a	2-0	10,000	Copland; Shaw o.g.
24th	L	Third Lanark	h	2-1	20,000	Ewen; Andrews
Mar 3rd	L	St Mirren	a	2-2	10,000	Ewen; Irvine
10th	SCQ	Raith Rovers	h	1-2	40,920	Christie
17th	L	East Fife	h	2-4	15,000	Ewen; Williams
24th	L	Airdrie	a	0-2	10,000	-
31st	L	Clyde	h	1-1	9,000	Steel
Apr 2nd	L	Raith Rovers	h	2-0	15,000	Williams; Hill
7th	L	Hibernian	h	2-2	21,000	Hill; Steel
11th	FCS1	Montrose	h	5-1	1,500	Beaton (pen); Ewen; Williams 2; Andrews
21st	FCS2	Montrose	a	1-2 (6-3)	800	Beaton
28th	L	Partick Thistle	a	1-1	20,000	Andrews
May 19th	FCF	Dundee United	h	2-3	12,500	Gallacher; Ewen

* 1948-49 Forfarshire Cup Final. ** Abandoned after 68 mts and not replayed.
Cup Cash v. D. Utd (h) £2,850^; v. St Johns. £1,985; v. Raith £2,800^ (^ exc. stand + enclos.)

Billy Steel - the famous Scots international inspired Dundee to trophy success.

The Record

League	-	Third Place, 'A' Division
League Cup	-	Qualifying stages only
Scottish Cup	-	Quarter-final
Forfarshire Cup	-	Runners-up
Top Scorer	-	Alfie Boyd (8 goals)
Av. Home Gate	-	23,500
Players used	-	30
Sent off	-	None

Appearances

	League	L/Cup	S/Cup	Total
Alfie Boyd	28 (6)	5 (1)	4 (2)	37 (9)
Gerry Follon	27	4 (1)	4	35 (1)
Doug Cowie	25	5	4	34
Jack Cowan	25	5	3	33
Billy Steel	26 (7)	0	4 (1)	30 (8)
George Hill	15 (3)	4	3	22 (3)
Andy Irvine	18 (1)	0	4	22 (1)
Stan Williams	21 (3)	1	0	22 (3)
Johnny Lynch	19	0	2	21
Ernie Ewen	15 (5)	0	4 (2)	19 (7)
Tommy Gallacher	13	5	1	19
Johnny Pattillo	·13 (4)	3	1	17 (4)
George Christie	13 (2)	0	3 (2)	16 (4)
Jimmy Andrews	15 (2)	1	0	16 (2)
Bill Brown	11	0	2	13
Ally Gunn	13 (3)	0	0	13 (3)
Syd Gerrie	5 (2)	4 (2)	0	9 (4)
Jimmy Toner	8 (3)	0	0	8 (3)
Ernie Copland	5 (1)	1	1	7 (1)
Gordon Rennie	0	5	0	5
Ken Ziesing	3 (3)	0	2	5 (3)
Willie Craig	4	0	0	4
Gordon Frew	2	0	2	4
Jimmy McIlhatton	0	4	0	4
Alan Massie	2	1	0	3
Alec Beaton	2	0	0	2
Jimmy Fraser	0	2	0	2
Peter Rattray	0 (3)	2	0	2 (3)
Willie Roy	2	0	0	2
George Stewart	0	2	0	2

Scottish League 'A' Division

		Home			Away			Goals		
	P	W	D	L	W	D	L	F A	PTS
Hibernian	30	13	1	1	9	3	3	78-26	48
Rangers	30	10	3	2	7	1	7	64-37	38
Dundee	**30**	**11**	**3**	**1**	**4**	**5**	**6**	**47-30**	**38**
Hearts	30	10	3	2	6	2	7	72-45	37
Aberdeen	30	9	2	4	6	3	6	61-50	35
Partick Thistle	30	9	4	2	4	3	8	57-48	33
Celtic	30	6	3	6	6	2	7	48-46	29
Raith Rovers	30	8	2	5	5	0	10	52-52	28
Motherwell	30	7	3	5	4	3	8	58-65	28
East Fife	30	7	4	4	3	4	8	48-66	28
St Mirren	30	7	3	5	2	4	9	35-51	25
Morton	30	6	0	9	4	4	7	47-59	24
Third Lanark	30	7	1	7	4	1	10	40-51	24
Airdrie	30	6	3	6	4	1	10	52-67	24
Clyde	30	6	4	5	2	3	10	37-57	23
Falkirk	30	6	3	6	1	1	13	35-81	18

League Cup Section

	P	W	D	L	F A	PTS
Hibernian	5	5	0	0	22-4	10
St Mirren	6	2	1	3	7-16	5
Dundee	**5**	**2**	**0**	**3**	**8-10**	**4**
Falkirk	6	1	1	4	8-15	3

Dundee F.C. Line-Ups 1950-51

	1	2	3	4	5	6	7	8	9	10	11
Aug 12th	Rennie	Massie	Cowan	Gallacher	Cowie	Boyd	McIlhatton	Pattillo	Fraser	Gerrie	Andrews
16th	Rennie	Follon	Cowan	Gallacher	Cowie	Boyd	McIlhatton	Pattillo	Fraser	Gerrie	Hill
19th	Rennie	Follon	Cowan	Gallacher	Cowie	Boyd	McIlhatton	Rattray	Copland	Gerrie	Hill
26th*	Rennie	Follon	Cowan	Gallacher	Cowie	Boyd	McIlhatton	Rattray	Copland	Gerrie	Hill
30th	Rennie	Follon	Cowan	Gallacher	Cowie	Boyd	McIlhatton	Rattray	Stewart	Gerrie	Hill
Sep 2nd	Rennie	Follon	Cowan	Gallacher	Cowie	Boyd	Pattillo	Williams	Gerrie	Stewart	Hill
9th	Lynch	Follon	Cowan	Gallacher	Cowie	Boyd	Gunn	Toner	Williams	Gerrie	Andrews
16th	Brown	Follon	Cowan	Gallacher	Cowie	Boyd	Gunn	Toner	Williams	Gerrie	Andrews
23rd	Brown	Follon	Cowan	Gallacher	Cowie	Boyd	Gunn	Toner	Williams	Steel	Andrews
30th	Lynch	Follon	Cowan	Gallacher	Roy	Boyd	Gunn	Toner	Williams	Steel	Andrews
Oct 7th	Lynch	Follon	Cowan	Gallacher	Cowie	Boyd	Gunn	Toner	Williams	Steel	Andrews
14th	Lynch	Follon	Cowan	Gallacher	Cowie	Boyd	Gunn	Toner	Williams	Steel	Andrews
21st	Lynch	Follon	Cowan	Cowie	Boyd	Craig	Gunn	Toner	Williams	Gerrie	Andrews
28th	Lynch	Follon	Cowan	Craig	Cowie	Boyd	Williams	Ewen	Gerrie	Steel	Andrews
Nov 4th	Lynch	Follon	Cowan	Craig	Cowie	Boyd	Gunn	Ewen	Gerrie	Steel	Andrews
11th	Lynch	Follon	Cowan	Craig	Cowie	Boyd	Williams	Ewen	Copland	Steel	Andrews
18th	Lynch	Follon	Cowan	Pattillo	Roy	Boyd	Gunn	Toner	Copland	Steel	Christie
25th	Lynch	Follon	Cowan	Irvine	Cowie	Boyd	Hill	Pattillo	Williams	Steel	Christie
Dec 2nd	Lynch	Follon	Cowan	Irvine	Cowie	Boyd	Hill	Pattillo	Williams	Steel	Christie
9th	Lynch	Follon	Cowan	Irvine	Cowie	Boyd	Hill	Pattillo	Williams	Steel	Christie
16th	Lynch	Follon	Cowan	Irvine	Cowie	Boyd	Hill	Pattillo	Williams	Steel	Christie
23rd	Lynch	Follon	Cowan	Irvine	Cowie	Boyd	Gunn	Pattillo	Williams	Steel	Christie
30th	Lynch	Follon	Cowan	Irvine	Cowie	Boyd	Gunn	Ewen	Williams	Steel	Christie
Jan 1st	Lynch	Follon	Cowan	Irvine	Cowie	Boyd	Hill	Pattillo	Williams	Steel	Christie
2nd	Lynch	Follon	Cowan	Irvine	Cowie	Boyd	Gunn	Pattillo	Ziesing	Ewen	Christie
6th	Lynch	Follon	Cowan	Irvine	Cowie	Boyd	Gunn	Ewen	Ziesing	Steel	Christie
20th	Lynch	Frew	Cowan	Irvine	Cowie	Boyd	Hill	Ewen	Ziesing	Steel	Christie
27th	Lynch	Follon	Cowan	Irvine	Cowie	Boyd	Hill	Ewen	Pattillo	Steel	Christie
31st	Lynch	Frew	Cowan	Irvine	Cowie	Boyd	Follon	Ewen	Ziesing	Steel	Hill
Feb 10th	Brown	Frew	Cowan	Irvine	Cowie	Boyd	Follon	Ewen	Ziesing	Steel	Christie
17th	Brown	Follon	Cowan	Irvine	Cowie	Boyd	Hill	Ewen	Copland	Steel	Christie
24th	Brown	Follon	Cowan	Irvine	Cowie	Boyd	Hill	Ewen	Copland	Steel	Andrews
Mar 3rd	Brown	Follon	Cowan	Gallacher	Cowie	Irvine	Hill	Ewen	Copland	Steel	Boyd
10th	Brown	Follon	Irvine	Gallacher	Cowie	Boyd	Hill	Ewen	Copland	Steel	Christie
17th	Brown	Follon	Frew	Gallacher	Cowie	Irvine	Hill	Ewen	Williams	Steel	Christie
24th	Brown	Follon	Massie	Gallacher	Pattillo	Irvine	Hill	Beaton	Ewen	Steel	Boyd
31st	Brown	Irvine	Follon	Gallacher	Pattillo	Boyd	Hill	Ewen	Williams	Steel	Andrews
Apr 2nd	Brown	Irvine	Follon	Gallacher	Pattillo	Boyd	Hill	Beaton	Williams	Steel	Andrews
7th	Brown	Irvine	Boyd	Gallacher	Pattillo	Cowie	Hill	Ewen	Williams	Steel	Andrews
28th	Brown	Massie	Cowan	Gallacher	Pattillo	Cowie	Hill	Ewen	Williams	Steel	Andrews

* Not included in appearances

Gunn glory - Ally Gunn beats Jock Shaw to a Billy Steel cross to head past Bobby Brown in Dundee's 2-0 win over Rangers at Dens. Ibrox defenders Willie Woodburn and Ian McColl are helpless as Dundee's Stan Williams and Ernie Ewen look on.   DC Thomson

Season 1951-52

Date		Opponents		Score	Crowd	Scorers
Aug 11th	LC	St Mirren	a	2-2	12,000	Toner; Flavell
15th	LC	Hearts	h	2-1	22,500	Ziesing 2
18th	LC	Raith Rovers	h	5-0	21,000	Steel; Toner 3; Colville o.g.
25th	LC	St Mirren	h	0-1	21,000	-
29th	LC	Hearts	a	2-5	30,000	Toner; Ziesing
Sep 1st	LC	Raith Rovers	a	3-1	12,400	Christie 2; Williams
8th	L	Stirling Albion	a	2-2	11,000	Copland 2
15th	LCQ	Falkirk	a	0-0	12,000	-
20th	LCQ	Falkirk	h	2-1 (2-1)	20,000	Ziesing; Steel
22nd	L	Aberdeen	a	1-3	26,000	Irvine
29th	L	Rangers	h	1-0	31,000	Steel
Oct 6th	L	Hearts	a	2-4	40,000	Toner; Flavell
13th	LCS	Motherwell	Ibrox	5-1	25,000	Christie; Flavell 3; Pattillo
20th	L	Celtic	h	2-1	32,000	Christie; Pattillo
27th	LCF	Rangers	Hamp	3-2	92,325	Flavell; Pattillo; Boyd
Nov 3rd	L	Raith Rovers	h	2-0	21,000	Flavell 2
10th	L	Motherwell	a	1-2	7,000	Flavell
17th	L	QOS	h	0-0	15,000	-
24th	L	St Mirren	a	1-1	12,000	Flavell
Dec 1st	L	Hibernian	a	1-4	26,000	Ewen
8th	L	East Fife	h	3-4	23,000	Pattillo; Flavell 2
15th	L	Airdrie	a	3-4	9,000	Burrell; Steel; Flavell
22nd	L	Stirling Albion	h	4-1	17,000	Cowan; Boyd; Flavell; Henderson
25th	L	Partick Thistle	a	3-1	17,000	Henderson; Ziesing
29th	L	Third Lanark	a	2-0	8,000	Flavell; Steel
Jan 1st	L	Aberdeen	h	3-2	26,000	Pattillo; Hill; Flavell
2nd	L	Rangers	a	2-1	35,000	Steel; Christie
5th	L	Hearts	h	3-3	32,000	Henderson; Steel; Christie
12th	L	Morton	a	0-3	12,000	-
19th	L	Celtic	a	1-1	25,000	Steel
26th	SC1	Ayr United	h	4-0	20,000	Irvine 2; Pattillo; Steel
Feb 9th	SC2	Wigtown	a	7-1	4,500	Steel 2; Pattillo 2; Hill 2; Christie
13th	L	Raith Rovers	a	2-1	4,200	Toner; Ewen
16th	L	Motherwell	h	1-2	21,000	Williams
23rd	SC3	Berwick Rangers	h	1-0	15,000	Pattillo
27th	L	QOS	a	0-1	5,000	-
Mar 1st	L	St Mirren	h	3-0	12,000	Burrell; Henderson; Ziesing
8th	SCQ	Aberdeen	h	4-0	41,000	Ziesing; Steel 2; Boyd (pen)
15th	L	East Fife	a	1-3	12,000	Henderson
22nd	L	Airdrie	h	0-1	17,000	-
29th	SCS	Third Lanark	E.Rd	2-0	23,615	Burrell; Steel
Apr 2nd	L	Morton	h	2-2	7,500	Ziesing; Hill
9th	L	Hibernian	a	1-3	26,000	Christie
12th	L	Partick Thistle	h	0-2	16,000	-
19th	SCF	Motherwell	Hamp	0-4	136,990	-
26th	L	Third Lanark	h	6-0	10,500	Christie; Flavell 3; Henderson 2

Bobby Flavell - the ace scorer forged a great partnership with Billy Steel.

The Record

League	-	Eighth Place, 'A' Division
League Cup	-	Winners
Scottish Cup	-	Runners-up
Forfarshire Cup	-	Withdrew from Comp. until 1954-55
Top Scorer	-	Bobby Flavell (19 goals)
Av. Home Gate	-	20,500
Players used	-	26
Sent off	-	None

Appearances

	League		L/Cup		S/Cup		Total	
Alfie Boyd	26	(1)	10	(1)	6	(1)	42	(3)
Gerry Follon	24		10		6		40	
Doug Cowie	23		9		6		38	
George Christie	24	(5)	6	(3)	6	(1)	36	(9)
Tommy Gallacher	22		7		6		35	
Billy Steel	21	(6)	8	(2)	6	(6)	35	(14)
Jack Cowan	23	(1)	3		6		32	(1)
Bobby Flavell	21	(14)	8	(5)	3		32	(19)
Bobby Henderson (g)	14		5		6		25	
Johnny Pattillo	15	(3)	2	(2)	6	(4)	23	(9)
Bill Brown	16		5		0		21	
Jimmy Toner	11	(2)	9	(5)	0		20	(7)
Ken Ziesing	12	(3)	7	(4)	1	(1)	20	(8)
George Hill	12	(2)	1		4	(2)	17	(4)
Gordon Frew	9		7		0		16	
Gerry Burrell	12	(2)	0		2	(1)	14	(3)
Bert Henderson	11	(8)	0		0		11	(8)
Andy Irvine	7	(1)	3		2	(2)	12	(3)
George Merchant	11		0		0		11	
Stan Williams	7	(1)	3	(1)	0		10	(2)
Ernie Ewen	7	(2)	1		0		8	(2)
Jimmy Andrews	4		0		0		4	
Ernie Copland	1	(2)	1		0		2	(2)
Jimmy Fraser	1		0		0		1	
Bob Henderson (ch)	0		1		0		1	

Scottish League 'A' Division

		Home			Away			Goals		
	P	W	D	L	W	D	L	F	A	PTS
Hibernian	30	12	2	1	8	3	4	92-36		45
Rangers	30	10	4	1	6	5	4	61-31		41
East Fife	30	11	2	2	6	1	8	71-49		37
Hearts	30	9	5	1	5	2	8	69-53		35
Raith Rovers	30	9	2	4	5	3	7	43-42		33
Partick Thistle	30	7	3	5	5	4	6	40-51		31
Motherwell	30	8	4	3	4	3	8	51-57		31
Dundee	**30**	**7**	**3**	**5**	**4**	**3**	**8**	**53-52**		**28**
Celtic	30	7	5	3	3	3	9	52-55		28
QOS	30	10	3	2	0	5	10	50-60		28
Aberdeen	30	7	4	4	3	3	9	65-58		27
Third Lanark	30	7	3	5	2	5	8	51-62		26
Airdrie	30	7	3	5	4	1	10	54-69		26
St Mirren	30	9	2	4	1	3	11	43-58		25
Morton	30	7	1	7	2	5	8	49-56		24
Stirling Albion	30	4	4	7	1	1	13	36-99		15

League Cup Section

	P	W	D	L	F A	PTS
Dundee	**6**	**3**	**1**	**2**	**14-10**	**7**
Hearts	6	3	1	2	15-12	7
St Mirren	6	2	2	2	13-13	6
Raith Rovers	6	2	0	4	6-13	4

Dundee F.C. Line-Ups 1951-52

		1	2	3	4	5	6	7	8	9	10	11
Aug	11th	Henderson	Follon	Frew	Gallacher	Boyd	Cowie	Flavell	Toner	Ziesing	Steel	Andrews
	15th	Henderson	Follon	Cowan	Gallacher	Cowie	Boyd	Flavell	Toner	Ziesing	Steel	Andrews
	18th	Henderson	Follon	Frew	Gallacher	Cowie	Boyd	Flavell	Toner	Ziesing	Steel	Andrews
	25th	Henderson	Follon	Frew	Gallacher	Henderson B	Boyd	Flavell	Toner	Ziesing	Steel	Andrews
	29th	Henderson	Follon	Frew	Gallacher	Cowie	Boyd	Flavell	Toner	Ziesing	Steel	Christie
Sep	1st	Brown	Follon	Frew	Irvine	Cowie	Boyd	Ewen	Toner	Ziesing	Williams	Christie
	8th	Brown	Follon	Frew	Irvine	Cowie	Boyd	Flavell	Toner	Copland	Williams	Christie
	15th	Brown	Follon	Frew	Irvine	Cowie	Boyd	Flavell	Toner	Copland	Williams	Christie
	20th	Brown	Follon	Frew	Irvine	Cowie	Boyd	Hill	Williams	Ziesing	Steel	Christie
	22nd	Brown	Follon	Frew	Irvine	Cowie	Boyd	Flavell	Williams	Ziesing	Steel	Christie
	29th	Brown	Follon	Frew	Gallacher	Cowie	Boyd	Hill	Pattillo	Flavell	Steel	Christie
Oct	6th	Brown	Follon	Frew	Gallacher	Cowie	Boyd	Hill	Toner	Flavell	Ewen	Christie
	13th	Brown	Follon	Cowan	Gallacher	Cowie	Boyd	Toner	Pattillo	Flavell	Steel	Christie
	20th	Brown	Follon	Cowan	Gallacher	Merchant	Cowie	Toner	Pattillo	Flavell	Steel	Christie
	27th	Brown	Follon	Cowan	Gallacher	Cowie	Boyd	Toner	Pattillo	Flavell	Steel	Christie
Nov	3rd	Brown	Follon	Cowan	Gallacher	Cowie	Boyd	Toner	Pattillo	Flavell	Steel	Christie
	10th	Brown	Follon	Cowan	Gallacher	Cowie	Boyd	Toner	Pattillo	Flavell	Williams	Christie
	17th	Brown	Follon	Cowan	Gallacher	Cowie	Boyd	Toner	Pattillo	Flavell	Steel	Christie
	24th	Brown	Follon	Cowan	Gallacher	Cowie	Boyd	Toner	Pattillo	Flavell	Ewen	Christie
Dec	1st	Brown	Follon	Frew	Gallacher	Cowie	Boyd	Hill	Toner	Flavell	Ewen	Christie
	8th	Henderson	Frew	Cowan	Gallacher	Cowie	Boyd	Follon	Pattillo	Flavell	Ewen	Hill
	15th	Brown	Irvine	Cowan	Gallacher	Cowie	Boyd	Burrell	Ewen	Flavell	Steel	Christie
	22nd	Brown	Frew	Cowan	Gallacher	Merchant	Boyd	Burrell	Henderson A	Flavell	Steel	Christie
	25th	Henderson	Follon	Cowan	Gallacher	Merchant	Boyd	Burrell	Henderson A	Ziesing	Steel	Christie
	29th	Henderson	Follon	Cowan	Gallacher	Merchant	Boyd	Hill	Henderson A	Ziesing	Steel	Flavell
Jan	1st	Brown	Follon	Cowan	Gallacher	Merchant	Boyd	Hill	Pattillo	Flavell	Steel	Christie
	2nd	Brown	Follon	Cowan	Gallacher	Merchant	Boyd	Hill	Pattillo	Flavell	Steel	Christie
	5th	Brown	Follon	Cowan	Gallacher	Merchant	Boyd	Hill	Henderson A	Flavell	Steel	Christie
	12th	Henderson	Pattillo	Frew	Cowie	Merchant	Boyd	Hill	Henderson A	Ziesing	Steel	Christie
	19th	Brown	Pattillo	Frew	Gallacher	Cowie	Boyd	Burrell	Henderson A	Flavell	Steel	Hill
	26th	Henderson	Follon	Cowan	Gallacher	Cowie	Boyd	Hill	Pattillo	Irvine	Steel	Christie
Feb	9th	Henderson	Follon	Cowan	Gallacher	Cowie	Boyd	Hill	Pattillo	Irvine	Steel	Christie
	13th	Henderson	Follon	Cowan	Gallacher	Cowie	Irvine	Toner	Ewen	Williams	Steel	Christie
	16th	Henderson	Follon	Cowan	Gallacher	Cowie	Boyd	Hill	Toner	Williams	Steel	Christie
	23rd	Henderson	Follon	Cowan	Gallacher	Cowie	Boyd	Hill	Pattillo	Flavell	Steel	Christie
	27th	Henderson	Follon	Cowan	Cowie	Merchant	Irvine	Toner	Henderson A	Flavell	Ziesing	Burrell
Mar	1st	Henderson	Pattillo	Cowan	Cowie	Merchant	Irvine	Burrell	Ziesing	Henderson A	Steel	Williams
	8th	Henderson	Follon	Cowan	Gallacher	Cowie	Boyd	Burrell	Pattillo	Ziesing	Steel	Christie
	15th	Henderson	Follon	Cowan	Gallacher	Cowie	Boyd	Burrell	Henderson A	Ziesing	Williams	Christie
	22nd	Henderson	Follon	Cowan	Gallacher	Cowie	Boyd	Burrell	Henderson A	Ziesing	Steel	Christie
	29th	Henderson	Follon	Cowan	Gallacher	Cowie	Boyd	Burrell	Pattillo	Flavell	Steel	Christie
Apr	2nd	Henderson	Follon	Cowan	Irvine	Merchant	Boyd	Burrell	Pattillo	Ziesing	Ewen	Hill
	9th	Henderson	Follon	Cowan	Gallacher	Cowie	Boyd	Burrell	Ziesing	Flavell	Steel	Christie
	12th	Henderson	Follon	Cowan	Ziesing	Cowie	Boyd	Burrell	Pattillo	Fraser	Steel	Christie
	19th	Henderson	Follon	Cowan	Gallacher	Cowie	Boyd	Hill	Pattillo	Flavell	Steel	Christie
	26th	Henderson	Pattillo	Cowan	Ziesing	Boyd	Cowie	Burrell	Henderson A	Flavell	Steel	Christie

Souvenir - the match programme from the Dundee v. Rangers League Cup Final of October 1951.

Glory day - director-manager George Anderson joins the celebrations after Dundee's 3-2 League Cup triumph over Rangers at Hampden. From left - Pattillo, Cowan, Toner, Follon, Steel, Boyd (with cup), Gallacher, Flavell, Cowie, Christie, Smith (coach), Brown and Frew.

113

Season 1952-53

Date		Opponents		Score	Crowd	Scorers
Aug 9th	LC	Raith Rovers	h	2-1	20,000	Burrell; Christie
13th	LC	Airdrie	a	3-1	12,000	Flavell 3
16th	LC	Clyde	h	2-2	21,000	Flavell; Steel
23rd	LC	Raith Rovers	a	2-1	17,000	Steel 2
27th	LC	Airdrie	h	3-2	19,000	Flavell 2; Toner
30th	LC	Clyde	a	3-3	18,000	Christie; Boyd (pen); Toner
Sep 6th	L	Motherwell	h	0-0	24,000	-
13th	LCQ	Stirling Albion	a	1-3	8,000	Burrell
17th	LCQ	Stirling Albion	h	5-0 (6-3)	24,000	Flavell 2; Steel 2; Boyd (pen)
20th	L	Aberdeen	h	3-1	23,000	Flavell; Burrell; Harris o.g.
27th	L	Clyde	a	1-1	12,000	Christie
Oct 4th	LCS	Hibernian	Tync.	2-1	44,200	Steel; Flavell
11th	L	Raith Rovers	a	1-1	11,000	Henderson
18th	L	Hearts	h	2-1	21,000	Cowie; Henderson
25th	LCF	Kilmarnock	Hamp	2-0	51,000	Flavell 2
Nov 1st	L	East Fife	a	2-3	14,000	Flavell; Steel
8th	L	St Mirren	h	0-0	16,500	-
15th	L	Hibernian	a	0-3	25,000	-
22nd	L	Third Lanark	a	0-0	6,000	-
29th	L	Airdrie	h	0-2	13,000	-
Dec 6th	L	Partick Thistle	h	6-0	15,500	Flavell 2; Stables; Steel 3
13th	L	Celtic	a	0-5	25,000	-
20th	L	Motherwell	a	1-2	9,000	Flavell
27th	L	QOS	h	0-0	15,000	-
Jan 1st	L	Aberdeen	a	2-2	21,000	Flavell 2
3rd	L	Clyde	h	4-1	18,000	Burrell 2; Flavell; Hill
10th	L	Falkirk	a	1-2	8,000	Flavell
17th	L	Raith Rovers	h	2-3	22,500	Steel; Boyd (pen)
31st	L	Hearts	a	1-1	16,000	Henderson
Feb 7th	SC2	Rangers	h	0-2	43,024	-
14th	L	Rangers	h	1-1	24,000	Ziesing
21st	L	East Fife	h	1-1	23,000	Burrell
28th	L	St Mirren	a	0-0	14,000	-
Mar 7th	L	Hibernian	h	2-0	30,000	Flavell; Steel
14th	L	Falkirk	h	2-1	15,000	Boyd (pen); Steel
18th	L	Third Lanark	h	3-0	6,000	Boyd 2; Toner
21st	L	Airdrie	a	1-2	6,000	Flavell
28th	L	Partick Thistle	a	3-0	12,000	Henderson; Steel; Flavell
Apr 4th	L	Celtic	h	4-0	28,000	Flavell; Toner; Henderson 2
18th	L	QOS	a	0-1	10,000	-
May 2nd	L	Rangers	a	1-3	60,000	Gallacher

Cup Cash v. Rangers £3,270

Alfie Boyd - the Dundee skipper is on a high after Dundee's League Cup success over Kilmarnock.

Appearances

	League		L/Cup		S/Cup	Total	
Doug Cowie	29	(1)	9		1	39	(1)
Bobby Flavell	27	(14)	10	(11)	1	38	(25)
Jack Cowan	26		9		1	36	
Billy Steel	22	(8)	10	(6)	1	33	(14)
Ken Ziesing	23	(1)	10		0	33	(1)
Bobby Henderson (g)	22		10		0	32	
Alfie Boyd	22	(3)	8	(2)	1	31	(5)
Gerry Follon	22		7		1	30	
Tommy Gallacher	24	(1)	4		1	29	(1)
Bert Henderson	22	(6)	4		0	26	(6)
Jimmy Toner	16	(2)	8	(2)	1	25	(4)
George Christie	13	(1)	10	(2)	1	24	(3)
Gerry Burrell	14	(4)	5	(2)	1	20	(6)
Gordon Frew	10		4		0	14	
George Hill	10	(1)	0		0	10	(1)
Bill Brown	8		0		1	9	
Ian Stables	6	(1)	0		0	6	(1)
Andy Irvine	5		0		0	5	
George Merchant	3		2		0	5	
Bob Henderson (ch)	3		0		0	3	
Jack Johnsen	1		0		0	1	
Alan Massie	1		0		0	1	
Bert Walker	1		0		0	1	

The Record		
League	-	Seventh Place, 'A' Division
League Cup	-	Winners
Scottish Cup	-	Second round
Top Scorer	-	Bobby Flavell (25 goals)
Av. Home Gate	-	19,600
Players used	-	23
Sent off	-	None

Scottish League 'A' Division

		Home			Away			Goals		
	P	W	D	L	W	D	L	F A	PTS	
Rangers	30	12	1	2	6	6	3	80-39	43	
Hibernian	30	10	3	2	9	2	4	93-51	43	
East Fife	30	11	2	2	5	5	5	72-48	39	
Hearts	30	8	3	4	4	3	8	59-50	30	
Clyde	30	8	2	5	5	2	8	78-78	30	
St Mirren	30	6	6	3	5	2	8	52-58	30	
Dundee	**30**	**8**	**5**	**2**	**1**	**6**	**9**	**44-37**	**29**	
Celtic	30	7	3	5	4	4	7	51-54	29	
Partick Thistle	30	6	4	5	4	5	6	55-63	29	
QOS	30	8	3	4	2	5	8	43-61	28	
Aberdeen	30	8	5	2	3	0	12	64-68	27	
Raith Rovers	30	5	7	3	4	1	10	47-53	26	
Falkirk	30	7	1	7	4	3	8	53-63	26	
Airdrie	30	6	4	5	4	2	9	53-75	26	
Motherwell	30	7	2	6	3	3	9	57-80	25	
Third Lanark	30	6	2	7	2	2	11	52-75	20	

League Cup Section

	P	W	D	L	F A	PTS
Dundee	**6**	**4**	**2**	**0**	**14-10**	**10**
Clyde	6	1	3	2	15-15	5
Raith Rovers	6	2	1	3	9-14	5
Airdrie	6	1	2	4	9- 9	4

They Wore The Dark Blue

Dundee F.C. Line-Ups 1952-53

		1	2	3	4	5	6	7	8	9	10	11
Aug	9th	Henderson B	Frew	Cowan	Ziesing	Boyd	Cowie	Burrell	Toner	Flavell	Steel	Christie
	13th	Henderson B	Frew	Cowan	Ziesing	Merchant	Cowie	Burrell	Toner	Flavell	Steel	Christie
	16th	Henderson B	Frew	Cowan	Ziesing	Merchant	Cowie	Burrell	Toner	Flavell	Steel	Christie
	23rd	Henderson B	Follon	Cowan	Ziesing	Boyd	Cowie	Burrell	Gallacher	Flavell	Steel	Christie
	27th	Henderson B	Follon	Cowan	Ziesing	Boyd	Cowie	Toner	Gallacher	Flavell	Steel	Christie
	30th	Henderson B	Follon	Cowan	Ziesing	Boyd	Cowie	Toner	Gallacher	Flavell	Steel	Christie
Sep	6th	Henderson B	Follon	Cowan	Ziesing	Boyd	Cowie	Burrell	Toner	Flavell	Henderson A	Christie
	13th	Henderson B	Follon	Cowan	Gallacher	Boyd	Ziesing	Burrell	Henderson A	Flavell	Steel	Christie
	17th	Henderson B	Follon	Cowan	Ziesing	Boyd	Cowie	Toner	Henderson A	Flavell	Steel	Christie
	20th	Henderson B	Follon	Cowan	Ziesing	Boyd	Cowie	Toner	Henderson A	Flavell	Steel	Burrell
	27th	Henderson B	Follon	Cowan	Ziesing	Boyd	Cowie	Burrell	Gallacher	Flavell	Toner	Christie
Oct	4th	Henderson B	Follon	Cowan	Ziesing	Boyd	Cowie	Toner	Henderson A	Flavell	Steel	Christie
	11th	Henderson B	Follon	Cowan	Ziesing	Merchant	Cowie	Burrell	Henderson A	Flavell	Steel	Christie
	18th	Henderson B	Follon	Cowan	Ziesing	Boyd	Cowie	Toner	Gallacher	Flavell	Henderson A	Christie
	25th	Henderson B	Follon	Frew	Ziesing	Boyd	Cowie	Toner	Henderson A	Flavell	Steel	Christie
Nov	1st	Henderson B	Follon	Frew	Ziesing	Merchant	Cowie	Toner	Henderson A	Flavell	Steel	Hill
	8th	Henderson B	Frew	Cowan	Ziesing	Merchant	Cowie	Toner	Gallacher	Flavell	Steel	Christie
	15th	Henderson B	Follon	Cowan	Ziesing	Boyd	Cowie	Stables	Gallacher	Flavell	Steel	Christie
	22nd	Henderson B	Follon	Cowan	Ziesing	Boyd	Cowie	Stables	Gallacher	Henderson A	Steel	Christie
	29th	Henderson B	Follon	Cowan	Ziesing	Boyd	Cowie	Stables	Gallacher	Henderson A	Steel	Christie
Dec	6th	Henderson B	Follon	Cowan	Ziesing	Boyd	Cowie	Stables	Henderson A	Flavell	Steel	Christie
	13th	Henderson B	Follon	Cowan	Gallacher	Boyd	Cowie	Stables	Henderson A	Flavell	Steel	Christie
	20th	Henderson B	Follon	Massie	Ziesing	Henderson B	Cowie	Burrell	Henderson A	Flavell	Steel	Christie
	27th	Henderson B	Follon	Cowan	Cowie	Henderson B	Boyd	Stables	Galacher	Flavell	Steel	Burrell
Jan	1st	Henderson B	Follon	Cowan	Cowie	Henderson B	Boyd	Christie	Gallacher	Flavell	Steel	Burrell
	3rd	Henderson B	Frew	Cowan	Irvine	Boyd	Cowie	Burrell	Gallacher	Flavell	Henderson A	Hill
	10th	Henderson B	Follon	Cowan	Irvine	Boyd	Cowie	Burrell	Gallacher	Flavell	Henderson A	Hill
	17th	Henderson B	Follon	Cowan	Irvine	Boyd	Cowie	Toner	Gallacher	Johnson	Steel	Burrell
	31st	Brown	Follon	Cowan	Gallacher	Cowie	Boyd	Burrell	Henderson A	Flavell	Steel	Toner
Feb	7th	Brown	Follon	Cowan	Gallacher	Cowie	Boyd	Burrell	Toner	Flavell	Steel	Christie
	14th	Brown	Follon	Cowan	Gallacher	Cowie	Boyd	Toner	Henderson A	Ziesing	Steel	Flavell
	21st	Brown	Follon	Cowan	Gallacher	Cowie	Irvine	Burrell	Henderson A	Ziesing	Steel	Flavell
	28th	Henderson B	Follon	Cowan	Gallacher	Cowie	Boyd	Burrell	Henderson A	Ziesing	Steel	Flavell
Mar	7th	Brown	Frew	Cowan	Gallacher	Cowie	Ziesing	Hill	Henderson A	Flavell	Toner	Steel
	14th	Henderson	Frew	Boyd	Gallacher	Cowie	Ziesing	Hill	Henderson A	Flavell	Toner	Steel
	18th	Henderson	Frew	Cowan	Gallacher	Cowie	Boyd	Toner	Henderson A	Flavell	Ziesing	Hill
	21st	Brown	Frew	Cowan	Gallacher	Cowie	Boyd	Burrell	Toner	Flavell	Ziesing	Hill
	28th	Henderson	Follon	Boyd	Gallacher	Cowie	Ziesing	Toner	Henderson A	Flavell	Steel	Hill
Apr	4th	Brown	Follon	Cowan	Gallacher	Cowie	Ziesing	Toner	Henderson A	Flavell	Steel	Hill
	18th	Brown	Frew	Cowan	Gallacher	Irvine	Ziesing	Follon	Henderson A	Flavell	Hill	Toner
May	2nd	Brown	Follon	Cowan	Ziesing	Cowie	Boyd	Christie	Gallacher	Flavell	Steel	Walker

Heads you win - Jimmy Toner (right) watches left-half Doug Cowie beat team-mate Bobby Flavell (no 9) to a cross to head Dundee's opener against Hearts at Dens. The following week, Flavell netted twice in the League Cup triumph over Kilmarnock.

Season 1953-54

Date		Opponents		Score	Crowd	Scorers
Aug 8th	LC	Stirling Albion	h	6-1	21,000	Flavell 4; Steel 2
12th	LC	Clyde	a	4-2		Ziesing; Christie; Flavell; Turnbull
15th	LC	Partick Thistle	h	1-1	19,500	Turnbull
22nd	LC	Stirling Albion	a	2-0	11,000	Christie 2
26th	LC	Clyde	h	4-2	20,000	Turnbull 2 (1 pen); Christie; Steel
29th	LC	Partick Thistle	a	0-4	30,000	-
Sep 5th	L	Falkirk	a	0-4	15,000	-
12th	L	Raith Rovers	h	0-0	23,000	-
19th	L	Aberdeen	a	1-1	20,000	Flavell
26th	L	Clyde	h	2-0	18,000	Turnbull (pen); Steel
Oct 3rd	L	Hamilton	a	3-2	10,000	Turnbull 2; Carmichael
10th	L	QOS	h	4-1	22,000	Cowie; Christie; Turnbull; Steel
17th	L	Hearts	a	1-2	26,000	Flavell
24th	L	Rangers	h	1-0	34,000	Henderson
31st	L	Celtic	h	1-1	27,000	Cowie
Nov 7th	L	Partick Thistle	a	0-1	16,000	-
14th	L	Airdrie	a	2-2	9,000	Steel; Henderson
21st	L	Stirling Albion	h	2-1	15,000	Henderson; Turnbull
28th	L	Hibernian	h	1-0	26,000	Cowie
Dec 12th	L	East Fife	h	1-1	15,000	Henderson
19th	L	Falkirk	h	1-0	13,000	Henderson
26th	L	Raith Rovers	a	2-1	10,000	Toner 2
Jan 1st	L	Aberdeen	h	4-2	28,000	Toner 2; Steel; Malloy (pen)
2nd	L	Clyde	a	0-2	18,000	-
9th	L	Hamilton	h	3-2	14,000	Steel; Carmichael 2
16th	L	QOS	a	1-5	8,500	Merchant
23rd	L	Hearts	h	2-4	25,000	Cowie; Steel
Feb 6th	L	Rangers	a	0-2	30,000	-
13th	SC2	Albion Rovers	a	1-1	9,000	Merchant
17th	SC2R	Albion Rovers	h	4-0	12,256	Merchant 4 (1 pen)
20th	L	Celtic	a	1-5	32,000	Merchant
27th	SC3	Berwick Rangers	a	0-3	9,000	-
Mar 10th	L	Airdrie	h	1-0	5,500	Merchant
13th	L	Stirling Albion	a	3-2	7,000	Merchant; Christie; Henderson
20th	L	Hibernian	a	0-2	23,000	-
27th	L	St Mirren	h	2-0	10,000	Gallacher; Christie
Apr 3rd	l	East Fife	a	1-1	3,000	Merchant
10th	L	St Mirren	a	0-3	7,000	-
17th	L	Partick Thistle	h	6-0	11,000	Merchant; Henderson 3;

Cup Cash v. Albion Rovers (a) £660; (h) £993

Doug Cowie - the Scottish international half-back was a key man for Dundee.

The Record		
League	-	Seventh Place, 'A' Division
League Cup	-	Qualifying stages only
Scottish Cup	-	Third round
Top Scorer	-	George Merchant (11 goals)
Av. Home Gate	-	19,100
Players used	-	24
Sent off	-	None

Appearances

	League	L/Cup	S/Cup	Total
Doug Cowie	27 (4)	6	3	36 (4)
Billy Steel	25 (6)	6 (3)	2	33 (9)
Danny Malloy	29 (1)	0	3	32 (1)
Tommy Gallacher	22 (1)	6	3	31 (1)
George Christie	24 (3)	6 (4)	0	30 (7)
Bill Brown	20	6	3	29
Gordon Frew	23	2	3	28
Jack Cowan	20	4	1	25
Bert Henderson	21 (9)	2	0	23 (9)
George Hill	15 (1)	6	2	23 (1)
Ronnie Turnbull	16 (5)	6 (4)	1	23 (9)
Gerry Follon	10	6	3	19
Bobby Flavell	12 (2)	4 (5)	2	18 (7)
Ken Ziesing	7	6 (1)	3	16 (1)
George Merchant	10 (6)	0	3 (5)	13 (11)
George Carmichael	10 (3)	0	0	10 (3)
Bobby Henderson	10	0	0	10
Andy Irvine	8	0	1	9
Jackie Stewart	7	0	0	7
Jimmy Toner	6 (4)	0	0	6 (4)
Gerry Burrell	5	0	0	5
Archie Simpson	1	0	0	1
Willie Craig	1	0	0	1
Bert Walker	1 (1)	0	0	1 (1)

Scottish League 'A' Division

		Home			Away			Goals		
	P	W	D	L	W	D	L	F A		PTS
Celtic	30	14	1	0	6	2	7	72-29		43
Hearts	30	9	3	3	7	3	5	70-45		38
Partick Thistle	30	9	0	6	8	1	6	76-54		35
Rangers	30	9	4	2	4	4	7	56-35		34
Hibernian	30	9	1	5	6	3	6	72-51		34
East Fife	30	11	3	1	2	5	8	55-45		34
Dundee	**30**	**11**	**3**	**1**	**3**	**3**	**9**	**46-47**		**34**
Clyde	30	8	1	6	7	3	5	64-67		34
Aberdeen	30	10	2	3	5	1	9	66-51		33
Queen of the South	30	10	2	3	4	2	9	72-58		32
St Mirren	30	7	3	5	5	1	9	44-54		28
Raith Rovers	30	7	3	5	3	3	9	56-60		26
Falkirk	30	5	5	5	4	2	9	47-61		25
Stirling Albion	30	8	1	6	2	3	10	39-62		24
Airdrie	30	4	5	6	1	0	14	41-92		15
Hamilton	30	4	1	10	0	2	13	29-94		11

League Cup Section

	P	W	D	L	F A	PTS
Partick Thistle	6	4	1	1	15- 7	9
Dundee	**6**	**4**	**1**	**1**	**19-10**	**9**
Clyde	6	1	1	4	14-19	3
Stirling Albion	6	1	1	4	8-18	3

Dundee F.C. Line-Ups 1953-54

		1	2	3	4	5	6	7	8	9	10	11
Aug	8th	Brown	Follon	Cowan	Gallacher	Cowie	Ziesing	Hill	Turnbull	Flavell	Steel	Christie
	12th	Brown	Follon	Cowan	Gallacher	Cowie	Ziesing	Hill	Turnbull	Flavell	Steel	Christie
	15th	Brown	Follon	Cowan	Gallacher	Cowie	Ziesing	Hill	Turnbull	Flavell	Steel	Christie
	22nd	Brown	Follon	Cowan	Gallacher	Cowie	Ziesing	Hill	Turnbull	Flavell	Steel	Christie
	26th	Brown	Follon	Frew	Gallacher	Cowie	Ziesing	Hill	Turnbull	Henderson	Steel	Christie
	29th	Brown	Follon	Frew	Gallacher	Cowie	Ziesing	Hill	Turnbull	Henderson	Steel	Christie
Sep	5th	Brown	Follon	Frew	Gallacher	Cowie	Ziesing	Toner	Turnbull	Henderson	Steel	Christie
	12th	Henderson B	Frew	Cowan	Ziesing	Malloy	Cowie	Burrell	Henderson	Flavell	Steel	Christie
	19th	Henderson B	Frew	Cowan	Ziesing	Malloy	Cowie	Turnbull	Gallacher	Flavell	Steel	Hill
	26th	Henderson B	Frew	Cowan	Stewart J	Malloy	Cowie	Carmichael	Turnbull	Flavell	Steel	Christie
Oct	3rd	Henderson B	Frew	Cowan	Gallacher	Malloy	Stewart J	Carmichael	Turnbull	Flavell	Steel	Christie
	10th	Henderson B	Frew	Cowan	Stewart J	Malloy	Cowie	Carmichael	Turnbull	Flavell	Steel	Christie
	17th	Henderson B	Frew	Cowan	Stewart J	Malloy	Cowie	Carmichael	Turnbull	Flavell	Henderson	Christie
	24th	Brown	Frew	Cowan	Gallacher	Malloy	Cowie	Burrell	Henderson A	Turnbull	Steel	Christie
	31st	Brown	Frew	Cowan	Gallacher	Malloy	Cowie	Burrell	Henderson A	Turnbull	Steel	Christie
Nov	7th	Brown	Frew	Cowan	Gallacher	Malloy	Cowie	Burrell	Henderson A	Turnbull	Steel	Christie
	14th	Brown	Frew	Cowan	Stewart J	Malloy	Ziesing	Carmichael	Cowie	Henderson A	Steel	Burrell
	21st	Brown	Frew	Cowan	Stewart J	Malloy	Ziesing	Carmichael	Henderson A	Turnbull	Cowie	Christie
	28th	Brown	Frew	Cowan	Gallacher	Malloy	Cowie	Hill	Turnbull	Flavell	Henderson A	Christie
Dec	12th	Brown	Frew	Cowan	Gallacher	Malloy	Irvine	Hill	Turnbull	Flavell	Henderson A	Christie
	19th	Henderson B	Frew	Cowan	Gallacher	Malloy	Cowie	Hill	Turnbull	Flavell	Henderson A	Christie
	26th	Brown	Frew	Cowan	Gallacher	Malloy	Cowie	Hill	Toner	Henderson A	Steel	Christie
Jan	1st	Brown	Frew	Cowan	Gallacher	Malloy	Cowie	Hill	Toner	Henderson A	Steel	Christie
	2nd	Brown	Frew	Cowan	Gallacher	Malloy	Cowie	Hill	Simpson	Henderson A	Steel	Christie
	9th	Brown	Frew	Cowan	Gallacher	Malloy	Cowie	Carmichael	Toner	Turnbull	Steel	Christie
	16th	Henderson B	Frew	Cowan	Stewart J	Malloy	Cowie	Flavell	Turnbull	Merchant	Steel	Carmichael
	23rd	Henderson B	Frew	Cowan	Gallacher	Malloy	Cowie	Carmichael	Toner	Turnbull	Steel	Flavell
Feb	6th	Henderson B	Follon	Frew	Ziesing	Malloy	Cowie	Hill	Toner	Merchant	Steel	Christie
	13th	Brown	Follon	Frew	Gallacher	Malloy	Ziesing	Hill	Turnbull	Merchant	Cowie	Flavell
	17th	Brown	Follon	Frew	Ziesing	Malloy	Cowie	Hill	Gallacher	Merchant	Steel	Flavell
	20th	Brown	Follon	Frew	Ziesing	Malloy	Cowie	Carmichael	Gallacher	Merchant	Steel	Flavell
	27th	Brown	Frew	Cowan	Gallacher	Malloy	Cowie	Follon	Irvine	Merchant	Ziesing	Steel
Mar	10th	Brown	Follon	Irvine	Gallacher	Malloy	Craig	Hill	Henderson A	Merchant	Steel	Christie
	13th	Brown	Follon	Irvine	Gallacher	Malloy	Cowie	Hill	Henderson A	Merchant	Steel	Christie
	20th	Brown	Follon	Irvine	Gallacher	Malloy	Cowie	Hill	Henderson A	Merchant	Steel	Christie
	27th	Brown	Follon	Irvine	Gallacher	Malloy	Cowie	Hill	Henderson A	Merchant	Steel	Christie
Apr	3rd	Brown	Follon	Irvine	Gallacher	Malloy	Cowie	Hill	Henderson A	Merchant	Steel	Christie
	10th	Brown	Follon	Irvine	Gallacher	Malloy	Cowie	Hill	Henderson A	Merchant	Steel	Christie
	17th	Brown	Follon	Irvine	Gallacher	Malloy	Cowie	Hill	Henderson A	Merchant	Steel	Walker

Dundee F.C. Season 1953-54. (BACK, left to right) Tommy Gallacher, Gordon Frew, Jackie Stewart, Bobby Henderson, Danny Malloy, Doug Cowie, Jack Cowan, Reggie Smith (trainer). FRONT - George Carmichael, Ronnie Turnbull, Bobby Flavell, Billy Steel and George Christie.

Season 1954-55

Date		Opponents		Score	Crowd	Scorers
Aug 14th	LC	Hearts	a	1-3	30,000	Hill
18th	LC	Celtic	h	3-1	29,000	Merchant; Henderson; Roy
21st	LC	Falkirk	h	3-1	16,500	Merchant 3
28th	LC	Hearts	h	4-1	29,500	Merchant; Roy 2; Gallacher
Sep 1st	LC	Celtic	a	1-0	30,000	Malloy
4th	LC	Falkirk	a	0-4	15,000	-
11th	L	Raith Rovers	a	0-3	14,000	-
18th	L	Aberdeen	h	0-2	21,000	-
25th	L	Kilmarnock	a	2-0	15,000	Walker; Henderson
Oct 2nd	L	Hearts	h	3-2	20,000	Dunsmuir; Malloy (pen); Henderson
9th	L	Clyde	a	0-2	11,000	-
16th	L	Falkirk	h	2-0	18,500	Henderson; Walker
23rd	L	Rangers	a	0-3	30,000	-
30th	L	QOS	h	3-1	13,500	Carmichael; Dunsmuir; Flavell
Nov 6th	L	East Fife	a	1-4	9,000	Flavell
13th	L	St Mirren	h	0-1	12,500	-
20th	L	Hibernian	a	1-3	30,000	Roy
27th	L	Stirling Albion	a	2-0	4,000	Merchant; Henderson
Dec 4th	L	Motherwell	h	4-1	14,000	Malloy (pen); Merchant 3
11th	L	Partick Thistle	h	3-1	16,000	Carmichael 2; Merchant
18th	L	Celtic	a	1-4	14,000	Merchant
25th	L	Raith Rovers	h	4-1	13,000	Merchant 2; Henderson; Christie
Jan 1st	L	Aberdeen	a	0-1	25,000	-
3rd	L	Kilmarnock	h	2-5	17,000	Cowie; Merchant
8th	L	Hearts	a	1-2	20,000	Christie
29th	L	Rangers	h	2-1	25,000	Christie; Merchant
Feb 5th	SC5	Rangers	a	0-0	58,000	-
9th	SC5R	Rangers	h	0-1	25,600	-
12th	L	QOS	a	1-1	6,500	Chalmers
Mar 5th	L	St Mirren	a	2-0	12,000	Dunsmuir; Henderson
7th	FCS	Forfar Athletic	h	1-0		Roy
9th	L	East Fife	h	1-1	7,000	Dunsmuir
12th	L	Hibernian	h	2-2	18,000	Merchant; Christie
19th	L	Stirling Albion	h	4-1	8,000	Chalmers 3; Malloy (pen)
26th	L	Motherwell	a	2-0	9,000	Henderson 2
Apr 2nd	L	Partick Thistle	a	1-2	9,000	Chalmers
9th	L	Celtic	h	0-1	23,000	-
11th	L	Clyde	h	2-1	12,010	Cowie; Chalmers
30th	L	Falkirk	a	2-2	12,000	Henderson; Christie

Cup Cash v. Rangers (h) £1,960

Bill Brown - the Dundee keeper went on to became a regular for Scotland.

Appearances

	League	L/Cup	S/Cup	Total
Danny Malloy	30 (3)	6 (1)	2	38 (4)
Bert Henderson	29 (9)	6 (1)	2	37 (10)
Bill Brown	28	6	2	36
Tommy Gallacher	27	6 (1)	2	35 (1)
Andy Irvine	28	6	0	34
George Christie	22 (5)	4	2	28 (5)
Doug Cowie	26 (2)	0	2	28 (2)
George Merchant	18 (11)	3 (5)	2	23 (16)
Joe Roy	15 (1)	6 (3)	2	23 (4)
Davie Gray	12	6	2	20
Gerry Follon	17	1	0	18
Willie Craig	8	5	2	15
George Hill	10	6 (1)	0	16 (1)
Jimmy Chalmers	12 (6)	0	2	14 (6)
Davie Dunsmuir	14 (4)	0	0	14 (4)
George Carmichael	11 (3)	0	0	11 (3)
Bobby Flavell	8 (2)	2	0	10 (2)
Bert Walker	7 (2)	1	0	8 (2)
Davie Easson	1	2	0	3
Bobby Henderson	2	0	0	2
Alan Massie	1	0	0	1
Jimmy Mason	1	0	0	1
Hugh Reid	1	0	0	1
Dave Sneddon	1	0	0	1
Jake Young	1	0	0	1

The Record		
League	-	Eighth Place, 'A' Division
League Cup	-	Qualifying stages only
Scottish Cup	-	Fifth round
Forfarshire Cup	-	Winners (Final on 30-05-56)
Top Scorer	-	George Merchant (16 goals)
Av. Home Gate	-	15,900
Players used	-	20
Sent off	-	One

Scottish League 'A' Division

		Home			Away			Goals	
	P	W	D	L	W	D	L	F A	PTS
Aberdeen	30	14	0	1	10	1	4	73-26	49
Celtic	30	10	4	1	9	4	2	76-37	46
Rangers	30	13	2	0	6	1	8	67-33	41
Hearts	30	10	2	3	6	5	4	74-45	39
Hibernian	30	8	2	5	7	2	6	64-54	34
St Mirren	30	8	3	4	4	5	6	55-54	32
Clyde	30	6	7	2	5	3	7	59-50	31
Dundee	**30**	**9**	**2**	**4**	**4**	**2**	**9**	**48-48**	**30**
Partick Thistle	30	5	5	5	6	2	7	49-61	29
Kilmarnock	30	5	3	7	5	3	7	46-58	26
East Fife	30	6	1	8	3	5	7	51-62	24
Falkirk	30	6	6	3	2	2	11	42-54	24
Queen of the South	30	7	2	6	2	4	9	38-56	24
Raith Rovers	30	9	1	5	1	2	12	49-57	23
Motherwell	30	5	2	8	4	2	9	42-62	22
Stirling Albion	30	2	1	12	0	1	14	29-105	6

League Cup Section

	P	W	D	L	F A	PTS
Hearts	6	5	0	1	19-11	10
Dundee	**6**	**4**	**0**	**2**	**12-10**	**8**
Celtic	6	1	1	4	9-11	3
Falkirk	6	1	1	4	10-18	3

Dundee F.C. Line-Ups 1954-55

		1	2	3	4	5	6	7	8	9	10	11
Aug	14th	Brown	Follon	Gray D	Gallacher	Malloy	Irvine	Walker	Henderson A	Flavell	Roy	Hill
	18th	Brown	Gray D	Irvine	Gallacher	Malloy	Craig	Christie	Henderson A	Merchant	Roy	Hill
	21st	Brown	Gray D	Irvine	Gallacher	Malloy	Craig	Christie	Henderson A	Merchant	Roy	Hill
	28th	Brown	Gray D	Irvine	Gallacher	Malloy	Craig	Christie	Henderson A	Merchant	Roy	Hill
Sep	1st	Brown	Gray D	Irvine	Gallacher	Malloy	Craig	Christie	Easson	Henderson A	Roy	Hill
	4th	Brown	Gray D	Irvine	Gallacher	Malloy	Craig	Flavell	Easson	Henderson A	Roy	Hill
	11th	Brown	Gray D	Irvine	Gallacher	Malloy	Craig	Hill	Henderson A	Massie	Roy	Christie
	18th	Henderson B	Follon	Irvine	Gallacher	Malloy	Craig	Christie	Easson	Henderson A	Roy	Hill
	25th	Brown	Follon	Irvine	Gallacher	Malloy	Cowie	Walker	Henderson A	Flavell	Dunsmuir	Hill
Oct	2nd	Brown	Follon	Irvine	Gallacher	Malloy	Cowie	Walker	Henderson A	Flavell	Dunsmuir	Hill
	9th	Brown	Follon	Irvine	Gallacher	Malloy	Cowie	Walker	Henderson A	Flavell	Dunsmuir	Hill
	16th	Brown	Follon	Irvine	Gallacher*	Malloy	Craig	Walker	Henderson A	Flavell	Dunsmuir	Hill
	23rd	Brown	Follon	Irvine	Gallacher	Malloy	Cowie	Walker	Henderson A	Flavell	Dunsmuir	Hill
	30th	Henderson B	Follon	Irvine	Craig	Malloy	Cowie	Carmichael	Henderson A	Flavell	Dunsmuir	Christie
Nov	6th	Brown	Follon	Irvine	Craig	Malloy	Cowie	Carmichael	Henderson A	Flavell	Dunsmuir	Christie
	13th	Brown	Follon	Irvine	Gallacher	Malloy	Cowie	Carmichael	Henderson A	Flavell	Dunsmuir	Christie
	20th	Brown	Follon	Irvine	Gallacher	Malloy	Cowie	Carmichael	Henderson A	Merchant	Roy	Hill
	27th	Brown	Follon	Irvine	Gallacher	Malloy	Cowie	Carmichael	Henderson A	Merchant	Roy	Hill
Dec	4th	Brown	Follon	Irvine	Gallacher	Malloy	Cowie	Carmichael	Henderson A	Merchant	Roy	Hill
	11th	Brown	Follon	Irvine	Gallacher	Malloy	Cowie	Carmichael	Henderson A	Merchant	Roy	Christie
	18th	Brown	Follon	Irvine	Gallacher	Malloy	Cowie	Carmichael	Henderson A	Merchant	Roy	Christie
	25th	Brown	Follon	Irvine	Craig	Malloy	Cowie	Carmichael	Henderson A	Merchant	Roy	Christie
Jan	1st	Brown	Follon	Irvine	Gallacher	Malloy	Cowie	Carmichael	Henderson A	Merchant	Roy	Christie
	3rd	Brown	Follon	Irvine	Gallacher	Malloy	Cowie	Carmichael	Henderson A	Merchant	Roy	Christie
	8th	Brown	Gray	Craig	Gallacher	Malloy	Cowie	Walker	Chalmers	Merchant	Dunsmuir	Christie
	29th	Brown	Gray	Craig	Gallacher	Malloy	Cowie	Chalmers	Henderson A	Merchant	Roy	Christie
Feb	5th	Brown	Gray	Craig	Gallacher	Malloy	Cowie	Chalmers	Henderson A	Merchant	Roy	Christie
	9th	Brown	Gray	Craig	Gallacher	Malloy	Cowie	Chalmers	Henderson A	Merchant	Roy	Christie
	12th	Brown	Gray	Irvine	Gallacher	Malloy	Cowie	Chalmers	Henderson A	Merchant	Dunsmuir	Christie
Mar	5th	Brown	Gray	Irvine	Gallacher	Malloy	Cowie	Chalmers	Henderson A	Merchant	Dunsmuir	Christie
	9th	Brown	Gray	Irvine	Gallacher	Malloy	Cowie	Chalmers	Henderson A	Merchant	Dunsmuir	Christie
	12th	Brown	Gray	Irvine	Gallacher	Malloy	Cowie	Chalmers	Henderson A	Merchant	Dunsmuir	Christie
	19th	Brown	Reid	Irvine	Gallacher	Malloy	Cowie	Chalmers	Henderson A	Merchant	Sneddon	Christie
	26th	Brown	Gray	Irvine	Gallacher	Malloy	Cowie	Chalmers	Roy	Merchant	Henderson A	Christie
Apr	2nd	Brown	Gray	Young	Gallacher	Malloy	Irvine	Chalmers	Roy	Merchant	Henderson A	Christie
	9th	Brown	Gray	Irvine	Gallacher	Malloy	Cowie	Walker	Roy	Chalmers	Henderson A	Christie
	11th	Brown	Gray	Irvine	Gallacher	Malloy	Cowie	Chalmers	Dunsmuir	Mason	Henderson A	Christie
	30th	Brown	Gray	Irvine	Gallacher	Malloy	Cowie	Chalmers	Roy	Merchant	Henderson A	Christie

Spot the ball - Dundee's Jimmy Toner, Doug Cowie, Bert Henderson and George Christie and Willie Redpath and Charlie Cox of Motherwell all appear baffled as to the whereabouts of the ball in this match at Dens in 1952.

D. Cowie Jnr.

119

Season 1955-56

Date		Opponents		Score	Crowd	Scorers
Aug 13th	LC	Airdrie	a	0-4		-
17th	LC	Kilmarnock	h	1-2	16,000	Anderson
20th	LC	St Mirren	h	2-0	16,000	Chalmers; Henderson
27th	LC	Airdrie	h	2-2	15,000	Chalmers; McIvor
31st	LC	Kilmarnock	a	0-0	15,000	
Sep 3rd	LC	St Mirren	a	3-0	15,000	Roy; Ritchie 2
10th	L	Hearts	a	0-4	26,000	-
17th	L	Dunfermline	h	3-0	11,000	Henderson; Ritchie 2
24th	L	Aberdeen	a	0-2	20,000	-
Oct 1st	L	Clyde	h	2-1	13,000	Chalmers; Malloy (pen)
8th	L	Dunfermline	a	1-2	7,000	Gallacher
15th	L	Raith Rovers	h	6-3	13,000	Smith 4; Malloy (pen); Chalmers
22nd	L	Kilmarnock	a	0-0	12,000	-
29th	L	Falkirk	h	0-0	11,000	-
Nov 5th	L	Airdrie	a	3-3	8,000	Ritchie 2; Anderson
12th	L	Celtic	h	1-2	24,000	Malloy (pen)
19th	L	Partick Thistle	a	2-1	12,000	Smith; Ritchie
26th	L	East Fife	h	1-0	12,500	Smith
Dec 3rd	L	QOS	h	3-0	10,000	Stables 2; Smith
10th	L	Hibernian	a	3-6	7,000	Merchant; Smith; Christie
17th	L	St Mirren	h	5-1	8,000	Stables; Smith; Merchant 2; Christie
24th	L	Stirling Albion	a	0-0	5,000	-
31st	L	Motherwell	h	2-1	13,000	Henderson; Stables
Jan 2nd	L	Aberdeen	h	2-4	29,000	Christie; Merchant
7th	L	Rangers	a	1-3		Ritchie
14th	L	Hearts	h	0-2	17,000	
21st	L	Clyde	a	1-4	6,000	Christie
Feb 4th	SC5	Dundee United	a	2-2	20,000	Stables; Merchant
8th	SC5R	Dundee United	h	3-0	17,000	Merchant; Stables; Henderson
11th	L	Raith Rovers	a	1-1		O'Hara
18th	SC6	Rangers	h	0-1	42,500	
25th	L	Kilmarnock	h	1-1	11,000	Henderson
Mar 3rd	L	Falkirk	a	1-3	10,000	Stables
10th	L	Airdrie	h	1-3	11,000	O'Hara
17th	L	Celtic	a	0-1	25,000	
24th	L	Partick Thistle	h	3-0	7,500	Merchant; Gallacher 2
31st	L	East Fife	a	4-5	6,000	Merchant 3; O'Hara
Apr 2nd	L	Rangers	h	0-3	18,500	-
7th	L	QOS	a	1-2	5,500	Merchant
13th	L	Stirling Albion	h	2-1	4,000	Merchant (pen); O'Hara
21st	L	St Mirren	a	1-3	7,000	Christie
24th	L	Hibernian	h	3-2	10,000	Merchant 2; Christie
25th	FC1	Forfar Athletic	a	4-2	2,000	Birse 2; O'Hara; Christie
28th	L	Motherwell	h	2-1	8,000	Cousin; O'Hara
May 5th	FCS	Dundee United	h	2-1	6,000	Chalmers; Birse
12th	FCF	Arbroath	h	2-0	4,500	Merchant 2 (1 pen)
30th	FCF*	Montrose	h	6-0	1,500	Merchant 4; Stables 2

Appearances

* 1954-55 Final; Cup Cash v. Dundee Utd. (h) £1,850

	League		L/Cup	S/Cup	Total	
Andy Irvine	32		6	3	41	
George Christie	31	(6)	6	3	40	(6)
Bill Brown	30		6	1	37	
Gordon Black	32		1	3	36	
Doug Cowie	27		6	3	36	
Bert Henderson	21	(3)	6 (1)	3 (1)	30	(5)
Hugh Reid	27		1	1	29	
Tommy Gallacher	18	(3)	5	3	26	(3)
George Merchant	20	(12)	1	3 (2)	24	(14)
Ian Stables	20	(5)	0	3 (2)	23	(7)
Jimmy Chalmers	13	(2)	6 (2)	0	19	(4)
Danny Malloy	13	(3)	5	0	18	(3)
Ivor Smith	15	(9)	1	0	16	(9)
Davie Gray	8		5	2	15	
George O'Hara	12	(5)	0	1	13	(5)
Billy Ritchie	12	(6)	1 (2)	0	13	(8)
Jimmy Stevenson	10		0	0	10	
Willie Craig	7		1	0	8	
Joe Roy	4		1 (1)	2	7	(1)
Alan Cousin	6	(1)	0	0	6	(1)
Bobby Henderson	4		0	2	6	
Arthur McIvor	3		3 (1)	0	6	(1)
Johnny Anderson	3	(1)	2 (1)	0	5	(2)
Davie Dunsmuir	0		3	0	3	
Billy Birse	2		0	0	2	
George Carmichael	1		0	0	1	
Dave Easson	1		0	0	1	
Dave Sneddon	1		0	0	1	
Jim Watt	1		0	0	1	

Jimmy Chalmers - brought power and pace to Dundee's front line.

The Record

League	-	13th Place, Division One
League Cup	-	Qualifying stages only
Scottish Cup	-	Fifth round
Forfarshire Cup	-	Winners
Top Scorer	-	George Merchant (14 goals)
Av. Home Gate	-	13,100
Players used	-	29
Sent off	-	None

Scottish League Division One

		Home			Away			Goals		
	P	W	D	L	W	D	L	F	A	PTS
Rangers	34	12	4	1	10	4	3	88-27		52
Aberdeen	34	11	3	3	7	7	3	87-50		46
Hearts	34	13	2	2	6	5	6	99-47		45
Hibernian	34	11	4	2	8	3	6	86-50		45
Celtic	34	9	4	4	7	5	5	55-39		41
Queen of the South	34	12	2	3	4	3	10	69-73		37
Airdrie	34	8	4	5	6	4	7	85-96		36
Kilmarnock	34	7	6	4	5	4	8	52-45		34
Partick Thistle	34	8	4	5	5	3	9	62-60		33
Motherwell	34	7	6	4	4	5	8	53-59		33
Raith Rovers	34	6	7	4	6	2	9	58-75		33
East Fife	34	11	3	3	2	2	13	60-69		31
Dundee	**34**	**10**	**2**	**5**	**2**	**4**	**11**	**56-65**		**30**
Falkirk	34	9	2	6	2	4	11	58-75		28
St Mirren	34	9	2	6	1	5	11	57-70		27
Dunfermline	34	6	4	7	4	2	11	42-82		26
Clyde	34	2	4	11	6	2	9	50-74		22
Stirling Albion	34	4	3	10	0	2	15	23-82		13

League Cup Section

	P	W	D	L	F	A	PTS
St Mirren	6	3	1	2	10	-9	7
Kilmarnock	6	2	3	1	7	-7	7
Dundee	**6**	**2**	**2**	**2**	**8**	**-8**	**6**
Airdrie	6	1	2	3	13	-14	4

Dundee F.C. Line-Ups 1955-56

		1	2	3	4	5	6	7	8	9	10	11
Aug	13th	Brown	Gray	Irvine	Gallacher	Cowie	Craig	Chalmers	Anderson	Henderson A	Smith	Christie
	17th	Brown	Gray	Irvine	Gallacher	Malloy	Cowie	Chalmers	Anderson	Merchant	Henderson A	Christie
	20th	Brown	Gray	Irvine	Gallacher	Malloy	Cowie	McIvor	Dunsmuir	Chalmers	Henderson A	Christie
	27th	Brown	Gray	Irvine	Black	Malloy	Cowie	McIvor	Dunsmuir	Chalmers	Henderson A	Christie
	31st	Brown	Gray	Irvine	Gallacher	Malloy	Cowie	Chalmers	Dunsmuir	McIvor	Henderson A	Christie
Sep	3rd	Brown	Reid	Irvine	Gallacher	Malloy	Cowie	Chalmers	Roy	Ritchie	Henderson A	Christie
	10th	Brown	Gray	Craig	Gallacher	Malloy	Cowie	Chalmers	Roy	Ritchie	Henderson A	Christie
	17th	Brown	Reid	Irvine	Black	Malloy	Cowie	McIvor	Roy	Ritchie	Henderson A	Christie
	24th	Brown	Reid	Irvine	Black	Malloy	Cowie	Chalmers	Roy	Easson	Henderson A	Christie
Oct	1st	Brown	Reid	Irvine	Black	Malloy	Cowie	Christie	Gallacher	Chalmers	Smith	McIvor
	8th	Brown	Reid	Irvine	Black	Malloy	Craig	Carmichael	Gallacher	Chalmers	Henderson A	Christie
	15th	Brown	Reid	Irvine	Black	Malloy	Craig	Chalmers	Gallacher	Ritchie	Smith	Christie
	22nd	Brown	Reid	Irvine	Black	Malloy	Craig	Chalmers	Gallacher	Ritchie	Smith	Christie
	29th	Brown	Reid	Irvine	Black	Malloy	Craig	McIvor	Gallacher	Ritchie	Henderson A	Christie
Nov	5th	Brown	Reid	Irvine	Black	Malloy	Cowie	Chalmers	Anderson	Ritchie	Smith	Christie
	12th	Brown	Reid	Irvine	Black	Malloy	Cowie	Chalmers	Stables	Ritchie	Smith	Christie
	19th	Brown	Reid	Irvine	Black	Malloy	Cowie	Chalmers	Henderson A	Ritchie	Smith	Christie
	26th	Brown	Reid	Irvine	Black	Malloy	Cowie	Chalmers	Henderson A	Ritchie	Smith	Christie
Dec	3rd	Brown	Reid	Irvine	Black	Malloy	Cowie	Stables	Henderson A	Ritchie	Smith	Christie
	10th	Brown	Reid	Irvine	Gallacher	Black	Cowie	Stables	Henderson A	Merchant	Smith	Christie
	17th	Brown	Reid	Irvine	Black	Stevenson	Cowie	Stables	Henderson A	Merchant	Smith	Christie
	24th	Brown	Reid	Irvine	Gallacher	Black	Cowie	Stables	Henderson A	Merchant	Smith	Christie
	31st	Brown	Reid	Irvine	Gallacher	Black	Cowie	Stables	Henderson A	Merchant	Smith	Christie
Jan	2nd	Brown	Reid	Irvine	Gallacher	Black	Cowie	Stables	Henderson A	Merchant	Smith	Christie
	7th	Brown	Reid	Irvine	Black	Merchant	Cowie	Stables	Henderson A	Ritchie	Smith	Christie
	14th	Henderson B	Reid	Irvine	Black	Merchant	Cowie	Anderson	Henderson A	Stables	O'Hara	Christie
	21st	Henderson B	Reid	Gray	Black	Merchant	Cowie	Stables	Henderson A	Watt	Smith	Christie
Feb	4th	Henderson B	Reid	Irvine	Gallacher	Black	Cowie	Stables	Henderson A	Merchant	Roy	Christie
	8th	Henderson B	Gray	Irvine	Gallacher	Black	Cowie	Stables	Henderson A	Merchant	Roy	Christie
	11th	Henderson B	Reid	Irvine	Stevenson	Black	Craig	Stables	Henderson A	Merchant	O'Hara	Christie
	18th	Brown	Gray	Irvine	Gallacher	Black	Cowie	Stables	Henderson A	Merchant	O'Hara	Christie
	25th	Brown	Gray	Irvine	Gallacher	Black	Cowie	Stables	Henderson A	Merchant	O'Hara	Christie
Mar	3rd	Brown	Reid	Irvine	Gallacher	Black	Craig	Stables	Roy	Cousin	O'Hara	Christie
	10th	Brown	Reid	Irvine	Gallacher	Merchant	Black	Stables	Anderson	Cousin	O'Hara	Christie
	17th	Brown	Gray	Irvine	Gallacher	Black	Cowie	Stables	Henderson	Merchant	O'Hara	Chalmers
	24th	Brown	Gray	Irvine	Black	Stevenson	Cowie	Stables	Gallacher	Merchant	O'Hara	Christie
	31st	Brown	Gray	Irvine	Black	Stevenson	Cowie	Stables	Gallacher	Merchant	O'Hara	Christie
Apr	2nd	Brown	Gray	Irvine	Black	Stevenson	Cowie	Stables	Gallacher	Merchant	O'Hara	Christie
	7th	Brown	Gray	Irvine	Black	Stevenson	Cowie	Chalmers	Gallacher	Merchant	O'Hara	Christie
	13th	Brown	Reid	Irvine	Black	Stevenson	Cowie	Stables	Cousin	Merchant	O'Hara	Ritchie
	21st	Brown	Reid	Irvine	Black	Stevenson	Cowie	Stables	Cousin	Merchant	Sneddon	Christie
	24th	Brown	Reid	Irvine	Black	Stevenson	Cowie	Birse	Cousin	Merchant	Henderson A	Christie
	28th	Brown	Reid	Irvine	Henderson	Stevenson	Cowie	Chalmers	Cousin	Merchant	O'Hara	Birse

Deadly finish - Dundee United defenders are helpless as George Merchant beats Edmiston to set Dundee on the road to a 3-0 win in the Scottish Cup replay at Dens. Dundee's Ian Stables is on the left.

Season 1956-57

Date		Opponents		Score	Crowd	Scorers
Aug 11th	LC	Motherwell	a	1-0		Christie
15th	LC	Raith Rovers	h	1-0	16,000	Merchant
18th	LC	Airdrie	h	3-1	13,000	Merchant; Christie; Chalmers
25th	LC	Motherwell	h	2-1	15,000	Merchant 2
30th	LC	Raith Rovers	a	2-2	8,500	Black; Merchant
Sep 1st	LC	Airdrie	a	7-1	6,000	Merchant 2; Cowie; O'Hara 2; Chalmers; Shanks o.g.
8th	L	Kilmarnock	h	1-1	13,000	Merchant
12th	LCQ	Dundee United	h	7-3	20,000	Black; Christie; Chalmers 3; O'Hara; Merchant
15th	LCQ	Dundee United	a	1-2 (8-5)	14,000	Merchant
22nd	L	Aberdeen	h	4-2	20,000	Christie 2; Chalmers; O'Hara
29th	L	Hearts	a	1-2	30,000	Birse
Oct 6th	LCS	Partick Thistle	Ibr	0-0	22,000	-
9th	LCSR	Partick Thistle	Ibr	2-3	18,000	Christie; O'Hara
13th	L	QOS	a	1-3	7,500	Watt
20th	L	Queens Park	h	3-1	8,500	O'Hara; Watt; Chalmers
Nov 3rd	L	Celtic	h	2-1	22,000	Black; O'Hara
10th	L	Hibernian	a	1-1	12,000	Watt
17th	L	St Mirren	a	3-2	9,000	Christie; Watt 2
24th	L	Airdrie	h	2-1	7,000	Christie; Watt
Dec 1st	L	Falkirk	a	1-1	6,000	O'Hara
8th	L	Dunfermline	h	2-0	11,000	Christie; Merchant
15th	L	Ayr United	h	5-0	8,500	Cousin 3; Watt; O'Hara
22nd	L	East Fife	a	0-2	3,500	-
29th	L	Raith Rovers	a	2-1	16,000	Christie; Reid
Jan 1st	L	Aberdeen	a	1-2	20,000	Chalmers
2nd	L	Rangers	h	1-3	28,500	O'Hara
5th	L	Kilmarnock	a	0-4	13,000	-
12th	L	Hearts	h	0-3	20,000	-
19th	L	Motherwell	a	2-4	10,000	Chalmers; Birse
26th	L	QOS	h	5-2	9,000	Chalmers 3; Birse 2
Feb 2nd	SC5	Clyde	h	0-0	22,000	-
6th	SC5R	Clyde	a	1-2	12,000	Cowie
9th	L	Queens Park	a	0-2	10,000	-
16th	L	Ayr United	a	1-0	8,000	Cousin
23rd	L	Partick Thistle	h	5-1	5,000	Cousin 2; Chalmers 2; Birse
Mar 2nd	L	Dunfermline	a	1-1	6,000	Birse
6th	L	Celtic	a	1-1	4,000	O'Hara
9th	L	Hibernian	h	0-3	13,000	-
16th	L	St Mirren	h	1-1	10,000	Cousin
20th	L	Rangers	a	0-4	25,000	-
23rd	L	Airdrie	a	2-3	7,000	Cousin; O'Hara
30th	L	Falkirk	h	1-2	10,000	O'Hara
Apr 8th	L	Motherwell	h	3-1	7,000	Easson 2; Sneddon
16th	FCS	Brechin City	h	2-5	2,000	Easson; Birse
20th	L	East Fife	h	0-1	3,000	-
23rd	L	Partick Thistle	a	0-5	6,000	-
27th	L	Raith Rovers	h	3-0	7,000	Cowie; Black; Easson

Albert Henderson - a great servant to the club at half-back and inside-forward.

Appearances

	League	L/Cup	S/Cup	Total
Jimmy Chalmers	32 (9)	10 (5)	2	44 (14)
George Christie	32 (6)	10 (4)	2	44 (10)
Hugh Reid	32 (1)	10	2	44 (1)
Bill Brown	31	10	2	43
Ralph McKenzie	30	10	2	42
Gordon Black	33 (2)	6 (2)	1	40 (4)
Bert Henderson	28	10	2	40
George O'Hara	28 (9)	10 (4)	2	40 (13)
Bobby Cox	28	0	2	30
Doug Cowie	17 (1)	10 (1)	2 (1)	29 (3)
Alan Cousin	23 (8)	0	2	25 (8)
Billy Birse	16 (6)	0	1	17 (6)
George Merchant	3 (2)	10 (9)	0	13 (11)
Andy Irvine	3	9	0	12
Jim Watt	12 (7)	0	0	12 (7)
Dave Easson	3 (3)	4	0	7 (3)
Jim Ferguson (def)	5	0	0	5
George McGeachie	4	0	0	4
Ian Smith	3	0	0	3
Dave Sneddon	3 (1)	0	0	3 (1)
Jim Ferguson (gk)	2	0	0	2
Dave Skinner	1	1	0	2
Dougie Alexander	1	0	0	1
Dave McLaren	1	0	0	1
Felix Reilly	1	0	0	1
Jackie Stewart	1	0	0	1
Jake Young	1	0	0	1

The Record		
League	-	Tenth Place, Division One
League Cup	-	Semi-final
Scottish Cup	-	Fifth round
Forfarshire Cup	-	Semi-final
Top Scorer	-	Jimmy Chalmers (14)
Av. Home gate	-	11,900
Players used	-	27
Sent off	-	None

Scottish League Division One

		Home			Away			Goals		
	P	W	D	L	W	D	L	F	A	PTS
Rangers	34	13	2	2	13	1	3	96-48		55
Hearts	34	11	3	3	13	2	2	81-48		53
Kilmarnock	34	9	6	2	7	4	6	57-39		42
Raith Rovers	34	10	2	5	6	5	6	84-58		39
Celtic	34	9	6	2	6	2	9	58-43		38
Aberdeen	34	10	1	6	8	1	8	79-59		38
Motherwell	34	9	2	6	7	3	7	72-66		37
Partick Thistle	34	11	3	3	2	5	10	53-51		34
Hibernian	34	6	8	3	6	1	10	69-56		33
Dundee	**34**	**10**	**2**	**5**	**3**	**4**	**10**	**55-61**		**32**
Airdrie	34	8	2	7	5	2	10	77-89		30
St Mirren	34	8	3	6	4	3	10	58-72		30
Queens Park	34	5	2	10	6	5	6	55-59		29
Falkirk	34	5	2	10	5	6	6	51-70		28
East Fife	34	7	3	7	3	3	11	59-82		26
Queen of the South	34	8	3	6	2	2	13	54-96		25
Dunfermline	34	6	3	8	3	3	11	54-74		24
Ayr United	34	5	2	10	2	3	12	48-89		19

League Cup Section

	P	W	D	L	F	A	PTS
Dundee	**6**	**5**	**1**	**0**	**16- 5**		**11**
Raith Rovers	6	3	1	2	12-10		7
Motherwell	6	2	0	4	12-10		4
Airdrie	6	1	0	5	9-24		2

Dundee F.C. Line-Ups 1956-57

		1	2	3	4	5	6	7	8	9	10	11
Aug	11th	Brown	Reid	Irvine	Henderson	McKenzie	Cowie	Chalmers	Easson	Merchant	O'Hara	Christie
	15th	Brown	Reid	Irvine	Henderson	McKenzie	Cowie	Chalmers	Easson	Merchant	O'Hara	Christie
	18th	Brown	Reid	Irvine	Henderson	McKenzie	Cowie	Chalmers	Easson	Merchant	O'Hara	Christie
	25th	Brown	Reid	Irvine	Henderson	McKenzie	Cowie	Chalmers	Easson	Merchant	O'Hara	Christie
	30th	Brown	Reid	Irvine	Henderson	McKenzie	Cowie	Chalmers	Black	Merchant	O'Hara	Christie
Sep	1st	Brown	Reid	Irvine	Henderson	McKenzie	Cowie	Chalmers	Black	Merchant	O'Hara	Christie
	8th	Brown	Reid	Irvine	Henderson	McKenzie	Cowie	Chalmers	Black	Merchant	O'Hara	Christie
	12th	Brown	Reid	Irvine	Henderson	McKenzie	Cowie	Chalmers	Black	Merchant	O'Hara	Christie
	15th	Brown	Reid	Irvine	Henderson	McKenzie	Cowie	Chalmers	Black	Merchant	O'Hara	Christie
	22nd	Brown	Reid	Irvine	Henderson	McKenzie	Cowie	Chalmers	Black	Birse	O'Hara	Christie
	29th	McLaren	Reid	Irvine	Henderson	McKenzie	Cowie	Chalmers	Black	Birse	O'Hara	Christie
Oct	6th	Brown	Reid	Irvine	Henderson	McKenzie	Cowie	Chalmers	Black	Merchant	O'Hara	Christie
	9th	Brown	Reid	Skinner	Henderson	McKenzie	Cowie	Chalmers	Black	Merchant	O'Hara	Christie
	13th	Brown	Reid	Skinner	Henderson	McKenzie	Cowie	Chalmers	Black	Watt	Sneddon	Christie
	20th	Brown	Reid	Cox	Henderson	McKenzie	Black	Chalmers	O'Hara	Watt	Smith	Christie
Nov	3rd	Brown	Reid	Cox	Henderson	McKenzie	Cowie	Chalmers	Black	Watt	O'Hara	Christie
	10th	Brown	Reid	Cox	Henderson	McKenzie	Black	Chalmers	Cousin	Watt	O'Hara	Christie
	17th	Brown	Reid	Cox	Henderson	McKenzie	Black	Chalmers	Cousin	Watt	O'Hara	Christie
	24th	Brown	Reid	Cox	Henderson	McKenzie	Black	Chalmers	Cousin	Watt	O'Hara	Christie
Dec	1st	Brown	Reid	Cox	Henderson	McKenzie	Black	Chalmers	Cousin	Merchant	O'Hara	Christie
	8th	Brown	Reid	Cox	Henderson	McKenzie	Black	Chalmers	Cousin	Watt	O'Hara	Christie
	15th	Brown	Reid	Cox	Henderson	McKenzie	Black	Chalmers	Cousin	Merchant	O'Hara	Christie
	22nd	Brown	Reid	Cox	Henderson	McKenzie	Black	Chalmers	Black	Birse	O'Hara	Christie
	29th	Brown	Reid	Cox	Henderson	McKenzie	Cowie	Chalmers	Black	Birse	O'Hara	Christie
Jan	1st	Brown	Reid	Cox	Henderson	McKenzie	Cowie	Chalmers	Black	Birse	O'Hara	Christie
	2nd	Brown	Reid	Cox	Henderson	McKenzie	Cowie	Chalmers	Black	Watt	O'Hara	Christie
	5th	Brown	Reid	Cox	Henderson	McKenzie	Cowie	Chalmers	Black	Watt	O'Hara	Christie
	12th	Brown	Reid	Cox	Black	McKenzie	Smith	Chalmers	Cousin	Watt	O'Hara	McGeachie
	19th	Brown	Reid	Cox	Henderson	McKenzie	Black	Chalmers	O'Hara	Birse	Cowie	Christie
	26th	Brown	Reid	Cox	Henderson	McKenzie	Cowie	Chalmers	Cousin	Birse	O'Hara	Christie
Feb	2nd	Brown	Reid	Cox	Henderson	McKenzie	Cowie	Chalmers	Cousin	Birse	O'Hara	Christie
	6th	Brown	Reid	Cox	Henderson	McKenzie	Black	Chalmers	Cousin	O'Hara	Cowie	Christie
	9th	Brown	Ferguson J	Cox	Henderson	Black	Alexander	Chalmers	Cousin	O'Hara	Cowie	McGeachie
	16th	Brown	Reid	Cox	Henderson	McKenzie	Black	Chalmers	Cousin	Birse	O'Hara	Christie
	23rd	Brown	Reid	Cox	Henderson	McKenzie	Black	Chalmers	Cousin	Birse	O'Hara	Christie
Mar	2nd	Brown	Reid	Cox	Henderson	McKenzie	Black	Chalmers	Cousin	Birse	O'Hara	Christie
	6th	Brown	Reid	Cox	Henderson	Ferguson J	Black	Chalmers	Cousin	Birse	O'Hara	Christie
	9th	Brown	Reid	Cox	Henderson	McKenzie	Black	Chalmers	Cousin	Birse	O'Hara	Christie
	16th	Brown	Reid	Cox	Henderson	McKenzie	Black	Chalmers	Cousin	Birse	McGeachie	Christie
	20th	Brown	Ferguson J	Cox	Henderson	Ferguson J	Black	Chalmers	Cousin	Birse	O'Hara	Christie
	23rd	Brown	Ferguson J	Cox	Henderson	McKenzie	Black	Chalmers	Cousin	Watt	O'Hara	Christie
	30th	Brown	Ferguson J	Cox	Black	McKenzie	Cowie	Chalmers	Cousin	Watt	O'Hara	Christie
Apr	8th	Brown	Reid	Cox	Black	McKenzie	Cowie	McGeachie	Cousin	Easson	Sneddon	Christie
	20th	Brown	Reid	Cox	Black	McKenzie	Cowie	Chalmers	Cousin	Birse	Smith	Christie
	23rd	Brown	Reid	Young	Stewart J	Black	Cowie	Birse	Cousin	Easson	Sneddon	Christie
	27th	Brown	Reid	Ferguson J	Black	McKenzie	Cowie	Chalmers	Cousin	Easson	Reilly	Christie

The Dundee F.C. team which reached the 1956 League Cup semi-final (BACK, left to right) Hugh Reid, Andy Irvine, Bill Brown, Ralph McKenzie, Bert Henderson, Doug Cowie. FRONT - Jimmy Chalmers, Gordon Black, George Merchant, George O'Hara and George Christie.

DC Thomson

Season 1957-58

Date		Opponents		Score	Crowd	Scorers
Aug	10th	LC	Queens Park	a	5-2	10,000	Easson 2; Cousin 3
	14th	LC	Kilmarnock	h	0-3	15,000	-
	20th	LC	Hearts	h	2-2*	16,200	Chalmers; Cousin
	24th	LC	Queens Park	h	1-1	10,000	Cousin
	28th	LC	Kilmarnock	a	1-1		Chalmers
	31st	LC	Hearts	a	2-4	18,000	Cousin 2
Sep	7th	L	Hearts	a	0-6	19,000	-
	14th	L	Raith Rovers	h	0-2	13,000	-
	21st	L	Aberdeen	a	0-3	10,000	-
Oct	5th	L	Clyde	a	1-3	7,000	Christie
	12th	L	Motherwell	h	3-0	10,000	O'Hara; Henderson 2
	19th	L	Hibernian	h	3-0	16,000	Sneddon; Christie; Black
	26th	L	East Fife	a	1-3	6,000	Chalmers
Nov	2nd	L	QOS	h	2-1	9,000	Henderson; Cousin
	9th	L	Third Lanark	a	1-5	8,000	O'Hara
	16th	L	Partick Thistle	h	5-0	9,000	Cousin; O'Hara 3; Robertson
	23rd	L	St Mirren	a	1-1	10,000	Cousin
	30th	L	Queens Park	h	1-0	7,500	Cowie (pen)
Dec	7th	L	Celtic	a	0-0	12,000	-
	14th	L	Rangers	h	1-2	21,000	Cousin
	21st	L	Falkirk	h	2-4	7,000	Cousin; Robertson
	26th	L	Kilmarnock	h	2-0	9,000	Cousin; McGrory
	28th	L	Airdrie	a	1-7	6,000	Black (pen)
Jan	1st	L	Aberdeen	h	1-2	18,000	Sneddon
	2nd	L	Raith Rovers	a	0-4	10,000	-
	4th	L	Hearts	h	0-5	20,000	-
	11th	L	Kilmarnock	a	1-1	11,000	Cousin
	18th	L	Clyde	h	2-0	15,000	Chalmers; Cousin
Feb	1st	FC1	Dundee United	a	1-0	7,500	O'Hara
	15th	SC2	Raith Rovers	a	1-0	12,649	Cousin
	22nd	L	QOS	a	0-4	7,000	-
Mar	1st	SC3	Aberdeen	h	1-3	28,000	Robertson
	5th	L	Third Lanark	h	2-0	4,000	Robertson; Sneddon
	8th	L	Partick Thistle	a	0-2	10,000	-
	15th	L	St Mirren	h	0-0	10,000	-
	22nd	L	Queens Park	a	7-2	4,000	Sneddon 2; Cousin 3; Christie; Bonthrone
	29th	L	Celtic	h	5-3	5,000	Sneddon; Bonthrone; Cousin; Curlett 2
Apr	12th	L	Falkirk	a	2-0	7,000	Cousin 2
	16th	L	Hibernian	a	1-1	10,000	Bonthrone
	26th	L	Airdrie	h	1-3	6,500	Curlett
	28th	L	Motherwell	a	0-1	5,000	-
	30th	L	East Fife	h	2-0	5,000	Cowie (pen); Curlett
May	5th	FCS	Arbroath	h	3-4	1,400	Bonthrone; Sneddon 2 (1 pen)
	10th	L	Rangers	a	1-0	10,000	Cousin

* Earlier match on August 17th abandoned at half-time at 0-0 due to flooding. Cup Cash v Raith £1,095

Alan Cousin - was top marksman for Dundee between 1957 and 1960.

The Record

League	-	11th Place, Division One
League Cup	-	Qualifying stages only
Scottish Cup	-	Third round
Forfarshire Cup	-	Semi-final
Top Scorer	-	Alan Cousin (23 goals)
Av. Home Gate	-	10,900
Players used	-	29
Sent off	-	None

Appearances

	League	L/Cup	S/Cup	Total
Bobby Cox	34	6	2	42
Bill Brown	31	6	2	39
Alan Cousin	31 (15)	6 (7)	2 (1)	39 (23)
Doug Cowie	31 (2)	6	2	39 (2)
Ralph McKenzie	31	0	2	33
George Christie	25 (3)	6	1	32 (3)
Bert Henderson	26 (3)	4	2	32 (3)
Hugh Robertson	23 (3)	0	2 (1)	25 (4)
Dave Sneddon	23 (6)	0	2	25 (6)
Gordon Black	20 (2)	4	0	24 (2)
Alex Hamilton	18	1	2	21
Hugh Reid	16	5	0	21
George O'Hara	15 (5)	3	1	19 (5)
Jimmy Chalmers	9 (2)	6 (2)	2	17 (4)
George McGeachie	5	4	0	9
Dave Curlett	8 (4)	0	0	8 (4)
Jimmy Bonthrone	7 (3)	0	0	7 (3)
Felix Reilly	4	3	0	7
Frank McGrory	5 (1)	0	0	5 (1)
Danny McLennan	0	4	0	4
Dave Easson	1	2 (2)	0	3 (2)
Arthur McIvor	3	0	0	3
Jim Ferguson (gk)	2	0	0	2
Dougie Alexander	1	0	0	1
Alec Glen	1	0	0	1
Pat Liney	1	0	0	1
Gordon Tosh	1	0	0	1
Clive Wallace	1	0	0	1
Don Watt	1	0	0	1

Scottish League Division One

		Home			Away			Goals		
	P	W	D	L	W	D	L	F	A	PTS
Hearts	34	15	2	0	14	2	1	132-29		62
Rangers	34	10	2	5	12	3	5	89-49		49
Celtic	34	7	6	4	12	2	3	86-47		46
Clyde	34	13	1	3	5	5	7	84-61		42
Kilmarnock	34	8	6	3	6	3	8	60-55		37
Partick Thistle	34	11	1	5	6	2	9	69-71		37
Raith Rovers	34	10	2	5	4	5	8	66-56		35
Motherwell	34	8	3	6	4	5	8	68-67		32
Hibernian	34	6	4	7	7	1	9	59-60		31
Falkirk	34	6	5	6	5	4	8	64-82		31
Dundee	**34**	**10**	**1**	**6**	**3**	**4**	**10**	**49-65**		**31**
Aberdeen	34	8	0	9	6	2	9	68-76		30
St Mirren	34	7	4	6	4	4	9	59-66		30
Third Lanark	34	6	2	9	7	2	8	69-88		30
Queen of the South	34	6	4	7	6	1	10	61-72		29
Airdrie	34	8	2	7	5	0	12	71-92		28
East Fife	34	5	2	10	5	1	11	45-88		23
Queens Park	34	1	0	16	3	1	13	41-114		9

League Cup Section

	P	W	D	L	F	A	PTS
Kilmarnock	6	3	3	0	11- 5		9
Hearts	6	2	3	1	17- 9		7
Dundee	**6**	**1**	**3**	**2**	**11-13**		**5**
Queens Park	6	0	3	3	8-20		3

Dundee F.C. Line-Ups 1957-58

		1	2	3	4	5	6	7	8	9	10	11
Aug	10th	Brown	Reid	Cox	Black	Cowie	McLennan	Chalmers	Easson	Cousin	Reilly	Christie
	14th	Brown	Reid	Cox	Black	Cowie	McLennan	Chalmers	Easson	Cousin	O'Hara	Christie
	20th	Brown	Reid	Cox	Henderson	Cowie	McLennan	McGeachie	Cousin	Chalmers	O'Hara	Christie
	24th	Brown	Reid	Cox	Henderson	Cowie	McLennan	McGeachie	Cousin	Chalmers	O'Hara	Christie
	28th	Brown	Reid	Cox	Henderson	Cowie	Black	McGeachie	Cousin	Chalmers	Reilly	Christie
	31st	Brown	Hamilton	Cox	Henderson	Cowie	Black	McGeachie	Cousin	Chalmers	Reilly	Christie
Sep	7th	Brown	Reid	Cox	Henderson	Cowie	Black	Watt D	Cousin	Chalmers	Reilly	McGeachie
	14th	Brown	Reid	Cox	Henderson	McKenzie	Cowie	McGeachie	Black	Cousin	O'Hara	Christie
	21st	Brown	Reid	Cox	Henderson	McKenzie	Cowie	Wallace	Reilly	Cousin	O'Hara	Robertson
Oct	5th	Brown	Reid	Cox	Henderson	McKenzie	Black	Chalmers	Reilly	O'Hara	Sneddon	Christie
	12th	Brown	Reid	Cox	Black	McKenzie	Cowie	Chalmers	Cousin	Henderson	O'Hara	Christie
	19th	Brown	Reid	Cox	Black	McKenzie	Cowie	Chalmers	Sneddon	Cousin	O'Hara	Christie
	26th	Brown	Reid	Cox	Black	McKenzie	Cowie	Chalmers	Sneddon	Cousin	O'Hara	Christie
Nov	2nd	Brown	Reid	Cox	Black	McKenzie	Cowie	Chalmers	Cousin	Henderson	O'Hara	Christie
	9th	Brown	Reid	Cox	Black	McKenzie	Cowie	Chalmers	Cousin	Henderson	O'Hara	Christie
	16th	Brown	Reid	Cox	Black	McKenzie	Cowie	Christie	Cousin	Henderson	O'Hara	Robertson
	23rd	Brown	Reid	Cox	Black	McKenzie	Cowie	Christie	Cousin	Henderson	O'Hara	Robertson
	30th	Brown	Reid	Cox	Black	McKenzie	Cowie	Christie	Cousin	Henderson	O'Hara	Robertson
Dec	7th	Brown	Reid	Cox	Black	McKenzie	Cowie	Christie	Cousin	Henderson	Sneddon	Robertson
	14th	Brown	Reid	Cox	Black	McKenzie	Cowie	Christie	Cousin	Henderson	Sneddon	Robertson
	21st	Brown	Reid	Cox	Black	McKenzie	Cowie	Christie	Cousin	Easson	Sneddon	Robertson
	26th	Brown	Reid	Cox	Black	McKenzie	Cowie	Christie	Cousin	McGrory	Sneddon	Robertson
	28th	Brown	Hamilton	Cox	Black	Tosh	Glen	McIvor	Cousin	McGrory	Sneddon	Robertson
Jan	1st	Ferguson J	Hamilton	Cox	Black	McKenzie	Cowie	McIvor	Cousin	O'Hara	Sneddon	Robertson
	2nd	Ferguson J	Hamilton	Cox	Black	McKenzie	Cowie	McIvor	Cousin	O'Hara	Sneddon	Robertson
	4th	Brown	Hamilton	Cox	Black	McKenzie	Cowie	Christie	Cousin	Henderson	Sneddon	Robertson
	11th	Brown	Hamilton	Cox	Henderson	McKenzie	Cowie	Christie	Cousin	O'Hara	Sneddon	Robertson
	18th	Brown	Hamilton	Cox	Henderson	McKenzie	Cowie	Chalmers	Cousin	O'Hara	Reilly	Christie
Feb	15th	Brown	Hamilton	Cox	Henderson	McKenzie	Cowie	Christie	Cousin	Chalmers	Sneddon	Robertson
	22nd	Brown	Hamilton	Cox	Henderson	McKenzie	Cowie	Christie	Cousin	Chalmers	Sneddon	Robertson
Mar	1st	Brown	Hamilton	Cox	Henderson	McKenzie	Cowie	Chalmers	Cousin	O'Hara	Sneddon	Robertson
	5th	Brown	Hamilton	Cox	Henderson	McKenzie	Cowie	Christie	Cousin	McGrory	Sneddon	Robertson
	8th	Brown	Hamilton	Cox	Henderson	McKenzie	Cowie	Curlett	Cousin	McGrory	Bonthrone	Robertson
	15th	Brown	Hamilton	Cox	Henderson	McKenzie	Cowie	Curlett	Bonthrone	Cousin	Sneddon	Robertson
	22nd	Brown	Hamilton	Cox	Henderson	McKenzie	Cowie	Curlett	Bonthrone	Cousin	Sneddon	Christie
	29th	Brown	Hamilton	Cox	Henderson	McKenzie	Cowie	Curlett	Bonthrone	Cousin	Sneddon	Christie
Apr	12th	Brown	Hamilton	Cox	Henderson	McKenzie	Cowie	Robertson	Bonthrone	Cousin	Sneddon	Christie
	16th	Brown	Hamilton	Cox	Henderson	McKenzie	Cowie	Robertson	Bonthrone	Cousin	Sneddon	Christie
	26th	Brown	Hamilton	Cox	Black	McKenzie	Cowie	Christie	Curlett	Cousin	Sneddon	Robertson
	28th	Brown	Hamilton	Cox	Henderson	Cowie	Alexander	Christie	McGeachie	Curlett	Sneddon	Robertson
	30th	Brown	Hamilton	Cox	Henderson	McKenzie	Cowie	Curlett	McGeachie	McGrory	Sneddon	Robertson
May	10th	Liney	Hamilton	Cox	Henderson	McKenzie	Curlett	Robertson	Bonthrone	Cousin	Sneddon	Christie

Totally relaxed - that's Dundee skipper Doug Cowie as his penalty leaves QOS keeper Bert Gebbie helpless in a League Cup tie at Dens in August 1958. Ally Hill moves in but the immaculate Cowie has made no mistake.

D. Cowie Jnr.

Season 1958-59

Date		Opponents		Score	Crowd	Scorers
Aug 9th	LC	Partick Thistle	h	2-3	11,000	Cowie (pen); Sneddon
13th	LC	Motherwell	a	2-1		H. Robertson; Bonthrone
16th	LC	QOS	a	0-1	6,500	-
20th	L	Falkirk	a	5-2	13,000	Cousin 3; Hill; Curlett
23rd	LC	Partick Thistle	a	2-3	12,000	Cousin; Hill
27th	LC	Motherwell	h	2-3	8,000	Hill 2
30th	LC	QOS	h	2-0	8,000	Cowie (pen); Hill
Sep 6th	L	Aberdeen	h	2-1	12,000	H. Robertson; McGeachie
13th	L	Raith Rovers	a	1-4	10,000	Hill
20th	L	Kilmarnock	h	1-0	12,000	Sneddon
27th	L	Rangers	a	2-1	32,000	Telfer o.g.; Hill
29th	FC1	Brechin City	a	0-1		-
Oct 4th	L	Motherwell	h	1-1	10,000	H. Robertson
11th	L	Hearts	h	3-3	18,000	Cousin 2; Cowie (pen)
18th	L	Clyde	a	2-3	11,000	Curlett ; H. Robertson
25th	L	St Mirren	a	2-2	8,000	Crossan 2
Nov 1st	L	Celtic	h	1-1	22,500	McNeill o.g.
8th	L	Stirling Albion	h	3-0	12,500	Curlett; Cousin; H. Robertson
15th	L	QOS	a	3-1	5,500	Cousin 2; H. Robertson
22nd	L	Third Lanark	h	3-0	10,500	Henderson; Curlett 2
29th	L	Partick Thistle	a	0-3		-
Dec 6th	L	Hibernian	h	2-1	13,000	H. Robertson; Cousin
13th	L	Dunfermline	a	1-2	8,000	Sneddon
20th	L	Airdrie	h	1-1	10,000	H.Robertson
27th	L	Falkirk	h	3-2	8,000	Sneddon 3
Jan 1st	L	Aberdeen	a	1-1	12,000	Curlett
3rd	L	Raith Rovers	h	2-0	14,000	Curlett; Bonthrone
10th	L	Kilmarnock	a	0-1	7,000	-
24th	L	Motherwell	a	0-2	11,000	-
28th	L	Rangers	h	1-3	14,000	Sneddon
31st	SC1	Fraserburgh	a	0-1	4,500	-
Feb 7th	L	Hearts	a	0-1	18,000	-
21st	L	St Mirren	h	4-6	6,500	Bonthrone 2; Cowie (pen); Henderson
28th	L	Clyde	h	2-1	7,000	Cousin 2
Mar 4th	L	Celtic	a	1-1	7,500	Bonthrone
7th	L	Stirling Albion	a	1-0	5,500	Cousin
14th	L	QOS	h	2-1	5,000	Cousin 2
21st	L	Third Lanark	a	3-0	6,000	Cousin 2; McGeachie
28th	L	Partick Thistle	h	3-2	8,000	H. Robertson; McGeachie; Cousin
Apr 4th	L	Hibernian	a	2-1	10,000	Grant o.g.; T. Robertson
13th	L	Dunfermline	h	2-2	5,000	H. Robertson; Sweeney o.g.
18th	L	Airdrie	a	1-1	5,000	T. Robertson

Cup Cash v. Fraserburgh £630

Bobby Cox - the hard-tackling left-back was an inspirational player for the Dark Blues.

The Record

League	-	Fourth Place, Division One
League Cup	-	Qualifying stages only
Scottish Cup	-	First round
Forfarshire Cup	-	First round
Top Scorer	-	Alan Cousin (18 goals)
Av. Home Gate	-	11,100
Players used	-	23
Sent off	-	None

Appearances

	League	L/Cup	S/Cup	Total
Bobby Cox	34	6	1	41
Jimmy Gabriel	34	5	1	40
Alan Cousin	32 (17)	6 (1)	1	39 (18)
Dave Sneddon	32 (6)	6 (1)	1	39 (7)
Hugh Robertson	32 (9)	5 (1)	1	38 (10)
Bill Brown	30	6	1	37
Bert Henderson	30 (2)	6	1	37 (2)
Doug Cowie	27	6	1	34
George McGeachie	23 (3)	4	0	27 (3)
Dave Curlett	21 (7)	3	1	25 (7
Alex Hamilton	15	6	1	22
Ally Hill	16 (3)	3 (4)	0	19 (7)
Hugh Reid	19	0	0	19
Jimmy Bonthrone	13 (4)	3 (1)	1	17 (5)
Tommy Robertson	4 (2)	0	0	4 (2)
Frank Crossan	2 (2)	0	0	2 (2)
Pat Liney	2	0	0	2
Andy Penman	2	0	0	2
Ian Ure	2	0	0	2
Mike Watson	2	0	0	2
Hugh Drennan	1	0	0	1
Fred Jardine	1	0	0	1
Ralph McKenzie	0	1	0	1

Scottish League Division One

		Home			Away			Goals		
	P	W	D	L	W	D	L	F A	PTS
Rangers	34	13	2	2	8	6	3	92-51	50
Hearts	34	12	2	3	9	4	4	92-51	48
Motherwell	34	11	4	2	7	4	6	83-50	44
Dundee	34	10	5	2	6	4	7	61-51	41
Airdrie	34	8	3	6	7	4	6	64-62	37
Celtic	34	11	4	2	3	4	10	70-53	36
St Mirren	34	8	4	5	6	3	8	71-74	35
Kilmarnock	34	10	3	4	3	5	9	58-51	34
Partick Thistle	34	8	4	5	6	2	9	59-66	34
Hibernian	34	8	3	6	5	3	9	68-70	32
Third Lanark	34	6	5	6	5	5	7	74-83	32
Stirling Albion	34	6	5	6	5	3	9	54-64	30
Aberdeen	34	7	4	6	5	1	11	63-66	29
Raith Rovers	34	9	3	5	1	6	10	60-70	29
Clyde	34	8	2	7	4	2	11	62-66	28
Dunfermline	34	7	3	7	3	5	9	68-87	28
Falkirk	34	6	4	7	4	3	10	58-79	27
Queen of the South	34	4	5	8	2	1	14	38-101	18

League Cup Section

	P	W	D	L	F A	PTS
Partick Thistle	6	4	1	1	17-11	9
Motherwell	6	3	1	2	13-11	7
Dundee	6	2	0	4	10-11	4
Queen of the South	6	2	0	4	6-13	4

Dundee F.C. Line-Ups 1958-59

		1	2	3	4	5	6	7	8	9	10	11
Aug	9th	Brown	Hamilton	Cox	Henderson	McKenzie	Cowie	Curlett	Bonthrone	Cousin	Sneddon	McGeachie
	13th	Brown	Hamilton	Cox	Henderson	Gabriel	Cowie	Curlett	Bonthrone	Cousin	Sneddon	Robertson
	16th	Brown	Hamilton	Cox	Henderson	Gabriel	Cowie	Curlett	Bonthrone	Cousin	Sneddon	Robertson
	20th	Brown	Hamilton	Cox	Henderson	Gabriel	Cowie	Curlett	Cousin	Hill	Sneddon	Robertson
	23rd	Brown	Hamilton	Cox	Henderson	Gabriel	Cowie	McGeachie	Cousin	Hill	Sneddon	Robertson
	27th	Brown	Hamilton	Cox	Henderson	Gabriel	Cowie	McGeachie	Cousin	Hill	Sneddon	Robertson
	30th	Brown	Hamilton	Cox	Henderson	Gabriel	Cowie	McGeachie	Cousin	Hill	Sneddon	Robertson
Sep	6th	Brown	Hamilton	Cox	Henderson	Gabriel	Cowie	McGeachie	Cousin	Hill	Sneddon	Robertson
	13th	Brown	Hamilton	Cox	Henderson	Gabriel	Cowie	McGeachie	Cousin	Hill	Sneddon	Robertson
	20th	Brown	Reid	Cox	Henderson	Gabriel	Cowie	McGeachie	Cousin	Hill	Sneddon	Robertson
	27th	Brown	Reid	Cox	Henderson	Gabriel	Cowie	McGeachie	Cousin	Hill	Sneddon	Robertson
Oct	4th	Brown	Reid	Cox	Henderson	Gabriel	Cowie	McGeachie	Cousin	Hill	Sneddon	Robertson
	11th	Brown	Reid	Cox	Henderson	Gabriel	Cowie	McGeachie	Cousin	Hill	Sneddon	Robertson
	18th	Liney	Reid	Cox	Henderson	Gabriel	Cowie	McGeachie	Cousin	Curlett	Sneddon	Robertson
	25th	Liney	Reid	Cox	Henderson	Gabriel	Curlett	McGeachie	Cousin	Crossan	Sneddon	Robertson
Nov	1st	Brown	Reid	Cox	Henderson	Gabriel	Cowie	McGeachie	Cousin	Curlett	Sneddon	Robertson
	8th	Brown	Reid	Cox	Henderson	Gabriel	Cowie	McGeachie	Cousin	Curlett	Sneddon	Robertson
	15th	Brown	Reid	Cox	Henderson	Gabriel	Cowie	Curlett	Cousin	Hill	Sneddon	Robertson
	22nd	Brown	Reid	Cox	Henderson	Gabriel	Cowie	Curlett	Cousin	Hill	Sneddon	Robertson
	29th	Brown	Reid	Cox	Henderson	Gabriel	Cowie	Curlett	Cousin	Hill	Sneddon	Robertson
Dec	6th	Brown	Reid	Cox	Henderson	Gabriel	Cowie	McGeachie	Cousin	Hill	Sneddon	Robertson
	13th	Brown	Reid	Cox	Henderson	Gabriel	Cowie	Curlett	Cousin	Hill	Sneddon	McGeachie
	20th	Brown	Reid	Cox	Henderson	Gabriel	Cowie	McGeachie	Cousin	Hill	Sneddon	Robertson
	27th	Brown	Reid	Cox	Henderson	Gabriel	Ure	McGeachie	Cousin	Hill	Sneddon	Robertson
Jan	1st	Brown	Reid	Cox	Henderson	Gabriel	Cowie	Curlett	Bonthrone	Cousin	Sneddon	Robertson
	3rd	Watson	Reid	Cox	Henderson	Gabriel	Cowie	Curlett	Bonthrone	Cousin	Sneddon	Robertson
	10th	Brown	Reid	Cox	Henderson	Gabriel	Cowie	Hill	Bonthrone	Cousin	Sneddon	Robertson
	24th	Brown	Reid	Cox	Henderson	Gabriel	Cowie	Curlett	Bonthrone	Cousin	Sneddon	Robertson
	28th	Brown	Hamilton	Cox	Henderson	Gabriel	Cowie	Curlett	Bonthrone	Cousin	Sneddon	Robertson
	31st	Brown	Hamilton	Cox	Henderson	Gabriel	Cowie	Curlett	Bonthrone	Cousin	Sneddon	Robertson
Feb	7th	Brown	Hamilton	Cox	Henderson	Gabriel	Cowie	Penman	Bonthrone	Hill	Sneddon	Jardine
	21st	Brown	Hamilton	Cox	Henderson	Gabriel	Cowie	Penman	Bonthrone	Crossan	Sneddon	Robertson
	28th	Brown	Hamilton	Cox	Henderson	Gabriel	Curlett	McGeachie	Bonthrone	Cousin	Sneddon	Robertson
Mar	4th	Brown	Hamilton	Cox	Henderson	Gabriel	Curlett	McGeachie	Bonthrone	Cousin	Sneddon	Robertson
	7th	Brown	Hamilton	Cox	Henderson	Gabriel	Curlett	McGeachie	Bonthrone	Cousin	Sneddon	Robertson
	14th	Brown	Hamilton	Cox	Henderson	Gabriel	Ure	McGeachie	Bonthrone	Cousin	Sneddon	Robertson
	21st	Brown	Hamilton	Cox	Henderson	Gabriel	Curlett	McGeachie	Bonthrone	Cousin	Sneddon	Robertson
	28th	Brown	Hamilton	Cox	Gabriel	Cowie	Curlett	McGeachie	Robertson T	Cousin	Sneddon	Robertson H
Apr	4th	Brown	Hamilton	Cox	Gabriel	Cowie	Curlett	McGeachie	Robertson T	Cousin	Sneddon	Robertson H
	13th	Brown	Hamilton	Cox	Gabriel	Cowie	Curlett	McGeachie	Robertson T	Cousin	Bonthrone	Robertson H
	18th	Watson	Hamilton	Cox	Gabriel	Cowie	Curlett	McGeachie	Robertson T	Cousin	Drennan	Robertson H

Dundee F.C. 1958-59. (BACK, left to right) Willie Thornton (manager), Bobby Cox, Jimmy Gabriel, Bert Henderson, Doug Cowie, Bill Brown, Pat Liney, Alex. Stuart, Ian Ure, Hugh Reid, Sammy Kean (coach). FRONT - George McGeachie, Alex. Hamilton, Davie Sneddon, Jimmy Bonthrone, Alan Cousin, Ally Hill, Hugh Robertson, Jimmy Stevenson and Davie Curlett.

Stephen Borland

127

Season 1959-60

Date		Opponents		Score	Crowd	Scorers
Aug 8th	LC	Motherwell	a	2-4	15,500	Cousin; Bonthrone
12th	LC	Hibernian	h	4-3	17,000	Cowie; Cousin 2; Robertson
15th	LC	Rangers	a	0-2	37,000	-
19th	L	Hearts	h	1-3	18,500	Cousin
22nd	LC	Motherwell	h	1-4	18,000	Hill
26th	LC	Hibernian	a	3-1		Robertson 2; McGeachie
29th	LC	Rangers	h	2-3	20,000	Waddell; Cousin
Sep 5th	L	Aberdeen	a	3-0	12,000	Cousin; Waddell; Hill
12th	L	Raith Rovers	h	0-2	11,000	-
19th	L	Clyde	a	1-1	10,000	Henderson
26th	L	Motherwell	h	1-1	14,000	Robertson
Oct 3rd	L	Kilmarnock	a	2-2	9,000	McGeachie; Robertson
10th	L	Rangers	h	1-3	22,000	Robertson
17th	L	Ayr United	h	3-1	9,000	Bonthrone; Curlett; Cousin
24th	L	St Mirren	a	3-2	12,000	Bonthrone; Robertson; Curlett
31st	L	Arbroath	h	5-0	12,000	Logie o.g.; Bonthrone 2; Cousin; Cowie (pen)
Nov 7th	L	Dunfermline	h	3-2	11,000	Bonthrone; Curlett; Robertson
14th	L	Partick Thistle	a	5-0	8,000	Curlett 2; Bonthrone; Cousin 2
21st	L	Hibernian	a	2-4	16,000	Cousin 2
28th	L	Airdrie	h	1-2	10,000	McGeachie
Dec 5th	L	Celtic	a	3-2	12,000	Bonthrone; Robertson; Henderson
12th	L	Stirling Albion	a	1-0	5,000	Cousin
19th	L	Third Lanark	h	2-1	9,000	Henderson; Cowie
26th	L	Hearts	a	0-3	16,000	-
Jan 1st	L	Aberdeen	h	4-1	16,000	Henderson 2; Robertson; Penman
2nd	L	Raith Rovers	a	1-1	11,000	Bonthrone
9th	L	Clyde	h	2-0	11,000	Penman; Robertson
16th	L	Motherwell	a	0-0	10,000	-
23rd	L	Kilmarnock	h	0-4	15,000	-
Feb 9th	L	Rangers	a	0-0	20,000	-
27th	L	St Mirren	h	3-1	11,000	McGeachie; Gilzean; Cousin
29th	SC2	Hibernian	a	0-3	30,419	-
Mar 5th	L	Arbroath	a	1-1	5,200	Cowie (pen)
10th	L	Ayr United	a	0-1	4,500	-
12th	L	Dunfermline	a	2-2	7,000	Cousin; Waddell
19th	L	Partick Thistle	h	3-0	7,500	Robertson 2; Cousin
26th	L	Hibernian	h	6-3	8,000	Gilzean; Penman 3; McGeachie; Robertson
Apr 2nd	L	Airdrie	a	3-3	4,500	Gilzean; Robertson; Cowie (pen)
6th	FCS	Brechin City	h	6-0	5,000	Cowie; Robertson 2; McGeachie; Gilzean 2
16th	L	Celtic	h	2-0	16,000	Gilzean; Robertson
23rd	L	Stirling Albion	h	4-1	7,000	Gilzean 3; McGeachie
30th	L	Third Lanark	a	2-2	5,000	Gilzean; Cousin
May 7th	FCF	Forfar Athletic	h	3-2	6,500	Penman 2; Henderson

Cup Cash v. Hibernian (a) £3,487

Hugh Robertson - the left-wing speed-merchant cracked in 16 goals.

Appearances

	League	L/Cup	S/Cup	Total
Alan Cousin	34 (13)	6 (4)	1	41 (17)
Bobby Cox	34	6	1	41
Alex Hamilton	34	6	1	41
Hugh Robertson	32 (13)	6 (3)	1	39 (16)
George McGeachie	31 (5)	5 (1)	1	37 (6)
Pat Liney	33	2	1	36
Doug Cowie	29 (4)	4 (1)	1	34 (5)
Jimmy Gabriel	21	5	1	27
Billy Smith	26	0	1	27
Bert Henderson	18 (5)	6	0	24 (5)
Davie Curlett	18 (5)	4	0	22 (5)
Andy Penman	19 (5)	1	1	21 (5)
Jimmy Bonthrone	10 (8)	3 (1)	0	13 (9)
Alan Gilzean	8 (8)	1	1	10 (8)
Ally Hill	7 (1)	3 (1)	0	10 (2)
Billy McMillan	6	2	0	8
Ian Ure	7	0	0	7
John Horsburgh	1	4	0	5
Bobby Waddell	3 (2)	1 (1)	0	4 (3)
Fred Jardine	2	0	0	2
Tom Robertson	1	1	0	2

The Record

League	-	Fourth Place, Division One
League Cup	-	Qualifying stages only
Scottish Cup	-	Second round
Forfarshire Cup	-	Winners
Top Scorer	-	Alan Cousin (17 goals)
Av. Home Gate	-	12,000
Players used	-	21
Sent off	-	None

Scottish League Division One

		Home			Away			Goals		
	P	W	D	L	W	D	L	F A	PTS
Hearts	34	14	2	1	9	6	2	102-51	54
Kilmarnock	34	13	2	2	11	0	6	67-45	50
Rangers	34	5	6	6	12	2	3	72-38	42
Dundee	**34**	**11**	**1**	**5**	**5**	**9**	**3**	**70-49**	**42**
Motherwell	34	9	4	4	7	4	6	71-61	40
Clyde	34	7	5	5	8	4	5	77-69	39
Hibernian	34	8	4	5	6	3	8	106-85	35
Ayr United	34	9	4	4	5	2	10	65-73	34
Celtic	34	7	5	5	5	4	8	73-59	33
Partick Thistle	34	10	0	7	4	4	9	54-78	32
Raith Rovers	34	7	3	7	7	0	10	64-62	31
Third Lanark	34	7	3	7	6	1	10	75-83	30
Dunfermline	34	7	5	5	3	4	10	72-80	29
St Mirren	34	5	3	9	6	3	8	78-86	28
Aberdeen	34	8	4	5	3	2	12	54-72	28
Airdrie	34	5	1	11	6	5	6	56-80	28
Stirling Albion	34	4	3	10	3	5	9	55-72	22
Arbroath	34	4	5	8	0	2	15	38-106	15

League Cup Section

	P	W	D	L	F A	PTS
Motherwell	6	6	0	0	19- 8	12
Rangers	6	4	0	2	18- 8	8
Dundee	**6**	**2**	**0**	**4**	**12-17**	**4**
Hibernian	6	0	0	6	9-25	0

Dundee F.C. Line-Ups 1959-60

		1	2	3	4	5	6	7	8	9	10	11
Aug	8th	Horsburgh	Hamilton	Cox	Henderson	Gabriel	Curlett	McGeachie	Robertson T	Cousin	Bonthrone	Robertson H
	12th	Horsburgh	Hamilton	Cox	Curlett	Gabriel	Cowie	McGeachie	Bonthrone	Cousin	Henderson	Robertson H
	15th	Horsburgh	Hamilton	Cox	Curlett	Gabriel	Cowie	McGeachie	Bonthrone	Cousin	Henderson	Robertson H
	19th	Horsburgh	Hamilton	Cox	Henderson	Cowie	Curlett	Penman	Cousin	Hill	Robertson T	Robertson H
	22nd	Horsburgh	Hamilton	Cox	Henderson	Cowie	Curlett	Penman	Cousin	Hill	Gilzean	Robertson H
	26th	Liney	Hamilton	Cox	Gabriel	McMillan	Cowie	Hill	Henderson	Cousin	McGeachie	Robertson H
	29th	Liney	Hamilton	Cox	Gabriel	McMillan	Henderson	Hill	Cousin	Waddell	McGeachie	Robertson H
Sep	5th	Liney	Hamilton	Cox	Henderson	McMillan	Cowie	Hill	Cousin	Waddell	McGeachie	Robertson H
	12th	Liney	Hamilton	Cox	Henderson	McMillan	Cowie	Hill	Cousin	Waddell	McGeachie	Robertson H
	19th	Liney	Hamilton	Cox	Gabriel	McMillan	Curlett	Hill	Henderson	Cousin	McGeachie	Robertson H
	26th	Liney	Hamilton	Cox	Gabriel	McMillan	Curlett	Hill	Henderson	Cousin	McGeachie	Robertson H
Oct	3rd	Liney	Hamilton	Cox	Gabriel	McMillan	Curlett	McGeachie	Cousin	Hill	Henderson	Robertson H
	10th	Liney	Hamilton	Cox	Gabriel	Smith	Curlett	McGeachie	Cousin	Hill	Henderson	Robertson H
	17th	Liney	Hamilton	Cox	Gabriel	Smith	Cowie	McGeachie	Cousin	Curlett	Bonthrone	Robertson H
	24th	Liney	Hamilton	Cox	Gabriel	Smith	Cowie	McGeachie	Cousin	Curlett	Bonthrone	Robertson H
	31st	Liney	Hamilton	Cox	Gabriel	Smith	Cowie	McGeachie	Cousin	Curlett	Bonthrone	Robertson H
Nov	7th	Liney	Hamilton	Cox	Gabriel	Smith	Cowie	McGeachie	Cousin	Curlett	Bonthrone	Robertson H
	14th	Liney	Hamilton	Cox	Gabriel	Smith	Cowie	McGeachie	Cousin	Curlett	Bonthrone	Robertson H
	21st	Liney	Hamilton	Cox	Gabriel	Smith	Cowie	McGeachie	Cousin	Curlett	Bonthrone	Robertson H
	28th	Liney	Hamilton	Cox	Gabriel	Smith	Cowie	McGeachie	Cousin	Curlett	Bonthrone	Robertson H
Dec	5th	Liney	Hamilton	Cox	Gabriel	Smith	Cowie	Penman	Bonthrone	Cousin	Henderson	Robertson H
	12th	Liney	Hamilton	Cox	Gabriel	Smith	Cowie	Penman	Cousin	Curlett	Henderson	Robertson H
	19th	Liney	Hamilton	Cox	Gabriel	Smith	Cowie	Penman	Cousin	Curlett	Henderson	Robertson H
	26th	Liney	Hamilton	Cox	Gabriel	Smith	Cowie	Penman	McGeachie	Henderson	Cousin	Robertson H
Jan	1st	Liney	Hamilton	Cox	Gabriel	Smith	Cowie	Penman	McGeachie	Cousin	Henderson	Robertson H
	2nd	Liney	Hamilton	Cox	Gabriel	Smith	Cowie	McGeachie	Bonthrone	Cousin	Henderson	Robertson H
	9th	Liney	Hamilton	Cox	Gabriel	Smith	Cowie	Penman	McGeachie	Cousin	Henderson	Robertson H
	16th	Liney	Hamilton	Cox	Gabriel	Smith	Cowie	Penman	McGeachie	Cousin	Henderson	Robertson H
	23rd	Liney	Hamilton	Cox	Curlett	Smith	Cowie	Penman	McGeachie	Cousin	Bonthrone	Robertson H
Feb	9th	Liney	Hamilton	Cox	Gabriel	Smith	Cowie	Penman	McGeachie	Cousin	Gilzean	Robertson H
	27th	Liney	Hamilton	Cox	Gabriel	Smith	Cowie	Penman	McGeachie	Cousin	Gilzean	Robertson H
	29th	Liney	Hamilton	Cox	Gabriel	Smith	Cowie	Penman	McGeachie	Cousin	Gilzean	Robertson H
Mar	5th	Liney	Hamilton	Cox	Henderson	Smith	Cowie	Penman	McGeachie	Curlett	Cousin	Jardine
	10th	Liney	Hamilton	Cox	Ure	Smith	Cowie	Penman	McGeachie	Cousin	Gilzean	Jardine
	12th	Liney	Hamilton	Cox	Henderson	Smith	Cowie	Penman	McGeachie	Waddell	Cousin	Robertson H
	19th	Liney	Hamilton	Cox	Ure	Smith	Cowie	Penman	Cousin	Henderson	McGeachie	Robertson H
	26th	Liney	Hamilton	Cox	Ure	Smith	Curlett	Penman	McGeachie	Gilzean	Cousin	Robertson H
Apr	2nd	Liney	Hamilton	Cox	Ure	Smith	Cowie	Penman	McGeachie	Gilzean	Cousin	Robertson H
	16th	Liney	Hamilton	Cox	Ure	Smith	Cowie	Penman	McGeachie	Gilzean	Cousin	Robertson H
	23rd	Liney	Hamilton	Cox	Ure	McMillan	Cowie	Penman	McGeachie	Gilzean	Cousin	Robertson H
	30th	Liney	Hamilton	Cox	Curlett	Ure	Cowie	Penman	McGeachie	Gilzean	Cousin	Robertson H

Great tackle - Motherwell inside-right Pat Quinn was set to score when Doug Cowie slid in with a last-ditch tackle in the League Cup tie at Dens. The Dundee players in the background are Alan Gilzean - in his debut game - and Davie Curlett.

D. Cowie Jnr.

Season 1960-61

Date		Opponents		Score	Crowd	Scorers
Aug 13th	LC	Raith Rovers	h	5-0	16,000	Penman; Gilzean 3; Robertson
17th	LC	Ayr United	a	2-1	9,000	Gilzean; Cousin
20th	LC	Aberdeen	a	4-1	18,000	Gilzean 2; Cousin; Penman
24th	L	Raith Rovers	a	1-2	7,000	Cousin
27th	LC	Raith Rovers	a	3-0	8,000	Gilzean 3
31st	LC	Ayr United	h	3-0	10,500	Waddell; Gilzean; Robertson
Sep 3rd	LC	Aberdeen	h	6-0	12,000	Gilzean 3; McGeachie 2; Waddell
10th	L	Aberdeen	h	3-3	12,000	Gilzean 3
14th	LCQ	Rangers	a	0-1	45,000	-
17th	L	Dundee United	a	1-3	20,000	Penman
21st	LCQ	Rangers	h	3-4(3-5)	33,000	Cousin 2; Penman (pen)
24th	L	Clyde	h	4-1	13,700	Cousin; Gilzean; Robertson; Seith
Oct 1st	L	St Johnstone	h	2-1	12,000	Waddell; Robertson
8th	L	Rangers	a	1-0	43,000	Cousin
15th	L	Kilmarnock	h	1-0	16,000	Penman (pen)
19th	FC1	Arbroath	h	6-2	3,000	Cowie; Henderson 3; Gilzean 2
22nd	L	St Mirren	a	2-1	10,000	Waddell; Cousin
29th	L	Dunfermline	a	2-4	9,000	Cousin; Gilzean
Nov 5th	L	Hibernian	h	0-1	13,000	-
12th	L	Third Lanark	h	0-2	10,000	-
19th	L	Ayr United	a	4-2	6,000	Gilzean 3; Cousin
26th	L	Partick Thistle	h	1-2	10,000	Cowie (pen)
Dec 10th	L	Airdrie	h	2-1	8,000	Cousin; Henderson
17th	L	Motherwell	a	0-2	11,000	-
24th	L	Hearts	h	2-2	13,000	Gilzean 2
26th	L	Celtic	a	1-2	11,000	Robertson
31st	L	Raith Rovers	h	2-3	8,000	Henderson; Cousin
Jan 2nd	L	Aberdeen	a	1-2	23,000	Gilzean
7th	L	Dundee United	h	3-0	22,000	Wishart 2; Adamson
14th	L	Clyde	a	0-0	7,000	-
21st	L	St Johnstone	a	1-1	10,000	Gilzean
28th	FCS	Dundee United	a	1-2	12,000	Penman (pen)
Feb 8th	L	Rangers	h	4-2	22,000	Wishart; Cousin; Gilzean 2
11th	SC2	Rangers	h	1-5	32,000	Cousin
18th	L	Kilmarnock	a	1-2	10,000	Gilzean
Mar 4th	L	Dunfermline	h	4-1	11,000	Seith; Cowie; Gilzean; Cox (pen)
8th	L	St Mirren	h	2-0	12,000	Robertson; Cousin
18th	L	Third Lanark	a	1-2	7,000	Cousin
20th	L	Hibernian	a	0-1	8,000	-
25th	L	Ayr United	h	6-1	8,000	Robertson 2; Crichton; Gilzean 2; Cousin
Apr 1st	L	Partick Thistle	a	2-2	7,000	Penman; Robertson
8th	L	Celtic	h	0-1	17,500	-
12th	L	Airdrie	a	4-2	3,500	Waddell; Robertson; Penman; Gilzean
22nd	L	Motherwell	h	2-2	10,000	Waddell; Robertson
29th	L	Hearts	a	1-2	10,000	Wishart

Cup Cash v. Rangers £4,372

Alex. Hamilton - the classy right-back went on to gain 24 full Scotland caps.

The Record

League	-	Tenth Place, Division One
League Cup	-	Quarter-final
Scottish Cup	-	Second round
Forfarshire Cup	-	Semi-final
Top Scorer	-	Alan Gilzean (32 goals)
Av. Home Gate	-	12,800
Players used	-	22
Sent off	-	One

Appearances

	League	L/Cup	S/Cup	Total
Hugh Robertson	34 (9)	8 (2)	1	43 (11)
Alan Gilzean	33 (19)	8 (13)	1	42 (32)
Bobby Seith	33 (2)	8	1	42 (2)
Ian Ure	32	8	1	41
Pat Liney	30	8	1	39
Bobby Cox	30 (1)	7	1	38 (1)
Alex. Hamilton	28	8	1	37
Alan Cousin	29 (12)	4 (4)	1 (1)	34 (17)
Andy Penman	16 (4)	8 (3)	1	25 (7)
Doug Cowie	17 (2)	1	0	18 (2)
George McGeachie	10	7 (2)	0	17 (2)
Bobby Wishart	15	0	1	16
Billy Smith	6	8	1	15
Bobby Waddell	8 (4)	4 (2)	0	12 (6)
Ronnie Crichton	11 (1)	0	0	11 (1)
Bert Henderson	11 (2)	0	0	11 (2)
Hugh Reid	10	1	0	11
Bobby Adamson	8 (1)	0	0	8 (1)
John Horsburgh	4	0	0	4
Alex. Stuart	3	0	1	4
Fred Jardine	3	0	0	3
Dave Curlett	2	0	0	2

Scottish League Division One

		Home			Away			Goals		
	P	W	D	L	W	D	L	F A		PTS
Rangers	34	14	1	2	9	4	4	88-46		51
Kilmarnock	34	12	4	1	9	4	4	77-45		50
Third Lanark	34	11	2	4	9	0	8	100-80		42
Celtic	34	9	4	4	6	5	6	64-46		39
Motherwell	34	9	3	5	6	5	6	70-57		38
Aberdeen	34	9	2	6	5	6	6	72-72		36
Hibernian	34	10	3	4	5	1	11	66-69		34
Hearts	34	8	3	6	5	5	7	51-53		34
Dundee United	34	9	3	5	4	4	9	60-58		33
Dundee	**34**	**9**	**3**	**5**	**4**	**3**	**10**	**61-53**		**32**
Partick Thistle	34	8	4	5	5	2	10	59-69		32
Dunfermline	34	8	4	5	4	3	10	65-81		31
Airdrie	34	9	4	4	1	6	10	61-71		30
St Mirren	34	6	5	6	5	2	10	53-50		29
St Johnstone	34	7	5	5	3	4	10	47-63		29
Raith Rovers	34	5	4	8	5	3	9	46-67		27
Clyde	34	5	7	5	1	4	12	55-77		23
Ayr United	34	5	6	6	0	6	11	51-81		22

League Cup Section

	P	W	D	L	F A		PTS
Dundee	**6**	**6**	**0**	**0**	**23- 2**		**12**
Raith Rovers	6	2	1	3	7-14		5
Aberdeen	6	2	1	3	10-18		5
Ayr United	6	0	2	4	7-13		2

Dundee F.C. Line-Ups 1960-61

		1	2	3	4	5	6	7	8	9	10	11
Aug	13th	Liney	Hamilton	Cox	Seith	Smith B	Ure	Penman	McGeachie	Gilzean	Cousin	Robertson
	17th	Liney	Hamilton	Cox	Seith	Smith B	Ure	Penman	McGeachie	Gilzean	Cousin	Robertson
	20th	Liney	Hamilton	Cox	Seith	Smith B	Ure	Penman	McGeachie	Gilzean	Cousin	Robertson
	24th	Liney	Hamilton	Cox	Seith	Smith B	Ure	Penman	McGeachie	Gilzean	Cousin	Robertson
	27th	Liney	Hamilton	Cox	Seith	Smith B	Ure	Penman	McGeachie	Waddell	Gilzean	Robertson
	31st	Liney	Hamilton	Cox	Seith	Smith B	Ure	Penman	McGeachie	Waddell	Gilzean	Robertson
Sep	3rd	Liney	Hamilton	Cox	Seith	Smith B	Ure	Penman	McGeachie	Waddell	Gilzean	Robertson
	10th	Liney	Hamilton	Cox	Seith	Smith B	Ure	Penman	McGeachie	Cousin	Gilzean	Robertson
	14th	Liney	Hamilton	Cox	Seith	Smith B	Ure	Penman	McGeachie	Gilzean	Cowie	Robertson
	17th	Liney	Hamilton	Stuart	Seith	Smith B	Ure	Penman	McGeachie	Gilzean	Henderson	Robertson
	21st	Liney	Hamilton	Reid	Seith	Smith B	Ure	Penman	Cousin	Waddell	Gilzean	Robertson
	24th	Liney	Hamilton	Reid	Seith	Ure	Henderson	Penman	Cousin	Waddell	Gilzean	Robertson
Oct	1st	Liney	Reid	Cox	Seith	Ure	Henderson	Penman	Cousin	Waddell	Gilzean	Robertson
	8th	Liney	Reid	Cox	Seith	Ure	Henderson	Penman	McGeachie	Cousin	Gilzean	Robertson
	15th	Liney	Reid	Cox	Seith	Ure	Henderson	Penman	McGeachie	Cousin	Gilzean	Robertson
	22nd	Liney	Hamilton	Reid	Curlett	Ure	Cowie	McGeachie	Cousin	Waddell	Gilzean	Robertson
	29th	Liney	Hamilton	Reid	Seith	Ure	Cowie	McGeachie	Cousin	Waddell	Gilzean	Robertson
Nov	5th	Liney	Hamilton	Cox	Seith	Smith B	Ure	Curlett	McGeachie	Gilzean	Cousin	Robertson
	12th	Horsburgh	Hamilton	Cox	Seith	Smith B	Ure	Adamson	Cousin	Gilzean	Robertson	Jardine
	19th	Liney	Hamilton	Cox	Seith	Ure*	Stuart	Robertson	Henderson	Cousin	Gilzean	Jardine
	26th	Liney	Hamilton	Cox	Seith	Ure	Cowie	Robertson	Reid	Cousin	Gilzean	Jardine
Dec	10th	Liney	Hamilton	Cox	Seith	Smith B	Cowie	McGeachie	Henderson	Cousin	Gilzean	Robertson
	17th	Liney	Hamilton	Cox	Seith	Smith B	Cowie	McGeachie	Henderson	Cousin	Gilzean	Robertson
	24th	Horsburgh	Hamilton	Cox	Seith	Ure	Cowie	Crichton	Henderson	Cousin	Gilzean	Robertson
	26th	Horsburgh	Reid	Cox	Seith	Ure	Cowie	Crichton	Cousin	Waddell	Gilzean	Robertson
	31st	Liney	Reid	Cox	Seith	Ure	Cowie	Crichton	Henderson	Cousin	Gilzean	Robertson
Jan	2nd	Liney	Reid	Cox	Seith	Ure	Cowie	Crichton	Henderson	Adamson	Gilzean	Robertson
	7th	Liney	Hamilton	Cox	Seith	Ure	Cowie	Crichton	Gilzean	Adamson	Wishart	Robertson
	14th	Liney	Hamilton	Cox	Seith	Ure	Cowie	Penman	Gilzean	Adamson	Wishart	Robertson
	21st	Liney	Hamilton	Cox	Seith	Ure	Cowie	Crichton	Gilzean	Adamson	Wishart	Robertson
Feb	8th	Liney	Hamilton	Cox	Seith	Ure	Cowie	Crichton	Gilzean	Cousin	Wishart	Robertson
	11th	Liney	Hamilton	Cox	Ure	Smith	Stuart	Penman	Gilzean	Cousin	Wishart	Robertson
	18th	Horsburgh	Hamilton	Cox	Seith	Ure	Stuart	Penman	Gilzean	Cousin	Wishart	Robertson
Mar	4th	Liney	Hamilton	Cox	Seith	Ure	Cowie	Adamson	Cousin	Gilzean	Wishart	Robertson
	8th	Liney	Hamilton	Cox	Seith	Ure	Cowie	Adamson	Cousin	Gilzean	Wishart	Robertson
	18th	Liney	Hamilton	Cox	Seith	Ure	Cowie	Adamson	Cousin	Gilzean	Wishart	Robertson
	20th	Liney	Hamilton	Cox	Seith	Ure	Wishart	Penman	Crichton	Gilzean	Cousin	Robertson
	25th	Liney	Hamilton	Cox	Seith	Ure	Wishart	Penman	Crichton	Gilzean	Cousin	Robertson
Apr	1st	Liney	Hamilton	Cox	Seith	Ure	Wishart	Penman	Crichton	Gilzean	Cousin	Robertson
	8th	Liney	Hamilton	Cox	Seith	Ure	Cowie	Penman	Cousin	Gilzean	Wishart	Robertson
	12th	Liney	Hamilton	Cox	Seith	Ure	Wishart	Penman	Cousin	Waddell	Gilzean	Robertson
	22nd	Liney	Hamilton	Cox	Seith	Ure	Wishart	Penman	Cousin	Waddell	Gilzean	Robertson
	29th	Liney	Hamilton	Cox	Seith	Ure	Wishart	Penman	Crichton	Waddell	Cousin	Robertson

On the deck - the lively Hugh Robertson has just been brought down by a Kilmarnock defender at Dens and Ian Ure, Andy Penman, Bobby Seith, Bert Henderson, Bobby Cox and Alan Gilzean look on anxiously. The Killie men are Frank O'Connor, Frank Beattie, Matt Watson and Jimmy Brown.

DC Thomson

They Wore The Dark Blue

Season 1961-62

Date			Opponents		Score	Crowd	Scorers
Aug 12th	LC	Airdrie	h	2-0	13,000	Wishart; Cousin
16th	LC	Rangers	a	2-4	40,000	Penman; Cousin
19th	LC	Third Lanark	a	2-3	12,000	Smith; Gilzean
23rd	L	Falkirk	a	3-1	7,000	Smith; Cousin; Wishart
26th	LC	Airdrie	a	5-0	4,500	Cousin; Smith; Penman; Gilzean 2
30th	LC	Rangers	h	1-1	24,000	Robertson
Sep 2nd	LC	Third Lanark	h	2-2	9,000	Cousin; Penman
9th	L	Dundee United	h	4-1	20,000	Penman; Smith; Briggs o.g.; Robertson
16th	L	Aberdeen	a	1-3	12,000	Gilzean
23rd	L	Hearts	h	2-0	12,000	Gilzean 2
30th	L	Third Lanark	a	3-1	9,500	Gilzean 2; Cousin
Oct 7th	L	Kilmarnock	h	5-3	14,000	Watson o.g.; Penman 3; Gilzean
14th	L	Motherwell	a	4-2	15,000	Penman (pen); Cousin; Smith; Gilzean
21st	L	Dunfermline	a	2-1	10,000	Cousin 2
28th	L	Partick Thistle	h	3-2	16,000	Cousin 2; Penman (pen)
Nov 4th	L	Celtic	h	2-1	24,500	Wishart; Gilzean
11th	L	Rangers	a	5-1	38,000	Gilzean 4; Penman
18th	L	Raith Rovers	h	5-4	15,000	Gilzean 2; Wishart; Seith; Smith
25th	L	Hibernian	a	3-1	16,000	Gilzean; Penman; Smith
Dec 2nd	L	Stirling Albion	h	2-2	11,500	Robertson; Cousin
16th	L	Airdrie	h	5-1	11,500	Wishart; Smith; Cousin; Robertson 2
23rd	L	St Mirren	a	1-1	11,000	Wishart
30th	L	Falkirk	h	2-1	15,000	Gilzean 2
Jan 13th	L	Hearts	a	2-0	25,000	Cousin; Gilzean
17th	L	Aberdeen	h	2-1	16,000	Cousin; Penman (pen)
20th	L	Third Lanark	h	2-1	17,500	Penman (pen); Robertson
24th	L	St Johnstone	h	2-1	16,000	Gilzean; Penman
27th	SC2	St Mirren	h	0-1	22,834	-
Feb 3rd	L	Kilmarnock	a	1-1	14,000	Cousin
10th	L	Motherwell	h	1-3	19,000	Robertson
24th	L	Partick Thistle	a	0-3	15,000	-
Mar 3rd	L	Celtic	a	1-2	39,000	Wishart
7th	L	Dunfermline	h	1-2	17,500	Seith
14th	L	Rangers	h	0-0	35,000	-
17th	L	Raith Rovers	a	3-2	5,000	Cousin; Penman 2
24th	L	Hibernian	h	1-0	12,000	Waddell
31st	L	Stirling Albion	a	3-2	4,500	Cousin; Smith; Gilzean
Apr 7th	L	Airdrie	a	2-1	7,000	Penman 2 (1 pen)
9th	L	Dundee United	a	2-1	20,000	Gilzean 2
25th	L	St Mirren	h	2-0	20,000	Cousin; Penman
28th	L	St Johnstone	a	3-0	26,500	Gilzean 2; Penman

Cup Cash v. St Mirren (h) £3,490

Gordon Smith - his experience was key factor in Dundee's title success.

The Record		
League	-	Division One Champions
League Cup	-	Qualifying stages only
Scottish Cup	-	Second round
Forfarshire Cup	-	Unable to fit in
Top Scorer	-	Alan Gilzean (27 goals)
Av. Home Gate	-	17,200
Players used	-	15
Sent off	-	None

Magic moment - Hugh Robertson blasts Dundee ahead in the League Cup tie against Rangers at Dens. The game ended 1-1 and the battle for the League title was to prove just as close.

DC Thomson

Scottish League Division One

		Home			Away			Goals		
	P	W	D	L	W	D	L	F A	PTS	
Dundee	34	13	2	2	12	2	3	80-46	54	
Rangers	34	12	2	3	10	5	2	84-31	51	
Celtic	34	12	4	1	7	4	6	81-37	46	
Dunfermline	34	13	1	3	6	4	7	77-46	43	
Kilmarnock	34	10	4	3	6	6	5	74-58	42	
Hearts	34	7	5	5	9	1	7	54-49	38	
Partick Thistle	34	12	0	5	4	3	10	60-55	35	
Hibernian	34	7	5	5	7	0	10	58-72	33	
Motherwell	34	7	3	7	6	3	8	66-62	32	
Dundee United	34	8	3	6	5	3	9	70-71	32	
Third Lanark	34	8	3	6	5	2	10	59-60	31	
Aberdeen	34	6	6	5	4	3	10	60-73	29	
Raith Rovers	34	5	5	7	5	2	10	51-73	27	
Falkirk	34	6	2	9	5	2	10	45-68	26	
Airdrie	34	7	2	8	2	5	10	57-78	25	
St Mirren	34	7	3	7	3	2	12	52-80	25	
St Johnstone	34	4	2	11	5	5	7	35-61	25	
Stirling Albion	34	5	3	9	1	3	13	34-76	18	

League Cup Section

	P	W	D	L	F A	PTS
Rangers	6	5	1	0	18- 5	11
Dundee	6	2	2	2	**14-10**	6
Third Lanark	6	2	2	2	10-14	6
Airdrie	6	0	1	5	5-18	1

Dundee F.C. Line-Ups 1961-62

		1	2	3	4	5	6	7	8	9	10	11
Aug	12th	Liney	Hamilton	Cox	Seith	Ure	Wishart	McGeachie	Penman	Cousin	Gilzean	Robertson
	16th	Liney	Hamilton	Cox	Seith	Ure	Wishart	McGeachie	Penman	Waddell	Cousin	Robertson
	19th	Liney	Hamilton	Cox	Seith	Ure	Wishart	Smith	Penman	Gilzean	Cousin	Robertson
	23rd	Liney	Hamilton	Cox	Seith	Ure	Wishart	Smith	Penman	Gilzean	Cousin	Robertson
	26th	Liney	Hamilton	Cox	Seith	Ure	Wishart	Smith	Penman	Gilzean	Cousin	Robertson
	30th	Liney	Hamilton	Cox	Seith	Ure	Wishart	Smith	Penman	Gilzean	Cousin	Robertson
Sep	2nd	Liney	Hamilton	Cox	Seith	Ure	Wishart	Smith	Penman	Gilzean	Cousin	Robertson
	9th	Liney	Hamilton	Cox	Seith	Ure	Stuart	Smith	Penman	Gilzean	Cousin	Robertson
	16th	Liney	Hamilton	Cox	Seith	Ure	Stuart	Smith	Penman	Gilzean	Cousin	Robertson
	23rd	Liney	Hamilton	Cox	Seith	Ure	Wishart	Smith	Penman	Cousin	Gilzean	Robertson
	30th	Liney	Hamilton	Cox	Seith	Ure	Wishart	Smith	Penman	Cousin	Gilzean	Robertson
Oct	7th	Liney	Hamilton	Cox	Seith	Ure	Wishart	Smith	Penman	Cousin	Gilzean	Robertson
	14th	Liney	Hamilton	Cox	Seith	Ure	Wishart	Smith	Penman	Cousin	Gilzean	Robertson
	21st	Liney	Hamilton	Cox	Seith	Ure	Wishart	Smith	Penman	Cousin	Gilzean	Robertson
	28th	Liney	Hamilton	Cox	Seith	Ure	Wishart	McGeachie	Penman	Cousin	Gilzean	Robertson
Nov	4th	Liney	Hamilton	Cox	Seith	Ure	Wishart	Smith	Penman	Cousin	Gilzean	Robertson
	11th	Liney	Hamilton	Cox	Seith	Ure	Wishart	Smith	Penman	Cousin	Gilzean	Robertson
	18th	Liney	Hamilton	Cox	Seith	Ure	Wishart	Smith	Penman	Cousin	Gilzean	Robertson
	25th	Liney	Hamilton	Cox	Seith	Ure	Wishart	Smith	Penman	Cousin	Gilzean	Robertson
Dec	2nd	Liney	Hamilton	Cox	Seith	Ure	Wishart	Smith	Penman	Cousin	Gilzean	Robertson
	9th	Liney	Hamilton	Cox	Seith	Ure	Wishart	Smith	Penman	Cousin	McGeachie	Robertson
	23rd	Liney	Hamilton	Cox	Seith	Ure	Wishart	Smith	Penman	Cousin	McGeachie	Robertson
	30th	Liney	Hamilton	Cox	Seith	Ure	Wishart	Smith	Penman	Cousin	Gilzean	Robertson
Jan	13th	Liney	Hamilton	Cox	Seith	Ure	Wishart	Smith	Penman	Cousin	Gilzean	Robertson
	17th	Liney	Hamilton	Cox	Seith	Ure	Wishart	Smith	Penman	Cousin	Gilzean	Robertson
	20th	Liney	Hamilton	Cox	Seith	Ure	Wishart	Smith	Penman	Cousin	Gilzean	Robertson
	23rd	Liney	Hamilton	Cox	Seith	Ure	Wishart	Smith	Penman	Cousin	Gilzean	Robertson
	27th	Liney	Hamilton	Cox	Seith	Ure	Wishart	Smith	Penman	Cousin	Gilzean	Robertson
Feb	3rd	Liney	Hamilton	Brown	Seith	Ure	Wishart	Smith	Penman	Cousin	Gilzean	Robertson
	10th	Liney	Hamilton	Brown	Seith	Ure	Wishart	Smith	Penman	Cousin	Gilzean	Robertson
	24th	Liney	Hamilton	Brown	Seith	Ure	Wishart	Smith	Penman	Cousin	Gilzean	Robertson
Mar	3rd	Liney	Hamilton	Cox	Seith	Ure	Brown	Smith	Wishart	Cousin	Gilzean	Robertson
	7th	Liney	Hamilton	Cox	Seith	Ure	Brown	Penman	Wishart	Cousin	Gilzean	Robertson
	14th	Liney	Hamilton	Cox	Seith	Ure	Brown	Smith	Penman	Waddell	Cousin	Robertson
	17th	Liney	Hamilton	Cox	Seith	Ure	Brown	Smith	Penman	Waddell	Cousin	Robertson
	24th	Liney	Hamilton	Cox	Seith	Ure	Brown	Smith	Penman	Waddell	Cousin	Wishart
	31st	Liney	Hamilton	Cox	Seith	Ure	Brown	Smith	Gilzean	Waddell	Cousin	Robertson
Apr	7th	Liney	Hamilton	Cox	Seith	Ure	Wishart	Smith	Penman	Cousin	Gilzean	Robertson
	9th	Liney	Hamilton	Cox	Seith	Ure	Wishart	Smith	Penman	Cousin	Gilzean	Robertson
	25th	Liney	Hamilton	Cox	Seith	Ure	Wishart	Smith	Penman	Cousin	Gilzean	Robertson
	28th	Liney	Hamilton	Cox	Seith	Ure	Wishart	Smith	Penman	Cousin	Gilzean	Robertson

Pride of Dundee - the Dark Blues have beaten St Johnstone 3-0 on the last day of the season and players and officials celebrate their League Championship win in the Muirton stand. BACK - Alex. Hamilton, Pat Liney, Bobby Seith, Ian Ure, Bobby Wishart, Bobby Cox. FRONT - Gordon Smith, Andy Penman, Sammy Kean (coach), Bob Shankly (manager), Alan Cousin, Alan Gilzean and Hugh Robertson.

Alex. Benvie

OCTOBER 1961 - Pat Liney is beaten by Motherwell's Willie Hunter at Fir Park but Dundee recovered to win 4-2. Looking on are Bobby Roberts, Pat Quinn and Willie Hunter (Motherwell) and Dundee's Alex. Hamilton, Bobby Seith, Ian Ure and Bobby Wishart.

NOVEMBER 1961 - Alan Gilzean beats Celtic keeper Frank Haffey only for Duncan McKay to clear off the line at Dens with Jim Kennedy and Pat Crerand watching anxiously. Later on Gilzean headed the winner in a 2-1 Dundee triumph. DC Thomson

NOVEMBER 1961 - Billy Ritchie sprawls at Andy Penman's feet after Alan Gilzean has netted Dundee's fourth in the 5-1 win over Rangers at Ibrox.

DECEMBER 1961 - a powerfully stuck free-kick by Bobby Wishart earns the Dark Blues a 1-1 draw with St Mirren at Love Street .

Appearances

	League	L/Cup	S/Cup	Total
Alan Cousin	34 (15)	6 (4)	1	41 (19)
Alex Hamilton	34	6	1	41
Pat Liney	34	6	1	41
Bobby Seith	34 (2)	6	1	41 (2)
Ian Ure	34	6	1	41
Hugh Robertson	33 (6)	6 (1)	1	40 (7)
Andy Penman	32 (17)	6 (3)	1	39 (20)
Bobby Cox	31	6	1	38
Gordon Smith	32 (7)	4 (2)	1	37 (9)
Bobby Wishart	29 (6)	6 (1)	1	36 (7)
Alan Gilzean	29 (24)	5 (3)	1	35 (27)
Craig Brown	9	0	0	9
George McGeachie	3	2	0	5
Bobby Waddell	4 (1)	1	0	5 (1)
Alex Stuart	2	0	0	2

JANUARY 1962 - Alan Cousin outjumps Bobby Kirk for the opener as Dundee continue their winning form with a 2-0 triumph over Hearts at Tynecastle.

FEBRUARY 1962 - Pat Liney and Ian Ure watch an Andy Kerr header skim the bar in a hard-fought 1-1 draw at Kilmarnock.

MARCH 1962 - Drama at Dens as Ian Ure steps in to clear a header from Doug Baillie of Rangers. Dundee's spirited display against the Ibrox men marked a resurgence in their fortunes after only one point was taken from their previous five games.
DC Thomson

APRIL 1962 - Joyous scenes after Alan Gilzean's winner in the 2-1 victory against Dundee United at Tannadice, a result which took Dundee back to the top alongside Rangers.
DC Thomson

April 1962 - Alan Cousin's shot beats keeper Bobby Williamson for the Dundee opener against St Mirren at Dens. Later, Andy Penman made it 2-0 as Dundee moved two points clear.
DC Thomson

APRIL 1962 - Ace marksman Alan Gilzean bursts through to crash the ball past St Johnstone keeper Bill Taylor for Dundee's second goal at Muirton. Andy Penman added a third and the 1961-62 League Championship belonged to Dundee!

Hail, Hail, the Dee are here - there were thousands of exultant fans in Dundee's City Square to welcome the Dens Park players and officials when they appeared on the balcony of the City Chambers.

DC Thomson

Season 1962-63

Date		Opponents		Score	Crowd	Scorers
Aug 11th	LC	Dundee United	a	2-3	25,300	Gilzean 2
15th	LC	Celtic	h	1-0	21,000	Smith
18th	LC	Hearts	h	0-2	20,000	-
22nd	L	Hearts	a	1-3	18,000	Houston
25th	LC	Dundee United	h	2-1	19,500	Smith 2
29th	LC	Celtic	a	0-3	28,000	-
Sep 1st	LC	Hearts	a	0-2	15,000	-
5th	EC1	Cologne	h	8-1	25,000	Hemmersbach o.g.; Wishart; Robertson; Gilzean 3; Smith; Penman
8th	L	Aberdeen	h	2-2	18,000	Penman; Gilzean
15th	L	Dundee United	a	1-1	18,000	Cousin
22nd	L	Clyde	h	2-0	12,000	Penman 2
26th	EC1	Cologne	a	0-4 (8-5)	40,000	-
29th	L	Rangers	a	1-1	46,000	Robertson
Oct 1st	FC1	Forfar Athletic	a	4-2	3,500	Penman; Gilzean 2; Waddell
6th	L	Falkirk	h	2-1	12,000	Cousin; Gilzean
13th	L	Hibernian	a	2-2	5,000	Penman; Cousin
20th	L	Kilmarnock	h	1-0	16,000	Gilzean
24th	EC2	Sporting Lisbon	a	0-1	50,000	-
27th	L	Dunfermline	a	0-2	9,000	-
31st	EC2	Sporting Lisbon	h	4-1 (4-2)	32,000	Gilzean 3; Cousin
Nov 3rd	L	Airdrie	h	2-1	12,000	Houston; Gilzean
10th	L	Partick Thistle	a	0-1	18,000	-
17th	L	Celtic	h	0-0	18,000	-
24th	L	Third Lanark	a	3-4	5,000	Cousin; Gilzean 2
Dec 1st	L	Q.O.S.	h	10-2	12,000	Gilzean 7; Penman; Houston; Ryden
8th	L	St Mirren	a	3-0		Campbell o.g.; Cousin; Penman
15th	L	Motherwell	h	2-2	13,000	Gilzean; Wishart
22nd	L	Raith Rovers	a	4-2		Gilzean 3; Penman (pen)
Jan 1st	L	Aberdeen	a	0-1		-
5th	L	Clyde	a	2-3	7,000	Gilzean 2
12th	SC1	Inverness Caley	a	5-1	4,632	Penman 2; Robertson; Gilzean; Cousin
Feb 5th	SC2	Montrose	h	8-0	12,062	Cousin 2; Gilzean 2; Wishart; Robertson; Waddell; Smith
Mar 6th	ECQ	Anderlecht	a	4-1	60,000	Gilzean 2; Cousin; Smith
9th	L	Airdrie	a	0-1	3,000	-
13th	ECQ	Anderlecht	h	2-1 (6-2)	40,000	Cousin; Smith
16th	L	Partick Thistle	h	2-1	12,000	Hogan o.g.; Cameron
18th	SC3	Hibernian	h	1-0	16,000	Gilzean
23rd	L	Celtic	a	1-4	42,000	Gilzean
30th	SCQ	Rangers	h	1-1	36,839	Penman (pen)
Apr 3rd	SCQ	Rangers	a	2-3	82,000	Gilzean 2
5th	L	Q.O.S.	a	0-1	5,500	-
8th	L	Hibernian	h	1-3	10,000	Penman (pen)
13th	L	St Mirren	h	5-1	10,000	Houston; Waddell; Gilzean
15th	L	Dundee United	h	1-2	16,000	Waddell
20th	L	Motherwell	a	1-2	8,500	Gilzean
24th	ECS	AC Milan	a	1-5	78,000	Cousin
27th	L	Raith Rovers	h	1-1	9,000	Gilzean
May 1st	ECS	AC Milan	h	1-0 (2-5)	38,000	Gilzean
6th	L	Hearts	h	2-2	10,000	Penman 2 (1 pen)
11th	L	Kilmarnock	a	0-1	6,000	-
13th	L	Third Lanark	h	5-2	6,000	Smith 2; Cameron 2; Ryden
16th	L	Dunfermline	h	1-0	12,000	Cousin
18th	L	Falkirk	a	2-0	2,000	Gilzean; Smith
22nd	FCS	Dundee United	a	0-2	15,000	-
25th	L	Rangers	h	0-0	17,000	-

Ian Ure - the Scottish international pivot was a defensive colossus.

The Record		
League	-	Ninth Place, Division One
League Cup	-	Qualifying stages only
Scottish Cup	-	Quarter-final
European Cup	-	Semi-final
Forfarshire Cup	-	Semi-final
Top scorer	-	Alan Gilzean (41 goals)
Av. Home gate	-	12,700
Players used	-	21
Sent off	-	One

Cup Cash v. Montrose £1,708; v. Hibs £2,254

Hit man - Alan Gilzean beats the diving Carvalho with a low shot for Dundee's third in the 4-1 European Cup win over Sporting Lisbon at Dens.

Dundee F.C. Line-Ups 1962-63

		1	2	3	4	5	6	7	8	9	10	11
Aug	11th	Slater	Hamilton	Cox	Brown	Ure	Wishart	Smith	Penman	Cousin	Gilzean	Robertson
	15th	Slater	Hamilton	Cox	Seith	Ure	Wishart	Smith	Penman	Cousin	Gilzean	Robertson
	18th	Slater	Hamilton	Cox	Seith	Ure	Wishart	Smith	Penman	Cousin	Houston	Robertson
	22nd	Slater	Hamilton	Cox	Seith	Ure	Wishart	Smith	Penman	Waddell	Cousin	Houston
	25th	Slater	Hamilton	Cox	Seith	Ure	Wishart	Smith	Penman	Cameron	Cousin	Houston
	29th	Slater	Hamilton	Cox	Seith	Ure	Wishart	Smith	Penman	Cameron	Cousin	Robertson
Sep	1st	Slater	Hamilton	Cox	Seith	Ure	Stuart	Smith	Penman	Gilzean	Houston	Robertson
	5th	Slater	Hamilton	Cox	Seith	Ure	Wishart	Smith	Penman	Cousin	Gilzean	Robertson
	8th	Slater	Hamilton	Cox	Seith	Ure	Wishart	Smith	Penman	Cousin	Gilzean	Robertson
	15th	Slater	Hamilton	Cox	Seith	Ure	Wishart	Smith	Penman	Cousin	Gilzean	Robertson
	22nd	Slater	Hamilton	Cox	Seith	Ure	Stuart	Smith	Penman	Cousin	Gilzean	Robertson
	26th	Slater	Hamilton	Cox	Seith	Ure	Wishart	Smith	Penman	Cousin	Gilzean	Robertson
	29th	Liney	Hamilton	Cox	Seith	Ure	Wishart	Smith	Penman	Cousin	Gilzean	Robertson
Oct	6th	Slater	Hamilton	Cox	Seith	Ure	Wishart	Smith	Penman	Cousin	Gilzean	Robertson
	13th	Slater	Hamilton	Cox	Seith	Ure	Wishart	Smith	Penman	Cousin	Gilzean	Robertson
	20th	Slater	Reid	Cox	Seith	Ryden	Wishart	Smith	Penman	Cousin	Gilzean	Robertson
	24th	Slater	Hamilton	Cox	Seith	Ure	Wishart	Smith	Penman	Cousin	Gilzean	Houston
	27th	Slater	Hamilton	Cox	Seith	Ure	Wishart	Smith	Penman	Cousin	Gilzean	Houston
	31st	Slater	Hamilton	Cox	Seith	Ure	Wishart	Smith	Penman	Cousin	Gilzean	Robertson
Nov	3rd	Slater	Hamilton	Cox	Seith	Ure	Wishart	Smith	Penman	Cousin	Gilzean	Houston
	10th	Slater	Hamilton	Cox	Seith	Ure	Wishart	Smith	Penman	Cousin	Gilzean	Houston
	17th	Slater	Hamilton	Cox	Seith	Ure	Wishart	Smith	Penman	Gilzean	Cousin	Houston
	24th	Slater	Hamilton	Cox	Seith	Ure	Wishart	Smith	Penman	Cousin	Gilzean	Houston
Dec	1st	Slater	Hamilton	Cox	Ryden	Ure	Wishart	Smith	Penman	Cousin	Gilzean	Houston
	8th	Slater	Hamilton	Cox	Ryden	Ure	Wishart	McGeachie	Penman	Cousin	Gilzean	Houston
	15th	Slater	Hamilton	Cox	Ryden	Ure	Wishart	Smith	Penman	Cousin	Gilzean	Houston
	22nd	Slater	Hamilton	Cox	Ryden	Ure	Wishart	Smith	Penman	Gilzean	Houston	Robertson
Jan	1st	Slater	Hamilton	Cox	Ryden	Ure	Wishart	Smith	Penman	Cousin	Gilzean	Houston
	5th	Slater	Hamilton	Cox	Seith	Ure	Wishart	Smith	Penman	Cousin	Gilzean	Robertson
	12th	Slater	Hamilton	Cox	Seith	Ryden	Wishart	Smith	Penman	Cousin	Gilzean	Robertson
Feb	5th	Slater	Hamilton	Cox	Seith	Ure	Wishart	Smith	Waddell	Cousin	Gilzean	Robertson
Mar	6th	Slater	Hamilton	Cox	Seith	Ure	Wishart	Smith	Penman	Cousin	Gilzean	Robertson
	9th	Slater	Hamilton	Cox	Seith	Ure	Wishart	Smith	Penman	Waddell	Cousin	Robertson
	13th	Slater	Hamilton	Cox	Seith	Ure	Wishart	Smith	Penman	Cousin	Gilzean	Robertson
	16th	Slater	Hamilton	Cox	Seith	Ure	Wishart	Penman	Waddell	Cameron	Cousin	Robertson
	18th	Slater	Hamilton	Cox	Seith	Ure	Wishart	Smith	Penman	Cousin	Gilzean	Robertson
	23rd	Slater	Hamilton	Cox	Seith	Ure	Wishart	Smith	Penman	Cousin	Gilzean	Robertson
	30th	Slater	Hamilton	Cox	Seith	Ure	Wishart	Smith	Penman	Cousin	Gilzean	Robertson
Apr	1st	Slater	Hamilton	Cox	Seith	Ure	Wishart	Smith	Penman	Cousin	Gilzean	Robertson
	5th	Slater	Reid	Cox	Seith	Ryden	Wishart	Smith	Penman	Cousin	Gilzean	Robertson
	8th	Slater	Hamilton	Cox	Seith	Ure	Wishart	Smith	Penman	Gilzean	Cousin	Robertson
	13th	Slater	Reid	Cox	Seith	Ure	Wishart	Smith	Penman	Waddell	Gilzean	Houston
	15th	Slater	Hamilton	Cox	Seith	Ure	Wishart	Smith	Penman	Waddell	Gilzean	Houston
	20th	Slater	Hamilton	Cox	Seith	Ure	Wishart	Smith	Penman	Cousin	Gilzean	Houston
	24th	Slater	Hamilton	Stuart	Seith	Ure	Wishart	Smith	Penman	Cousin	Gilzean	Houston
	27th	Slater	Reid	Stuart	Seith	Ure	Wishart	Penman	Waddell	Cousin	Gilzean	Robertson
May	1st	Slater	Hamilton	Stuart	Seith	Ure	Wishart	Smith	Penman	Cousin	Gilzean*	Houston
	6th	Liney	Hamilton	Stuart	Seith	Ure	Wishart	Smith	Penman	Waddell	Gilzean	Houston
	11th	Slater	Hamilton	Stuart	Seith	Ure	Ryden	Penman	Cousin	Waddell	Houston	Robertson
	13th	Slater	Hamilton	Stuart	Ryden	Ure	Brown	Smith	Penman	Cameron	Cousin	Mackle
	16th	Slater	Hamilton	Stuart	Seith	Ure	Brown	Smith	Penman	Cameron	Cousin	Mackle
	18th	Slater	Hamilton	Stuart	Seith	Ure	Brown	Smith	Penman	Gilzean	Cousin	Mackle
	25th	Slater	Hamilton	Stuart	Seith	Ure	Brown	Penman	Cousin	Waddell	Wishart	Houston

Rangers Billy Ritchie is helpless as Andy Penman fires Dundee ahead from the penalty spot in the Scottish Cup quarter-final at Dens.

Handy Andy - Andy Penman sends a header past the Cologne keeper for Dundee's sixth goal in their 8-1 triumph at Dens.

Heroic and sure - Ian Ure breaks up an attack by Sporting Lisbon at Dens with Bert Slater and Alex. Hamilton in attendance.

Appearances

	League	L/Cup	S/Cup	E/Cup	Total
Andy Penman	34 (10)	6	4 (3)	8 (1)	52 (14)
Bert Slater	32	6	5	8	51
Ian Ure	32	6	4	8	50
Alex Hamilton	30	6	5	8	49
Gordon Smith	29 (3)	6 (3)	5 (1)	8 (3)	48 (10)
Alan Cousin	30 (6)	5	5 (3)	8 (4)	48 (13)
Bobby Wishart	29 (1)	5	5 (1)	8 (1)	47 (3)
Bobby Seith	28	5	5	8	46
Bobby Cox	27	6	5	6	44
Alan Gilzean	27 (24)	3 (2)	5 (6)	8 (9)	43 (41)
Hugh Robertson	16 (1)	5	5 (2)	5 (1)	31 (4)
Doug Houston	17 (4)	3	0	3	23 (4)
Alex Stuart	8	1	0	2	11
George Ryden	9 (2)	0	1	0	10 (2)
Bobby Waddell	9 (4)	0	1 (1)	0	10 (5)
Craig Brown	4	1	0	0	5
Kenny Cameron	3 (3)	2	0	0	5 (3)
Hugh Reid	4	0	0	0	4
Tommy Mackle	3	0	0	0	3
Pat Liney	2	0	0	0	2
George McGeachie	1	0	0	0	1

Scottish League Division One

		Home			Away			Goals	
	P	W	D	L	W	D	L	F A	PTS
Rangers	34	13	4	0	12	3	2	94-28	57
Kilmarnock	34	12	4	1	8	4	5	92-40	48
Partick Thistle	34	11	1	5	9	5	3	66-44	46
Celtic	34	10	3	4	9	3	5	76-44	44
Hearts	34	10	4	3	7	5	5	85-59	43
Aberdeen	34	10	2	5	7	5	5	70-47	41
Dundee United	34	10	6	1	5	5	7	67-52	41
Dunfermline	34	9	6	2	4	2	11	50-47	34
Dundee	**34**	**9**	**6**	**2**	**3**	**3**	**11**	**60-49**	**33**
Motherwell	34	6	7	4	4	4	9	60-63	31
Airdrie	34	10	0	7	4	2	11	52-76	30
St Mirren	34	6	4	7	4	4	9	52-72	28
Falkirk	34	8	1	8	4	2	11	54-69	27
Third Lanark	34	6	4	7	3	4	10	56-68	26
Queen of the South	34	6	3	8	4	3	10	36-75	26
Hibernian	34	4	5	8	4	4	9	47-67	25
Clyde	34	6	1	10	3	4	10	49-83	23
Raith Rovers	34	0	4	13	2	1	14	35-118	9

League Cup Section

	P	W	D	L	F A	PTS
Hearts	6	4	0	2	11-8	8
Celtic	6	3	1	2	12-5	7
Dundee United	6	2	1	3	7-11	5
Dundee	**6**	**2**	**0**	**4**	**5-11**	**4**

Close call - watched by Bobby Cox, Bert Slater and Bobby Wishart, Bobby Seith gives the all clear as the ball whistles past the post after an Anderlecht attack at Dens. The Dark Blues beat their clever opponents 2-1 to reach the semi-final 6-2 on aggregate. DC Thomson

Head man - Alan Gilzean became feared by continental opponents as the Dark Blues progressed to the European Cup semi-final. AC Milan kept a tight rein on the inside-left but the deadly striker eludes Benitez to head the winner in Dundee's 1-0 victory at Dens. DC Thomson

Season 1963-64

Date		Opponents		Score	Crowd	Scorers
Aug 10th	LC	Third Lanark	a	2-1	5,000	Cousin; Gilzean
14th	LC	Airdrie	h	2-1	15,000	Penman; Houston
17th	LC	Dunfermline	h	4-1	16,500	Penman 2 (1 pen); Gilzean; Robertson
21st	L	Rangers	h	1-1	34,500	Seith
24th	LC	Third Lanark	h	3-2	14,500	Gilzean 3
28th	LC	Airdrie	a	1-4	7,000	Penman
31st	LC	Dunfermline	a	4-3	13,000	Gilzean 2; Cameron 2
Sep 7th	L	Aberdeen	a	4-2	12,500	Gilzean 2; Cameron; Penman
11th	LCQ	Hibernian	h	3-3	25,000	Gilzean; Penman; Waddell
14th	L	Dundee United	h	1-1	22,000	Gilzean
18th	LCQ	Hibernian	a	0-2 (3-5)	30,000	-
21st	L	Third Lanark	a	2-1	6,000	Waddell; Gilzean
28th	L	East Stirling	h	3-1	11,000	Gilzean; Penman; Collumbine o.g.
Oct 5th	L	QOS	a	5-0	5,500	Waddell 2; Cousin; Gilzean 2
12th	L	Motherwell	h	1-3	15,000	Waddell
19th	L	Hibernian	a	4-0	10,000	Gilzean 4
26th	L	Dunfermline	h	2-1	17,000	Cousin; Gilzean
Nov 2nd	L	St Mirren	a	1-2	7,500	Waddell
9th	L	Airdrie	h	4-0	10,500	Cox; Penman; Gilzean 2 (1 pen)
16th	L	St Johnstone	a	6-1	12,000	Gilzean; Penman 2; Stuart; Richmond o.g.; Waddell
23rd	L	Hearts	a	3-1	10,000	Gilzean; Penman (pen); Waddell
30th	L	Celtic	h	1-1	28,000	Penman (pen)
Dec 7th	L	Kilmarnock	a	1-1	8,000	Gilzean
14th	L	Partick Thistle	a	0-2	10,000	-
21st	L	Falkirk	h	4-3	9,000	Waddell; Gilzean; Robertson; Hamilton
28th	L	Rangers	a	1-2	43,000	Penman
Jan 1st	L	Aberdeen	h	1-4	15,000	Gilzean
2nd	L	Dundee United	a	1-2	22,500	Gilzean
4th	L	Third Lanark	h	6-0	8,000	Gilzean 2; Penman; Waddell; Cousin; Cameron
11th	SC1	Forres Mechanics	a	6-3	5,681	Waddell; Gilzean; Penman (pen); Stuart; Cousin; Cameron
18th	L	East Stirling	a	5-1	3,500	Cousin 2; Waddell 2; Gilzean
25th	SC2	Brechin City	a	9-2	8,022	Penman 2 (1 pen); Waddell; Cousin 2; Gilzean 3; Cameron
Feb 1st	L	QOS	h	6-2	11,000	Cameron 2; Gilzean 3; Penman
8th	L	Motherwell	a	2-2	7,000	Cousin; Cameron
15th	SC3	Forfar Athletic	h	6-1	17,574	Waddell 2; Gilzean 2; Cousin; Cameron
19th	L	Hibernian	h	3-0	12,000	Penman; Cameron 2
22nd	L	Dunfermline	a	2-1	9,000	Cousin; Penman
29th	L	St Mirren	h	9-2	13,000	Gilzean 3; Waddell 2; Cousin; Cameron 2; Penman
Mar 7th	SCQ	Motherwell	h	1-1	30,443	Cameron
11th	SCQ	Motherwell	a	4-2	26,280	Cameron 2; Gilzean; Waddell
18th	L	Airdrie	a	1-3	802	Stuart
21st	L	Hearts	h	2-4	13,000	Waddell; Cameron
28th	SCS	Kilmarnock	Ibrox	4-0	32,664	Gilzean 2; Penman; McFadzean o.g.
Apr 1st	L	Celtic	a	1-2	7,000	Gilzean
4th	L	Kilmarnock	h	2-1	13,000	Cameron; Gilzean
13th	L	St Johnstone	h*	2-1	13,000	Stuart; Robertson
18th	L	Partick Thistle	h	5-2	12,000	Stuart 2; Penman; Gilzean 2
25th	SCF	Rangers	Hamp	1-3	120,982	Cameron
29th	L	Falkirk	a	2-0	3,000	Penman 2
May 1st	Su	Dundee United	a	0-0	13,500	-
6th	Su	Aberdeen	h	1-0	5,000	Cousin
9th	Su	St Johnstone	a	2-2	7,000	Penman; Cameron
13th	Su	Dundee United	h	3-3	16,000	Penman (2 pens); Cameron
16th	Su	Aberdeen	a	1-3	9,000	Gilzean
20th	Su	St Johnstone	h	5-1	6,000	Penman 2 (1 pen); Gilzean; Tinney, Cousin

Alan Gilzean - Dundee's all-time top scorer with 165 goals in his seven years at Dens.

The Record

League	-	Sixth Place, Division One
League Cup	-	Quarter-final
Scottish Cup	-	Runners-up
Summer Cup	-	Qualifying stages only
Forfarshire Cup	-	Unable to fit in
Top Scorer	-	Alan Gilzean (52 goals)
Av. Home Gate	-	14,900
Players used	-	21
Sent off	-	None

* Earlier game on March 14th abandoned after 63 minutes due to flooding with St Johnstone leading 1-0.

Up for the Cup - a joyous Kenny Cameron runs the ball into the net to put Dundee ahead in the quarter-final against Motherwell at Dens.

They Wore The Dark Blue

Dundee F.C. Line-Ups 1963-64

		1	2	3	4	5	6	7	8	9	10	11
Aug	10th	Slater	Hamilton	Stuart	Seith	Ryden	Houston	Smith	Penman	Cousin	Gilzean	Robertson
	14th	Slater	Hamilton	Cox	Seith	Ryden	Stuart	Smith	Penman	Cousin	Houston	Robertson
	17th	Slater	Hamilton	Cox	Seith	Ryden	Stuart	Penman	Houston	Cousin	Gilzean	Robertson
	21st	Slater	Hamilton	Cox	Seith	Ryden	Stuart	Penman	Houston	Cousin	Gilzean	Robertson
	24th	Slater	Hamilton	Cox	Seith	Ryden	Stuart	Penman	Houston	Cousin	Gilzean	Robertson
	28th	Slater	Hamilton	Cox	Seith	Ryden	Houston	Smith	Penman	Cousin	Gilzean	Robertson
	31st	Slater	Hamilton	Cox	Seith	Ryden	Brown	Penman	Cousin	Cameron	Gilzean	Houston
Sep	7th	Slater	Hamilton	Cox	Seith	Ryden	Houston	Penman	Cousin	Cameron	Gilzean	Robertson
	11th	Slater	Hamilton	Cox	Houston	Ryden	Wishart	Penman	Cousin	Waddell	Gilzean	Robertson
	14th	Slater	Hamilton	Cox	Seith	Ryden	Houston	Penman	Cousin	Waddell	Gilzean	Robertson
	18th	Slater	Hamilton	Cox	Seith	Ryden	Stuart	Penman	Waddell	Gilzean	Cousin	Robertson
	21st	Slater	Hamilton	Cox	Seith	Ryden	Stuart	Smith	Penman	Waddell	Gilzean	Cousin
	28th	Slater	Hamilton	Cox	Seith	Ryden	Stuart	Smith	Penman	Waddell	Gilzean	Houston
Oct	5th	Slater	Hamilton	Cox	Seith	Ryden	Stuart	Smith	Waddell	Cousin	Gilzean	Houston
	12th	Slater	Reid	Cox	Seith	Ryden	Stuart	Penman	Waddell	Cousin	Gilzean	Houston
	19th	Slater	Hamilton	Cox	Seith	Ryden	Stuart	Smith	Cousin	Waddell	Gilzean	Robertson
	26th	Slater	Hamilton	Cox	Seith	Ryden	Stuart	Smith	Cousin	Waddell	Gilzean	Robertson
Nov	2nd	Slater	Hamilton	Cox	Seith	Ryden	Stuart	Smith	Cousin	Waddell	Gilzean	Robertson
	9th	Slater	Hamilton	Cox	Seith	Ryden	Stuart	Smith	Penman	Cousin	Gilzean	Robertson
	16th	Slater	Hamilton	Cox	Seith	Ryden	Stuart	Penman	Waddell	Cousin	Gilzean	Robertson
	23rd	Slater	Hamilton	Cox	Seith	Ryden	Stuart	Penman	Waddell	Cousin	Gilzean	Robertson
	30th	Slater	Hamilton	Cox	Seith	Ryden	Stuart	Penman	Waddell	Cousin	Gilzean	Robertson
Dec	7th	Slater	Hamilton	Cox	Seith	Ryden	Stuart	Penman	Waddell	Cousin	Gilzean	Robertson
	14th	Slater	Hamilton	Cox	Seith	Ryden	Stuart	Penman	Waddell	Cousin	Gilzean	Robertson
	21st	Slater	Hamilton	Cox	Seith	Stuart	Wishart	Penman	Cousin	Waddell	Gilzean	Robertson
	28th	Slater	Hamilton	Cox	Seith	Stuart	Wishart	Smith	Penman	Waddell	Cousin	Robertson
Jan	1st	Slater	Hamilton	Cox	Seith	Stuart	Wishart	Smith	Waddell	Cousin	Gilzean	Robertson
	2nd	Slater	Hamilton	Cox	Seith	Ryden	Stuart	Penman	Waddell	Cameron	Gilzean	Houston
	4th	Slater	Hamilton	Cox	Seith	Ryden	Stuart	Penman	Cousin	Waddell	Gilzean	Cameron
	11th	Slater	Hamilton	Cox	Seith	Ryden	Stuart	Penman	Cousin	Waddell	Gilzean	Cameron
	18th	Slater	Hamilton	Cox	Seith	Ryden	Stuart	Penman	Cousin	Waddell	Gilzean	Cameron
	25th	Slater	Hamilton	Cox	Seith	Ryden	Stuart	Penman	Cousin	Waddell	Gilzean	Cameron
Feb	1st	Slater	Hamilton	Cox	Seith	Ryden	Stuart	Penman	Cousin	Waddell	Gilzean	Cameron
	8th	Slater	Hamilton	Cox	Seith	Ryden	Stuart	Penman	Cousin	Waddell	Gilzean	Cameron
	15th	Slater	Hamilton	Cox	Seith	Ryden	Stuart	Penman	Cousin	Waddell	Gilzean	Cameron
	19th	Slater	Hamilton	Cox	Seith	Ryden	Stuart	Penman	Cousin	Waddell	Gilzean	Cameron
	22nd	Slater	Hamilton	Cox	Seith	Ryden	Stuart	Penman	Waddell	Cameron	Cousin	Robertson
	29th	Slater	Hamilton	Cox	Seith	Ryden	Stuart	Penman	Cousin	Waddell	Gilzean	Cameron
Mar	7th	Slater	Hamilton	Cox	Seith	Ryden	Stuart	Penman	Cousin	Waddell	Gilzean	Cameron
	11th	Slater	Hamilton	Cox	Seith	Ryden	Stuart	Penman	Cousin	Waddell	Gilzean	Cameron
	18th	Slater	Reid	Cox	Seith	Ryden	Stuart	Penman	Murray	Waddell	Cousin	Cameron
	21st	Slater	Hamilton	Cox	Seith	Ryden	Stuart	Penman	Cousin	Waddell	Gilzean	Cameron
	28th	Slater	Hamilton	Cox	Seith	Ryden	Stuart	Penman	Cousin	Cameron	Gilzean	Robertson
Apr	1st	Slater	Hamilton	Cox	Seith	Ryden	Stuart	Penman	Cousin	Cameron	Gilzean	Robertson
	4th	Slater	Hamilton	Cox	Seith	Ryden	Stuart	Penman	Cousin	Cameron	Gilzean	Robertson
	13th	Slater	Hamilton	Brown	Cousin	Ryden	Stuart	Penman	Waddell	Cameron	Gilzean	Robertson
	18th	Slater	Hamilton	Reid	Cousin	Ryden	Stuart	Penman	Murray	Cameron	Gilzean	Robertson
	25th	Slater	Hamilton	Cox	Seith	Ryden	Stuart	Penman	Cousin	Cameron	Gilzean	Robertson
	29th	Slater	Hamilton	Cox	Seith	Ryden	Stuart	Penman	Cousin	Waddell	Houston	Robertson
May	1st	Slater	Hamilton	Cox	Seith	Ryden	Stuart	Penman	Reid	Waddell	Cousin	Cameron
	6th	Slater	Hamilton	Cox	Seith	Ryden	Stuart	Penman	Cousin	Waddell	Gilzean	Cameron
	9th	Slater	Hamilton	Cox	Seith	Ryden	Stuart	Penman	Cousin	Waddell	Gilzean	Cameron
	13th	Slater	Reid	Cox	Seith	Ryden	Stuart	Penman	Cousin	Waddell	Murray	Cameron
	16th	Slater	Hamilton	Cox	Seith	Ryden	Stuart	Penman	Cousin	Gilzean	Murray	Cameron
	20th	Donaldson	Reid	Cox	Kinninmonth	Seith	Stuart	Penman	Cousin	Gilzean	Murray	Tinney

Andy Penman crashes home Dundee's seventh from the penalty spot in a 9-2 second round romp over Brechin City at Glebe Park.

143

Scoring aces - Dundee's first-team squad which netted an amazing 156 goals in the 1963-64 season. (Left to right) Alan Gilzean, Craig Brown, Bobby Waddell, George Ryden, Bobby Seith, Bobby Wishart, Alan Cousin, Bobby Cox, Andy Penman, Hugh Robertson, Doug Houston, Alex. Stuart, Alex Hamilton, Gordon Smith and Bert Slater.

DC Thomson

Appearances

	League	L/Cup	S/Cup	Sum/Cup	Total
Bert Slater	34	8	7	5	54
Alan Cousin	32 (8)	8 (1)	7 (4)	6 (2)	53 (15)
Bobby Cox	32 (1)	7	7	6	52 (1)
Bobby Seith	32 (1)	7	7	6	52 (1)
Alex Hamilton	32 (1)	8	7	4	51 (1)
George Ryden	31	8	7	5	51
Andy Penman	29 (16)	8 (5)	7 (4)	6 (5)	50 (30)
Alex Stuart	32 (5)	5	7 (1)	6	50 (6)
Alan Gilzean	30 (33)	7 (8)	7 (9)	4 (2)	48 (52)
Bobby Waddell	28 (14)	2 (1)	5 (5)	4	39 (20)
Hugh Robertson	21 (2)	6 (1)	2	0	29 (3)
Kenny Cameron	15 (11)	1 (2)	7 (7)	5 (2)	28 (22)
Doug Houston	8	8 (1)	0	0	16 (1)
Gordon Smith	9	3	0	0	12
Bobby Wishart	3	1	0	0	4
Hugh Reid	3	0	0	3	6
Craig Brown	1	1	0	0	2
Steve Murray	2	0	0	3	5
Ally Donaldson	0	0	0	1	1
Alex Kinninmonth	0	0	0	1	1
Hugh Tinney	0	0	0	1 (1)	1 (1)

Scottish League Division One

		Home			Away			Goals		
	P	W	D	L	W	D	L	F A		PTS
Rangers	34	13	1	3	12	4	1	85-21		55
Kilmarnock	34	14	2	1	8	3	6	77-40		49
Celtic	34	13	3	1	6	6	5	89-34		47
Hearts	34	8	5	4	11	4	2	74-40		47
Dunfermline	34	11	3	3	7	6	4	64-33		45
Dundee	**34**	**11**	**3**	**3**	**9**	**2**	**6**	**94-50**		**45**
Partick Thistle	34	11	3	3	4	2	11	55-54		35
Dundee United	34	10	2	5	3	6	8	65-49		34
Aberdeen	34	5	5	7	7	3	7	43-43		32
Hibernian	34	9	4	4	3	2	12	59-66		30
Motherwell	34	7	5	5	2	6	9	51-62		29
St Mirren	34	9	4	4	3	1	13	44-74		29
St Johnstone	34	6	2	8	5	3	9	54-70		28
Falkirk	34	7	4	6	4	2	11	54-84		28
Airdrie	34	7	3	7	4	1	12	52-97		26
Third Lanark	34	5	3	9	4	4	9	47-74		25
Queen of the South	34	3	3	11	2	3	12	40-92		16
East Stirling	34	4	2	11	1	0	16	37-91		12

League Cup Section

	P	W	D	L	F A	PTS
Dundee	**6**	**5**	**0**	**1**	**16-12**	**10**
Dunfermline	6	3	3	0	13-13	6
Third Lanark	6	3	3	0	11-13	6
Airdrie	6	1	5	0	10-12	2

Killer goal - Scottish international goalkeeper Campbell Forsyth pushes away a Kenny Cameron shot but Andy Penman is on the spot to ram home Dundee's all-important second goal against Kilmarnock in the Scottish Cup semi-final at Ibrox.

DC Thomson

Hampden showdown - 120,982 fans saw the Dundee v. Rangers Scottish Cup Final. Referee Hugh Phillips (Wishaw) brings together Dundee skipper Bobby Cox and Rangers captain Bobby Shearer to choose ends prior to kick-off. DC Thomson

Courageous keeper - Dundee lost 3-1 but Bert Slater performed heroically in goal. Here he prepares for action as Jimmy Millar of Rangers heads goalwards. Bobby Cox covers the line as Ralph Brand (Rangers) and Alex. Stuart look on.

Season 1964-65

Date		Opponents		Score	Crowd	Scorers
Aug 8th	LC	Dundee United	h	2-3	17,500	Penman; Waddell
12th	LC	Motherwell	a	0-3	8,000	-
15th	LC	Falkirk	h	4-1	9,000	Penman; Houston; Waddell; Kinninmonth
19th	L	Morton	a	2-3	15,000	Cousin; Penman
22nd	LC	Dundee United	a	1-2	18,000	Stuart
26th	LC	Motherwell	h	6-0	9,000	Waddell 3; Penman 2; Cousin
29th	LC	Falkirk	a	3-1	3,500	Penman; Waddell; Cousin
Sep 5th	L	Aberdeen	h	3-1	8,000	Penman 2; Stuart
12th	L	Dundee United	h	4-1	17,500	Cousin; Waddell; Scott 2
19th	L	Rangers	h	4-1	28,000	Stuart; Cousin; Robertson 2
26th	L	Motherwell	a	1-2	7,000	Penman
Oct 3rd	L	Clyde	h	1-2	10,000	Cameron
7th	FC1	Brechin City	h	6-1	3,000	Murray 2; Cousin; Robertson; Cameron; Penman
10th	L	Falkirk	a	2-4	4,000	Stuart; Cameron
17th	L	Kilmarnock	h	1-3	14,000	Murray
24th	L	Hearts	h	1-2	16,000	Waddell
31st	L	St Mirren	a	2-0	2,500	Gilzean 2
Nov 7th	L	Dunfermline	h	3-1	14,000	Penman 2; Cousin
14th	L	Celtic	a	2-0	14,500	Penman; Murray
18th	ECW2	Zarragoza	h	2-2	21,000	Murray; Houston
21st	L	Partick Thistle	h	3-3	11,000	Penman; Stuart; Robertson
28th	L	Hibernian	a	2-2	16,000	Murray; Penman
Dec 5th	L	St Johnstone	h	4-4	12,000	Gilzean 3; Penman
8th	ECW2	Zarragoza	a	1-2 (3-4)	23,000	Robertson
12th	L	Third Lanark	a	1-0	2,500	Baillie o.g.
19th	L	Airdrie	h	4-0	9,000	Harley 3; Cooke
26th	L	Morton	h	1-1	10,000	Harley
Jan 1st	L	Aberdeen	a	1-1	8,000	Penman
9th	L	Rangers	a	0-4	28,000	-
16th	L	Motherwell	h	4-2	10,500	Cousin; Cooke; Cameron; Robertson
Feb 6th	SC1	St Johnstone	a	0-1	17,000	-
10th	L	Falkirk	h	3-2	5,300	Penman 2; Cooke
13th	L	Kilmarnock	a	4-1	6,000	Cooke 2; Murray; Robertson
20th	L	Clyde	a	0-1	4,500	-
27th	L	Hearts	a	7-1	12,000	Penman 3 (1 pen); Cameron 3; Cousin
Mar 6th	L	St Mirren	h	2-1	11,000	Penman 2
13th	L	Dunfermline	a	3-3	10,000	Murray; Cameron; Cousin
20th	L	Celtic	h	3-3	18,000	Cameron 2; Murdoch o.g.
24th	L	Dundee United	h	2-4	18,000	Cooke; Cameron
27th	L	Partick Thistle	a	4-4	6,000	Cameron 2; Penman 2
31st	FCS	Arbroath	h	6-0	3,500	Scott 2; Cooke; Murray; Stuart; Penman
Apr 3rd	L	Hibernian	h	2-1	15,890	Scott 2
9th	L	St Johnstone	a	2-2	7,500	Penman 2 (1 pen)
17th	L	Third Lanark	h	6-1	8,000	Scott 2; Penman 2; Cousin; Cooke
21st	FCF	Dundee United	a	0-1	15,000	-
24th	L	Airdrie	a	2-2	1,000	Cameron 2
May 1st	SU	Dundee United	h	1-4	12,000	Stuart
5th	SU	Aberdeen	a	1-3	5,000	Cameron
8th	SU	St Johnstone	h	2-1	5,000	Cameron; Penman
12th	SU	Dundee United	a	2-3	12,000	Penman 2
15th	SU	Aberdeen	h	1-2	4,000	Penman
19th	SU	St Johnstone	a	3-2	2,000	Cameron 2; Richmond o.g.

Andy Penman - a clever forward who scored many vital goals for Dundee.

Appearances

	League	L/Cup	S/Cup	CWC	Sum/C	Total	
Andy Penman	34 (24)	6 (5)	1	2	6 (4)	49 (33)	
Alex Stuart	34 (4)	6 (1)	1	2	6 (1)	49 (6)	
Alan Cousin	34 (8)	6 (2)	1	2	1	44 (10)	
Hugh Robertson	32 (5)	3	1	2 (1)	4	42 (6)	
Ally Donaldson	30	2	0	2	6	40	
Alex. Hamilton	29	6	1	2	2	40	
Jim Easton	26	0	1	0	6	33	
Steve Murray	23 (5)	2	0	2 (1)	0	27 (6)	
Kenny Cameron	16 (14)	2	1	1	6 (4)	26 (18)	
Charlie Cooke	18 (7)	0	1	0	6	25 (7)	
Bobby Cox	15	4	1	2	0	22	
George Ryden	8	6	0	1	5	20	
Bobby Waddell	8 (2)	5 (6)	0	1	0	14 (8)	
Norrie Beattie	6	0	0	1	6	13	
Bobby Seith	7	4	1	0	0	12	
Alec Totten	9	2	0	0	0	11	
Doug Houston	5	3 (1)	0	2 (1)	1	11 (2)	
Hugh Reid	7	0	0	0	4	11	
Jocky Scott	6 (6)	2	0	0	3	11 (6)	
Alec Harley	10 (4)	0	0	0	0	10 (4)	
Bert Slater	4	4	1	0	0	9	
Alan Gilzean	7 (5)	0	0	0	0	7 (5)	
John Phillips	4	2	0	0	0	6	
Tony Harvey	0	0	0	0	0	4	
Alex. Kinninmonth	2	1 (1)	0	0	0	3 (1)	

The Record

League	-	Sixth Place, Division One
League Cup	-	Qualifying stages only
Scottish Cup	-	First round
European Cup Winners' Cup	-	Second round
Summer Cup	-	Qualifying stages only
Forfarshire Cup	-	Runners up
Top Scorer	-	Andy Penman (33 goals)
Av. Home Gate	-	12,900
Players used	-	25
Sent off	-	Two

Scottish League Division One

	P	Home W	D	L	Away W	D	L	Goals F	A	PTS
Kilmarnock	34	12	4	1	10	2	5	62-33		50
Hearts	34	11	3	3	11	3	3	90-49		50
Dunfermline	34	14	2	1	8	3	6	83-36		49
Hibernian	34	11	2	4	10	2	5	75-47		46
Rangers	34	9	5	3	9	3	5	78-35		44
Dundee	**34**	**9**	**4**	**4**	**6**	**6**	**5**	**86-63**		**40**
Clyde	34	10	3	4	7	3	7	64-58		40
Celtic	34	9	2	6	7	3	7	76-57		37
Dundee United	34	10	1	6	5	5	7	59-51		36
Morton	34	9	4	4	4	3	10	54-54		33
Partick Thistle	34	5	5	7	6	5	6	57-58		32
Aberdeen	34	8	5	4	4	3	10	59-75		32
St Johnstone	34	6	5	6	3	6	8	57-62		29
Motherwell	34	4	9	4	6	4	7	45-54		28
St Mirren	34	8	2	7	1	4	12	38-70		24
Falkirk	34	6	5	6	1	2	14	43-85		21
Airdrie	34	3	3	11	2	1	14	48-110		14
Third Lanark	34	2	0	15	1	1	15	26-99		7

League Cup Section

	P	W	D	L	F A	PTS
Dundee United	6	5	0	1	13- 9	10
Dundee	**6**	**3**	**0**	**3**	**16-10**	**6**
Motherwell	6	2	1	3	8-11	5
Falkirk	6	1	1	4	9-16	3

Dundee F.C. Line-Ups 1964-65

		1	2	3	4	5	6	7	8	9	10	11
Aug	8th	Slater	Hamilton	Cox	Seith	Ryden	Stuart	Penman	Murray	Waddell	Cousin	Cameron
	12th	Slater	Hamilton	Cox	Seith	Ryden	Stuart	Murray	Penman	Cousin	Houston	Robertson
	15th	Slater	Hamilton	Cox	Seith	Ryden	Stuart	Penman	Cousin	Waddell	Kinninmonth	Houston
	19th	Slater	Hamilton	Cox	Seith	Ryden	Stuart	Penman	Waddell	Cousin	Kinninmonth	Houston
	22nd	Slater	Hamilton	Cox	Seith	Ryden	Stuart	Penman	Waddell	Cameron	Cousin	Houston
	26th	Donaldson	Hamilton	Totten	Phillips	Ryden	Stuart	Penman	Scott	Waddell	Cousin	Robertson
	29th	Donaldson	Hamilton	Totten	Phillips	Ryden	Stuart	Penman	Scott*	Waddell	Cousin	Robertson
Sep	5th	Donaldson	Hamilton	Totten	Seith	Ryden	Stuart	Penman	Scott	Waddell	Cousin	Robertson
	12th	Donaldson	Hamilton	Totten	Seith	Ryden	Stuart	Penman	Scott	Waddell	Cousin	Robertson
	19th	Donaldson	Hamilton	Totten	Houston	Ryden	Stuart	Penman	Cameron	Waddell	Cousin	Robertson
	26th	Donaldson	Hamilton	Totten	Kinninmonth	Ryden	Stuart	Penman	Cameron	Waddell	Cousin	Robertson
Oct	3rd	Donaldson	Reid	Totten	Houston	Ryden	Stuart	Penman	Scott	Cameron	Cousin	Robertson
	10th	Slater	Reid	Totten	Seith	Beattie	Stuart	Penman	Murray	Cameron	Cousin	Robertson
	17th	Donaldson	Hamilton	Totten	Seith	Ryden	Stuart	Penman	Murray	Waddell	Cousin	Robertson
	24th	Donaldson	Hamilton	Cox	Phillips	Easton	Stuart	Penman	Cousin	Waddell	Gilzean	Robertson
	31st	Slater	Hamilton	Totten	Seith	Easton	Stuart	Penman	Cousin	Waddell	Gilzean	Robertson
Nov	7th	Donaldson	Reid	Totten	Cousin	Easton	Stuart	Murray	Penman	Harley	Gilzean	Robertson
	14th	Donaldson	Hamilton	Beattie	Cousin	Easton	Stuart	Murray	Penman	Harley	Gilzean	Robertson
	18th	Donaldson	Hamilton	Cox	Cousin	Beattie	Stuart	Penman	Murray	Waddell	Houston	Robertson
	21st	Donaldson	Hamilton	Beattie	Cousin	Easton	Stuart	Murray	Penman	Harley	Gilzean	Robertson
	28th	Donaldson	Reid	Cox	Cousin	Easton	Stuart	Murray	Penman	Harley	Gilzean	Robertson
Dec	5th	Donaldson	Hamilton	Cox	Cousin	Easton	Stuart	Murray	Penman	Harley	Gilzean	Robertson
	8th	Donaldson	Hamilton	Cox	Cousin	Ryden	Stuart	Murray	Penman	Cameron	Houston	Robertson
	12th	Donaldson	Hamilton	Phillips	Ryden	Easton	Stuart	Murray	Penman	Harley	Cousin	Cameron
	19th	Donaldson	Hamilton	Phillips	Cousin	Easton	Stuart	Murray	Penman	Harley	Cooke	Robertson
	26th	Donaldson	Hamilton	Phillips	Cousin	Easton	Stuart	Murray	Penman	Harley	Cooke	Robertson
Jan	1st	Donaldson	Hamilton	Reid	Cousin	Easton	Stuart	Murray	Penman	Harley	Cooke	Robertson
	9th	Donaldson	Hamilton	Reid	Cousin	Easton	Stuart	Murray	Penman	Harley	Cooke	Robertson
	16th	Donaldson	Hamilton	Beattie	Seith	Easton	Stuart	Penman	Cousin	Cameron	Cooke	Robertson
Feb	6th	Slater	Hamilton	Cox	Seith	Easton	Stuart	Penman	Cousin	Cameron	Cooke	Robertson
	10th	Donaldson	Hamilton	Cox	Cousin	Easton	Stuart	Murray	Penman	Cameron	Cooke	Robertson
	13th	Donaldson	Hamilton	Cox	Cousin	Easton	Stuart	Murray	Penman	Cameron	Cooke	Robertson
	20th	Slater	Hamilton	Cox	Cousin	Easton	Stuart	Murray	Penman	Cameron	Cooke	Robertson
	27th	Donaldson	Hamilton	Cox	Cousin	Easton	Stuart	Murray	Penman	Cameron	Cooke	Robertson
Mar	6th	Donaldson	Hamilton	Cox	Cousin	Easton	Stuart	Murray	Penman	Cameron	Cooke	Robertson
	13th	Donaldson	Hamilton	Cox*	Cousin	Easton	Stuart	Murray	Penman	Cameron	Cooke	Robertson
	20th	Donaldson	Hamilton	Cox	Cousin	Easton	Stuart	Murray	Penman	Cameron	Cooke	Robertson
	24th	Donaldson	Hamilton	Cox	Cousin	Easton	Stuart	Murray	Penman	Cameron	Cooke	Robertson
	27th	Donaldson	Hamilton	Cox	Cousin	Easton	Stuart	Murray	Penman	Cameron	Cooke	Robertson
Apr	3rd	Donaldson	Hamilton	Cox	Cousin	Easton	Stuart	Murray	Penman	Scott	Cooke	Robertson
	9th	Donaldson	Reid	Cox	Cousin	Easton	Stuart	Murray	Penman	Scott	Cooke	Robertson
	17th	Donaldson	Hamilton	Beattie	Cousin	Easton	Stuart	Robertson	Penman	Scott	Cooke	Houston
	24th	Donaldson	Hamilton	Beattie	Cousin	Easton	Stuart	Robertson	Penman	Cameron	Cooke	Houston
May	1st	Donaldson	Hamilton	Beattie	Cousin	Easton	Stuart	Robertson	Penman	Cameron	Cooke	Houston
	5th	Donaldson	Hamilton	Beattie	Ryden	Easton	Stuart	Scott	Penman	Cameron	Cooke	Robertson
	8th	Donaldson	Reid	Beattie	Ryden	Easton	Stuart	Harvey	Penman	Cameron	Cooke	Robertson
	12th	Donaldson	Reid	Beattie	Ryden	Easton	Stuart	Harvey	Penman	Cameron	Cooke	Robertson
	15th	Donaldson	Reid	Beattie	Ryden	Easton	Stuart	Harvey	Penman	Scott	Cooke	Cameron
	19th	Donaldson	Reid	Beattie	Ryden	Easton	Stuart	Harvey	Penman	Cameron	Cooke	Scott

Sweet revenge - five months after losing the Scottish Cup Final, Dundee gained revenge with a 4-1 win over Rangers at Dens. Left-winger Hugh Robertson fires home his second goal to complete a splendid afternoon for the Dark Blues.

DC Thomson

They Wore The Dark Blue

Season 1965-66

Date		Opponents		Score	Crowd	Scorers
Aug 14th	LC	Motherwell	a	0-1	6,000	-
18th	LC	Dundee United	h	0-0	25,000	-
21st	LC	Celtic	a	2-0	34,000	Cameron 2
25th	L	Clyde	a	2-0	2,500	Penman; Bertelsen
28th	LC	Motherwell	h	1-2	12,000	Cameron
Sep 1st	LC	Dundee United	a	3-1	20,000	Cameron 2; Murray
4th	LC	Celtic	h	1-3	28,000	Penman
11th	L	Dundee United	h	0-5	16,000	-
18th	L	Aberdeen	a	3-2	8,000	Penman; Cooke; Bertelsen
25th	L	Rangers	h	1-1	24,000	Bertelsen
Oct 2nd	L	Hearts	a	0-0	10,000	-
9th	L	Falkirk	h	2-0	8,000	McLean; Murray
16th	L	Kilmarnock	a	3-5	8,000	McLean; Penman; Cameron
23rd	FC1	Dundee United	h	1-0	14,000	Cameron
27th	L	Celtic	h	1-2	17,000	Penman
30th	L	St Mirren	a	5-2	2,500	Murray 2; Cameron; Stuart; Bertelsen
Nov 6th	L	Morton	a	2-2	6,000	Cameron; Penman
13th	L	Hibernian	h	4-3	14,000	Cooke; Houston; Bertelsen; Murray
20th	L	St Johnstone	h	3-1	9,000	Cameron; Penman; Houston
27th	L	Stirling Albion	a	4-1	2,000	Cameron; Penman; Houston; Murray
Dec 18th	L	Partick Thistle	a	0-2	3,500	-
25th	L	Motherwell	h	4-0	8,000	Cameron 3; Bertelsen
Jan 3rd	L	Dundee United	a	1-2	24,000	Murray
8th	L	Clyde	h	1-4	9,000	Harvey
29th	L	Falkirk	a	1-3	5,000	Penman (pen)
Feb 9th	SC1	East Fife	h	9-1	8,000	Penman 3; Cox; McLean 2; Cameron; Stuart 2
12th	L	Kilmarnock	h	0-2	8,000	-
23rd	SC2	Celtic	h	0-2	29,000	-
26th	L	St Mirren	h	3-2	7,000	Penman; Cameron 2
28th	L	Celtic	a	0-5	23,000	-
Mar 5th	L	Morton	h	5-1	8,000	Stuart; McLean 2; Penman; S. Wilson
9th	L	Hamilton	h	2-1	7,000	McLean; S. Wilson
12th	L	Hibernian	a	1-1	9,000	S. Wilson
16th	FCS	Montrose	h	7-1	3,000	Cameron 2; S. Wilson 2; Scott 2; Harvey
19th	L	St Johnstone	a	0-1	7,000	-
26th	L	Stirling Albion	h	6-2	6,000	Penman 3; Cooke 2; Cameron
Apr 4th	L	Rangers	a	0-1	15,000	-
9th	L	Dunfermline	a	2-2		Stuart; Cameron
13th	L	Hearts	h	1-0	8,000	Penman
16th	L	Hamilton	a	2-1	750	Murray; Penman
20th	L	Aberdeen	h	1-2	5,000	Murray
23rd	L	Partick Thistle	h	1-1	4,000	McLean
27th	L	Dunfermline	h	0-2	3,500	-
30th	L	Motherwell	a	0-2	3,000	-
May 4th	FCF	Brechin City	h	2-1	1,500	Houston; Scott

Cup Cash v. East Fife £1,414; v. Celtic £5,719

Appearances

	League	L/Cup	S/Cup	Total
Jim Easton	34	6	2	42
Steve Murray	33 (8)	6 (1)	2	41 (9)
Andy Penman	33 (15)	6 (1)	2 (3)	41 (19)
Alex. Stuart	32 (3)	5	2 (2)	39 (5)
Kenny Cameron	28 (12)	6 (5)	2 (1)	36 (18)
Ally Donaldson	29	6	1	36
Charlie Cooke	29 (4)	6	2	34 (4)
Alex. Hamilton	22	6	2	30
Jim McLean	27 (6)	0	2 (2)	29 (8)
Bobby Cox	27	0	1 (1)	28 (1)
Carl Bertelsen	15 (6)	6	1	22 (6)
Doug Houston	15 (3)	6	0	21 (3)
Bobby Wilson	11	0	0	11
Alan Cousin	3	6	0	9
Jocky Scott	7	0	0	7
Sammy Wilson	7 (3)	0	0	7 (3)
John Arrol	5	0	1	6
Alex. Kinninmonth	6	0	0	6
George Ryden	4	1	1	6
Tony Harvey	5 (1)	0	0	5 (1)
Norrie Beattie	2	0	1	3
Davie Swan	3	0	0	3

Kenny Cameron - always a danger in the opposition penalty area.

The Record

League	-	Ninth Place, Division One
League Cup	-	Qualifying stages only
Scottish Cup	-	Second round
Forfarshire Cup	-	Winners
Top Scorer	-	Andy Penman (19 goals)
Av. Home Gate	-	9,500
Players used	-	22
Sent off	-	None

Scottish League Division One

	P	Home W	D	L	Away W	D	L	Goals F	A	PTS
Celtic	34	16	1	0	11	2	4	106-30		57
Rangers	34	15	1	1	10	4	3	91-29		55
Kilmarnock	34	12	2	3	8	3	6	37-28		45
Dunfermline	34	11	2	4	8	6	5	94-55		44
Dundee United	34	10	3	4	9	2	6	79-51		43
Hibernian	34	8	6	3	8	0	9	81-55		38
Hearts	34	7	5	5	6	7	4	56-48		38
Aberdeen	34	8	3	6	7	3	7	61-54		36
Dundee	34	9	2	6	5	4	8	61-61		34
Falkirk	34	10	1	6	5	1	11	48-72		31
Clyde	34	7	2	8	6	2	9	62-64		30
Partick Thistle	34	9	5	4	1	5	10	55-64		30
Motherwell	34	9	0	8	3	4	10	52-69		28
St Johnstone	34	6	6	5	3	2	12	58-81		26
Stirling Albion	34	7	2	8	2	6	9	40-68		26
St Mirren	34	6	3	8	3	1	13	44-82		22
Morton	34	4	5	8	4	0	13	42-84		21
Hamilton	34	3	1	13	0	1	16	27-117		8

League Cup Section

	P	W	D	L	F	A	PTS
Celtic	6	4	2	0	11- 7		8
Motherwell	6	3	0	3	9-11		6
Dundee	6	2	1	3	7- 7		5
Dundee United	6	2	1	3	9-11		5

Dundee F.C. Line-Ups 1965-66

		1	2	3	4	5	6	7	8	9	10	11
Aug	14th	Donaldson	Hamilton	Ryden	Cousin	Easton	Houston	Murray	Penman	Bertelsen	Cooke	Cameron
	18th	Donaldson	Hamilton	Stuart	Cousin	Easton	Houston	Murray	Penman	Bertelsen	Cooke	Cameron
	21st	Donaldson	Hamilton	Stuart	Cousin	Easton	Houston	Murray	Penman	Bertelsen	Cooke	Cameron
	25th	Donaldson	Hamilton	Stuart	Cousin	Easton	Houston	Murray	Penman	Bertelsen	Cooke	Cameron
	28th	Donaldson	Hamilton	Stuart	Cousin	Easton	Houston	Murray	Penman	Bertelsen	Cooke	Cameron
Sep	1st	Donaldson	Hamilton	Stuart	Cousin	Easton	Houston	Murray	Penman	Cameron	Cooke	Bertelsen
	4th	Donaldson	Hamilton	Stuart	Cousin	Easton	Houston	Murray	Penman	Cameron	Cooke	Bertelsen
	11th	Donaldson	Hamilton	Cox	Houston	Easton	Stuart	Bertelsen	Cousin	Cameron	Cooke	McLean
	18th	Donaldson	Hamilton	Cox	Cooke	Easton	Houston	Murray	Penman	Bertelsen	McLean	Scott
	25th	Donaldson	Hamilton	Cox	Cooke	Easton	Stuart	Murray	Penman	Bertelsen	McLean	Houston
Oct	2nd	Donaldson	Ryden	Cox	Cooke	Easton	Stuart	Murray	Penman	Bertelsen	McLean	Houston
	9th	Donaldson	Hamilton	Cox	Cooke	Easton	Stuart	Murray	Penman	Bertelsen	McLean	Cameron
	16th	Donaldson	Hamilton	Cox	Cooke	Easton	Stuart	Murray	Penman	Cameron	McLean	Harvey
	27th	Donaldson	Ryden	Cox	Cousin	Easton	Houston	Murray	Penman	Cameron	McLean	Cooke
	30th	Donaldson	Hamilton	Cox	Cooke	Easton	Stuart	Penman	Murray	Cameron	Houston	Bertelsen
Nov	6th	Donaldson	Hamilton	Cox	Cooke	Easton	Stuart	Penman	Murray	Cameron	Houston	Bertelsen
	13th	Donaldson	Hamilton	Cox	Cooke	Easton	Stuart	Penman	Murray	Cameron	Houston	Bertelsen
	20th	Donaldson	Hamilton	Cox	Cooke	Easton	Stuart	Penman	Murray	Cameron	Houston	Bertelsen
	27th	Donaldson	Hamilton	Cox	Cooke	Easton	Stuart	Penman	Murray	Cameron	Houston	Bertelsen
Dec	18th	Donaldson	Hamilton	Cox	Cooke	Easton	Stuart	Penman	Murray	Cameron	Houston	Bertelsen
	25th	Donaldson	Hamilton	Cox	Cooke	Easton	Stuart	Penman	Murray	Cameron	McLean	Bertelsen
Jan	3rd	Donaldson	Hamilton	Cox	Cooke	Easton	Stuart	Penman	Murray	Bertelsen	McLean	Harvey
	8th	Donaldson	Hamilton	Cox	Cooke	Easton	Stuart	Penman	Murray	Cameron	McLean	Harvey
	29th	Donaldson	Hamilton	Cox	Beattie	Easton	Stuart	Penman	Murray	Cameron	McLean	Harvey
Feb	9th	Donaldson	Hamilton	Cox	Beattie	Easton	Stuart	Penman	Murray	McLean	Cooke	Cameron
	12th	Donaldson	Hamilton	Cox	Beattie	Easton	Stuart	Scott	Murray	McLean	Penman	Cameron
	21st	Arrol	Hamilton	Ryden	Cooke	Easton	Stuart	Penman	Murray	Bertelsen	McLean	Cameron
	26th	Arrol	Ryden	Swan	Cooke	Easton	Stuart	Penman	Murray	Kinninmonth	McLean	Cameron
	28th	Arrol	Ryden	Swan	Murray	Easton	Stuart	Penman	Bertelsen	Cameron	McLean	Harvey
Mar	5th	Donaldson	Cox	Swan	Cooke	Easton	Stuart	Penman	Murray	Wilson S	McLean	Cameron
	9th	Donaldson	Wilson B	Cox	Cooke	Easton	Stuart	Penman	Murray	Wilson S	McLean	Cameron
	12th	Donaldson	Wilson B	Cox	Murray	Easton	Stuart	Penman	Cooke	Wilson S	McLean	Cameron
	19th	Donaldson	Wilson B	Cox	Murray	Easton	Stuart	Penman	Scott	Wilson S	McLean	Cameron
	26th	Donaldson	Wilson B	Cox	Murray	Easton	Stuart	Penman	Cooke	Wilson S	McLean	Cameron
Apr	4th	Donaldson	Wilson B	Cox	Murray	Easton	Stuart	Penman	Cooke	Cameron	McLean	Kinninmonth
	9th	Donaldson	Wilson B	Cox	Murray	Easton	Stuart	Penman	Cooke	Cameron	McLean	Kinninmonth
	13th	Donaldson	Wilson B	Cox	Murray	Easton	Stuart	Penman	Cooke	Cameron	McLean	Kinninmonth
	16th	Donaldson	Wilson B	Hamilton	Murray	Easton	Stuart	Penman	Cooke	Wilson S	McLean	Cameron
	20th	Donaldson	Wilson B	Hamilton	Murray	Easton	Stuart	Penman	Scott	Wilson S	McLean	Cameron
	23rd	Arrol	Hamilton	Cox	Murray	Easton	Stuart	Penman	McLean	Scott	Houston	Cameron
	27th	Arrol	Wilson B	Hamilton	Murray	Easton	Stuart	Penman	McLean	Scott	Houston	Kinninmonth
	30th	Arrol	Wilson B	Hamilton	Murray	Easton	Stuart	Penman	McLean	Scott	Houston	Kinninmonth

Great save Ally - Ally Donaldson pushes the ball away from Bertie Auld watched by Dundee's Charlie Cooke and Doug Houston and Bobby Lennox and Joe McBride of Celtic. His efforts were worthwhile with the Dark Blues going on to win 2-0 in this League Cup tie at Parkhead.

Season 1966-67

Date		Opponents		Score	Crowd	Scorers
Aug 13th	LC	Dundee United	a	0-2	15,000	-
17th	LC	Aberdeen	h	3-4	8,000	Scott; McLean 2
20th	LC	St Johnstone	h	2-0	8,000	McLean; Cameron
27th	LC	Dundee United	h	1-1	16,000	Penman
31st	LC	Aberdeen	a	0-2	11,000	-
Sep 3rd	LC	St Johnstone	a	2-2	3,200	McLean; Cameron
10th	L	Aberdeen	h	2-1	8,000	Cameron; Penman (pen)
17th	L	Dundee United	a	4-1	14,000	Cameron; Penman 2; McKay
24th	L	Celtic	h	1-2	28,500	Penman
26th	FC1	Forfar Athletic	a	3-0		Scott; S. Wilson; Cameron
Oct 1st	L	Hearts	a	1-3	8,000	Stuart
8th	L	Kilmarnock	h	1-1	9,000	Kinninmonth
15th	L	Falkirk	a	2-3	4,500	Cameron; Penman
22nd	L	Motherwell	h	3-0	8,500	Penman; McLean; Scott
24th	FCS	Arbroath	h	2-1	2,000	McLean; Penman
29th	L	Partick Thistle	a	0-0	3,500	-
Nov 5th	L	St Johnstone	h	4-0	10,000	Penman 3; McLean
12th	L	Ayr United	a	1-1	5,000	S. Wilson
19th	L	Hibernian	h	2-1	5,000	McLean 2
26th	L	Stirling Albion	a	3-2	4,000	McLean 2 (1 pen); Kinninmonth
Dec 3rd	L	St Mirren	h	2-0	6,000	McLean; Stuart
10th	L	Clyde	h	3-4	6,000	S. Wilson; Campbell; Kinninmonth
17th	L	Dunfermline	a	1-0	5,000	Campbell
24th	L	Airdrie	h	0-0	7,000	-
31st	L	Rangers	a	2-2	25,000	Bryce; Cameron
Jan 1st	L	Aberdeen	a	2-5	17,000	Cameron 2
3rd	L	Dundee United	h	2-3	18,000	Scott; Bryce
7th	L	Celtic	a	1-5	37,000	Cameron
14th	L	Hearts	h	1-1	8,500	Houston
21st	L	Kilmarnock	a	4-4	4,000	Kinninmonth 2; Bryce 2
28th	SC1	Aberdeen	h	0-5	23,000	-
Feb 4th	L	Falkirk	h	4-1	6,500	Scott 2; McLean 2
11th	L	Motherwell	a	3-5	4,500	Murray; Scott 2
25th	L	Partick Thistle	h	0-0	6,000	-
Mar 4th	L	St Johnstone	a	3-0	5,000	Scott; Bryce; S. Wilson
10th	L	Ayr United	h	3-0	5,000	Bryce; Scott; Stuart
18th	L	Hibernian	a	1-2	10,500	S. Wilson
25th	L	Stirling Albion	h	2-0	4,500	Scott 2 (1 pen)
Apr 1st	L	St Mirren	a	5-0	3,000	McLean 2; Campbell; S. Wilson; Stuart
8th	L	Clyde	a	3-1	2,500	Scott; S. Wilson 2
12th	L	Dunfermline	h	3-1	8,000	McLean 2; Stuart
22nd	L	Airdrie	a	4-1	2,000	S. Wilson 2; Campbell; Cameron
29th	L	Rangers	h	1-1	18,000	Scott

Cup Cash v. Aberdeen £5,400; nb. subs. only listed in totals if they came on.

Jim McLean - the ex-Clyde inside-forward was Dundee's top scorer.   DC Thomson

The Record

League	-	Sixth Place, Division One.
League Cup	-	Qualifying stages only.
Scottish Cup	-	First round.
Forfarshire Cup	-	Winners (Final 04-05-68)
Top Scorer	-	Jim McLean (17 goals)
Av. Home Gate	-	10,000
Players used	-	21
Sent off	-	None

Appearances

	League	L/Cup	S/Cup	Total	
Steve Murray	32 (1)	6	1	39	(1)
Jim McLean	29 (13)	6 (4)	1	36	(17)
Alex. Stuart	30 (5)	5	1	36	(5)
Bobby Cox	29	4	0	33	
Jim Easton	25	5	1	31	
John Arrol	28	1	1	30	
Jocky Scott	20 (12)	5 (1)	1	26	(13)
Billy Campbell	24 (4)	1	0	25	(4)
Alex. Bryce	22 (6)	1	1	24	(6)
Alex. Hamilton	19	2	1	22	
Andy Penman	16 (9)	5 (1)	0	21+1s	(10)
Alex. Kinninmonth	17 (5)	1	1	19+4s	(5)
Bobby Wilson	15	4	0	19	
Kenny Cameron	13 (8)	4 (2)	1	18+5s	(10)
Sammy Wilson	18 (9)	0	0	18+1s	(9)
Doug Houston	11 (1)	4	1	16	(1)
Ally Donaldson	6	5	0	11	
Ron Selway	9	0	0	9	
George Stewart	9	0	0	9	
Derek McKay	7 (1)	1	0	8+2s	(1)
Tony Harvey	0	0	0	0+1s	

Scottish League Division One

		Home			Away			Goals		
	P	W	D	L	W	D	L	F	A	PTS
Celtic	34	14	2	1	12	4	1	111-33		58
Rangers	34	13	3	1	11	4	2	92-31		55
Clyde	34	10	2	5	10	4	3	64-48		46
Aberdeen	34	11	3	3	6	5	6	72-38		42
Hibernian	34	10	3	4	9	1	7	72-49		42
Dundee	**34**	**9**	**5**	**3**	**7**	**4**	**6**	**74-51**		**41**
Kilmarnock	34	9	5	3	7	3	7	59-46		40
Dunfermline	34	9	4	4	5	6	6	72-52		38
Dundee United	34	7	5	5	7	4	6	68-62		37
Motherwell	34	7	6	4	3	5	9	59-60		31
Hearts	34	7	6	4	4	2	11	39-48		30
Partick Thistle	34	5	8	5	4	4	8	49-68		30
Airdrie	34	7	1	9	4	5	8	41-53		28
Falkirk	34	8	1	8	3	3	11	33-70		26
St Johnstone	34	8	3	6	2	2	13	53-73		25
Stirling Albion	34	3	6	8	2	3	12	31-85		19
St Mirren	34	4	1	12	0	6	11	25-81		15
Ayr United	34	1	4	12	0	3	14	20-86		9

League Cup Section

	P	W	D	L	F	A	PTS
Aberdeen	6	6	0	0	20-7		12
Dundee United	6	2	2	2	13-13		6
Dundee	**6**	**1**	**2**	**3**	**8-11**		**4**
St Johnstone	6	0	2	4	6-16		2

Dundee F.C. Line-Ups 1966-67

	1	2	3	4	5	6	7	8	9	10	11	12
Aug 13th	Arrol	Hamilton	Cox	Murray	Easton	Selway	Bryce	McLean	Penman	Houston	Campbell	Cameron (7)
17th	Donaldson	Hamilton	Cox	Selway	Easton	Stuart	Penman	Murray	McLean	Scott	Cameron	Kinninmonth
20th	Donaldson	Wilson B	Cox	Houston	Selway	Stuart	Penman	Murray	McLean	Scott	Cameron	Easton
27th	Donaldson	Wilson B	Selway	Houston	Easton	Stuart	Penman	Murray	McLean	Scott	Cameron	Hamilton
31st	Donaldson	Wilson B	Selway	Houston	Easton	Stuart	McKay	Murray	McLean	Scott	Kinninmonth	Cox
Sep 3rd	Donaldson	Wilson B	Cox	Selway	Easton	Stuart	Penman	Murray	McLean	Scott	Cameron	Harvey (9)
10th	Donaldson	Wilson B	Cox	Selway	Easton	Stuart	McKay	Penman	Cameron	Murray	Campbell	Scott
17th	Donaldson	Wilson B	Cox	Selway	Easton	Stuart	McKay	Penman	Cameron	Murray	Campbell	Scott
24th	Donaldson	Wilson B	Cox	Houston	Easton	Stuart	McKay	Penman	Cameron	Murray	Campbell	Kinninmonth (2)
Oct 1st	Donaldson	Hamilton	Stuart	Murray	Easton	Houston	McKay	Penman	Cameron	Kinninmonth	Campbell	Cameron
8th	Donaldson	Hamilton	Cox	Murray	Easton	Houston	Penman	Bryce	McLean	Kinninmonth	Campbell	Cameron (4)
15th	Donaldson	Hamilton	Cox	Kinninmonth	Easton	Houston	Murray	Penman	Cameron	McLean	Scott	McKay (7)
22nd	Arrol	Hamilton	Cox	Kinninmonth	Easton	Stuart	Penman	McLean	Wilson S	Houston	Scott	McKay (9)
29th	Arrol	Hamilton	Cox	Selway	Easton	Houston	McKay	Penman	McLean	Kinninmonth	Scott	Cameron
Nov 5th	Arrol	Hamilton	Cox	Selway	Easton	Stuart	Penman	Murray	Wilson S	McLean	Kinninmonth	Cameron (4)
12th	Arrol	Hamilton	Cox	Murray	Easton	Stuart	Penman	Kinninmonth	Cameron	Wilson S	Campbell	Bryce
19th	Arrol	Hamilton	Cox	Murray	Easton	Stuart	Penman	Kinninmonth	Wilson S	McLean	Campbell	Cameron
26th	Arrol	Hamilton	Cox	Murray	Easton	Stuart	Bryce	Kinninmonth	Wilson S	McLean	Campbell	Cameron
Dec 3rd	Arrol	Hamilton	Cox	Murray	Easton	Stuart	Bryce	Kinninmonth	Wilson S	McLean	Campbell	Scott
10th	Arrol	Hamilton	Cox	Murray	Easton	Stuart	Penman	Kinninmonth	Wilson S	McLean	Campbell	Bryce
17th	Arrol	Hamilton	Cox	Murray	Easton	Stuart	Penman	Kinninmonth	Wilson S	McLean	Campbell	Cameron (7)
24th	Arrol	Hamilton	Cox	Murray	Easton	Stuart	Bryce	Kinninmonth	Cameron	McLean	Campbell	Wilson S (11)
31st	Arrol	Hamilton	Cox	Murray	Easton	Stuart	Bryce	Kinninmonth	Wilson S	McLean	Scott	Cameron (9)
Jan 1st	Arrol	Hamilton	Cox	Murray	Easton	Stuart	Bryce	Kinninmonth	Cameron	McLean	Scott	McKay
3rd	Arrol	Wilson B	Cox	Murray	Easton	Stuart	Bryce	Scott	Cameron	McLean	McKay	Kinninmonth
7th	Arrol	Wilson B	Cox	Murray	Easton	Houston	Bryce	Scott	Cameron	McLean	Kinninmonth	McKay
14th	Arrol	Hamilton	Stuart	Murray	Easton	Houston	McKay	Scott	Cameron	McLean	Bryce	Kinninmonth
21st	Arrol	Hamilton	Stuart	Murray	Easton	Houston	Scott	Kinninmonth	Cameron	McLean	Bryce	Cox
28th	Arrol	Hamilton	Stuart	Murray	Easton	Houston	Scott	Kinninmonth	Cameron	McLean	Bryce	Penman (7)
Feb 4th	Arrol	Hamilton	Stuart	Murray	Easton	Houston	Bryce	Penman	McLean	Scott	Campbell	Kinninmonth
11th	Arrol	Hamilton	Stuart	Murray	Easton	Houston	Bryce	Penman	McLean	Scott	Campbell	Cameron
25th	Arrol	Wilson B	Cox	Murray	Stewart	Stuart	Penman	Bryce	McLean	Scott	Campbell	Cameron (7)
Mar 4th	Arrol	Wilson B	Cox	Murray	Stewart	Stuart	Bryce	McLean	Wilson S	Scott	Campbell	Kinninmonth (9)
10th	Arrol	Wilson B	Cox	Murray	Stewart	Stuart	Bryce	McLean	Wilson S	Scott	Campbell	Kinninmonth
18th	Arrol	Wilson B	Cox	Murray	Stewart	Stuart	Bryce	McLean	Wilson S	Scott	Campbell	Houston
25th	Arrol	Wilson B	Cox	Murray	Stewart	Stuart	Bryce	McLean	Wilson S	Scott	Campbell	Kinninmonth
Apr 1st	Arrol	Wilson B	Cox	Murray	Stewart	Stuart	Campbell	McLean	Wilson S	Scott	Bryce	Kinninmonth
8th	Arrol	Wilson B	Cox	Murray	Stewart	Stuart	Campbell	McLean	Wilson S	Scott	Bryce	Kinninmonth (9)
12th	Arrol	Wilson B	Cox	Murray	Stewart	Stuart	Campbell	McLean	Wilson S	Scott	Bryce	Kinninmonth
22nd	Arrol	Wilson B	Cox	Murray	Stewart	Stuart	Campbell	McLean	Wilson S	Cameron	Bryce	Houston
29th	Arrol	Wilson B	Cox	Murray	Easton	Stuart	Campbell	Scott	Wilson S	McLean	Bryce	Kinninmonth(10)

No go Sammy - Northern Ireland international Sammy Wilson formed a fine partnership with Jim McLean as Dundee finished the season in style. This time the bustling centre-forward was foiled by Stirling Albion keeper Bill Taylor.

DC Thomson

They Wore The Dark Blue

Season 1967-68

Date		Opponents		Score	Crowd	Scorers
Aug 12th	LC	Hibernian	h	0-0	14,000	
16th	LC	Clyde	a	2-1	2,000	J. McLean; S. Wilson
19th	LC	Motherwell	h	2-1	10,000	G. McLean ; Campbell
26th	LC	Hibernian	a	4-2	13,317	G. McLean 2; J. McLean; S. Wilson
30th	LC	Clyde	h	1-0	10,000	S. Wilson
Sep 2nd	LC	Motherwell	a	5-2	3,000	J. McLean 2; Scott; Campbell; G. McLean
9th	L	Aberdeen	a	2-4	14,000	Campbell; Stuart
13th	LCQ	East Fife	a	1-0	8,553	Murray
16th	L	Dundee United	h	2-2	16,000	J. McLean; Scott
20th	LCQ	East Fife	h	4-0 (5-0)	9,000	J. McLean; G. McLean; Scott; Stuart
23rd	L	Hearts	a	0-1		-
27th	FA1	DWS Amsterdam	a	1-2	12,000	G. McLean
30th	L	Motherwell	h	2-1	7,000	G. McLean 2
Oct 4th	FA1	DWS Amsterdam	h	3-0 (4-2)	15,000	S.Wilson; J. McLean. 2
7th	L	Kilmarnock	a	0-0	5,000	-
11th	LCS	St Johnstone	Tan	3-1	18,000	Miller 2 o.g.'s; J. McLean (pen)
14th	L	St Johnstone	h	1-4	8,000	J. McLean
23rd	L	Rangers	a	0-2	30,000	-
28th	LCF	Celtic	Ham	3-5	66,660	G. McLean 2; J. McLean
Nov 1st	FA2	Royal Liege	h	3-1	12,000	Stuart 2; S. Wilson
4th	L	Airdrie	a	0-0	3,000	-
8th	L	Stirling Albion	h	4-2	4,000	Bryce; J. McLean; S. Wilson; B. Wilson
11th	L	Hibernian	h	1-4	7,000	G. McLean
15th	FA2	Royal Liege	a	4-1 (7-2)	12,000	G. McLean 4
18th	L	Dunfermline	h	4-0	8,000	G. McLean 2; J. McLean; S. Wilson
22nd	FC1	Brechin City	h	1-0	1,000	Kinninmonth
25th	L	Clyde	a	0-1	2,500	-
Dec 2nd	L	Partick Thistle	h	3-4	8,000	J. McLean; G. McLean; S. Wilson
9th	L	Morton	a	0-0	7,000	-
16th	L	Celtic	h	4-5	18,000	G. McLean; Scott; Campbell; S. Wilson
23rd	L	Raith Rovers	h	4-0	5,000	G. McLean; J. McLean; Houston; Campbell
30th	L	Falkirk	a	2-0	4,000	Stuart; J. McLean
Jan 1st	L	Aberdeen	h	0-2	10,000	-
2nd	L	Dundee United	a	0-0	15,000	-
20th	L	Kilmarnock	h	6-5	4,500	G. McLean 2; Campbell 2; Bryce; Stuart
27th	SC1	Cowdenbeath	a	1-0	5,633	Kinninmonth
Feb 3rd	L	St Johnstone	a	2-0	5,000	Campbell; Stuart
10th	L	Rangers	h	2-4	23,000	Scott 2
17th	SC2	Rangers	h	1-1	33,000	Campbell
Mar 2nd	L	Airdrie	h	6-2	8,000	G. McLean 3; S. Wilson 2; Scott
4th	SC2R	Rangers	a	1-4*	53,875	S. Wilson
6th	L	Stirling Albion	a	3-0	600	G. McLean 2; Campbell
9th	L	Hibernian	a	0-2	8,467	-
15th	L	Motherwell	h	4-2	2,600	G. McLean 2; Campbell 2
16th	L	Dunfermline	a	0-2	5,000	-
23rd	L	Clyde	h	3-0	8,000	G. McLean 3
27th	FAQ	FC Zurich	h	1-0	13,500	Easton
30th	L	Partick Thistle	a	1-1	3,000	J. McLean
Apr 3rd	FAQ	FC Zurich	a	1-0 (2-0)	25,000	S. Wilson
13th	L	Celtic	a	2-5	41,500	Scott; G. McLean
15th	L	Hearts	h	1-0	8,000	G. McLean
20th	L	Raith Rovers	a	2-0		G. McLean; Georgeson
24th	L	Morton	h^	0-3	6,000	-
27th	L	Falkirk	h	1-1	3,500	J. McLean
May 1st	FAS	Leeds United	h	1-1	24,371	B. Wilson
4th	FCF**	Dundee United	h	4-3	7,000	S. Wilson 3; Houston
11th	FCS	Montrose	h	2-1	2,000	S. Wilson; Scott
14th	FAS	Leeds United	a	0-1 (1-2)	28,830	

**Billy Campbell - Dundee's dazzling
Northern Ireland international winger**

* aet, 1-1 after 90 minutes ** 1966-67 Forfarshire Cup Final. ^ Earlier game on April 6th abandoned at ht. due to snow. Morton led 1-0; FA = Fairs Cup; Cup Cash v. Cowden £1,147; v. Rangers (a) £12,000

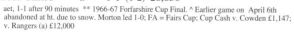

The Record		
League	-	Ninth Place, Division One.
League Cup	-	Runners-up
Scottish Cup	-	Second round
Fairs Cup	-	Semi-final
Forfarshire Cup	-	Finalists, Comp. unfinished
Top Scorer	-	George McLean (35 goals)
Av. Home Gate	-	8,900
Players used	-	21
Sent off	-	One

**Alex. Kinninmonth - long-serving
midfielder with bags of skill.**

Dundee F.C. Line-Ups 1967-68

		1	2	3	4	5	6	7	8	9	10	11	12
Aug	12th	Arrol	Wilson R	Cox	Murray	Stewart	Stuart	Campbell	McLean J	Wilson S	Scott	Bryce	McLean G (7)
	16th	Arrol	Wilson R	Cox	Murray	Stewart	Stuart	Campbell	McLean J	Wilson S	Scott	Bryce	McLean G
	19th	Arrol	Wilson R	Cox	Murray	Stewart	Stuart	Campbell	McLean J	Wilson S	McLean G	Bryce	Scott
	26th	Arrol	Wilson R	Cox	Murray	Stewart	Stuart	Campbell	McLean J	Wilson S	McLean G	Bryce	Scott
	30th	Arrol	Wilson R	Cox	Murray	Stewart	Stuart	Campbell	McLean J	Wilson S	McLean G	Bryce	Scott
Sep	2nd	Arrol	Wilson R	Cox	Murray	Stewart	Stuart	Campbell	McLean J	Wilson S	McLean G	Bryce	Scott (11)
	9th	Arrol	Wilson R	Cox	Murray	Stewart	Stuart	Campbell	McLean J	Wilson S	McLean G	Scott	Houston
	13th	Arrol	Wilson R	Cox	Murray	Stewart	Stuart	Campbell	McLean J	Wilson S	McLean G	Scott	Houston
	16th	Arrol	Wilson R	Cox	Murray	Stewart	Stuart	Campbell	McLean J	Wilson S	McLean G	Scott	Kinninmonth
	20th	Arrol	Wilson R	Cox	Murray	Stewart	Stuart	Campbell	McLean J	McLean G	Scott	Bryce	Selway
	23rd	Arrol	Wilson R	Cox	Murray	Stewart	Stuart	Campbell	McLean J	McLean G	Scott	Bryce	Selway
	27th	Arrol	Wilson R	Cox	Murray	Stewart	Stuart	Campbell	McLean J	Wilson S	McLean G	Bryce	Scott (7), Selway
	30th	Arrol	Wilson R	Selway	Murray	Stewart	Stuart	Campbell	McLean J	Wilson S	Bryce	McLean G	Scott (10)
Oct	4th	Donaldson	Wilson R	Selway	Murray	Stewart	Stuart	Campbell	McLean J	Wilson S	Bryce	McLean G	Kinninmonth (2),Scott
	7th	Donaldson	Wilson R	Houston	Murray	Stewart	Stuart	Campbell	McLean J	Wilson S	Scott	McLean G	Kinninmonth
	11th	Donaldson	Wilson R	Houston	Murray	Stewart	Stuart	Campbell	McLean J	Wilson S	McLean G	Bryce	Scott
	14th	Donaldson	Wilson R	Houston	Murray	Stewart	Stuart	Campbell	McLean J	Wilson S	Kinninmonth	McLean G	Cox (9)
	23rd	Donaldson	Wilson R	Cox	Murray	Stewart	Stuart	Campbell	McLean J	Wilson S	Houston	McLean G	Bryce (7)
	28th	Arrol	Wilson R	Houston	Murray	Stewart	Stuart	Campbell	McLean J	Wilson S	McLean G	Bryce	Cox
Nov	1st	Arrol	Wilson R	Cox	Murray	Stewart	Stuart	Campbell	McLean J	Wilson S	Houston	McLean G	Bryce, Kinninmonth
	4th	Arrol	Wilson R	Cox	Murray	Stewart	Stuart	Campbell	Bryce	McLean J	Houston	McLean G	Easton (2)
	8th	Arrol	Wilson R	Stuart	Murray	Stewart	Houston	Campbell	Bryce	Wilson S	McLean J	McLean G	Easton
	11th	Arrol	Wilson R	Stuart	Murray	Stewart	Houston	Campbell	Bryce	Wilson S	McLean J	McLean G	Cox
	15th	Arrol	Wilson R	Cox	Murray	Easton	Stuart	Campbell	McLean J	Wilson S	McLean G	Houston	Bryce, Kinninmonth
	18th	Arrol	Wilson R	Cox	Murray	Easton	Stuart	Campbell	McLean J	Wilson S	McLean G	Houston	Bryce
	25th	Arrol	Wilson R	Swan	Murray	Easton	Stuart	Bryce	Wilson S	McLean J	McLean G	Houston	Kinninmonth (2)
Dec	2nd	Arrol	Wilson R	Swan	Murray	Easton	Stuart	Campbell	McLean J	Wilson S	McLean G	Houston	Bryce
	9th	Donaldson	Wilson R	Swan	Murray	Easton	Stewart	Campbell	McLean J	McLean G	Houston	McKay	Rough
	16th	Donaldson	Wilson R	Houston	Murray	Easton	Stewart	Scott	McLean J	Wilson S	McLean G	Campbell	Stuart
	23rd	Donaldson	Wilson R	Houston	Murray	Easton	Stuart	Scott	McLean J	Wilson S	McLean G	Campbell	Swan
	30th	Donaldson	Wilson R	Houston	Murray	Easton	Stuart	Scott	McLean J	Wilson S	McLean G	Campbell	Kinninmonth
Jan	1st	Donaldson	Wilson R	Houston	Murray	Easton	Stuart	Scott	McLean J	Wilson S	McLean G	Campbell	Bryce
	2nd	Donaldson	Wilson R	Houston	Murray	Easton	Stuart	Bryce	McLean J	Wilson S	McLean G	McKay	Scott (7)
	20th	Donaldson	Wilson R	Houston	Murray	Easton	Stuart	Bryce	McLean J	McLean G	Kinninmonth	Campbell	McKay
	27th	Donaldson	Wilson R	Houston	Murray	Easton	Stuart	Bryce	McLean J	McLean G	Kinninmonth	Campbell	Scott
Feb	3rd	Donaldson	Wilson R	Houston	Murray	Easton	Stuart	Campbell	Scott	McLean G	McLean J	Kinninmonth	Wilson S
	10th	Donaldson	Wilson R	Houston	Murray	Easton	Stuart	Campbell	McLean J	McLean G	Scott	Kinninmonth	Georgeson
	17th	Donaldson	Wilson R	Houston	Murray	Easton	Stewart	Campbell	McLean J	Wilson S	McLean G	Scott	Stuart
Mar	2nd	Donaldson	Wilson R	Houston	Murray	Easton	Stewart	Campbell	McLean J	Wilson S	McLean G	Scott	Kinninmonth
	4th	Donaldson	Wilson R	Houston	Murray	Easton	Stewart	Campbell	McLean J	Wilson S	McLean G	Scott	Kinninmonth (11)
	6th	Donaldson	Wilson R	Houston	Murray	Stewart	Steele	Bryce	McLean J	Georgeson	McLean G	Campbell	Scott
	9th	Donaldson	Wilson R	Houston	Murray	Easton	Stewart	Bryce	McLean J	McLean G	Scott	Campbell	Georgeson (9)
	13th	Donaldson	Wilson R	Swan	Murray	Easton	Stewart	Campbell	McLean J	Wilson S	McLean G	Bryce	Scott
	16th	Donaldson	Wilson R	Houston	Murray	Easton	Stewart	Campbell	McLean J	Wilson S	McLean G	Bryce	Scott (6)
	23rd	Donaldson	Wilson R	Houston	Murray	Easton	Stewart	Campbell	McLean J	Wilson S	McLean G	Scott	Kinninmonth
	27th	Donaldson	Wilson R	Houston	Murray	Easton	Stewart	Campbell	McLean J	Wilson S	McLean G	Scott	Georgeson (9), Swan
	30th	Donaldson	Wilson R	Houston	Murray	Easton	Stewart	Campbell	McLean J	Wilson S	McLean G	Scott	Georgeson (7)
Apr	3rd	Donaldson	Wilson R	Houston	Murray	Easton	Stewart	Campbell	McLean J	Wilson S	McLean G	Scott	Georgeson Kinninmonth
	13th	Donaldson	Wilson R	Swan	Murray	Easton	Stewart	Campbell	McLean J	Wilson S	McLean G	Scott	Kinninmonth
	15th	Donaldson	Wilson R	Swan	Murray	Easton	Stewart	Campbell	McLean J	Wilson S	McLean G	Scott	Georgeson (9)
	20th	Donaldson	Wilson R	Swan	Murray	Easton	Stewart	Campbell	McLean J	Georgeson*	McLean G	Scott	Kinninmonth (10)
	24th	Donaldson	Wilson R	Swan	Murray	Easton	Stewart	Campbell	McLean J	Wilson S	Scott	Georgeson	Kinninmonth (6)
	27th	Donaldson	Wilson R	Swan	Selway	Easton	Houston	Campbell	Scott	McLean J	Kinninmonth	McKay	Georgeson (8)
May	1st	Donaldson	Wilson R	Swan	Murray	Easton	Stewart	Campbell	McLean J	Wilson S	McLean G	Kinninmonth	Scott, Houston
	14th	Donaldson	Selway	Houston	Murray	Easton	Stewart	Campbell	McLean J	Wilson S	McLean G	Scott	Stuart, Kinninmonth

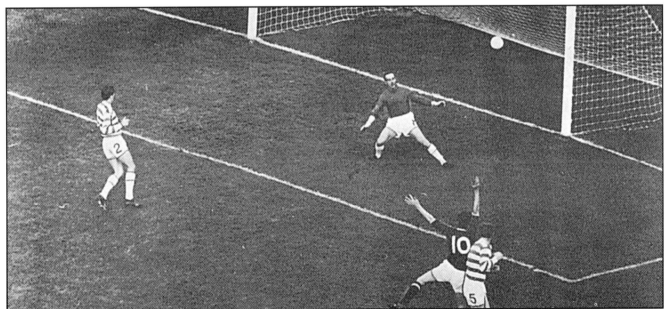

Fightback - George McLean pulls one back for the Dark Blues after Celtic had taken an early two-goal lead in the 1967 League Cup Final .

Goal grabber - George McLean was Dundee's top scorer with 35 goals. Watched by Jim McLean and Sammy Wilson, he sees his shot pushed wide by the Royal Liege keeper in the Fairs Cup second round tie at Dens. The big striker cracked home four goals in the second leg at Liege as Dundee qualified 7-2 on aggregate to reach their second European semi-final in five years.

DC Thomson

Appearances

	League		L/Cup		S/Cup	Fairs Cup		Total	
Jim McLean	34	(9)	10	(7)	3	8	(2)	55	(18)
Steve Murray	33		10	(1)	3	8		54	(1)
Bobby Wilson	34	(1)	10		3	7	(1)	54	(2)
George McLean	32	(23)	8	(7)	3	8	(5)	51+1s	(35)
Billy Campbell	32	(9)	10	(2)	3 (1)	8		45	(12)
Sammy Wilson	24	(6)	9	(3)	2 (1)	8	(3)	43	(13)
George Stewart	23		10		2	7		42	
Doug Houston	25	(1)	2		3	5		35	(1)
Alex. Stuart	20	(4)	10	(1)	1	4	(2)	35	(7)
Ally Donaldson	24		1		3	5		33	
Jim Easton	23		0		3	5	(1)	31+1s	(1)
Jocky Scott	19	(6)	4	(2)	2	3		28+5s	(8)
Alex. Bryce	12	(2)	9		1	2		24+1s	(2)
John Arrol	10		9		0	3		22	
Bobby Cox	6		8		0	3		17+1s	
Davie Swan	9		0		0	1		10	
Alex. Kinninmonth	5		0		1 (1)	1		7+5s	(1)
Derek McKay	3		0		0	0		3	
Roddy Georgeson	3	(1)	0		0	0		3+5s	(1)
Ron Selway	2		0		0	1		3	
Jim Steele	1		0		0	1		1	

Scottish League Division One

		Home			Away			Goals		
	P	W	D	L	W	D	L	F A		PTS
Celtic	34	14	3	0	16	0	1	106-24		63
Rangers	34	14	2	1	14	3	0	93-34		61
Hibernian	34	12	2	3	8	3	6	67-49		45
Dunfermline	34	9	1	7	8	4	5	64-41		39
Aberdeen	34	11	1	5	5	4	8	65-48		37
Morton	36	10	4	3	5	2	10	57-53		36
Kilmarnock	34	9	4	4	4	4	9	59-57		34
Clyde	34	9	3	5	6	1	10	55-55		34
Dundee	**34**	**8**	**2**	**7**	**5**	**5**	**7**	**62-59**		**33**
Partick Thistle	34	6	5	6	6	2	9	51-67		31
Dundee United	34	7	7	3	3	4	10	53-72		31
Hearts	34	9	1	7	4	3	10	56-61		30
Airdrie	34	7	5	5	3	4	10	45-58		29
St Johnstone	34	6	2	9	4	5	8	43-52		27
Falkirk	34	3	6	8	4	6	7	36-45		26
Raith Rovers	34	5	4	8	4	3	10	58-86		25
Motherwell	34	4	3	10	2	4	11	40-66		19
Stirling Albion	34	4	3	10	0	1	16	29-105		12

League Cup Section

	P	W	D	L	F A	PTS
Dundee	**6**	**5**	**1**	**0**	**14- 6**	**11**
Hibernian	6	3	1	2	9- 7	7
Motherwell	6	1	1	4	8-13	3
Clyde	6	1	1	4	6-11	3

The Dundee F.C. squad which reached the League Cup Final in October 1967. (BACK, left to right) Bobby Wilson, Ally Donaldson, John Arrol, Steve Murray, Jocky Scott, Alex. Stuart, Doug Houston. FRONT - Sammy Wilson, Jim McLean, Bobby Cox, George Stewart, Alex. Bryce and George McLean. Inset - Billy Campbell.

DC Thomson

Goals galore at Hampden - Celtic's Jim Craig, John Clark and keeper Ronnie Simpson are helpless as Jim McLean nets the Dark Blues second in the high-scoring 1967 League Cup Final.

They Wore The Dark Blue

Season 1968-69

Date		Opponents		Score	Crowd	Scorers
Aug 10th	LC	Kilmarnock	h	4-0	8,500	Scott 2; Duncan; Stuart
14th	LC	Hearts	a	1-2	11,000	Stuart
17th	LC	Airdrie	h	1-1	7,000	G. McLean
24th	LC	Kilmarnock	a	2-2	6,000	G. McLean; Stewart
28th	LC	Hearts	h	4-0	8,300	Duncan 3; G. McLean
31st	LC	Airdrie	a	3-0	6,000	G. McLean 2; Duncan
Sep 7th	L	Aberdeen	h	4-4	10,000	Scott; Campbell; B. Wilson; Duncan
11th	LCQ	Stranraer	a	4-0	4,000	Duncan 2; Scott; Georgeson
14th	L	Dundee United	a	1-3	14,000	Georgeson
18th	LCQ	Stranraer	h	6-0 (10-0)	3,000	Scott 3; G. McLean 3
21st	L	St Johnstone	h	2-3	8,000	Scott; Duncan
28th	L	Airdrie	h	3-0	3,000	Campbell; Scott; Black o.g.
Oct 5th	L	Clyde	h	2-3	7,000	Duncan; Bryce
9th	LCS	Hibernian	Tyn	1-2	19,572	G. McLean
12th	L	St Mirren	h	0-0	5,000	-
19th	L	Arbroath	a	2-1	5,307	G. McLean; Gilroy
26th	L	Hearts	h	3-1	8,000	Gilroy; Campbell; Kinninmonth
Nov 2nd	L	Celtic	a	1-3	37,000	Campbell
9th	L	Dunfermline	h	1-0	7,500	Gilroy
16th	L	Falkirk	a	1-0	4,500	Campbell
23rd	L	Kilmarnock	a	0-1		
30th	L	Partick Thistle	h	1-1	6,000	Scott
Dec 7th	L	Morton	a	1-2	4,500	Gilroy
14th	L	Hibernian	h	0-0	8,000	-
Jan 1st	L	Aberdeen	a	0-0	11,000	-
2nd	L	Dundee United	h	1-2	21,000	Bryce
4th	L	St Johnstone	a	1-3	8,000	Kinninmonth
11th	L	Airdrie	h	1-1	5,000	G. McLean
18th	L	Clyde	a	0-0	3,000	-
25th	SC1	Hearts	h	1-2	14,000	Scott
Feb 1st	L	St Mirren	a	3-2	6,000	Gilroy; Bryce; Stewart
8th	L	Arbroath	h	3-0	5,000	Campbell; Bryce; Scott (pen)
Mar 5th	L	Dunfermline	a	0-2	6,000	-
8th	L	Falkirk	h	0-0	-	-
12th	L	Hearts	a	2-2	6,000	Kinninmonth; Scott
15th	L	Kilmarnock	h	0-0	5,000	-
22nd	L	Partick Thistle	a	4-0	2,500	Scott 2; Kinninmonth; Bryce
26th	L	Raith Rovers	h	2-2	6,000	Bryce; Duncan
29th	L	Morton	h	0-2	5,000	-
Apr 8th	L	Hibernian	a	3-1	5,000	Kinninmonth; Scott 2
16th	FC1	Dundee United	a	0-1	7,000	-
19th	L	Raith Rovers	a	0-4	5,000	-
22nd	L	Rangers	h	3-2	9,000	Bryce 2; Gilroy
28th	L	Rangers	a	1-1	6,800	Steele
30th	L	Celtic	h	1-2	14,000	Murray

Jim Easton - the former Hibs defender was a stalwart for the Dark Blues.

The Record

League	-	Ninth Place, Division One.
League Cup	-	Semi-final.
Scottish Cup	-	First round.
Forfarshire Cup	-	First round
Top Scorer	-	Jocky Scott (17 goals).
Av. Home Gate	-	7,900
Players used	-	23
Sent Off	-	One

Appearances

	League	L/Cup	S/Cup	Total
Ally Donaldson	33	9	1	43
Doug Houston	32	9	1	42
Jocky Scott	32 (10)	9 (6)	1 (1)	42+1s (17)
Bobby Wilson	34 (1)	7	1	42 (1)
Steve Murray	31 (1)	8	1	40 (1)
Billy Campbell	28 (6)	9	1	38+1s (6)
George Stewart	24 (1)	9 (1)	1	38 (2)
Jim Easton	21	8	0	29
George McLean	20 (2)	8 (9)	1	29+2s (11)
Alex. Bryce	24 (8)	2	1	27+2s (8)
Joe Gilroy	24 (6)	0	1	25 (6)
Alex Kinninmonth	20 (5)	1	0	21+2s (5)
Davie Swan	18	0	1	19
John Duncan	11 (4)	7 (7)	0	18+1s (11)
Alex. Stuart	5	4 (2)	0	9 (2)
Roddy Georgeson	4 (1)	4 (1)	0	8+1s (2)
Dave Johnston	4	0	0	4
Ron Selway	4	0	0	4+1s
Jim Steele	3 (1)	1	0	4+1s (1)
Bobby Cox	0	2	0	2
Derek McKay	1	1	0	2
John Arrol	1	0	0	1
Sammy Wilson	0	1	0	1

Scottish League Division One

		Home			Away			Goals		
	P	W	D	L	W	D	L	F A	PTS
Celtic	34	12	3	2	11	5	1	89-32	54
Rangers	34	13	3	1	8	4	5	81-32	49
Dunfermline	34	12	4	1	7	3	7	63-45	45
Kilmarnock	34	10	6	1	5	8	4	50-32	44
Dundee United	34	12	3	2	5	6	6	61-49	43
St Johnstone	34	11	2	4	5	3	9	66-59	37
Airdrie	34	10	5	2	3	6	8	46-44	37
Hearts	34	7	7	3	7	1	9	52-54	36
Dundee	**34**	**4**	**8**	**5**	**6**	**4**	**7**	**47-48**	**32**
Morton	34	8	5	4	4	3	10	58-68	32
St Mirren	34	7	4	6	4	6	7	40-54	32
Hibernian	34	9	2	6	3	5	9	60-59	31
Clyde	34	6	7	4	3	6	8	35-50	31
Partick Thistle	34	7	3	7	2	7	8	39-53	28
Aberdeen	34	6	5	6	3	3	11	50-59	26
Raith Rovers	34	6	2	9	2	3	12	45-67	21
Falkirk	34	4	6	7	1	2	14	33-69	18
Arbroath	34	4	3	10	1	3	13	41-102	16

League Cup Section

	P	W	D	L	F A	PTS
Dundee	**6**	**3**	**2**	**1**	**15- 5**	**8**
Airdrie	6	3	1	2	10- 7	7
Hearts	6	2	2	2	8-12	6
Kilmarnock	6	0	3	3	5-14	3

Dundee F.C. Line-Ups 1968-69

		1	2	3	4	5	6	7	8	9	10	11	12
Aug	10th	Donaldson	Wilson B	Houston	Murray	Easton	Stewart	McKay	Scott	Duncan	Stuart	Campbell	McLean J
	14th	Donaldson	Cox	Houston	Murray	Easton	Stewart	Campbell	Stuart	Duncan	Scott	McLean G	McKay
	17th	Donaldson	Cox	Houston	Murray	Easton	Stewart	Campbell	Stuart	Duncan	Scott	McLean G	Georgeson (9)
	24th	Donaldson	Wilson B	Houston	Murray	Easton	Stewart	Scott	Kinninmonth	Georgeson	McLean G	Campbell	Duncan (8)
	28th	Donaldson	Wilson B	Houston	Murray	Easton	Stewart	Campbell	Scott	Duncan	McLean G	Georgeson	Stuart
	31st	Donaldson	Wilson B	Houston	Murray	Easton	Stewart	Campbell	Scott	Duncan	McLean G	Georgeson	Stuart
Sep	7th	Donaldson	Wilson B	Houston	Murray	Easton	Stewart	Campbell	McLean G	Duncan	Scott	Georgeson	Bryce (11)
	11th	Donaldson	Wilson B	Houston	Murray	Easton	Stewart	Campbell	McLean G	Duncan	Scott	Georgeson	Stuart
	14th	Donaldson	Wilson B	Houston	Murray	Easton	Stewart	Campbell	McLean G	Duncan	Scott	Georgeson	Bryce
	18th	Donaldson	Wilson B	Houston	Steele	Stewart	Stuart	Campbell	Scott	Duncan	McLean G	Bryce	Georgeson
	21st	Donaldson	Wilson B	Houston	Murray	Easton	Stewart	Campbell	McLean G	Duncan	Scott	Georgeson	Wilson S (6)
	28th	Donaldson	Wilson B	Houston	Selway	Easton	Stewart	Campbell	McLean G	Duncan	Scott	Bryce	Georgeson
Oct	5th	Donaldson	Wilson B	Houston	Murray	Easton	Selway	Campbell	Scott	Duncan	McLean G	Bryce	Wilson S (9)
	9th	Donaldson	Wilson B	Houston	Murray	Easton	Stewart	Campbell	McLean G	Wilson S	Scott	Bryce	Selway
	12th	Donaldson	Wilson B	Houston	Murray	Easton	Stewart	Scott	McLean G	Duncan	Georgeson	Bryce	Steele
	19th	Donaldson	Wilson B	Houston	Murray	Easton	Stewart	Campbell	McLean G	Gilroy	Steele	Scott	Bryce (10)
	26th	Donaldson	Wilson B	Houston	Murray	Easton	Stewart	Campbell	McLean G	Gilroy	Kinninmonth	Scott	Stuart
Nov	2nd	Donaldson	Wilson B	Houston	Murray	Easton	Stewart	Campbell	McLean G	Gilroy	Kinninmonth	Scott	Bryce
	9th	Donaldson	Wilson B	Swan	Murray	Stewart	Houston	Campbell	McLean G	Gilroy	Kinninmonth	Scott	Bryce
	16th	Donaldson	Wilson B	Swan	Murray	Stewart	Houston	Campbell	McLean G	Gilroy	Kinninmonth	Scott	Bryce
	23rd	Donaldson	Wilson B	Swan	Murray	Stewart	Houston	Campbell	McLean G	Gilroy*	Kinninmonth	Scott	Bryce
	30th	Donaldson	Wilson B	Swan	Murray	Stewart	Houston	Campbell	McLean G	Gilroy	Kinninmonth	Scott	McKay
Dec	7th	Donaldson	Wilson B	Swan	Murray	Easton	Stewart	Campbell	Scott	Gilroy	Houston	Bryce	McLean G (6)
	14th	Donaldson	Wilson B	Swan	Murray	Stuart	Houston	Campbell	Gilroy	McLean G	Bryce	Scott	Kinninmonth
Jan	1st	Donaldson	Wilson B	Swan	Murray	Stuart	Houston	Campbell	Gilroy	Kinninmonth	Bryce	Scott	McLean G
	2nd	Donaldson	Wilson B	Swan	Murray	Stuart	Houston	Campbell	Duncan	Gilroy	Bryce	Scott	McLean G (8)
	4th	Donaldson	Wilson B	Houston	Murray	Stuart	Stewart	Campbell	McLean G	Gilroy	Bryce	Kinninmonth	Steele (5)
	11th	Donaldson	Wilson B	Swan	Murray	Easton	Houston	Bryce	Gilroy	McLean G	Stuart	Scott	Campbell (10)
	18th	Donaldson	Wilson B	Swan	Murray	Stewart	Houston	Campbell	McLean G	Gilroy	Scott	Bryce	Kinninmonth
	25th	Donaldson	Wilson B	Swan	Murray	Stewart	Houston	Campbell	McLean G	Gilroy	Scott	Bryce	Kinninmonth
Feb	1st	Donaldson	Wilson B	Johnston	Murray	Stewart	Houston	Campbell	Kinninmonth	Gilroy	McLean G	Bryce	Scott (10)
	8th	Donaldson	Wilson B	Johnston	Selway	Stewart	Houston	Scott	Bryce	Gilroy	Kinninmonth	Campbell	McKay
Mar	5th	Donaldson	Wilson B	Johnston	Kinninmonth	Stewart	Houston	Scott	McLean G	Gilroy	Bryce	Campbell	Swan
	8th	Donaldson	Wilson B	Johnston	Murray	Stewart	Houston	Campbell	Bryce	Gilroy	Swan	Scott	Kinninmonth (3)
	12th	Donaldson	Wilson B	Houston	Murray	Easton	Stewart	Campbell	McLean G	Gilroy	Scott	Bryce	Kinninmonth (9)
	15th	Donaldson	Wilson B	Houston	Murray	Easton	Stewart	Campbell	Scott	Duncan	Kinninmonth	Bryce	Selway
	22nd	Donaldson	Wilson B	Swan	Murray	Easton	Stewart	Campbell	Scott	Duncan	Kinninmonth	Bryce	Selway (4)
	26th	Donaldson	Wilson B	Swan	Murray	Easton	Stewart	Campbell	Scott	Duncan	Kinninmonth	Bryce	Houston
	29th	Donaldson	Wilson B	Houston	Murray	Easton	Stewart	Campbell	Scott	Duncan	Kinninmonth	Bryce	Swan
Apr	8th	Donaldson	Wilson B	Swan	Murray	Easton	Houston	Campbell	Scott	Gilroy	Kinninmonth	Bryce	Selway
	19th	Arrol	Wilson B	Swan	Murray	Easton	Selway	Bryce	Scott	Gilroy	Kinninmonth	Houston	Steele
	22nd	Donaldson	Wilson B	Swan	Murray	Easton	Houston	McKay	Scott	Gilroy	Kinninmonth	Bryce	Selway
	28th	Donaldson	Wilson B	Swan	Murray	Easton	Houston	Steele	Scott	Gilroy	Kinninmonth	Bryce	Selway
	30th	Donaldson	Wilson B	Swan	Murray	Easton	Houston	Steele	Scott	Gilroy	Kinninmonth	Bryce	Selway

Up in attack - that's Dundee right-back Bobby Wilson in this derby match with Dundee United at Tannadice. The defender's shot is saved by United keeper Don Mackay watched by John Duncan and George McLean and United's Dennis Gillespie.

DC Thomson

Season 1969-70

Date		Opponents		Score	Crowd	Scorers
Aug 9th	LC	St Johnstone	a	1-3	6,600	Scott
13th	LC	Partick Thistle	h	4-0	7,000	Campbell; Gilroy 2; Stewart
16th	LC	Kilmarnock	h	0-0	10,000	-
20th	LC	Partick Thistle	a	1-0	2,000	Gilroy
23rd	LC	St Johnstone	h	1-2	13,400	Scott
27th	LC	Kilmarnock	a	0-1	3,000	-
Sep 3rd	L	Motherwell	h	1-3	5,400	Scott
6th	L	Ayr United	h	1-0	5,000	Georgeson
13th	L	Raith Rovers	a	0-0	4,000	-
20th	L	Dundee United	h	1-2	12,500	Wallace
27th	L	Aberdeen	a	1-1	13,000	Wilson
Oct 4th	L	Airdrie	h	4-2	5,000	Scott 2; Gilroy 2
11th	L	Kilmarnock	a	0-3		-
18th	L	Clyde	h	3-0	4,000	Murray 2; Wallace
25th	L	Morton	a	1-0	5,000	Walace
Nov 1st	L	Rangers	a	1-3	30,000	Wallace
8th	L	Dunfermline	h	1-1	7,000	Wallace
15th	L	St Johnstone	a	4-1	6,000	Wallace 3; Scott
22nd	L	Hearts	h	2-0	5,500	Gilroy 2
29th	L	St Mirren	h	1-0	5,000	Wallace
Dec 6th	L	Celtic	a	0-1	31,000	-
20th	L	Motherwell	a	1-1	4,500	Wallace
27th	L	Hibernian	h	1-0	12,000	Houston
Jan 1st	L	Aberdeen	h	2-0	12,000	Steele; Bryce
3rd	L	Dundee United	a	1-4	18,000	Wallace
17th	L	Raith Rovers	h	0-0	5,500	-
24th	SC1	Albion Rovers	a	2-1	2,710	Bryce; Kinninmonth
31st	L	Ayr United	a	2-3	5,000	Kinninmonth; Wallace
Feb 7th	SC2	Airdrie	h	3-0	10,000	Kinninmonth 2; Wallace
9th	L	Hibernian	a	1-4	6,400	Steele
21st	SCQ	East Fife	a	1-0	14,994	Bryce
25th	L	Airdrie	a	1-0		Kinninmonth
28th	L	Kilmarnock	h	3-0	9,000	Houston; Scott; Wallace
Mar 7th	L	Clyde	a	1-1	2,000	Wallace
11th	L	St Mirren	a	1-2	4,800	Scott
14th	SCS	Celtic	Ham	1-2	64,000	Wallace
21st	L	Rangers	h	2-1	15,000	Wallace; Scott
25th	L	Morton	h	2-1	6,000	Wallace 2
28th	L	Dunfermline	a	2-3	4,000	Wallace; Johnston
Apr 1st	L	Partick Thistle	h	4-1	3,000	Wallace; Scott; Bryce; Kinninmonth
4th	L	St Johnstone	h	0-2	6,500	-
8th	L	Celtic	h	1-2	13,000	Wallace
12th	L	Hearts	a	3-1	7,500	Wallace 2; Scott

Cup Cash v.Airdrie £2,070

Gordon Wallace - the free scoring striker rates as one of Dundee's best-ever buys.

The Record		
League	-	Sixth Place, Division One.
League Cup	-	Qualifying stages only.
Scottish Cup	-	Semi-final.
Forfarshire Cup	-	Did not play (Comp. unfinished)
Top Scorer	-	Gordon Wallace (23 goals)
Av. Home Gate	-	8,000
Players used	-	19.
Sent off	-	One.

Appearances

	League	L/Cup	S/Cup	Total
Ally Donaldson	34	6	4	44
Jocky Scott	32 (9)	6 (2)	4	42 (11)
Doug Houston	30 (2)	6	4	40 (2)
Alex Bryce	27 (2)	6	4 (2)	37+1s (4)
Alex Kinninmonth	26 (3)	4	4 (3)	34+4s (6)
Steve Murray	25 (3)	6	3	34 (3)
Ron Selway	29	1	4	34
Gordon Wallace	30 (21)	0	4 (2)	34 (23)
Jim Steele	23 (2)	1	4	28 (2)
Bobby Wilson	22 (1)	5	1	28 (1)
Billy Campbell	18	6 (1)	3	27+1s (1)
Jim Easton	23	0	4	27
George Stewart	21	5 (1)	1	27+1s (1)
Joe Gilroy	14 (4)	6 (3)	0	20 (7)
Davie Swan	11	1	0	12
Jim Fraser	2	6	0	8
John Duncan	2	1	0	3
Dave Johnston	3 (1)	0	0	3 (1)
Roddy Georgeson	2 (1)	0	0	2 (1)

Scottish League Division One

	P	Home W	D	L	Away W	D	L	Goals F	A	PTS
Celtic	34	12	2	3	15	1	1	96-33		57
Rangers	34	13	1	3	6	6	5	67-40		45
Hibernian	34	12	3	2	7	3	7	65-40		44
Hearts	34	6	7	4	7	5	5	50-36		38
Dundee United	34	10	3	4	6	3	8	62-64		38
Dundee	**34**	**11**	**2**	**4**	**4**	**4**	**9**	**49-44**		**36**
Kilmarnock	34	10	5	2	3	5	9	62-57		36
Aberdeen	34	6	6	5	8	1	8	55-45		35
Dunfermline	34	12	2	3	1	7	9	52-52		35
Morton	34	9	5	3	6	0	11	45-45		35
Motherwell	34	8	4	5	3	6	8	49-51		32
Airdrie	34	8	3	6	4	5	8	59-64		32
St Johnstone	34	9	4	4	2	5	10	50-62		31
Ayr United	34	10	3	4	2	3	12	37-52		30
St Mirren	34	6	5	6	2	4	11	39-54		25
Clyde	34	8	4	5	1	3	13	34-56		25
Raith Rovers	34	4	6	7	1	5	11	32-69		21
Partick Thistle	34	4	4	9	1	3	13	41-82		17

League Cup Section

	P	W	D	L	F	A	PTS
St Johnstone	6	6	0	0	22-6		12
Kilmarnock	6	3	1	2	12-5		7
Dundee	**6**	**2**	**3**	**1**	**7-6**		**5**
Partick Thistle	6	0	0	6	1-25		0

Dundee F.C. Line-Ups 1969-70

		1	2	3	4	5	6	7	8	9	10	11	12
Aug	9th	Donaldson	Wilson B	Swan	Murray	Fraser	Houston	Campbell	Scott	Gilroy	Bryce	Steele	Kinninmonth
	13th	Donaldson	Wilson B	Houston	Murray	Fraser	Stewart	Scott	Kinninmonth	Gilroy	Bryce	Campbell	Steele
	16th	Donaldson	Wilson B	Houston	Murray	Fraser	Stewart	Scott	Kinninmonth	Gilroy	Bryce	Campbell	Steele
	20th	Donaldson	Wilson B	Houston	Murray	Fraser	Stewart	Scott	Kinninmonth	Gilroy	Bryce	Campbell	Selway
	23rd	Donaldson	Selway	Houston	Murray	Fraser	Stewart	Campbell	Gilroy	Duncan	Bryce	Scott	Kinninmonth (2)
	27th	Donaldson	Wilson B	Houston	Murray	Fraser	Stewart	Campbell	Kinninmonth	Gilroy	Scott	Bryce	Georgeson
	30th	Donaldson	Wilson B	Houston	Murray	Fraser	Stewart	Campbell	Kinninmonth	Gilroy	Scott	Bryce	Steele (6)
Sep	3rd	Donaldson	Wilson B	Houston	Murray	Fraser	Stewart	Campbell	Scott	Duncan	Bryce	Steele	Kinninmonth (11)
	6th	Donaldson	Wilson B	Swan	Murray	Stewart	Houston	Campbell	Scott	Gilroy	Bryce	Georgeson	Kinninmonth
	13th	Donaldson	Wilson B	Swan	Murray	Stewart	Houston	Duncan	Scott	Gilroy	Bryce	Campbell	Kinninmonth (11)
	20th	Donaldson	Wilson B	Swan	Murray	Stewart	Houston	Gilroy	Bryce	Wallace	Scott	Kinninmonth	Duncan
	27th	Donaldson	Wilson B	Swan	Selway	Stewart	Houston	Murray	Scott	Gilroy	Bryce	Wallace	Kinninmonth (6)
Oct	4th	Donaldson	Wilson B	Swan	Selway	Stewart	Houston	Murray	Gilroy	Wallace	Scott	Bryce	Steele
	11th	Donaldson	Wilson B	Swan	Selway	Stewart	Houston	Murray	Gilroy	Wallace	Scott	Bryce	Steele
	18th	Donaldson	Wilson B	Selway	Steele	Stewart	Houston	Murray	Gilroy	Wallace	Bryce	Campbell	Scott
	25th	Donaldson	Wilson B	Selway	Steele	Stewart	Houston	Murray	Scott	Wallace	Bryce	Campbell	Kinninmonth
Nov	1st	Donaldson	Wilson B	Swan	Selway	Stewart	Houston	Murray	Gilroy	Wallace	Kinninmonth	Bryce	Scott
	8th	Donaldson	Wilson B	Swan	Murray	Easton	Selway	Campbell	Gilroy	Wallace	Scott	Kinninmonth	Houston
	15th	Donaldson	Wilson B	Houston	Murray	Easton	Selway	Gilroy	Kinninmonth	Wallace	Scott	Bryce	Steele
	22nd	Donaldson	Wilson B	Houston	Murray	Easton	Selway	Gilroy	Kinninmonth	Wallace	Scott	Steele	Campbell
	29th	Donaldson	Wilson B	Swan	Murray	Easton	Selway	Gilroy	Kinninmonth	Wallace	Scott*	Steele	Campbell
Dec	6th	Donaldson	Wilson B	Houston	Murray	Easton	Selway	Gilroy	Kinninmonth	Wallace	Scott	Steele	Campbell (7)
	20th	Donaldson	Wilson B	Houston	Murray	Easton	Selway	Bryce	Kinninmonth	Wallace	Scott	Steele	Campbell
	27th	Donaldson	Wilson B	Houston	Murray	Easton	Selway	Steele	Kinninmonth	Wallace	Scott	Bryce	Georgeson
Jan	1st	Donaldson	Wilson B	Houston	Murray	Easton	Selway	Steele	Kinninmonth	Wallace	Scott	Bryce	Georgeson
	3rd	Donaldson	Wilson B	Houston	Murray	Easton	Selway	Steele	Kinninmonth	Wallace	Scott	Bryce	Georgeson
	17th	Donaldson	Wilson B	Houston	Murray	Easton	Selway	Steele	Kinninmonth	Wallace	Scott	Bryce	Campbell
	24th	Donaldson	Wilson B	Houston	Murray	Easton	Selway	Steele	Kinninmonth	Wallace	Scott	Bryce	Campbell
	31st	Donaldson	Wilson B	Houston	Steele	Easton	Selway	Campbell	Kinninmonth	Wallace	Scott	Bryce	Swan
Feb	7th	Donaldson	Steele	Houston	Murray	Easton	Selway	Campbell	Kinninmonth	Wallace	Scott	Bryce	Johnston
	9th	Donaldson	Swan	Houston	Murray	Easton	Selway	Steele	Kinninmonth	Wallace	Scott	Bryce	Campbell
	21st	Donaldson	Selway	Houston	Murray	Easton	Steele	Campbell	Kinninmonth	Wallace	Scott	Bryce	Swan
	25th	Donaldson	Selway	Houston	Murray	Easton	Stewart	Campbell	Kinninmonth	Wallace	Scott	Steele	Georgeson
	28th	Donaldson	Selway	Houston	Murray	Easton	Stewart	Campbell	Kinninmonth	Wallace	Scott	Steele	Bryce
Mar	7th	Donaldson	Selway	Houston	Murray	Easton	Stewart	Campbell	Kinninmonth	Wallace	Scott	Bryce	Steele
	11th	Donaldson	Selway	Swan	Kinninmonth	Easton	Houston	Campbell	Bryce	Wallace	Scott	Steele	Stewart (3)
	14th	Donaldson	Selway	Houston	Steele	Easton	Stewart	Bryce	Kinninmonth	Wallace	Scott	Campbell	Georgeson
	21st	Donaldson	Selway	Johnston	Steele	Easton	Stewart	Campbell	Kinninmonth	Wallace	Scott	Bryce	Georgeson
	25th	Donaldson	Selway	Johnston	Steele	Easton	Stewart	Campbell	Kinninmonth	Wallace	Scott	Bryce	Houston
	28th	Donaldson	Selway	Johnston	Houston	Easton	Stewart	Campbell	Kinninmonth	Wallace	Scott	Steele	Bryce (6)
Apr	1st	Donaldson	Selway	Houston	Steele	Easton	Stewart	Campbell	Kinninmonth	Wallace	Scott	Bryce	Johnston
	4th	Donaldson	Selway	Houston	Steele	Easton	Stewart	Campbell	Kinninmonth	Wallace	Scott	Bryce	Georgeson
	8th	Donaldson	Selway	Houston	Kinninmonth	Easton	Stewart	Campbell	Bryce	Wallace	Scott	Steele	Johnston
	12th	Donaldson	Selway	Houston	Kinninmonth	Easton	Stewart	Georgeson	Bryce	Wallace	Scott	Steele	Duncan

Dundee F.C. Season 1969-70. (BACK, left to right) Bobby Wilson, John Duncan, Doug Houston, Iain Phillip, Jim Easton, Jim Fraser, Alex. Kinninmonth. MIDDLE - Maurice Friel (physio), Jim Steele, George Stewart, Ally Donaldson, Ron Selway, Davie Swan, Joe Gilroy, Bruce Hay (coach). FRONT - Alex. Bryce, Roddy Georgeson, Gordon Wallace, John Prentice (manager), Steve Murray, Ian Chalmers and Jocky Scott.

DC Thomson

They Wore The Dark Blue

Season 1970-71

Jim Steele - an influential performer for Dundee either at the back or in midfield.

Date				Score	Crowd	Scorers
Aug	8th	LC	St Mirren	h	1-0	6,000	Kinninmonth
	12th	LC	Ayr United	a	2-1	6,500	Duncan 2
	15th	LC	Kilmarnock	h	2-0	8,000	Scott 2
	19th	LC	Ayr United	h	4-1	6,000	Steele; Wallace; Scott; J. Wilson
	22nd	LC	St Mirren	a	2-0	4,000	Duncan; Scott
	26th	LC	Kilmarnock	a	1-2	3,000	Duncan
	29th	L	Cowdenbeath	a	1-0	5,500	Duncan
Sep	5th	L	Aberdeen	h	1-2	9,000	Duncan
	9th	LCQ	Celtic	h	2-2	23,000	Kinninmonth; Scott
	12th	L	Dundee United	a	2-3	13,000	Gilroy; Scott
	16th	TC1	Wolves	h	1-2	11,500	Wallace
	19th	L	St Mirren	h	2-2	5,000	Wallace 2
	23rd	LCQ	Celtic	a	1-5 (3-7)	41,000	Wallace
	26th	L	Celtic	a	0-3	28,000	-
	29th	TC1	Wolves	a	0-0 (1-2)	13,042	-
Oct	3rd	L	Falkirk	h	1-2	4,000	Scott
	10th	L	Ayr United	a	1-0	5,500	Duncan
	17th	L	Hearts	h	1-0	6,000	Scott
	24th	L	St Johnstone	a	3-3	6,500	Wallace 2; Duncan
	31st	L	Kilmarnock	h	3-0	4,000	Wallace; Johnston; Kinninmonth
Nov	7th	L	Hibernian	a	2-1	7,210	Wallace; Shevlane o.g.
	14th	L	Airdrie	h	3-0	5,500	Wallace; Scott 2
	21st	L	Dunfermline	a	0-0	5,000	-
	28th	L	Clyde	h	1-3	5,500	Scott
Dec	5th	L	Rangers	a	0-0	30,000	-
	12th	L	Morton	h	2-0	4,000	Scott; Gilroy
	19th	L	Motherwell	a	1-1	7,000	Wallace
	26th	L	Cowdenbeath	h	5-1	5,000	Wallace; Scott 2; Gilroy; Kinninmonth
Jan	1st	L	Aberdeen	a	0-3	24,000	-
	9th	L	St Mirren	a	4-2	3,500	Duncan 2; Scott 2
	16th	L	Celtic	h	1-8	21,000	Duncan
	23rd	SC1	Partick Thistle	h	1-0	8,000	Johnston
	30th	L	Falkirk	a	2-2	6,000	Duncan; B. Wilson
Feb	6th	L	Ayr United	a	2-1	4,500	Wallace; B. Wilson
	13th	SC2	Stirling Albion	h	2-0	6,000	Johnston; B. Wilson
	20th	L	Hearts	a	0-0	8,000	-
	27th	L	St Johnstone	h	0-1	9,500	-
Mar	6th	SCQ	Hibernian	a	0-1	21,710	-
	10th	L	Kilmarnock	a	1-1		Scott
	13th	L	Hibernian	h	1-0	6,500	B. Wilson
	20th	L	Airdrie	a	6-2	5,000	Duncan 3; Scott; Bryce 2
	27th	L	Dunfermline	h	0-0	6,500	-
Apr	3rd	L	Clyde	a	0-0	1,000	-
	7th	L	Dundee United	h	2-3	12,500	Scott; Steele
	10th	L	Rangers	h	1-0	13,000	Scott
	12th	FC1	Forfar Athletic	h	6-1	1,500	Easton; J. Scott (pen)Wallace; Kinninmonth 2; Grimshaw o.g.
	17th	L	Morton	a	0-1	2,500	-
	19th	FCS	Brechin City	a	2-1	750	Wallace; Gilroy
	24th	L	Motherwell	h	4-0	4,500	Easton; Kinninmonth;

Cup Cash v. Stirling Albion £1,400

The Record

League	-	Fifth Place, Division One.
League Cup	-	Quarter-final
Scottish Cup	-	Quarter-final
Texaco Cup	-	First round
Forfarshire Cup	-	Winners (Final 18-03-72)
Top Scorer	-	Jocky Scott (21 goals)
Av. Home Gate	-	7,400
Players used	-	21
Sent off	-	Two

Appearances

	League	L/Cup	S/Cup	T/Cup	Total	
Gordon Wallace	33 (11)	8 (2)	3	2 (1)	46	(14)
Doug Houston	32	8	3	2	45+1s	
Jocky Scott	33 (16)	7 (5)	3	2	45	(21)
Bobby Wilson	32 (3)	7	3 (1)	2	44	(4)
Ally Donaldson	29	8	3	2	42	
Jim Steele	28 (1)	7 (1)	3	2	40	(2)
Alex Kinninmonth	25 (3)	6 (2)	2	1	34+2s	(5)
Iain Phillip	29	0	3	0	32+2s	
Dave Johnston	25 (1)	3	3 (2)	0	31+4s	(3)
Jimmy Wilson	19	5 (1)	2	2	28+2s	(1)
Alex Bryce	14 (2)	7	1	1	22+3s	(2)
John Duncan	13 (11)	6 (4)	0	1	20+5s	(15)
Ronnie Selway	15	2	1	2	20+2s	
George Stewart	9	8	1	2	20	
Joe Gilroy	14 (3)	1	1	1	17+1s	(3)
Dave Souter	9	1	1	0	11+1s	
Jim Easton	6 (1)	3	0	0	9	(1)
Mike Hewitt	5	0	0	0	5	
Jim Fraser	2	1	0	0	3	
George Falconer	1	0	0	0	1+2s	
Duncan Lambie	1	0	0	0	1	

Scottish League Division One

		Home			Away			Goals		
	P	W	D	L	W	D	L	F	A	PTS
Celtic	34	15	1	1	11	5	2	89-23		56
Aberdeen	34	11	6	0	13	0	4	68-18		54
St Johnstone	34	10	3	4	9	3	5	59-44		44
Rangers	34	10	5	2	6	4	7	58-34		41
Dundee	**34**	**9**	**2**	**6**	**5**	**8**	**4**	**53-45**		**38**
Dundee United	34	8	4	5	6	4	7	53-54		36
Falkirk	34	8	5	4	5	4	8	46-53		35
Morton	34	9	4	4	4	4	9	44-44		34
Airdrie	34	8	3	6	5	5	7	60-65		34
Motherwell	34	7	4	6	6	4	7	43-47		34
Hearts	34	8	5	4	5	2	10	41-40		33
Hibernian	34	8	4	5	2	6	9	47-53		30
Kilmarnock	34	5	6	6	5	2	10	43-67		28
Ayr United	34	7	5	5	2	3	12	37-54		26
Clyde	34	5	5	7	3	5	9	33-59		26
Dunfermline	34	6	5	6	0	6	11	44-56		23
St Mirren	34	4	3	10	3	6	8	38-56		23
Cowdenbeath	34	1	2	14	6	1	10	33-77		17

League Cup Section

	P	W	D	L	F A	PTS
Dundee	**6**	**5**	**0**	**1**	**12- 4**	**10**
Kilmarnock	6	4	1	1	8- 4	9
Ayr United	6	1	2	3	6-10	4
St Mirren	6	0	1	5	4-12	1

Dundee F.C. Line-Ups 1970-71

		1	2	3	4	5	6	7	8	9	10	11	12
Aug	8th	Donaldson	Wilson B	Houston	Kinninmonth	Easton	Stewart	Duncan	Bryce	Wallace	Scott	Wilson J	Johnston
	12th	Donaldson	Wilson B	Souter	Johnston	Stewart	Houston	Duncan	Kinninmonth	Wallace	Bryce	Steele	Gilroy
	15th	Donaldson	Wilson B	Houston	Kinninmonth	Easton	Stewart	Duncan	Bryce	Wallace	Scott	Steele	Gilroy
	19th	Donaldson	Wilson B	Johnston	Steele	Stewart	Houston	Duncan	Bryce	Wallace	Scott	Wilson J	Kinninmonth
	22nd	Donaldson	Wilson B	Johnston	Steele	Stewart	Houston	Duncan	Bryce	Wallace	Scott	Wilson J	Selway
	26th	Donaldson	Wilson B*	Houston	Steele	Fraser	Stewart	Duncan	Kinninmonth	Wallace	Scott	Bryce	Phillip (10)
	29th	Donaldson	Selway	Houston	Kinninmonth	Easton	Stewart	Duncan	Bryce	Wallace	Steele	Wilson J	Gilroy
Sep	5th	Donaldson	Wilson B	Johnston	Selway	Stewart	Houston	Kinninmonth	Bryce	Duncan	Scott	Wilson J	Phillip
	9th	Donaldson	Selway	Houston	Kinninmonth	Easton	Stewart	Wilson J	Steele	Wallace	Scott	Bryce	Gilroy
	12th	Donaldson	Selway	Houston	Steele	Fraser	Stewart	Duncan	Bryce	Wallace	Scott	Wilson J	Gilroy (7)
	16th	Donaldson	Wilson B	Houston	Selway	Stewart	Steele	Gilroy	Kinninmonth	Wallace	Scott	Wilson J	Duncan (7)
	19th	Donaldson	Wilson B	Houston	Selway	Stewart	Phillip	Duncan	Bryce	Wallace	Scott	Wilson J	Kinninmonth (6)
	23rd	Donaldson	Wilson B	Houston	Selway	Stewart	Steele	Gilroy	Kinninmonth	Wallace	Scott	Wilson J	Duncan (7)
	26th	Donaldson	Wilson B	Houston	Selway*	Easton	Stewart	Duncan	Kinninmonth	Wallace	Scott	Steele	Johnston (6)
	29th	Donaldson	Wilson B	Houston	Selway	Stewart	Steele	Duncan	Bryce	Wallace	Scott	Wilson J	Johnston (7)
Oct	3rd	Donaldson	Wilson B	Houston	Selway	Easton	Steele	Duncan	Bryce	Wallace	Scott	Wilson J	Phillip (5)
	10th	Donaldson	Wilson B	Souter	Phillip	Stewart	Steele	Duncan	Bryce	Wallace	Scott	Johnston	Houston (10)
	17th	Donaldson	Wilson B	Souter	Steele	Phillip	Houston	Duncan	Kinninmonth	Wallace	Scott	Johnston	Wilson J
	24th	Donaldson	Wilson B	Houston	Phillip	Fraser	Steele	Wilson J	Bryce	Wallace	Scott	Johnston	Duncan (7)
	31st	Donaldson	Wilson B	Houston	Phillip	Easton	Steele	Wilson J	Kinninmonth	Wallace	Scott	Johnston	Duncan
Nov	7th	Donaldson	Wilson B	Souter	Steele	Phillip	Houston	Wilson J	Kinninmonth	Wallace	Scott	Johnston	Gilroy
	14th	Donaldson	Wilson B	Souter	Steele	Phillip	Houston	Wilson J	Kinninmonth	Wallace	Scott	Johnston	Gilroy
	21st	Donaldson	Wilson B	Souter	Steele	Phillip	Houston	Wilson J	Kinninmonth	Wallace	Scott	Johnston	Gilroy
	28th	Hewitt	Wilson B	Souter	Steele	Phillip	Houston	Wilson J	Kinninmonth	Wallace	Scott	Johnston	Selway (8)
Dec	5th	Hewitt	Wilson B	Houston	Selway	Phillip	Steele	Gilroy	Kinninmonth	Wallace	Scott	Johnston	Duncan (7)
	12th	Hewitt	Wilson B	Houston	Kinninmonth	Phillip	Selway	Wilson J	Gilroy	Wallace	Scott	Johnston	Falconer
	19th	Hewitt	Wilson B	Houston	Selway	Phillip	Steele	Wilson J	Kinninmonth	Wallace	Scott	Johnston	Gilroy
	26th	Hewitt	Wilson B	Houston	Selway	Phillip	Steele	Gilroy	Kinninmonth	Wallace	Scott	Johnston	Bryce (6)
Jan	1st	Donaldson	Wilson B	Souter	Selway	Phillip	Houston	Gilroy	Kinninmonth	Wallace	Scott	Johnston	Falconer (11)
	9th	Donaldson	Wilson B	Souter	Steele	Phillip	Houston	Duncan	Gilroy	Wallace	Scott	Kinninmonth	Johnston
	16th	Donaldson	Wilson B	Souter	Steele	Phillip	Houston	Duncan	Gilroy	Wallace	Scott	Kinninmonth	Johnston (2)
	23rd	Donaldson	Wilson B	Souter	Houston	Phillip	Steele	Wilson J	Kinninmonth	Wallace	Scott	Johnston	Duncan (3)
	30th	Donaldson	Wilson B	Houston	Selway	Phillip	Steele	Duncan	Gilroy	Wallace	Scott	Bryce	Johnston (6)
Feb	6th	Donaldson	Wilson B	Johnston	Phillip	Stewart	Steele	Wilson J	Gilroy	Wallace	Scott	Bryce	Duncan
	13th	Donaldson	Wilson B	Johnston	Houston	Phillip	Steele	Wilson J	Gilroy	Wallace	Scott	Bryce	Selway (8)
	20th	Donaldson	Wilson B	Houston	Selway	Phillip	Steele	Wilson J	Kinninmonth	Wallace	Scott	Johnston	Bryce (7)
	27th	Donaldson	Wilson B	Johnston	Selway	Phillip	Houston	Gilroy	Kinninmonth	Wallace	Scott	Steele	Falconer (7)
Mar	6th	Donaldson	Wilson B	Johnston	Selway	Stewart	Houston	Kinninmonth	Phillip	Wallace	Scott	Steele	Bryce (5)
	9th	Donaldson	Wilson B	Houston	Selway	Stewart	Steele	Falconer	Phillip	Wallace	Scott	Johnston	Kinninmonth (4)
	13th	Donaldson	Wilson B	Johnston	Houston	Phillip	Steele	Gilroy	Bryce	Wallace	Duncan	Wilson J	Stewart
	20th	Donaldson	Wilson B	Johnston	Phillip	Steele	Houston	Kinninmonth	Wallace	Duncan	Scott	Bryce	Souter (9)
	27th	Donaldson	Wilson B	Johnston	Phillip	Steele	Houston	Kinninmonth	Wallace	Duncan	Scott	Bryce	Wilson J (9)
Apr	3rd	Donaldson	Wilson B	Johnston	Phillip	Steele	Houston	Kinninmonth	Wallace	Gilroy	Scott	Bryce	Wilson J
	5th	Donaldson	Wilson B	Johnston	Phillip	Steele	Houston	Kinninmonth	Bryce	Wallace	Scott	Wilson J	Gilroy
	10th	Donaldson	Wilson B	Houston	Stewart	Phillip	Steele	Kinninmonth	Gilroy	Wallace	Scott	Wilson J	Bryce
	17th	Donaldson	Wilson B	Johnston	Phillip	Easton	Houston	Kinninmonth	Gilroy	Wallace	Scott	Lambie	Wilson J (11)
	24th	Donaldson	Wilson B	Johnston	Phillip	Easton	Houston	Kinninmonth	Gilroy	Wallace	Scott	Wilson J	Bryce

Head start - Dundee striker Gordon Wallace is on hand to nod the ball past Parkes after the Wolves keeper had parried a 25-yard free kick from Jocky Scott in the first-leg of the Texaco Cup first round tie at Dens.

DC Thomson

Season 1971-72

Date			Opponents		Score	Crowd	Scorers
Aug	14th	LC	Aberdeen	a	1-1	20,000	Duncan
	18th	LC	Falkirk	h	2-2	8,500	Johnston; Wallace
	21st	LC	Clyde	a	1-0	2,000	B. Wilson
	25th	LC	Falkirk	a	0-1	6,000	-
	28th	LC	Aberdeen	h	3-1	13,000	Wallace 2; Houston
Sep	1st	LC	Clyde	h	3-0	6,030	J. Scott 2; Bryce
	4th	L	Aberdeen	a	0-3	15,000	-
	11th	L	Dundee United	h	6-4	16,500	Bryce 2; Wallace 2; J. Scott 2
	15th	UE1	AB Copenhagen	h	4-2	9,000	Bryce 2; Wallace; Lambie
	18th	L	East Fife	a	5-2	5,331	Wallace 4; Johnston
	25th	L	Hearts	h	0-0	10,500	-
	29th	UE1	AB Copenhagen	a	1-0 (5-2)	2,000	Duncan
Oct	2nd	L	Ayr United	a	0-0	6,000	-
	9th	L	Falkirk	h	4-0	7,500	Duncan; Wallace 2; Lambie
	16th	L	Celtic	a	1-3	32,000	Duncan
	20th	UE2	Cologne	a	1-2	15,000	Kinninmonth
	25th	L	Partick Thistle	h	0-0	10,000	-
	30th	L	Motherwell	a	3-1	3,812	Wallace; Duncan 2
Nov	3rd	UE2	Cologne	h	4-2 (5-4)	15,500	Duncan 3; Wallace
	6th	L	Morton	h	0-1	6,000	-
	13th	L	Rangers	a	3-2	35,000	Kinninmonth; Wallace; Johnston
	20th	L	Clyde	h	0-0	4,700	-
	24th	UE3	AC Milan	a	0-3	25,000	-
	27th	L	Dunfermline	a	2-1	5,000	Wallace; Duncan
Dec	4th	L	Airdrie	h	4-1	5,000	J. Scott 3; Duncan
	8th	UE3	AC Milan	h	2-0 (2-3)	15,500	Wallace; Duncan
	11th	L	Hibernian	a	0-1	10,000	-
	18th	L	Kilmarnock	h	2-0	4,800	J. Scott; Wallace
	25th	L	St Johnstone	a	0-0	6,800	-
Jan	1st	L	Aberdeen	h	1-1	19,000	Duncan
	3rd	L	Dundee United	a	1-1	19,000	Steele
	8th	L	East Fife	h	0-0	6,500	-
	15th	L	Hearts	a	5-2	9,000	Duncan 2; Wallace 2; I. Scott
	22nd	L	Ayr United	h	5-1	5,500	Duncan; J. Scott
	29th	L	Falkirk	a	1-1	5,000	Duncan
Feb	9th	SC3	QOS	h	3-0	8,500	B. Wilson; Johnston; J. Scott
	19th	L	Partick Thistle	a	0-0	7,000	-
	26th	SC4	Celtic	a	0-4	47,000	-
Mar	4th	L	Motherwell	h	2-0	5,000	Wallace; Muir o.g.
	11th	L	Morton	a	2-2	3,200	J. Scott; Wallace
	18th	FCF*	Dundee United	a	2-0	8,000	Stewart; J. Scott
	25th	L	Clyde	a	1-1	1,500	Johnston
Apr	1st	L	Dunfermline	h	1-0	5,000	J. Scott
	5th	FCS	Brechin City	h	9-1	1,000	J. Scott 4; Duncan 2; I. Scott; J. Wilson; Houston
	8th	L	Airdrie	a	2-4	4,200	I. Scott; J. Scott
	10th	L	Rangers	h	2-0	12,000	I. Scott; Stewart
	17th	L	Hibernian	h	1-2	9,500	J. Wilson
	22nd	L	Kilmarnock	a	3-0	4,000	Johnston; Duncan; J. Scott
	29th	L	St Johnstone	h	1-3	5,500	Duncan
May	1st	L	Celtic	h	1-1	10,500	I. Scott

* 1970-71 Competition

Dundee skipper Doug Houston with Ally Donaldson just behind.

The Record		
League	-	Fifth Place, Division One
League Cup	-	Qualifying stages only
Scottish Cup	-	Second round
UEFA Cup	-	Third round
Forfarshire Cup	-	Runners up (Final 23-10-72)
Top Scorer	-	Gordon Wallace (21 goals)
Av. Home gate	-	8,400
Players used	-	18
Sent off	-	One

Appearances

	League	L/Cup	S/Cup	UEFA	Total	
Jocky Scott	34 (12)	6 (2)	2 (1)	6	48	(15)
Dave Johnston	33 (4)	6 (1)	2 (1)	5	46+1s	(6)
Bobby Wilson	32	6 (1)	2 (1)	6 (1)	46	(3)
Iain Phillip	32	6	2	5	45	
John Duncan	32 (13)	6 (1)	2	4 (5)	44+1s	(19)
Gordon Wallace	30 (16)	6 (3)	2	6 (2)	44+2s	(21)
Mike Hewitt	31	6	2	3	42	
Doug Houston	28	6 (1)	2	6	42	(1)
Jim Steele	19 (1)	6	0	6	31	(1)
Duncan Lambie	20 (1)	2	2	3 (1)	27+4s	(2)
Jimmy Wilson	15 (1)	4	0	4	23+5s	(1)
Bobby Ford	19	0	0	2	21+1s	
George Stewart	16 (1)	0	0	3	19	(1)
Alex. Kinninmonth	9 (1)	4	0	5 (1)	18+7s	(2)
Ian Scott	14 (6)	2	2	0	18+5s	(6)
Ally Donaldson	3	0	0	3	6	
Alex. Bryce	4 (2)	0 (1)	0	1 (2)	5+3s	(5)
Ronnie Selway	3	0	0	0	3+3s	

Scottish League Division One

	P	Home W	Home D	Home L	Away W	Away D	Away L	Goals F A	PTS
Celtic	34	15	1	1	13	3	1	96-28	60
Aberdeen	34	13	3	1	8	5	4	80-26	50
Rangers	34	11	0	6	10	2	5	71-38	44
Hibernian	34	11	2	4	8	4	5	62-34	44
Dundee	**34**	**8**	**6**	**3**	**6**	**7**	**4**	**59-38**	**41**
Hearts	34	10	5	2	3	8	6	53-49	39
Partick Thistle	34	9	6	2	3	5	4	53-54	34
St Johnstone	34	7	5	5	5	3	9	52-58	32
Dundee United	34	7	5	5	5	2	10	55-70	31
Motherwell	34	9	3	5	2	4	11	49-69	28
Kilmarnock	34	7	3	7	4	3	10	49-64	28
Ayr United	34	5	6	6	4	4	8	40-58	28
Morton	34	5	7	5	5	0	12	46-52	27
Falkirk	34	7	4	6	3	3	11	44-60	27
Airdrie	34	4	6	7	3	6	8	44-76	26
East Fife	34	2	7	8	3	8	6	34-61	25
Clyde	34	5	4	8	2	6	9	33-66	24
Dunfermline	34	5	5	7	2	4	11	31-50	23

League Cup Section

	P	W	D	L	F A	PTS
Falkirk	6	4	1	1	12-6	9
Dundee	**6**	**3**	**2**	**1**	**10-5**	**8**
Aberdeen	6	3	1	2	11-7	7
Clyde	6	0	0	6	2-17	0

Dundee F.C. Line-Ups 1971-72

		1	2	3	4	5	6	7	8	9	10	11	12
Aug	14th	Hewitt	Wilson B	Johnston	Steele	Phillip	Houston	Duncan	Scott I	Wallace	Scott J	Lambie	Bryce (11)
	18th	Hewitt	Wilson B	Johnston	Steele	Phillip	Houston	Duncan	Scott I	Wallace	Scott J	Lambie	Kinninmonth (10)
	21st	Hewitt	Wilson B	Johnston	Steele	Phillip	Houston	Duncan	Kinninmonth	Wallace	Scott J	Wilson J	Bryce
	25th	Hewitt	Wilson B	Johnston	Steele	Phillip	Houston	Duncan	Kinninmonth	Wallace	Scott J	Wilson J	Bryce
	28th	Hewitt	Wilson B	Johnston	Steele	Phillip	Houston	Duncan	Kinninmonth	Wallace	Scott J	Wilson J	Bryce
Sep	1st	Hewitt	Wilson B	Johnston	Steele	Phillip	Houston	Duncan	Kinninmonth	Wallace	Scott J	Wilson J	Bryce (8)
	4th	Hewitt	Wilson B	Johnston	Steele	Phillip	Houston	Duncan	Kinninmonth	Wallace	Scott J	Lambie	Bryce (7)
	11th	Hewitt	Wilson B	Johnston	Steele	Phillip	Houston	Kinninmonth	Bryce	Wallace	Scott J	Wilson J	Duncan
	15th	Hewitt	Wilson B	Johnston	Steele	Phillip	Houston	Kinninmonth	Bryce	Wallace	Scott J	Wilson J	Lambie (7)
	18th	Hewitt	Wilson B	Johnston	Steele	Phillip	Houston	Duncan	Bryce	Wallace	Scott J	Wilson J	Kinninmonth (4)
	25th	Hewitt	Wilson B	Johnston	Steele	Phillip	Houston	Duncan	Bryce	Wallace	Scott J	Wilson J	Lambie
	29th	Hewitt	Wilson B	Johnston	Steele	Phillip	Houston	Duncan	Kinninmonth	Wallace	Scott J	Wilson J	Selway (4)
Oct	2nd	Hewitt	Wilson B	Johnston	Stewart	Phillip	Houston	Wilson J	Scott I	Duncan	Scott J	Lambie	Bryce
	9th	Hewitt	Wilson B	Johnston	Steele	Phillip	Houston	Duncan	Bryce	Wallace	Scott J	Lambie	Scott I
	16th	Hewitt	Wilson B	Johnston	Steele	Phillip	Houston	Duncan	Selway	Wallace	Scott J	Lambie	Kinninmonth (10)
	20th	Donaldson	Wilson B	Johnston	Steele	Stewart	Houston	Duncan	Kinninmonth	Wallace	Scott J	Lambie	Selway (5)
	25th	Hewitt	Wilson B	Johnston	Steele	Selway	Houston	Duncan	Kinninmonth	Wallace	Scott J	Lambie	Scott I
	30th	Hewitt	Wilson B	Johnston	Steele	Phillip	Houston	Duncan	Kinninmonth	Wallace	Scott J	Lambie	Selway (4)
Nov	3rd	Donaldson	Wilson B	Johnston	Steele	Phillip	Houston	Duncan	Kinninmonth	Wallace	Scott J	Lambie	Scott I (8) Wilson J (11)
	6th	Donaldson	Wilson B	Selway	Steele	Phillip	Houston	Duncan	Wilson J	Wallace	Scott J	Lambie	Scott I (11)
	13th	Donaldson	Wilson B	Johnston	Steele	Phillip	Ford	Duncan	Kinninmonth	Wallace	Scott J	Wilson J	Scott I
	20th	Donaldson	Wilson B	Johnston	Steele	Phillip	Houston	Duncan	Kinninmonth	Wallace	Scott J	Lambie	Ford (11)
	24th	Donaldson	Wilson B	Johnston	Steele	Phillip	Houston	Wilson J	Kinninmonth	Wallace	Scott J	Stewart	Scott I (8), Duncan (10)
	27th	Hewitt	Wilson B	Johnston	Steele	Phillip	Houston	Duncan	Ford	Wallace	Scott J	Wilson J	Robinson
Dec	4th	Hewitt	Wilson B	Johnston	Steele	Phillip	Houston	Duncan	Ford	Wallace	Scott J	Wilson J	Kinninmonth (8)
	8th	Hewitt	Wilson B	Houston	Steele	Phillip	Stewart	Duncan	Lambie	Wallace	Scott J	Wilson J	Johnston (11),Scott I (10)
	11th	Hewitt	Wilson B	Houston	Steele	Phillip	Stewart	Duncan	Lambie	Wallace	Scott J	Johnston	Wilson J (6)
	18th	Hewitt	Wilson B	Johnston	Stewart	Phillip	Houston	Duncan	Kinninmonth	Wallace	Scott J	Lambie	Wilson J (11)
	25th	Hewitt	Wilson B	Johnston	Steele	Phillip	Ford	Duncan	Kinninmonth	Wallace	Scott J	Wilson J	Lambie (4)
Jan	1st	Hewitt	Wilson B	Johnston	Stewart	Phillip	Ford	Duncan	Lambie	Wallace	Scott J	Wilson J	Kinninmonth (6)
	3rd	Hewitt	Wilson B	Johnston	Steele	Phillip	Ford	Duncan	Scott I	Wallace	Scott J	Lambie	Kinninmonth
	8th	Hewitt	Wilson B	Johnston	Steele	Phillip	Ford	Duncan	Scott I	Wallace	Scott J	Kinninmonth	Lambie (8)
	15th	Hewitt	Wilson B	Johnston	Steele	Phillip	Ford	Duncan	Scott I	Wallace	Scott J	Lambie	Kinninmonth (2)
	22nd	Hewitt	Johnston	Houston	Steele	Phillip	Ford	Duncan	Scott I	Wallace	Scott J	Lambie	Kinninmonth
	29th	Hewitt	Johnston	Houston	Ford	Phillip	Stewart	Duncan	Scott I	Wallace	Scott J	Lambie	Kinninmonth
Feb	9th	Hewitt	Wilson B	Johnston	Ford	Phillip	Houston	Duncan	Scott I	Wallace	Scott J	Lambie	Kinninmonth (2)
	19th	Hewitt	Wilson B	Johnston	Houston	Stewart	Ford	Duncan	Scott I	Wallace	Scott J	Lambie	Kinninmonth
	26th	Hewitt	Wilson B	Johnston	Houston	Phillip	Ford	Duncan	Scott I	Wallace	Scott J	Lambie	Kinninmonth
Mar	4th	Hewitt	Wilson B	Johnston	Stewart	Phillip	Houston	Duncan	Scott I	Wallace	Scott J	Lambie	Wilson J (7)
	11th	Hewitt	Wilson B	Johnston	Stewart	Phillip	Houston	Wilson J	Ford	Wallace	Scott J	Lambie	Selway
	25th	Hewitt	Wilson B	Johnston	Stewart	Phillip	Houston	Duncan	Ford	Wallace	Scott J	Wilson J	Scott I (11)
Apr	1st	Hewitt	Wilson B	Johnston	Stewart	Phillip	Houston	Duncan	Ford	Wallace	Scott J	Lambie	Scott I
	8th	Hewitt	Wilson B	Johnston	Stewart*	Phillip	Houston	Duncan	Ford	Wallace	Scott J	Scott I	Wilson J
	10th	Hewitt	Wilson B	Johnston	Stewart	Phillip	Houston	Duncan	Ford	Scott I	Scott J	Lambie	Wilson J (11)
	17th	Hewitt	Wilson B	Johnston	Stewart	Phillip	Houston	Duncan	Ford	Scott I	Scott J	Wilson J	Wallace (4)
	22nd	Hewitt	Wilson B	Johnston	Phillip	Stewart	Houston	Ford	Duncan	Scott I	Scott J	Wilson J	Wallace (7)
	29th	Hewitt	Wilson B	Johnston	Phillip	Stewart	Houston	Wallace	Duncan	Scott I	Scott J	Wilson J	Ford
May	1st	Hewitt	Wilson B	Johnston	Stewart	Phillip	Houston	Scott I	Duncan	Wallace	Scott J	Ford	Lambie (9)

John Duncan (out of picture) has put Dundee ahead against Motherwell at Fir Park and Gordon Wallace follows up to make sure. Duncan Lambie and Jocky Scott raise their arms in joy while Iain Phillip and Alex. Kinninmonth rush in to add their congratulations. DC Thomson

Season 1972-73

Date			Opponents		Score		Crowd	Scorers
Aug	12th	LC	East Stirling	a	8-2		1,500	Duncan 5; Stein o.g; Robinson; J. Wilson;
	16th	LC	Clyde	h	2-1		4,900	Duncan; I. Scott
	19th	LC	Motherwell	a	3-1		5,000	J. Wilson; Duncan 2
	23rd	LC	Clyde	a	1-0		2,000	Phillip
	26th	LC	East Stirling	h	3-0		4,700	Duncan; J.Scott; Robinson
	30th	LC	Motherwell	h	2-1		4,000	Wallace; Duncan
Sep	2nd	L	Motherwell	a	2-2		5,000	J. Wilson; Duncan
	9th	L	Aberdeen	h	0-0		15,000	-
	13th	TC	Norwich City	h	2-1		8,000	I. Scott; Lambie
	16th	L	Dundee United	a	1-2		13,000	Ford
	20th	LC2	Dumbarton	a	0-3		4,000	-
	23rd	L	Celtic	h	2-0		18,300	I. Scott; Gray
	27th	TC	Norwich City	a	0-2	(2-3)	18,339	-
	30th	L	Airdrie	a	1-0		2,500	Robinson
Oct	4th	LC2	Dumbarton	h	4-0	(4-3)	7,200	I. Scott; Wallace 2; Duncan
	7th	L	Hibernian	h	1-0		11,700	Ford
	11th	LCQ	Celtic	h	1-0		22,000	Wallace
	14th	L	Dumbarton	a	2-2		4,000	Wallace; Cushley o.g.
	21st	L	Kilmarnock	h	1-0		5,600	Duncan
	23rd	FCF*	Dundee United	a	0-4		6,500	-
	28th	L	Morton	a	2-5		2,500	Rowan o.g.; Duncan
Nov	1st	LCQ	Celtic	a**	2-3	(3-3)	39,000	Wallace; J. Scott
	4th	L	Rangers	h	1-1		19,600	Wallace
	11th	L	Arbroath	a	1-2		5,149	Duncan
	18th	L	St Johnstone	h	3-0		6,000	Duncan; Robinson; Houston
	20th	LCQR	Celtic	Ham	1-4		36,483	J. Scott
	25th	L	Ayr United	a	1-2		5,000	Anderson
Dec	2nd	L	East Fife	h	4-0		5,300	Duncan 2; Wallace; J. Scott
	9th	L	Falkirk	a	2-2		4,000	Duncan; I Scott
	16th	L	Partick Thistle	h	4-1		3,900	Duncan 3; Johnston
	23rd	L	Hearts	a	2-1		9,000	Stewart; Duncan
	30th	L	Motherwell	h	2-0		5,600	Duncan; J. Scott
Jan	1st	L	Aberdeen	a	1-3		14,000	J. Scott
	6th	L	Dundee United	h	3-0		13,600	Duncan 2; Houston
	13th	L	Celtic	a	1-2		27,000	Houston
	27th	L	Hibernian	a	1-1		15,896	Duncan
Feb	3rd	SC3	Dunfermline	a	3-0		10,618	J. Wilson; Duncan; J. Scott
	10th	L	Dumbarton	h	2-1		4,500	J. Scott; Wallace
	20th	L	Airdrie	h	1-1		3,650	Stewart
	24th	SC4	Stranraer	a	9-2		3,350	Duncan 4; Wallace 3; Houston; I. Scott
	27th	L	Kilmarnock	a	2-1		2,000	I. Scott; J Scott
Mar	3rd	L	Morton	h	6-0		5,000	J .Wilson; J. Scott; Duncan 3
	10th	L	Rangers	a	1-3		30,000	Duncan
	17th	SCQ	Montrose	a	4-1		8,893	Wallace; J. Scott 2; Duncan
	21st	L	Arbroath	h	6-0		5,950	J. Scott 3; Duncan 2; Wallace
	24th	L	St Johnstone	a	1-4		4,500	Lambie o.g.
	31st	L	Ayr United	h	2-1		5,050	J. Scott; Houston
Apr	7th	SCS	Celtic	Ham	0-0		53,428	-
	11th	SCSR	Celtic	Ham	0-3***		47,384	-
	14th	L	Falkirk	h	5-3		4,000	Wallace 2; Duncan; J. Scott 2
	18th	L	East Fife	h	1-0		4,304	Semple
	21st	L	Partick Thistle	a	1-1		5,000	Wallace
	23rd	FC1	Dundee United	a	2-4		5,000	Gray; Wallace
	28th	L	Hearts	h	2-2		6,400	Wallace; Houston

* 1971-72 competition; ** a.e.t, 2-3 after 90 minutes; *** a.e.t, 0-0 after 90 mts

Jimmy Wilson - experience helped Dundee's talented youngsters

The Record		
League	-	**Fifth Place, Division One**
League Cup	-	**Quarter-final**
Scottish Cup	-	**Semi-final**
Texaco Cup	-	**First round**
Forfarshire Cup	-	**First round**
Top Scorer	-	**John Duncan (40 goals)**
Av. Home Gate	-	**8,200**
Players used	-	**22**
Sent off (booked)	-	**One (15)**

Cup Cash v. Dunferm. £2,577; Stranraer £748; Montrose £2,637

Eyes down for the Dundee derby - John Duncan is on the spot to send a Doug Houston (on left) cross into the net for Dundee's second goal in the 3-0 victory at Dens. The Dundee United players are George Fleming, Hamish McAlpine, Frank Kopel and Andy Rolland.

DC Thomson

They Wore The Dark Blue

Dundee F.C. Line-Ups 1972-73

	1	2	3	4	5	6	7	8	9	10	11	12
Aug 12th	Allan	Wilson B	Johnston	Robinson	Phillip	Houston	Ford	Duncan	Wallace	Scott J	Scott I	Wilson J (9)
16th	Allan	Wilson B	Houston	Ford	Phillip	Robinson	Wilson J	Duncan	Wallace	Scott J	Scott I	Anderson (11)
19th	Allan	Wilson B	Houston	Robinson	Phillip	Ford	Wilson J	Duncan	Wallace	Scott J	Scott I	Anderson
23rd	Allan	Wilson B	Houston	Robinson	Phillip	Ford	Wilson J	Duncan	Anderson	Scott J	Scott I	Gray (11)
26th	Allan	Ford	Houston	Wilson B	Phillip	Stewart	Duncan	Robinson	Wallace	Scott J	Wilson J	Anderson (2)
30th	Hewitt	Ford	Houston	Robinson	Phillip	Stewart	Wilson J	Duncan	Wallace	Scott J	Scott I	Anderson (10)
Sep 2nd	Hewitt	Ford	Houston	Wilson B	Phillip	Stewart	Robinson	Duncan	Wallace	Scott J	Wilson J	Anderson (2)
9th	Hewitt	Wilson B	Houston	Robinson	Phillip	Stewart	Wilson J	Duncan	Wallace	Scott J	Scott I	Ford (11)
13th	Hewitt	Wilson B	Houston	Robinson	Phillip	Stewart	Wilson J	Scott I	Wallace	Scott J	Lambie	Smith I, Knowles
16th	Hewitt	Wilson B	Houston	Robinson	Phillip	Stewart	Wilson J	Ford	Gray	Scott J	Lambie	Anderson
20th	Hewitt	Wilson B	Houston	Robinson	Phillip	Stewart	Wilson J	Ford	Gray	Scott J	Lambie	Anderson (11)
23rd	Hewitt	Wilson B	Houston	Robinson	Phillip	Stewart	Wilson J	Wallace	Gray	Scott J	Scott I	Pringle (8)
27th	Hewitt	Wilson B	Houston	McLeod	Robinson	Stewart	Wilson J	Wallace	Gray	Scott J	Scott I	Mathieson Allan
30th	Hewitt	Wilson B	Mathieson	Robinson	Stewart	Ford	Wilson J	Duncan	Gray	Scott J	Scott I	Smith I
Oct 4th	Hewitt	Wilson B	Johnston	Robinson	Stewart	Houston	Wilson J	Duncan	Wallace	Scott J	Scott I	Smith I
7th	Allan	Wilson B	Houston	Robinson	Stewart	Ford	Wilson J	Duncan	Wallace	Scott J	Lambie	Smith I
11th	Allan	Wilson B	Houston	Robinson	Stewart	Ford	Scott I	Duncan	Wallace	Scott J	Lambie	Gray
14th	Allan	Wilson B	Houston	Robinson	Stewart	Ford	Scott I	Duncan	Wallace	Scott J	Lambie	Smith I
21st	Allan	Wilson B	Houston	Robinson	Stewart	Ford	Smith	Duncan	Wallace	Scott J	Scott I	Mathieson
28th	Allan	Wilson B	Houston	Robinson	Stewart	Ford	Wilson J	Duncan	Wallace	Scott J	Scott I	Gray (10)
Nov 1st	Allan	Wilson B	Houston	Robinson	Stewart	Ford	Wilson J	Duncan	Wallace	Scott J	Scott I	Gray
4th	Allan	Wilson B	Houston	Robinson	Stewart	Ford	Wilson J	Duncan	Wallace	Scott J	Scott I	Gray
11th	Allan	Wilson B	Houston	Robinson	Stewart	Ford	Wilson J	Duncan	Wallace	Scott J	Scott I	Gray (10)
18th	Allan	Wilson B	Houston	Robinson	Stewart	Pringle	Wilson J	Duncan	Wallace	Scott J	Lambie	Gray
20th	Allan	Wilson B	Houston	Robinson	Stewart	Pringle	Wilson J	Duncan	Wallace	Scott J	Scott I	Gray (11)
25th	Allan	Wilson B	Houston	Robinson	Stewart	Ford	Wilson J	Duncan	Wallace	Anderson	Lambie	Scott J (7)
Dec 2nd	Allan	Wilson B	Houston	Robinson	Stewart	Pringle	Wallace	Scott I	Duncan	Scott J	Anderson	Ford
9th	Allan	Wilson B	Houston	Robinson	Stewart	Pringle	Wallace	Scott I	Duncan	Scott J	Anderson	Ford (11)
16th	Allan	Wilson B	Johnston	Houston	Stewart	Pringle	Ford	Wallace	Duncan	Scott J	Scott I	Semple (7)
23rd	Allan	Ford	Johnston	Houston	Stewart	Pringle	Robinson	Wallace	Duncan	Scott J	Scott I	Lambie (7)
30th	Allan	Ford	Johnston	Houston	Stewart	Pringle	Scott I	Wallace	Duncan	Scott J	Lambie	Wilson B (8)
Jan 1st	Allan	Wilson B	Johnston	Houston	Stewart	Pringle*	Scott I	Wallace	Duncan	Scott J	Lambie	Ford
6th	Allan	Wilson B	Johnston	Houston	Stewart	Pringle	Robinson	Scott I	Duncan	Wallace	Lambie	Anderson
13th	Allan	Ford	Johnston	Houston	Robinson	Pringle	Wilson R	Scott I	Duncan	Wallace	Lambie	Semple
27th	Allan	Wilson B	Johnston	Houston	Stewart	Robinson	Wilson J	Wallace	Duncan	Scott J	Lambie	Semple (11)
Feb 3rd	Allan	Wilson B	Johnston	Houston	Stewart	Robinson	Wilson J	Wallace	Duncan	Scott J	Scott I	Semple (11)
10th	Allan	Wilson B	Johnston	Robinson	Stewart	Houston	Wilson J	Wallace	Duncan	Scott J	Scott I	Lambie (11)
20th	Allan	Wilson B	Johnston	Houston	Stewart	Robinson	Wilson J	Wallace	Duncan	Scott J	Anderson	Scott I
24th	Allan	Wilson B	Johnston	Robinson	Stewart	Ford	Wilson J	Wallace	Duncan	Scott J	Anderson	Scott I (8)
27th	Allan	Wilson B	Johnston	Robinson	Stewart	Houston	Wilson J	Wallace	Duncan	Scott J	Scott I	Lambie
Mar 3rd	Allan	Wilson B	Johnston	Robinson	Stewart	Houston	Wilson J	Scott I	Duncan	Scott J	Lambie	Wallace (11)
10th	Allan	Wilson B	Houston	Robinson	Stewart	Anderson	Wilson J	Wallace	Duncan	Scott J	Scott I	Ford (6)
17th	Allan	Wilson B	Johnston	Robinson	Stewart	Houston	Wilson J	Wallace	Duncan	Scott J	Scott I	Ford (11)
21st	Allan	Wilson B	Johnston	Robinson	Stewart	Houston	Wilson J	Wallace	Duncan	Scott J	Scott I	Ford (11)
24th	Allan	Wilson B	Johnston	Robinson	Stewart	Houston	Ford	Wallace	Duncan	Scott J	Wilson J	Scott I (5)
31st	Allan	Wilson B	Johnston	Robinson	Stewart	Houston	Wilson J	Wallace	Duncan	Scott J	Scott I	Ford
Apr 7th	Allan	Wilson B	Johnston	Robinson	Stewart	Houston	Wilson J	Wallace	Duncan	Scott J	Scott I	Ford (7)
11th	Allan	Wilson B	Johnston	Robinson	Stewart	Houston	Ford	Wallace	Duncan	Scott J	Scott I	Semple (8)
14th	Allan	Wilson B	Johnston	Robinson	Stewart	Houston	Ford	Wallace	Duncan	Scott J	Scott I	Semple (3)
18th	Allan	Wilson B	Johnston	Robinson	Stewart	Houston	Ford	Wallace	Duncan	Scott J	Semple	Wilson J (9)
21st	Allan	Wilson B	Johnston	Robinson	Stewart	Houston	Ford	Wallace	Scott I	Scott J	Semple	Duncan (11)
28th	Allan	Wilson B	Johnston	Robinson	Stewart	Houston	Ford	Wallace	Scott I	Scott J	Lambie	Semple

Dundee F.C. Season 1972-73. BACK (left to right) Davie White (manager), Alex. Pringle, Bobby Wilson, Dave Johnston, Mike Hewitt, Thomson Allan, Bobby Robinson, John Duncan, George Stewart. FRONT- Eric Ferguson (physio), Ian Scott, Gordon Wallace, Doug Houston, John Gray, Duncan Lambie, Jocky Scott, Jimmy Wilson and Harold Davis (coach).

DC Thomson

Heads you win - always dangerous at dead-ball situations, George Stewart demonstrates his heading ability by outjumping Dundee United's Donald Mackay and Stewart Markland to score in a 2-0 Forfarshire Cup Final win in 1972.

DC Thomson

Appearances

	League		L/Cup		S/Cup		T/Cup	Total	
Doug Houston	33	(5)	11		4	(1)	2	50	(6)
Bobby Robinson	31	(2)	11	(2)	5		2	49	(4)
Jocky Scott	31	(12)	11	(3)	5	(3)	2	49+1s	(18)
Bobby Wilson	32		10		5		2	49+1s	
George Stewart	33	(2)	7		5		2	47	(2)
Gordon Wallace	31	(9)	9	(5)	5	(4)	2	47+1s	(18)
John Duncan	30	(23)	10	(11)	5	(6)	0	45+1s	(40)
Thomson Allan	29		9		5		0	43	
Ian Scott	25	(3)	9	(2)	4	(1)	2	40+2s	(6)
Jimmy Wilson	20	(3)	9	(2)	4	(1)	2	35+2s	(6)
Bobby Ford	19	(2)	9		2		0	30+6s	(2)
Dave Johnston	18	(1)	2		5		0	25	(1)
Duncan Lambie	12		2		0		1	15+2s	
Iain Phillip	4		7		0		1	12	
Alec Pringle	9		1		0		0	10+1s	
Ian Anderson	5	(1)	1		1		0	7+5s	(1)
Mike Hewitt	5		2		0		2	9	
John Gray	3	(1)	1		0		1	5+4s	(1)
Billy Semple	2		0		0		0	2+5s	
Ian Mathieson	1		0		0		0	1	
Ian Smith	1		0		0		0	1	
Duncan McLeod	0		0		0		1	1	

Scottish League Division One

		Home			Away			Goals		
	P	W	D	L	W	D	L	F	A	PTS
Celtic	34	14	3	0	12	2	3	93-28		57
Rangers	34	14	2	1	12	2	3	74-30		56
Hibernian	34	12	2	3	7	5	5	74-33		45
Aberdeen	34	10	6	1	6	5	6	61-34		43
Dundee	**34**	**13**	**4**	**0**	**4**	**5**	**8**	**68-43**		**43**
Ayr United	34	11	4	2	5	4	8	50-51		40
Dundee United	34	11	3	3	6	2	9	56-51		39
Motherwell	34	5	6	6	6	3	8	38-48		31
East Fife	34	8	3	6	3	5	9	46-54		30
Hearts	34	7	4	6	5	2	10	39-50		30
St Johnstone	34	8	3	6	2	6	9	52-67		29
Morton	34	8	4	5	2	4	11	47-53		28
Partick Thistle	34	4	5	8	6	3	8	40-43		28
Falkirk	34	6	4	7	1	8	8	38-56		26
Arbroath	34	8	3	6	1	5	11	39-63		26
Dumbarton	34	3	9	5	3	2	12	43-72		23
Kilmarnock	34	6	3	8	1	5	11	40-71		22
Airdrie	34	2	4	11	2	4	11	34-75		16

League Cup Section

	P	W	D	L	F	A	PTS
Dundee	**6**	**6**	**0**	**0**	**19- 5**		**12**
Motherwell	6	2	2	2	11- 9		6
Clyde	6	2	2	2	9- 7		6
East Stirling	6	0	0	6	4-22		0

Dundee reached the semi-final of the Scottish Cup. TOP - Ian Scott crashes the ball past right-back Duffy for Dundee's eighth in their 9-2 second round triumph at Stranraer. BOTTOM - End of the road for the Dark Blues. Jimmy Johnstone has just made it 3-0 for Celtic in extra-time of the semi-final replay with Celtic at Hampden. Bobby Robinson, Thomson Allan and Dave Johnston are disconsolate. DC Thomson

Season 1973-74

Date			Opponents		Score	Crowd	Scorers
Jul	28th	DC	Raith Rovers	h	1-0 (a.e.t.)	5,500	Selway o.g.
Aug	8th	DCS	Celtic	a	0-4	26,000	-
	11th	LC	St Johnstone	h	1-0	6,400	B. Wilson
	15th	LC	Partick Thistle	a	3-0	6,000	Gray; Anderson; J. Scott
	18th	LC	Hearts	h	2-1	8,000	Wallace; J. Scott
	22nd	LC	Partick Thistle	h	4-0	6,000	J. Scott; Gray; Wallace 2
	25th	LC	Hearts	a	0-0	13,500	-
	29th	LC	St Johnstone	a	1-1	6,000	Wallace
Sep	1st	L	Falkirk	h	4-0	4,500	J. Scott 2; Wallace; Lambie
	8th	L	Aberdeen	a	0-0	10,000	-
	12th	LC2	Dunfermline	a	3-2	6,000	J. Scott; Gray; Lambie
	15th	L	Dundee United	h	0-1	12,086	-
	19th	UE1	Twente Enschede	h	1-3	11,210	Stewart
	22nd	L	Hearts	a	2-2	14,000	Duncan; Lambie
	29th	L	East Fife	h	0-1	3,483	-
Oct	3rd	UE1	Twente Enschede	a	2-4 (3-7)	15,000	Johnston; I. Scott
	6th	L	Partick Thistle	a	0-1	3,500	-
	10th	LC2	Dunfermline	h	2-2 (5-4)	4,868	B. Wilson; Wallace
	13th	L	Celtic	h	0-1	17,500	-
	20th	L	Arbroath	a	4-2	3,120	Wallace; B. Wilson; J. Scott; Robinson
	27th	L	Ayr United	h	2-1	5,611	Duncan; J. Scott (pen)
	31st	LCQ	Clyde	h	1-0	4,609	Duncan
Nov	3rd	L	St Johnstone	a	4-1	3,800	J. Wilson; Wallace 2; Duncan
	10th	L	Dumbarton	h	2-1	4,465	Wallace 2
	17th	L	Hibernian	a	1-2	11,348	Wallace
	21st	LCQ	Clyde	a	2-2 (3-2)	5,000	J. Wilson; Wallace
	24th	L	Dunfermline	h	1-5	3,550	J. Scott
	28th	LCS	Kilmarnock	Ham	1-0	4,682	Gemmell
Dec	15th	LCF	Celtic	Ham	1-0	27,974	Wallace
	22nd	L	Motherwell	h	0-1	6,000	-
	29th	L	Falkirk	a	3-3	2,500	J. Wilson; J. Scott; Lambie
Jan	1st	L	Aberdeen	h	1-1	9,451	J. Wilson
	5th	L	Dundee United	a	2-1	11,800	Duncan 2
	19th	L	East Fife	a	3-0	2,927	J. Scott 3
	27th	SC3	Aberdeen	a	2-0	23,574	Johnston; Robinson
Feb	3rd	L	Partick Thistle	h	4-1	7,526	Robinson; Lambie; Duncan; J. Scott
	10th	L	Celtic	a	2-1	40,000	Lambie; Duncan
	17th	SC4	Rangers	a	3-0	65,000	J. Scott; Duncan 2
	23rd	L	Arbroath	h	5-2	7,676	J. Scott 4 (1 pen); Lambie
Mar	2nd	L	Ayr United	a	2-4	6,500	J. Scott (pen); Gemmell
	9th	SCQ	Hibernian	a	3-3	28,236	J. Scott; J Wilson; Duncan
	18th	SCQR	Hibernian	h	3-0	30,888	J. Scott; Duncan; B Wilson
	30th	L	Dunfermline	a	5-1	4,000	J. Scott (pen); Ford; J. Wilson; Pringle; Wallace
Apr	3rd	SCS	Celtic	Ham	0-1	58,250	-
	6th	L	Morton	h	2-1	4,0001	J. Scott; Wallace
	10th	L	Hibernian	h	1-3	7,300	J. Scott
	13th	L	Rangers	a	2-1	23,000	J. Scott 2
	17th	L	Clyde	a	2-0	1,000	Duncan; Wallace
	20th	L	Clyde	h	6-1	4,027	Robinson; Wallace 2; Duncan 2; J. Scott (pen)
	22nd	L	St Johnstone	h	2-2	5,184	Wallace; Duncan
	27th	L	Motherwell	a	2-2	3,902	Wallace; J. Scott
	29th	L	Rangers	h	2-3	10,578	Duncan 2
May	3rd	L	Morton	a	1-0	3,100	Wallace
	6th	L	Hearts	h	0-0	5,056	-
	10th	L	Dumbarton	a	0-2	1,000	-

Thomson Allan - the keeper was in Scotland's 1974 World Cup squad.

The Record		
League	-	Fifth Place, Division One
League Cup	-	Winners
Scottish Cup	-	Semi-final
UEFA Cup	-	First round
Drybrough Cup	-	Semi-final
Forfarshire Cup	-	Unable to compete
Top Scorer	-	Jocky Scott (29 goals)
Av. Home Gate	-	7,000
Players used	-	21
Sent off (booked)	-	One (13)

Cup Cash v. Aberdeen £7,287; Hibs (h) £10,814

Dandy double - it's John Duncan's first as he places a low shot past Dundee United's Hamish McAlpine at Tannadice. Duncan Lambie looks on while Jackie Copland is helpless to intervene. The Dark Blues went on to win 2-1.

Dundee F.C. Line-Ups 1973-74

	1	2	3	4	5	6	7	8	9	10	11	12	13
Jul 28th	Allan	Gemmell	Johnston	Wilson B	Stewart	Robinson	Anderson	Scott I	Duncan	Semple	Lambie	Strachan (10)	Grimmond
Aug 1st	Allan	Gemmell	Johnston	Wilson B	Stewart	Robinson	Semple	Ford	Duncan	Scott J	Lambie	Anderson (8)	Pringle (9)
11th	Allan	Wilson B	Johnston	Robinson	Gemmell	Pringle	Ford	Gray	Wallace	Scott J	Lambie	Strachan	Grimmond
15th	Allan	Ford	Johnston	Robinson	Gemmell	Pringle	Gray	Anderson	Wallace	Scott J	Lambie	Strachan (7)	Robertson
18th	Allan	Ford	Johnston	Robinson	Gemmell	Pringle	Gray	Anderson	Wallace	Scott J	Lambie	Semple (7)	Strachan
22nd	Allan	Gemmell	Johnston	Ford	Stewart	Robinson	Gray	Anderson	Wallace	Scott J	Lambie	Wilson J (11)	Semple
25th	Allan	Ford	Johnston	Gemmell	Stewart	Pringle	Robinson	Wilson B	Wallace	Scott J	Anderson	Lambie	Semple
29th	Allan	Ford	Johnston	Gemmell	Stewart	Pringle	Robinson	Wilson B	Wallace	Scott J	Anderson	Lambie (6)	Gray
Sep 1st	Allan	Ford	Johnston	Robinson	Stewart	Gemmell	Duncan	Anderson	Wallace	Scott J	Lambie	Pringle (3)	Wilson B (7)
8th	Allan	Ford	Johnston	Robinson	Stewart	Gemmell	Duncan	Anderson	Wallace	Scott J	Lambie	Pringle (5)	Wilson B (8)
12th	Allan	Ford	Johnston	Wilson B	Gemmell	Pringle	Robinson	Gray	Wallace	Scott J	Lambie	Anderson	Semple (8)
15th	Allan	Ford	Johnston	Wilson B	Stewart	Gemmell	Robinson	Lambie	Wallace	Scott J	Semple	Pringle (2)	Gray (9)
19th	Allan	Wilson B	Johnston	Ford	Stewart	Gemmell	Robinson	Gray	Wallace	Scott J	Lambie	Pringle (7)	Scott I (8)
22nd	Allan	Wilson B	Johnston	Ford	Stewart	Gemmell	Anderson	Scott I	Duncan	Scott J	Lambie	Pringle (5)	Robinson (8)
29th	Allan	Wilson B	Johnston	Ford	Gemmell	Pringle	Anderson	Scott I	Duncan	Scott J	Lambie	Robinson (7)	Semple
Oct 3rd	Allan	Wilson B	Johnston	Ford	Gemmell	Pringle	Robinson	Gray	Scott I	Scott J	Lambie	Semple (8)	Anderson (11)
6th	Allan	Wilson B	Johnston	Ford	Gemmell	Pringle	Wilson J	Robinson	Wallace	Duncan	Scott I	Gray (11)	Lambie (10)
10th	Allan	Wilson B	Johnston	Ford	Gemmell	Pringle	Wilson J	Robinson	Wallace	Scott J	Scott I	Semple (10)	Gray
13th	Allan	Wilson B	Johnston	Ford	Gemmell	Pringle	Wilson J	Robinson	Wallace	Scott I	Lambie	Semple (7)	Gray
20th	Allan	Wilson B	Johnston	Ford	Gemmell	Pringle	Duncan	Robinson	Wallace	Scott J	Scott I	Wilson J (11)	Semple (6)
27th	Allan	Wilson B	Johnston	Ford	Phillip	Gemmell	Duncan	Robinson	Wallace	Scott J	Wilson J	Scott I	Semple
31st	Allan	Wilson B	Johnston	Ford	Phillip	Gemmell	Duncan	Robinson	Wallace	Scott J	Wilson J	Semple	Scott I
Nov 3rd	Allan	Wilson B	Johnston	Ford	Phillip	Gemmell	Wilson J	Robinson	Wallace	Duncan	Scott I	Semple (6)	Lambie (11)
10th	Allan	Wilson B	Johnston	Ford	Phillip	Gemmell	Wilson J	Robinson	Wallace	Scott J	Lambie	Scott I (10)	Semple
17th	Allan	Wilson B	Johnston	Ford	Phillip	Gemmell	Wilson J	Robinson	Wallace	Duncan	Lambie	Semple (7)	Scott I
21st	Allan	Wilson B	Johnston	Ford	Phillip	Gemmell	Wilson J	Robinson	Wallace	Duncan	Lambie	Scott ?	Semple
24th	Allan	Wilson B	Johnston	Ford	Phillip	Gemmell	Wilson J	Robinson	Scott I	Scott J	Lambie	Semple (7)	Gray (10)
28th	Allan	Wilson B	Gemmell	Ford	Stewart	Phillip	Wilson J	Robinson	Duncan	Scott J	Lambie	Johnston (5)	Scott I (7)
Dec 15th	Allan	Wilson B	Gemmell	Ford	Stewart	Phillip	Duncan	Robinson	Wallace	Scott J	Lambie	Johnston	Scott I
22nd	Allan	Wilson B	Gemmell*	Ford	Stewart	Phillip	Duncan	Robinson	Wallace	Scott J	Lambie	Johnston	Scott I
29th	Allan	Wilson B	Gemmell	Ford	Stewart	Phillip	Wilson J	Robinson	Duncan	Scott J	Lambie	Johnston (5)	Strachan
Jan 1st	Allan	Wilson B	Johnston	Ford	Gemmell	Phillip	Wilson J	Robinson	Duncan	Scott J	Lambie	Pringle	Strachan
5th	Allan	Wilson B	Johnston	Phillip	Stewart	Gemmell	Wilson J	Ford	Duncan	Scott J	Lambie	Pringle	Strachan
19th	Allan	Wilson B	Gemmell	Ford	Phillip	Robinson	Wilson J	Duncan	Wallace	Scott J	Lambie	Pringle	Johnston
27th	Allan	Wilson B	Johnston	Ford	Phillip	Gemmell	Wilson J	Robinson	Duncan	Scott J	Lambie	Pringle (2)	Scott I
Feb 3rd	Allan	Wilson B	Johnston	Ford	Phillip	Gemmell	Wilson J	Robinson	Duncan	Scott J	Lambie	Pringle	Scott I
10th	Allan	Wilson B	Johnston	Ford	Phillip	Gemmell	Wilson J	Robinson	Duncan	Scott J	Lambie	Pringle	Scott I
17th	Allan	Wilson B	Gemmell	Ford	Stewart	Phillip	Wilson J	Robinson	Duncan	Scott J	Lambie	Pringle	Scott I
23rd	Allan	Wilson B	Gemmell	Ford	Stewart	Phillip	Wilson J	Robinson	Duncan	Scott J	Lambie	Pringle	Scott I
Mar 2nd	Allan	Wilson B	Gemmell	Ford	Stewart	Phillip	Wilson J	Robinson	Duncan	Scott J	Lambie	Scott I (7)	Pringle
9th	Allan	Wilson B	Gemmell	Ford	Stewart	Phillip	Wilson J	Robinson	Duncan	Scott J	Lambie	Scott I (6)	Wallace
18th	Allan	Wilson B	Gemmell	Ford	Stewart	Phillip	Wilson J	Robinson	Duncan	Scott J	Lambie	Scott I (11)	Wallace
30th	Allan	Wilson B	Gemmell	Ford	Stewart	Phillip	Wilson J	Robinson	Duncan	Scott J	Wallace	Scott I (2)	Pringle (5)
Apr 3rd	Allan	Wilson B	Gemmell	Ford	Stewart	Phillip	Wilson J	Robinson	Duncan	Scott J	Lambie	Wallace (11)	Pringle
6th	Allan	Gemmell	Johnston	Pringle	Caldwell	Phillip	Wilson R	Wallace	Duncan	Scott J	Lambie	Scott I	Strachan
10th	Allan	Wilson B	Johnston	Ford	Gemmell	Phillip	Wallace	Robinson	Duncan	Scott J	Wilson J	Lambie (3)	Caldwell
13th	Allan	Gemmell	Johnston	Ford	Stewart	Phillip	Wilson J	Robinson	Duncan	Scott J	Lambie	Wallace (7)	Caldwell (5)
17th	Allan	Wilson B	Gemmell	Ford	Caldwell	Phillip	Wallace	Robinson	Duncan	Scott J	Lambie	Wilson J	Johnston
20th	Allan	Wilson B	Gemmell	Robinson	Caldwell	Phillip	Wilson J	Wallace	Duncan	Scott J	Lambie	Scott I (11)	Johnston (2)
22nd	Allan	Wilson B	Gemmell	Ford	Caldwell	Phillip	Robinson	Wallace	Duncan	Scott J	Wilson J	Lambie (11)	Scott I
27th	Allan	Wilson B	Johnston	Ford	Caldwell	Phillip	Scott I	Robinson	Wallace	Scott J	Lambie	Wilson J	Pringle
29th	Allan	Wilson B	Gemmell	Ford	Caldwell	Phillip	Wallace	Robinson	Duncan	Scott J	Johnston	Scott I (4)	Lambie (3)
May 3rd	Allan	Wilson B	Johnston	Ford	Caldwell	Phillip	Wallace	Robinson	Duncan	Scott J	Scott I	Lambie (11)	Hendrie
6th	Allan	Wilson B	Johnston	Ford	Caldwell	Phillip	Wilson J	Robinson	Duncan	Scott J	Wallace	Lambie (6)	Scott I
10th	Hewitt	Wilson B	Johnston	Robinson	Caldwell	Phillip	Wilson J	Wallace	Duncan	Scott J	Lambie	Scott I (8)	Ford

Joy for the Dark Blues - Jimmy Wilson (on knees) cracks in a 25 yarder to make it 2-2 in the six goal Scottish Cup thriller against Hibs at Easter Road. John Duncan, Bobby Robinson and Tommy Gemmell are jubilant while Bobby Ford and Iain Phillip run to congratulate Wilson.

Jocky Scott controls a header from the grounded Gordon Wallace before beating Dunfermline keeper John Arrol for Dundee's first goal in their 3-2 win at East End Park in the second round of the League Cup. DC Thomson

Appearances

	League	L/Cup	S/Cup	UEFA	D/Cup	Total	
Thomson Allan	33	12	5	2	2	54	
Bobby Ford	31 (1)	12	5	2	1	51	(1)
Tommy Gemmell	30 (1)	12 (1)	5	2	2	51	(2)
Bobby Robinson	30 (4)	12	5 (1)	2	2	51+2s	(5)
Jocky Scott	30 (22)	11 (4)	5 (3)	2	1	49	(29)
Bobby Wilson	31 (1)	9 (2)	5 (1)	2	2	49+2s	(4)
Duncan Lambie	24 (6)	8 (1)	5	2	2	41+8s	(7)
John Duncan	29 (13)	4 (1)	5 (4)	0	2	40	(18)
Dave Johnston	25	10	1 (1)	2	2	40+3s	(1)
Iain Phillip	26	4	5	0	0	35	
Gordon Wallace	23 (14)	11 (7)	0	1	0	35+2s	(21)
Jimmy Wilson	22 (4)	4 (1)	5 (1)	0	0	31+2s	(6)
George Stewart	11	5	4	1 (1)	2	23	
Alec Pringle	5 (1)	7	0	1	0	13+8s	(1)
Ian Scott	9	1	0	1 (1)	1	12+10s	(1)
Ian Anderson	4	5 (1)	0	0	1	10+2s	(1)
Alec Caldwell	9	0	0	0	0	9+1s	
John Gray	0	5 (3)	0	0	2	7+3s	(3)
Mike Hewitt	1	0	0	0	0	1	
Billy Semple	1	0	0	0	2	3+9s	
Gordon Strachan	0	0	0	0	0	0+2s	

Scottish League Division One

	P	Home W D L	Away W D L	Goals F A	PTS
Celtic	34	12 4 1	11 3 3	82-27	53
Hibernian	34	14 2 1	6 7 4	75-42	49
Rangers	34	9 3 5	12 3 2	67-34	48
Aberdeen	34	7 9 1	6 7 4	46-26	42
Dundee	**34**	**7 3 7**	**9 4 4**	**67-48**	**39**
Hearts	34	6 6 5	8 4 5	54-43	38
Ayr United	34	9 4 4	6 4 7	44-40	38
Dundee United	34	7 3 7	8 4 5	55-41	37
Motherwell	34	8 5 4	6 2 9	45-40	35
Dumbarton	34	7 3 7	4 4 9	43-58	29
Partick Thistle	34	7 4 6	2 6 9	33-46	28
St Johnstone	34	3 6 8	6 4 7	41-60	28
Arbroath	34	5 2 10	5 5 7	52-69	27
Morton	34	4 5 8	4 5 8	37-49	26
Clyde	34	5 2 10	3 7 7	29-65	25
Dunfermline	34	3 5 9	5 3 9	43-65	24
East Fife	34	3 2 12	6 4 7	26-51	24
Falkirk	34	1 11 5	3 3 11	33-58	22

League Cup Section

	P	W	D	L	F A	PTS
Dundee	6	4	2	0	11- 2	10
St Johnstone	6	3	1	2	12- 9	7
Hearts	6	2	2	2	8- 5	6
Partick Thistle	6	0	1	5	2-17	1

Only 14 minutes remain as Dundee strike gold in the 1973 League Cup Final. Gordon Wallace finds the net with a brilliantly executed turn and shot leaving Celtic's Ally Hunter clutching at thin air. There was no further scoring as Dundee claimed their third League Cup success. DC Thomson

The following Saturday the League Cup was on display before the game with Motherwell at Dens. Parading the trophy are (left to right) John Duncan, Thomson Allan, Bobby Ford, Iain Phillip, Gordon Wallace, Jocky Scott and George Stewart. DC Thomson

The Dark Blues also had a great run to the semi-final of the Scottish Cup beating Aberdeen, Rangers and Hibernian. Scottish international midfielder Bobby Robinson crashes the ball home for Dundee's opener in the Scottish Cup tie against Aberdeen at Pittodrie. DC Thomson

Season 1974-75

Date			Opponents		Score	Crowd	Scorers
July	31st	DC1	QOS	a	3-2 a.e.t.	3,000	Duncan 3 (2-2 after 90 mts.)
Aug	3rd	DCS	Celtic	h	1-2	15,000	Hutchinson
	10th	LC	St Johnstone	a	1-2	4,500	Duncan
	14th	LC	Hibernian	h	2-1	6,829	J. Scott; Spalding o.g.
	17th	LC	Rangers	h	0-2	18,548	-
	21st	LC	Hibernian	a	2-4	13,913	I. Scott; Duncan
	24th	LC	Rangers	a	0-4	35,000	-
	28th	LC	St Johnstone	h	6-1	2,903	J. Scott 2; I. Scott 2; Hutchinson; Ford
	31st	L	Airdrie	a	1-0	5,000	Lambie
Sep	7th	L	Aberdeen	h	0-1	6,396	-
	14th	L	Dundee United	a	0-3	11,000	-
	18th	UE1	RWD Molenbeek	a	0-1	15,000	-
	21st	L	Arbroath	h	0-1	4,672	-
	28th	L	Motherwell	a	1-0		Robinson
Oct	2nd	UE1	RWD Molenbeek		2-4 (2-5)	12,000	Duncan; J. Scott
	5th	L	Hibernian	h	0-0	8,252	-
	12th	L	Kilmarnock	a	1-1	6,000	Robinson
	19th	L	Morton	h	3-0	4,578	J. Scott 2 (1 pen); I. Scott
	26th	L	Dunfermline	a	1-3	5,000	Robinson
Nov	2nd	L	Clyde	h	4-1	3,435	J. Scott 2 (1 pen); Hutchinson; Hoggan
	9th	L	Rangers	a	0-1	15,000	-
	16th	L	St Johnstone	h	4-0	5,933	Hutchinson 2; Stewart; Robinson
	23rd	L	Dumbarton	a	0-0	2,900	-
	30th	L	Partick Thistle	h	1-0	4,495	Hoggan
Dec	7th	L	Ayr United	a	1-2	3,900	Hutchinson
	14th	L	Celtic	h	0-6	14,901	-
	21st	L	Hearts	a	0-0	11,000	-
	28th	L	Airdrie	h	1-0	5,500	Gordon
Jan	1st	L	Aberdeen	a	0-4	12,000	-
	4th	L	Dundee United	h	2-0	16,184	Wallace; Anderson
	11th	L	Arbroath		2-2	4,292	Gordon; Hutchinson
	25th	SC3	Clyde	a	1-0	4,500	Gordon
Feb	1st	L	Hibernian	a	1-2	9,788	Anderson
	8th	L	Kilmarnock	h	4-1	4,835	Wallace 2; Gordon; J. Scott
(pen)							
	10th	L	Motherwell	h	4-1	5,300	I. Scott 2; J. Scott; Wallace
	15th	SC4	St Johnstone	a	1-0	11,840	Anderson
	22nd	L	Morton	a	2-1	3,000	Wallace 2
Mar	1st	L	Dunfermline	h	2-0	4,491	Ford; Gordon
	8th	SCQ	Hearts	a	1-1	27,000	Wallace
	12th	SCQR	Hearts	h	3-2	22,197	Stewart; Hutchinson; Robinson
	15th	L	Rangers	h	1-2	22,738	Hutchinson
	18th	L	Clyde	a	1-0	2,500	Robinson
	22nd	L	St Johnstone	a	1-3	4,400	S. Smith o.g.
	29th	L	Dumbarton	h	2-1	4,411	Stewart; Hutchinson
Apr	2nd	SCS	Celtic	Ham	0-1	40,720	-
	5th	L	Partick Thistle	a	2-2	3,500	Gordon; Hoggan
	12th	l	Ayr United	h	2-3	3,599	J. Scott; B. Wilson
	19th	L	Celtic	a	2-1	13,000	Robinson; Hoggan
	23rd	L	Hearts	h	2-0	4,949	Anderson; J. Scott

John Duncan - the free-scoring striker joined Spurs and was badly missed.

The Record

League	-	Fifth Place, Division One
League Cup	-	Qualifying stages only
Scottish Cup	-	Semi-final
UEFA Cup	-	First round
Drybrough Cup	-	Semi-final
Forfarshire Cup	-	First round
Top Scorer	-	Jocky Scott (12 goals)
Av. Home Gate	-	7,400
Players used	-	23
Sent off (booked)	-	None (12)

Cup Cash v. Hearts (a) £9,498

Scottish League Division One

		Home			Away			Goals		
	P	W	D	L	W	D	L	F	A	PTS
Celtic	34	14	3	0	12	2	3	93-28		57
Rangers	34	14	2	1	12	2	3	74-30		56
Hibernian	34	12	2	3	7	5	5	74-33		45
Aberdeen	34	10	6	1	6	5	6	61-34		43
Dundee	34	13	4	0	4	5	8	68-43		43
Ayr United	34	11	4	2	5	4	8	50-51		40
Dundee United	34	11	3	3	6	2	9	56-51		39
Motherwell	34	5	6	6	6	3	8	38-48		31
East Fife	34	8	3	6	3	5	9	46-54		30
Hearts	34	7	4	7	5	2	10	39-50		30
St Johnstone	34	8	3	6	2	6	9	52-67		29
Morton	34	8	4	5	2	4	11	47-53		28
Partick Thistle	34	4	5	8	6	3	8	40-43		28
Falkirk	34	6	4	7	1	8	8	38-56		26
Arbroath	34	8	3	6	1	5	11	39-63		26
Dumbarton	34	3	9	5	3	2	12	43-72		23
Kilmarnock	34	6	3	8	1	5	11	40-71		22
Airdrie	34	2	4	11	2	4	11	34-75		16

League Cup Section

	P	W	D	L	F	A	PTS
Hibernian	6	5	0	1	16-16		10
Rangers	6	4	0	2	16-9		8
Dundee	6	2	0	4	11-14		4
St Johnstone	6	1	0	5	9-23		2

Alan Gordon scores the winner in the 1-0 Scottish Cup win against Clyde.

Dundee F.C. Line-Ups 1974-75

	1	2	3	4	5	6	7	8	9	10	11	12	13
Jul 27th	Allan	Gemmell	Johnston	Phillip	Stewart	Pringle	Ford	Robinson	Duncan	Scott J	Lambie	Caldwell (5)	Scott I (11)
31st	Allan	Gemmell	Johnston	Ford	Stewart	Phillip	Scott I	Robinson	Hutchinson	Scott J	Wilson J	Caldwell (5)	Lambie (11)
Aug 10th	Allan	Wilson B	Johnston	Ford	Stewart	Phillip	Wilson J	Robinson	Duncan	Scott J	Hutchinson	Gemmell	Scott I (9)
14th	Allan	Wilson B	Gemmell	Ford	Stewart	Phillip	Wilson J	Robinson	Hutchinson	Scott J	Scott I	Caldwell	Strachan
17th	Allan	Wilson B	Gemmell	Ford	Stewart	Phillip	Wilson J	Robinson	Hutchinson	Scott J	Scott I	Duncan (7)	Johnston (3)
21st	Allan	Wilson B	Johnston	Ford	Stewart	Phillip	Strachan	Robinson	Duncan	Scott J	Hutchinson	Gemmell (6)	Scott I (11)
24th	Allan	Wilson B	Johnston	Ford	Stewart	Gemmell	Caldwell	Robinson	Hutchinson	Scott J	Wilson J	Anderson (5)	Scott I (10)
28th	Allan	Wilson B	Johnston	Ford	Stewart	Gemmell	Laing	Hutchinson	Duncan	Scott J	Scott I	Wilson J	McPhail
31st	Allan	Wilson B	Johnston	Ford	Stewart	Gemmell	Laing	Robinson	Hutchinson	Scott J	Lambie	Wilson	Anderson(11
Sep 7th	Allan	Wilson B	Johnston	Ford	Stewart	Gemmell	Wilson J	Robinson	Hutchinson	Scott J	Scott I	Laing	Lambie
14th	Allan	Wilson B	Gemmell	Caldwell	Stewart	Phillip	Wilson J	Robinson	Hutchinson	Scott J	Scott I	Lambie (4)	Laing
18th	Allan	Wilson B	Gemmell	Caldwell	Stewart	Phillip	Scott I	Robinson	Hutchinson	Scott J	Johnston	Anderson (4)	Wilson J
21st	Allan	Wilson B	Gemmell	Robinson	Stewart	Phillip	Wilson J	Hutchinson	Duncan	Scott J	Johnston	Scott I	Caldwell
28th	Allan	Wilson B	Gemmell	Ford	Stewart	Phillip	Robinson	Hutchinson	Duncan	Scott J	Johnston	Caldwell (5)	Scott I
Oct 2nd	Allan	Wilson B	Gemmell	Ford	Caldwell	Phillip	Robinson	Duncan	Hutchinson	Scott J	Johnston	Wilson J (2)	Anderson
5th	Allan	Wilson B	Johnston	Ford	Gemmell	Phillip	Caldwell	Robinson	Duncan	Scott J	Hutchinson	Lambie	Scott I (5)
12th	Allan	Wilson B	Gemmell	Ford	Caldwell	Phillip	Hoggan	Robinson	Duncan	Scott J	Johnston	Stewart	Scott I
19th	Allan	Wilson B	Gemmell	Ford	Stewart	Phillip	Hoggan	Robinson	Scott I	Scott J	Caldwell	Johnston (6)	Wilson J (7)
26th	Allan	Wilson B	Gemmell	Ford	Stewart	Phillip	Hoggan	Robinson	Scott I	Scott J	Johnston	Wilson J (11)	Caldwell (6)
Nov 2nd	Allan	Wilson B	Gemmell	Ford	Stewart	Phillip	Hoggan	Robinson	Hutchinson	Scott J	Caldwell	Scott I (4)	Johnston
9th	Allan	Wilson B	Gemmell	Ford	Stewart	Phillip	Hoggan	Robinson	Hutchinson	Scott J	Caldwell	Scott I (1)	Johnston (3)
16th	Allan	Wilson B	Johnston	Ford	Stewart	Phillip	Hoggan	Robinson	Hutchinson	Scott J	Caldwell	Gemmell	Scott I
23rd	Allan	Wilson B	Johnston	Ford	Stewart	Phillip	Hoggan	Robinson	Hutchinson	Scott J	Caldwell	Scott I (7)	Gemmell
30th	Allan	Wilson B	Johnston	Ford	Stewart	Phillip	Hoggan	Robinson	Hutchinson	Scott J	Caldwell	Scott I	Gemmell
Dec 7th	Allan	Wilson B	Johnston	Ford	Stewart	Phillip	Hoggan	Robinson	Hutchinson	Scott J	Caldwell	Scott I (4)	Gemmell
14th	Allan	Wilson B	Johnston	Ford	Stewart	Phillip	Hoggan	Robinson	Hutchinson	Scott J	Caldwell	Gordon (11)	Gemmell
21st	Allan	Wilson B	Gemmell	Robinson	Stewart	Caldwell	Hoggan	Gordon	Hutchinson	Scott J	Johnston	Anderson (3)	Hendrie
28th	Allan	Ford	Gemmell	Caldwell	Stewart	Anderson	Hoggan	Robinson	Gordon	Scott J	Hutchinson	Wallace	Scott I
Jan 1st	Allan	Wilson B	Gemmell	Ford	Stewart	Phillip	Gordon	Robinson	Wallace	Scott J	Caldwell	Johnston (5)	Hutchinson (9)
4th	Allan	Wilson B	Gemmell	Phillip	Stewart	Anderson	Robinson	Gordon	Wallace	Scott J	Johnston	Wilson J	Hutchinson
11th	Allan	Wilson B	Johnston	Anderson	Stewart	Gemmell	Robinson	Gordon	Wallace	Scott J	Hutchinson	Hendrie	Wilson J
25th	Allan	Wilson B	Johnston	Ford	Stewart	Gemmell	Hoggan	Robinson	Wallace	Gordon	Anderson	Scott I	Hutchinson
Feb 1st	Allan	Wilson B	Ford	Robinson	Stewart	Caldwell	Hoggan	Gordon	Wallace	Scott J	Anderson	Scott I	Hutchinson
8th	Allan	Wilson B	Ford	Robinson	Stewart	Gemmell	Hoggan	Gordon	Wallace	Scott J	Anderson	Caldwell (3)	Hutchinson (8)
10th	Allan	Wilson B	Gemmell	Anderson	Stewart	Ford	Hoggan	Robinson	Wallace	Scott J	Scott I	Laing	Hendrie
15th	Allan	Wilson B	Gemmell	Anderson	Stewart	Ford	Hoggan	Robinson	Wallace	Scott J	Scott I	Laing (7)	Hutchinson (5)
22nd	Allan	Wilson B	Gemmell	Robinson	Stewart	Ford	Hoggan	Gordon	Wallace	Scott J	Anderson	Scott I	Hutchinson
Mar 1st	Allan	Wilson B	Gemmell	Robinson	Stewart	Ford	Hoggan	Gordon	Wallace	Scott J	Anderson	Scott I	Hutchinson
8th	Allan	Wilson B	Gemmell	Robinson	Stewart	Ford	Hoggan	Gordon	Wallace	Scott J	Anderson	Scott I	Johnston
12th	Allan	Wilson B	Gemmell	Robinson	Stewart	Ford	Hoggan	Hutchinson	Wallace	Scott J	Anderson	Scott I	Johnston
15th	Allan	Wilson B	Gemmell	Robinson	Stewart	Ford	Hoggan	Hutchinson	Wallace	Scott J	Anderson	Gordon	Johnston
18th	Allan	Wilson B	Johnston	Caldwell	Stewart	Ford	Hoggan	Robinson	Hutchinson	Gordon	Scott I	Scott J	Wallace (9)
22nd	Allan	Wilson B	Johnston	Robinson	Caldwell	Gemmell	Hoggan	Hutchinson	Wallace	Scott J	Scott I	Gordon (9)	Stewart
29th	Allan	Wilson B	Johnston	Phillip	Caldwell	Gemmell	Hoggan	Ford	Wallace	Scott J	Hutchinson	Gordon (9)	Robinson
Apr 2nd	Allan	Wilson B	Gemmell	Anderson	Stewart	Ford	Hoggan	Robinson	Wallace	Scott J	Hutchinson	Gordon (11)	Johnston
5th	Allan	Wilson B	Johnston	Caldwell	Stewart	Ford	Hoggan	Robinson	Gordon	Scott J	Anderson	Wallace	Hutchinson
12th	Allan	Wilson B	Johnston	Robinson	Caldwell	Ford	Hoggan	Gordon	Wallace	Scott J	Anderson	Gemmell	Hutchinson
19th	Allan	Wilson B	Johnston	Anderson	Ford	Gemmell	Hoggan	Robinson	Gordon	Scott J	Hutchinson	Caldwell	Scott I
23rd	Allan	Wilson B	Johnston	Anderson	Ford	Gemmell	Hoggan	Robinson	Wallace	Strachan	Sinclair	Scott J (9)	Mackie

Appearances

	League	L/Cup	S/Cup	UEFA	D/Cup	Total	
Thomson Allan	34	6	5	2	2	49	
Bobby Robinson	33 (6)	5	5 (1)	2	2	47	(7)
Bobby Wilson	33 (1)	6	5	2	0	46	(1)
Jocky Scott	32 (8)	6 (3)	4	2 (1)	2	46+1s	(12)
Bobby Ford	28 (1)	6 (1)	5	2	2	43	(2)
George Stewart	28 (2)	6	5 (1)	1	2	42	(3)
Tommy Gemmell	25	4	5	2	2	38+1s	
Bobby Hutchinson	21 (7)	6 (1)	2 (1)	2	1 (1)	32+3s	(10)
Dave Johnston	22	4	1	2	2	31+4s	
Wilson Hoggan	25 (4)	0	5	0	0	30	(4)
Iain Phillip	17	4	0	2	2	25	
Alec Caldwell	19	1	0	1	0	21+5s	
Ian Anderson	13 (3)	0	5 (1)	0	0	18+4s	(4)
Gordon Wallace	13 (6)	0	5 (1)	0	0	18+1s	(7)
Alan Gordon	13 (5)	0	2 (1)	0	0	15+4s	(6)
Ian Scott	7 (3)	3 (3)	1	1	1	13+9s	(6)
John Duncan	4	3 (2)	0	1 (1)	1 (3)	9+1s	(6)
Jimmy Wilson	3	4	0	0	1	8+3s	
Derek Laing	1	1	0	0	0	2+1s	
Gordon Strachan	1	1	0	0	0	2	
Duncan Lambie	1 (1)	0	0	0	1	2+2s	(1)
Eric Sinclair	1	0	0	0	0	1	
Alec Pringle	0	0	0	0	1	1	

Iain Phillip looks on as Jim O'Rourke of Hibs goes down after a tackle by Dundee left-back Dave Johnston. DC Thomson

Season 1975-76

Date			Opponents		Score	Crowd	Scorers
Aug	4th	AS1	Motherwell	a	1-1	3,799	B. Wilson
	6th	AS1	Motherwell	h	0-1 (1-2)	4,881	-
	9th	LC	Hibernian	a	0-2	10,851	-
	13th	LC	Dunfermline	h	4-0	4,000	Gemmell 2 (1 pen); Wallace; Gordon
	16th	LC	Ayr United	a	1-1	5,000	Gordon
	20th	LC	Dunfermline	a	1-1	3,000	Caldwell
	23rd	LC	Ayr United	h	2-4	5,248	Wallace; Hoggan
	27th	LC	Hibernian	h	1-2	4,982	Munro o.g.
	30th	L	Aberdeen	h	3-2	6,067	Ford; Gemmell (pen); Hoggan
Sep	6th	L	Celtic	a	0-4	25,000	-
	13th	L	Hearts	h	2-3	6,700	Martin; Johnston
	20th	L	Ayr United	a	1-2	4,024	Wallace
	27th	L	Rangers	h	0-0	15,000	-
Oct	4th	L	Hibernian	a	1-1	8,708	Wallace
	8th	FCS	Forfar Athletic	h	2-0 a.e.t	2,000	Caldwell; Anderson
	11th	L	St Johnstone	h	4-3	5,300	Hoggan 2 (1 pen); Gordon; Wallace
	18th	L	Dundee United	a	2-1	11,327	Wallace; Hoggan (pen)
	25th	L	Motherwell	h	3-6	6,850	Gordon; Strachan (pen); Wallace
Nov	1st	L	Aberdeen	a	0-2	6,313	-
	8th	L	Celtic	h	1-0	16,456	Robinson
	15th	L	Hearts	a	1-1	10,000	Strachan
	22nd	L	Ayr United	h	2-2	5,100	Gordon; Strachan
	29th	L	Rangers	a	1-2	16,500	Wallace
Dec	6th	L	Hibernian	h	2-0	7,350	Caldwell 2
	13th	L	St Johnstone	a	3-1	3,500	Wallace 3
	20th	L	Dundee United	h	0-0	9,950	-
	27th	L	Motherwell	a	2-3	7,169	Wallace; Laing
Jan	1st	L	Aberdeen	h	1-3	10,000	Hutchinson
	3rd	L	Celtic	a	3-3	21,000	Lynch o.g.; Hoggan; McIntosh
	10th	L	Hearts	h	4-1	6,550	Wallace; Martin; Hutchinson; Robinson
	17th	L	Ayr United	a	1-3	4,100	Hutchinson
	24th	SC3	Falkirk	h	1-2	5,600	Laing
	31st	L	Rangers	h	1-1	14,400	Johnston
Feb	7th	L	Hibernian	a	0-4	9,241	-
	21st	L	St Johnstone	h	3-0	4,100	Strachan 2 (1 pen); Wallace
Mar	13th	L	Aberdeen	a	1-0	6,460	Hutchinson
	20th	L	Celtic	h	0-1	14,830	-
	27th	L	Hearts	a	0-3	8,500	-
Apr	3rd	L	Ayr United	h	1-2	4,150	Strachan (pen)
	10th	L	Rangers	a	0-3	24,000	-
	14th	L	Hibernian	h	1-1	6,050	Ford
	17th	L	St Johnstone	a	1-1	3,410	Gemmell (pen)
	21st	L	Dundee United	h	2-1	13,800	Gemmell (pen); Sinclair
	24th	L	Motherwell	a	1-1	4,675	Hutchinson
May	1st	L	Motherwell	h	1-0	7,661	Sinclair

Bobby Ford - the busy midfielder was a popular figure at Dens.

Appearances

	League	L/Cup	S/Cup	AS/Cup	Total
Thomson Allan	36	6	1	2	45
Dave Johnston	32 (2)	5	0	2	39 (2)
Bobby Ford	29 (2)	6	1	2	38+1s (2)
Gordon Wallace	29 (12)	4 (2)	1	1	35+3s (14)
George Stewart	25	3	0	0	28
Iain Phillip	23	1	1	2	27+5s
Ian Purdie	22	3	0	0	25+4s
Gordon Strachan	17 (6)	6	1	1	25+6s (6)
Tommy Gemmell	16 (3)	5 (2)	0	0	21+3s (5)
Wilson Hoggan	16 (5)	6 (1)	1	1	24+3s (6)
Alec Caldwell	18 (2)	5 (1)	1	2	26+4s (3)
Alan Gordon	17 (3)	5 (2)	0	2	24+3s (5)
Bobby Robinson	17 (2)	4	1	2	24+5s (2)
Bobby Hutchinson	18 (5)	0	1	0	19+3s (5)
Derek Laing	18 (1)	0	1 (1)	0	19 (2)
Bobby Wilson	17	2	0	1	20
George Mackie	14	0	1	0	15+1s
John Martin	10 (2)	4	0	1	15+1s (2)
Eric Sinclair	9 (2)	0	0	1	10+3s (2)
John McPhail	5	0	0	0	5
Dave McIntosh	4 (1)	0	0	0	4 (1)
Ian Anderson	2	0	0	1	3
Tom Hendrie	2	0	0	0	2+1s
Mitch Bavidge	0	1	0	0	1+4s
Jocky Scott	0	0	0	1	1

The Record

League	-	Ninth Place, Premier Division
League Cup	-	Qualifying stages only
Scottish Cup	-	First round
Anglo Scottish Cup	-	First round
Forfarshire Cup	-	Runners up (Final 01-05-78)
Top Scorer	-	Gordon Wallace (14 goals)
Av. Home Gate	-	8,900
Players used	-	24
Sent Off (booked)	-	None (20)

Scottish League Premier Division

		Home			Away			Goals		
	P	W	D	L	W	D	L	F	A	PTS
Rangers	36	14	2	2	8	6	4	58-26		52
Celtic	36	10	5	3	11	1	6	71-42		48
Hibernian	36	13	2	3	5	5	8	55-43		43
Motherwell	36	11	4	3	5	4	9	57-48		40
Hearts	36	7	5	6	6	5	8	39-45		35
Ayr United	36	10	3	5	5	2	11	48-57		35
Aberdeen	36	8	5	5	3	5	10	49-50		32
Dundee United	36	9	3	6	3	5	10	46-48		32
Dundee	**36**	**8**	**5**	**5**	**3**	**5**	**10**	**49-72**		**32**
St Johnstone	36	3	4	11	0	1	17	28-79		11

League Cup Section

	P	W	D	L	F	A	PTS
Hibernian	6	5	0	1	14-4		10
Ayr United	6	2	3	1	11-9		7
Dundee	**6**	**1**	**2**	**3**	**9-10**		**4**
Dunfermline	6	0	3	3	4-15		3

Dundee F.C. Line-Ups 1975-76

	1	2	3	4	5	6	7	8	9	10	11	12	13
Aug 4th	Allan	Wilson B	Johnston	Ford	Phillip	Caldwell	Hoggan	Robinson	Wallace	Gordon	Anderson	Strachan	Gemmell
6th	Allan	Martin	Johnston	Ford	Caldwell	Phillip	Strachan	Robinson	Gordon	Sinclair	Scott J	Gemmell	Hoggan
9th	Allan	Wilson B	Johnston	Ford	Caldwell	Phillip	Strachan	Robinson	Wallace	Gordon	Hoggan	Martin (6)	Bavidge (7)
13th	Allan	Martin	Johnston	Ford	Caldwell	Gemmell	Strachan	Robinson	Wallace	Gordon	Hoggan	Wilson	Sinclair
16th	Allan	Wilson B	Johnston	Caldwell	Stewart	Gemmell	Strachan	Ford	Wallace	Gordon	Hoggan	Purdie (2)	Robinson (5)
20th	Allan	Martin	Johnston	Caldwell	Stewart	Gemmell	Hoggan	Ford	Wallace	Strachan	Purdie	Bavidge (9)	Robinson (2)
23rd	Allan	Martin	Gemmell	Ford	Stewart	Caldwell	Hoggan	Robinson	Gordon	Strachan	Purdie	Bavidge (9)	Wallace (6)
27th	Allan	Martin	Johnston	Robinson	Gemmell	Ford	Hoggan	Strachan	Bavidge	Gordon	Purdie	Phillip (4)	Caldwell (9)
30th	Allan	Wilson B	Johnston	Ford	Stewart	Phillip	Hoggan	Martin	Gordon	Anderson	Purdie	Sinclair (3)	Gemmell (5)
Sep 6th	Allan	Wilson B	Johnston	Ford	Stewart	Phillip	Hoggan	Martin	Gordon	Anderson	Purdie	Sinclair (8)	Gemmell (10)
13th	Allan	Martin	Johnston	Ford	Stewart	Phillip	Hoggan	Strachan	Sinclair	Gordon	Purdie	Wallace (8)	Caldwell (11)
20th	Allan	Martin	Johnston	Ford	Stewart	Phillip	Hoggan	Sinclair	Wallace	Gordon	Purdie	Strachan (7)	Caldwell
27th	Allan	Martin	Johnston	Ford	Stewart	Robinson	Hoggan	Wallace	Sinclair	Gordon	Purdie	Strachan (10)	Phillip
Oct 4th	Allan	Wilson B	Johnston	Robinson	Stewart	Ford	Hoggan	Sinclair	Wallace	Gordon	Purdie	Phillip	Caldwell (8)
11th	Allan	Wilson B	Johnston	Robinson	Stewart	Ford	Laing	Hoggan	Wallace	Gordon	Purdie	Strachan	Phillip (10)
18th	Allan	Wilson B	Johnston	Robinson	Stewart	Ford	Laing	Hoggan	Wallace	Gordon	Purdie	Phillip (5)	Strachan
25th	Allan	Wilson B	Johnston	Robinson	Stewart	Ford	Laing	Strachan	Wallace	Gordon	Purdie	Phillip (4)	Sinclair (8)
Nov 1st	Allan	Wilson B	Johnston	Robinson	Stewart	Ford	Laing	Strachan	Wallace	Gordon	Purdie	Phillip (8)	Caldwell (3)
8th	Allan	Caldwell	Johnston	Ford	Stewart	Gemmell	Strachan	Robinson	Wallace	Gordon	Purdie	Mackie	Sinclair
15th	Allan	Caldwell	Johnston	Ford	Stewart	Gemmell	Strachan	Robinson	Wallace	Gordon	Purdie	Mackie	Hutchinson
22nd	Allan	Caldwell	Johnston	Ford	Stewart	Gemmell	Strachan	Robinson	Wallace	Gordon	Purdie	Hoggan (2)	Hutchinson (8)
29th	Allan	Caldwell	Johnston	Ford	Stewart	Gemmell	Hoggan	Strachan	Wallace	Gordon	Purdie	Mackie (8)	Hutchinson (7)
Dec 6th	Allan	Caldwell	Johnston	Mackie	Stewart	Gemmell	Hoggan	Strachan	Wallace	Ford	Purdie	Gordon	Hutchinson
13th	Allan	Caldwell	Johnston	Mackie	Stewart	Gemmell	Hoggan	Strachan	Wallace	Ford	Purdie	Gordon	Hutchinson
20th	Allan	Caldwell	Johnston	Mackie	Stewart	Gemmell	Hoggan	Strachan	Wallace	Ford	Purdie	Gordon (8)	Hutchinson (7)
27th	Allan	Caldwell	Johnston	Mackie	Stewart	Gemmell	Hoggan	Phillip	Wallace	Hutchinson	Laing	Strachan (7)	Ford (3)
Jan 1st	Allan	Caldwell	Gemmell	Ford	Stewart	Phillip	Laing	Strachan	Wallace	Mackie	Hutchinson	Robinson (3)	Purdie (11)
3rd	Allan	Caldwell	Mackie	McIntosh	Stewart	Phillip	Laing	Ford	Wallace	Strachan	Hutchinson	Hoggan (2)	Gordon (5)
10th	Allan	Martin	Mackie	Phillip	Stewart	McIntosh	Laing	Ford	Wallace	Strachan	Hutchinson	Hoggan (2)	Robinson (2)
17th	Allan	Martin	Mackie	Phillip	Stewart	McIntosh	Laing	Ford	Wallace	Strachan	Hutchinson	Hoggan (2)	Robinson (6)
24th	Allan	Ford	Mackie	Robinson	Phillip	Caldwell	Hoggan	Hutchinson	Wallace	Strachan	Laing	Martin	Hendrie (7)
31st	Allan	Caldwell	Johnston	Phillip	Stewart	McIntosh	Hendrie	Ford	Wallace	Hutchinson	Laing	Strachan	Gordon
Feb 7th	Allan	Martin	Johnston	Ford	Stewart	Phillip	Hendrie	Robinson	Wallace	Strachan	Laing	Purdie (9)	Gordon (10)
21st	Allan	Martin	Johnston	Ford	Caldwell	Phillip	Strachan	Robinson	Wallace	Hutchinson	Laing	Purdie	McIntosh
28th	Allan	Martin	Johnston	Phillip	Caldwell	Gemmell	Strachan	Robinson	Wallace	Hutchinson	Laing	Purdie (9)	Mackie
Mar 13th	Allan	Wilson B	Johnston	Robinson	Phillip	Caldwell	Mackie	Gordon	Wallace	Hutchinson	Laing	Strachan (11)	Ford
20th	Allan	Wilson B	Johnston	Robinson	Phillip	Caldwell	Mackie	Gordon	Wallace	Hutchinson	Laing	Strachan	Gemmell (2)
27th	Allan	Wilson B	Johnston	Robinson	Phillip	Caldwell	Laing	Gordon	Hutchinson	Mackie	Purdie	Strachan (3)	Wallace (11)
Apr 3rd	Allan	Wilson B	Johnston	Caldwell	Stewart	Phillip	Mackie	Robinson	Wallace	Hutchinson	Laing	Strachan (4)	Bavidge (7)
10th	Allan	Wilson B	Johnston	Caldwell	Phillip	Gemmell	Laing	Robinson	Wallace	Mackie	Hutchinson	McPhail (4)	Bavidge
14th	Allan	Wilson B	Johnston	McPhail	Phillip	Gemmell	Ford	Sinclair	Wallace	Mackie	Hutchinson	Purdie (10)	Laing (9)
17th	Allan	Wilson B	Johnston	McPhail	Phillip	Gemmell	Ford	Sinclair	Wallace	Hutchinson	Purdie	Laing (9)	Hoggan (11)
21st	Allan	Wilson B	Johnston	McPhail	Phillip	Gemmell	Hoggan	Ford	Sinclair	Hutchinson	Purdie	Martin	Bavidge
24th	Allan	Wilson B	Johnston	McPhail	Phillip	Gemmell	Hoggan	Ford	Sinclair	Hutchinson	Purdie	Martin	Bavidge (7)
May 1st	Allan	Wilson B	Johnston	McPhail	Phillip	Gemmell	Hoggan	Ford	Sinclair	Hutchinson	Purdie	Martin	Bavidge

Hip, hip for Henry - Wilson Hoggan beats Dundee United keeper Hamish McAlpine with a 74th minute penalty at Tannadice to give Dundee a 2-1 win in the first-ever Premier League derby between the clubs.

DC Thomson

Season 1976-77

Date			Opponents		Score	Crowd	Scorers
Aug	14th	LC	Hearts	a	0-2	10,000	
	18th	LC	Motherwell	h	2-1	6,000	Sinclair; Hutchinson
	21st	LC	Partick Thistle	h	0-2	5,837	-
	25th	LC	Motherwell	a	3-3	4,258	Pirie 3 (1 pen)
	28th	LC	Partick Thistle	a	1-0	5,000	Hoggan
Sep	1st	LC	Hearts	h	3-2	4,733	Robinson; Pirie; Purdie
	4th	L	Dumbarton	h	2-1	4,619	Hutchinson; Pirie
	8th	L	East Fife	a	4-2	2,083	Strachan; Sinclair; Pirie 2
	11th	L	Morton	h	2-2	1,800	Hutchinson; Sinclair
	15th	L	Arbroath	h	2-1	4,229	Carson o.g.; Pirie
	18th	L	QOS	h	1-1	5,061	Pirie
	22nd	L	Airdrie	a	2-2	3,000	Pirie; Hutchinson
	25th	L	Falkirk	a	6-1	2,500	Hutchinson 2; Purdie; Pirie 2; Strachan
	29th	L	Hamilton	h	5-1	3,500	Pirie 3 (1 pen); Purdie; Hutchinson
Oct	2nd	L	St Mirren	a	0-4	4,000	
	6th	L	Hamilton	a	2-4	1,000	Pirie (pen); Purdie
	9th	L	Raith Rovers	h	3-1	5,372	Ford; Pirie 2
	16th	L	Clydebank	a	1-2	2,000	Pirie
	23rd	L	Montrose	h	6-1	4,941	Sinclair 3; Pirie 2; Hutchinson
	30th	L	St Johnstone	h	1-0	5,329	Pirie
Nov	10th	L	Dumbarton	a	1-1	500	Hutchinson
	13th	L	Morton	h	1-1	4,948	Gemmell (pen)
	20th	L	QOS	a	2-2	2,000	Purdie 2
	27th	L	Falkirk	h	2-0	4,287	Sinclair; Ford
Dec	15th	L	Raith Rovers	a	2-1	1,645	Hutchinson; Robinson
	25th	L	Montrose	a	1-0	3,500	Purdie
Jan	8th	L	Morton	a	3-2	2,000	Pirie 2; Hoggan
	22nd	L	Falkirk	a	8-0	2,500	Pirie 4; Sinclair 3; Purdie
Feb	5th	L	St Mirren	a	1-3	10,000	Strachan
	7th	SC3	St Johnstone	a	1-1	7,000	Purdie
	8th	SC3R	St Johnstone	h	4-2	8,197	Pirie 2; Purdie; Hutchinson
	12th	L	Raith Rovers	h	4-0	5,088	Hoggan; Pirie 2; Sinclair
	15th	L	QOS	h	0-2	4,635	-
	19th	L	Clydebank	a	0-3	3,900	-
	26th	SC4	Aberdeen	h	0-0	16,999	-
Mar	2nd	SC4R	Aberdeen	a	2-1	18,373	Hutchinson 2
	5th	L	Montrose	h	3-2	4,333	Strachan 2; Pirie
	12th	SCQ	Arbroath	a	3-1	9,558	Strachan; Sinclair 2
	15th	L	St Johnstone	h	2-0	2,849	Gemmell (pen); Laing
	19th	L	Arbroath	a	0-1	2,330	-
	23rd	L	Dumbarton	h	4-0	2,401	Pirie 4
	26th	L	Arbroath	h	5-2	4,006	Strachan; Pirie 3; Sinclair
	30th	L	St Johnstone	a	0-0	2,048	-
Apr	2nd	L	Airdrie	a	2-2	1,500	Pirie; Gemmell (pen)
	6th	SCS	Celtic	Hamp	0-2	29,900	-
	9th	L	Airdrie	h	3-1	3,926	Phillip; Pirie; Strachan
	12th	L	Clydebank	h	2-3	8,707	Hutchinson; Ford
	16th	L	East Fife	h	2-2	2,887	Gemmell (pen); Hutchinson
	19th	L	St Mirren	h	0-4	4,386	-
	23rd	L	East Fife	a	2-0	2,263	Pirie; Robinson
	30th	L	Hamilton		3-0	400	Hutchinson; Caldwell; Pirie

Cup Cash v. St Johns. (a) £3,840, (h) £4,116; Aberdeen (h) £11,926, (a) £11,220;

Billy Pirie - the Dundee striker proved a prolific scorer in the First Division.

The Record		
League	-	Third Place, Division One
League Cup	-	Qualifying stages only
Scottish Cup	-	Semi-final
Forfarshire Cup	-	Unable to compete.
Top Scorer	-	Billy Pirie (44 goals)
Av. Home Gate	-	4,500
Players used	-	21
Sent off (bookings)	-	Two (unknown)

Appearances

	League	L/Cup	S/Cup	Total	
Iain Phillip	36 (1)	6	6	48	(1)
Ian Purdie	33 (7)	6 (1)	6 (2)	45+1s	(10)
Billy Pirie	33 (38)	6 (4)	6 (2)	45	(44)
Bobby Hutchinson	35 (12)	5 (1)	5 (3)	45	(16)
Bobby Ford	34 (3)	3	6	43+4s	(3)
Alec Caldwell	31 (1)	5	5	41+4s	(1)
Gordon Strachan	33 (7)	0	6 (1)	39+3s	(8)
Eric Sinclair	30 (11)	4 (1)	2 (2)	36+3s	(14)
Ally Donaldson	29	0	6	35	
John McPhail	23	6	4	33+2s	
Wilson Hoggan	23 (2)	3 (1)	4	30+5s	(3)
Dave Johnston	21	1	5	27+1s	
Tommy Gemmell	20 (4)	3	2	25	(4)
Bobby Robinson	20 (2)	2 (1)	2	24+16s	(3)
John Martin	12	6	1	19+2s	
Thomson Allan	10	6	0	16	
Dave McKinnon	2	3	0	5+4s	
Derek Laing	2 (1)	1	0	3+9s	(1)
Dave McIntosh	2	0	0	2+3s	
Paddy Morris	0	0	0	0+1s	
Ian Redford	0	0	0	0+1s	

Scottish League Division One

		Home			Away			Goals		
	P	W	D	L	W	D	L	F A		PTS
St Mirren	39	15	4	0	10	8	2	91-38		62
Clydebank	39	16	1	2	8	9	3	88-38		58
Dundee	**39**	**13**	**3**	**3**	**8**	**6**	**6**	**90-55**		**51**
Morton	39	11	4	5	9	6	4	77-52		48
Montrose	39	10	6	4	6	3	10	61-62		41
Airdrie	39	7	8	5	6	4	9	63-58		38
Dumbarton	39	6	8	6	8	1	10	63-68		37
Arbroath	39	11	3	5	6	0	14	46-62		37
Queen of the South	39	7	5	8	4	7	8	56-64		34
Hamilton	39	7	4	9	5	5	9	43-57		33
St Johnstone	39	5	7	7	3	6	11	42-64		29
East Fife	39	6	6	7	2	7	11	40-71		29
Raith Rovers	39	7	7	6	1	4	14	45-68		27
Falkirk	39	5	4	10	1	4	15	36-85		20

League Cup Section

	P	W	D	L	F A	PTS
Hearts	6	4	1	1	15- 8	9
Dundee	**6**	**3**	**1**	**2**	**9-10**	**7**
Partick Thistle	6	2	2	2	8- 7	6
Motherwell	6	0	2	4	7-14	2

Dundee F.C. Line-Ups 1976-77

		1	2	3	4	5	6	7	8	9	10	11	12	13
Aug	14th	Allan	Martin	Johnston	McPhail	Phillip	Gemmell	Ford	Robinson	Pirie	Hutchinson	Purdie	Laing (2)	Caldwell (8)
	18th	Allan	Martin	Caldwell	McPhail	Phillip	Gemmell	Ford	Sinclair	Pirie	Hutchinson	Purdie	McKinnon (7)	Hoggan (9)
	21st	Allan	Martin	Caldwell	McPhail	Phillip	Gemmell	Laing	Ford	Sinclair	McKinnon	Purdie	Hoggan (7)	Morris (11)
	25th	Allan	Martin	Caldwell	McPhail	Phillip	McKinnon	Hoggan	Sinclair	Pirie	Hutchinson	Purdie	Robinson	Ford (8)
	28th	Allan	Martin	Caldwell	McPhail	Phillip	McKinnon	Hoggan	Sinclair	Pirie	Hutchinson	Purdie	Robinson (6)	Ford
Sep	1st	Allan	Martin	Caldwell	McPhail	Phillip	Robinson	Hoggan	Sinclair	Pirie	Hutchinson	Purdie	Ford	McKinnon
	4th	Allan	Martin	Caldwell	McPhail	Phillip	Robinson	Hoggan	Sinclair	Pirie	Hutchinson	Purdie	Ford	McKinnon
	8th	Allan	Martin	Caldwell	McPhail	Phillip	Strachan	Hoggan	Sinclair	Pirie	Hutchinson	Purdie	Ford (7)	Robinson (9)
	11th	Allan	Martin	Caldwell	McPhail	Phillip	Strachan	Hoggan	Sinclair	Pirie	Hutchinson	Purdie	Ford (11)	Robinson (4)
	15th	Allan	Martin	Caldwell	McPhail	Phillip	Strachan	Hoggan	Sinclair	Pirie	Hutchinson	Purdie	Ford (2)	Robinson (4)
	18th	Allan	Ford	Johnston	Caldwell	Phillip	Strachan	Hoggan	Sinclair	Pirie	Hutchinson	Purdie	McKinnon	Robinson (6)
	22nd	Allan	Ford	Johnston	Caldwell	Phillip	Robinson	Hoggan	Sinclair	Pirie	Hutchinson	Purdie	McKinnon	Strachan (11)
	25th	Allan	Ford	Johnston	Caldwell	Phillip	Robinson	Hoggan	Strachan	Pirie	Hutchinson	Purdie	McKinnon (5)	Sinclair (8)
	29th	Allan	Ford	Johnston	Caldwell	Phillip	Robinson	Hoggan	Strachan	Pirie	Hutchinson	Purdie	McPhail (3)	Laing
Oct	2nd	Allan	Ford	Johnston	Caldwell	Phillip	Robinson	Hoggan	Strachan	Pirie	Hutchinson	Purdie	McPhail (3)	Laing
	6th	Allan	Ford	Caldwell	McKinnon	Phillip	McPhail	Hoggan	Strachan	Pirie	Hutchinson	Purdie	Martin (11)	Robinson (4)
	9th	Donaldson	Martin	Caldwell	Robinson	Phillip	McIntosh	Strachan	Ford	Pirie	Hutchinson	Purdie	Laing (9)	Sinclair
	16th	Donaldson	Caldwell	Gemmell	Robinson	Phillip	McIntosh	Strachan	Ford	Pirie	Hutchinson	Purdie	Sinclair (5)	Hoggan (6)
	23rd	Donaldson	Martin	Caldwell	Ford	McPhail	Gemmell	Hoggan	Sinclair	Pirie	Strachan	Hutchinson	Robinson (4)	Laing (10)
	30th	Donaldson	Martin	Caldwell	Ford	McPhail	Gemmell	Hoggan	Sinclair	Pirie	Strachan	Hutchinson	Robinson (10)	Purdie (9)
Nov	10th	Donaldson	Martin	Caldwell	Gemmell	McPhail	Phillip	Hoggan	Sinclair	Pirie	Ford	Hutchinson	Robinson (9)	Strachan
	13th	Donaldson	Martin	Gemmell	Robinson	McPhail	Phillip	Hoggan	Strachan	Hutchinson	Ford	Purdie	Sinclair (5)	Laing
	20th	Donaldson	Martin	Gemmell	Robinson	Phillip	Caldwell	Hoggan	Sinclair	Hutchinson*	Ford	Purdie	Laing	Strachan
	27th	Donaldson	Martin	Gemmell	Robinson	Phillip	Caldwell	Hoggan	Sinclair	Hutchinson	Ford	Purdie	Laing (4)	Strachan (2)
Dec	15th	Donaldson	Gemmell	Johnston	Robinson	Phillip	Caldwell	Hoggan	Sinclair	Hutchinson	Ford	Purdie	Strachan (3)	McKinnon
	27th	Donaldson	Martin	Johnston	Robinson	Phillip	Caldwell	Hoggan	Strachan	Sinclair	Ford	Purdie	Pirie	McPhail
Jan	8th	Donaldson	Ford	Johnston	Strachan	Phillip	Caldwell	Hoggan	Sinclair	Pirie	Hutchinson	Purdie	Robinson	Martin
	22nd	Donaldson	Ford	Johnston	Strachan	Phillip	Caldwell	Hoggan	Sinclair	Pirie	Hutchinson	Purdie	Martin (3)	Robinson (10)
Feb	5th	Donaldson	Ford	Johnston	Strachan	Phillip	Caldwell	Hoggan	Sinclair	Pirie	Hutchinson	Purdie	McIntosh	Martin
	7th	Donaldson	Martin	Johnston	Strachan	Phillip	Caldwell	Hoggan	Sinclair	Pirie	Ford	Purdie	McIntosh (4)	McKinnon
	8th	Donaldson	Ford	Johnston	Robinson	Phillip	Caldwell	Hoggan	Strachan	Pirie	Hutchinson	Purdie	McIntosh (9)	McKinnon (10)
	12th	Donaldson	Ford	Johnston	Strachan	Phillip	Caldwell	Hoggan	Sinclair	Pirie	Hutchinson	Purdie	Robinson (4)	McKinnon (10)
	15th	Donaldson	Ford	Johnston	McKinnon	Phillip	Caldwell	Hoggan	Sinclair	Pirie	Strachan	Purdie	Robinson (4)	McIntosh (10)
	19th	Donaldson	Ford	Gemmell	Caldwell	Phillip	McPhail	Strachan	Sinclair	Pirie	Hutchinson	Purdie	Hoggan (10)	Robinson (8)
	26th	Donaldson	Ford	Johnston	Caldwell	Phillip	McPhail	Hoggan	Strachan	Pirie	Hutchinson	Purdie	Robinson (10)	Sinclair (7)
Mar	2nd	Donaldson	Ford	Johnston	Caldwell	Phillip	McPhail	Robinson	Strachan	Pirie	Hutchinson	Purdie	Laing (4)	Sinclair (9)
	5th	Donaldson	Ford	Gemmell	Caldwell	Phillip	McPhail	Robinson	Strachan	Pirie	Sinclair	Purdie	Laing	Hoggan
	12th	Donaldson	Ford	Gemmell	Caldwell	Phillip	McPhail	Hoggan	Strachan	Pirie	Hutchinson	Purdie	Robinson (4)	Sinclair (7)
	15th	Donaldson	Ford	Gemmell	Robinson	Caldwell	McPhail	Laing	Strachan	Sinclair	Hutchinson	Purdie	Hoggan	Redford I
	19th	Donaldson	Caldwell	Gemmell	Ford	Phillip	McPhail	Strachan	Sinclair*	Pirie	Hutchinson	Purdie	Laing (9)	Robinson (2)
	23rd	Donaldson	Gemmell	Johnston	Ford	Phillip	McPhail	Strachan	Sinclair	Pirie	Hutchinson	Purdie	Hoggan (8)	Caldwell (3)
	26th	Donaldson	Gemmell	Johnston	Ford	Phillip	McPhail	Strachan	Sinclair	Pirie	Hutchinson	Purdie	Robinson	Caldwell
	30th	Donaldson	Gemmell	Johnston	Ford	Phillip	McPhail	Strachan	Sinclair	Pirie	Hutchinson	Purdie	Robinson	Caldwell
Apr	2nd	Donaldson	Gemmell	Johnston	Ford	Phillip	McPhail	Strachan	Sinclair	Pirie	Caldwell	Purdie	Robinson	Laing (11)
	6th	Donaldson	Gemmell	Johnston	Ford	Phillip	McPhail	Strachan	Sinclair	Pirie	Hutchinson	Purdie	Caldwell (3)	Robinson
	9th	Donaldson	Ford	Johnston	Robinson	Phillip	McPhail	Strachan	Sinclair	Pirie	Hutchinson	Purdie	Laing (11)	Caldwell (8)
	12th	Donaldson	Gemmell	Johnston	Ford	Phillip	McPhail	Strachan	Robinson	Pirie	Hutchinson	Purdie	Laing	Caldwell
	16th	Donaldson	Gemmell	Johnston	Robinson	Phillip	McPhail	Strachan	Sinclair	Pirie	Hutchinson	Laing	Morris	Redford I (8)
	19th	Donaldson	Gemmell	Johnston	Ford	Phillip	McPhail	Strachan	Robinson	Pirie	Hutchinson	Caldwell	Laing (9)	Morris
	23rd	Donaldson	Caldwell	Johnston	Ford	Phillip	McPhail	Strachan	Sinclair	Pirie	Hutchinson	Robinson	Laing	Morris
	30th	Donaldson	Ford	Gemmell	Robinson	Phillip	McPhail	Strachan	Sinclair	Pirie	Hutchinson	Purdie	Johnston (11)	Caldwell

Dundee F.C. 1976-77 (BACK, left to right) D. McKinnon, D. Johnston, E. Sinclair, T. Allan, A. Donaldson, G. Arthur, D. McIntosh, I. Phillip, I. Redford. MIDDLE - E. Ferguson (physio), B. Ford, J. Cord, I. Purdie, J. Leonard, A. Caldwell, P. Smith, J. McPhail, G. Redford, G. Strachan, D. Thomson, B. Robinson, G. Blues (coach). FRONT - D. White (manager), W. Hoggan, D. Laing, B. Hutchinson, P. Morris, T. Gemmell, M. Bavidge, B. Pirie, G. Nisbet, J. Martin, H. Robertson (coach).

Season 1977-78

Date			Opponents		Score	Crowd	Scorers
Aug	13th	L	Airdrie	h	3-0	5,467	Hutchinson; Pirie (pen); Sinclair
	17th	LC1	Montrose	a	3-1		Pirie; Strachan; Hutchinson
	20th	L	Hearts	a	1-2	12,000	Pirie
	24th	LC1	Montrose	h	1-0 (4-1)	3,653	Pirie (pen)
	27th	L	Stirling Albion	h	0-1	5,082	-
	31st	LC2	Berwick Rangers	h	4-0	3,183	Sinclair 2; McDougall; Pirie
Sep	3rd	LC2	Berwick Rangers	a	1-1 (5-1)	1,000	McDougall
	10th	L	St Johnstone	a	2-1	3,900	Sinclair; Pirie
	14th	L	Alloa Athletic	a	5-3	1,200	Pirie 3; Sinclair; Redford
	17th	L	Dumbarton	h	2-1	4,725	Sinclair 2
	24th	L	Hamilton Accies	a	1-1	2,500	Williamson
	28th	L	QOS	a	2-0	2,000	Pirie; Williamson
Oct	1st	L	Kilmarnock	h	2-1	4,700	Williamson 2
	th	LC3	QOS	h	0-0	4,647	-
	8th	L	Montrose	a	2-1	2,000	Williamson; Pirie
	15th	L	East Fife	h	2-1	5,000	Pirie; McKinnon
	19th	L	Arbroath	h	2-3	4,123	Pirie 2
	22nd	L	Airdrie	a	0-3	2,000	-
	26th	LC3	QOS	a	0-6 (0-6)	3,500	-
	29th	L	Hearts	h	1-1	9,074	Williamson
Nov	5th	L	Stirling Albion	a	2-0		Simpson; Pirie
	12th	L	St Johnstone	h	5-3	5,753	Pirie 3 (1 pen); Sinclair 2
	19th	L	Dumbarton	a	0-0	1,700	
	26th	L	Hamilton Accies	h	3-0	6,686	Williamson; Shirra; Sinclair
Dec	3rd	L	Kilmarnock	a	0-1	4,500	-
	10th	L	Montrose	h	4-1	5,108	Pirie 2; Sinclair; Williamson
	17th	L	East Fife	a	3-0	2,860	Pirie; Williamson; Scott
	24th	L	Morton	h	3-1	12,458	Pirie 2; McLean o.g.
	31st	L	Stirling Albion	a	3-2	4,000	Pirie 2; Sinclair
Jan	2nd	L	St Johnstone	h	3-4	12,785	Scott; Williamson 2
	7th	L	Hearts	a	2-2	19,720	Pirie; McDougall
	14th	L	Alloa Athletic	h	6-0	6,582	Pirie 4; Scott; Shirra
Feb	6th	SC3	Celtic	a	1-7	22,000	Schaedler
	25th	L	East Fife	h	2-0	4,765	Pirie; Redford
Mar	1st	L	Montrose	a	3-0	1,450	Williamson; McKinnon; Redford
	4th	L	Airdrie	a	3-3	4,000	Redford; McGeachie; Williamson
	8th	L	Hamilton Accies	a	1-0	1,200	Pirie
	11th	L	QOS	h	3-0	5,222	Pirie 2; Redford
	18th	L	Arbroath	a	0-0	4,104	-
	22nd	L	Kilmarnock	h	5-2	5,295	Redford 2; Williamson 2; Scott
	25th	L	Arbroath	h	2-0	6,605	Williamson; Sinclair
Apr	8th	L	Morton	h	1-1	12,305	Redford
	12th	L	Dumbarton	a	1-2	2,000	Redford
	15th	L	Alloa	a	5-1	2,000	Pirie 3; McGeachie; Sinclair
	22nd	L	QOS	h	3-0	6,152	Sinclair; McKinnon; Williamson
	29th	L	Morton	a	3-2	8,000	Redford; Glennie; Pirie
May	1st`	FCF*	Dundee United	a	1-3	10,778	Pirie

* 1975-76 Competition, a.e.t., 1-1 after 90 mts.

Billy Williamson - the ex-Don made a telling contribution from midfield.

Appearances

	League		L/Cup		S/Cup	Total	
Billy Pirie	39	(35)	6	(3)	1	46	(38)
Billy Williamson	37	(17)	6		1	44	(17)
Ian McDougall	36	(1)	6	(2)	1	43+1s	(3)
John McPhail	34		4		1	39	
Eric Sinclair	27	(13)	3	(2)	1	31+6s	(15)
Ian Redford	25	(10)	5		0	30+11s	(10)
Ally Donaldson	22		4		1	27	
Dave Johnston	22		5		0	27+6s	
Dave McKinnon	25	(3)	2		0	27	(3)
Alec Caldwell	18		4		1	23+3s	
Jim Shirra	22	(2)	0		1	23+1s	(2)
Iain Phillip	14		5		1	20+1s	
Jocky Scott	19	(4)	0		1	20+1s	(4)
Thomson Allan	17		2		0	19	
Bobby Ford	13		4		0	17+5s	
Eric Schaedler	15		0		1	16	(1)
Bobby Glennie	13	(1)	0		0	13	(1)
George McGeachie	12	(2)	1		0	13+3s	(2)
Bobby Hutchinson	8	(1)	3	(1)	0	11+2s	(2)
Gordon Strachan	5		4	(1)	0	9+5s	(1)
Jimmy Johnstone	2		0		0	2+1s	
Alan Simpson	2	(1)	0		0	2+2s	(1)
Stuart Turnbull	2		0		0	2	
Derek Laing	0		1		0	1+4s	
John Martin	0		1		0	1+1s	
Roy McCormack	0		0		0	0+3s	
Wilson Hoggan	0		0		0	0+2s	
John Cord	0		0		0	0+2s	

The Record

League	-	Third Place, Division One
League Cup	-	Third round
Scottish Cup	-	First round
Forfarshire Cup	-	Unable to play (Comp. unfinished)
Top Scorer	-	Billy Pirie (38 goals)
Av. Home Gate	-	6,700
Players used	-	30
Sent off (bookings)	-	One (unknown)

Scottish League Division One

		Home			Away			Goals		
	P	W	D	L	W	D	L	F	A	PTS
Morton	39	12	3	5	13	5	1	85-42		58
Hearts	39	13	4	2	11	6	3	77-41		58
Dundee	**39**	**14**	**2**	**3**	**11**	**5**	**4**	**91-44**		**57**
Dumbarton	39	11	8	1	5	9	5	65-48		49
Stirling Albion	39	7	6	7	8	6	5	59-52		42
Kilmarnock	39	8	7	4	6	5	9	52-46		40
Hamilton	39	10	5	5	2	7	10	54-55		36
St Johnstone	39	7	2	10	8	4	8	52-64		36
Arbroath	39	7	7	6	4	6	9	41-56		35
Airdrie	39	8	5	7	4	5	10	50-64		34
Montrose	39	7	5	7	3	4	13	55-71		29
Queen of the South	39	6	7	6	2	6	12	44-68		29
Alloa Athletic	39	4	6	9	4	2	14	71-84		24
East Fife	39	4	7	9	0	4	15	39-74		19

They Wore The Dark Blue

Dundee F.C. Line-Ups 1977-78

Date	1	2	3	4	5	6	7	8	9	10	11	12	13
Aug 13th	Donaldson	Ford	Johnston	McDougall	McGeachie	Phillip	Johnstone	Strachan	Pirie	Sinclair	Hutchinson	Robinson (4)	Redford (10)
17th	Donaldson	Ford	Johnston	McDougall	Caldwell	Phillip	Strachan	Williamson	Pirie	Sinclair	Hutchinson	Laing	Redford (11)
20th	Donaldson	Williamson	Johnston	McDougall	Caldwell	Phillip	Johnstone	Strachan	Pirie	Sinclair	Hutchinson	Ford (7)	Redford (4)
24th	Donaldson	Ford	Williamson	McDougall	Caldwell	Phillip	Strachan	Sinclair	Pirie	Hutchinson	Redford	Johnston (4)	Laing (8)
27th	Donaldson	Ford	Williamson	McDougall	Caldwell	Phillip	Strachan	Sinclair	Pirie	Hutchinson	Redford	Johnston (10)	Johnstone (7)
31st	Donaldson	Ford	Williamson	McDougall	McPhail	Phillip	Laing	Strachan	Pirie	Johnston	Redford	Hoggan (7)	Martin (8)
Sep 3rd	Donaldson	Martin	Williamson	Caldwell	McPhail	Phillip	Ford	McDougall	Pirie	Johnston	Redford	Morris (10)	Strachan (6)
10th	Donaldson	Ford	Johnston	McGeachie	McPhail	Phillip	McDougall	Sinclair	Pirie	Williamson	Redford	Strachan	Laing
14th	Donaldson	Ford	Johnston	McGeachie	McPhail	Phillip	McDougall	Sinclair	Pirie	Williamson	Redford	Strachan (4)	Laing (11)
17th	Donaldson	Ford	Johnston	McGeachie	McPhail	Phillip	McDougall	Sinclair	Pirie	Williamson	Redford	Strachan (7)	Hoggan (11)
24th	Donaldson	Ford	Caldwell	McGeachie	McPhail	Phillip	McDougall	Sinclair	Pirie	Williamson	Redford	Laing (11)	Johnston (4)
28th	Allan	McKinnon	Johnston	McDougall	McPhail	Phillip	Williamson	Caldwell	Pirie	Sinclair	Redford	Strachan	Hutchinson
Oct 1st	Allan	McKinnon	Johnston	McDougall	McPhail	Phillip	Williamson	Caldwell	Pirie	Sinclair	Redford	Strachan (4)	Davidson
5th	Allan	McKinnon	Johnston	McDougall	McPhail	Phillip	Williamson	Caldwell	Pirie	Sinclair	Redford	Laing (10)	Hutchinson (8)
8th	Allan	McKinnon	Johnston	Williamson	McPhail	Phillip	McDougall	Sinclair	Pirie	Hutchinson	Redford	Caldwell (11)	Cord
15th	Allan	Johnston	Caldwell	McKinnon	McPhail	Phillip	McDougall	Sinclair	Pirie	Williamson	Hutchinson	Redford (8)	Cord
19th	Allan	Caldwell	Johnston	McKinnon	McPhail	Phillip	McDougall	Hutchinson	Pirie	Williamson	Redford	Cord (6)	Strachan (5)
22nd	Allan	McKinnon	Johnston	Caldwell	McGeachie	Williamson	McDougall	Strachan	Pirie	Sinclair	Redford	Hutchinson(11)	Cord
26th	Allan	McKinnon	Johnston	McDougall	McPhail	McGeachie	Strachan	Hutchinson	Pirie	Williamson	Redford	Simpson (9)	Cord (4)
29th	Allan	McKinnon	Johnston	McDougall	McPhail	Phillip	Strachan •	Hutchinson	Pirie	Williamson	Simpson	McGeachie(6)	Redford (11)
Nov 5th	Allan	McKinnon	Johnston	Shirra	McPhail	McGeachie	McDougall	Hutchinson	Pirie	Williamson	Redford	Simpson (11)	Cord
12th	Allan	McKinnon	Johnston	Shirra	McPhail	McGeachie	McDougall	Sinclair	Pirie	Williamson	Simpson	Redford (1)	Ford (4)
19th	Allan	McKinnon	Schaedler	Shirra	McPhail	Johnston	McDougall	Sinclair	Pirie	Williamson	Redford	Caldwell (11)	Ford
26th	Allan	McKinnon	Schaedler	Shirra	McPhail	Johnston	McDougall	Sinclair	Pirie	Williamson	Scott	Redford	Ford (10)
Dec 3rd	Allan	McKinnon	Schaedler	Shirra	McPhail	Johnston	McDougall	Sinclair	Pirie	Williamson	Scott	Redford	Ford (10)
10th	Allan	McKinnon	Schaedler	Shirra	McPhail	Ford	McDougall	Sinclair	Pirie	Williamson	Scott	Redford (8)	McGeachie
17th	Allan	McKinnon	Schaedler	Shirra	McPhail	Johnston	McDougall	Sinclair	Pirie	Williamson	Scott	Redford	Turnbull
24th	Allan	McKinnon	Schaedler	Shirra	McPhail	Johnston	McDougall	Sinclair	Pirie	Williamson	Scott	Redford	Turnbull
31st	Allan	McKinnon	Schaedler	Shirra	Caldwell	Johnston	McDougall	Sinclair	Pirie	Williamson	Scott	Redford (3)	Turnbull
Jan 2nd	Allan	McKinnon	Schaedler	Shirra	McPhail	Johnston	McDougall	Sinclair	Pirie	Williamson	Scott	Redford (8)	Caldwell (5)
7th	Donaldson	Turnbull	Schaedler	Shirra	McPhail	Caldwell	McDougall	Sinclair	Pirie	Williamson	Scott	Redford	McKinnon
14th	Donaldson	Turnbull	Johnston	Shirra	McPhail	Caldwell	McDougall	Sinclair	Pirie	Williamson	Scott	Redford (8)	Phillip (3)
Feb 6th	Donaldson	Caldwell	Schaedler	Shirra	McPhail	Phillip	McDougall	Sinclair	Pirie	Williamson	Scott	Redford (8)	McKinnon
25th	Donaldson	Ford	McKinnon	Shirra	McPhail	Glennie	McDougall	Redford	Pirie	Williamson	Scott	Johnston (7)	Sinclair (11)
Mar 1st	Donaldson	Ford	McKinnon	Shirra	McPhail	Glennie	McDougall	Redford	Pirie	Williamson	Scott	McGeachie	Sinclair
4th	Donaldson	Ford	McKinnon	Shirra	McPhail	Glennie	McGeachie	Scott	Pirie	Williamson	Redford	Sinclair (8)	Turnbull
8th	Donaldson	Ford	McKinnon	Shirra	McPhail	Glennie	McDougall	Redford	Pirie	Williamson	Scott	Sinclair	McGeachie (2)
11th	Donaldson	McKinnon	Phillip	Shirra	McPhail	Glennie	McDougall	Scott	Pirie	Williamson	Redford	McGeachie(11)	Sinclair (8)
18th	Donaldson	McPhail	Schaedler	McDougall	Glennie	Shirra	Sinclair	Scott	Pirie	Williamson	Redford	Ford (11)	Phillip
22nd	Donaldson	Ford	Caldwell	Shirra	Glennie	McPhail	McDougall	Redford	Pirie	Williamson	Scott	McCormack(7)	Sinclair (2)
25th	Donaldson	Ford	Caldwell	Shirra	Glennie	McPhail	McDougall	Redford	Pirie	Williamson	Scott	McCormack(11)	Sinclair (2))
Apr 8th	Donaldson	Williamson	Shaedler	Shirra	Glennie	McPhail	Scott	McDougall	Pirie	Caldwell	Redford	Sinclair (4)	Phillip
12th	Donaldson	Caldwell	Schaedler	Shirra	Glennie	McPhail	McDougall	Scott	Pirie	Williamson	Redford	Sinclair	Phillip
15th	Donaldson	Caldwell	Schaedler	McGeachie	Glennie	McPhail	Williamson	McKinnon	Pirie	Sinclair	Redford	McCormack(10)	Johnston (7)
22nd	Donaldson	Caldwell	Schaedler	McGeachie*	Glennie	McPhail	Williamson	McKinnon	Pirie	Sinclair	Redford	McDougall (8)	Scott (7)
29th	Donaldson	Caldwell	Schaedler	McGeachie	Glennie	McPhail	McDougall	McKinnon	Pirie	Sinclair	Redford	Johnston (11)	Shirra (12)

Deadly finisher - McKeil has no chance as Billy Pirie hammers home a penalty kick in a Scottish Cup tie against Falkirk at Dens. The former Arbroath and Aberdeen striker hit an incredible 100 goals in his first three seasons with Dundee.

DC Thomson

Season 1978-79

Date			Opponents		Score	Crowd	Scorers
July	29th	FC1	Arbroath	a	2-1	1,780	Shirra; Morris
Aug	12th	L	Ayr United	a	1-0	3,875	Redford
	16th	LC	Celtic	a	1-3	12,000	Sinclair
	19th	L	Arbroath	h	2-0	6,826	Sinclair; Pirie
	23rd	LC	Celtic	h	0-3 (1-6)	12,698	-
	26th	L	St Johnstone	a	2-0	3,875	Pirie 2
Sep	6th	L	Montrose	h	1-1	4,708	Phillip
	9th	L	Kilmarnock	a	1-1		Lamb
	13th	L	Raith Rovers	a	4-2	4,488	Barr; McDougall; Redford 2
	16th	L	Clyde	h	2-0	6,899	Redford; Williamson
	23rd	L	Clydebank	h	2-0	7,272	Pirie 2
	27th	l	Dumbarton	a	0-0	1,700	-
	30th	L	Hamilton	a	2-1	3,000	Shirra; McGhee
Oct	7th	L	QOS	h	5-0	5,837	Redford; Williamson 2; McGhee; Sinclair
	14th	L	Stirling Albion	a	0-1	2,000	-
	21st	L	Airdrie	h	1-0	5,600	Shirra
	28th	L	Arbroath	a	1-0	3,852	Wells og
Nov	4th	L	St Johnstone	h	1-1	5,918	Caldwell
	11th	L	Kilmarnock	h	0-0	5,620	-
	18th	L	Clyde	a	1-2	2,368	Glennie
	25th	L	Clydebank	a	1-2		Sinclair
Dec	2nd	L	Hamilton	h	1-1	4,646	Pirie
	9th	L	QOS	a	1-3	1,350	Williamson
	16th	L	Stirling Albion	h	2-1	4,641	Pirie; Redford
	23rd	L	Airdrie	a	2-0		Pirie; Murphy
Feb	21st	L	Clydebank	h	2-1	5,901	Redford 2
	25th	SC3	Falkirk	h	1-0	9,671	Pirie (pen)
Mar	3rd	SC4	St Mirren	h	4-1	11,140	Lamb; Sinclair 2; Pirie (pen)
	10th	SCQ	Rangers	a	3-6	23,000	MacLaren 2; Shirra
	14th	L	Montrose	a	2-0	1,800	Redford; Lamb
	24th	L	Dumbarton	h	2-0	5,547	Shirra; Pirie (pen)
	28th	L	Stirling Albion	a	1-0	2,000	Pirie
	31st	L	Ayr United	a	2-1	2,970	Sinclair; Pirie (pen)
Apr	4th	L	QOS	h	4-0	4,546	Sinclair 2; Pirie 2 (1 pen)
	7th	L	Dumbarton	a	2-3	1,500	Pirie; Redford
	11th	L	Raith Rovers	a	2-1	2,769	MacLaren; Redford
	14th	L	Hamilton	h	4-3	5,804	Sinclair 2; MacLaren; Shirra
	18th	L	Clyde	h	2-0	5222	MacLaren; Pirie
	21st	L	Airdrie	a	4-2	2,500	Sinclair; Shirra; Redford 2
	25th	L	Kilmarnock	a	1-2	5,000	Murphy
	28th	L	Montrose	h	1-0	5,941	Pirie (pen)
May	2nd	L	St Johnstone	a	2-3	5,840	Sinclair; Schaedler
	6th	L	Arbroath	h	0-2	8,385	-
	8th	L	Raith Rovers	h	2-0	6,450	Redford; MacLaren
	10th	L	Ayr United	h	2-2	7,692	Redford 2
	13th	FCS	Dundee United	a	2-2*	12,170	Shirra; Murphy

* a.e.t. 1-1 after 90 mts. Dundee won 3-2 on pens. Cup Cash v. Falkirk £6,737; St Mirren £9,473

Jim Shirra - battling qualities added bite to the Dundee midfield.

Appearances

	League	L/Cup	S/Cup	Total	
Ally Donaldson	39	2	3	44	
Bobby Glennie	36 (1)	2	3	41+1s	(1)
Willie Watson	34	2	3	39	
Ian Redford	33 (16)	2	1	36+5s	(16)
Billy Pirie	30 (16)	1	3 (2)	34+1s	(18)
Jim Shirra	30 (5)	1	1 (1)	32+3s	(6)
Eric Sinclair	27 (10)	2 (1)	2 (2)	31+4s	(13)
Eric Schaedler	27 (1)	0	3	30+1s	(1)
Alan Lamb	22 (2)	2	3 (1)	27+2s	(3)
Les Barr	21 (1)	2	3	26	(1)
Stewart MacLaren	21 (4)	0	3 (2)	24	(6)
Alec McGhee	20 (2)	2	2	24	(2)
Billy Williamson	20 (4)	0	0	20+3s	(4)
Peter Millar	16	0	0	16	
Alec Caldwell	14 (1)	0	0	14+2s	(1)
Jimmy Murphy	10 (2)	0	3	13+6s	(2)
Ian McDougall	8 (1)	1	0	9+9s	(1)
Iain Phillip	8 (1)	1	0	9	(1)
Gerry Davidson	3	0	0	3+4s	
George McGeachie	3	0	0	3+2s	
John McPhail	2	1	0	3+1s	
Brian Scrimgeour	3	0	0	3+1s	
Dave McKinnon	1	1	0	2	
Jocky Scott	1	0	0	1+4s	
Chic Bradley	0	0	0	0+1s	
Norrie Brown	0	0	0	0+1s	

The Record

League	-	Division One Champions
League Cup	-	First round
Scottish Cup	-	Quarter-final
Forfarshire Cup	-	Runners up (Final on 28-07-79)
Top Scorer	-	Billy Pirie (18 goals)
Av. Home Gate	-	6,000
Players used	-	26
Sent off (bookings)	-	One (unknown)

Scottish League Division One

		Home			Away			Goals		
	P	W	D	L	W	D	L	F	A	PTS
Dundee	39	13	5	1	11	2	7	69-36		55
Kilmarnock	39	13	5	1	9	5	6	72-36		54
Clydebank	39	15	2	3	9	4	6	78-50		54
Ayr United	39	12	3	5	9	2	8	73-54		47
Hamilton	39	13	4	2	4	5	11	63-61		43
Airdrie	39	9	4	7	7	4	8	72-61		40
Dumbarton	39	9	3	8	5	8	6	58-50		39
Stirling Albion	39	6	4	9	7	5	8	43-55		35
Clyde	39	8	3	8	5	5	10	54-65		34
Arbroath	39	8	6	6	3	5	11	50-61		33
Raith Rovers	39	8	3	8	4	5	11	45-55		32
St Johnstone	39	6	8	6	4	3	12	57-66		31
Montrose	39	4	6	9	4	3	13	55-92		25
Queen of the South	39	8	4	8	0	4	15	43-90		24

Dundee F.C. Line-Ups 1978-79

	1	2	3	4	5	6	7	8	9	10	11	12	13
Aug 12th	Donaldson	Barr	Watson	McDougall	McPhail	Phillip	Lamb	McKinnon	Sinclair	McGhee	Redford I	Williamson	Redford G
16th	Donaldson	Barr	Watson	Glennie	McPhail	McDougall	Lamb	McKinnon	Sinclair	McGhee	Redford I	Shirra (7)	Williamson
19th	Donaldson	Barr	Watson	Lamb	Glennie	Phillip	McGhee	Shirra	Pirie	Sinclair	Redford I	McDougall	Scott (8)
23rd	Donaldson	Barr	Watson	Lamb	Glennie	Phillip	McGhee	Shirra	Pirie	Sinclair	Redford I	Williamson	Scott
26th	Donaldson	Barr	Watson	Lamb	Glennie	Phillip	McGhee	Shirra	Pirie	Sinclair	Redford I	Scott	McDougall (11)
Sep 6th	Donaldson	Barr	Schaedler	Phillip	Glennie	Watson	Lamb	Sinclair	McGhee	Shirra	Redford I	Scott (11)	Caldwell (3)
9th	Donaldson	Barr	Schaedler	Caldwell	Glennie	Watson	Lamb	Shirra	Pirie	Sinclair	McGhee	Phillip	Redford (8)
13th	Donaldson	Barr	Schaedler	Shirra	Watson	Phillip	Lamb	Sinclair	Pirie	Williamson	McGhee	Redford I (8)	McDougall (4)
16th	Donaldson	Barr	Schaedler	McDougall	Glennie	Watson	Lamb	Redford I	Pirie	Williamson	McGhee	Shirra	Bradley
23rd	Donaldson	Barr	Schaedler	McDougall	Glennie	Watson	Lamb	Redford I	Pirie	Williamson	McGhee	Shirra (4)	Sinclair (7)
27th	Donaldson	Barr	Schaedler	Watson	Glennie	Shirra	McDougall	Caldwell	Redford	Williamson	McGhee	Pirie (10)	Phillip
30th	Donaldson	Barr	Schaedler	McDougall	Glennie	Watson	Lamb	Redford	Pirie	Shirra	McGhee	Sinclair	Williamson
Oct 7th	Donaldson	Barr	Schaedler	McDougall	Glennie	Watson	Lamb	Redford	Pirie	Shirra	McGhee	Sinclair (10)	Williamson (4)
14th	Donaldson	Barr	Schaedler	Williamson	Glennie	Watson	Lamb	Redford	Pirie	Shirra	McGhee	Sinclair (4)	Bradley (10)
21st	Donaldson	Barr	Caldwell	Williamson	Glennie	Watson	Lamb	Redford	Pirie	Shirra	McGhee	McPhail (2)	Sinclair (9)
28th	Donaldson	Barr	Caldwell	Williamson	Glennie	Watson	Lamb	Redford	Sinclair	Shirra	McGhee	Schaedler (3)	McDougall (10)
Nov 4th	Donaldson	Barr	Schaedler	Watson	Glennie	Caldwell	Lamb	Redford	Sinclair	McDougall	McGhee	Phillip	McPhail
11th	Donaldson	Barr	Schaedler	Watson	Glennie	Caldwell	Williamson	Redford	Sinclair	Phillip	McGhee	McDougall	McPhail
18th	Donaldson	Glennie	Schaedler	Watson	McPhail	Phillip	Williamson	Lamb	McGhee	Sinclair	Caldwell	McDougall (5)	Brown (7)
25th	Donaldson	Barr	Schaedler	MacLaren	Glennie	Watson	McGhee	Phillip	Sinclair	Redford	Caldwell	McDougall	Williamson
Dec 2nd	Donaldson	Barr	Schaedler	MacLaren	Glennie	Watson	Williamson	Sinclair	Pirie	Redford	McGhee	Shirra (9)	McDougall
9th	Donaldson	Barr	Schaedler	MacLaren	Glennie	Watson	Lamb	Redford	Shirra	Williamson	McGhee	Scott (11)	Caldwell
16th	Donaldson	Barr	Caldwell	MacLaren	Glennie	Watson	Lamb	Redford	Pirie	Shirra	Williamson	Scott (4)	McDougall (2)
23rd	Donaldson	Watson	Caldwell	MacLaren	Glennie	Shirra	McDougall	Redford	Pirie	Scott	Williamson	Murphy (10)	Lamb
Feb 21st	Donaldson	Barr	Schaedler	MacLaren	Scrimgeour	Watson	Murphy	Lamb	Pirie	Shirra	Redford	Glennie (5)	Davidson
25th	Donaldson	Barr	Schaedler	MacLaren	Glennie	Watson	Murphy	Lamb	Pirie	Shirra	Redford	Scrimgeour(11)	Davidson (7)
Mar 3rd	Donaldson	Barr	Schaedler	MacLaren	Glennie	Watson	Murphy	Lamb	Pirie	Sinclair	Shirra	Scrimgeour	Davidson
10th	Donaldson	Barr	Schaedler	MacLaren	Glennie	Watson	Lamb	Sinclair	Pirie	Shirra	Murphy	Scrimgeour	Redford (7)
14th	Donaldson	MacLaren	Schaedler	Lamb	Glennie	Shirra	Murphy	Millar	Pirie	Sinclair	Redford	Scrimgeour	Davidson (10)
24th	Donaldson	Millar	Watson	MacLaren	Glennie	Shirra	Murphy	Sinclair	Pirie	Lamb	Redford	Scrimgeour	Davidson (7)
28th	Donaldson	Millar	Watson	MacLaren	Glennie	Shirra	Davidson	Lamb	Pirie	Sinclair	Redford	Scrimgeour	Murphy
31st	Donaldson	MacLaren	Schaedler	Watson	Glennie	Shirra	Davidson	Millar	Pirie	Sinclair	Redford	Lamb (6)	Murphy
Apr 4th	Donaldson	Millar	Schaedler	Watson	Glennie	Shirra	Murphy	MacLaren	Pirie	Sinclair	Redford	Lamb (9)	Davidson (10)
7th	Donaldson	Millar	Schaedler	Watson	Glennie	Shirra	Davidson	MacLaren	Pirie	Sinclair	Redford	Murphy (7)	Lamb
11th	Donaldson	Caldwell	Schaedler	MacLaren	Glennie	Shirra	Murphy	Miller	Pirie	Lamb	Redford	Williamson(11)	Davidson
14th	Donaldson	Millar	Schaedler	Watson	Glennie	Shirra	Williamson	MacLaren	Pirie	Sinclair	Murphy	Caldwell (3)	Davidson
18th	Donaldson	Millar	Caldwell	Watson	Glennie	Shirra	Williamson	MacLaren	Pirie	Sinclair	Murphy	Redford I (6)	McDougall (8)
21st	Donaldson	Millar	Caldwell	Watson	Glennie	Shirra	Williamson	MacLaren	Pirie	Sinclair	Murphy	McDougall	Redford I (11)
25th	Donaldson	Millar	Caldwell	Watson	Glennie	Shirra	Williamson	MacLaren	Pirie	Sinclair	Redford	Murphy (7)	Schaedler
28th	Donaldson	Millar	Schaedler	MacLaren	Glennie	Watson	Sinclair	Redford	Pirie	Shirra	Murphy	Williamson	McGeachie (11
May 2nd	Donaldson	Millar	Schaedler	MacLaren	Glennie	Watson	Sinclair	Redford	Pirie	Shirra	Murphy	Williamson(11)	McGeachie (6)
6th	Donaldson	Millar	Schaedler	MacLaren	Glennie	McGeachie	Sinclair	Redford	Pirie	Williamson	Shirra*	McDougall (2)	Murphy (8)
8th	Donaldson	Millar	Schaedler	McGeachie	Glennie	Scrimgeour	Williamson	MacLaren	Pirie	Sinclair	Redford	Murphy (10)	McDougall (4)
10th	Donaldson	Millar	Schaedler	McGeachie	Glennie	Scrimgeour	Williamson	Shirra	Pirie	Sinclair	Redford	Murphy (10)	McDougall (9)

Stewart MacLaren watches as Bobby Glennie and Les Barr clear from Jimmy Bone and Jacky Copland of St Mirren in the Scottish Cup tie at Dens. Billy Stark and Lex Richardson are the other Saints.

DC Thomson

They Wore The Dark Blue

Season 1979-80

Date			Opponents		Score	Crowd	Scorers
July	28th	FCF*	Forfar Athletic	a	1-3	2,000	Pirie
Aug	1st	FCS	Brechin City	a	2-1	700	Sinclair 2
	6th	AS1	Kilmarnock	h	1-1	3,832	Shirra
	8th	AS1	Kilmarnock	a	3-3 (4-4)**4,000		Sinclair; Redford 2 (1 pen)
	11th	L	Dundee United	a	0-3	17,968	-
	18th	L	St Mirren	h	4-1	8,350	Redford 4
	25th	L	Hibernian	a	2-5	7,344	Paterson o.g.; Redford (pen)
	29th	LC1	Cowdenbeath	a	4-1	1,551	Sinclair 2; Shirra; Redford (pen)
Sep	1st	LC1	Cowdenbeath	h	3-1 (7-2)	4,553	Sinclair; Shirra 2
	4th	AS2	Sheffield United	a	1-2	7,596	Williamson
	8th	L	Partick Thistle	h	2-2	6,400	Sinclair; Redford
	11th	AS2	Sheffield United	h	0-1 (1-3)	6,866	-
	15th	L	Morton	h	4-3	7,243	MacLaren; Sinclair; Murphy; Redford
	22nd	L	Rangers	a	0-2	23,000	-
	26th	LC2	Ayr United	h	2-1	5,133	Sinclair; Murphy
	29th	L	Aberdeen	h	0-4	11,800	-
Oct	6th	L	Kilmarnock	a	1-3	5,500	MacLaren
	10th	LC2	Ayr United	a	1-0 (3-1)		Redford
	13th	L	Celtic	a	0-3	25,000	-
	20th	L	Dundee United	h	1-0	16,300	Sinclair
	27th	L	St Mirren	a	2-4	6,000	McGeachie; Murphy
	31st	LCQ	Hamilton	a	1-3	3,871	Sinclair
Nov	3rd	L	Hibernian	h	2-1	6,879	Millar; Fletcher
	10th	L	Partick Thistle	a	3-2	5,500	Miller; Pirie; Sinclair
	14th	LCQ	Hamilton	h	1-0 (2-3)	5,696	Pirie
	17th	L	Morton	a	0-2	6,500	-
	24th	L	Rangers	h	3-1	13,342	Pirie; Sinclair; Shirra
Dec	15th	L	Kilmarnock	h	3-1	6,000	Mackie; Ferguson; Pirie
	22nd	L	Dundee United	a	0-2	15,431	-
Jan	5th	L	Partick Thistle	h	1-1	6,788	Pirie
	12th	L	Morton	h	1-0	7,922	Redford
	30th	SC3	Dundee United	a	1-5	18,604	Pirie
Feb	2nd	L	Aberdeen	h	1-3	7,661	Redford
	9th	L	Kilmarnock	a	1-1	4,500	Fleming
	23rd	L	Celtic	a	2-2	23,000	Murphy; Aitken o.g.
Mar	1st	L	Dundee United	h	1-1	15,110	Shirra
	8th	L	St Mirren	a	1-2	6,000	Sinclair
	12th	L	Rangers	a	0-1	15,000	-
	15th	L	Hibernian	h	3-0	8,100	Corrigan; Shirra; Ferguson
	19th	L	Aberdeen	a	0-3	8,000	-
	25th	L	Hibernian	a	0-2	5,000	-
	29th	L	Morton	a	1-1	3,500	MacLaren
Apr	2nd	L	St Mirren	h	1-3	6,031	Ferguson
	5th	L	Rangers	h	1-4	12,948	Sinclair
	9th	L	Aberdeen	a	1-2	12,000	Fleming
	12th	L	Partick Thistle	a	0-3	5,000	-
	19th	L	Celtic	h	5-1	14,633	Ferguson 2 (1 pen); Fleming; Sinclair; Mackie
	26th	L	Kilmarnock	h	0-2	4,600	-
	30th	L	Celtic	h	0-2	10,500	-

*1978-79 Final; ** Dundee qualified on "away goals". Cup Cash v. Dundee Utd £22,000

Ian Redford - the talented striker joined Rangers for a record fee of £210,000.

Appearances

	League	L/Cup	S/Cup	AS/Cup	Total	
Ally Donaldson	36	6	1	3	46	
Eric Sinclair	35 (8)	6 (5)	1	4 (1)	46	(14)
Bobby Glennie	35	5	1	4	45+1s	
Stewart MacLaren	28 (3)	5	1	2	36	(3)
Jimmy Murphy	28 (3)	5 (1)	1	4	38+3s	(4)
George McGeachie	28 (1)	5	0	2	35+1s	(1)
Les Barr	26	5	0	4	35+4s	
Peter Millar	26 (2)	4	1	0	31+2s	(2)
Jim Shirra	27 (3)	3 (3)	1	4	35+6s	(6)
Eric Schaedler	27	2	1	0	30	
Peter Mackie	22 (2)	0	1	0	23	(2)
Ian Redford	13 (9)	3 (2)	1	4 (2)	21	(13)
Ian Fleming	16 (3)	0	0	0	16	(3)
John Fletcher	12 (1)	4	0	3	19+5s	(1)
Stuart Turnbull	8	6	0	4	18	
Billy Pirie	9 (4)	2 (1)	1 (1)	0	12	(6)
Iain Ferguson	9 (5)	0	0	0	9+4s	(5)
Willie Watson	4	2	0	2	8+1s	
Billy Williamson	3	2	0	3 (1)	8+4s	(1)
Alec Caldwell	2	1	0	0	3+2s	
Dennis Corrigan	2 (1)	0	0	0	2+4s	(1)
Bobby Geddes	0	0	0	0	1	
Alec McGhee	0	0	0	0	0+2s	
Gerry Davidson	0	0	0	0	0+1s	

The Record

League	-	Ninth Place, Premier Division
League Cup	-	Quarter-final
Scottish Cup	-	First round
Anglo Scottish Cup	-	First round
Forfarshire Cup	-	Runners-up (Final 07-08-82)
Top Scorer	-	Eric Sinclair (14 goals)
Av. Home Gate	-	9,900
Players Used	-	24
Sent off (booked)	-	Five (20)

Scottish League Premier Division

		Home			Away			Goals		
	P	W	D	L	W	D	L	F A	PTS
Aberdeen	36	10	4	4	9	6	3	68-36	48
Celtic	36	13	3	2	4	8	5	61-38	47
St Mirren	36	11	5	2	4	7	7	56-49	42
Dundee United	36	9	7	2	3	6	9	43-30	37
Rangers	36	11	5	2	4	2	12	50-46	37
Morton	36	9	4	5	5	4	9	51-46	36
Partick Thistle	36	6	8	4	5	6	7	43-47	36
Kilmarnock	36	7	6	5	4	5	9	36-52	33
Dundee	**36**	**9**	**3**	**6**	**1**	**3**	**14**	**47-73**	**26**
Hibernian	36	6	4	8	0	2	16	29-67	18

Dundee F.C. Line-Ups 1979-80

	1	2	3	4	5	6	7	8	9	10	11	12	13
Aug 6th	Donaldson	Barr	Turnbull	Williamson	Glennie	Watson	Fletcher	Shirra	Sinclair	Redford	Murphy	McGhee	Caldwell
8th	Donaldson	Barr	Turnbull	MacLaren	Glennie	Watson	Fletcher	Shirra	Sinclair	Redford	Murphy	McGhee	Williamson (8)
11th	Donaldson	Barr	Turnbull	MacLaren	Glennie	Watson	Fletcher	Shirra	Sinclair	Redford	Murphy	McGhee	Williamson (8)
18th	Donaldson	Barr	Turnbull	Williamson	Glennie	MacLaren	Fletcher	Shirra	Sinclair	Redford	Murphy	McGhee (7)	Caldwell
25th	Donaldson	Barr	Turnbull	MacLaren	Glennie	Fletcher	Shirra	Williamson	Sinclair	Redford	Murphy	Millar	McGeachie
29th	Donaldson	Barr	Turnbull	MacLaren	Glennie	Watson	Williamson	Shirra	Sinclair	Redford	Murphy	Fletcher (9)	McGeachie (5)
Sep 1st	Donaldson	Barr	Turnbull	MacLaren	Glennie	McGeachie	Fletcher	Williamson	Sinclair	Shirra	Murphy	McGhee (9)	Watson
4th	Donaldson	Barr	Turnbull	MacLaren	Glennie	McGeachie	Williamson	Redford I	Sinclair	Shirra	Murphy	Geddes	Caldwell (9)
8th	Donaldson	Barr	Turnbull	MacLaren	Glennie	McGeachie	Fletcher	Shirra	Sinclair	Redford	Murphy	Watson (3)	Williamson (4)
11th	Geddes	Barr	Turnbull	Williamson	Glennie	McGeachie	Fletcher	Shirra	Sinclair	Redford	Murphy	Donaldson	Caldwell (7)
15th	Donaldson	Millar	Schaedler	Barr	Glennie	Watson	Murphy	MacLaren	Sinclair	Redford	Fletcher	McGeachie	Shirra
22nd	Donaldson	Barr	Turnbull	Watson	Glennie	McGeachie	Murphy	Millar	Sinclair	MacLaren	Redford	Shirra	Fletcher
26th	Donaldson	Barr	Turnbull	Millar	Glennie	McGeachie	Fletcher	MacLaren	Sinclair	Redford	Murphy	Shirra (10)	Watson
29th	Donaldson	Turnbull	Schaedler	Watson	Glennie	McGeachie	Murphy	Millar	Sinclair	MacLaren	Shirra	Fletcher (4)	Davidson
Oct 6th	Donaldson	Turnbull	Schaedler	Millar	Glennie	McGeachie	MacLaren	Shirra*	Sinclair	Redford	Murphy	Watson	Fletcher (7)
10th	Donaldson	Turnbull	Schaedler	McGeachie	Glennie	Watson	Fletcher	Millar	Sinclair	Redford	Murphy	Williamson	Davidson
13th	Donaldson	Turnbull	Schaedler	Millar	Glennie	McGeachie	Fletcher	MacLaren*	Sinclair	Redford	Murphy	Barr (2)	Shirra (7)
20th	Donaldson	Barr	Schaedler	Millar	Glennie	Caldwell	Fletcher	McGeachie	Sinclair	Redford	Murphy	Shirra (10)	Turnbull
27th	Donaldson	Barr	Schaedler	Millar	Glennie	Caldwell	Fletcher	McGeachie	Sinclair	Redford	Murphy	Shirra	Turnbull
31st	Donaldson	Turnbull	Schaedler	Millar	Caldwell	Barr	McGeachie	MacLaren	Pirie	Sinclair	Shirra	Glennie (2)	Murphy
Nov 3rd	Donaldson	Barr	Schaedler	Millar	Glennie	McGeachie	Fletcher	MacLaren	Pirie	Sinclair	Murphy	Shirra	Ferguson
10th	Donaldson	Barr	Schaedler	Millar	Glennie	McGeachie	Fletcher	MacLaren	Pirie	Sinclair	Murphy	Shirra (7)	Turnbull
14th	Donaldson	Barr	Turnbull	Millar	Glennie	McGeachie	Fletcher	MacLaren	Pirie	Sinclair	Murphy	Shirra (3)	Davidson (11)
17th	Donaldson	Barr	Schaedler	Millar	Glennie	McGeachie	Murphy	MacLaren	Pirie	Sinclair	Shirra	Williamson(11)	Davidson
24th	Donaldson	McGeachie	Schaedler	Millar	Glennie	MacLaren	Mackie	Sinclair	Pirie	Shirra	Murphy	Fletcher	Turnbull
Dec 15th	Donaldson	McGeachie	Schaedler	Mackie	Glennie	MacLaren	Ferguson	Sinclair	Pirie	Shirra	Murphy	Barr	Fletcher (7)
22nd	Donaldson	McGeachie	Schaedler*	Mackie	Glennie	MacLaren	Ferguson	Sinclair	Pirie	Shirra	Murphy	Barr (7)	Smith P
Jan 5th	Donaldson	Barr	Shirra	MacLaren	Glennie	Williamson	Mackie	Redford	Pirie	Sinclair	Murphy	Fletcher	Ferguson
12th	Donaldson	Barr	Schaedler	MacLaren	Glennie	Shirra	Mackie	Redford	Pirie	Sinclair	Murphy	Fletcher (8)	Williamson (3)
30th	Donaldson	Millar	Schaedler	MacLaren*	Glennie	Shirra	Murphy	Mackie	Pirie	Sinclair*	Redford	Barr (7)	Fletcher
Feb 2nd	Donaldson	Barr	Schaedler	Millar	Glennie	Shirra	Fletcher	Mackie	Pirie	Redford	Murphy	Williamson	Ferguson
9th	Donaldson	Barr	Schaedler	MacLaren	Glennie	Shirra	Mackie	Millar	Fleming	Sinclair	Redford	Williamson	Murphy (9)
23rd	Donaldson	Millar	Schaedler	McGeachie	Glennie	Shirra	Fletcher	Mackie	Fleming	Sinclair	Murphy	Barr (7)	Ferguson
Mar 1st	Donaldson	Barr	Schaedler	McGeachie	Glennie	Shirra	Mackie	Millar	Fleming	Sinclair	Murphy	Fletcher	Ferguson
8th	Donaldson	Barr	Schaedler	McGeachie	Glennie	Shirra	Mackie	Millar	Fleming	Sinclair	Murphy	Fletcher	Ferguson (11)
12th	Donaldson	Millar	Schaedler	MacLaren	Glennie	McGeachie	Mackie	Sinclair	Fleming	Shirra	Murphy	Barr	Corrigan (11)
15th	Donaldson	MacLaren	Schaedler	Millar	Glennie	McGeachie	Mackie	Sinclair	Fleming	Shirra	Corrigan	Ferguson (8)	Murphy (11)
18th	Donaldson	Barr	Schaedler	MacLaren	Glennie	McGeachie	Mackie	Millar	Fleming	Sinclair	Murphy	Corrigan (10)	Ferguson (11)
25th	Donaldson	Barr	Schaedler	MacLaren	McGeachie	Shirra	Mackie	Millar	Fleming	Sinclair	Corrigan	Turnbull	Murphy (11)
29th	Donaldson	Barr	Schaedler	MacLaren	Glennie	McGeachie	Ferguson	Mackie	Fleming	Sinclair	Murphy	Shirra (8)	Millar (11)
Apr 2nd	Donaldson	Barr	Schaedler	MacLaren	Glennie	McGeachie	Mackie	Sinclair	Fleming	Shirra	Murphy	Ferguson (11)	Millar (3)
5th	Donaldson	Barr	Millar	MacLaren	Glennie	McGeachie	Mackie	Sinclair	Fleming	Shirra	Ferguson	Murphy	Corrigan
9th	Donaldson	Barr	Millar	MacLaren	Glennie	McGeachie	Mackie	Sinclair	Fleming	Shirra	Ferguson	Murphy	Corrigan (8)
12th	Donaldson	MacLaren	Millar	Mackie	Glennie	McGeachie	Ferguson	Sinclair	Fleming	Shirra	Murphy	Corrigan (11)	Barr
19th	Donaldson	Barr	Schaedler	Millar	Glennie	McGeachie	Mackie	Sinclair	Fleming	Shirra	Ferguson	Fletcher	Corrigan
26th	Donaldson	Barr	Schaedler	Millar	Glennie	McGeachie	Mackie	Sinclair	Fleming	Shirra	Ferguson	Williamson(10)	Corrigan (11)
30th	Donaldson	Barr	Schaedler	Millar	Glennie	McGeachie	Mackie	Sinclair	Fleming	Shirra	Ferguson	Murphy	Williamson

Dens delight - one of the few highlights of a disappointing season was the 3-1 win over Rangers at Dens. Ibrox goalkeeper Peter McCloy lies spreadeagled and left-back Ally Dawson is helpless as Eric Sinclair nets Dundee's second goal. DC Thomson

Season 1980-81

Date			Opponents		Score	Crowd	Scorers
Aug	9th	L	Dunfermline	a	0-1	3,660	-
	16th	L	Ayr United	h	0-0	5,328	-
	23rd	L	St Johnstone	a	0-1	4,197	-
	26th	LC1	Arbroath	h	2-0	3,745	Fletcher 2
	30th	LC1	Arbroath	a	3-0 (5-0)	2,855	MacLaren; Sinclair; Fletcher
Sep	3rd	LC2	Kilmarnock	h	0-0	4,388	-
	6th	L	Clydebank	a	0-3	1,296	-
	9th	L	Hibernian	h	1-2	5,304	Scrimgeour
	13th	L	Berwick Rangers	h	2-2	3,782	Fraser; Shirra (pen)
	17th	L	Motherwell	a	2-3	2,300	Fraser; McGeachie
	20th	L	Falkirk	h	4-0	3,993	Fletcher; Mackie; Sinclair 2
	24th	LC2	Kilmarnock	a	0-0 (0-0)*	2,401	-
	27th	L	Stirling Albion	a	1-1	1,557	Shirra (pen)
Oct	4th	L	Dumbarton	h	3-1	3,553	Sinclair; Fleming; Shirra
	8th	LCQ	Aberdeen	h	0-0	10,308	-
	11th	L	Raith Rovers	a	0-0	3,255	-
	14th	L	Hamilton	h	2-0	3,170	Fraser; Sinclair
	18th	L	East Stirling	h	2-0	3,771	Murphy; Sinclair
	25th	L	Berwick Rangers	a	1-0	1,080	Sinclair
	29th	LCQ	Aberdeen	a	1-0 (1-0)	14,060	Fraser
Nov	1st	L	Clydebank	h	2-1	4,700	Fraser; Stephen
	5th	LCS	Ayr United	a	1-1	6,801	Sinclair
	8th	L	Motherwell	h	2-1	5,112	Ferguson (pen); Shirra (pen)
	15th	L	Falkirk	a	3-0	2,800	Sinclair 2; McGeachie
	19th	LCS	Ayr United	h	3-2 (4-3)	9,438	Williamson; Fraser; Sinclair
	22nd	L	Stirling Albion	h	5-1	4,815	Sinclair; Stephen 2; Mackie 2
	29th	L	Dumbarton	a	2-1	958	Stephen 2
Dec	6th	LCF	Dundee United	Dens	0-3	24,446	-
	13th	L	East Stirling	a	2-0	1,026	A. Geddes; Murphy
	19th	L	Hibernian	h	1-0	7,454	Sinclair
	26th	L	Ayr United	a	0-1	4,026	-
Jan	1st	L	St Johnstone	h	2-2	8,573	Stephen; Sinclair
	3rd	L	Hamilton	a	2-4	2,381	Stephen; A. Geddes
	24th	SC3	Falkirk	a	0-1	4,486	-
	31st	L	Ayr United	h	2-4	4,724	Scrimgeour; Sinclair
Feb	7th	L	Hibernian	a	0-0	4,989	-
	21st	L	Motherwell	a	1-4	2,072	Williamson
Mar	11th	L	Dumbarton	h**	2-1	2,812	Scrimgeour; Sinclair
	14th	L	Raith Rovers	h	3-1	6,315	A. Geddes 2; Scrimgeour
	18th	L	Dunfermline	h	2-0	3,153	A. Geddes 2
	21st	L	Hamilton	a	3-1	1,492	Sinclair 2; Murphy
	24th	L	Stirling Albion	a	1-0	752	Murphy
	28th	L	Berwick Rangers	h	0-0	3,509	-
Apr	1st	L	Raith Rovers	h	2-1	6,178	Sinclair; Fraser
	4th	L	St Johnstone	h	4-1	8,586	Sinclair 2; Scrimgeour; Mackie
	11th	L	Dunfermline	a	1-1	3,000	Mackie
	18th	L	Clydebank	h	1-0	4,771	A. Geddes
	25th	L	Falkirk	a	2-1	4,500	Murphy; Stephen
May	2nd	L	East Stirling	a	1-0	5,762	Sinclair

*After extra-time. Dundee won 5-4 on penalties.** Earlier game on February 28th abandoned after 63 minutes due to flooding at 0-0.

Jimmy Murphy - the wee winger was a great crowd pleaser for the Dark Blues.

The Record		
League	-	Runners-up, Division One
League Cup	-	Runners-up
Scottish Cup	-	First round
Forfarshire Cup	-	Unable to fit in
Top Scorer	-	Eric Sinclair (22)
Av. Home Gate	-	4,900
Players used	-	24
Sent off (booked)	-	One (19)

Appearances

	League		L/Cup		S/Cup	Total	
Bobby Glennie	39		9		1	49	
Eric Sinclair	36	(19)	9	(3)	1	46	(22)
Stewart MacLaren	31		8	(1)	1	40	(1)
Erich Schaedler	31		8		1	40+1s	
Cammy Fraser	30	(5)	6	(2)	1	37	(7)
Les Barr	30		5		0	35+3s	
George McGeachie	26	(2)	8		1	35+3s	(2)
Peter Mackie	25	(5)	7		1	33+11s	(5)
Bobby Geddes	21		9		0	30	
Jimmy Murphy	20	(5)	4		0	24+19s	(5)
Ray Stephen	19	(8)	2		1	22+5s	(8)
Jim Shirra	15	(4)	6		0	21+7s	(4)
Andy Geddes	18	(7)	1		1	20	(7)
Billy Williamson	15	(1)	5	(1)	0	20+7s	(2)
Brian Scrimgeour	17	(5)	1		0	18+5s	(5)
Stewart McKimmie	15		0		0	15+2s	
Alan Blair	14		0		0	14	
Ian Fleming	7	(1)	4		0	11+1s	(1)
John Fletcher	6	(1)	4	(3)	0	10+3s	(4)
Ian Ferguson	7	(1)	0		1	8+4s	(1)
Jocky Scott	2		3		0	5	

Scottish League Division One

		Home			Away			Goals		
	P	W	D	L	W	D	L	F A		PTS
Hibernian	39	14	4	2	10	5	4	67-24		57
Dundee	**39**	**14**	**4**	**2**	**8**	**4**	**7**	**64-40**		**52**
St Johnstone	39	12	3	5	8	8	3	64-45		51
Raith Rovers	39	11	7	1	9	3	8	49-32		50
Motherwell	39	14	5	1	5	6	8	65-51		49
Ayr United	39	11	5	3	6	6	8	59-42		45
Hamilton	39	9	5	6	6	2	11	61-57		37
Dumbarton	39	8	5	6	5	6	9	49-50		37
Falkirk	39	7	4	8	6	4	10	39-52		34
Clydebank	39	8	6	5	2	7	11	48-59		33
East Stirling	39	4	10	6	2	7	10	41-56		29
Dunfermline	39	6	3	11	4	4	11	41-58		27
Stirling Albion	39	4	6	9	2	5	13	18-48		23
Berwick Rangers	39	5	6	8	0	6	14	31-82		22

Appearances (Ctd.)

	League	L/Cup	S/Cup	Total
Evan Williams	4	0	1	5
Dennis Corrigan	1	0	0	1
Gerry Davidson	0	0	0	0+1s

They Wore The Dark Blue

Dundee F.C. Line-Ups 1980-81

Date	1	2	3	4	5	6	7	8	9	10	11	12	13
Aug 9th	Geddes B	Barr	Schaedler	MacLaren	Glennie	McGeachie	Mackie	Fleming	Ferguson	Corrigan	Murphy	Shirra (11)	Fletcher
16th	Geddes B	Barr	Schaedler	MacLaren	Glennie	McGeachie	Mackie	Fleming	Ferguson	Shirra	Murphy	Corrigan (4)	Fletcher (7)
23rd	Geddes B	Barr	Schaedler	MacLaren	Glennie	McGeachie	Mackie	Ferguson	Sinclair	Shirra	Murphy	Fleming (2)	Corrigan (8)
26th	Geddes B	MacLaren	Schaedler	Glennie	McGeachie	Shirra	Scott	Fleming	Fletcher	Sinclair	Murphy	Mackie (7)	Stephen (11)
30th	Geddes B	McGeachie	Schaedler	MacLaren	Glennie	Shirra	Mackie	Fleming	Sinclair	Scott		Murphy (9)	Barr (7)
Sep 3rd	Geddes B	McGeachie	Schaedler	MacLaren	Glennie	Shirra	Scott	Fleming	Sinclair	Mackie	Fletcher	Murphy (8)	Barr (2)
6th	Geddes B	McGeachie	Schaedler	MacLaren	Glennie	Shirra	Mackie	Scrimgeour	Sinclair	Scott	Fletcher	Murphy (10)	Barr
9th	Geddes B	Barr	Schaedler	Scrimgeour	Glennie	McGeachie	Mackie	Scott	Sinclair	Ferguson	Shirra	Murphy (10)	Williamson (8)
13th	Geddes B	Barr	Schaedler	Fraser	Glennie	McGeachie	Fletcher	Williamson	Sinclair	Scrimgeour	Shirra	Mackie (10)	Murphy (11)
17th	Geddes B	Barr	Schaedler	Fraser	Glennie	McGeachie	Fletcher	MacLaren	Sinclair	Scrimgeour	Williamson	Mackie	Shirra
20th	Geddes B	Barr	Schaedler	Fraser	Glennie	McGeachie	Fletcher	MacLaren	Sinclair	Mackie	Williamson	Shirra (11)	Murphy (10)
24th	Geddes B	Barr	Schaedler	Fraser	Glennie	MacLaren	Mackie	Scrimgeour	Sinclair	Fletcher	Shirra	Murphy (7)	Williamson(10)
27th	Geddes B	Barr	Schaedler	Fraser	Glennie	MacLaren	Mackie	Scrimgeour	Sinclair	Fletcher	Shirra	Murphy (10)	Williamson
Oct 4th	Geddes B	Barr	Williamson	Fraser	Glennie	MacLaren	Mackie	Scrimgeour	Sinclair	Fleming	Shirra	Murphy (4)	Schaedler (8)
8th	Geddes B	Barr	Schaedler	Fraser	Glennie	MacLaren	Mackie	McGeachie	Sinclair	Fleming	Shirra	Murphy (10)	Schaedler
11th	Geddes B	Barr	Schaedler	Fraser	Glennie	MacLaren	Mackie	McGeachie	Sinclair	Fleming	Shirra	Murphy (7)	Williamson (3)
14th	Geddes B	Barr	McKimmie	Fraser	Glennie	MacLaren	Murphy	McGeachie	Sinclair	Fleming	Shirra	Mackie (4)	Williamson(11)
18th	Geddes B	Barr	McKimmie	Fraser	Glennie	MacLaren	Murphy	McGeachie	Sinclair	Fleming	Williamson	Mackie (10)	Shirra (2)
25th	Geddes B	Barr	McKimmie	Fraser	Glennie	MacLaren	Murphy	McGeachie	Sinclair	Fleming	Williamson	Mackie (10)	Shirra (8)
29th	Geddes B	Barr	Schaedler	Fraser	Glennie	MacLaren	Murphy	McGeachie	Sinclair	Mackie	Williamson	Shirra	Fletcher (10)
Nov 1st	Geddes B	Barr	Schaedler	Fraser	Glennie	MacLaren	Murphy	McGeachie	Sinclair	Mackie	Williamson	Stephen (7)	Shirra (8)
5th	Geddes B	Barr	Schaedler	Fraser	Glennie	MacLaren	Murphy	McGeachie	Sinclair	Mackie	Williamson	Shirra (8)	Fletcher (10)
8th	Geddes B	Barr	Schaedler	Fraser	Glennie	MacLaren	Fletcher	Stephen	Sinclair	Shirra	Williamson	Ferguson (7)	Scrimgeour (10)
15th	Geddes B	Barr	Schaedler	Fraser	Glennie	MacLaren	Mackie	Stephen	Sinclair	Shirra	Williamson	McGeachie(2)	Murphy (7)
19th	Geddes B	McGeachie	Schaedler	Fraser	Glennie	MacLaren	Murphy	Stephen	Sinclair	Williamson	Shirra	Mackie (6)	Barr (3)
22nd	Geddes B	Barr	Schaedler	Fraser	Glennie	McGeachie	Mackie	Stephen	Sinclair	Williamson	Geddes A	Murphy (8)	Shirra
29th	Geddes B	Barr	Schaedler	Fraser	Glennie	McGeachie	Mackie	Stephen	Sinclair	Williamson	Geddes A	Murphy	Shirra
Dec 6th	Geddes B	Barr	Schaedler	Fraser	Glennie	McGeachie	Mackie	Stephen	Sinclair	Williamson	Geddes A	Scrimgeour 11	Shirra (10)
13th	Geddes B	Barr	Schaedler	Fraser	Glennie	McGeachie	Mackie	Geddes A	Sinclair	Shirra	Murphy	Ferguson	Williamson
19th	Geddes B	Barr	Schaedler	Fraser	Glennie	McGeachie	Mackie	Stephen	Sinclair	Shirra	Geddes A	Murphy (7)	Williamson
26th	Williams	Barr	Schaedler	Fraser	Glennie	McGeachie	Mackie	Stephen	Sinclair	Shirra*	Geddes A	Murphy (2)	Williamson(11)
Jan 1st	Williams	Barr	Schaedler	Fraser	Glennie	MacLaren	Mackie	Stephen	Sinclair	Geddes A	Murphy	Scrimgeour(5)	Williamson (4)
3rd	Williams	Barr	Schaedler	Williamson	Glennie	Scrimgeour	Geddes A	Stephen	Sinclair	Shirra	Murphy	Mackie (2)	Ferguson (10)
24th	Williams	McGeachie	Schaedler	Fraser	Glennie	MacLaren	Mackie	Ferguson	Sinclair	Stephen	Geddes A	Barr	Williamson (8)
31st	Williams	Barr	Schaedler	Fraser	Glennie	MacLaren	Mackie	Scrimgeour	Sinclair	Williamson	Murphy	Stephen (10)	Ferguson
Feb 7th	Blair	McGeachie	Schaedler	Fraser	Glennie	MacLaren	Mackie	Scrimgeour	Sinclair	Williamson	Murphy	Stephen (7)	McKimmie (3)
21st	Blair	McGeachie	Schaedler	Fraser	Glennie	MacLaren	Mackie	Scrimgeour	Ferguson	Williamson	Murphy	Stephen (11)	McKimmie (2)
Mar 11th	Blair	McGeachie	Schaedler	McKimmie	Glennie	MacLaren	Mackie	Scrimgeour	Sinclair	Stephen	Ferguson	Geddes A	Davidson (11)
14th	Blair	McGeachie	Schaedler	McKimmie	Glennie	MacLaren	Mackie	Scrimgeour	Sinclair	Stephen	Geddes A	Ferguson	Murphy (11)
18th	Blair	McGeachie	Schaedler	McKimmie	Glennie	MacLaren	Mackie	Scrimgeour	Sinclair	Stephen	Geddes A	Ferguson (10)	Murphy (2)
21st	Blair	McGeachie	Schaedler	Fraser	Glennie	MacLaren	Mackie	Stephen	Sinclair	McKimmie	Geddes A	Murphy (7)	Scrimgeour
24th	Blair	McGeachie	Schaedler	Fraser	Glennie	MacLaren	Murphy	Stephen	Sinclair	McKimmie	Geddes A	Mackie	Scrimgeour
28th	Blair	Barr	Schaedler	Fraser	Glennie	MacLaren	Murphy	Stephen	Sinclair	McKimmie	Geddes A	Mackie (8)	Scrimgeour (3)
Apr 1st	Blair	Barr	Schaedler	Fraser	Glennie	MacLaren	Murphy	Stephen	Sinclair	McKimmie	Geddes A	Mackie	Scrimgeour
4th	Blair	Barr	Schaedler	Fraser	Glennie	MacLaren	Murphy	Stephen	Sinclair	McKimmie	Geddes A	Mackie (7)	Scrimgeour(10)
11th	Blair	Barr	McKimmie	Fraser	Glennie	MacLaren	Mackie	Stephen	Sinclair	Scrimgeour	Geddes A	Murphy (7)	McGeachie11
18th	Blair	McGeachie	McKimmie	Fraser	Glennie	MacLaren	Murphy	Ferguson	Sinclair	Scrimgeour	Geddes A	Mackie (2)	Stephen (11)
25th	Blair	Barr	McKimmie	Fraser	Glennie	MacLaren	Murphy	Stephen	Sinclair	Scrimgeour	Geddes A	Mackie	McGeachie
May 2nd	Blair	Barr	McKimmie	Fraser	Glennie	MacLaren	Murphy	Stephen	Sinclair	Scrimgeour	Geddes A	Mackie (8)	McGeachie (11)

Young blood - Bobby Geddes was one of Dundee's successes in the 1980 League Cup Final against Dundee United at Dens. Andy Geddes and George McGeachie look on as the young keeper saves from Paul Sturrock.

DC Thomson

185

Season 1981-82

Date			Opponents		Score	Crowd	Scorers
Aug	1st	FC1	Brechin City	h	2-0	2,000	Sinclair; Mackie
	8th	LC	Raith Rovers	h	1-2	5,362	Fleming
	12th	LC	Rangers	a	1-4	13,039	Fleming
	15th	LC	Morton	h	1-2	4,710	Fleming
	19th	LC	Rangers	h	1-2	9,124	MacDonald
	22nd	LC	Raith Rovers	a	1-1	1,844	Stephen
	26th	LC	Morton	a	2-3	1,675	Cameron; Fleming
	29th	L	Hibernian	a	0-2	5,738	
Sep	5th	L	Partick Thistle	h	4-2	4,653	Fraser; Ferguson; MacDonald; McKinnon o.g.
	12th	L	Dundee United	a	2-5	16,500	Ferguson (pen); Mackie
	19th	L	St Mirren	h	3-0	5,257	Ferguson 2 (1 pen); Sinclair
	26th	L	Morton	a	0-2	2,763	-
Oct	3rd	L	Celtic	h	1-3	13,254	McGeachie
	10th	L	Airdrie	a	2-4	2,500	Ferguson 2 (1 pen)
	17th	L	Rangers	h	2-3	11,956	Cameron; Ferguson
	24th	L	Aberdeen	a	1-2	11,893	Stephen
	31st	L	Hibernian	h	0-0	6,011	-
Nov	7th	L	Partick Thistle	a	2-1	3,337	Mackie 2
	14th	L	Dundee United	h	1-3	15,578	Ferguson
	21st	L	St Mirren	a	0-4	3,600	-
	28th	L	Morton	h	4-1	3,598	Ferguson; Bell; Sinclair; Mackie
Dec	5th	L	Celtic	a	1-3	14,570	Sinclair
	12th	L	Airdrie	h	3-1	3,988	MacDonald; Sinclair; Fraser
	19th	L	Rangers	a	1-2	8,500	McGeachie
Jan	2nd	L	Hibernian	a	1-2	8,281	Sinclair
	23rd	SC3	Raith Rovers	h	1-0	5,474	Stephen
	30th	L	St Mirren	h	0-2	4,628	-
Feb	6th	L	Celtic	h	1-3	11,377	Kidd
	14th	SC4	Meadowbank	h	3-0	4,453	Smith; Ferguson; Mackie
	20th	L	Morton	a	0-2	2,000	-
	27th	L	Aberdeen	a	0-0	9,000	-
Mar	6th	SCQ	Rangers	a	0-2	16,072	-
	10th	L	Dundee United	a	1-1	13,790	Ferguson (pen)
	13th	L	Airdrie	a	2-0	2,000	Fleming; Fraser
	17th	L	Aberdeen	h	0-3	6,126	-
	20th	L	Hibernian	h	2-2	4,345	Fraser; Stephen
	27th	L	Partick Thistle	a	2-0	2,500	Sinclair; Fraser
Apr	3rd	L	Dundee United	h	0-2	12,602	-
	10th	L	St Mirren	a	1-0	3,804	Kidd
	14th	L	Rangers	h	3-1	7,975	Stephen 2; Ferguson
	17th	L	Celtic	a	2-4	14,288	Smith; Ferguson
	21st	L	Partick Thistle	h	1-2	6,463	Sinclair
	25th	L	Morton	h	2-1	5,346	McGeachie; Fraser
May	1st	L	Aberdeen	h	0-5	6,415	-
	8th	L	Rangers	a	0-4	8,500	-
	15th	L	Airdrie	h	1-0	6,600	Ferguson

Cup Cash v. Meadowbank £4,624

Appearances

	League	L/Cup	S/Cup	Total
Bobby Glennie	35	6	3	44
Iain Ferguson	34 (13)	1	3 (1)	38+1s (14)
Cammy Fraser	31 (6)	4	2	37 (6)
George McGeachie	28 (3)	4	3	35+2s (3)
Bobby Geddes	28	4	2	35
Eric Sinclair	24 (7)	5	1	30+1s (7)
Albert Kidd	21 (2)	6	2	29+10s (2)
Danny Cameron	25 (1)	1 (1)	2	28+4s (2)
Les Barr	23	2	0	25+1s
Peter Mackie	22 (4)	1	2 (1)	25+12s (5)
Iain MacDonald	17 (2)	6 (1)	0	23 (3)
Stewart McKimmie	16	4	2	22
Ian Fleming	13 (1)	6 (4)	2	21+3s (5)
Davie Bell	15 (1)	4	1	20+1s (1)
Chic McLelland	15	1	3	19
Jim Smith	17 (1)	0	2 (1)	19 (2)
Ray Stephen	9 (4)	3 (1)	0 (1)	12+18s (6)
Alan Blair	8	2	1	11
Jimmy Murphy	7	3	1	11
Brian Scrimgeour	6	2	1	9+8s
Erich Schaedler	1	1	0	2
Gerry Davidson	1	0	0	1+3s

Albert Kidd - the mercurial midfielder cost Dundee a new record fee of £80,000.

The Record

League	-	Eighth Place, Premier Division
League Cup	-	Qualifying stages only
Scottish Cup	-	Quarter-final
Forfarshire Cup	-	Semi-final (Comp. unfinished)
Top Scorer	-	Iain Ferguson (14 goals)
Av. Home Gate	-	7,600
Players used	-	22
Sent off (booked)	-	Four (21)

Scottish League Premier Division

		Home			Away			Goals		
	P	W	D	L	W	D	L	F	A	PTS
Celtic	36	12	5	1	12	2	4	79-33		55
Aberdeen	36	12	4	2	11	3	4	71-29		53
Rangers	36	10	5	3	6	6	6	57-45		43
Dundee United	36	10	4	4	5	6	7	61-38		40
St Mirren	36	8	4	6	6	5	7	49-52		37
Hibernian	36	8	7	3	3	7	8	38-40		36
Morton	36	9	6	3	0	6	12	31-54		30
Dundee	**36**	**7**	**2**	**9**	**4**	**2**	**12**	**46-71**		**26**
Partick Thistle	36	4	5	9	2	5	11	35-59		22
Airdrie	36	5	4	9	0	4	14	31-76		18

League Cup Section

	P	W	D	L	F	A	PTS
Rangers	6	5	1	0	19-5		11
Morton	6	4	1	1	13-7		9
Raith Rovers	6	1	1	4	7-20		3
Dundee	**6**	**0**	**1**	**5**	**7-14**		**1**

Dundee F.C. Line-Ups 1981-82

		1	2	3	4	5	6	7	8	9	10	11	12	13
Aug	8th	Geddes B	Barr	McKimmie	Fraser	Glennie	MacDonald	Murphy	Kidd	Sinclair	Fleming	Scrimgeour	McGeachie (4)	Stephen (9)
	12th	Geddes B	Barr	McKimmie	Kidd	Glennie	MacDonald	Murphy	McGeachie	Sinclair	Fleming	Scrimgeour	Stephen	Mackie
	15th	Geddes B	McGeachie	McKimmie	Fraser	Glennie	MacDonald	Bell	Kidd	Sinclair	Fleming	Stephen	Mackie (4)	Scrimgeour (8)
	19th	Geddes B	McGeachie	McKimmie	Fraser	Glennie	MacDonald	Bell	Kidd	Sinclair	Fleming	Stephen	Mackie	Scrimgeour
	22nd	Blair	McGeachie	McLelland	Kidd	Glennie	MacDonald	Mackie	Stephen	Fleming	Bell	Murphy	Ferguson (11)	Scrimgeour (3)
	26th	Blair	Cameron	Schaedler	Fraser	Glennie	MacDonald	Ferguson	Bell	Sinclair	Fleming	Kidd	Barr	Stephen
	29th	Geddes B	Cameron	Schaedler	Fraser	Glennie	MacDonald	Ferguson	Bell	Sinclair	Fleming	Kidd	Stephen (9)	Barr (4)
Sep	5th	Geddes B	Barr	Cameron	Fraser	Glennie	MacDonald	Ferguson	Bell	Sinclair	Fleming	McGeachie	Stephen (10)	Mackie
	12th	Geddes B	Barr	Cameron	Fraser	Glennie	MacDonald	Ferguson	Bell	Sinclair	Fleming	McGeachie	Stephen	Mackie (10)
	19th	Geddes B	Barr	Cameron	Fraser	Glennie	MacDonald	Ferguson	Bell	Sinclair	Fleming	McGeachie	Kidd (11)	Mackie
	26th	Geddes B	Barr	Cameron	Kidd*	Glennie	MacDonald	Ferguson	Bell	Sinclair	Fleming	McGeachie	Stephen (11)	Mackie (9)
Oct	3rd	Geddes B	Barr	Cameron	Fraser	Glennie	MacDonald	Ferguson	Bell	Sinclair	Fleming	McGeachie	Scrimgeour (10)	Mackie (11)
	10th	Geddes B	Barr	Cameron	Fraser	Glennie	MacDonald	Ferguson	Bell	Sinclair	Fleming*	McGeachie	Kidd (4)	Mackie (9)
	17th	Geddes B	Cameron	McKimmie	Fraser	Smith	MacDonald	Ferguson	Bell	Mackie	Kidd	McGeachie	Barr	Stephen (11)
	24th	Geddes B	Barr	Cameron	Kidd	Glennie	MacDonald	Ferguson	Bell	Mackie	McGeachie	Murphy	Scrimgeour	Stephen (4)
	31st	Geddes B	Barr	Cameron	Kidd	Glennie	MacDonald	Ferguson	Bell	Mackie	McGeachie	Murphy	Scrimgeour (5)	Stephen (4)
Nov	7th	Geddes B	Barr	Cameron	Fraser	Glennie	MacDonald	Ferguson	Bell	Mackie	McGeachie	Murphy	Scrimgeour	Fleming (11)
	14th	Geddes B	Barr	Cameron	Fraser	Glennie	MacDonald	Mackie	Bell	Ferguson	McGeachie	Murphy	Scrimgeour (4)	Smith
	21st	Geddes B	Barr	McLelland	Fraser	Glennie	MacDonald	Ferguson	Bell	Mackie	Cameron	Murphy	Scrimgeour	Kidd (11)
	28th	Blair	Barr	McLelland	Fraser	Glennie	McGeachie	Ferguson	Bell	Sinclair	Mackie	Cameron	Stephen* (6)	Kidd (4)
Dec	5th	Blair	Barr	McLelland	Fraser	Glennie	MacDonald	Ferguson	Bell	Sinclair	Mackie	Cameron	Scrimgeour (5)	Kidd (8)
	12th	Blair	Barr	McLelland	Fraser	Glennie	MacDonald	Ferguson	Kidd	Sinclair	Mackie	Cameron	Murphy	Scrimgeour
	19th	Blair	Barr	McLelland	Fraser	Glennie	MacDonald	Ferguson	McGeachie	Sinclair	Mackie	Cameron	Kidd	Bell
Jan	2nd	Blair	Barr	McLelland	Fraser	Glennie	MacDonald	Ferguson	McGeachie	Sinclair	Mackie	Cameron	Kidd (11)	Stephen (5)
	23rd	Blair	Scrimgeour	McLelland	Fraser	Glennie	McGeachie	Ferguson	Bell	Sinclair	Mackie	Cameron	Kidd (2)	Stephen (8)
	30th	Blair	Cameron	McLelland	Fraser	Glennie	McGeachie	Ferguson	Kidd	Sinclair	Mackie	Stephen	Scrimgeour	Bell (4)
Feb	6th	Blair	Cameron	McLelland	Kidd	Glennie	McGeachie	Ferguson	Scrimgeour	Sinclair	McKimmie	Stephen	Mackie (2)	Fleming (9)
	14th	Geddes B	McKimmie	McLelland	Kidd	Smith	Glennie	Ferguson	McGeachie	Fleming	Cameron	Murphy	Mackie (4)	Stephen
	20th	Geddes B	McKimmie	Cameron	Mackie	Smith	Glennie	Ferguson	McGeachie	Fleming	Scrimgeour	Murphy	Kidd (2)	Stephen (9)
	27th	Geddes B	McKimmie	McLelland	Fraser	Smith	Glennie	Ferguson	Kidd	Fleming	McGeachie	Mackie	Cameron (10)	Stephen (9)
Mar	6th	Geddes B	McKimmie	McLelland	Fraser	Smith	Glennie	Ferguson	Kidd	Fleming	McGeachie	Mackie	Cameron (8)	Stephen (9)
	10th	Geddes B	McKimmie	McLelland	Fraser	Smith	Glennie	Ferguson	Kidd	Fleming	McGeachie	Mackie	Cameron (9)	Stephen (8)
	13th	Geddes B	McKimmie	McLelland	Fraser	Smith	Glennie	Ferguson	Kidd	Fleming	McGeachie	Mackie	Cameron (2)	Stephen
	17th	Geddes B	Cameron	McLelland	Fraser	Smith	Glennie	Mackie	Kidd	Fleming	McGeachie	Murphy	Sinclair (11)	Scrimgeour
	20th	Geddes B	McKimmie	Cameron	Fraser	Smith	Glennie	Mackie	Kidd	Sinclair	McGeachie	Ferguson	Fleming (11)	Stephen (6)
	27th	Geddes B	McKimmie	Cameron	Fraser	Smith	Glennie	Mackie	Fleming	Sinclair	McGeachie*	Kidd	McLelland	Stephen (8)
Apr	3rd	Geddes B	Barr	Cameron	Fraser	Smith	Glennie	Ferguson	McKimmie	Sinclair	Kidd	Mackie	Scrimgeour (2)	Stephen (10)
	10th	Geddes B	Barr	McLelland	Fraser	Smith	Glennie	Ferguson	McGeachie	Kidd	Scrimgeour	Mackie	Sinclair	Stephen (8)
	14th	Geddes B	Barr	McKimmie	Fraser	Smith	Glennie	Ferguson	Stephen	Sinclair	Kidd	Scrimgeour	Mackie (7)	Davidson (4)
	17th	Geddes B	Barr	McKimmie	Fraser	Smith	Glennie	Ferguson	Kidd	Sinclair	Scrimgeour	Stephen	Mackie (8)	McGeachie (10)
	21st	Geddes B	Barr	McKimmie	Fraser	Smith	Glennie	Ferguson	Stephen	Sinclair	Scrimgeour	Kidd	Mackie (7)	Davidson (10)
	25th	Geddes B	Barr	McKimmie	Fraser	Smith	Glennie	Ferguson	Stephen	Sinclair	Kidd	McGeachie	Mackie (10)	Scrimgeour (11)
May	1st	Geddes B	Barr	McKimmie	Fraser	Smith	Glennie	Ferguson	Stephen	Sinclair	Kidd	McGeachie	Mackie (7)	Scrimgeour
	8th	Geddes B	McKimmie	McLelland	Fraser	Smith	Glennie	Ferguson	Stephen	Sinclair	McGeachie	Mackie	Kidd (5)	Davidson (3)
	15th	Blair	McKimmie	McLelland	Fraser	Smith	Glennie	Ferguson	Stephen	Sinclair	Davidson	McGeachie	Kidd (2)	Mackie

Dundee F.C. Season 1981-82. (BACK, left to right) Eric Sinclair, George McGeachie, Iain MacDonald, Bobby Geddes, Bobby Glennie, Brian Scrimgeour, Les Barr. MIDDLE - Peter Mackie, Ray Stephen, Iain Ferguson, Chic McLelland, John Fletcher, Jimmy Murphy, Ian Fleming. FRONT - Stewart McKimmie, Andy Geddes, Ken Wimhurst (coach), Donald Mackay (manager), Eric Ferguson (physio), Erich Schaedler and Cammy Fraser.

DC Thomson

They Wore The Dark Blue

Season 1982-83

Date			Opponents		Score	Crowd	Scorers
Aug	7th	FCF*	Dundee United	h	1-2	9,027	MacDonald
	14th	LC	Aberdeen	a	3-3	9,002	Ferguson 2; Stephen
	18th	LC	Dumbarton	h	3-2	3,174	Ferguson 2; Mackie
	21st	LC	Morton	a	1-4	1,992	Davidson
	25th	LC	Dumbarton	a	3-2	433	Sinclair; Stephen; Ferguson
	28th	LC	Aberdeen	h	1-5	6,977	Stephen
Sep	1st	LC	Morton	h	3-3	1,888	Ferguson; Kidd; Mackie
	4th	L	Celtic	a	0-2	19,122	-
	11th	L	Motherwell	h	3-1	4,621	Ferguson (2 pens); Stephen
	18th	L	Morton	h	2-0	3,977	Sinclair 2
	25th	L	Kilmarnock	a	0-0	2,105	-
Oct	2nd	L	Rangers	a	1-1	16,797	Fraser
	9th	L	Hibernian	h	2-1	5,287	Smith; Ferguson
	16th	L	Aberdeen	a	0-1	10,863	-
	23rd	L	St Mirren	h	1-1	4,831	Stephen
	30th	L	Dundee United	a	0-1	14,959	-
Nov	6th	L	Celtic	h	2-3	11,681	Fraser 2
	13th	L	Motherwell	a	0-1	3,295	-
	21st	L	Morton	a	2-1	1,984	Bell; Mackie
	27th	L	Kilmarnock	h	5-2	4,311	Fraser; Murphy 2; Bell; Mackie
Dec	11th	L	Hibernian	a	1-1	5,150	Mackie
	18th	L	Aberdeen	h	0-2	6,528	-
	27th	L	St Mirren	a	0-0	4,412	-
Jan	1st	L	Dundee United	h	0-2	18,109	-
	3rd	L	Celtic	a	2-2	16,615	Sinclair 2
	8th	L	Motherwell	h	3-1	5,131	Ferguson; Mackie; Stephen
	15th	L	Morton	h	3-3	4,557	Ferguson; Sinclair; Stephen
	22nd	L	Kilmarnock	a	0-2	1,900	-
	29th	SC3	Brora Rangers	h	2-1	5,823	Ferguson; Sinclair
Feb	5th	L	Rangers	a	1-1	7,096	Bell
	19th	SC4	Aberdeen	a	0-1	19,070	-
	22nd	L	Hibernian	h	0-1	4,363	-
	26th	L	Aberdeen	a	1-3	11,314	Stephen
Mar	2nd	L	Rangers	h	1-0	6,624	Kidd
	5th	L	St Mirren	h	2-5	4,161	Scrimgeour; Kidd
	12th	L	Dundee United	a	3-5	13,433	Fraser; Ferguson (pen); Kidd
	19th	L	Celtic	h	2-1	11,196	Scrimgeour; Kidd
	26th	L	Motherwell	a	1-1	3,222	Ferguson
Apr	2nd	L	Morton	a	0-1	3,000	-
	9th	L	Kilmarnock	a	0-0	3,376	-
	23rd	L	Hibernian	a	0-0	4,000	-
	30th	L	Aberdeen	h	0-2	10,076	-
May	4th	L	Rangers	h	2-1	4,778	Ferguson; Sinclair
	9th	L	St Mirren	a**	1-2	6,000	Mackie
	14th	L	Dundee United	h	1-2	29,016	Ferguson

*1979-80 competition. ** Earlier game on May 7th abandoned after 23 minutes due to flooding with the score 1-1. Fraser scored for Dundee. Cup Cash v. Abdn. £40,000

Iain Ferguson - Dundee's top scorer between 1981 to 1984.

The Record		
League	-	Sixth Place, Premier Division
League Cup	-	Qualifying stages only
Scottish Cup	-	Second round
Forfarshire Cup	-	Unable to fit in
Top Scorer	-	Iain Ferguson (16 goals)
Av. Home Gate	-	8,000
Players used	-	22
Sent off (bookings)	-	None (28)

Appearances

	League	L/Cup	S/Cup	Total	
Cammy Fraser	34 (5)	6	2	42	(5)
Peter Mackie	32 (5)	6 (2)	2	40+4s	(7)
Jim Smith	36 (1)	1	2	39	(1)
Colin Kelly	35	1	2	38	
Iain MacDonald	34	2	1	37	
Stewart McKimmie	28	6	2	36+3s	
Ray Stephen	27 (5)	6 (3)	2	35+3s	(8)
Iain Ferguson	25 (9)	6 (6)	2 (1)	33+4s	(16)
Eric Sinclair	25 (6)	5 (1)	2 (1)	32+7s	(8)
Bobby Glennie	23	6	1	30+3s	
George McGeachie	20	6	2	28+2s	
Davie Bell	21 (3)	0	2	23+7s	(3)
Brian Scrimgeour	19 (2)	1	0	20+4s	(2)
Albert Kidd	15 (4)	1 (1)	0	16+5s	(5)
Ian Fleming	8	0	0	8+4s	
Gerry Davidson	6	1 (1)	0	7+5s	(1)
Chic McLelland	0	5	0	5+1s	
Jimmy Murphy	6 (2)	0	0	6+6s	(2)
Alan Blair	0	3	0	3	
Bobby Geddes	1	2	0	3	
Andy Geddes	0	2	0	2	
Tosh McKinlay	1	0	0	1	
Colin McGlashan	0	0	0	0+2s	

Scottish League Premier Division

		Home			Away			Goals		
	P	W	D	L	W	D	L	F	A	PTS
Dundee United	36	13	4	1	11	4	3	90-35		56
Celtic	36	12	3	3	13	2	3	90-36		55
Aberdeen	36	14	0	4	11	5	2	76-24		55
Rangers	36	9	6	3	4	6	8	52-41		38
St Mirren	36	8	5	5	3	7	8	47-51		34
Dundee	**36**	**8**	**3**	**7**	**1**	**8**	**9**	**42-53**		**29**
Hibernian	36	3	11	4	4	4	10	35-51		29
Motherwell	36	9	3	6	2	2	14	39-73		27
Morton	36	4	4	10	2	4	12	30-74		20
Kilmarnock	36	3	7	8	0	4	14	28-91		17

League Cup Section

	P	W	D	L	F	A	PTS
Aberdeen	6	4	2	0	18- 7		10
Morton	6	3	2	1	16-11		8
Dundee	**6**	**2**	**2**	**2**	**14-19**		**6**
Dumbarton	6	0	0	6	7-18		0

Dundee F.C. Line-Ups 1982-83

	1	2	3	4	5	6	7	8	9	10	11	12	13
Aug 14th	Blair	McKimmie	McLelland	Fraser	MacDonald	Glennie	Ferguson	McGeachie	Sinclair	Mackie	Stephen	Fleming	Davidson (9)
18th	Blair	McKimmie	McLelland	Fraser	MacDonald	Glennie	Ferguson	McGeachie	Sinclair	Mackie	Stephen	Fleming (7)	Davidson (9)
21st	Blair	McKimmie	McLelland	Fraser	Scrimgeour	Glennie	Ferguson	McGeachie	Sinclair	Mackie	Stephen	Fleming (8)	Davidson (3)
25th	Geddes B	McKimmie	McLelland	Fraser	Glennie	McGeachie	Ferguson	Geddes A	Sinclair	Mackie	Stephen	Fleming (8)	Davidson
28th	Geddes B	McKimmie	McLelland	Fraser	Glennie	McGeachie	Ferguson	Geddes A	Sinclair	Mackie	Stephen	Kidd (8)	Davidson (9)
Sep 1st	Kelly	McGeachie	McKimmie	Fraser	Smith	Glennie	Ferguson	Kidd	Davidson	Mackie	Stephen	Sinclair (11)	Fleming (7)
4th	Kelly	McGeachie	McKimmie	Fraser	Smith	Glennie	Mackie	Bell	Davidson	Kidd	Fleming	Sinclair (10)	Scrimgeour
11th	Kelly	McGeachie	McKimmie	Fraser	Smith	MacDonald	Ferguson	Fleming	Davidson	Mackie	Stephen	Kidd (9)	Sinclair (2)
18th	Kelly	Glennie	McKimmie	Fraser	Smith	MacDonald	Ferguson	Fleming	Sinclair	Mackie	Stephen	Bell (5)	Davidson
25th	Kelly	Glennie	McKimmie	Fraser	Smith	MacDonald	Ferguson	Fleming	Sinclair	Mackie	Stephen	Bell	Davidson
Oct 2nd	Kelly	Glennie	Scrimgeour	Fraser	Smith	MacDonald	Ferguson	Fleming	Davidson	Mackie	Stephen	Sinclair (9)	Bell
9th	Kelly	Glennie	McKimmie	Fraser	Smith	MacDonald	Ferguson	Fleming	Sinclair	Mackie	Stephen	Davidson	Bell
16th	Kelly	Glennie	McKimmie	Fraser	Smith	MacDonald	Ferguson	Fleming	Bell	Mackie	Stephen	Sinclair (9)	Scrimgeour (5)
23rd	Kelly	Glennie	McKimmie	Fraser	Smith	MacDonald	Ferguson	Fleming	Sinclair	Mackie	Stephen	Bell (3)	Davidson (7)
30th	Kelly	Glennie	McKimmie	Fraser	Smith	MacDonald	Ferguson	Scrimgeour	Davidson	Mackie	Stephen	Bell (8)	Kidd (11)
Nov 6th	Kelly	Glennie	McKimmie	Fraser	Smith	MacDonald	Ferguson	Scrimgeour	Davidson	Mackie	Stephen	Kidd (7)	Bell (2)
13th	Kelly	Glennie	Scrimgeour	Fraser	Smith	MacDonald	Kidd	Bell	Sinclair	Mackie	Stephen	McKimmie	Murphy (7)
21st	Kelly	Glennie	Scrimgeour	Fraser	Smith	MacDonald	Kidd	Bell	Sinclair	Mackie	Stephen	Murphy (8)	McKimmie (7)
27th	Kelly	Glennie	Scrimgeour	Fraser	Smith	MacDonald	Murphy	Bell	Sinclair	Mackie	Stephen	McKimmie	Kidd
Dec 11th	Kelly	Glennie	Scrimgeour	Fraser	Smith	MacDonald	Murphy	Bell	Sinclair	Mackie	Stephen	McKimmie (3)	McGlashan
18th	Kelly	Glennie	McKimmie	Fraser	Smith	MacDonald	Murphy	Bell	Sinclair	Mackie	Stephen	McGeachie(11)	McGlashan (2)
27th	Kelly	Glennie	McKimmie	Fraser	Smith	MacDonald	Murphy	Bell	Sinclair	Mackie	McGeachie	Ferguson (7)	Stephen
Jan 1st	Kelly	Glennie	McKimmie	Bell	Smith	MacDonald	Ferguson	McGeachie	Stephen	Mackie	Murphy	Scrimgeour (2)	Sinclair (4)
3rd	Kelly	Glennie	Scrimgeour	Bell	Smith	MacDonald	Ferguson	Stephen	Sinclair	Mackie	Murphy	McGeachie	McKimmie
8th	Kelly	Glennie	Scrimgeour	Fraser	Smith	MacDonald	Ferguson	Bell	Sinclair	Mackie	Stephen	Murphy	McKimmie (3)
15th	Kelly	McGeachie	McKimmie	Fraser	Smith	MacDonald	Ferguson	Bell	Sinclair	Mackie	Stephen	Murphy (5)	Scrimgeour(2)
22nd	Kelly	Glennie	Scrimgeour	Fraser	Smith	MacDonald	Ferguson	Bell	Sinclair	Mackie	Stephen	Murphy (11)	McGeachie (6)
29th	Kelly	Glennie	McKimmie	Fraser	Smith	McGeachie	Ferguson	Bell	Sinclair	Mackie	Stephen	Murphy	Scrimgeour
Feb 5th	Kelly	McGeachie	McKimmie	Fraser	Smith	MacDonald	Ferguson	Bell	Sinclair	Mackie	Stephen	Murphy	Scrimgeour
19th	Kelly	McGeachie	McKimmie	Fraser	Smith	MacDonald	Ferguson	Bell	Sinclair	Mackie	Stephen	Glennie (8)	Murphy (11)
22nd	Kelly	McGeachie	McKimmie	Fraser	Smith	MacDonald	Ferguson	Bell	Sinclair	Mackie	Stephen	Glennie	Murphy (9)
26th	Kelly	McGeachie	McKimmie	Fraser	Smith	MacDonald	Ferguson	Scrimgeour	Kidd	Mackie	Stephen	Bell (8)	Glennie (9)
Mar 2nd	Kelly	McGeachie	McKimmie	Fraser	Smith	MacDonald	Ferguson	Scrimgeour	Sinclair	Mackie	Kidd	Glennie (2)	Bell (9)
5th	Kelly	McGeachie	McKimmie	Fraser	Smith	MacDonald	Ferguson	Scrimgeour	Bell	Mackie	Kidd	Glennie	McGlashan (7)
12th	Geddes B	McGeachie	McKimmie	Fraser	Smith	MacDonald	Ferguson	Bell	Sinclair	Scrimgeour	Kidd	Mackie (1)	McLelland (8)
19th	Kelly	McGeachie	McKimmie	Fraser	Smith	MacDonald	Mackie	Bell	Sinclair	Scrimgeour	Kidd	Ferguson (11)	Stephen
26th	Kelly	McGeachie	McKimmie	Fraser	Smith	MacDonald	Mackie	Bell	Sinclair	Scrimgeour	Kidd	Ferguson (11)	Stephen (10)
Apr 2nd	Kelly	McGeachie	McKimmie	Fraser	Smith	MacDonald	Mackie	Bell	Sinclair	Scrimgeour	Kidd	Ferguson (11)	Stephen (8)
9th	Kelly	McGeachie	McKimmie	Fraser	Smith	MacDonald	Mackie	Bell	Ferguson	Kidd	Stephen	Sinclair (9)	Scrimgeour (2)
23rd	Kelly	McGeachie	McKimmie	Fraser	Smith	MacDonald	Mackie	Scrimgeour	Sinclair	Stephen	Kidd	Bell (11)	Glennie
30th	Kelly	McGeachie	McKimmie	Fraser	Smith	MacDonald	Mackie	Glennie	Davidson	Scrimgeour	Ferguson	Kidd (2)	Stephen (10)
May 4th	Kelly	Glennie	McKimmie	Fraser	Smith	MacDonald	Ferguson	McGeachie	Sinclair	Stephen	Kidd	Mackie (9)	McGlashan
9th	Kelly	Glennie	McKinlay	Fraser	Smith	McKimmie	Ferguson	McGeachie	Sinclair	Stephen	Kidd	Mackie (11)	Scrimgeour
14th	Kelly	Glennie	McKimmie	Fraser	Smith	MacDonald	Ferguson	McGeachie	Sinclair	Stephen	Kidd	Mackie (2)	Scrimgeour

Glee club - Albert Kidd celebrates after scoring the opener in the 2-1 win over Celtic at Dens. The grounded midfielder is congratulated by Brian Scrimgeour with Davie Bell and Peter Mackie about to join in. Despondent Celts are Roy Aitken and Pat Bonner.   DC Thomson

Season 1983-84

Date			Opponents		Score	Crowd	Scorers
Aug	3rd	FCS	Montrose	a	1-0	850	Kidd
	8th	FCF	Forfar Athletic	a	2-3	2,308	Stephen; Sinclair
	20th	L	Aberdeen	a	0-3	14,500	-
	24th	LC1	Montrose	a	3-1	844	Kidd; Ferguson; MacDonald
	27th	LC1	Montrose	h	4-1 (7-2)	2,516	MacDonald 2; McCall; Ferguson (pen)
	31st	LC2	St Johnstone	h	2-1	4,534	McCall; Mackie
Sep	3rd	L	Dundee United	h	1-4	13,656	McCall
	7th	LC2	Meadowbank	a	1-0	592	McCall
	10th	L	St Mirren	a	0-0	2,808	
	17th	L	Hearts	h	1-2	6,765	Ferguson (pen)
	24th	L	Celtic	h	2-6	11,467	Ferguson (2 pens)
Oct	1st	L	Motherwell	a	3-1	2,931	McCall; MacLeod o.g.; Carson o.g.
	5th	LC2	Aberdeen	h	0-0	13,200	-
	8th	L	St Johnstone	h	2-0	3,709	McCall; A. Geddes
	15th	L	Rangers	h	3-2	11,945	Ferguson 2; McCall
	22nd	L	Hibernian	a	1-2	6,838	Mackie
	25th	LC2	Meadowbank	h	1-1	1,853	Fraser
	29th	L	Aberdeen	h	1-3	7,849	Glennie
Nov	5th	L	Dundee United	a	1-0	14,813	Mackie
	9th	LC2	St Johnstone	a	3-0	2,458	Ferguson 2; McCall
	13th	L	Hearts	a	3-1	12,271	McKinlay; McCall 2
	19th	L	Motherwell	h	2-0	4,638	Fraser; Stephen
	26th	L	Celtic	a	0-1	14,583	-
Nov	30th	LC2	Aberdeen	h	1-2	11,019	Fraser
Dec	3rd	L	St Mirren	h	2-2	4,572	McCall; Stephen
	10th	L	Hibernian	h	0-3	4,628	-
	17th	L	Rangers	a	1-2	16,500	A. Geddes
	27th	L	St Johnstone	h	0-1	6,650	-
	31st	L	Aberdeen	a	2-5	19,000	Mackie; Ferguson
Jan	7th	L	Hearts	h	4-1	5,960	Glennie; McCall; Ferguson; Fraser
Feb	8th	SC3	Cowdenbeath	a	2-0	1,500	McCall 2
	11th	L	St Mirren	a	0-4	3,187	
	19th	SC4	Airdrie	h	2-1	5,107	Stephen; Ferguson
	25th	L	Rangers	h	1-3	11,750	Harris
	29th	L	Hibernian	a*	1-3	10,000	McCall
Mar	3rd	L	St Johnstone	a	0-1	2,824	-
	10th	SCQ	Rangers	h	2-2	17,097	Ferguson; Kidd
	17th	SCQR	Rangers	a	3-2	21,000	Smith; Ferguson 2
	20th	L	Celtic	h	3-2	7,746	McCall 2; Stephen
	28th	L	Motherwell	a	4-2	1,828	Kidd; MacDonald; McKinlay; Ferguson
	31st	L	Hibernian	h	1-2	4,355	McInally
Apr	2nd	L	Dundee United	h	2-5	12,732	Ferguson 2 (pens)
	7th	L	St Mirren	h	2-5	3,582	Harris; Fraser
	14th	SCS	Aberdeen	Tyn	0-2	17,654	-
	18th	L	Motherwell	h	1-0	4,190	McGlashan
	21st	L	Dundee United	a	1-1	13,244	McCall
	24th	L	Celtic	a	0-3	4,956	-
	28th	L	Aberdeen	h	0-1	6,663	-
May	5th	L	Rangers	a	2-2	17,000	McKinlay; McCall
	9th	L	Hearts	a	1-1	6,571	McInally
	12th	L	St Johnstone	h	2-0	4,879	Ferguson 2

* Earlier game on February 2nd abandoned after 20 minutes due to fog at 0-0.

Cammy Fraser was an inspirational midfielder for the Dark Blues.

The Record

League	-	Eighth Place, Premier Division
League Cup	-	Second qualifying round
Scottish Cup	-	Semi-final
Forfarshire Cup	-	Runners up
Top Scorer	-	Iain Ferguson (20 goals)
Av. Home Gate	-	7,500
Players used	-	24
Sent off (booked)	-	Four (45)

Appearances

	League	L/Cup	S/Cup	Total
Iain Ferguson	33 (12)	8 (4)	4 (4)	45 (20)
Tosh McKinlay	36 (3)	5	4	45+1s (3)
Cammy Fraser	29 (3)	8 (2)	5	42 (5)
Jim Smith	32	4	5 (1)	41+2s (1)
Walker McCall	30 (13)	6 (4)	3 (2)	39+1s (19)
Bobby Glennie	26 (2)	6	4	36+1s (2)
Lex Richardson	28	0	4	32+1s
George McGeachie	21	6	4	31+1s
Bobby Geddes	24	4	1	29
Peter Mackie	18 (3)	7 (1)	4	29+10s (4)
Ray Stephen	18 (3)	7	3 (1)	28+4s (4)
Albert Kidd	18 (1)	5 (1)	4 (1)	27+8s (3)
Iain MacDonald	18 (1)	5 (3)	3	26+3s (4)
Stewart McKimmie	16	8	0	24
Colin Kelly	10	4	2	16
Andy Geddes	9 (2)	3	0	12+2s (2)
Colin Harris	9 (2)	0	3	12+5s (2)
Jim McInally	11 (2)	0	0	11 (2)
Rab Shannon	5	1	0	6+1s
Alan Blair	2	0	2	4
Colin McGlashan	2 (1)	0	0	2+9s (1)
Colin Hendry	1	0	0	1+3s
Eric Sinclair	0	1	0	1+1s
Derek Paterson	0	0	0	0+2s

Scottish League Premier Division

		Home			Away			Goals		
	P	W	D	L	W	D	L	F	A	PTS
Aberdeen	36	14	3	1	11	4	3	78-21		57
Celtic	36	13	5	0	8	3	7	80-41		50
Dundee United	36	11	3	4	7	8	3	67-39		47
Rangers	36	7	8	3	8	4	6	43-41		42
Hearts	36	5	9	4	5	7	6	38-47		36
St Mirren	36	8	6	4	1	8	9	55-59		32
Hibernian	36	7	4	7	5	3	10	45-55		31
Dundee	**36**	**6**	**1**	**11**	**5**	**4**	**9**	**50-74**		**27**
St Johnstone	36	6	1	11	4	2	12	36-81		23
Motherwell	36	2	5	11	2	2	14	31-75		15

League Cup Section

	P	W	D	L	F	A	PTS
Aberdeen	6	5	1	0	11-2		11
Dundee	**6**	**3**	**2**	**1**	**8-4**		**8**
Meadowbank	6	1	2	3	4-10		4
St Johnstone	6	0	1	5	2- 9		1

Dundee F.C. Line-Ups 1983-84

		1	2	3	4	5	6	7	8	9	10	11	12	13
Aug	20th	Kelly	McGeachie	McKinlay	Fraser	Smith	Glennie	Mackie	Geddes A	Stephen	McKimmie	Kidd	Sinclair (8)	MacDonald
	24th	Kelly	McGeachie	McKimmie	Fraser	Glennie	MacDonald	Ferguson	Stephen	Sinclair	Mackie	Kidd	Smith	McKinlay
	27th	Kelly	McGeachie	McKimmie	Fraser	Glennie	MacDonald	Ferguson	Stephen	McCall	Mackie	Kidd	Sinclair	McKinlay (4)
	31st	Kelly	McGeachie	McKimmie	Fraser	Glennie	MacDonald	Ferguson	Stephen	McCall	Mackie	Kidd	Sinclair	McKinlay
Sep	3rd	Kelly	McKimmie	McKinlay	Fraser	Glennie	MacDonald	Ferguson	McGeachie	McCall	Mackie	Kidd	Smith	Stephen (8)
	7th	Kelly	McKimmie	McKinlay	Fraser	Glennie	MacDonald	Ferguson	McGeachie	McCall	Mackie	Kidd	Smith	Stephen
	10th	Kelly	McGeachie	McKinlay	Fraser	Glennie	MacDonald	Ferguson	McKimmie	McCall	Stephen	Kidd	Mackie	Smith
	17th	Kelly	McGeachie	McKinlay	Fraser	Glennie	MacDonald	Ferguson	McKimmie	McCall	Stephen	Kidd	Mackie (9)	Smith (2)
	24th	Kelly	McGeachie	McKinlay	Fraser*	Glennie	MacDonald	Ferguson	McKimmie	McCall	Richardson	Kidd	Mackie (8)	Smith (9)
Oct	1st	Geddes B	McGeachie	McKimmie	Geddes A	Smith	MacDonald	Ferguson	Stephen	McCall	Richardson	McKinlay	Kidd	Glennie
	5th	Geddes B	McGeachie	McKimmie	Geddes A	Smith	MacDonald	Ferguson	Stephen	McCall	Fraser	McKinlay	Kidd	Glennie
	8th	Geddes B	McGeachie	McKimmie	Geddes A	Smith	MacDonald	Ferguson	Fraser	Stephen	Richardson	McKinlay	Kidd	McCall (2)
	15th	Geddes B	McKimmie	McKinlay	Geddes A	Smith	MacDonald	Ferguson	Fraser	McCall	Richardson	Stephen	Glennie	Mackie (4)
	22nd	Geddes B	McGeachie	McKinlay	Geddes A	Smith	MacDonald	Ferguson	Fraser	McCall	Richardson	McKimmie	Stephen (2)	McGlashan
	25th	Geddes B	McKimmie	McKinlay	Fraser	Smith	McGeachie	Mackie	Shannon	Ferguson	Stephen	Kidd	Glennie	Mackie (9)
	29th	Geddes B	McKimmie	McKinlay	Fraser	Smith	Glennie	Mackie	Stephen	Ferguson	Richardson	Geddes A	Kidd (11)	McGeachie(6)
Nov	5th	Geddes B	McKimmie	McKinlay	Fraser	Smith	Glennie	Mackie	Richardson	Ferguson	McCall	Stephen	Geddes A	Kidd
	9th	Geddes B	McKimmie	McKinlay	Fraser	Smith	Glennie	Mackie	Geddes A	Ferguson	McCall	Stephen	Kidd	McGlashan
	13th	Geddes B	McKimmie	McKinlay	Fraser	Smith	Glennie	Mackie	Richardson	Ferguson	McCall	Stephen	Kidd	McGlashan
	19th	Geddes B	McKimmie	McKinlay	Fraser	Smith	Glennie	Mackie	Richardson	Ferguson	McCall	Stephen	Kidd	McGlashan
	26th	Geddes B	McKimmie	McKinlay	Fraser	Smith	Glennie	Mackie	Richardson	Ferguson	McCall	Stephen	Kidd	McGlashan(11)
	30th	Geddes B	McKimmie	McKinlay	Fraser	Smith	Glennie	Mackie	Geddes A	Ferguson	McCall	Stephen	McGlashan(8)	Kidd (1)
Dec	3rd	Geddes B	McKimmie	McKinlay	Fraser	Smith	Glennie	Mackie	Richardson	McCall	Kidd	Stephen	McGlashan	Geddes A (10)
	10th	Geddes B	McKimmie	McKinlay	Kidd	Smith	Glennie	Mackie	Richardson	Ferguson	McCall	Stephen	MacDonald	McGlashan(11)
	17th	Geddes B	Glennie*	McKinlay	Richardson	Smith	Macdonald	Mackie	Stephen	Ferguson	McCall	Geddes A	Kidd	McGlashan
	27th	Geddes B	McGeachie	McKinlay	Fraser	Smith	MacDonald	Mackie	Richardson	Ferguson	McCall	Geddes A	Kidd (7)	McGlashan (2)
	31st	Geddes B	Glennie	McKinlay	Fraser	Smith	MacDonald	Mackie	Richardson	Ferguson	McCall	Geddes A	Kidd (8)	Paterson (11)
Jan	7th	Geddes B	McGeachie	McKinlay	Fraser	Smith	Glennie	Mackie	Richardson	Ferguson	McCall	Kidd	Paterson (2)	Hendry (10)
Feb	8th	Blair	McGeachie	McKinlay	Fraser	Smith	Glennie	Mackie	Richardson	Ferguson	McCall	Kidd	Stephen (2)	Geddes A
	11th	Blair	McGeachie	McKinlay	Fraser	Smith	Glennie	Mackie	Richardson	Ferguson	Stephen	Kidd	Geddes A(11)	MacDonald(8)
	19th	Blair	McGeachie	McKinlay	Fraser	Smith	Glennie	Mackie	Richardson	Ferguson	Stephen	Kidd	MacDonald	McGlashan (7)
	25th	Blair	McGeachie	McKinlay	Fraser	Smith	Glennie	Mackie	Harris	Ferguson	Stephen	McGlashan	Kidd	MacDonald(7)
	29th	Kelly	McGeachie*	Glennie	Fraser	Smith	MacDonald	Shannon	Ferguson	McCall	Harris	McKinlay	McGlashan	Mackie (5)
Mar	3rd	Kelly	Glennie	McKinlay	Fraser	Smith	MacDonald	Shannon	Richardson	Ferguson	McCall	Harris	Kidd (9)	McGlashan (7)
	10th	Kelly	Glennie	McKinlay	Fraser	Smith	MacDonald	Stephen	McGeachie	Ferguson	McCall	Harris	Kidd (9)	McGlashan
	17th	Kelly	Mackie	Richardson	Fraser	Smith	MacDonald	Kidd	Ferguson	McCall	Stephen	Harris	Hendry (11)	Shannon
	20th	Kelly	McGeachie	McKinlay	Fraser	Smith	MacDonald	Kidd	Ferguson	McCall	Richardson	Stephen	Harris (4)	Mackie (2)
	28th	Kelly	Richardson	McInally	Fraser	Smith	MacDonald	Ferguson	Kidd	McCall	McKinlay	Harris	Mackie (11)	McGlashan
	31st	Kelly	McGeachie	McInally	Fraser	Smith	MacDonald	Ferguson	Kidd	McCall	McKinlay	Harris	McGlashan(11)	Richardson (2)
Apr	2nd	Geddes B	McGeachie	McInally	Fraser	Smith	MacDonald	Ferguson	Richardson	McCall	McKinlay	Mackie	Kidd (10)	Glennie (6)
	7th	Geddes B	McGeachie	McInally	Fraser	Smith	Glennie	Ferguson	Richardson	McCall	McKinlay	Harris	Kidd (5)	Mackie (9)
	14th	Geddes B	Glennie	McKinlay	Fraser	Smith	MacDonald	Mackie	Richardson	Harris	McGeachie	Kidd	McGlashan 7	Stephen (8)
	18th	Geddes B	McInally	McKinlay	Fraser	Smith	Glennie	Mackie	Richardson	Harris	Kidd	Stephen	MacDonald (6	McGlashan (11
	21st	Geddes B	McInally	McKinlay	Fraser*	Smith	Glennie	Kidd	Richardson	McCall	Ferguson	Harris	Mackie (5)	McGlashan
	24th	Geddes B	McInally	McKinlay	Kidd	Smith	McGeachie	Mackie	Ferguson	McCall	Harris	McGlashan	Hendry (11)	Shannon (4)
	28th	Geddes B	McInally	McKinlay	Shannon	Smith	Glennie	Hendry	Richardson	McCall	McGeachie	Ferguson	Harris (7)	Kidd
May	5th	Geddes B	McInally	McKinlay	McGeachie	Smith	Glennie	Kidd	Richardson	McCall	Shannon	Ferguson	Harris (10)	Hendry
	9th	Geddes B	McInally	McKinlay	McGeachie	Smith	Glennie	Kidd	Richardson	McCall	Shannon	Ferguson	Harris (4)	Mackie (9)
	12th	Geddes B	McInally	McKinlay	Fraser	Smith	Glennie	Kidd	Richardson	McCall	McGeachie	Ferguson	Harris (10)	Shannon

Peter lays the bogey - Peter Mackie ends Dundee's dismal derby record of four years without a win over Dundee United by rounding Hamish McAlpine to net the only goal of a Tannadice thriller. Looking on are United's Maurice Malpas and Dundee's Cammy Fraser. DC Thomson

Season 1984-85

Date			Opponents		Score	Crowd	Scorers
Aug	7th	FC1	Arbroath	a	3-0	1,200	McWalter o.g.; Stephen; Harris
	11th	L	Aberdeen	a	2-3	14,700	Rafferty; Stephen
	18th	L	Hibernian	h	0-1	6,290	-
	22nd	LC1	Hamilton	h	3-0	2,916	Stephen; McCall; Connor
	25th	L	Dumbarton	a	1-2	2,000	Stephen
	29th	LC2	Kilmarnock	h	1-1*	3,367	Brown
Sep	1st	L	Rangers	h	0-2	14,156	-
	5th	LCQ	Hearts	h	0-1	8,818	-
	8th	L	Dundee United	a	4-3	14,190	McWilliams; McKinlay; Harris; Brown
	15th	L	St Mirren	h	2-0	5,913	Rafferty; Brown
	22nd	L	Hearts	a	2-0	7,511	McKinlay; Brown
	29th	L	Celtic	h	2-3	13,761	McCormack; Stephen
Oct	6th	L	Morton	a	1-1	2,000	McWilliams
	13th	L	Aberdeen	h	1-2	10,990	Connor
	20th	L	Hibernian	a	0-2	5,000	-
	27th	L	Dumbarton	h	1-1	4,375	Smith
Nov	3rd	L	Rangers	a	0-0	14,558	-
	10th	L	Dundee United	h	0-2	14,423	-
	17th	L	St Mirren	a	1-2	2,877	Stephen
	24th	L	Hearts	h	2-1	6,414	Richardson; Connor
Dec	1st	L	Celtic	a	1-5	15,887	Connor
	8th	L	Morton	h	5-1	3,525	Stephen; McCall; Connor; Kidd 2
	15th	L	Aberdeen	a	0-0	14,000	-
	29th	L	Hibernian	h	2-0	5,941	Stephen; Kidd
Jan	1st	L	Dumbarton	a	0-1	2,500	-
	5th	L	Rangers	h	2-2	11,911	McCormack 2
Feb	3rd	L	Hearts	a	3-3	10,063	McCormack; Brown; Harvey
	5th	SC3	St Johnstone	a	1-1	5,955	Brown
	6th	SC3R	St Johnstone	h	2-1	5,444	McWilliams; Connor (pen)
	9th	L	Celtic	h	2-0	12,087	Stephen; Connor (pen)
	16th	SC4	Rangers	a	1-0	26,619	Brown
	20th	L	St Mirren	h	1-0	5,142	Harvey
	23rd	L	Morton	a	1-0	2,200	McGeachie
Mar	2nd	L	Hibernian	a	1-0	5,500	Brown
	9th	SCQ	Celtic	h	1-1	21,300	Brown
	13th	SCQR	Celtic	a	1-2	37,390	Stephen
	16th	L	Aberdeen	h	0-4	9,161	-
	23rd	L	Rangers	a	3-1	9,554	Rafferty; Connor; Stephen
Apr	3rd	L	Dundee United	a	0-4	15,167	-
	6th	L	St Mirren	a	2-4	3,500	McCormack 2
	13th	L	Dumbarton	h	1-0	3,366	Rafferty
	20th	L	Hearts	h	3-0	7,421	McCormack; Brown; McKinlay
	27th	L	Morton	h	0-0	3,454	-
May	4th	L	Celtic	a	1-0	8,815	Brown
	11th	L	Dundee United	h	1-0	14,000	Connor
	13th	FCS	Dundee United	h	2-3	3,286	Stephen; McWilliams

*After extra-time. 1-1 at 90 mts. Dundee won 3-2 on pens.

Bobby Glennie - defensive lynchpin for the Dark Blues down the years.

Appearances

	League	L/Cup	S/Cup	Total	
George McGeachie	35 (1)	3	5	43	(1)
John McCormack	34 (7)	3	5	42	(7)
Stuart Rafferty	35 (4)	3	4	42+2s	(4)
Ray Stephen	34 (8)	3 (1)	5 (1)	42+1s	(10)
John Brown	33 (7)	3 (1)	5 (3)	41+1s	(11)
Bobby Connor	34 (7)	2 (1)	5 (1)	41	(9)
Tosh McKinlay	33 (3)	3	4	40+1s	(3)
Bobby Glennie	28	3	5	36+1s	
Tom Carson	20	3	0	23	
Jim Smith	19 (1)	0	4	23+4s	(1)
Bobby Geddes	16	0	5	21	
Walker McCall	14 (1)	3 (1)	0	17+13s	(2)
Colin Harris	13 (1)	1	0	14+3s	(1)
Albert Kidd	11 (3)	2	1	14+15s	(3)
Stewart Forsyth	10	0	2	12	
Graham Harvey	7 (2)	0	3	10	(2)
Derek McWilliams	7 (2)	1	1	9+9s	(2)
Lex Richardson	7 (1)	0	1	8+18s	(1)
Colin Hendry	3	0	0	3+1s	
Rab Shannon	2	0	0	2+1s	
John Waddell	1	0	0	1+2s	
John Docherty	0	0	0	0+1s	

The Record

League	-	Sixth Place, Premier Division
League Cup	-	Quarter-final
Scottish Cup	-	Quarter-final
Forfarshire Cup	-	Semi-final
Top Scorer	-	John Brown (11 goals)
Av. Home Gate	-	8,500
Players used	-	22
Sent off (booked)	-	Three (45)

Scottish League Premier Division

		Home			Away			Goals		
	P	W	D	L	W	D	L	F A		PTS
Aberdeen	36	13	4	1	14	1	3	89-26		59
Celtic	36	12	3	3	10	5	3	77-30		52
Dundee United	36	13	2	3	7	5	6	67-33		47
Rangers	36	7	6	5	6	6	6	47-38		38
St Mirren	36	10	2	6	7	2	9	51-56		38
Dundee	**36**	**9**	**3**	**6**	**6**	**4**	**8**	**48-50**		**37**
Hearts	36	6	3	9	7	2	9	47-64		31
Hibernian	36	5	4	9	5	3	10	38-61		27
Dumbarton	36	4	4	10	2	3	13	29-64		19
Morton	36	3	1	14	2	1	15	29-100		12

Dundee F.C. Line-Ups 1984-85

	1	2	3	4	5	6	7	8	9	10	11	12	13
Aug 11th	Geddes	McGeachie	McKinlay	Rafferty	McCormack	Glennie	Kidd	Stephen	McCall	Connor	Harris	Smith (8)	McWilliams (7)
18th	Carson	McGeachie	McKinlay	Rafferty	McCormack	Brown	Kidd	Stephen	McCall	Connor	McWilliams	Harris (7)	Glennie (2)
22nd	Carson	McGeachie	McKinlay	Rafferty	McCormack	Glennie	Stephen	Brown	McCall*	Connor	Kidd	Harris (4)	Richardson (3)
25th	Carson	McGeachie	Brown	Rafferty	McCormack	Glennie	Stephen	Richardson	Harris	Connor	Kidd	McKinlay (6)	Docherty (11)
29th	Carson	McGeachie	McKinlay	Rafferty	McCormack	Glennie	Stephen	Brown	McCall	Connor	McWilliams	Smith	Kidd (11)
Sep 1st	Carson	McGeachie	McKinlay	Rafferty	McCormack	Glennie	Stephen	Brown	McCall	Connor	Kidd	Smith (10)	McWilliams (4)
5th	Carson	McGeachie	McKinlay	Rafferty	McCormack	Glennie	Stephen	Brown	McCall	Harris	Kidd	Smith	McWilliams (11
8th	Carson	McGeachie	McKinlay	Rafferty	McCormack	Glennie	Stephen	Brown	Harris	Connor	McWilliams	Kidd (11)	Richardson
15th	Carson	McGeachie	McKinlay	Rafferty	McCormack	Glennie	Stephen	Brown	Harris	Connor	McWilliams	McCall (11)	Richardson (9)
22nd	Carson	McGeachie	McKinlay	Rafferty	McCormack	Glennie	Stephen	Brown	Harris	Connor	McWilliams	Kidd (11)	Richardson (4)
29th	Carson	McGeachie	McKinlay	Rafferty	McCormack	Glennie	Stephen	Brown	McCall	Connor	Harris	Kidd (9)	Richardson (11)
Oct 6th	Carson	McGeachie	McKinlay	Rafferty	McCormack	Glennie	Stephen	Brown	Harris	Connor	McWilliams	McCall (8)	Forsyth (9)
13th	Carson	McGeachie	McKinlay	Rafferty	McCormack	Glennie	Forsyth	Brown	McCall	Connor	Stephen	Kidd (11)	McWilliams (7)
20th	Carson	McGeachie	McKinlay	Rafferty	McCormack	Glennie	Forsyth	Brown	McCall	Connor	Richardson	Kidd (10)	Smith (5)
27th	Carson	McGeachie	McKinlay	Rafferty	McCormack	Brown	Forsyth	Stephen	Harris	Connor	McWilliams	Kidd (11)	Smith (7)
Nov 3rd	Carson	McGeachie	McKinlay	Rafferty	McCormack	Glennie	Forsyth	Brown	Stephen	Connor	Kidd	McCall (11)	McWilliams
10th	Carson	McGeachie	McKinlay	Rafferty	McCormack	Glennie	Forsyth	Brown	Stephen	Connor*	Kidd	McCall (7)	Harris (11)
17th	Carson	McGeachie	McKinlay	Rafferty	McCormack	Glennie	Forsyth	Smith	Stephen	McCall	Harris	Brown (6)	Richardson (11)
24th	Geddes	McGeachie	McKinlay	Rafferty	McCormack	Smith	Stephen	Richardson	McCall	Connor	Harris	Forsyth (7)	McWilliams (9)
Dec 1st	Geddes	McGeachie	McKinlay	Rafferty	Smith	Glennie	Richardson	Brown	Stephen	Connor	Harris	Forsyth (8)	McCall (7)
8th	Geddes	McGeachie	McKinlay	Rafferty	Smith	Glennie	Stephen	Brown	McCall	Connor	Kidd	Forsyth	Richardson
15th	Carson	McGeachie	McKinlay	McCormack	Smith	Glennie	Stephen	Brown	McCall	Connor	Rafferty	Forsyth	Richardson (9)
29th	Carson	McGeachie	Brown	McCormack	Smith	Glennie	Stephen	Rafferty	Harris	Connor	Kidd	McWilliams	Richardson (11)
Jan 1st	Carson	McGeachie	Brown	McCormack	Smith	Glennie	Stephen	Rafferty	Harris	Connor	Kidd	Richardson (9)	McWilliams (11
5th	Carson	McGeachie	McKinlay	McCormack	Smith	Glennie	Rafferty	Brown	McCall	Connor	Harvey	Stephen (5)	Richardson (11)
Feb 3rd	Carson	McGeachie	McKinlay	McCormack	Smith	Glennie	Rafferty	Brown	Harvey	Connor	Stephen	Kidd (9)	Richardson (8)
5th	Geddes	McGeachie	McKinlay	McCormack	Smith	Glennie	Rafferty	Brown	Harvey	Connor	Stephen	Kidd (9)	Richardson (6)
6th	Geddes	McGeachie	Forsyth	McCormack	Glennie	Brown	McWilliams	Richardson	Stephen	Connor	Kidd	McCall (2)	Rafferty (6)
9th	Geddes	McGeachie	McKinlay	McCormack	Smith	Glennie	Stephen	Brown	Harvey	Connor	Kidd	McCall (11)	Rafferty (9)
16th	Geddes	McGeachie	McKinlay	McCormack	Smith	Glennie	Rafferty	Brown	Harvey	Connor	Stephen	Kidd (9)	Richardson (2)
20th	Geddes	Forsyth	McKinlay	McCormack	Smith	Glennie	Rafferty	Brown	Harvey	Connor	Stephen	Kidd (11)	Richardson (8)
23rd	Geddes	McGeachie	McKinlay	McCormack	Smith	Forsyth	Rafferty	Brown	Harvey	Connor	Stephen	Richardson(6)	McWilliams (9)
Mar 2nd	Geddes	McGeachie	McKinlay	McCormack	Smith	Glennie	Rafferty	Brown	Harvey	Connor	Stephen	McCall (9)	Richardson
9th	Geddes	McGeachie	McKinlay	McCormack	Smith	Glennie	Rafferty	Brown	Harvey	Connor	Stephen	McCall (9)	Forsyth
13th	Geddes	McGeachie	McKinlay	McCormack	Smith	Glennie*	Rafferty	Brown	Forsyth	Connor	Stephen	McCall (9)	Richardson
16th	Geddes	McGeachie	McKinlay	Rafferty	Smith	McCormack	Stephen	Brown	Harvey	Connor	McWilliams	McCall (9)	Richardson (6)
23rd	Geddes	McGeachie	McKinlay	McCormack	Smith	Glennie	Rafferty	Brown	Hendry	Connor	Stephen	Shannon (10)	Richardson (9)
Apr 3rd	Geddes	McGeachie	McKinlay	McCormack	Smith	Brown	Forsyth	Richardson	Hendry	Rafferty	Stephen	McCall (9)	Kidd (8)
6th	Carson	Forsyth	McKinlay	McCormack	Smith	McGeachie	Rafferty	Brown	McCall	Connor	Stephen	Hendry (11)	Richardson (2)
13th	Geddes	Waddell	McKinlay	McCormack	Smith	McGeachie	Rafferty	Brown	Stephen	Connor	Kidd	McCall (11)	Richardson (8)
20th	Geddes	McGeachie	McKinlay	McCormack	Smith	Glennie	Rafferty	Brown	Richardson	Connor	Stephen	Waddell (5)	Harvey
27th	Geddes	McGeachie	McKinlay	McCormack	Glennie	Brown	Rafferty	Hendry	Richardson	Connor	Stephen	Waddell (10)	Kidd (8)
May 4th	Geddes	McGeachie	McKinlay	McCormack	Glennie	Shannon	Rafferty	Brown	McCall	Connor	Stephen	Kidd (11)	McWilliams (2)
11th	Geddes	McGeachie	McKinlay	McCormack	Glennie	Shannon	Rafferty	Brown	McCall	Connor	Stephen	Kidd (8)	McWilliams (9)

True grit - John McCormack added a competitive edge and was particularly strong in the air. Here he outjumps Sandy Clark to head home the first in Dundee's 3-0 home win over Hearts watched by team-mate Jim Smith and Roddy McDonald of Hearts.
DC Thomson

Season 1985-86

Date		Opponents		Score	Crowd	Scorers
Aug 10th	L	St Mirren	h	2-1	6,474	Connor 2 (1 pen)
12th	FCS	Brechin City	a	4-0		Rafferty; McCormack; Harvey; Jack (pen)
17th	L	Clydebank	a	0-4	2,500	-
21st	LC1	Stranraer	a	3-2	1,554	Smith; Stephen 2
24th	L	Dundee United	a	0-2	14,000	
28th	LC2	Hamilton Accies	a	1-2*	2,234	Kidd
31st	L	Aberdeen	h	1-3	7,592	Black
Sep 7th	L	Motherwell	a	3-1	2,607	McCormack; Brown; Harvey
14th	L	Hibernian	h	1-0	5,410	Brown
21st	L	Rangers	a	1-0	23,600	Rafferty
28th	L	Celtic	h	0-2	15,387	
Oct 5th	L	Hearts	a	1-1	8,500	McWilliams
12th	L	St Mirren	a	0-1	4,250	-
19th	L	Clydebank	h	2-0	4,160	Stephen 2
26th	L	Motherwell	h	3-1	4,628	Harvey; Stephen; McCormack
Nov 2nd	L	Hibernian	a	1-2	6,500	Glennie
9th	L	Aberdeen	a	1-4	12,000	Stephen
16th	L	Dundee United	h	0-3	11,736	-
23rd	L	Rangers	h	3-2	10,798	Brown 3 (1 pen)
30th	FCF	Dundee United	a	2-0	5,201	Jack; Brown
Dec 7th	L	Hearts	h	1-1	10,780	Brown
14th	L	St Mirren	h	3-1	4,290	Brown; Harvey; Stephen
23rd	L	Clydebank	a	0-0	1,350	-
28th	L	Dundee United	h	0-0	14,869	-
Jan 1st	L	Aberdeen	h	0-0	9,096	-
4th	L	Rangers	a	0-5	13,954	-
11th	L	Hibernian	h	3-1	5,073	Brown (pen); Stephen 2
18th	L	Motherwell	a	2-2	2,204	Rafferty; Brown (pen)
25th	SC3	Nairn County	a	7-0	3,600	Rafferty; Shannon 2; Harvey 3; Hendry
Feb 1st	L	Celtic	h	1-3	12,295	Stephen (pen)
8th	L	Hearts	a	1-3	15,365	Mennie
19th	SC4	Airdrie	h	2-0	4,010	Stephen; Mennie
22nd	L	St Mirren	a	2-1	3,123	Stephen 2
Mar 1st	L	Clydebank	h	4-0	4,033	Harvey; Stephen 3
8th	SCQ	Aberdeen	h	2-2	13,188	Brown; Harvey
12th	SCQR	Aberdeen	a	1-2*	21,000	Stephen
15th	L	Rangers	h	2-1	10,965	Brown (pen); Harvey
22nd	L	Aberdeen	a	0-0	13,000	-
29th	L	Dundee United	h	0-1	15,079	-
Apr 2nd	L	Celtic	a	1-2	12,506	Stephen
12th	l	Hibernian	a	0-1	4,500	-
19th	L	Motherwell	h	4-0	3,745	Forsyth; Glennie; Rafferty; Brown
26th	L	Celtic	a	0-2	22,000	-
May 3rd	L	Hearts	h	2-0	19,567	Kidd 2

* After extra-time. Both ties 1-1 after 90 minutes. Cup Cash v. Aberdeen £26,000

Bobby Connor - classy midfielder made Scotland breakthrough while at Dens.

Appearances

	League		L/Cup		S/Cup		Total	
Jim Duffy	36		2		4		42	
Bobby Geddes	36		2		4		42	
Bobby Connor	35	(2)	2		4		41	(2)
Rab Shannon	33		2		4	(2)	39	(2)
Jim Smith	32		2	(1)	3		37	(1)
Ray Stephen	32	(14)	2	(2)	3	(2)	37	(18)
Bobby Glennie	32	(2)	2		1		35+2s	(2)
John Brown	28	(11)	1		2	(1)	31+1s	(12)
Graham Harvey	25	(5)	1		3	(4)	29+7s	(9)
Tosh McKinlay	22		0		4		26	
Stuart Rafferty	23	(3)	2		1	(1)	26+8s	(4)
John McCormack	15	(2)	2		1		18+13s	(2)
Vince Mennie	11	(1)	0		3		14	(1)
Colin Hendry	10		0		2	(1)	12+10s	(1)
Stewart Forsyth	7	(1)	0		4		11+2s	(1)
Ross Jack	5		1		1		7+1s	
Derek McWilliams	6	(1)	0		0		6+5s	(1)
Albert Kidd	4	(2)	1	(1)	0		5+9s	(3)
Steve Campbell	2		0		0		2+3s	
Russell Black	1	(1)	0		0		1	(1)
George McGeachie	1		0		0		1+1s	
Danny Crainie	0		0		0		0+3s	
Walker McCall	0		0		0		0+2s	
John Waddell	0		0		0		0+2s	

The Record		
League	-	Sixth Place, Premier Division
League Cup	-	Second round
Scottish Cup	-	Quarter-final
Forfarshire Cup	-	Winners
Top Scorer	-	Ray Stephen (18 goals)
Av. Home Gate	-	9,000
Players used	-	24
Sent off (booked)	-	Three (44)

Scottish League Premier Division

		Home			Away			Goals		
	P	W	D	L	W	D	L	F	A	PTS
Celtic	36	10	6	2	10	4	4	67-38		50
Hearts	36	13	5	0	7	5	6	59-33		50
Dundee United	36	10	6	2	8	5	5	59-31		47
Aberdeen	36	11	4	3	5	8	5	62-31		44
Rangers	36	10	4	4	3	5	10	53-45		35
Dundee	**36**	**11**	**2**	**5**	**3**	**5**	**10**	**45-51**		**35**
St Mirren	36	9	2	7	4	3	11	42-63		31
Hibernian	36	6	4	8	5	2	11	49-63		28
Motherwell	36	7	3	8	0	3	15	33-66		20
Clydebank	36	4	6	8	2	2	14	29-77		20

Dundee F.C. Line-Ups 1985-86

		1	2	3	4	5	6	7	8	9	10	11	12	13
Aug	10th	Geddes	Shannon	Glennie	McCormack	Smith	Duffy	Rafferty	Brown	Jack	Connor	Stephen	McCall (8)	Harvey
	17th	Geddes	Shannon	Glennie	McCormack	Smith	Duffy	Rafferty	Brown	Jack	Connor	Stephen	McCall (7)	Harvey (11)
	21st	Geddes	Shannon	Glennie	McCormack	Smith	Duffy	Rafferty	Brown	Jack	Connor	Stephen	Harvey (4)	Forsyth
	24th	Geddes	Shannon	Glennie	Rafferty	Smith	Duffy	Jack	Brown	Harvey	Connor	Stephen	McCormack (8)	Kidd (7)
	28th	Geddes	Shannon	Glennie	McCormack	Smith	Duffy	Rafferty	Stephen	Harvey	Connor	Kidd	McCall	Brown
	31st	Geddes	Shannon	Glennie	McCormack	Smith	Duffy	Stephen	Brown	Black	Connor	Jack	McWilliams (7)	Waddell (11)
Sep	7th	Geddes	Shannon	Glennie	McCormack	Smith	Duffy	Rafferty	Brown	Harvey	Connor	Stephen	Hendry (8)	Black
	14th	Geddes	Shannon	Glennie	McCormack	Smith	Duffy	Rafferty	Brown	Harvey	Connor	Stephen	McWilliams (8)	Hendry (8)
	21st	Geddes	Shannon	Glennie	McCormack	Smith	Duffy	Rafferty	Brown	Harvey	Connor	Stephen	Hendry (8)	Jack
	28th	Geddes	Shannon	Glennie	McCormack	Smith	Duffy	Rafferty	Brown	Harvey	Connor	Stephen	Jack (9)	Hendry (5)
Oct	5th	Geddes	Shannon	Glennie	McCormack	Smith	Duffy	Rafferty	Hendry	Harvey	Connor	McWilliams	Forsyth (2)	Waddell (8)
	12th	Geddes	Shannon	Glennie	McCormack	Smith	Duffy	Rafferty	McKinlay	Stephen	Connor	McWilliams	Hendry (7)	Harvey (9)
	19th	Geddes	Shannon	Glennie	McCormack	Smith	Duffy	McWilliams	Brown	Hendry	Connor	McKinlay	Stephen (7)	Kidd (9)
	26th	Geddes	Shannon	Glennie	McCormack	Smith	Duffy	Stephen	Brown	Harvey	Connor	McKinlay	McWilliams (8)	Rafferty (10)
Nov	2nd	Geddes	Shannon	Glennie	McCormack	Smith	Duffy	Stephen	Brown	Harvey	Connor	McKinlay	McWilliams (9)	Rafferty (4)
	9th	Geddes	Shannon	Glennie	McCormack	Smith	Duffy	McWilliams	Brown	Stephen	Connor	McKinlay	Harvey (8)	Hendry
	16th	Geddes	Shannon	Glennie	McCormack	Smith	Duffy	McWilliams	Forsyth	Stephen	Connor	McKinlay	Brown (4)	Kidd (6)
	23rd	Geddes	Shannon	McKinlay*	Duffy	Smith	Glennie	Rafferty	Brown	Harvey	Connor	Stephen	Forsyth (9)	Kidd (7)
Dec	7th	Geddes	Shannon	Glennie	Rafferty	Smith	Duffy	Stephen	Brown	Harvey	Connor	Jack	Hendry (8)	Kidd (11)
	14th	Geddes	Glennie	McKinlay	Rafferty	Smith	Duffy	Shannon	Brown	Harvey	Connor	Stephen	Kidd (9)	Hendry (11)
	23rd	Geddes	Glennie	McKinlay	Rafferty	Smith	Duffy	Shannon	Brown	Harvey	Connor	Stephen	Kidd	Hendry
	28th	Geddes	Glennie	McKinlay	Kidd	Smith	Duffy	Shannon	Brown	Harvey	Connor	Stephen	Rafferty	Hendry
Jan	1st	Geddes	Glennie	McKinlay	Kidd	Smith	Duffy	Shannon	Brown	Harvey	Connor	Stephen	Rafferty (4)	Hendry (9)
	4th	Geddes	Glennie	McKinlay	Kidd	Smith	Duffy	Shannon	Brown	Harvey	Connor	Stephen	Rafferty (4)	McGeachie (5)
	11th	Geddes	Glennie	McKinlay	Shannon	Smith	Duffy	Rafferty	Brown	Hendry	Connor	Stephen	McCormack (5)	Kidd (11)
	18th	Geddes	Glennie	McKinlay	Shannon	McGeachie	Duffy	Rafferty	Brown	Hendry	Connor	Stephen	McCormack (5)	Harvey (9)
	25th	Geddes	Forsyth	McKinlay	Rafferty	Glennie	Duffy	Shannon	Stephen	Harvey	Connor	Hendry	McCormack (10)	Kidd (8)
Feb	1st	Geddes	Forsyth	McKinlay	Kidd	Glennie	Duffy	Shannon	Mennie	Harvey	Connor	Stephen	Rafferty (4)	McCormack (7)
	8th	Geddes	Glennie*	McKinlay	Forsyth	Smith	Duffy	Hendry	Brown	Mennie	Connor	Harvey	McWilliams (3)	McCormack (8)
	19th	Geddes	Forsyth	McKinlay	McCormack	Smith	Duffy	Shannon	Stephen	Mennie	Connor	Jack	Rafferty (10)	Harvey (7)
	22nd	Geddes	Forsyth	Shannon	Rafferty	Smith	Duffy	Hendry	Stephen	Mennie	Harvey	McWilliams	McCormack (7)	Campbell (8)
Mar	1st	Geddes	Forsyth	McKinlay	Shannon	Smith	Duffy	Hendry	Mennie	Harvey	Connor	Stephen	McCormack (10)	Rafferty (11)
	8th	Geddes	Forsyth	McKinlay	Shannon	Smith	Duffy	Hendry	Brown	Harvey	Connor	Mennie	McCormack	Rafferty (7)
	12th	Geddes	Forsyth	McKinlay	Shannon	Smith	Duffy	Stephen	Brown	Harvey	Connor	Mennie	Hendry (7)	Glennie (2)
	15th	Geddes	Shannon	McKinlay	Rafferty	Smith	Duffy	Mennie	Brown	Harvey	Connor	Stephen	McCormack (7)	Glennie (5)
	22nd	Geddes	Shannon	McKinlay	Rafferty	Smith	Duffy	Mennie	Brown	Harvey	Connor	Stephen	McCormack (5)	Campbell (8)
	29th	Geddes	Shannon	Glennie	Rafferty	McCormack	Duffy	Stephen	Mennie	Harvey	Connor	Hendry	Crainie (8)	Campbell (11)
Apr	2nd	Geddes	Shannon	Glennie	Rafferty	Hendry	Duffy	Stephen	Mennie	Harvey	Connor	Campbell	Crainie (5)	McCormack (4)
	12th	Geddes	Shannon	Glennie	Rafferty	Smith	Duffy	Stephen	Brown	Harvey	Connor	Campbell	Crainie (4)	Hendry (9)
	19th	Geddes	Forsyth	McKinlay	Glennie	Smith	Duffy	Rafferty	Brown	Mennie	Connor	Stephen	Harvey	McCormack
	26th	Geddes	Forsyth	McKinlay	Glennie	Smith	Duffy	Rafferty	Brown	Mennie	Connor	Stephen*	Harvey (8)	McCormack (3)
May	3rd	Geddes	Shannon	McKinlay	Glennie	Smith	Duffy	Mennie	Brown	Harvey	Connor	Hendry	McCormack (5)	Kidd (3

Power game- John Brown thunders home a penalty for his third goal in Dundee's 3-2 triumph over Rangers at Dens. Dave McPherson and Bobby Russell of Rangers, Dundee's Graham Harvey and referee George Smith watch as the ball rages into the net. DC Thomson

195

They Wore The Dark Blue

Season 1986-87

Date			Opponents		Score	Crowd	Scorers
Aug	2nd	FC1	Dundee United	h	0-1	4,250	-
	9th	L	Celtic	a	0-1	35,443	-
	13th	L	St Mirren	h	2-1	4,212	Ferguson; Stephen
	16th	L	Hibernian	h	3-0	7,216	Ferguson; Angus; Harvey
	20th	LC2	Morton	a	5-2*	2,097	Harvey 2; Stephen; Angus 2
	23rd	L	Falkirk	a	1-0	5,000	Stephen
	27th	LC3	Montrose	h	4-0	3,851	Jack; Shannon; Harvey; Brown (pen)
	30th	L	Aberdeen	a	0-2	12,500	-
Sep	3rd	LCQ	Rangers	a	1-3**	33,750	Forsyth
	6th	L	Dundee United	h	0-2	12,079	-
	13th	L	Motherwell	a	0-0	2,880	-
	20th	L	Rangers	h	1-0	17,132	Brown
	27th	L	Hearts	h	0-0	9,847	-
Oct	4th	L	Clydebank	a	2-0	1,507	Harvey; Stephen
	8th	L	Hamilton	a	3-0	1,941	Brown (pen); Stephen; Harvey
	11th	L	Celtic	h	0-3	15,351	-
	18th	L	St Mirren	a	1-4	3,032	Hendry
	25th	L	Falkirk	h	3-0	3,715	Harvey; Angus; Hendry
	29th	L	Hibernian	a	3-0	3,500	Jack; Stephen; Rafferty
Nov	1st	L	Aberdeen	h	0-2	8,200	-
	8th	L	Dundee United	a	3-0	11,733	Harvey 2; Shannon
	15th	L	Motherwell	h	1-1	4,167	Harvey
	19th	L	Rangers	a	1-2	22,992	Shannon
	22nd	L	Hearts	a	1-3	12,094	Angus
	29th	L	Clydebank	h	3-3	2,947	Rafferty; Harvey 2
Dec	3rd	L	Hamilton	h	3-3	2,525	Brown 2; Duffy (pen)
	6th	L	Celtic	a	0-2	19,300	-
	13th	L	St Mirren	h	6-3	3,498	Wright 2; Brown; Duffy (pen); Harvey 2
	27th	L	Hibernian	h	2-0	6,251	Shannon; Angus
Jan	1st	L	Aberdeen	a	1-2	11,000	Jack
	24th	L	Hearts	h	0-1	8,377	-
	27th	L	Motherwell	a	0-2	2,340	-
Feb	4th	SC3	East Fife	h	2-2	4,856	Smith; Coyne
	7th	L	Clydebank	a	1-1	1,037	Coyne
	9th	SC3R	East Fife	a	4-1	4,958	Harvey; Wright; Coyne; Jack
	14th	L	Hamilton	a	1-1	2,019	Coyne (pen)
	21st	SC4	Meadowbank	h	1-1	3,592	Harvey
	25th	SC4R	Meadowbank	a	1-1**	4,000	Jack
	28th	L	Celtic	h	4-1	12,455	Mennie; Shannon; Brown; Jack
Mar	2nd	SC4R	Meadowbank	h	2-0	4,516	Coyne 2 (1 pen)
	7th	L	St Mirren	a	1-0	2,294	McKinlay
	10th	L	Dundee United	h	1-1	11,615	Brown
	14th	SCQ	Clydebank	a	4-0	5,222	Wright; Coyne; Brown 2
	17th	L	Rangers	h	0-4	18,723	-
	21st	L	Hibernian	a	2-2	4,300	Coyne; Mitchell o.g.
	25th	L	Falkirk	h	4-0	2,997	Lawrence; Jack (pen); Wright; Brown
	28th	L	Dundee United	a	1-1	12,220	Rafferty
Apr	4th	L	Aberdeen	h	1-1	4,346	Brown
	11th	SCS	Dundee United	Tyn	2-3	13,913	Coyne; Wright
	14th	L	Rangers	a	0-2	42,427	-
	18th	L	Motherwell	h	4-1	3,080	Wright; McKinlay; Coyne 2
	21st	L	Falkirk	a	0-0		-
	25th	L	Clydebank	h	4-1	2,598	Coyne 3; Wright
May	2nd	L	Hearts	a	3-1	7,818	Wright 2; Rafferty
	9th	L	Hamilton	h	7-3	3,536	Brown; Wright 3; Shannon; Coyne (pen); Harvey

* a.e.t., 2-2 after 90 mts. ** a.e.t., 1-1 after 90 mts. Cup Cash v. Clydebank £10,000

Jim Duffy - the classy defender was to become a legendary figure at Dens.

Ray Stephen - last season's top scorer moved to Nancy in a big money deal.

The Record

League	-	Sixth Place, Premier Division
League Cup	-	Quarter-final
Scottish Cup	-	Semi-final
Forfarshire Cup	-	First round
Top Scorer	-	Graham Harvey (17 goals)
Av. Home Gate	-	7,500
Players used	-	24
Sent off (booked)	-	One (39)

Scottish League Premier Division

		Home			Away			Goals		
	P	W	D	L	W	D	L	F A	PTS
Rangers	44	18	2	2	13	5	4	85-23	69
Celtic	44	16	5	1	11	4	7	90-41	63
Dundee United	44	15	5	2	9	7	6	66-36	60
Aberdeen	44	13	6	3	8	10	4	63-28	58
Hearts	44	13	6	2	8	7	7	63-42	55
Dundee	**44**	**11**	**6**	**5**	**7**	**6**	**9**	**74-57**	**48**
St Mirren	44	9	5	8	3	7	12	36-51	36
Motherwell	44	7	5	10	4	7	11	43-64	34
Hibernian	44	6	8	8	4	5	13	44-70	33
Falkirk	44	4	9	9	4	1	17	31-70	26
Clydebank	44	3	7	12	3	5	14	35-93	24
Hamilton	44	2	4	16	4	5	13	39-93	21

Dundee F.C. Line-Ups 1986-87

		1	2	3	4	5	6	7	8	9	10	11	12	13
Aug	9th	Geddes	Forsyth	McKinlay	McGeachie	Smith	Duffy	Kidd	Shannon	Harvey	Connor	Stephen	Jack (2)	Ferguson (7)
	13th	Geddes	Forsyth	McKinlay	McGeachie	Smith	Duffy	Ferguson	Shannon	Harvey	Connor	Stephen	Kidd	Jack (9)
	16th	Geddes	McGeachie	McKinlay	Shannon	Smith	Duffy	Ferguson	Brown	Kidd	Angus	Stephen	Forsyth (8)	Harvey (2)
	20th	Geddes	Forsyth	McKinlay	McGeachie	Smith	Duffy	Shannon	Brown	Harvey	Angus	Stephen	Jack (4)	Kidd (8)
	23rd	Geddes	Forsyth	McKinlay	McGeachie	Smith	Duffy	Shannon	Brown	Angus	Stephen	Harvey	Jack (4)	Hendry
	27th	Geddes	Forsyth	McKinlay	Shannon	Smith	Duffy	Jack	Brown	Harvey	Angus	McGeachie	McGeachie (2)	Kidd (11)
	30th	Geddes	McGeachie	McKinlay	Shannon	Smith	Duffy	Jack	Brown	Harvey	Angus	Stephen	Hendry (7)	Mennie (8)
Sep	3rd	Geddes	Forsyth	McKinlay	Shannon	Smith*	Duffy	Rafferty	Brown	Harvey	Angus	Stephen	McWilliams	Jack (9)
	6th	Geddes	McGeachie	McKinlay	Shannon	Hendry	Duffy	McWilliams	Brown	Jack	Angus	Stephen	Rafferty (4)	Forsyth (2)
	13th	Geddes	Forsyth	McKinlay	McGeachie	Smith	Duffy	Shannon	Brown	Harvey	Angus	Stephen	Rafferty	Jack (9)
	20th	Geddes	McGeachie	McKinlay	Shannon	Smith	Duffy	Jack	Brown	Harvey	Angus	Stephen	Rafferty	Mennie (2)
	27th	Geddes	Forsyth	McKinlay	Shannon	Smith	Duffy	Mennie	Brown	Jack	Kidd	Stephen	Harvey (7)	Rafferty (10)
Oct	4th	Geddes	Shannon	McKinlay	Rafferty	Smith	Duffy	Jack	Brown	Harvey	Angus	Stephen	McGeachie (7)	Hendry
	8th	Geddes	Shannon	McKinlay	Rafferty	Smith	Duffy	Jack	Brown	Harvey	Angus	Stephen	Hendry	McGeachie
	11th	Geddes	Shannon	McKinlay	McGeachie	Smith	Duffy	Jack	Brown	Harvey	Angus	Stephen	Hendry (4)	Rafferty (8)
	18th	Geddes	Shannon	McKinlay	McGeachie	Smith	Duffy	Rafferty	Jack	Harvey	Angus	Stephen	Hendry (11)	Mennie (8)
	25th	Geddes	Shannon	McKinlay	McGeachie	Smith	Duffy	Rafferty	Brown	Harvey	Angus	Stephen	Mennie (8)	Hendry (2)
	29th	Geddes	Shannon	McKinlay	McGeachie	Smith	Duffy	Mennie	Kidd	Jack	Angus	Stephen	Rafferty (6)	Hendry (9)
Nov	1st	Geddes	Shannon	McKinlay	McGeachie	Smith	Duffy	Mennie	Kidd	Harvey	Angus	Stephen	Hendry (8)	Rafferty (7)
	8th	Geddes	Shannon	McKinlay	McGeachie	Smith	Duffy	Rafferty	Jack	Harvey	Angus	Stephen	Mennie	Campbell (3)
	15th	Geddes	Shannon	Campbell	Forsyth	Smith	Duffy	Rafferty	Jack	Harvey	Angus	Mennie	Hendry (3)	McWilliams (11
	19th	Geddes	Shannon	McWilliams	Forsyth	Smith	Duffy	Rafferty	Jack	Harvey	Angus	Mennie	Campbell	Davidson (11)
	22nd	Geddes	Shannon	McWilliams	Forsyth	Smith	Duffy	Rafferty	Jack	Harvey	Angus	Mennie	Kidd (11)	Campbell
	29th	Geddes	Forsyth	Shannon	Mennie	Smith	Duffy	Rafferty	Jack	Harvey	Angus	Kidd	McWilliams (8)	McGeachie (11)
Dec	3rd	Geddes	Forsyth	Shannon	Mennie	Smith	Duffy	Rafferty	Brown	Harvey	Angus	McWilliams	Campbell (8)	McGeachie (11)
	6th	Geddes	Forsyth	Shannon	McGeachie	Smith	Hendry	Rafferty	Brown	Harvey	Angus	Mennie	Glennie	Wright (8)
	13th	Geddes	Forsyth	Shannon	Rafferty	Smith	Duffy	Coyne	Brown	Harvey	Angus	Wright	Hendry (11)	Mennie (8)
	27th	Geddes	Forsyth	Shannon	Hendry	Smith	Duffy	Coyne	Rafferty	Harvey	Angus	Wright	Jack (11)	Glennie (4)
Jan	1st	Geddes	Glennie	Shannon	Rafferty	Smith	Duffy	Coyne	Brown	Harvey	Angus	Wright	Jack (11)	Forsyth
	24th	Geddes	Forsyth	Shannon	Glennie	Smith	Duffy	Coyne	Rafferty	Harvey	Angus	Jack	Wright (9)	Mennie
	27th	Geddes	Forsyth	Shannon	Glennie	Smith	Duffy	Coyne	Brown	Harvey	Angus	Rafferty	Jack (3)	Hendry (9)
Feb	4th	Geddes	Forsyth	McKinlay	Shannon	Smith	Duffy	Coyne	Brown	Harvey	Rafferty	Jack	Wright (9)	Angus
	7th	Geddes	Shannon	McKinlay	Rafferty	Glennie	Duffy	Coyne	Brown	Harvey	Angus	Wright	Forsyth	Mennie
	9th	Geddes	Shannon	Glennie	Rafferty	Smith	Duffy	Coyne	Mennie	Harvey	Angus	Wright	Jack (11)	Forsyth
	14th	Geddes	Shannon	Glennie	Rafferty	Smith	Duffy	Coyne	Mennie	Harvey	Angus	Wright	Jack	Forsyth
	21st	Geddes	Shannon	Mckinlay	Rafferty	Glennie	Duffy	Coyne	Mennie	Harvey	Angus	Wright	Brown (4)	Forsyth (2)
	25th	Geddes	Shannon	McKinlay	Rafferty	Glennie	Smith	Coyne	Mennie	Harvey	Angus	Jack	Forsyth (11)	Hendry (9)
	28th	Geddes	Shannon	McKinlay	Glennie	Smith	Duffy	Forsyth	Brown	Mennie	Coyne	Jack	Rafferty (9)	Wright (11)
Mar	2nd	Geddes	Shannon	McKinlay	Glennie	Smith	Duffy	Forsyth	Brown	Mennie	Coyne	Jack	Rafferty (9)	Wright
	7th	Geddes	Shannon	McKinlay	Glennie	Smith	Duffy	Forsyth	Brown	Mennie	Coyne	Wright	Rafferty	Jack
	10th	Geddes	McGeachie	McKinlay	Rafferty	Smith	Duffy	Forsyth	Brown	Harvey	Coyne	Jack	Wright (2)	Campbell
	14th	Geddes	Shannon	McKinlay	Glennie	Smith	Duffy	Forsyth	Brown	Mennie	Coyne	Wright	Rafferty (9)	Harvey (11)
	17th	Geddes	Shannon	McKinlay	Glennie	Smith	Duffy	Forsyth	Brown	Mennie	Coyne	Jack	Rafferty (8)	Wright (9)
	21st	Geddes	McGeachie	McKinlay	Rafferty	Glennie	Duffy	Lawrence	Brown	Harvey	Coyne	Angus	Mennie (7)	Wright
	25th	Geddes	Forsyth	McKinlay	Rafferty	Glennie	Smith	McGeachie	Lawrence	Brown	Jack	Wright	Mennie (6)	Harvey (11)
	28th	Geddes	Forsyth	McKinlay	Rafferty	Glennie	Duffy	Shannon	Brown	Jack	Coyne	Wright	McGeachie (8)	Lawrence (11)
Apr	4th	Geddes	Forsyth	McKinlay	McGeachie	Smith	Duffy	Rafferty	Brown	Jack	Coyne	Wright	Angus	Glennie
	11th	Geddes	Forsyth	McKinlay	Shannon	Smith	Duffy	Rafferty	Brown	Jack	Coyne	Wright	Angus (9)	Glennie (3)
	14th	Geddes	McGeachie	McKinlay	Glennie	Smith	Duffy	Rafferty	Brown	Shannon	Coyne	Wright	Forsyth (8)	Jack
	18th	Geddes	McGeachie	McKinlay	Glennie	Smith	Duffy	Rafferty	Brown	Shannon	Coyne	Wright	Forsyth	Jack
	21st	Geddes	McGeachie	McKinlay	Glennie	Smith	Duffy	Rafferty	Brown	Shannon	Coyne	Wright	Angus	Lawrence
	25th	Geddes	McGeachie	McKinlay	Glennie	Smith	Duffy	Forsyth	Brown	Lawrence	Coyne	Wright	Rafferty (4)	Harvey (9)
May	2nd	Geddes	Forsyth	McKinlay	Glennie	Smith	Duffy	Rafferty	Brown	Shannon	Coyne	Wright	Angus	Harvey
	9th	Geddes	Forsyth	McKinlay	Rafferty	Glennie	Duffy	Campbell	Brown	Shannon	Coyne	Wright	Angus (7)	Harvey (9)

Appearances

	League	L/Cup	S/Cup	Total
Bobby Geddes	44	3	7	54
Jim Duffy	42 (2)	3	6	51 (2)
Rab Shannon	39 (5)	3 (1)	7	49 (6)
Jim Smith	39	3	6 (1)	48 (1)
Tosh McKinlay	32 (2)	3	6	41 (2)
John Brown	31 (10)	3 (1)	4 (2)	38+1s (13)
Graham Harvey	28 (12)	3 (3)	4 (2)	35+6s (17)
Ian Angus	28 (4)	3 (2)	3	34+2s (6)
Stuart Rafferty	28 (4)	1	5	34+10s (4)
Stewart Forsyth	25	3 (1)	4	32+5s (1)
Tommy Coyne	20 (9)	0	7 (6)	27 (15)
Ross Jack	21 (4)	1 (1)	4 (2)	26+10s (7)
George McGeachie	23	2	0	25+5s
Bobby Glennie	17	0	5	22+2s
Ray Stephen	17 (5)	2 (1)	0	19 (6)
Keith Wright	15 (10)	0	4 (3)	19+6s (13)
Vince Mennie	13 (1)	0	5	18+7s (1)
Albert Kidd	6	0	0	6+3s
Derek McWilliams	4	0	0	4+2s
Colin Hendry	3 (2)	0	0	3+10s (2)
Alan Lawrence	3 (1)	0	0	3+1s (1)
Steve Campbell	2	0	0	2+2s
Bobby Connor	2	0	0	2
Iain Ferguson	2 (2)	0	0	2+1s (2)

Graham Harvey (front) celebrates but the top scorer in 1986-87 later made way for the prolific Coyne-Wright partnership. DC Thomson

Season 1987-88

Date			Opponents		Score	Crowd	Scorers
July	26th	FC1	Arbroath	h	6-2		Coyne; Brown; Grant 2; Angus; Chisholm
Aug	8th	L	Aberdeen	h	1-1	10,223	Angus
	12th	L	Falkirk	a	3-0	2,800	Brown 2; Wright
	15th	L	Hibernian	a	4-0	8,200	Coyne 2 (1 pen); Wright; Brown
	19th	LC2	Queens Park	a	3-0	1,140	McKinlay; Wright; Coyne
	22nd	L	St Mirren	h	0-2	5,969	-
	26th	LC3	Meadowbank	a	3-0	2,500	Coyne 2; Wright
	29th	L	Dunfermline	h	5-0	7,564	Coyne 4 (1 pen); Wright
Sep	2nd	LCQ	Dundee United	h	2-1*	19,724	Coyne; Wright
	5th	L	Rangers	a	1-2	38,312	Harvey
	12th	L	Morton	a	3-4	4,026	Angus; Coyne 2 (1 pen)
	19th	L	Hearts	h	1-3	9,199	Smith
	23rd	LCS	Aberdeen	Tan	0-2	22,034	-
	26th	L	Motherwell	a	2-0	2,656	Harvey; Coyne
Oct	3rd	L	Dundee United	h	1-1	11,497	Coyne
	7th	L	Celtic	h	1-1	11,238	Angus
	10th	L	Aberdeen	a	0-0	12,500	-
	17th	L	Dunfermline	a	1-0	6,890	Lawrence
	28th	L	Morton	h	1-0	3,829	Harvey
	31st	L	Hearts	a	2-4	13,806	Coyne; Wright
Nov	3rd	FCS	Brechin City	a	3-1	700	S. Campbell; Mennie 2
	7th	L	Falkirk	h	3-1	4,324	Coyne 2 (1 pen); Wright
	14th	L	Celtic	a	0-5	31,684	-
	18th	L	St Mirren	a	2-1	3,328	Coyne (pen); Smith
	21st	L	Hibernian	h	2-1	6,583	Coyne 2
	24th	L	Motherwell	h	2-0	3,695	Coyne; Mennie
	28th	L	Dundee United	a	3-1	13,625	Coyne 2; Wright
Dec	5th	L	Aberdeen	h	1-2	8,799	Forsyth
	12th	L	Falkirk	a	6-0	4,500	Coyne 2; Wright 2; Manley 2 o.g.'s
	16th	L	Morton	a	7-1	3,500	Wright 2; Coyne 3; McGeachie; Harvey
	19th	L	Hearts	h	0-0	10,806	-
	26th	L	Rangers	a	0-2	40,938	-
	28th	FCF	Dundee United	h	2-3	4,773	Grant; Harvey
Jan	1st	L	Dunfermline	h	2-0	8,527	Coyne 2 (1 pen)
	6th	L	Rangers	h	0-1	17,400	-
	9th	L	Motherwell	a	3-3	2,785	Coyne 2 (1 pen); Angus
	16th	L	Dundee United	h	0-2	13,651	-
	30th	SC3	Brechin City	h	0-0	5,040	-
Feb	3rd	SC3R	Brechin City	a	3-0	3,012	Harvey 2; Wright
	6th	L	Hibernian	a	1-2	8,000	Wright
	13th	L	Celtic	h	1-2	17,106	Angus
	20th	SC4	Motherwell	h	2-0	7,243	Angus; Rafferty
	27th	L	Aberdeen	a	0-1	13,500	-
Mar	1st	L	St Mirren	h	2-1	4,265	Coyne 2 (1 pen)
	5th	L	Morton	h	1-0	4,319	Coyne
	12th	SCQ	Dundee United	h	0-0	19,355	-
	15th	SCQR	Dundee United	a	2-2**	17,055	Harvey 2
	19th	L	Dunfermline	a	1-6	5,507	Wright
	26th	L	Rangers	h	2-3	14,879	Angus; Coyne
	28th	SCQR	Dundee United	h	0-3	19,152	-
	30th	L	Hearts	a	0-2	9,649	-
Apr	2nd	L	Dundee United	a	0-1	13,874	-
	6th	L	Motherwell	h	1-2	3,732	Campbell
	16th	L	Falkirk	h	4-1	4,970	Wright 3; Coyne
	23rd	L	Celtic	a	0-3	60,800	-
	30th	L	Hibernian	h	0-0	4,609	-
May	7th	L	St Mirren	a	0-1	5,746	-

* a.e.t., 1-1 after 90 mts. ** a.e.t., 2-2 after 90 mts.
Cup Cash v. Motherwell £13,600

The Record

League	-	**Seventh Place, Premier Division**
League Cup	-	**Semi-final**
Scottish Cup	-	**Quarter-final**
Forfarshire Cup	-	**Runners up**
Top Scorer	-	**Tommy Coyne (37 goals)**
Av. Home Gate	-	**8,600**
Players used	-	**26**
Sent off (booked)	-	**Three (53)**

Tommy Coyne - earned UEFA's Bronze Boot after netting 37 goals in 1987-88.

Rab Shannon - the Dundee defender gained seven Scottish Under-21 caps.

Scottish League Premier Division

		Home			Away			Goals		
	P	W	D	L	W	D	L	F A	PTS
Celtic	44	16	5	1	15	5	2	79-23	72
Hearts	44	13	8	1	10	8	4	74-32	62
Rangers	44	14	4	4	12	4	6	85-34	60
Aberdeen	44	11	7	4	10	10	2	56-25	59
Dundee United	44	8	7	7	8	8	6	54-47	47
Hibernian	44	8	8	6	4	11	7	41-42	43
Dundee	**44**	**9**	**5**	**8**	**8**	**2**	**12**	**70-64**	**41**
Motherwell	44	10	2	10	3	8	11	37-56	36
St Mirren	44	5	11	6	5	4	13	41-64	35
Falkirk	44	8	4	10	2	7	13	41-75	31
Dunfermline	44	6	6	10	2	4	16	41-84	26
Morton	44	3	7	12	0	3	19	27-100	16

Dundee F.C. Line-Ups 1987-88

		1	2	3	4	5	6	7	8	9	10	11	12	13
Aug	8th	Geddes	Forsyth	McKinlay	Shannon	Glennie	Duffy	Mennie	Brown	Wright	Coyne	Angus	Lawrence (7)	Rafferty
	12th	Geddes	Forsyth	McKinlay	Shannon	Glennie	Duffy*	Mennie	Brown	Wright	Coyne	Angus	Smith (7)	Jack (9)
	15th	Geddes	Forsyth	McKinlay	Shannon	Smith	Glennie	Rafferty	Brown	Wright	Coyne	Angus	McGeachie (7)	Harvey (8)
	19th	Geddes	Glennie	McKinlay	Shannon	Smith	Duffy	Forsyth	Brown	Wright	Coyne	Angus	McGeachie (8)	Jack (4)
	22nd	Geddes	McGeachie	McKinlay	Shannon	Smith	Duffy	Forsyth	Mennie	Wright	Coyne	Angus	Lawrence (2)	Harvey (11)
	26th	Geddes	Forsyth	McKinlay	Glennie	Smith	Duffy	Mennie	Shannon	Wright	Coyne	Angus	Lawrence	Harvey
	29th	Geddes	Forsyth	McKinlay	Glennie	Smith	Duffy	Mennie	Shannon	Wright	Coyne	Angus	Harvey (9)	Jack (10)
Sep	2nd	Geddes	Forsyth	McKinlay	Glennie	Smith	Duffy	Mennie	Shannon	Wright	Coyne	Angus	Harvey (7)	Jack (10)
	5th	Geddes	Forsyth	McKinlay	Glennie	Smith	Duffy	Mennie	Shannon	Wright	Coyne	Angus	Jack (6)	Harvey (8)
	12th	Geddes	Forsyth	McKinlay	Shannon	Smith	Glennie	Lawrence	Mennie	Wright	Coyne	Angus	McGeachie (7)	Harvey (8)
	19th	Geddes	Forsyth	McKinlay	McGeachie	Smith	Glennie	Shannon*	Brown	Wright	Coyne	Angus	Lawrence (2)	Harvey
	23rd	Geddes	McGeachie	McKinlay	Mennie	Smith	Glennie	Harvey	Brown	Wright	Coyne	Angus	Forsyth	Jack (4)
	26th	Geddes	McGeachie	McKinlay	Glennie	Smith	Chisholm	Mennie	Brown	Harvey	Coyne	Shannon	Jack (7)	Angus
Oct	3rd	Geddes	McGeachie	McKinlay	Glennie	Smith	Chisholm	Shannon	Brown	Wright	Coyne	Lawrence	Angus (3)	Harvey (2)
	7th	Geddes	Forsyth	Angus	Glennie	Smith	Chisholm	Shannon	Brown	Wright	Coyne	Lawrence	Mennie (11)	Harvey
	10th	Geddes	Forsyth	Angus	Glennie	Smith	Chisholm	Shannon	Brown	Wright	Coyne	Lawrence	Mennie	Harvey
	17th	Geddes	Forsyth	Angus	Glennie	Smith	Chisholm	Shannon	Brown	Wright	Coyne	Lawrence	Mennie (8)	Harvey (11)
	28th	Geddes	Forsyth	Glennie	Shannon	Smith	Chisholm	Mennie	Brown	Harvey	Coyne	Wright	Rafferty (9)	Lawrence
	31st	Geddes	Forsyth	Glennie	Shannon	Smith	Chisholm	Mennie	Brown	Wright	Coyne	Angus	Rafferty (3)	Harvey
Nov	7th	Geddes	Forsyth	Glennie	Shannon	Smith	Chisholm	Mennie	Brown	Wright	Coyne	Angus	Rafferty	Harvey
	14th	Geddes	Forsyth	Glennie	Shannon	Smith	Chisholm	Mennie	Brown	Wright	Coyne	Angus	Rafferty (8)	McGeachie
	18th	Geddes	Forsyth	McGeachie	Shannon	Smith	Chisholm	Mennie	Rafferty	Wright	Coyne	Angus	Lawrence	Harvey
	21st	Geddes	Forsyth	McGeachie	Shannon	Smith	Chisholm	Mennie	Rafferty	Wright	Coyne	Angus	Brown	Harvey
	24th	Geddes	Forsyth	McGeachie	Shannon	Smith	Chisholm	Mennie	Rafferty	Wright	Coyne	Angus	Brown (2)	Harvey (9)
	28th	Geddes	Forsyth	McGeachie	Shannon	Smith	Chisholm	Mennie	Rafferty	Wright	Coyne	Angus	Glennie	Harvey
Dec	5th	Geddes	Forsyth	McGeachie	Shannon	Smith	Chisholm	Mennie	Rafferty	Wright	Coyne	Angus	Lawrence (3)	Harvey (7)
	12th	Geddes	Forsyth	McGeachie	Shannon	Smith	Chisholm	Mennie	Rafferty	Wright	Coyne	Angus	Brown	Harvey
	16th	Geddes	Forsyth	McGeachie	Shannon	Smith	Rafferty	Mennie	Brown	Wright	Coyne	Angus	Harvey (3)	Frail (7)
	19th	Geddes	Forsyth	McKinlay	Shannon	Smith	Rafferty	Mennie	Brown	Wright	Coyne	Angus	Harvey	Frail
	26th	Geddes	Forsyth	McKinlay	Shannon	Smith	Rafferty	McGeachie	Brown	Wright	Coyne	Angus	Harvey (7)	Glennie
Jan	1st	Geddes	Forsyth	McKinlay	Shannon	Smith	Rafferty	Harvey	Brown	Wright	Coyne	Angus	Glennie	Lawrence
	6th	Geddes	Forsyth	Glennie	Shannon	Smith	Rafferty	Harvey	Brown	Wright	Coyne	Angus	Lawrence	Campbell
	9th	Geddes	Forsyth	Glennie	Shannon	Smith	Rafferty	Harvey	Brown	Wright	Coyne	Angus	Lawrence (8)	Campbell
	16th	Geddes	Forsyth	McKinlay	Shannon	Smith	Glennie	Harvey	Rafferty	Wright	Coyne	Angus	McFarlane (4)	Lawrence (7)
	30th	Geddes	Forsyth	McKinlay	Shannon	Smith	Glennie	Harvey	Rafferty	Wright	Coyne	Angus	McFarlane (6)	Campbell (11)
Feb	3rd	Geddes	McFarlane	McKinlay	Shannon	Smith	Mennie	Harvey	Rafferty	Wright	Coyne	Angus	Ogilvie	Campbell
	6th	Geddes	McFarlane	McKinlay	Shannon	Smith	Mennie	Harvey	Rafferty	Wright	Coyne	Angus	Ogilvie	Campbell
	13th	Geddes	Forsyth	McKinlay	Shannon	Smith	Saunders	Mennie	Rafferty	Wright	Coyne	Angus	Harvey (6)	McFarlane
	20th	Geddes	Forsyth	McKinlay	McFarlane	Smith	Glennie	Mennie	Rafferty	Wright	Coyne	Angus	Lawrence (6)	Harvey
	27th	Geddes	Forsyth	McKinlay	Kirkwood	Smith	Mennie	Lawrence	Rafferty	Wright	Coyne	Angus	Harvey (7)	McFarlane
Mar	1st	Geddes	Forsyth	McKinlay	Shannon	Smith	Kirkwood	Mennie	Rafferty	Wright	Coyne	Angus	Rowell (4)	Lawrence
	5th	Geddes	Forsyth	McKinlay	Kirkwood	Smith	Saunders	Mennie	Rafferty	Wright	Coyne	Angus	Harvey (6)	Lawrence (9)
	12th	Carson	Forsyth	McKinlay	Shannon	Smith	Saunders	Mennie	Rafferty	Wright	Coyne	Angus	Lawrence (6)	Harvey
	15th	Carson	Forsyth	McKinlay	Shannon	Smith	Saunders	Mennie	Rafferty	Wright	Coyne	Angus	Harvey (3)	Lawrence
	19th	Carson	Forsyth	Kirkwood	Shannon	Smith	Saunders	Mennie	Rafferty	Wright	Harvey	Angus	Lawrence (6)	Rowell
	26th	Geddes	Forsyth	Kirkwood	Shannon	Smith	Saunders	Lawrence	Rafferty	Harvey	Coyne	Angus	Wright	Mennie
	28th	Geddes	Forsyth	Mennie	Shannon	Smith	Saunders	Lawrence	Rafferty*	Wright	Coyne	Angus	Harvey (4)	Frail
	30th	Geddes	Forsyth	Angus	Mennie	Kirkwood	Saunders	Lawrence	Frail	Wright	Coyne	Campbell	Harvey (8)	Craib
Apr	2nd	Geddes	Kirkwood	Campbell	Shannon	Forsyth	Saunders	Lawrence	Rafferty	Harvey	Coyne	Mennie	Wright (11)	Frail
	6th	Carson	Kirkwood	McSkimming	Shannon	Forsyth	Saunders	Lawrence	Rafferty	Frail	Coyne	Campbell	Wright (7)	Mennie
	16th	Carson	Forsyth	Campbell	Shannon	Smith	Saunders	Lawrence	Rafferty	Wright	Coyne	Angus	Frail	Harvey
	23rd	Carson	Forsyth	Angus	Shannon	Smith	Saunders	Lawrence	Rafferty	Wright	Coyne	Campbell	Harvey (4)	Frail (7)
	30th	Carson	Forsyth	Angus	Shannon	Smith	Saunders*	Lawrence	Harvey	Wright	Coyne	Campbell	Harvey (5)	Frail
May	7th	Carson	Forsyth	Angus	Shannon	Smith	Saunders	Lawrence	Rafferty	Wright	Coyne	Kirkwood	Campbell (7)	Harvey (8)

Appearances

	League		L/Cup		S/Cup		Total	
Tommy Coyne	43	(33)	4	(4)	6		53	(37)
Keith Wright	40	(15)	4	(3)	6	(1)	50+2s	(19)
Ian Angus	39	(6)	4		6	(1)	49	(7)
Stewart Forsyth	41	(1)	3		5		49+1s	(1)
Jim Smith	39	(2)	4		6		49+1s	(2)
Rab Shannon	40		3		5		48	
Bobby Geddes	38		4		4		46	
Vince Mennie	27	(1)	3		5		35+2s	(1)
Stuart Rafferty	27		0		6	(1)	33+3s	(1)
Tosh McKinlay	19		4	(1)	5		28	(1)
Bobby Glennie	19		4		2		25	
John Brown	19	(3)	2		0		21+1s	(3)
Gordon Chisholm	15		0		0		15	
Alan Lawrence	14	(1)	0		1		15+10s	(1)
Wes Saunders	11		0		3		14	
Graham Harvey	10	(4)	1		2	(4)	13+21s	(8)
George McGeachie	12	(1)	1		0		13+3s	(1)
Jim Duffy	5		3		0		8	
Billy Kirkwood	9		0		0		9	
Tom Carson	6		0		2		8	
Steve Campbell	6	(1)	0		0		6+2s	(1)
Dave McFarlane	1		0		2		3+2s	
Steve Frail	2		0		0		2+2s	
Shaun McSkimming	1		0		0		1	

George McGeachie is just too late to prevent Rangers Scottish international winger Davie Cooper getting over a cross. DC Thomson

Appearances

	League	L/Cup	S/Cup	Total
Ross Jack	0	0	0	0+7s
Gary Rowell	0	0	0	0+1s

Season 1988-89

Date			Opponents		Score	Crowd	Scorers
Aug	13th	L	Aberdeen	h	1-1	12,222	Chisholm
	17th	LC2	QOS	h	5-1	3,846	McGeachie; Harvey 3; Wright
	20th	L	Motherwell	a	1-1	3,803	Wright
	24th	LC3	Falkirk	h	2-1	4,962	Wright; Lawrence
	27th	L	St Mirren	a	0-0	3,805	-
	31st	LCQ	Rangers	a	1-4	39,667	Rafferty
Sep	3rd	L	Dundee United	h	0-3	14,927	-
	17th	L	Hamilton	a	0-1	2,194	-
	24th	L	Celtic	h	1-0	15,574	Coyne
	28th	L	Hearts	a	1-1	8,392	Shannon
Oct	1st	L	Rangers	a	0-2	40,768	-
	8th	L	Hibernian	h	2-1	8,127	Chisholm; Coyne
	12th	L	Motherwell	h	1-1	4,161	Wright
	24th	FCS	Forfar Athletic	a	4-3*	767	Lawrence; Coyne; Harvey 2
	29th	L	Celtic	a	3-2	25,843	Frail; Harvey; Rafferty
Nov	2nd	L	Hamilton	h	5-2	3,857	Harvey; Wright; Coyne 3
	5th	L	Dundee United	a	0-2	14,882	-
	12th	L	St Mirren	h	0-1	4,657	-
	16th	L	Aberdeen	a	0-1	11,000	-
	19th	L	Rangers	h	0-0	16,514	-
	26th	L	Hibernian	a	1-1	9,000	Coyne
Dec	3rd	L	Hearts	h	1-1	6,902	Harvey
	10th	L	Hamilton	a	0-1	2,083	-
	12th	FCF	Arbroath	a	3-0	n/a	Shannon; D. Campbell; Kirkwood
	17th	L	Motherwell	a	0-1	4,560	-
	31st	L	Aberdeen	h	2-0	9,828	Coyne 2
Jan	3rd	L	St Mirren	a	1-1	4,920	Wright
	7th	L	Dundee United	h	0-1	16,332	-
	14th	L	Hibernian	h	1-2	7,261	McBride
	21st	L	Rangers	a	1-3	43,202	Wright
	28th	SC3	Dundee United	h	1-2	18,117	Angus
Feb	11th	L	Hearts	a	1-3	10,432	Lawrence
	25th	L	Celtic	h	0-3	14,559	-
Mar	11th	L	Aberdeen	a	0-2	11,800	-
	25th	L	Motherwell	h	2-1	3,718	McBride; Chisholm
Apr	1st	L	St Mirren	h	2-1	3,824	Craig; D. Campbell
	8th	L	Dundee United	a	1-2	11,910	Saunders
	15th	L	Hearts	h	2-1	6,993	Chisholm; Wright
	22nd	L	Celtic	a	1-2	19,105	Harvey (pen)
	29th	L	Hamilton	h	1-0	4,100	Craig
May	6th	L	Rangers	h	1-2	14,889	Wright

Ian Angus - industrious midfielder was signed from Aberdeen in 1986.

* After extra-time, 2-2 after 90 mts. Cup Cash v. Dundee Unoited £50,000

Appearances

	League	L/Cup	S/Cup	Total	
Keith Wright	35 (8)	3 (2)	1	39	(10)
Bobby Geddes	34	3	1	38	
Gordon Chisholm	33 (4)	3	1	37+1s	(4)
Stewart Forsyth	33	3	1	37	
Wes Saunders	30 (1)	3	1	34	(1)
Tommy Coyne	26 (8)	2	1	29+1s	(8)
Rab Shannon	29 (1)	0	0	29	(1)
Stuart Rafferty	26 (1)	0 (1)	0	26+8s	(2)
Steve Frail	21 (1)	0	1	22+2s	(1)
Steve Campbell	18	3	0	21+6s	
Tosh McKinlay	18	3	0	21	
Graham Harvey	11 (4)	3 (3)	0	14+9s	(7)
Joe McBride	13 (2)	0	1	14+4s	(2)
Ian Angus	12 (1)	0	1	13+3s	(1)
Billy Kirkwood	10	2	1	13+3s	
John Holt	10	0	1	11+1s	
Jim Smith	7	3	0	10+1s	
Alan Lawrence	8 (1)	1 (1)	0	9+3s	(2)
George McGeachie	6	1 (1)	0	7	(1)
Duncan Campbell	6 (1)	0	0	6+2s	(1)
Albert Craig	6 (2)	0	0	6	(2)
Mark Craib	2	0	0	2+2s	
Tom Carson	2	0	0	2	
Vince Mennie	0	0	0	0+4s	
John Hendry	0	0	0	0+2s	

The Record		
League	-	Eighth Place, Premier Division
League Cup	-	Quarter-final
Scottish Cup	-	Third round
Forfarshire Cup	-	Winners
Top Scorer	-	Keith Wright (10 goals)
Av. Home Gate	-	9,400
Players used	-	25
Sent off (booked)	-	One (51)

Scottish League Premier Division

		Home			Away			Goals		
	P	W	D	L	W	D	L	F	A	PTS
Rangers	36	15	1	2	11	3	4	62-26		56
Aberdeen	36	10	7	1	8	7	3	51-25		50
Celtic	36	13	1	4	8	3	7	66-44		46
Dundee United	36	6	8	4	10	4	4	44-26		44
Hibernian	36	8	4	6	5	5	8	37-36		35
Hearts	36	7	6	5	2	7	9	35-42		31
St Mirren	36	5	6	7	6	1	11	39-55		29
Dundee	**36**	**8**	**4**	**6**	**1**	**6**	**11**	**34-48**		**28**
Motherwell	36	5	7	6	2	6	10	35-44		27
Hamilton	36	5	0	13	1	2	15	19-76		14

Dundee F.C. Line-Ups 1988-89

		1	2	3	4	5	6	7	8	9	10	11	12	13
Aug	13th	Geddes	Forsyth	McKinlay	Chisholm	Smith	Saunders	Lawrence	Angus	Wright	Harvey	Campbell S	Rafferty (8)	Mennie (11)
	17th	Geddes	Forsyth	McKinlay	Chisholm	Smith	Saunders	Lawrence	McGeachie	Wright	Harvey	Campbell S	Kirkwood (8)	Coyne (10)
	20th	Geddes	Forsyth	McKinlay	Chisholm	Smith	Saunders	Campbell S	Kirkwood	Coyne	Harvey	Wright	Mennie (9)	Craib
	24th	Geddes	Forsyth	McKinlay	Chisholm	Smith	Saunders	Campbell S	Kirkwood	Coyne	Harvey	Wright	Lawrence (7)	Craib
	27th	Geddes	Forsyth	McKinlay	Chisholm	Smith	Saunders	Harvey	Kirkwood	Wright	Coyne	Lawrence	Campbell (10)	Craib
	31st	Geddes	Forsyth	McKinlay	Chisholm	Smith	Saunders	Harvey	Kirkwood	Wright	Coyne	Campbell S	Shannon (5)	Rafferty (3)
Sep	3rd	Geddes	Forsyth	McKinlay	Chisholm	Saunders	Shannon	Harvey	Kirkwood	Wright	Coyne	Rafferty	Campbell (7)	Hendry (10)
	17th	Geddes	Forsyth	McKinlay	Chisholm	Kirkwood	Saunders	Rafferty	Shannon	Wright	Coyne	Campbell S	Harvey (11)	Frail (7)
	24th	Geddes	Kirkwood	McKinlay	Chisholm	Forsyth	Saunders	Rafferty	Shannon	Wright	Coyne	Campbell S	Harvey	Smith
	28th	Geddes	Kirkwood	McKinlay	Chisholm	Forsyth	Saunders	Rafferty	Shannon	Wright	Coyne	Campbell S	Frail	Smith
Oct	1st	Geddes	Kirkwood	McKinlay	Chisholm	Forsyth	Saunders	Rafferty	Shannon	Wright	Coyne	Campbell S	Frail	Craib
	8th	Geddes	Kirkwood	McKinlay	Chisholm	Forsyth	Saunders	Rafferty	Shannon	Wright	Coyne	Campbell S	Angus (8)	Hendry
	12th	Geddes	Kirkwood	McKinlay	Chisholm	Forsyth	Saunders	Rafferty	Shannon	Wright	Coyne	Campbell S	Hendry (7)	Smith
	29th	Geddes	Shannon	McKinlay	Chisholm	Forsyth	Frail	Rafferty	Harvey	Wright	Coyne	Lawrence	Mennie (11)	Smith
Nov	2nd	Geddes	Shannon	McKinlay	Chisholm	Smith	Saunders	Rafferty	Harvey	Wright	Coyne	Frail	Mennie (6)	Lawrence (7)
	5th	Geddes	Shannon	McKinlay	Chisholm	Smith	Saunders	Rafferty	Harvey	Wright	Coyne	Frail	Campbell (7)	Mennie
	12th	Geddes	Forsyth	McKinlay	Shannon	Smith	Saunders	Rafferty	Frail	Wright	Coyne	Campbell S	Harvey (7)	Mennie
	16th	Geddes	Shannon	McKinlay	Frail	Forsyth	Saunders	Lawrence	Rafferty	Wright	Coyne	Campbell S	Harvey (11)	Kirkwood (7)
	19th	Geddes	Shannon	McKinlay	Frail	Forsyth	Saunders	Lawrence	Rafferty	Wright	Coyne	Campbell S	Chisholm (7)	Harvey
	26th	Geddes	Shannon	McKinlay	Chisholm	Forsyth	Saunders	Frail	Rafferty	Wright	Coyne	Campbell S	Harvey	Kirkwood
Dec	3rd	Geddes	Shannon	McKinlay	Chisholm	Forsyth	Saunders	Frail	Rafferty	Wright	Coyne	Campbell S	Harvey (7)	Kirkwood
	10th	Geddes	Shannon*	Saunders	Chisholm	Forsyth	Frail	Harvey	Rafferty	Wright	Coyne	Campbell S	Kirkwood (12)	Lawrence (6)
	17th	Geddes	Kirkwood	Holt	Chisholm	Forsyth	Saunders	Campbell S	Rafferty	Wright	Coyne	McBride	Angus (7)	Harvey (9)
	31st	Geddes	Shannon	Holt	Chisholm	Forsyth	Saunders	Frail	Rafferty	Wright	Coyne	McBride	Kirkwood	Campbell S
Jan	3rd	Geddes	Shannon	Holt	Chisholm	Forsyth	Saunders	Frail	Rafferty	Wright	Coyne	McBride	Kirkwood	Campbell S
	7th	Geddes	Shannon	Holt	Chisholm	Forsyth	Saunders	Frail	Rafferty	Wright	Coyne	McBride	Kirkwood	Campbell S
	14th	Geddes	Shannon	Holt	Chisholm	Forsyth	Saunders	Frail	Rafferty	Wright	Coyne	McBride	Campbell S (7)	Angus (3)
	21st	Geddes	Smith	Angus	Chisholm	Forsyth	Saunders	Frail	Rafferty	Wright	Coyne	McBride	Campbell S (7)	Harvey (6)
	28th	Geddes	Holt	Kirkwood	Chisholm	Forsyth	Saunders	Frail	Angus	Wright	Coyne	McBride	Smith (3)	Rafferty (11)
Feb	11th	Geddes	Shannon	Angus	Chisholm	Holt	Frail	Lawrence	Rafferty	Wright	Coyne	Campbell S	McBride (6)	Craib
	25th	Geddes	Shannon	Holt	Forsyth	Chisholm	Rafferty	Frail	Angus	Lawrence	Coyne	McBride	Campbell S (9)	Craib (11)
Mar	11th	Geddes	Forsyth	Holt	Chisholm	Craib	Saunders	Frail	McGeachie	Lawrence	Wright	Campbell S	McBride (9)	Rafferty (11)
	25th	Geddes	Forsyth	Shannon	McGeachie	Chisholm	Saunders	Frail	Angus	Wright	Campbell D	McBride	Rafferty (7)	Holt (4)
Apr	1st	Geddes	Forsyth	Shannon	Holt	Chisholm	Saunders	Craig	Angus	Wright	Campbell D	McBride	Rafferty	Campbell S
	8th	Geddes	Forsyth	Shannon	Frail	Chisholm	Saunders	Craig	Angus	Wright	Campbell D	McBride	Rafferty (7)	Harvey (3)
	15th	Carson	McGeachie	Shannon	Holt	Chisholm	Forsyth	Rafferty	Angus	Wright	Campbell D	McBride	Frail (4)	Harvey (9)
	22nd	Carson	McGeachie	Saunders	Chisholm	Forsyth	Craig	Angus	Wright	Harvey	McBride	Campbell D 10	Rafferty (2)	
	29th	Geddes	Shannon	Angus	McGeachie	Chisholm	Forsyth	Craig	Frail	Wright	Harvey	Campbell D	Rafferty (8)	McBride (11)
May	6th	Geddes	Shannon	Angus	Saunders	Chisholm	Forsyth	Rafferty	Craig	Wright	Campbell D	McBride	Harvey (7)	Craib (8)
	13th	Geddes	Forsyth	Angus	McGeachie	Chisholm	Craib	Craig	Frail	Wright	Harvey	Campbell S	Campbell D (10)	McBride (4)

Dundee F.C. Season 1988-89. (BACK, left to right) Shaun McSkimming, Bobby Glennie, Keith Wright, Gordon Chisholm, Jim Smith, Wes Saunders, Steve Campbell. MIDDLE - Bert Slater (coach), Alan Lawrence, Steve Frail, Billy Kirkwood, Bobby Geddes, Tom Carson, Ian Angus, Stewart Forsyth, Stuart Rafferty, Eric Ferguson (physio). FRONT - Graham Harvey, Tommy Coyne, Tosh McKinlay, Dave Smith (manager), Rab Shannon, George McGeachie and Vince Mennie.

DC Thomson

Season 1989-90

Date			Opponents		Score	Crowd	Scorers
Aug	7th	FC1	Forfar Athletic	a	2-1		Frail; Harvey
	12th	L	Dunfermline	a	1-2	8,987	Beedie
	15th	LC2	Clyde	h	5-1	3,033	McBride 2; Wright; Harvey 2
	19th	L	Dundee United	h	4-3	13,616	Wright 3; McBride
	23rd	LC3	Dunfermline	a	0-1	8,076	-
	26th	L	Aberdeen	a	0-1	12,500	-
Sep	4th	FCS	Montrose	a	3-0		Harvey; Chisholm; Craig
	9th	L	Hearts	h	2-2	8,440	Wright; Harvey
	16th	L	Rangers	a	2-2	35,836	Craig; Wright
	23rd	L	Hibernian	h	0-0	6,842	-
	30th	L	Motherwell	a	0-3	4,463	-
Oct	4th	L	St Mirren	a	2-3	3,587	Wright; Dodds
	14th	L	Celtic	h	1-3	16,215	Craib
	21st	L	Dunfermline	h	1-2	7,058	Dodds (pen)
	28th	L	Dundee United	a	0-0	11,529	-
Nov	4th	L	Aberdeen	h	1-1	7,041	Dodds
	11th	L	Hearts	a	3-6	11,869	Saunders; Dodds 2
	18th	L	Rangers	h	0-2	14,536	-
	25th	L	Hibernian	a	2-3	6,000	Beedie; Dodds
Dec	2nd	L	Motherwell	h	2-1	4,099	Dodds (pen); Craig
	9th	L	St Mirren	h	3-3	4,043	Dodds (pen); Chisholm; Forsyth
	16th	L	Celtic	a	1-4	17,860	Beedie
	26th	L	Dunfermline	a	0-1	9,282	-
	30th	L	Dundee United	h	1-1	12,803	Chisholm
Jan	2nd	L	Aberdeen	a	2-5	16,054	Wright; D. Campbell
	6th	L	Hearts	h	0-1	8,300	-
	13th	L	Rangers	a	0-3	36,993	-
	20th	SC3	Dundee United	h	0-0	14,276	-
	23rd	SC3R	Dundee United	a	0-1	15,503	-
	27th	L	Hibernian	h	2-0	5,720	Wright; Chisholm
Feb	3rd	L	Celtic	h	0-0	14,100	-
	10th	L	St Mirren	a	0-0	5,010	-
	17th	L	Motherwell	a	1-3	5,508	Dodds
	24th	FCF	St Johnstone	a	3-2	4,786	Beedie; A. Campbell; Wright
Mar	3rd	L	Rangers	h	2-2	12,743	A. Campbell; Dodds
	10th	L	Dunfermline	h	1-0	7,243	Dodds
	24th	L	Dundee United	a	2-1	11,918	Wright; Shannon
	31st	L	Aberdeen	h	1-1	8,071	Wright
Apr	4th	L	Hearts	a	0-0	10,761	-
	14th	L	St Mirren	h	1-2	7,415	A. Campbell
	21st	L	Celtic	a	1-1	15,115	Dodds (pen)
	28th	L	Hibernian	a	1-1	4,665	Dodds
May	5th	L	Motherwell	h	1-2	2,846	Wright

Gordon Chisholm - the Dens skipper brought composure to central defence.

Appearances

	League		L/Cup		S/Cup	Total	
Rab Shannon	36	(1)	2		2	40	(1)
Gordon Chisholm	34	(3)	2		2	38	(3)
Keith Wright	34	(11)	2	(1)	2	38	(12)
Stewart Forsyth	33	(1)	2		2	37+1s	(1)
Billy Dodds	29	(13)	0		2	31+1s	(13)
Gordon McLeod	24		0		2	26+3s	
Mark Craib	21	(1)	1		2	24+3s	(1)
Alan Dinnie	21		0		2	23+1s	
Stuart Beedie	19	(3)	2		0	21+2s	(3)
Tom Carson	16		0		2	18	
Albert Craig	11	(2)	2		2	15+8s	(2)
Bobby Geddes	12		2		0	14	
Willie Jamieson	14		0		0	14	
Joe McBride	10	(1)	2	(2)	0	12+8s	(3)
Arthur Albiston	9		2		0	11	
Alan Campbell	8	(2)	0		0	8+9s	(2)
Jim Duffy	8		0		0	8	
Shaun McSkimming	6		0		2	8+1s	
Paul Mathers	8		0		0	8	
Steve Frail	6		1		0	7	
Wes Saunders	7	(1)	0		0	7+2s	(1)
Duncan Campbell	6	(1)	0		0	6+9s	(1)
Graham Harvey	4	(1)	2	(2)	0	6+2s	(3)
Ian Angus	4		0		0	4	
Derek Ferguson	4		0		0	4	
Jim Smith	4		0		0	4	
Grant McMartin	3		0		0	3+1s	
John Holt	2		0		0	2	

The Record		
League	-	Tenth Place, Premier Division
League Cup	-	Third round
Scottish Cup	-	Third round
Forfarshire Cup	-	Winners
Top Scorer	-	Billy Dodds (13 goals)
Av. Home Gate	-	9,000
Players used	-	32
Sent off (bookings)	-	One (51)

Scottish League Premier Division

	P	Home			Away			Goals		PTS
		W	D	L	W	D	L	F	A	
Rangers	36	14	2	2	6	9	3	48-19		51
Aberdeen	36	12	4	2	5	6	7	56-33		44
Hearts	36	8	6	4	8	6	4	54-35		44
Dundee United	36	8	8	2	3	5	10	36-39		35
Celtic	36	6	6	6	4	8	6	37-37		34
Motherwell	36	7	6	5	4	6	8	43-47		34
Hibernian	36	8	5	5	4	5	9	34-41		34
Dunfermline	36	5	6	7	6	2	10	37-50		30
St Mirren	36	6	6	6	4	4	10	28-48		30
Dundee	**36**	**4**	**8**	**6**	**1**	**6**	**11**	**41-65**		**24**

Appearances (Ctd.)

	League	L/Cup	S/Cup	Total
George McGeachie	2	0	0	2
John McQuillan	1	0	0	1
Steve Campbell	0	0	0	0+2s
Michael Kerr	0	0	0	0+2s
Kevin Bain	0	0	0	0+1s

Dundee F.C. Line-Ups 1989-90

		1	2	3	4	5	6	7	8	9	10	11	12	13
Aug	12th	Geddes	Forsyth	Albiston	McGeachie	Chisholm	Craib	Craig	Shannon	Wright	Campbell D	Beedie	Dodds (10)	McBride (4)
	15th	Geddes	Shannon	Albiston	Frail	Chisholm	Forsyth	Craig	Beedie	Wright	Harvey	McBride	Campbell A (9)	Craib (4)
	19th	Geddes	Shannon	Albiston	Craib	Chisholm	Forsyth	Craig	Beedie	Wright	Harvey	McBride	Campbell A (10)	McGeachie
	23rd	Geddes	Shannon	Albiston	Craib	Chisholm	Forsyth	Craig	Beedie	Wright	Harvey	McBride	Campbell A (10)	McGeachie
	26th	Geddes	Shannon	Albiston	Craib	Chisholm	Forsyth	McGeachie	Beedie	Wright	Campbell A	McBride	McLeod (4)	Harvey (10)
Sep	9th	Geddes	Shannon	Albiston	McLeod	Chisholm	Forsyth	Craig	Beedie	Wright	Campbell D	McBride	McGeachie	Harvey (10)
	16th	Geddes	Shannon	Albiston	Chisholm	Saunders	Forsyth	Craig	Beedie	Wright	Harvey	McLeod	Frail	McBride (6)
	23rd	Geddes	Shannon	Albiston	Chisholm	Saunders	Forsyth	Craig	Beedie	Wright	Harvey	McLeod	Dodds	McBride
	30th	Geddes	Shannon	Albiston	Saunders	Chisholm	Forsyth	Frail	Beedie	Wright	Harvey	McLeod	Craig (3)	McBride (10)
Oct	4th	Geddes	Shannon	Albiston	Saunders	Chisholm	Forsyth	Frail	Craig	Wright	Dodds	McLeod	Campbell A (10)	Beedie (4)
	14th	Geddes	Shannon	Angus	Craib	Chisholm	Smith	Frail	Craig	Wright	Dodds	McLeod	Saunders (3)	Campbell A (7)
	21st	Geddes	Shannon	Albiston	Craib	Chisholm	Smith	Frail	McLeod	Wright	Dodds	McBride	Forsyth (4)	Campbell A (7)
	28th	Carson	Forsyth	Shannon	Craib	Chisholm	Smith	Campbell A	Beedie	Wright	Dodds	McLeod	Craig (6)	McBride (7)
Nov	4th	Carson	Forsyth	Shannon	Beedie	Chisholm	Saunders	Frail	McLeod	Wright	Dodds	McBride	Albiston (7)	Campbell A (8)
	11th	Carson	Forsyth	Shannon	Beedie	Chisholm	Saunders	Frail	McLeod	Wright	Dodds	McBride	Campbell A (11)	Dinnie (3)
	18th	Carson	Dinnie	Shannon	Forsyth	Chisholm	Saunders*	Craig	Craib	Wright	Dodds	Beedie	McLeod (7)	McBride (5)
	25th	Carson	Dinnie	Shannon	Holt	Chisholm	Craib	Beedie	McLeod	Wright	Dodds	Angus	Craig	McBride (4)
Dec	2nd	Geddes	Dinnie	Shannon	Chisholm	Forsyth	Craib	Beedie	Angus	Wright	Dodds	McBride	McLeod	Craig (6)
	9th	Geddes	Dinnie	Shannon	Chisholm	Forsyth	Craib	Beedie	Angus	Wright	Dodds	McBride	Campbell D (11)	Craig (4)
	16th	Carson	Dinnie	Shannon	Chisholm	Forsyth	Craig	Beedie	Craib	Wright	Dodds	McBride	Campbell D11	McSkimming4
	26th	Carson	Dinnie	Shannon	Smith	Forsyth	Craib	Beedie	Craig	Wright	Dodds	McBride	Saunders (4)	Campbell D 11
	30th	Carson	Dinnie	Shannon	Chisholm	Forsyth	Craib	Campbell D	Beedie	Wright	Dodds	McLeod	Craig (3)	McBride (7)
Jan	2nd	Carson	Dinnie	Shannon	Chisholm	Forsyth	Craib	Campbell D	Beedie	Wright	Dodds	McLeod	Craig (8)	McBride
	6th	Carson	Dinnie	Shannon	Chisholm	Forsyth	Craib	Campbell D	Holt	Wright	Dodds	McSkimming	Campbell S (2)	Beedie (8)
	13th	Carson	Dinnie	Shannon	Chisholm	Jamieson	Forsyth	Craig	Craib	Wright	Dodds	McSkimming	McLeod (2)	McMartin (7)
	20th	Carson	Dinnie	Shannon	Chisholm	Forsyth	Craib	Craig	McLeod	Wright	Dodds	McSkimming	Frail	McBride
	23rd	Carson	Dinnie	Shannon	Chisholm	Forsyth	Craib	Craig	McLeod	Wright	Dodds	McSkimming	Frail (7)	McBride (11)
	27th	Carson	Dinnie	Shannon	Chisholm	Forsyth	Jamieson	Ferguson	Craib	Wright	Dodds	McLeod	McSkimming	Campbell D 10
Feb	3rd	Carson	Dinnie	Shannon	Chisholm	Forsyth	Jamieson	Ferguson	McLeod	Wright	Dodds	McSkimming	Craib (4)	Campbell D
	10th	Carson	Dinnie	Shannon	Craib	Forsyth	Jamieson	Ferguson	McLeod	Campbell D	Dodds	McSkimming	Craig (10)	Campbell A (9)
	17th	Carson	Dinnie	Shannon	Chisholm	Forsyth	Jamieson	Ferguson	McLeod	Craig	Dodds	McSkimming	Campbell S (2)	Campbell D (9)
Mar	3rd	Carson	Dinnie	Forsyth	Chisholm	Jamieson	Duffy	Campbell A	McLeod	Wright	Dodds	Beedie	Dinnie	Campbell D (7)
	10th	Mathers	Forsyth	Shannon	Chisholm	Jamieson	Duffy	Campbell A	McLeod	Wright	Dodds	Dinnie	McSkimming	Campbell D
	24th	Mathers	Forsyth	Shannon	Chisholm	Jamieson	Duffy	Campbell A	Dinnie	Wright	Dodds	McLeod	Craib	Campbell D
	31st	Mathers	Forsyth	Shannon	Chisholm	Jamieson	Duffy	Campbell A	McLeod	Wright	Dodds	Dinnie	Craib	Campbell D (7)
Apr	4th	Mathers	Forsyth	Shannon	Chisholm	Jamieson	Duffy	Campbell A	McLeod	Wright	Dodds	Dinnie	Craib (6)	Campbell D
	14th	Mathers	Forsyth	Shannon	Chisholm	Jamieson	Duffy	Campbell A	Craib	Wright	Dodds	McSkimming	Craig (8)	Campbell D 11
	21st	Mathers	Forsyth	Shannon	Chisholm	Jamieson	Craib	McMartin	Dinnie	Wright	Dodds	McLeod	Bain	Campbell D (7)
	28th	Mathers	Forsyth	Shannon	Chisholm	Jamieson	Duffy	McMartin	Dinnie	Wright	Dodds	McLeod	McQuillan	Kerr (7)
May	5th	Mathers	Forsyth	Shannon	Chisholm	Jamieson	Duffy	McQuillan	Dinnie	Wright	Dodds	McMartin	Bain (8)	Kerr (11)

Hat-trick hero - Dundee striker Keith Wright beats Dundee United's Maurice Malpas and heads the ball past goalkeeper Scott Thomson. It was the first of three for Wright as the Dark Blues fought back for a 4-3 derby win at Dens.

DC Thomson

Season 1990-91

Date			Opponents		Score	Crowd	Scorers
Aug	20th	LC2	QOS	a	2-2*	1,346	Chisholm; Forsyth
	25th	L	Partick Thistle	h	1-1	5,040	Dodds
Sep	1st	L	Morton	a	1-0	1,865	McSkimming
	8th	L	Clydebank	a	3-1	1,775	Wright 2; Dodds
	15th	L	Clyde	h	3-1	3,518	Wright 2; Dodds (pen)
	18th	L	Hamilton	a	0-1	1,773	-
	22nd	L	Forfar Athletic	a	1-1	3,053	McQuillan
	29th	L	Kilmarnock	h	1-1	4,573	Dodds (pen)
Oct	6th	L	Ayr United	a	4-2	2,493	McLeod; Chisholm; Dodds; Wright
	9th	L	Airdrie	h	0-1	6,360	-
	13th	L	Raith Rovers	a	1-1	3,494	S. Campbell 85
	16th	BQ2	Alloa Athletic	a	5-3	915	Dodds 2 (pens); S. Campbell; Wright; Shannon
	20th	L	Falkirk	h	2-2	4,013	Wright; Dodds
	23rd	BQ3	Raith Rovers	a	1-0**	4,061	Dodds
	27th	L	Brechin City	a	3-1	2,011	Wright 2; Dodds
	30th	BQS	Kilmarnock	a	2-0	7,933	Wright 2
Nov	3rd	L	Meadowbank	h	1-2	3,404	McSkimming
	11th	BQF	Ayr United	Fir	3-2**	11,506	Dodds 3 (1 pen)
	17th	L	Partick Thistle	a	3-1	5,476	McLeod; West; Wright
	20th	L	Morton	h	1-0	3,554	McBride
	24th	L	Airdrie	a	1-0	5,000	Chisholm
	26th	FCS	Forfar Athletic	a	2-2*	541	McQuillan 2
Dec	1st	L	Ayr United	h	1-0	3,416	Dodds
	8th	L	Kilmarnock	a	1-2	4,458	Wright
	18th	L	Forfar Athletic	h	4-1	3,102	Wright; Dodds; McBride; Dinnie
	22nd	L	Brechin City	h	1-2	3,172	Dinnie
	29th	L	Meadowbank	a	1-0	1,000	McSkimming
Jan	1st	L	Raith Rovers	h	2-1	4,815	Chisholm; Jamieson
	5th	L	Falkirk	a	0-1	7,672	-
	19th	SC3	Brechin City	h	1-0	3,446	West
Feb	2nd	L	Hamilton	h	3-2	3,153	West 2; Shannon
	5th	L	Clydebank	h	1-0	2,793	Craig
	23rd	SC4	Kilmarnock	h	2-0	9,195	McMartin; Dodds
Mar	2nd	L	Airdrie	a	1-0	4,500	Dodds (pen)
	5th	L	Ayr United	h	4-0	3,379	Wright 3; Dodds
	9th	L	Brechin City	h	0-1	3,051	-
	13th	SCQ	Dundee United	a	1-3	16,228	Dodds
	16th	L	Forfar Athletic	h	1-0	2,618	Craig
	23rd	L	Clyde	a	2-4	1,500	Craig 2
	26th	L	Partick Thistle	a	0-1	3,500	-
	30th	L	Clydebank	a	1-1	1,235	Wright
Apr	6th	L	Morton	h	1-0	2,515	Wright
	13th	L	Falkirk	a	0-0	9,300	-
	20th	L	Meadowbank	h	4-0	2,716	Dinnie; Dodds 2; Wright
	27th	L	Raith Rovers	h	2-0	3,756	Jamieson; McMartin
	30th	L	Clyde	a	1-0	2,500	Wright
May	3rd	L	Kilmarnock	a	0-0	5,712	-
	10th	L	Hamilton	a	2-1	3,136	Shannon (pen); Dodds

* a.e.t., 1-1 after 90 minutes, QOS won 4-1 on penalties. Forfar won 3-2 on penalties
** a.e.t., 2-2 v. Ayr after 90 minutes.

Billy Dodds - the dynamic striker was a regular scorer for the Dark Blues.

The Record

League	-	**Third Place, First Division**
League Cup	-	**Second round**
Scottish Cup	-	**Quarter-final**
B&Q Centenary Cup	-	**Winners**
Forfarshire Cup	-	**Semi-final**
Top Scorer	-	**Billy Dodds (22 goals)**
Av. Home Gate	-	**3,600**
Players used	-	**25**
Sent off (booked)	-	**Three (45)**

Appearances

	League		L/Cup		S/Cup		B&Q		Total	
Willie Jamieson	38	(2)	1		3		4		46	(2)
Billy Dodds	31	(14)	1		3	(2)	4	(6)	45	(22)
Rab Shannon	37	(2)	1		3		4	(1)	45	(3)
Keith Wright	36	(18)	1		2		4	(3)	43	(21)
Tom Carson	33		1		3		4		41	
Gordon Chisholm	34	(3)	1	(1)	2		3		40	(4)
Alan Dinnie	25	(3)	0		3		3		31	(3)
Steve Frail	25		0		3		3		31+1s	
Gordon McLeod	23	(2)	1		0		3		27+1s	(2)
Mark Craib	17		0		2		3		22+1s	
Stewart Forsyth	18		1	(1)	1		2		22+3s	(1)
Colin West	16	(3)	1		2	(1)	1		20+2s	(4)
Shaun McSkimming	15	(3)	1		1		2		19+2s	(3)
Grant McMartin	15	(1)	0		2	(1)	0		17+4s	(2)
Duncan Campbell	10		0		0		1		11+5s	
Kevin Bain	7		0		1		1		9	
John McQuillan	8	(1)	1		0		0		9+4s	(1)
Stuart Beedie	8		0		0		0		8+1s	
Cammy Fraser	7		0		0		0		7	
Paul Mathers	6		0		0		0		6	
Steve Campbell	3	(1)	0		1		1	(1)	5+3s	(2)

Scottish League First Division

		Home			Away			Goals		
	P	W	D	L	W	D	L	F A	PTS
Falkirk	39	12	4	4	9	8	2	70-35	54
Airdrie	39	9	5	5	12	6	2	69-43	53
Dundee	**39**	**12**	**3**	**4**	**10**	**5**	**5**	**59-33**	**52**
Partick Thistle	39	7	6	6	9	7	4	56-53	45
Kilmarnock	39	10	6	3	5	7	8	58-48	43
Hamilton	39	8	6	6	8	4	7	50-41	42
Raith Rovers	39	7	5	8	7	4	8	54-64	37
Clydebank	39	6	6	8	7	4	8	65-70	36
Morton	39	6	7	6	5	6	9	48-55	35
Forfar Athletic	39	6	9	5	3	6	10	50-57	33
Meadowbank	39	4	7	8	6	6	8	56-68	33
Ayr United	39	7	7	6	3	5	11	47-59	32
Clyde	39	6	4	10	3	5	11	41-61	27
Brechin City	39	3	4	12	4	6	10	44-80	24

Appearances (Ctd.)

	League		L/Cup	S/Cup	B&Q	Total	
Albert Craig	3	(4)	0	1	0	4+9s	(4)
Joe McBride	4	(2)	0	0	0	4+10s	(2)
Gary Lennox	0		0	0	0	0+1s	

Dundee F.C. Line-Ups 1990-91

		1	2	3	4	5	6	7	8	9	10	11	12	13
Aug	20th	Carson	McQuillan	McSkimming	Shannon	Jamieson	Chisholm	West*	Forsyth	Wright	Dodds	McLeod	Craib	McBride (11)
	25th	Carson	McQuillan	McSkimming	Chisholm	Jamieson	Forsyth	Campbell D	Shannon	Wright	Dodds	McLeod	Craib	McBride (7)
Sep	1st	Mathers	McQuillan	Shannon	Chisholm	Jamieson	Forsyth	West	McLeod	Wright	Dodds	McSkimming	Craib	McBride (7)
	8th	Mathers	McQuillan	Shannon	Chisholm	Jamieson	Forsyth	West	McLeod	Wright	Dodds	McSkimming	McMartin (7)	McBride
	15th	Mathers	McQuillan	Shannon	Chisholm	Jamieson	Forsyth	West	McLeod	Wright	Dodds	McSkimming	McMartin (7)	McBride
	18th	Mathers	McQuillan	Shannon	Chisholm	Jamieson	Forsyth	West	McLeod*	Wright	Dodds	McSkimming	McMartin (11)	McBride
	22nd	Mathers	McQuillan	Shannon	Chisholm	Jamieson	Forsyth	West	McMartin	Wright	Dodds	Campbell S	McSkimming (11)	McBride
	29th	Carson	Forsyth	Shannon	Chisholm	Jamieson	Craib	McBride	McLeod	Wright	Dodds	McSkimming	McQuillan (2)	Campbell S 7
Oct	6th	Carson	Forsyth	Shannon	Chisholm	Jamieson	Craib	Frail	McLeod	Wright	Dodds	McSkimming	McQuillan (7)	Campbell S
	9th	Carson	Forsyth	Shannon	Chisholm	Jamieson	Bain	Frail	McLeod	Wright	Dodds*	McSkimming	McQuillan (7)	Campbell D
	13th	Carson	McQuillan	Shannon	Holt	Jamieson	Bain	Frail	McLeod	Wright	West	McSkimming	Campbell S (10)	Campbell D
	16th	Carson	Frail	Shannon	Holt	Jamieson	Bain	Campbell D	McLeod	Wright	Dodds	Campbell S	McSkimming (8)	Lennox (7)
	20th	Carson	Frail	Shannon	Holt	Jamieson	Chisholm	Campbell S	McLeod	Wright	Dodds	McSkimming	Craib (8)	West (4)
	23rd	Carson	Dinnie	Shannon	Chisholm	Jamieson	Craib	Frail	McLeod	Wright	Dodds	McSkimming	Campbell S (4)	Campbell D
	27th	Carson	Dinnie	Shannon	Holt	Jamieson	Craib	Frail	McLeod	Wright	Dodds	McBride	Campbell S	Campbell D11
	30th	Carson	Dinnie	Shannon	Chisholm	Jamieson	Craib	Frail	Forsyth	Wright	Dodds	McSkimming	Holt (4)	Campbell D
Nov	3rd	Carson	Dinnie	Shannon	Chisholm	Jamieson	Craib	Frail	Forsyth	Wright	Dodds	McSkimming	Holt (4)	McBride
	11th	Carson	Dinnie	Shannon	Chisholm	Jamieson	Craib	West	Forsyth	Wright	Dodds	McLeod	Frail	McBride (7)
	17th	Carson	Dinnie	Shannon	Chisholm	Frail	Craib	West	Forsyth	Wright	Dodds	McLeod	Holt (12)	McBride
	20th	Carson	Forsyth	Shannon	Chisholm	Jamieson	Craib	West	Frail	Wright	Dodds	Campbell S	Holt (8)	McBride (7)
	24th	Carson	Forsyth	Shannon	Chisholm	Jamieson	Craib	Frail	Dinnie	Wright	Dodds	McLeod	Holt (7)	McBride
Dec	1st	Carson	Dinnie	Shannon	Chisholm	Jamieson	Craib	Frail	McLeod	Wright	Dodds	McBride	Forsyth (6)	Campbell D
	8th	Carson	Forsyth	Shannon	Chisholm	Jamieson	Holt	Frail	McLeod	Wright	Dodds	McSkimming	McQuillan (7)	McBride (8)
	19th	Carson	Forsyth	Shannon	Chisholm	Jamieson	Dinnie	Campbell D	Frail	Wright	Dodds	McLeod	McQuillan	McBride (7)
	22nd	Carson	Forsyth	Shannon	Chisholm	Jamieson	Dinnie	Campbell D	Frail	Wright	Dodds	McLeod	McQuillan	McBride (7)
	29th	Carson	Dinnie	Shannon	Chisholm	Jamieson	Bain	Frail	McLeod	Wright	Dodds	McSkimming	McQuillan (7)	Campbell D
Jan	1st	Carson	Dinnie	Shannon	Chisholm	Jamieson	Bain	Frail	McLeod	Wright	Dodds	McSkimming	McQuillan	Campbell D
	5th	Carson	Dinnie	Shannon	Chisholm	Jamieson	Bain	Frail	McLeod	Wright	Dodds	McSkimming	McQuillan	West
	26th	Carson	Forsyth	Shannon	Dinnie	Jamieson	Bain	West	Frail	Wright	Dodds	Campbell S	Craig	McBride
Feb	2nd	Carson	Dinnie	Shannon	Chisholm	Jamieson	Bain	West	Frail	Wright	Dodds	McMartin	Forsyth (4)	Craig
	5th	Carson	Dinnie	Shannon	McMartin	Jamieson	Bain	West	Frail	Wright	Dodds	McLeod	Forsyth	Craig (11)
	23rd	Carson	Dinnie	Shannon	Chisholm	Jamieson	Craib	West	Frail	Wright	Dodds	McMartin	McLeod	Craig (7)
Mar	2nd	Carson	Dinnie	Shannon	Chisholm	Jamieson	Craib	West	Frail	Wright	Dodds	McMartin	McLeod	Craig (7)
	5th	Carson	Dinnie	Shannon	Chisholm	Jamieson	Craib	West	Frail	Wright	Dodds	McMartin	McLeod (8)	Craig (7)
	9th	Carson	Dinnie	Shannon	Chisholm	Jamieson	Craib	West	Frail	McBride	Dodds	McMartin	Forsyth (7)	Craig (9)
	13th	Carson	Dinnie	Shannon	Chisholm	Jamieson	Craib	Frail	McMartin	Craig	Dodds	McSkimming	McBride	Campbell D 11
	16th	Carson	Forsyth	Shannon	Chisholm	Jamieson	Craib	Campbell D	McMartin	Craig	Dodds	McLeod	Frail (7)	McBride (8)
	23rd	Carson	Forsyth	Dinnie	Chisholm	Jamieson	Craib	Frail	Craig	Wright	Dodds	McMartin	Campbell S	Campbell D(2)
	27th	Carson	McQuillan	Dinnie	Chisholm	Jamieson	Craib	Frail	McMartin	Craig	Dodds	McLeod	Beedie (8)	West (9)
	30th	Carson	Dinnie	Shannon	Fraser	Jamieson	Craib	West	Frail	Wright	Campbell D	Beedie	McMartin	Craig (7)
Apr	6th	Mathers	Dinnie	Shannon	Fraser	Jamieson	Craib	Campbell D	Frail	Wright	Dodds	Beedie	McMartin (8)	Craig
	13th	Carson	Dinnie	Shannon	Chisholm	Jamieson	Fraser	Campbell D	McMartin	Wright	Dodds	Beedie	Craib	Craig (7)
	20th	Carson	Dinnie	Shannon	Chisholm	Jamieson	Fraser	Campbell D	McMartin	Wright	Dodds	Beedie	Craig (8)	McBride (7)
	27th	Carson	Dinnie	Shannon	Chisholm	Jamieson	Fraser	West	McMartin	Wright	Dodds	Beedie	Campbell D (7)	Craig
	30th	Carson	Dinnie	Shannon	Chisholm	Jamieson	Fraser	Campbell D	McMartin	Wright	Dodds	Beedie	Craig (10)	Craib
May	3rd	Carson	Dinnie	Shannon	Chisholm	Jamieson	Fraser	Campbell D	McMartin	Wright	Dodds	Beedie	Craig (7)	Craib (8)
	10th	Carson	Dinnie	Shannon	Chisholm	Jamieson	Craib	West	McMartin	Wright	Dodds	Beedie	Campbell D (7)	McBride

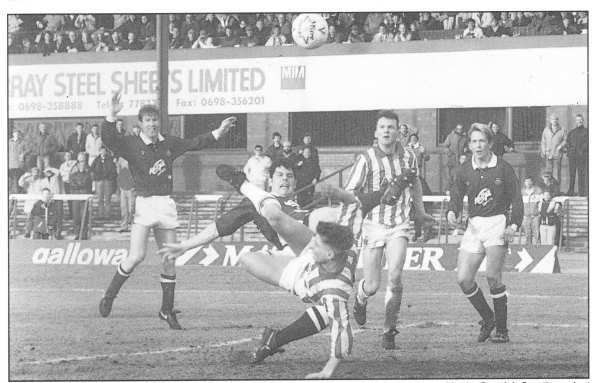

Close call - centre-half Willie Jamieson resists a desperate challenge and tries his luck at goal in the Scottish Cup tie against Kilmarnock at Dens. Team-mates Keith Wright and Billy Dodds await developments.

DC Thomson

Season 1991-92

Date			Opponents		Score	Crowd	Scorers
July	27th	FC1	Brechin City	a	4-3	700	Jamieson 2; Shannon; Wright
	29th	FCS	Forfar Athletic	a	1-2	898	D. Campbell
Aug	10th	L	Clydebank	a	2-1	1,527	Craig; D. Campbell
	13th	L	Forfar Athletic	a	4-2	2,458	McQuillan; Craig; Dodds 2
	17th	L	Meadowbank	h	3-1	2,860	Dodds 2; Craig
	21st	LC2	Ayr United	h	2-4**	3,084	Craig 2
	24th	L	Hamilton	h	4-1	2,751	Jamieson; Bremner; Craig; Dodds
	31st	L	Raith Rovers	a	1-0	3,122	Craig
Sep	7th	L	Morton	a	0-3	2,036	
	14th	L	Ayr United	h	3-1	3,410	West 2; Dodds
	21st	L	Kilmarnock	h	2-1	3,788	S. Campbell (pen); Jamieson
	28th	L	Montrose	a	2-1	2,147	Jamieson; S. Campbell (pen)
Oct	1st	BQ1	Ayr United	h	0-2	2,058	-
	5th	L	Partick Thistle	h	1-2	4,804	Beedie
	8th	L	Stirling Albion	a	1-1	1,450	McMartin
	12th	L	Clydebank	h	4-0	2,335	Chisholm; Dodds; Bremner; D. Campbell (pen)
	19th	L	Meadowbank	a	2-1	729	Bremner; Dodds
	26th	L	Morton	h	0-1	1,925	-
	29th	L	Ayr United	a	1-4	2,414	Dodds
Nov	2nd	L	Raith Rovers	h	1-1	2,397	Dodds
	9th	L	Hamilton	a	3-1	1,886	Gallagher 2; Dodds
	16th	L	Partick Thistle	a	6-2	5,441	Gallagher 3; Bremner 2; McQuillan
	19th	L	Stirling Albion	h	0-0	2,733	
	23rd	L	Kilmarnock	a	2-1	7,128	Chisholm; McCall
	30th	L	Forfar Athletic	a	4-0	2,976	McCall; Gallagher 2; Jamieson
Dec	3rd	L	Montrose	h	1-0	2,799	Beedie
	7th	L	Clydebank	a	2-2	1,425	Bremner; S. Campbell
	14th	L	Morton	a	0-0	1,567	-
	28th	L	Hamilton	h	1-2	4,595	Gallagher
Jan	1st	L	Raith Rovers	a	0-1	3,976	-
	4th	L	Partick Thistle	h	1-0	4,547	Chisholm
	7th	L	Ayr United	h	1-1	2,505	McCall
	11th	L	Stirling Albion	a	1-1	2,500	Craig
	18th	L	Forfar Athletic	a	3-0	2,212	Beedie; Craig; West
Feb	1st	L	Meadowbank	h	2-1	3,218	Dodds 2 (1 pen)
	3rd	SC3	Stirling Albion	h	1-1	3,851	Dinnie
	5th	SC3R	Stirling Albion	a**	1-0	3,418	McMartin
	8th	L	Kilmarnock	h	1-1	5,988	Gallagher
	15th	SC4	Falkirk	a	0-0	7,517	
	22nd	L	Montrose	a	3-2	2,361	Chisholm; Beedie; McCall
	24th	SC4R	Falkirk	h	0-1	7,722	
	29th	L	Partick Thistle	a	0-2	8,437	-
Mar	7th	L	Stirling Albion	h	5-0	3,202	Dodds; McCall 2; Stainrod; Gallagher
	14th	L	Hamilton	a	1-1	2,830	Dodds
	21st	L	Raith Rovers	h	3-2	4,458	McCall 2; Dodds
	28th	L	Clydebank	h	3-0	3,580	Chisholm; Stainrod; Dodds
Apr	4th	L	Meadowbank	a	0-0	1,222	
	7th	L	Morton	h	2-2	4,011	Dodds 2 (1 pen)
	18th	L	Kilmarnock	a	0-2	4,933	-
	25th	L	Forfar Athletic	h	3-1	5,144	McQuillan; Ritchie; Gallagher
May	2nd	L	Montrose	h	1-2	6,878	Gallagher

*After extra-time, 2-2 after 90 mts. ** At McDiarmid Park,

Wing wizard - Ian McCall was a real crowd-pleaser in his short spell at Dens.

The Record

League	-	First Division Champions
League Cup	-	Second round
Scottish Cup	-	Fourth round
B&Q Cup	-	First round
Forfarshire Cup	-	Semi-final
Top Scorer	-	Billy Dodds (19 goals)
Av. Home Gate	-	3,700
Players used	-	19
Sent off (booked)	-	Two (58)

Appearances

	League	L/Cup	S/Cup	B&Q	Total	
Billy Dodds	41 (19)	1	4	1	47	(19)
John McQuillan	39 (3)	1	4	1	45+1s	(3)
Stuart Beedie	39 (4)	1	2	0	42	(4)
Gordon Chisholm	37 (5)	0	4	1	42+2s	(5)
Willie Jamieson	38 (4)	1	2	0	41	(4)
Paul Mathers	31	1	2	0	34	
Steve Campbell	29 (3)	1	0	1	31+1s	(3)
Ian McCall	27 (8)	0	4	0	31+1s	(8)
Alan Dinnie	24 (1)	0	4	1	29+6s	(1)
Albert Craig	24 (7)	1 (2)	2	1	28+3s	(9)
Mark Craib	20	1	0	1	22	
Grant McMartin	18 (1)	0	3 (1)	1	22+9s	(2)
Eddie Gallagher	14 (12)	0	4	0	18+8s	(12)
Kevin Bremner	15 (6)	1	0	0	16 +10	(6)
Stewart Forsyth	11	0	4	0	15+4s	
Cammy Fraser	12	1	1	1	15	
Jim Leighton	13	0	2	0	15	
Duncan Campbell	11 (2)	1	0	1	13+2s	(2)
Gordon McLeod	11	0	1	0	12+4s	
Simon Stainrod	10 (2)	0	0	0	10+2s	(2)
Colin West	7 (3)	0	0	0	7+3s	(3)
Paul Ritchie	4 (1)	0	0	0	4+3s	(1)

Scottish League First Division

		Home			Away			Goals		
	P	W	D	L	W	D	L	F	A	PTS
Dundee	**44**	**13**	**5**	**4**	**10**	**7**	**5**	**80-48**		**58**
Partick Thistle	44	11	4	7	12	7	3	62-36		57
Hamilton	44	12	6	4	10	7	5	72-48		57
Kilmarnock	44	12	4	6	9	8	5	59-37		54
Raith Rovers	44	11	7	4	10	4	8	59-42		53
Ayr United	44	11	4	7	7	7	8	63-55		47
Morton	44	9	6	7	8	6	8	66-59		46
Stirling Albion	44	8	7	7	6	6	10	50-57		41
Clydebank	44	7	8	7	5	4	13	59-77		36
Meadowbank	44	4	8	10	3	8	11	37-59		30
Montrose	44	3	10	9	2	7	13	45-85		27
Forfar Athletic	44	3	7	12	2	5	15	36-85		22

	League	L/Cup	S/Cup	B&Q	Total
Steve Frail	2	0	1	0	3+1s
Graeme Forbes	3	0	0	0	3
Rab Shannon	3	0	0	0	3
Max Christie	1	0	0	0	1
Tom Carson	0	0	0	1	1
Andy Dow	0	0	0	0	0+5s

Dundee F.C. Line-Ups 1991-92

	1	2	3	4	5	6	7	8	9	10	11	12	13
Aug 10th	Mathers	McMartin	Campbell S	Forbes	McQuillan	Craib	Campbell D	Craig	Bremner	Dodds	Beedie	McLeod	Dow
13th	Mathers	McQuillan	Campbell S	Fraser	Forbes	Craib	Campbell D	Craig	Bremner	Dodds	Beedie	McMartin	Dow
17th	Mathers	McQuillan	Campbell S	Fraser	Forbes	Craib	Campbell D	Craig	Bremner	Dodds	Beedie	McMartin (11)	Dow
21st	Mathers	McQuillan	Campbell S	Fraser	Jamieson	Craib	Campbell D	Craig	Bremner	Dodds	Beedie	McMartin (3)	Chisholm (5)
24th	Mathers	McQuillan	Campbell S	Fraser	Jamieson	Craib	Campbell D	Craig	Bremner	Dodds	Beedie	Chisholm (4)	McMartin (7)
31st	Mathers	McQuillan	Campbell S	Fraser	Jamieson	Craib	Campbell D	Craig	Bremner	Dodds	Beedie	Chisholm	McMartin
Sep 7th	Mathers	McQuillan*	Campbell S	Fraser	Jamieson	Craib	Campbell D	Craig	Bremner	Dodds	Beedie	Chisholm (4)	McMartin (7)
14th	Mathers	Dinnie	Campbell S	Chisholm	Jamieson	Craib	West	Craig	McMartin	Dodds	Beedie	McLeod	Campbell D (10)
21st	Mathers	McQuillan	Campbell S	Chisholm	Jamieson	Craib	West	Craig	McMartin	Dodds	Beedie	Dinnie (7)	Campbell D
28th	Mathers	McQuillan	Campbell S	Chisholm	Jamieson	Craib	West	Craig	McMartin	Dodds	Beedie	Dinnie (7)	Campbell D
Oct 1st	Carson	Dinnie	Campbell S	Chisholm	McQuillan	Fraser	Craib	Craig	Campbell	Dodds	McMartin	McLeod (8)	West
5th	Mathers	McQuillan	Campbell S	Chisholm	Jamieson	Craib	West	McMartin	Campbell D	Dodds	Beedie	Dinnie (8)	Dow (9)
8th	Mathers	McQuillan	Campbell S	Chisholm	Jamieson	Craib	Campbell D	McLeod	McMartin	Dodds	Beedie	Dinnie (11)	Bremner (9)
12th	Mathers	McQuillan	Dinnie	Chisholm	Jamieson	Craib	Campbell D	McLeod	Bremner	Dodds	Beedie	McMartin (11)	Dow (9)
19th	Mathers	Dinnie	Campbell S	Chisholm	Jamieson	Craib	Campbell D	Shannon	Bremner	Dodds	McLeod	McMartin (2)	Dow (7)
26th	Mathers	McQuillan	Campbell S	Chisholm	Jamieson	Shannon	Campbell D	McLeod	Bremner	Dodds	Beedie	Craib	McMartin (8)
29th	Mathers	McQuillan	Shannon	Chisholm	Jamieson	Fraser	McMartin	Craig	Bremner	Dodds	Beedie	Craib	Campbell S (7)
Nov 2nd	Mathers	McQuillan	Campbell S	Craib	Jamieson	Fraser	Dinnie	Craig	Bremner	Dodds	Beedie	McMartin	Dow (9)
9th	Mathers	McQuillan	Campbell S	Chisholm	Jamieson	Fraser	Craig	McCall	Gallagher	Dodds	Beedie	Bremner	Dinnie (6)
16th	Mathers	McQuillan	Campbell S	Chisholm	Jamieson	Craib	Dinnie	McCall	Gallagher	Dodds	Beedie	Bremner (8)	Dow
19th	Mathers	McQuillan	Campbell S	Chisholm	Jamieson	Craib	Dinnie	McCall	Gallagher	Dodds	Beedie	Bremner (6)	Craig
23rd	Mathers	McQuillan	Campbell S	Chisholm	Jamieson	Craib	Dinnie	McCall	Gallagher	Dodds	Beedie	Bremner (9)	Craig (11)
30th	Mathers	McQuillan	Campbell S	Chisholm	Jamieson	Craib	Craig	McCall	Gallagher	Dodds	Beedie	Bremner (8)	McLeod (3)
Dec 3rd	Mathers	McQuillan	Campbell S	Chisholm	Jamieson	Craib	Craig	Bremner	Gallagher	McCall	Beedie	Dinnie (11)	Dow (8)
7th	Mathers	McQuillan	Campbell S	Chisholm	Jamieson	Fraser	Craig	Bremner	Gallagher	McCall	Beedie	Dinnie	Campbell D (5)
14th	Mathers	McQuillan	Campbell S	Chisholm	Jamieson	Fraser	Craig	McCall	Gallagher	Dodds	Beedie	Bremner (9)	Dinnie (11)
28th	Mathers	McQuillan	Dinnie	Chisholm	Jamieson	Fraser	Craig	McCall	Gallagher	Dodds	Beedie	Bremner (7)	McLeod (6)
Jan 1st	Mathers	McQuillan	Campbell S	Chisholm	Jamieson	McLeod	Dinnie	McCall	Gallagher	Dodds*	Beedie	West (8)	Forsyth (11)
4th	Mathers	McQuillan	Campbell S	Chisholm	Jamieson	McLeod	West	McCall	Gallagher	McCall	Beedie	Bremner (11)	Forsyth (8)
7th	Mathers	McQuillan	Campbell S	Chisholm	Jamieson	McLeod	Dinnie	McCall	Gallagher	Dodds	Beedie	Bremner (9)	West (11)
11th	Mathers	McQuillan	McLeod	Chisholm	Jamieson	Fraser	Craig	McCall	Gallagher	Dodds	Beedie	Dinnie	Bremner
18th	Mathers	Forsyth	McLeod	Chisholm	Jamieson	Craig	West	McCall	Bremner	Dodds	Beedie	Craib	Frail (9)
Feb 1st	Mathers	McQuillan	McLeod	Chisholm	Jamieson	Craig	West	Frail	Bremner	Dodds	McCall	Gallagher (9)	Forsyth (7)
3rd	Mathers	McQuillan	Dinnie	Chisholm	Forsyth	McLeod	Frail	Craig	Gallagher	Dodds	McCall	Bremner (6)	McMartin (7)
5th	Mathers	McQuillan	Dinnie	Chisholm	Forsyth	Fraser	McMartin	Craig	Gallagher	Dodds	McCall	Bremner	West (3)
8th	Leighton	McQuillan	Dinnie	Chisholm	Jamieson	Craib	McMartin	Craig	Stainrod	Dodds	McCall	Gallagher (6)	Forsyth (8)
15th	Leighton	McQuillan	Dinnie	Chisholm	Jamieson	Forsyth	McMartin	McCall	Gallagher	Dodds	Beedie	Craig (11)	Craib
22nd	Leighton	McQuillan	Dinnie	Chisholm	Jamieson	McMartin	Beedie	Stainrod	Gallagher	Dodds	McCall	Craig	Forsyth
24th	Leighton	McQuillan	Dinnie	Chisholm	Jamieson	Forsyth	Beedie	McMartin	Gallagher	Dodds	McCall	Craig (5)	McLeod (3)
29th	Leighton	McQuillan	Dinnie	Chisholm	Jamieson	McMartin	Beedie	Stainrod	Ritchie	Dodds	McLeod	Forsyth	McCall (3)
Mar 7th	Leighton	McQuillan	Dinnie	Chisholm	Forsyth	McMartin	Beedie	Craig	Stainrod	Dodds	McCall	Gallagher (9)	McLeod (7)
14th	Leighton	McQuillan	Dinnie	Chisholm	Forsyth	McMartin	Beedie	Craig	Stainrod	Dodds	McCall	Craib	Gallagher
21st	Leighton	McQuillan	Dinnie	Chisholm	Forsyth	McMartin	Beedie	Craig	Stainrod	Dodds	McCall	Ritchie (9)	Gallagher (11)
28th	Leighton	McQuillan	Dinnie	Chisholm	Jamieson	Forsyth	Beedie	McMartin	Stainrod	Dodds	McCall	Ritchie (9)	Gallagher (10)
Apr 4th	Leighton	McQuillan	Dinnie	Chisholm	Jamieson	Forsyth	Beedie	McMartin	Stainrod	Dodds	McCall	Ritchie (9)	Gallagher
7th	Leighton	McQuillan	Dinnie	Chisholm	Jamieson	Forsyth	Beedie	Frail	Ritchie	Dodds	McCall	McMartin (8)	Gallagher (9)
11th	Leighton	Dinnie	Campbell S	Chisholm	Jamieson	Forsyth	Beedie	McMartin	Stainrod	Dodds	McCall	Gallagher	McQuillan (7)
18th	Leighton	Dinnie	Campbell S	Chisholm	Jamieson	Forsyth	Christie	McMartin	Stainrod	Dodds	McCall	Gallagher (8)	McQuillan
25th	Leighton	Dinnie	Campbell S	Chisholm	Jamieson	Forsyth	McQuillan	Beedie	Ritchie	Dodds	McCall	Gallagher (10)	Stainrod (8)
May 2nd	Leighton	Dinnie	Campbell S	Chisholm	Jamieson	Forsyth	McQuillan	Beedie	Ritchie	Dodds	McCall	Gallagher (9)	Stainrod (3)

Simon lets fly - Dundee player-manager Simon Stainrod was an expert at dead ball situations. Mark Craib, Alan Dinnie and Ian McCall look on as the big Englishman sends in a thundering free-kick.

DC Thomson

They Wore The Dark Blue

Season 1992-93

Date			Opponents		Score	Crowd	Scorers
Aug	1st	L	Falkirk	h	1-2	5,960	Rix
	4th	L	St Johnstone	h	1-1	5,663	Dinnie
	8th	L	Airdrie	a	0-0	2,500	
	11th	LC2	Meadowbank	a	3-0	898	Dodds; McGowan; D. Campbell
	15th	L	Rangers	h	4-3	12,087	Den Bieman; Gilzean; Dodds 2 (1 pen)
	19th	LC3	Celtic	a	0-1	30,849	
	22nd	L	Aberdeen	a	1-2	12,000	Paterson
	29th	L	Partick Thistle	a	3-6	5,429	Dodds 2; Gilzean
Sep	1st	L	Hearts	h	1-3	5,878	Dodds
	12th	L	Motherwell	h	2-1	3,797	Dodds; Vrto
	19th	L	Dundee United	a	1-0	12,456	Dodds (pen)
	26th	L	Hibernian	a	0-0	7,300	-
Oct	3rd	L	Celtic	h	0-1	15,883	
	10th	L	Falkirk	a	2-2	4,818	Den Biemen; Dodds
	17th	L	Airdrie	h	2-0	4,092	McKeown; Dodds
	24th	L	Partick Thistle	h	0-2	5,633	
	31st	L	Hearts	a	0-1	7,452	
Nov	7th	L	Aberdeen	h	1-2	7,527	Dodds
	11th	L	Rangers	a	1-3	33,497	Den Bieman
	21st	L	Dundee United	h	1-3	12,018	Dodds
	28th	L	Motherwell	a	3-1	3,534	Gilzean 2; Stainrod
Dec	2nd	L	St Johnstone	a	4-4	5,766	Pittman; Wieghorst; Dodds 2
	5th	L	Hibernian	h	1-1	5,656	Stainrod
	12th	L	Celtic	a	0-1	16,797	
	19th	L	Falkirk	h	2-1	6,190	Dodds; Stainrod
	26th	L	Rangers	h	1-3	13,960	Stainrod
Jan	2nd	L	Aberdeen	a	0-0	13,200	-
	10th	SC3	Dumbarton	h	2-0	4,290	Wieghorst; Dodds (pen)
	27th	L	Partick Thistle	a	0-2	2,797	
	30th	L	Airdrie	a	2-2	2,500	Reid o.g.; Paterson
Feb	3rd	L	Hearts	h	1-0	4,335	McGowan
	6th	SC4	Hearts	a	0-2	12,021	
	13th	L	St Johnstone	h	1-0	5,031	Stainrod
	20th	L	Hibernian	a	3-1	5,681	Stainrod; Dow; Kiwomya
	23rd	L	Celtic	h	0-1	7,360	
	27th	L	Dundee United	a	0-1	12,140	
Mar	6th	L	Motherwell	h	1-1	3,370	Rix
	10th	L	Falkirk	a	0-1	3,452	
	13th	L	Airdrie	h	1-1	3,079	Dodds
	20th	L	Aberdeen	h	1-2	5,933	Stainrod
	27th	L	Rangers	a	0-3	40,294	-
Apr	3rd	L	Partick Thistle	h	0-1	3,998	-
	10th	L	Hearts	a	0-0	6,033	-
	17th	l	Motherwell	a	2-1	4,287	Ritchie; Dodds
	20th	L	Dundee United	h	0-4	9,739	-
May	1st	L	St Johnstone	a	1-1	4,471	Ritchie
	8th	L	Hibernian	h	3-1	5,265	Ritchie; Wieghorst; Gilzean
	15th	L	Celtic	a	0-2	19,436	

Paul Mathers - re-established himself as Dundee's top keeper.

* From this season, only reserve or youth teams to be used for Forfarshire Cup ties.

The Record

League	-	Tenth Place, Premier Division
League Cup	-	Third round
Scottish Cup	-	Fourth round
Forfarshire Cup	-	Did not participate
Top Scorer	-	Billy Dodds (18 goals)
Av. Home Gate	-	6,900
Players used	-	32
Sent off (booked)	-	Nine (77)

Appearances

	League		L/Cup		S/Cup		Total	
Billy Dodds	41	(16)	2	(1)	2	(1)	45	(18)
Jim Duffy	39		2		2		43	
Paul Mathers	36		0		2		38	
Dusan Vrto	32	(1)	2		2		36	(1)
Alan Dinnie	26	(1)	2		1		29	(1)
John McQuillan	27		0		2		29	
Kevin Bain	24		0		2		26	
Ivo Den Biemen	23	(3)	2		0		25+3s	(3)
Jamie McGowan	21	(1)	2	(1)	1		24+1s	(2)
Morten Wieghorst	22	(2)	0		1	(1)	23+1s	(3)
Steve Pittman	20	(1)	0		2		22	(1)
Gary McKeown	20	(1)	1		0		21	(1)
Steve Campbell	20		0		0		20	
Ian Gilzean	17	(5)	2		0		19+6s	(5)
Paul Ritchie	17	(3)	0		0		17+1s	(3)
Graham Rix	12	(2)	2		0		14+2s	(2)
Garry Paterson	11	(2)	0		1		12+8s	(2)
Andy Kiwomya	11	(1)	0		0		11+9s	(1)
Simon Stainrod	10	(7)	0		1		11+10s	(7)
Stuart Beedie	8		2		0		10+5s	
Jim Leighton	8		2		0		10	
Andy Dow	8	(1)	0		1		9+5s	(1)
Lionel David	8		0		0		8	(1)
Steve Frail	7		0		0		7	

Scottish League Premier Division

		Home			Away			Goals		
	P	W	D	L	W	D	L	F	A	PTS
Rangers	44	20	2	0	13	5	4	97-35		73
Aberdeen	44	13	7	2	14	3	5	87-36		64
Celtic	44	13	5	4	11	7	4	68-41		60
Dundee United	44	8	7	7	11	2	9	56-49		47
Hearts	44	12	6	4	3	8	11	46-51		44
St Johnstone	44	8	10	4	2	10	10	52-66		40
Hibernian	44	8	8	6	4	5	13	54-64		37
Partick Thistle	44	5	6	11	7	6	9	50-71		36
Motherwell	44	7	4	11	4	9	9	46-62		35
Dundee	**44**	**7**	**4**	**11**	**4**	**8**	**10**	**48-68**		**34**
Falkirk	44	7	5	10	4	2	16	60-86		29
Airdrie	44	4	9	9	2	8	12	35-70		29

Appearances (Ctd.)

	League		L/Cup		S/Cup		Total	
Kevin Ratcliffe	4		1		0		5	
Duncan Campbell	2		1	(1)	0		3+2s	(1)
Colin West	2		1		0		3+5s	
Eddie Gallagher	2		0		0		2+1s	
Neil McCann	2		0		0		2+1s	
Grant McMartin	2		0		0		2	
Lachie Armstrong	1		0		0		1	
Max Christie	1		0		0		1+1s	

Dundee F.C. Line-Ups 1992-93

	1	2	3	4	5	6	7	8	9	10	11	12	13
Aug 1st	Leighton	Dinnie	Campbell S	Duffy	McGowan	McKeown	Ritchie	McMartin	Gilzean	Dodds	Rix	Beedie	Gallagher
4th	Leighton	Dinnie	Campbell S	Duffy	McGowan	McKeown	Den Biemen	Beedie	Gilzean	Dodds	Rix	McMartin	Gallagher
8th	Leighton	Dinnie	Campbell S	Duffy	McGowan	McKeown	Den Biemen	Vrto	Gilzean	Dodds	Rix	Gallagher (10)	Beedie (11)
11th	Leighton	Dinnie	Beedie	Duffy	McGowan	McKeown	Den Biemen	Vrto	Gilzean	Dodds	Rix	Bain	Campbell D
15th	Leighton	Dinnie	Beedie	Duffy	McGowan	Ratcliffe	Den Biemen	Vrto	Gilzean	Dodds	Rix	Campbell D	Bain
19th	Leighton	Dinnie	Beedie	Duffy	McGowan	Ratcliffe	Den Biemen	Vrto	Gilzean*	Dodds	Rix	Bain	Campbell D
22nd	Leighton	Dinnie	Beedie	McKeown	McGowan	Ratcliffe	Den Biemen	Vrto	Paterson	Dodds	Rix	Campbell D (7)	Stainrod (9)
29th	Leighton	Dinnie	Ratcliffe	Duffy	McGowan	McKeown	Den Biemen	Vrto	Gilzean	Dodds	Rix	McQuillan (6)	Paterson (5)
Sep 1st	Mathers	Dinnie	Ratcliffe	Duffy	McGowan	Campbell S	Den Biemen	Vrto	Gilzean	Dodds	Rix	McQuillan	Paterson (5)
12th	Mathers	Dinnie	Campbell S	Duffy	Beedie	McKeown	McQuillan	Vrto	Den Biemen	Dodds	Rix	Bain	Dow
19th	Mathers	Dinnie	Campbell S	Duffy	Bain	McKeown	Den Biemen	Vrto	Gilzean	Dodds	McQuillan	Beedie	Dow
26th	Mathers	Dinnie	Campbell S	Duffy	Bain	McKeown	Den Biemen	Vrto	Gilzean	Dodds	McQuillan	Beedie (9)	Dow(7)
Oct 3rd	Mathers	Dinnie	Campbell S	Duffy	Bain	McKeown	Den Biemen	Vrto	Gilzean	Dodds	McQuillan	Kiwomya (7)	Beedie (5)
10th	Mathers	Dinnie	Campbell S	Duffy	Bain	McKeown	Den Biemen	Vrto	Gilzean	Dodds	McQuillan	Beedie (8)	Kiwomya
17th	Mathers	Dinnie	Campbell S	Duffy	Bain	McKeown	Den Biemen	Vrto	Kiwomya	Dodds	Beedie	Gilzean (7)	McGowan
24th	Mathers	Dinnie	Campbell S	Duffy	Bain	McKeown*	Den Biemen	Vrto	Kiwomya	Dodds	Beedie	Gilzean	McGowan
31st	Mathers	Dinnie	Beedie	Duffy	Bain	Christie	Den Biemen	Vrto*	Gallagher	Dodds	McQuillan	Stainrod (7)	Paterson (9)
Nov 7th	Mathers	Dinnie	Pittman	Duffy	Bain	Beedie	Den Biemen	McGowan	Gallagher	Dodds	McQuillan	Christie	Paterson
11th	Mathers	Dinnie	Campbell S	Duffy	McGowan	McQuillan	Den Biemen	Vrto	Gilzean	Dodds	Ritchie	Paterson (11)	Stainrod (9)
21st	Mathers	Dinnie	Campbell S	Duffy	McGowan	McQuillan	Den Biemen	Paterson	Stainrod	Dodds	Ritchie	Gilzean (8)	Beedie (9)
28th	Mathers	Dinnie	Pittman	McMartin	McGowan	Dow	Campbell D	Vrto	Gilzean	Dodds	McQuillan	Paterson	Stainrod (4)
Dec 2nd	Mathers*	Dinnie	Pittman	Wieghorst	McGowan	Dow	Campbell D	Vrto	Gilzean	Dodds	McQuillan	Paterson (11)	Stainrod (9)
5th	Leighton	Dinnie	Pittman	Wieghorst	Bain	Dow	Den Biemen	Vrto	Gilzean	Dodds	McQuillan	Campbell D (7)	Stainrod (5)
12th	Mathers	Dinnie	Pittman	Wieghorst	Duffy	Dow	Den Biemen	Vrto	Gilzean	Dodds	McQuillan	West (7)	Stainrod (4)
19th	Mathers	Dinnie	Pittman	Duffy	McQuillan	Wieghorst	Ritchie	Vrto	Stainrod	Dodds	Kiwomya	Dow	Bain
26th	Leighton	Dinnie	Pittman	Wieghorst	Duffy	Paterson	McQuillan	Vrto	Stainrod	Dodds	Kiwomya	Ritchie	Dow (4)
Jan 2nd	Mathers	Dinnie	Pittman	Wieghorst	Duffy	Dow	McQuillan	Vrto	Ritchie	Dodds	Kiwomya	Den Biemen (9)	Paterson 11
10th	Mathers	McQuillan	Pittman	Duffy	Wieghorst	Dow	Bain		Stainrod*	Dodds	Campbell D	Den Biemen (9)	McGowan 5
27th	Mathers	McQuillan	Pittman	Wieghorst	Duffy	Dow	McGowan*	Vrto	Den Biemen	Dodds	Kiwomya	Ritchie (2)	Rix (11)
30th	Mathers	Dinnie	Pittman	Wieghorst	Duffy	Bain	Den Biemen*	Vrto	Ritchie	Dodds	Rix*	Paterson (3)	Kiwomya (4
Feb 3rd	Mathers	McQuillan	Pittman	Bain	Duffy	McGowan	Ritchie	Vrto	Paterson	Dodds	McKeown	West (7)	Kiwomya
6th	Mathers	McQuillan	Pittman	Dinnie	Duffy	McGowan	Bain	Vrto	Paterson	Dodds	West	Den Biemen (4)	Kiwomya(3)
13th	Mathers	McQuillan	Pittman	Wieghorst	Duffy	Bain	McGowan	Vrto	Stainrod	Dodds	West	Kiwomya (11)	McKeown
20th	Mathers	McQuillan	Campbell S	Wieghorst	Duffy	Bain	McGowan	Vrto	Stainrod	Dodds	West	Kiwomya (11)	Dow (4)
23rd	Mathers	McQuillan	Pittman	Wieghorst	Duffy	Bain	McGowan	Vrto	Stainrod	Dodds	Kiwomya	West (9)	Rix (11)
27th	Mathers	McQuillan	Pittman	Wieghorst	Duffy	Bain	McGowan	Vrto	Den Biemen	Dodds	Kiwomya	West (9)	Dow (6)
Mar 6th	Mathers	McQuillan	Pittman	Wieghorst	Duffy	Bain	McKeown	Vrto	Stainrod	Dodds	Rix	Kiwomya (7)	Paterson
10th	Mathers	McQuillan	Pittman	Wieghorst	Duffy	Bain	McGowan	Vrto	Stainrod	Dodds	Rix	Dow (7)	West (4)
13th	Mathers	McQuillan	Pittman	Paterson	Duffy	Dow	McCann	Vrto	Ritchie	Dodds	Bain	Kiwomya (11)	Stainrod (4)
20th	Mathers	McQuillan	Pittman	Wieghorst	Duffy	Bain	Ritchie	Vrto	Stainrod	Dodds	Dow	Paterson (8)	McCann
27th	Mathers	McQuillan	Pittman	Wieghorst	McGowan	Bain	Ritchie	David	Den Biemen	Dodds	McCann	Dow	Stainrod
Apr 3rd	Mathers	Frail	Pittman	McGowan	Duffy	Bain	Ritchie	David	Stainrod	Dodds	Rix	Wieghorst (3)	McCann (11
10th	Mathers	Frail	Campbell S	Wieghorst	Duffy	Bain	Ritchie	David	Paterson	Dodds	McKeown	Gilzean (7)	Kiwomya
17th	Mathers	Frail	Campbell S	Wieghorst	Duffy	Bain	Ritchie	David	Paterson	Dodds	McKeown	Gilzean (4)	Kiwomya 4
20th	Mathers	Frail	Campbell S	Wieghorst	Duffy	Bain	Ritchie	David	Paterson	Dodds*	McKeown	Gilzean (4)	Kiwomya 6
May 1st	Mathers	Frail	Campbell S	Wieghorst	Duffy	Paterson	Ritchie	David	Gilzean	McKeown	Kiwomya	Stainrod (9)	Bain
8th	Mathers	Frail	Campbell S	Wieghorst	Duffy	Paterson	Ritchie	David	Gilzean	McKeown	Kiwomya	Stainrod (9)	Bain
15th	Mathers	Frail	Campbell S	Wieghorst	Duffy	Paterson	Ritchie	David	Armstrong	McKeown	Kiwomya	Gilzean (9)	Christie (4)

Flying Dutchman - pacy winger Ivo den Biemen drives over a cross in Dundee's 4-3 win over Rangers at Dens.

Den Biemen again - this time he accepts the plaudits from Jamie McGowan and Ian Gilzean after scoring the opener against the Ibrox men.

DC Thomson

Season 1993-94

Noel Blake - experienced defender brought steel to the heart of Dundee's defence.

Date			Opponents		Score	Crowd	Scorers
Aug	7th	L	Kilmarnock	a	0-1	8,162	
	10th	LC2	Meadowbank	a*	1-1	811	Davidson o.g.
	14th	L	Motherwell	h	1-2	4,356	Dykstra o.g.
	21st	L	Aberdeen	h	1-1	7,655	Dodds
	24th	LC3	Hibernian	a	1-2	6,473	Neilson
	28th	L	Hibernian	a	0-2	5,491	-
Sep	4th	L	Rangers	h	1-1	14,364	Paterson
	11th	L	Dundee United	a	0-1	10,664	-
	18th	L	Raith Rovers	h	0-1	4,654	-
	25th	L	St Johnstone	a	1-2	4,203	Ristic
Oct	2nd	L	Hearts	h	2-0	5,021	Paterson; Ristic
	5th	L	Partick Thistle	h	2-2	4,690	Dodds; Pittman
	9th	L	Celtic	a	1-2	16,994	Dodds (pen)
	16th	L	Motherwell	a	0-1	5,126	-
	23rd	L	Kilmarnock	h	1-0	4,537	Adamczuk
	30th	L	Aberdeen	a	0-1	11,886	-
Nov	6th	L	Hibernian	h	3-2	4,685	Pittman; Ristic; Ritchie
	10th	L	Rangers	a	1-3	39,477	Dodds
	13th	L	Hearts	a	2-1	7,884	Ritchie; Czachowski
	20th	L	St Johnstone	h	0-1	4,884	-
Dec	1st	L	Raith Rovers	a	1-2	3,609	Wieghorst
	4th	L	Partick Thistle	a	2-3	3,595	Tosh; Dodds
	7th	L	Dundee United	h	1-2	9,156	Farningham
	11th	L	Celtic	h	1-1	8,250	Ristic
	18th	L	Motherwell	h	1-3	4,337	Ristic
Jan	4th	L	Kilmarnock	a	0-1	7,406	-
	8th	L	Hibernian	a	0-2	7,415	-
	11th	L	Aberdeen	h	0-1	5,369	-
	15th	L	Rangers	h	1-1	11,014	Wieghorst
	22nd	L	Raith Rovers	h	2-2	3,934	Shaw (pen); Blake
	29th	SC3	Clydebank	a	1-1	2,170	Tosh
Feb	5th	L	Dundee United	a	1-1	10,622	Ristic
	8th	SC3R	Clydebank	n**	2-1	856	Britton; Shaw
	12th	L	St Johnstone	h	1-1	5,517	Farningham
	20th	SC4	St Mirren	h	3-1	6,040	Britton 2 (1 pen); Shaw
	26th	L	Hearts	h	0-2	4,115	-
Mar	5th	L	Partick Thistle	h	1-0	3,360	Shaw
	12th	SCQ	Kilmarnock	a	0-1	10,446	-
	19th	L	Motherwell	a	1-3	6,127	McQuillan
	26th	L	Kilmarnock	h	3-0	3,348	Britton; Blake; McCann
	29th	L	Dundee United	h	1-1	8,400	N. Duffy
Apr	2nd	L	Raith Rovers	a	1-1	2,200	Shaw
	6th	L	Celtic	a	1-1	16,552	Martin o.g.
	9th	L	St Johnstone	h	0-1	3,586	-
	16th	L	Hearts	a	2-0	6,000	Shaw 2
	23rd	L	Celtic	h	0-2	5,982	-
	27th	L	Partick Thistle	a	0-1	3,604	-
	30th	L	Aberdeen	a	1-1	7,000	N. Duffy
May	4th	FC1	St Johnstone	a	1-0	n/a	Ritchie
	7th	L	Hibernian	h	4-0	3,012	McKeown; Shaw; Pittman; Anderson (pen)
	14th	L	Rangers	a	0-0	41,620	-

The Record		
League	-	12th Place, Premier Division
League Cup	-	Third round
Scottish Cup	-	Quarter-final
Forfarshire Cup	-	Runners-up (final on 14-12-94)
Top Scorer	-	George Shaw (8 goals)
Av. Home gate	-	5,900
Players used	-	35
Sent off (booked)	-	Four (88)

* a.e.t., 1-1 at 90 mts, Dundee won 3-1 on penalties. ** At Forthbank Stadium after Kilbowie incident.

How did that get in - Hibs defenders Graeme Mitchell and Jim Leighton debate the issue after Steve Pittman's inswinging corner lands in the back of the net. Dragutin Ristic is on hand to make sure.

DC Thomson

Dundee F.C. Line-Ups 1993-94

	1	2	3	4	5	6	7	8	9	10	11	12	13
Aug 7th	Mathers	Frail	Pittman	Wieghorst	David	McGowan	McMartin	Vrto	Ritchie	Tosh	Christie	Paterson	McQuillan
10th	Mathers	Frail	Christie	Wieghorst	David	McGowan	McMartin	Vrto	Ritchie	Dodds	Tosh	McQuillan	Paterson
14th	Mathers	McQuillan	Pittman	Wieghorst	Paterson	McGowan	McKeown	Vrto	Stainrod	Dodds	Tosh	Ritchie (9)	Frail (5)
21st	Mathers	McQuillan	Pittman	Wieghorst	Paterson	McGowan	Adamczuk	Vrto	Tosh	Dodds	McKeown	Frail (7)	Armstrong
24th	Mathers	McQuillan	Pittman	Wieghorst	Paterson	McGowan	Adamczuk	Vrto	Tosh	Dodds	McKeown	Frail	Nielsen (9)
28th	Mathers	Frail	Pittman	Wieghorst	Duffy J	Paterson	McGowan	Adamczuk	Tosh	Dodds	McKeown	Armstrong (8)	Ritchie (4)
Sep 4th	Mathers	Frail	Pittman	Wieghorst	Duffy J	Paterson	McGowan	Vrto	Ritchie*	Dodds	McKeown	Farningham (5)	Tosh
11th	Mathers	Frail	Pittman	Farningham	Duffy J	Paterson	McGowan	Vrto	Tosh	Dodds	McKeown	Adamczuk (7)	McQuillan
18th	Mathers	Frail	Pittman	Farningham	Duffy J	Paterson	Adamczuk	Vrto	Ritchie	Dodds	McKeown	McGowan (5)	Tosh (11)
25th	Mathers	Frail	Pittman	Farningham	Duffy J	Paterson	McKeown	Vrto	Tosh	Ristic	Czachowski	Dodds (5)	McQuillan(4
Oct 2nd	Mathers	Frail	Pittman	McQuillan	Duffy J	Paterson	McKeown	Vrto	Ristic	Dodds	Czachowski	McCann	Adamczuk
5th	Mathers	Frail	Pittman	McQuillan	Paterson	Czachowski	McKeown	Vrto	Ristic	Dodds	McCann	Adamczuk (6)	Mobilio (11)
9th	Mathers	Frail	Pittman	McGowan	Paterson	Duffy	McKeown	Vrto	Ristic	Dodds	Czachowski	Adamczuk (7)	Mobilio (4)
16th	Mathers	Frail*	Pittman	Farningham	Duffy J	Adamczuk	McQuillan	Vrto	Ristic	Dodds	Czachowski	Ritchie (9)	McMartin(6)
23rd	Mathers	McQuillan	Pittman	Farningham	Paterson	Duffy J	Adamczuk	Vrto	Ristic	Dodds	Czachowski	Ritchie (3)	McMartin(9)
30th	Mathers	Frail	Adamczuk	Farningham	Paterson	Duffy J	Ritchie	Vrto	Ristic	Dodds	Czachowski	McQuillan (9)	McMartin
Nov 6th	Mathers	Frail	Pittman	Adamczuk*	Paterson	Duffy J	Ritchie	Vrto	Ristic	Dodds	Czachowski	McQuillan (3)	Tosh (9)
10th	Mathers	Frail	Pittman	McQuillan	Paterson	Duffy J	Ritchie	Wieghorst	Ristic	Dodds	Czachowski	McGowan (8)	Tosh (9)
13th	Mathers	Frail	Pittman	McKeown	Paterson	Duffy J	Ritchie	Vrto	Ristic	Dodds	Czachowski	McQuillan (4)	Tosh (7)
20th	Mathers	Frail	McQuillan	McKeown	Paterson	Duffy J	Ritchie	Vrto	Ristic	Dodds	Czachowski	Wieghorst (9)	Tosh (5)
Dec 1st	Mathers	Frail	McQuillan	Wieghorst	McCann	Duffy J	McKeown	Vrto	Ristic	Dodds	Czachowski	Ritchie (7)	McGowan (4
4th	Mathers	Frail	Pittman	Farningham	Paterson	McGowan	Tosh	Vrto	Ristic	Dodds	Czachowski	Wieghorst	McCann (4)
7th	Mathers	Frail	Pittman	McGowan	Bain	Duffy J	Tosh	Vrto	Farningham	Dodds	Czachowski	McQuillan (4)	Ristic
14th	Mathers	Frail	McCann	Farningham	Blake	Duffy J	Tosh	Vrto	Ristic	Dodds	Czachowski	Tosh	Pittman (3)
19th	Mathers	Frail	Pittman	McQuillan	Blake	Duffy J	McGowan	Vrto	Ristic	Dodds	Czachowski	Farningham	Tosh (2)
Jan 4th	Mathers	Frail	Duffy J	Farningham	Blake	McKeown	Ritchie	Vrto	Ristic	Dodds	Czachowski	McQuillan (9)	Wieghorst11
8th	Mathers	Frail	McCann	Bain	Blake	Duffy J	Ritchie	Wieghorst	McQuillan	Dodds	Dinnie	Farningham (3)	McMartin
11th	Mathers	Frail	Pittman	McQuillan	Blake	Duffy J	Shaw	Wieghorst	Britton	Dinnie	McCann	Ritchie (6)	Bain
15th	Mathers	Frail	Pittman	Wieghorst	Blake	Duffy J	Shaw	Vrto	Britton	Dinnie	McCann	McQuillan (2)	Ritchie (8)
22nd	Mathers	Frail	Pittman	Wieghorst	Blake	Duffy J	Shaw	McQuillan	Britton	Dinnie	McCann	Farningham	Ritchie
29th	Mathers	Frail	Pittman	McQuillan	Blake	Duffy J	Shaw	Vrto	Ritchie	Wieghorst	McCann	Farningham (6)	Tosh (9)
Feb 5th	Mathers	Frail	Pittman	McQuillan	Blake	Duffy J	Shaw	Vrto	Tosh	Wieghorst	McCann	Farningham (2)	Ristic (9)
8th	Mathers	McQuillan	Pittman	Duffy J	Blake	Dinnie	Shaw	Vrto	Britton	Wieghorst	McCann*	Farningham (9)	Ristic (10)
12th	Mathers	McQuillan	Pittman	Dinnie	Blake	Duffy J	Shaw	Vrto	Britton	Wieghorst	Farningham	Tosh	McKeown
20th	Mathers	McQuillan	Pittman	Dinnie	Blake	Duffy J	Shaw	Farningham	Britton	Wieghorst	McCann	Frail (8)	Tosh (9)
26th	Pageaud	Frail	Pittman	Dinnie	Blake	Duffy N	Shaw	McQuillan	Britton	Wieghorst	McCann	Tosh (9)	Bain (2)
Mar 5th	Pageaud	McQuillan	Pittman	Dinnie	Blake	Duffy N	Shaw	Vrto	Britton	Czachowski	McCann	Frail (10)	Tosh (4)
12th	Mathers	McQuillan	Pittman	Dinnie	Blake	Frail	Shaw	Vrto	Britton	Wieghorst	McCann	Farningham (6)	Tosh (4)
19th	Mathers	McQuillan	Pittman	Frail	Blake	Duffy N	Tosh	Vrto	Britton	Wieghorst	McCann	Farningham (6)	Teasdale (4)
26th	Pageaud	McQuillan	Pittman	Teasdale	Blake	Farningham	Shaw	Vrto	Britton	Wieghorst	McCann	Frail (4)	Tosh (7)
29th	Pageaud	McQuillan	Pittman	Duffy N	Blake	Farningham	Shaw	Vrto	Britton	Wieghorst	McCann	Tosh	Bain
Apr 2nd	Pageaud	McQuillan	Pittman	Duffy N	Blake	Farningham	Shaw	Vrto	Britton	Wieghorst	McCann	Tosh (9)	Bain (10)
6th	Mathers	McQuillan	Pittman	Farningham	Blake	Duffy J	Shaw	Vrto	Britton	Duffy N	Tosh	Bain (11)	Paterson
9th	Mathers	McQuillan	Pittman	Farningham	Blake	Duffy J	Tosh	Vrto	Britton	Duffy N	McCann	Bain	Teasdale (3)
16th	Pageaud	McQuillan	Pittman	Farningham	Blake	Duffy J	Shaw	Vrto	Britton	Bain	Tosh	Paterson (11)	Anderson (7)
23rd	Pageaud	Farningham	Tully	Duffy N	Blake	Duffy J	Shaw	Vrto	Britton	Bain	McCann	McKeown (10)	Tosh (3)
27th	Pageaud	Teasdale	Duffy J	Farningham	Blake	Duffy N	Shaw	Vrto	Britton	McKeown	McCann	Tosh (10)	Paterson (2)
30th	Pageaud	McQuillan	Duffy N	Wieghorst	Blake	Duffy J	Shaw	Vrto	Tosh	McKeown	McCann	Teasdale (10)	Britton (4)
May 7th	Pageaud	McQuillan	Pittman	Farningham	Blake	Duffy N	Shaw	Vrto	Wieghorst	McKeown	McCann	Hamilton (9)	Anderson (8)
14th	Pageaud	McQuillan	Pittman	Duffy N	Blake	Duffy J	Shaw	Vrto	Wieghorst	McKeown	McCann	Britton (9)	Anderson

Appearances

	League		L/Cup	S/Cup		Total	
Dusan Vrto	38		2	3		43	
Steve Pittman	35	(3)	1	4		40+1s	(3)
Paul Mathers	33		2	4		39	
Jim Duffy	32		0	3		35	
Steve Frail	28		1	2		31+5s	
John McQuillan	26		1	4		31+7s	
Noel Blake	23	(2)	0	4		27	(2)
Morten Wieghorst	21	(2)	2	4		27+2s	(2)
Billy Dodds	23	(5)	2	0		25+1s	(5)
Neil McCann	20	(1)	0	4		24	(1)
Ray Farningham	20	(2)	0	1		21+7s	(2)
George Shaw	17	(6)	0	4	(2)	21	(8)
Gary McKeown	18	(1)	1	0		19+1s	(1)
Gerry Britton	15	(1)	0	3	(3)	18+2s	(4)
Pietor Czachowkski	18	(1)	0	0		18	(1)
Garry Paterson	17	(2)	1	0		18+2s	(2)
Dragutin Ristic	16	(6)	0	0		16+2s	(6)
Paul Tosh	14	(1)	2	0	(1)	16+15s	(2)
Jamie McGowan	11		2	0		13+3s	
Neil Duffy	12	(2)	0	0		12	(2)
Paul Ritchie	10	(2)	1	1		12+7s	(2)
Alan Dinnie	7		0	3		10	
Michel Pageaud	11		0	0		11	
Dariusz Adamczuk	7	(1)	1	0		8+3s	(1)
Kevin Bain	4		0	0		4+3s	
Mike Teasdale	2		0	0		2+3s	
Grant McMartin	1		1	0		2+2s	

Scottish League Premier Division

		Home			Away			Goals		
	P	W	D	L	W	D	L	F A		PTS
Rangers	44	12	6	4	10	8	4	74-41		58
Aberdeen	44	11	9	2	6	12	4	58-36		55
Motherwell	44	11	7	4	9	7	6	58-43		54
Celtic	44	8	11	3	7	9	6	51-38		50
Hibernian	44	11	7	4	5	8	9	53-48		47
Dundee United	44	5	11	6	6	9	7	47-48		42
Hearts	44	6	9	7	5	11	6	37-43		42
Kilmarnock	44	6	10	6	6	6	10	36-45		40
Partick Thistle	44	9	8	5	3	8	11	46-57		40
St Johnstone	44	7	7	8	3	13	6	35-47		40
Raith Rovers	44	3	12	7	3	7	12	46-80		31
Dundee	**44**	**6**	**7**	**9**	**2**	**6**	**14**	**42-57**		**29**

Appearances (Ctd.)   (T = trialist)

	League		L/Cup		S/Cup	Total	
Max Christie	1		1		0	2	
Lionel David	1		1		0	2	
Simon Stainrod	1		0		0	1	
Craig Tully	1		0		0	1	
Ian Anderson	0	(1)	0		0	0+2s	(1)
Dom Mobilio	0		0		0	0+2s	
Lachie Armstrong	0		0		0	0+1s	
Jim Hamilton	0		0		0	0+1s	
Henrik Neilson (T)	0		0	(1)	0	0+1s	(1)

Season 1994-95

Date		Opponents		Score	Crowd	Scorers
Aug	13th	L	St Mirren	h	2-0	4,125	Shaw; Britton
	17th	LC2	Caley Thistle	h	3-0	3,112	Shaw; Tosh 2
	20th	L	Stranraer	h	3-1	3,186	Britton 2; McCaffrey o.g.
	27th	L	St Johnstone	a	1-0	6,021	Pittman
	31st	LC3	Celtic	h	1-2	11,700	Farningham
Sep	3rd	L	Airdrie	h	1-1	4,020	Farningham
	10th	L	Clydebank	a	2-5	1,593	Britton 2
	17th	BQ1	Arbroath	h	5-0	2,205	Britton 4; Shaw
	24th	L	Ayr United	a	2-3	1,901	Britton; Hamilton
	28th	BQ2	Caley Thistle	a	1-1*	2,000	Wieghorst
Oct	1st	L	Dunfermline	h	4-4	4,784	Shaw 2; Tosh; Britton
	4th	BQ3	Morton	h	2-1	2,199	Britton; Wieghorst
	8th	L	Hamilton	h	2-0	2,370	Hamilton; Britton
	15th	L	Raith Rovers	a	1-1	3,834	Anderson
	18th	BQS	Dunfermline	a	2-1	7,154	Bain (pen); McCann
	22nd	L	St Mirren	a	2-1	2,758	McCann 2
	29th	L	St Johnstone	h	1-0	4,160	Shaw
Nov	6th	BQF	Airdrie	n^	2-3**	8,844	Hay o.g.; Britton
	12th	L	Clydebank	h	2-0	2,240	Bain (pen); Shaw
	19th	L	Airdrie	a	1-2	2,051	Britton
	23rd	L	Stranraer	a	2-0	850	Tosh; Cargill
	26th	L	Ayr United	h	1-1	2,506	Tosh
Dec	3rd	L	Dunfermline	a	1-0	6,065	Ritchie
	10th	L	Raith Rovers	h	2-1	3,482	Hamilton (pen); Wieghorst
	14th	FCF^	Arbroath	a	0-2	n/a	-
	26th	L	Hamilton	a	1-0	1,552	Hamilton
	31st	L	St Mirren	h	4-0	3,500	Hamilton; Shaw 3
Jan	7th	L	Stranraer	h	2-0	2,615	N. Duffy; Ritchie
	11th	L	St Johnstone	a	2-2	5,632	Hamilton; Britton
	14th	L	Airdrie	h	0-1	4,030	
	21st	L	Clydebank	a	3-0	967	Jack o.g.; N. Duffy; Hamilton
	29th	SC3	Partick Thistle	h	2-1	6,320	Shaw; Hamilton
Feb	4th	L	Dunfermline	h	2-3	5,896	Tosh; Britton
	11th	L	Ayr United	a	0-1	2,042	-
	18th	SC4	Raith Rovers	h	1-2	7,622	Shaw
	25th	L	Raith Rovers	a	0-0	5,885	-
Mar	4th	L	Hamilton	h	2-0	2,342	Britton; Teasdale
	18th	L	Clydebank	h	3-2	1,788	Shaw 2; Farningham
	25th	L	Airdrie	a	3-0	2,528	Farningham; Shaw 2;
Apr	1st	L	Dunfermline	a	1-1	8,407	Shaw
	8th	L	Ayr United	h	1-1	2,765	N. Duffy
	15th	L	Hamilton	a	4-1	1,471	Shaw; Hamilton 3
	22nd	L	Raith Rovers	h	0-2	7,828	-
	29th	L	St Mirren	a	0-1	2,976	-
May	6th	L	St Johnstone	h	2-1	3,906	Hamilton (pen); Shaw
	13th	L	Stranraer	a	5-0	1,530	Hamilton (pen); Wieghorst 2; Shaw; Tosh

* a.e.t, 1-1 at 90 mts. Dundee won 4-3 on penalties; ** a.et. 2-2 at 90 mts. ^ 1993-4 Competition.

Ray Farningham - a local lad who gives his all in the Dark Blue of Dundee.

Appearances

	League		L/Cup		S/Cup		B&Q		Total	
George Shaw	33	(16)	2	(1)	2	(2)	5	(1)	42+1s	(20)
Michel Pageaud	34		2		2		4		42	
John McQuillan	30		2		1		4		37+2s	
Noel Blake	29		2		1		3		36+2s	
Morten Wieghorst	29	(3)	1		2		4	(2)	36	(5)
Neil McCann	29	(2)	2		2		2	(1)	35+3s	(3)
Gerry Britton	23	(12)	2		2		5	(6)	32+3s	(18)
Ray Farningham	25	(3)	1	(1)	1		5		32+3s	(4)
Neil Duffy	24	(3)	2		2		1		29+1s	(3)
Dusan Vrto	22		1		2		2		27+1s	
Kevin Bain	20	(1)	0		2		4	(1)	26	(2)
Jim Hamilton	23	(12)	0		1	(1)	1		25+8s	(13)
Jim Duffy	15		1		2		5		23	
Paul Tosh	13	(5)	0	(2)	0		4		17+16s	(7)
Mike Teasdale	13	(1)	0		0		1		14+6s	(1)
Andy Cargill	10	(1)	0		0		0		10+3s	(1)
Mark Hutchison	7		0		0		2		9+1s	
Paul Ritchie	6	(2)	0		0		0		6+9s	(2)
Ian Anderson	4	(1)	1		0		1		6+6s	(1)
Steve Pittman	3	(1)	1		0		0		4	(1)
Paul Mathers	2		0		0		1		2+1s	
Marcus Dailly	1		0		0		1		2	
Alan Dinnie	1		1		0		0		2	
Gary McKeown	0		1		0		0		1+1s	

The Record

League	-	Third Place, First Division
League Cup	-	Third round
Scottish Cup	-	Fourth round
B&Q Cup	-	Runners-up
Forfarshire Cup	-	Unable to fit in.
Top Scorer	-	George Shaw (20 goals)
Av. Home gate	-	3,641
Players used	-	24
Sent off (booked)	-	Six (68)

Scottish League First Division

		Home			Away			Goals		
	P	W	D	L	W	D	L	F	A	PTS
Raith Rovers	36	8	8	2	11	4	3	54-32		69
Dunfermline	36	11	5	2	7	9	2	63-32		68
Dundee	**36**	**11**	**4**	**3**	**9**	**4**	**5**	**65-36**		**68**
Airdrie	36	7	6	5	10	4	4	50-33		61
St Johnstone	36	10	6	2	4	8	6	59-39		56
Hamilton	36	9	3	6	5	4	9	42-48		49
St Mirren	36	7	5	6	1	7	10	34-50		36
Clydebank	36	4	6	8	4	5	9	33-47		35
Ayr United	36	6	5	7	0	6	12	31-58		29
Stranraer	36	3	4	11	1	1	16	25-81		17

Dundee F.C. Line-Ups 1994-95

	1	2	3	4	5	6	7	8	9	10	11	12	13
Aug 13th	Pageaud	McQuillan	Pittman^	Duffy N	Blake^	Duffy J^	Shaw	Dinnie	Wieghorst^	Britton^	McCann	McKeown	Tosh (2)
17th	Pageaud	McQuillan	Pittman	McKeown	Blake	Dinnie^	Shaw	Anderson	Duffy N	Britton	McCann	Farningham (12)	Tosh (14)
20th	Pageaud	McQuillan^	Farningham	Anderson	Blake	Duffy N	Shaw	Vrto^	Wieghorst^	Britton	McCann	McKeown (9)	Tosh (4)
27th	Pageaud	McQuillan^	Pittman	Farningham^	Blake	Duffy N	Shaw	Vrto	Wieghorst	Britton^	McCann	Teasdale (11)	Tosh (9)
31st	Pageaud	McQuillan	Duffy J	Duffy N	Blake	Farningham	Shaw	Vrto*	Wieghorst	Britton	McCann	Teasdale (5)	Tosh (9)
Sep 3rd	Pageaud	McQuillan	Pittman	Duffy N^	Blake	Duffy J	Shaw	Farningham	Wieghorst	Britton	McCann	Teasdale	Tosh (8)
10th	Pageaud	McQuillan	Hutchison	Duffy N	Blake	Farningham^	Shaw	Vrto	Wieghorst^	Britton	Anderson	Tosh (6)	Anderson (7)
17th	Pageaud	McQuillan	Hutchison	Teasdale	Blake^	Duffy J	Shaw	Farningham	Tosh	Britton	Anderson	Hamilton (10)	Vrto (11)
24th	Pageaud	McQuillan	Hutchison	Farningham	Blake^	Duffy N	Shaw	Vrto	Wieghorst	Britton	Tosh	Teasdale	Hamilton(11)
28th	Mathers	Farningham	Hutchison	Duffy N	Blake	Duffy J	Shaw	Dailly	Wieghorst^?	Britton	Bain	Hamilton ( )	Teasdale ( )
Oct 1st	Mathers^	Farningham	McQuillan	Bain	Blake	Duffy J	Shaw	Wieghorst	Tosh^	Britton	Hamilton	Hutchison	Teasdale (10)
4th	Pageaud	McQuillan	Bain	Farningham^	Blake	Duffy J	Shaw	Wieghorst	Tosh	Britton	Hamilton	Hutchison (6)	Anderson
8th	Pageaud	McQuillan	Vrto	Cargill	Blake	Bain	Shaw	Wieghorst	Tosh	Britton^	Hamilton	Hutchison	Teasdale
15th	Pageaud	McQuillan^	Bain	Farningham	Blake	Wieghorst	Shaw^	Vrto	Tosh	Britton	Hamilton	McCann (11)	Anderson (8)
18th	Pageaud	McQuillan^	Bain^	Farningham	Duffy J	Wieghorst^	Shaw^^*	Vrto	Tosh	Britton^	McCann	Blake	Anderson
22nd	Pageaud	McQuillan^	Bain	Farningham	Duffy J	Wieghorst	Anderson	Vrto	Hamilton	Britton	McCann	Tosh (7)	Blake (6)
29th	Pageaud	McQuillan	Hutchison	Farningham	Duffy J	Cargill	Shaw	Bain	Tosh	Britton	McCann	Hamilton (10)	Blake (3)
Nov 6th	Pageaud	McQuillan	Bain	Farningham^	Duffy J^	Wieghorst	Shaw	Vrto^	Tosh	Britton^	McCann	Hamilton (9)	Blake
12th	Pageaud	McQuillan	Bain	Cargill	Blake	Wieghorst	Shaw	Vrto	Hamilton	Britton	McCann	Tosh (3)	Teasdale (6)
19th	Pageaud	McQuillan	Dailly^	Farningham^	Blake	Duffy J	Shaw	Vrto^	Wieghorst	Britton^^*	McCann	Hamilton (3)	Tosh (7)
23rd	Pageaud	McQuillan	Teasdale	Cargill	Blake	Duffy J	Shaw	Wieghorst	Tosh	Hamilton	McCann	Dailly	Cadger
26th	Pageaud	McQuillan^	Teasdale	Cargill	Blake	Bain	Shaw	Wieghorst	Tosh	Britton	McCann	Hamilton (4)	Tully
Dec 3rd	Pageaud	McQuillan	Teasdale	Farningham^	Blake^	Bain	Shaw	Cargill	Tosh	Hamilton	McCann	Anderson (4)	Ritchie (11)
10th	Pageaud	McQuillan	Teasdale	Farningham^	Blake	Bain*	Shaw	Wieghorst	Tosh	Hamilton	McCann	Anderson (11)	Duffy N (9)
26th	Pageaud	Duffy N	Teasdale	Farningham^?	Blake	Wieghorst	Shaw	Vrto	Tosh	Hamilton^	McCann	Cargill	Ritchie
31st	Pageaud	Duffy N	Teasdale	Farningham^	Blake	Bain	Shaw	Vrto^	Wieghorst	Hamilton	McCann	Ritchie (9)	Britton (2)
Jan 7th	Pageaud	Duffy N	Teasdale	Cargill	Blake	Bain	Shaw	Vrto	Ritchie	Hamilton	McCann	McQuillan (4)	Britton (2)
11th	Pageaud	Duffy N^	Teasdale^	Cargill^	Blake^	Bain	Shaw	Vrto	Ritchie	Hamilton	McCann^	McQuillan (3)	Britton (9)
14th	Pageaud	McQuillan	Farningham^	Cargill	Blake^	Bain	Shaw	Vrto	Britton	Hamilton	McCann	Ritchie (4)	Teasdale
21st	Pageaud	McQuillan	Duffy N	Wieghorst	Blake	Bain	Shaw^	Vrto	Hamilton	Britton	McCann	Farningham (4)	Ritchie (3)
29th	Pageaud	McQuillan	Duffy N	Wieghorst	Duffy J	Bain^	Shaw	Vrto	Hamilton	Britton	McCann	Ritchie (4)	Tosh
Feb 4th	Pageaud*	McQuillan	Duffy N	Wieghorst	Blake	Bain	Tosh	Vrto	Hamilton	Britton	McCann	Ritchie Anderson (3)	Mathers
11th	Mathers	McQuillan^	Bain	Wieghorst	Blake	Anderson	Shaw	Vrto	Hamilton	Britton^	McCann	Tosh (2)	Ritchie (7)
18th	Pageaud	Farningham	Duffy J	Duffy N	Blake	Bain	Shaw	Vrto	Wieghorst	Britton^	McCann	Tosh (5)	Hamilton
25th	Pageaud	Duffy N	Teasdale	Farningham	Cargill	Bain	Shaw	Vrto	Wieghorst	Britton	McCann	Hamilton (2)	Ritchie (9)
Mar 4th	Pageaud	Duffy N	Hutchison	Farningham	Teasdale	Bain	Ritchie	Vrto	Wieghorst	Britton	Hamilton	McCann (7)	Shaw (10)
18th	Pageaud	McQuillan	Duffy J	Farningham	Bain	Duffy N	Shaw	Vrto	Hamilton	Britton	McCann	Tosh (9)	Wieghorst
25th	Pageaud	McQuillan	Teasdale	Duffy N	Blake	Duffy J	Wieghorst	Vrto	Ritchie	Farningham^	McCann	Britton	Tosh (10)
Apr 1st	Pageaud^	McQuillan	Duffy N	Duffy N^	Bain^	Farningham	Shaw	Vrto	Ritchie	Britton	McCann	Teasdale (3)	Tosh
8th	Pageaud	McQuillan	Hutchison	Duffy N	Blake	Duffy J	Shaw	Farningham	Wieghorst	Ritchie	Britton*	McCann (8)	Tosh (3)
15th	Pageaud	McQuillan	Hutchison	Duffy N	Blake	Duffy J	Shaw	Wieghorst	Tosh	Hamilton	McCann	Farningham (8)	Ritchie (9)
22nd	Pageaud	McQuillan	Hutchison	Duffy N	Blake	Duffy J	Shaw	Farningham	Wieghorst	Hamilton	McCann	Tosh	Teasdale
29th	Pageaud	McQuillan	Teasdale	Duffy N	Blake	Duffy J	Shaw	Farningham	Wieghorst	Hamilton	Tosh	Ritchie (9)	Cargill (7)
May 6th	Pageaud	McQuillan	Teasdale	Duffy N	Blake	Duffy J	Shaw	Farningham	Wieghorst	Hamilton	McCann	Anderson (4)	Cargill (3)
13th	Pageaud	McQuillan	Duffy J	Duffy N	Blake	Anderson	Shaw	Farningham	Wieghorst	Hamilton	McCann	Cargill (8)	Tosh (6)

* Pageaud sent off in 15 mts. Mathers replaced Wieghorst and went in goals. ^ = booked

Shell-shocked - that's Dunfermline keeper Guido Van De Kamp as a cross-cum-shot from George Shaw, wide on the touchline, sails beyond him and into the net in a promotion crunch game at East End Park. Gerry Britton can't believe his luck!

DC Thomson

Dundee F.C. Friendlies, Benefit Games and other Matches.

Davie McLean - six goals on Spanish tour of 1924.

Date	Opponents		Score	Crowd	Scorers
Jan 1st, 1894	Newton Heath	h	2-1	6,000	Dundas; Thomson
Apr 7th, 1894	Newcastle United	h	8-2	5,000	Thomson; Dundas 3; McInroy; Longair 2; Gilligan
Apr 9th, 1894	Sunderland	h	1-2	8,000	Dundas
Apr 21st, 1894	Stoke City	h	2-2	7,000	Dundas; C. Craig
Jan 2nd, 1895	Sheffield United	h	0-2	4,000	-
Apr 8th, 1895	Sunderland	h	0-2	3,000	-
Apr 20th, 1895	Blackburn Rovers	h	1-3	7,000	Richardson
Jan 4th, 1896	Corinthians	h	0-1	4,000	-
Apr 4th, 1896	Corinthians	a	1-3	60,000*	Keillor
Apr 11th, 1896	Sheffield United	a	0-4	1,000	-
Apr 25th, 1896	Burnley	h	2-1	5,000	Smith; Williamson
Apr 19th, 1897	Nottingham Forest	a**	1-2		Smith
Apr 21st, 1897	Preston North End	a	0-0	3,000	-
Oct 10th, 1898	Celtic	h	0-2	5,000	-
	(Sandy Keillor Benefit, £143)				
Mar 3rd, 1900	Everton	h	0-2	5,000	-
Apr 21st, 1900	Sunderland	h	1-1	5,000	McDermott
Dec 14th, 1901	Derby County	h	1-2	4,000	Lloyd
Apr 21st, 1905	Middlesbrough	a	0-1	3,000	-
Apr 22nd, 1905	New Brompton	a	3-1	2,000	MacFarlane 2; Bell
Apr 24th, 1905	Woolwich Arsenal	a	0-3^	5,000	-
Apr 25th, 1905	Bradford	a	3-3	5,000	Cowie 2; MacFarlane
Aug 30th, 1905	Rangers	h	1-4	4,000	McLuckie
	(Fred McDiarmid Benefit)				
Oct 9th, 1905	Newcastle United	h	1-1	6,000	McLuckie
Jan 1st, 1906	Derby County	h	1-1	10,000	Webb
Aug 16th, 1909	Falkirk	h	1-0	7,000	Bellamy
	(Jack Fraser Benefit/Robertson Cup)				
Aug 17th, 1910	Clyde	h	2-0	3,000	Graydon 2
	(Bert Lee Benefit)				
Aug 15th, 1911	Aberdeen	h	3-4	3,000	Walker 2 (1 pen); McLauchlan
	(Bert Neal Benefit)				
Sep 1st, 1920	Aberdeen	a	3-2	9,000	Philip 2; Bell
	(George Anderson Testimonial)				
Apr 13th, 1921	Celtic	h	0-2	15,000	-
	(Napper Thomson Benefit)				
Aug 31st, 1922	Forfar Athletic	a	4-2	1,500	Bell 2; Troup; D. McLean
	(George Langlands Benefit)				

* New British record crowd. ** At Crystal Palace.
Herbert Dainty and Sandy MacFarlane also had benefit games - details unknown.

Tour of Spain 1923

Date	Opponents	Score	Crowd	Scorers
May 20th, 1923	Bilbao Athletic	3-0	10,000	J. McDonald; Halliday 2
May 21st, 1923	Bilbao Athletic	1-1	9,000	D. McLean
May 24th, 1923	Real Madrid	2-0	11,000	Halliday 2
May 26th, 1923	Valencia	3-0	8,000	Halliday 2; Cowan
May 27th, 1923	Valencia	1-0	6,000	J. McDonald
Jun 3rd, 1923	Barcelona	1-3	20,000	D. McLean
Jun 4th, 1923	Barcelona	0-2	28,000	-

Tour of Spain 1924

Date	Opponents		Score	Crowd	Scorers
Jun 1st, 1924	Barcelona		2-0	25,000	Halliday 2
Jun 5th, 1924	Barcelona		2-1	10,000	D. McLean; Duncan
Jun 8th, 1924	Real Madrid		1-1	6,000	D. McLean
Jun 9th, 1924	Real Madrid		2-1	12,000	Duncan; Letham
Jun 15th, 1924	La Corunna		3-3	9,000	D. McLean 3 (1 pen)
Jun 20th, 1924	La Corunna		1-5	10,000	Gilmour (pen)
Jun 22nd, 1924	La Corunna		2-0	10,000	Brown; D. McLean
Oct 1st, 1924	Darlington	a	1-1	3,000	Duncan
	(George Stevens Benefit)				
Apr 12th, 1926	Sunderland	h	1-1	10,000	A. Campbell
	(Sam Irving Benefit)				
Oct 4th, 1926	Aberdeen	h	2-2	5,000	McGinn; Hunter
	(Napper Thomson 2nd Benefit)				
Sep 5th, 1928	St Johnstone	h	3-1	4,000	Smith 2; O'Hare
	(Jock Ross Benefit)				
Oct 5th, 1936	Portsmouth	h	3-0	12,000	Coats; Phillips; Kirby
	(Bill Marsh Benefit, £500)				
Aug 5th, 1944	British Army	h	0-7	14,000	-

Tour of West Germany, Austria and Italy v. British Army Teams

Date	Opponents	Score	Scorers
Jun 8th, 1946	B.A.O.R.(Hamburg, W. Ger)	2-2	Juliussen; Joyner
Jun 12th, 1946	British T.A. (Klagenfurt, Aus)	2-1	Pattillo; Joyner
Jun 15th, 1946	British T.A. (Graz, Aus)	2-1	Turnbull; Smith
Jun 17th, 1946	British T.A. (Vienna, Aus)	6-2	Juliussen 3; Smith; Rattray; Pattillo
Jun 22nd, 1946	B.T.A/13th Corps (Trieste, Ita)	4-3	Juliussen 2; Rattray 2
Jun 26th, 1946	B.T.A/13th Corps (Udine, Ita)	5-1	Juliussen 4; Ouchterlonie

Archie Coats - scored in Bill Marsh benefit game

They Wore The Dark Blue

Billy Steel - Dundee's star attraction in floodlit friendlies.

Date	Opponents		Score	Crowd	Scorers
Oct 14th, 1946	Silesia (Poland)	h	2-0	10,000	Turnbull; Smith

Tour of Denmark and Sweden 1947

Date	Opponents		Score	Crowd	Scorers
May 31st, 1947	Esbjerg (Den)		5-4	15,000	Juliussen 4; Gunn
Jun 3rd, 1947	Copenhagen Select (Den)		0-3	30,000	-
Jun 5th, 1947	Copenhagen Select (Den)		1-4	20,000	Boyd
Jun 7th, 1947	Malmo (Sweden)		0-1	9,000	-
Jun 10th, 1947	Zeeland X1 (Den)		5-2	10,000	Ewen 2; Juliussen 2; Pattillo
Jan 31st, 1948	Huddersfield Town	h	1-1	12,000	Gunn
Aug 16th, 1948	Frem Copenhagen (Den)	h	5-2	12,000	Ewen 3 (1 pen); Pattillo; Stewart

Tour of Belgium and Denmark

Date	Opponents		Score	Crowd	Scorers
May 22nd, 1949	Beerschot Antwerp (Bel)		1-2	15,000	Stott
May 26th, 1949	Red Devils (Bel)		2-1	8,000	Rattray; Stott
May 29th, 1949	Royal Liege (Bel)		1-3	6,000	Gunn
Jun 2nd, 1949	Copenhagen Select (Den)		4-2	20,000	Fraser 2; Gallacher; Stewart
Jun 4th, 1949	Zeeland Select (Den)		1-1	7,000	Fraser
Jun 5th, 1949	Jutland Select (Den)		3-2	10,000	Fraser 2; Boyd
Jun 9th, 1949	Odense Select (Den)		2-0	15,000	Stewart; Fraser
Feb 11th, 1950	Preston North End	h	2-6	13,000	Water o.g.; Court
Apr 26th, 1950	Newcastle United	a	3-2	17,000	Gunn; Ewen 2 (1 pen)
Apr 29th, 1950	Peterhead	a	4-2	2,000	Gerrie; Copland; Andrews
May 1st, 1950	Inverness Select	a	4-0	3,000	Gerrie 2; Rattray; Ewen
May 5th, 1950	Aberdeen*	a	2-2	5,000	Gerrie; Ewen
May 10th, 1950	Celtic*	h	0-3	11,000	-
Aug 17th, 1950	A.B. Copenhagen (Den)	h	3-5	11,000	Gerrie 2; Rattray
May 9th, 1951	Bolton Wanderers	a	1-2	10,000	Flavell
May 12th, 1951	Reading	h	2-6	10,000	Cowie; Copland
May 16th, 1951	Belfast Distillery	h	4-1	6,000	Flavell; Ewen 2; Copland

* Charity match

Tour of Israel and Turkey

Date	Opponents		Score	Crowd	Scorers
May 30th, 1951	Maccabi (Tel Aviv, Israel)		2-0	50,000	Flavell; Copland
Jun 3rd, 1951	Hapoel (Tel Aviv)		1-0	9,000	Cowie (pen)
Jun 6th, 1951	Maccabi-Hapoel Select (T/Av)		1-2	25,000	Copland
Jun 9th, 1951	Glenclerbirgi (Ankara, Turkey)		2-2	3,000	Irvine; Ewen
Jun 10th, 1951	Istanbul Select (Istanbul)		5-3	15,000	Andrews 2; Flavell* 2; Gallacher
Jun 17th, 1951	Galatasaray (Istanbul)		6-0	8,000	Flavell 3; Copland 3
Jun 23rd, 1951	Galatasaray (Istanbul)		1-2	11,000	Copland
Jun 24th, 1951	Istanbul Select (Istanbul)		2-2	10,000	Ewen; Flavell
Jul 15th, 1951	Motherwell	h**	3-4	10,568	Steel 2; Hill
Mar 17th, 1952	Southampton	a	3-2	17,594	Steel; Gallacher 2
Dec 10th, 1952	Sunderland	a	3-5	34,000	Henderson; Flavell 2
Jan 19th, 1953	Hull City	a	4-1	31,700	Flavell 2; Toner; Steel
Mar 23rd, 1953	Portsmouth	a	3-3	17,000	Flavell; Walker; Ziesing

* Sent off. ** 1st round of the St Mungo's Cup - Scotland's contribution to the Festival of Great Britain

Tour of South Africa

Date	Opponents		Score	Crowd	Scorers
May 16th, 1953	Southern Transvaal (Jo'burg)		1-1	22,000	Flavell
May 20th, 1953	Natal (Pietermarizburg)		4-1		Flavell 3; Hill
May 23rd, 1953	Natal (Durban)		5-0		Flavell 2; Steel; Cowie; Boyd (pen)
May 27th, 1953	Border X1 (East London)		5-0	4,000	Turnbull 2; Henderson; Steel (pen); Cowie
May 30th, 1953	Eastern Province (Pt Elizabeth)		5-0		Easson 2; Turnbull 2; Christie
Jun 6th, 1953	Western Province (Capetown)		4-0		Flavell; Turnbull; Henderson 2
Jun 10th, 1953	Griqualand (Kimberly)		2-0		Christie; Flavell
Jun 13th, 1953	Eastern Transvaal (Benoni)		4-2		Steel; Flavell 2; Christie
Jun 14th, 1953	Lourenco Marques X1 (Port East Africa)		3-1		Flavell; Cowie 2
Jun 17th, 1953	Orange Free State (Bloemfontein)		9-2		Turnbull 3; Christie 2; Steel 2; Flavell; Walker
Jun 20th, 1953	Northern Transvaal (Pretoria)		2-0		Hill; Henderson
Jun 23rd, 1953	Southern Transvaal (Jo'burg)^		4-0	10,000	Steel; Ziesing; Christie 2
Jun 27th, 1953	South Africa* (Durban)		0-1		-
Jul 1st, 1953	Southern Rhodesia (Salisbury)		4-1		Cowie 3; Hill
Jul 4th, 1953	Southern Rhodesia (Bulawayo)		8-0		Christie 2; Flavell 2; Cowan; Turnbull; Cowie; Steel
Jul 11th, 1953	South Africa* (Johannesburg)		5-0		Flavell 3; Turnbull; Ziesing
Jul 15th, 1953	South Africa* (Cape Town)		5-3		Turnbull 2; Cowie; Steel; Ziesing

* Test Matches, Dundee won Series 2-1.

^Under Floodlights

Date	Opponents		Score	Crowd	Scorers
Oct 21st, 1953	South Africa	h	3-1	5,000	Henderson 2; Burrell

George Hill - the ex-Dundee star shows the tartan strip worn in South Africa.

Dundee F.C. Friendlies, Benefit Games and other Matches.

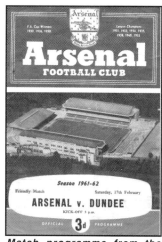

Date	Opponents		Score	Crowd	Scorers
Nov 16th, 1953	Leeds United	a	0-2	34,500	-
Apr 24th, 1954	Dundee United	h	9-3	3,500	Merchant 3; Simpson 2; Toner;
	(Joint Testimonial for Jimmy Toner				Hill; Christie; Sneddon (pen)
	and Dundee Utd's George Grant)				
Sep 22nd, 1954	Sparta Prague (Czec)	h	2-3	10,200	Mason; A. Henderson
Oct 19th, 1954	Brentford United	a	1-4	9,200	Dunsmuir
Oct 25th, 1954	Millwall	a	0-3	10,000	-
Oct 27th, 1954	Reading	a	0-4	10,739	-
Mar 29th, 1955	Sheffield United	a	1-3	10,000	Chalmers
May 5th, 1955	Preston North End	h	1-0	9,000	A. Brown *
Apr 9th, 1956	Manchester United	h	5-1	11,000	Merchant 3; Cousin; O'Hara
Oct 30th, 1956	Bury	a	1-3	3,557	Birse
Apr 12th, 1958	British Army	h	2-2	8,500	Cousin 2
Feb 14th, 1959	Rotherham	a	0-1	n/av	-
	* Guest from Blackpool				

Match programme from the Arsenal v. Dundee clash of 1962.

Tour of North America*

Date	Opponents	Score	Crowd	Scorers
May 17th, 1959	Fall River (Massachussetts)	3-1		Bonthrone 3
May 20th, 1959	Uhrik Truckers (Philadelphia)	7-2		McGeachie; H. Robertson; Bonthrone 2
				T. Robertson; Hill; Cowie (pen)
May 24th, 1959	West Brom (New York)	2-2	21,000	Henderson; T. Robertson
May 26th, 1959	St Louis Catholic Youth Select	7-0		T. Robertson 4; Bonthrone;
	(Missouri)			Gabriel (pen); Donovon o.g.
May 30th, 1959	West Brom (Vanvouver)	1-7	18,154	Cowie (pen)
Jun 3rd, 1959	North California All-Stars	6-2		Bonthrone 3; Cousin 2;
	(San Francisco)			Robertson
Jun 6th, 1959	West Brom (Toronto)	2-4		Hill 2
Jun 7th, 1959	Chicago X1	1-0	7,000	Cousin
Jun 10th, 1959	St Andrews Scots (Detroit)	3-2		Hill; Cowie (pen); Bonthrone
Jun 14th, 1959	Legia Warsaw (Pol) in N. Y.	3-3		Hill 2; Cousin
	* Sailed out on S.S. Mauretania on May 6th, returned by air			

Date	Opponents		Score	Crowd	Scorers
Oct 6th, 1959	Preston North End	a	1-0	11,906	Cousin
Jan 30th, 1960	Birmingham City	a	2-1	10,561	McGeachie; Gilzean
Mar 23st, 1960	Liverpool	h	1-0	12,000	Robertson
Aug 7th, 1960	Valenciennes (France)*	a	0-1	2,000	
Dec 7th, 1960	Valenciennes (France)*	h	4-2	7,000	Henderson; Gilzean 2; Cousin
Mar 17th, 1961	Southend	a	2-0	4,652	Gilzean; Robertson
	* Anglo-French Friendship Cup				

Tour of Iceland

Date	Opponents	Score	Scorers
Jul 6th, 1961	KR Reykyavik	3-1	Smith; Waddell; Penman
Jul 9th, 1961	Akranes	4-0	Cousin; Penman 2; Smith
Jul 12th, 1961	Iceland Select	3-1*	Gilzean; Robertson 2

* Cox went off, only to later find ref. had issued stern warning rather than a sending off.

Big switch on - the scene from the Provost Road terracing in April 1960 when Dundee staged a friendly against Liverpool - then in the English Second Division - for the official inaugeration of the Dens Park floodlights.

DC Thomson

Date	Opponents		Score	Crowd	Scorers
Nov 22nd, 1961	Elfsborg Boras (Swe)	h	8-1	11,000	Gilzean; Penman 5 (1 pen); Robertson; McGeachie
Feb 17th, 1962	Arsenal	a	2-2	15,000	Cousin; Gilzean
Mar 10th, 1962	Arsenal	h	0-1	10,000	-

New York Tourney*

May 20th, 1962	Reutlingen (W.Ger)		0-2	17,500	-
May 26th, 1962	Saarbrucken (W. Ger)**		1-5	5,311	Penman
May 30th, 1962	Hajduk Split (Yugos)		3-3		Gilzean 2; Penman
Jun 3rd, 1962	Guadalajara (Mexico)		3-2		Penman 2; Gilzean
Jun 10th, 1962	Palermo (Italy)		1-1		Waddell
Jun 16th, 1962	F.C. America (Brazil)		2-3		Waddell; Gilzean

(* See page 218. ** Friendly played in Detroit)

Nov 2nd, 1964	Arsenal	h	2-7	14,000	Penman; Gilzean
Aug 7th, 1965	Manchester City	a	2-1	10,000	Bertelsen; Penman
Aug 9th, 1965	Tranmere Rovers	a	2-0	7,100	Bertelsen; Murray

Tour of Eire

May 11th, 1966	Shelbourne		4-2		J. McLean 2; Murray; Cameron
May 13th, 1966	Cork Celtic		5-2		Cameron 2; Murray; Scott; Penman
May 15th, 1966	Limerick		1-0		Cameron

Aug 10th, 1966	Chelsea	h	1-2	15,000	J. McLean
Oct 10th, 1966	Tottenham Hotspur	h	2-3	12,000	Kinninmonth; J. McLean
Feb 17th, 1967	Plymouth Argyle	a	2-3	6,325	J. McLean; Campbell

Tour of North America

May 7th, 1967	Buffalo		12-1		Scott 3; J. McLean 3; G. McLean 2; Cameron; Stuart; Murray Hamilton
May 11th, 1967	Ukranian Select (New Jersey)		4-1	4,000	Panlyshyn o.g.; S. Wilson; Campbell 2
May 12th, 1967	Scottish American All-Stars (New Jersey)		15-1		G. McLean 7; Bryce 3; Scott 2; Kinninmonth 2; Cameron
May 14th, 1967	Ukranian All-Stars		1-0		G. McLean
May 17th, 1967	Boston Tigers		3-0	2,500	Stuart; Scott (pen); Bryce
May 19th, 1967	St Louis		8-0		J. McLean 3; G. McLean 2; Scott 2; Campbell
May 21st, 1967	Manchester United (S. Fran)		4-2	15,000	S. Wilson 2; Bryce; Campbell
May 25th, 1967	Chelsea (Los Angeles)		4-2	8,257	J. McLean 2; G. McLean; S. Wilson
May 30th, 1967	Orange County (San Diego)		6-0		J. McLean 3; S. Wilson 2; Bryce
Jun 2nd, 1967	Miami Cobras		3-1		Scott 2; J. McLean
Jun 4th, 1967	Chelsea (Miami)		2-2	3,500	S. Wilson; Scott

Aug 9th, 1967	Millwall	h	3-0	7,000	Bryce; J. McLean 2 (1 pen)
July 31st, 1968	Hull City	a	1-0	6,537	Scott
Aug 3rd, 1968	Queens Park Rangers	h	0-2	7,000	-
Aug 7th, 1968	Millwall	a	0-8	7,000	-
Aug 2nd, 1969	Southampton	a	1-5	9,083	Houston
Aug 5th, 1969	Southend United	a	5-1	3,459	Scott 4; Gilroy
Aug 2nd, 1970	Millwall	a	0-5	7,000	-
Aug 3rd, 1970	Walsall	a	0-2	2,500	-
Aug 5th, 1970	Southend United	h	5-0	2,000	Duncan; Wallace 2; J. Wilson

Mini-Tournament in Lisbon, Portugal

May 6th, 1971	Sporting Club Lisbon		0-3		-
May 8th, 1971	Norwich City		3-5		I. Scott; J. Scott; Selway
May 11th, 1971	Atletico Madrid (Spain)		2-0		Wallace 2
May 15th, 1971	Setubal* (Portugal)		0-1	10,000	-

* Friendly

Tour of Northern France and Belgium

Aug 1st, 1971	Boulogne (France)		3-0		Duncan 2; Kinninmonth
Aug 6th, 1971	Beerschot (Belgium)		2-1	6,000	Duncan 2
Aug 8th, 1971	La Louveroise (Belgium)		2-1	4,000	J. Scott; Wallace
Aug 10th, 1971	Royal Liege (Belgium)		2-0	6,000	Duncan; I. Scott

Alan Cousin and Alan Gilzean - a deadly double act up front for the Dark Blues. DC Thomson

Jocky Scott - Dens buzz bomb netted a bundle of goals in friendly games.

217

Arsenal's Jimmy Rimmer collects as Bobby Ford closes in at Dens. Terry Mancini and Pat Rice are the other Highbury defenders. Alex. Benvie

Dundee F.C. Friendlies, Benefit Games and other Matches.

Mar	3rd,	1972	Arbroath	a	5-0	2,287	Duncan 2; J. Scott; Wallace; Gray

(Official opening of the Gayfield Floodlights)

Tour of Australia and New Zealand

May	13th,	1972	Auckland X1 (N.Z)		7-0	11,000	Duncan 4; J. Scott 2; J. Wilson
May	14th,	1972	Victoria (Melbourne)		4-2	9,800	Lambie; Wallace; Houston; Robinson
May	17th,	1972	Australian X1 (Adelaide)		2-1		Own-goal; J. Scott
May	20th,	1972	A.C.T (Canberra)		9-1		J. Scott 3; J. Wilson; J. Duncan; Wallace
							Johnston; Gray; B. Wilson
May	21st,	1972	Queensland (Brisbane)		9-0	10,000	J. Scott 3; Duncan; Wallace; Phillip
							J. Wilson 2; I. Scott
May	24th,	1972	Northern Rivers (Lismore)		16-1	2,000	J. Scott 5; Gray 3; Duncan 2; I. Scott
							B. Wilson; Lambie; Houston; Wallace; Stewart
May	28th,	1972	New South Wales (Sydney)		6-1		Duncan 3; Johnston; B. Wilson; J. Scott

Aug	2nd,	1972	Preston North End	h	2-1	5,000	Duncan; J. Scott
Aug	5th,	1972	Crystal Palace	h	1-4	7,000	I. Scott
May	7th,	1973	Dundee United	a	1-2	10,500	J. Scott

(Dennis Gillespie** Testimonial)

Aug	3rd,	1974	Fulham	a	2-0	3,030	J. Scott; Hutchison
Aug	7th,	1974	Inverness Thistle	a	3-0		Hutchison; J. Scott; Ford

Tour of Sweden

Jul	22nd,	1975	IFK Oestersund	a	4-0	6,000	J. Scott; Robinson;
							Wallace; Gordon
Jul	24th,	1975	IFK Oskashamn	a	5-1		Martin 2; Phillip;
							Wallace; Sinclair
Jul	25th,	1975	Soelversburg	a	3-1		Stewart; Wallace 2
Jul	27th,	1975	IFK Ystad	a	3-2		J. Scott; Wallace; Johnston
Jul	29th,	1975	Inverness Thistle	a	2-0		Gordon; J. Scott
Jul	31st,	1975	Huntly	a	6-1		Sinclair 2; J. Scott 2;
							Gemmell; I. Scott
Aug	2nd,	1975	Arsenal	h	2-1	6,950	Ford; Gordon
Dec	6th,	1975	Celtic Select X1	h	5-1	5,790	J. Scott; G. McLean 2;
							Stewart; Wallace

(Bobby Wilson Testimonial)

Feb	14th,	1976	Everton	a	3-3	9,000	Martin; Wallace; Strachan
Aug	2nd,	1976	Inverness Thistle	a	3-2		Pirie; Martin; McKinnon
Aug	4th,	1976	Nairn County	a	1-1		Hoggan
Aug	7th,	1976	Elgin City	a	6-0	700	Hutchison; Johnston; Robinson;
							Purdie; McPhail; Laing
Oct	11th,	1976	Dundee United	a	7-7	5,057	J. Scott 3; Strachan 3; Laing

(Ian MacDonald** Testimonial)

Oct	20th,	1976	Arbroath X1	a	11-14	750	Pirie 4; J. Scott 2; Gemmell; Sellars*;
							Walker*; Strachan, Hutchison

* Guests from St Johnstone and Airdrie, respectively. ** Both Dundee United.

Dec	16th,	1976	Scotland Old Boys*	h	2-2	4,500	Waddell; Cameron
Aug	2nd,	1977	Rangers	h	1-1	7,904	McGeachie

* Dens Park Gala day game v. Dundee F.C. team of the 1960's. 40 mts duration.

Alan Gordon netted Dundee's winner against Arsenal in 1975. Alex. Benvie

They Wore The Dark Blue

Date		Opponents		Score	Crowd	Scorers
Aug 6th,	1977	Raith Rovers	a	0-1	1,000	-
Aug 8th,	1977	Aberdeen	h	0-4	4,468	-
Feb 22nd,	1978	Hibernian	h	1-2	1,725	Pirie
Apr 17th,	1978	Peter Lorimer X1	h	2-3	7,908	Sinclair; Pirie
		(Peter Lorimer of Leeds Utd. Testimonial)				

Tour of Australia, New Zealand and New Caledonia

Date		Opponents		Score	Crowd	Scorers
May 14th,	1978	Western Australia (Perth)		3-1		Pirie 2; McDougall
May 17th,	1978	Newcastle KB Utd. (NSW)		1-2		McGeachie
May 21st,	1978	Brisbane Lions/City Select		1-0		Williamson
May 23rd,	1978	Auckland X1 (NZ)		2-0	7,000	Redford; Sinclair
May 25th,	1978	Auckland X1 (NZ)		1-1	7,000	Sinclair
May 28th,	1978	Victoria (Melbourne)		1-2	9,000	Sinclair
May 31st,	1978	South Australia (Adelaide)		3-0	8,500	Williamson; McDougall; Sinclair
Jun 4th,	1978	New Caledonia X1 (Noumea)		1-2		Williamson (pen)
Jun 6th,	1978	New Caledonia X1 (Noumea)		2-1		Williamson (pen); Sinclair

Date		Opponents		Score	Crowd	Scorers
Jul 31st,	1978	Lossiemouth	a	3-0		Pirie; Williamson; Redford
Aug 1st,	1978	Rothes	a	5-4		Pirie 3; Williamson; Redford
Aug 3rd,	1978	Inverness Caley	a	2-1		Pirie; Redford
Aug 5th,	1978	Hibernian	Inv*	1-4		Scrimgeour
Oct 22nd,	1978	Keith	a	1-4		Caldwell
Nov 6th,	1978	Wigan Athletic	a	2-2	1,214	McGeachie; Barr (pen)
Feb 19th,	1979	St Mirren	a	0-1	2,000	-
Jul 24th,	1979	St Johnstone	a	3-1		Shirra; Pirie; Redford
Jul 30th,	1979	Preston North End	h	1-5	3,150	Pirie
Aug 4th,	1979	Brora Rangers	a	1-0		Norris o.g.
Oct 29th,	1979	New Zealand X1	h	8-1	2,133	Murphy; Shirra 2; Sinclair 2; Pirie 2 (1 pen); MacLaren
Feb 15th,	1980	Newcastle United	h	1-3	3,596	Ferguson
Feb 16th,	1980	East Fife	a	3-4		Pirie; Redford; Caldwell
May 4th,	1980	Dundee United	h	4-4	4,847	Williamson; Sinclair; Redford; Mackie
		(Ally Donaldson Testimonial)				
Jul 26th,	1980	Torquay United	a	1-1	1,454	Murphy
Jul 28th,	1980	Frome Town	a	2-1		Mackie 2
Jul 30th,	1980	Bristol Rovers	a	0-0		-
Jul 31st,	1980	Saltash United	a	3-1		Smith; Murphy; McGall
Feb 14th,	1981	Montrose	a	1-0		Sinclair
May 3rd,	1981	Aberdeen	h	0-3	4,000	-
		(Jocky Scott Testimonial)				
Aug 4th,	1981	Sunderland	h	2-2	3,580	Sinclair; Scrimgeour
Jul 31st,	1982	Arbroath	a	1-2	850	Fleming
Aug 4th,	1982	Swansea Town	h	2-4	4,000	A. Geddes 2
Aug 10th,	1982	Sunderland	h	2-2	1,982	Fraser; Stephen
Aug 10th,	1983	Queens Park Rangers	h	1-1	2,257	Sinclair
Mar 23rd,	1984	Norwich City	a	2-3	1,934	McKinlay; McCall
		* Inverness Trophy Final				

Match programme from Dundee's tour of Australia in 1978.

Bobby Glennie takes the field for his Testimonial game against Manchester City at Dens in 1986.

Time to celebrate - Manchester City keeper Nixon is helpless as Ray Stephen equalises for Dundee in the 2-2 draw.

Alex. Benvie

Dundee F.C. Friendlies, Benefit Games and Other Matches.

Tour of West Germany, Switzerland

Jul 17th, 1984	Borrussia Dortmund (W. Ger)	1-1		Harris
Jul 18th, 1984	SV Gottingen 05 (W. Ger)	5-1		Rafferty; Trialist; Brown; Richardson; McKinlay
Jul 23rd, 1984	Jestetten (W.Germany)	2-0		Rafferty; Kidd
Jul 24th, 1984	Horgen (Switzerland)	11-0		Harris 2; Stephen 2; Hendry 2; Docherty 2; Glennie; McKinlay; Richardson
Jul 25th, 1984	Eppstein (W.Ger)	9-1		Kidd 4; McCall 3; McKinlay; Docherty
Jul 28th, 1984	SV Elvesberg (W. Ger)	3-1		Kidd 2; Stephen
Aug 1st, 1984	Eintracht Badkreuznach (WG)	6-3		Harris 2; Kidd; Richardson; Stephen 2
Aug 3rd, 1984	Kusel (W. Germany)	2-1*		Rafferty; Hendry
Aug 4th, 1984	Bayer Leverkusen (W. Ger)	0-0		-

* Abandoned after 75 mts, thunderstorm

Apr 22nd, 1985	Eintracht Frankfurt	h	1-1	4,000	Hendry

Match programme from Dundee's match with Eintracht at Dens.

Tour of Tour of USA and Canada

Jun 2nd, 1985	F.C. Seattle (U.S.)	1-0*	4,487	McGeachie
Jun 6th, 1985	Vancouver Victoria (Can.)	2-1	1,500	McWilliams; Connor (pen)
Jun 13th, 1985	Portland (U.S.)	7-0*		McCormack 2; Harvey 2; Glennie; Connor; McWilliams
Jun 18th, 1985	Edmonton Brick Men (Can.)	5-1	2,436	Smith; Stephen; McGeachie; Harvey; McCormack

* Played on astroturf

Tour of West Germany

Jul 27th, 1985	FC Mayen	4-0		Stephen 3; McWilliams
Jul 30th, 1985	Pforzheim	4-1		Harvey; McKinlay; Jack 2
Jul 31st, 1985	FC Offenburg	0-0		-
Aug 2nd, 1985	Eintracht Frankfurt	0-2		-
Aug 3rd, 1985	Grundstadt	2-0		Harvey; own goal
Apr 6th, 1986	Manchester City h	2-2	3,000	Stephen; Glennie (pen)

(Bobby Glennie Testimonial)

Tour of USA and Canada

May 24th, 1986	Hollywood Kickers (L.A.)	1-3		Kidd
May 26th, 1986	L.A. Heat	0-0		-
May 27th, 1986	San Diego Nomads	1-2		Duffy (pen)
May 29th, 1986	San Hose Earthquakes	4-0		Kidd 2; Harvey; McWilliams
May 31st, 1986	Manchester City (at San Jose)	1-1*		Connor
Jun 4th, 1986	Edmonton Brick Men	3-1		McWilliams; Jack; Kidd
Jun 6th, 1986	Seattle Storm	2-1		Mennie; Harvey
Jun 7th, 1986	F.C. Portland	2-1		Harvey; McGeachie
Jun 11th, 1986	Orlando	1-0		Harvey
Jun 14th, 1986	Q.P.R. (at Tampa)	1-1		Connor

* Challenge match, Dundee lost on penalties)

Dundee met Liverpool in a testimonial for Bobby Geddes at Dens in 1989. However, the Dundee keeper was well beaten by a shot from Ray Houghton with another Irish international, John Aldridge, and Dundee's Steve Campbell looking on.

DC Thomson

They Wore The Dark Blue

Date	Opponents		Score	Crowd	Scorers
Jul 26th, 1986	Ross County	a	7-0		Jack 2; McKinlay; Harvey 3; Smith
Jul 28th, 1986	Inverness Thistle	a	5-0	579	Brown 2; Stephen 3
Jul 30th, 1986	Nairn County	a	0-0		-

Isle of Man International Football Festival

Date	Opponents		Score	Crowd	Scorers
Jul 28th, 1987	Oldham (Douglas Bowl)		1-0		Coyne
Jul 29th, 1987	Bury		0-0		-
Jul 31st, 1987	Galway United (Eire)		11-0		Wright 3; Jack 4; Rafferty; Duffy; McKinlay; Angus
Aug 1st, 1987	Stoke City		0-1		-
Aug 4th, 1987	Seattle Storm	h	3-0	1,665	Brown; Duffy (pen); Jack
Nov 19th, 1987	Liverpool	h	0-4	14,463	-
	(George McGeachie Testimonial)				
Dec 8th, 1987	Premier League Select	h	5-3	5,905	Wishart o.g.; Coyne; Brown; Duffy (pen); Nicholas
	(Jim Duffy Testimonial)				
Jul 30th, 1990	Inverness Caley	a	2-0		McGeachie; Lawrence
	(Bob Summers Testimonial)				
Aug 1st, 1988	Huntly	a	4-3		Chisholm 2; Rafferty; Wright
Aug 2nd, 1988	Morton	a	1-1		Wright
Aug 6th, 1988	St Johnstone	a	1-1	2,500	Angus
Aug 8th, 1988	Newcastle United*	h	2-0	4,820	Campbell 2
Feb 12th, 1989	Liverpool	h	1-3	9,311	Coyne (pen)
	(Bobby Geddes Testimonial)				
Feb 18th, 1989	Raith Rovers	a	2-2		Coyne; McBride
Mar 18th, 1989	Berwick Rangers	a	2-1		McBride; Harvey
Jul 26th, 1989	Gateshead	a	1-1		A. Campbell
Jul 28th, 1989	North Shields	a	0-0		-
Jul 29th, 1989	Brandon United	a	4-2		D. Campbell; S. Campbell 2; Dodds (pen)
Jul 31st, 1989	Billingham Symphonia	a	1-1		Dodds
Aug 3rd, 1989	Montrose	a	1-2		Craib
Aug 5th, 1989	Queens Park Rangers*	h	2-2	2,967	Craig 2 (1 pen)
Aug 4th, 1990	Rangers*	h	2-2	7,000	West^; Wright
Aug 6th, 1990	Stenhousemuir	a	1-2		Spiers o.g.
Aug 8th, 1990	East Fife	a	1-0	530	Dodds (pen)
Aug 9th, 1990	Cowdenbeath	a	1-0	150	Craig
Aug 11th, 1990	Arbroath	a	3-0	1,043	McLeod; McQuillan; Wright
Aug 16th, 1990	Aberdeen	h	0-1	1,789	-
Jul 30th, 1991	Cowdenbeath	a	2-1		Armstrong; Dow
Aug 3rd, 1991	Wimbledon*	h	0-0	725	-
Aug 5th, 1991	Celtic	h	1-1	2,318	Craig

* Dunclare Dispensers' Trophy ; ^ Sent off

Tour of Eire

Date	Opponents		Score	Crowd	Scorers
Jul 14th, 1992	Sligo Rovers		4-1		Dodds 3 (2 pens); Robson
Jul 15th, 1992	Athlone Town		0-0		-
Jul 16th, 1992	Limerick		1-1		Gilzean
Jul 17th, 1992	Ballinasloe		6-1		Bunberry 3 (1 pen); Jamieson; Dodds; Dinnie
Jul 18th, 1992	Galway United		3-3		McCann; McMartin; Dodds (pen)
Jul 20th, 1992	Deveronvale	a	4-1		Bunberry; Dodds 2; Dow
Jul 22nd, 1992	Elgin City	a	9-1		McMartin; Gilzean; Ritchie 3; Trialist; Gallagher 2; Bunberry
Jul 24th, 1992	Peterhead	a	9-1		Gilzean; Dodds 5 (1 pen); Ritchie 2; Tannock
Jul 27th, 1992	Wolverhampton Wand	h	2-1	2,259	Gilzean; McKeown
Apr 23rd, 1993	Elgin City	a	5-2	839	Marsh; David; Kiwomya 2; Stainrod
Jul 29th 1993	Lancaster City	a	0-0		-
Jul 31st 1993	Netherfield	a	6-2		McMartin 2; Dodds; McKeown; McQuillan; Paterson
Jul 24th, 1993	Clyde	h	1-0		McKeown
Aug 3rd, 1993	Airdrie	a	1-4		Christie
Jul 25th, 1994	Netherfield	a	4-1		Shaw 2; Britton; Wieghorst
Jul 27th, 1994	Morecambe	a	2-2		Shaw 2
Jul 29th, 1994	Lancaster City	a	3-1		Blake; Tosh; Britton
Jul 30th, 1994	Bangor	a	1-1		Tosh
Aug 1st, 1994	Portadown	a	2-1		McKeown; Teasdale
Aug 4th, 1994	Coleraine	a	2-2		Shaw 2
Aug 8th, 1994	Wolverhampton Wand	h	1-4	2,248	Britton
Mar 3rd, 1995	Celtic X1	h	4-2	500	N. Duffy; Tosh 2; Hamilton
Apr 25th, 1995	Forres Mechanics	a	5-1	250	Tosh; Ritchie; Green (trialist); Innes o.g.; Teasdale
	(Gerry Davidson Testimonial)				

Ian Gilzean - headed Dundee's opener against Wolves at Dens in 1992.

Paul Tosh - the former Arbroath striker grabbed double against Celtic X1.

Great was the joy - Dundee's new £23,500 record signing Billy Steel runs out for his debut against Aberdeen at Dens in September 1950. Stan Williams is in front with Jimmy Andrews bringing up the rear.

DC Thomson

Dewar Shield (for Aberdeenshire, Forfarshire, Perthshire and Stirlingshire Cup winners)

Date		Opponents		Score	Crowd	Scorers
1900-01						
23-03-01	SF	Dunblane	a	4-0	n/a	Boyd; McDiarmid; McGeoch; Gowans
13-04-01	F	East Stirling	h	6-1	n/a	McDiarmid; Halkett 2; McDermott; Steven; McGeoch
1902-03						
18-04-03	SF	St Johnstone	h	3-0	n/a	Dickson 2 (1 pen); Kerr
02-05-03	F	Victoria Utd	a	2-1	n/a	Dickson; Kerr
1904-05						
08-04-05	SF	Aberdeen	h	2-1	n/a	McHardy; Kerr
22-04-05	F	Alloa	h	4-0	n/a	Burnett 2; Findlay 2
1908-09						
27-03-09	SF	Aberdeen	a	0-0*	3,000	-

* Dundee refused to play extra-time and scratched after being unable to fit in replay

1911-12 and 1912-13 Dundee unable to participate since Forfarshire Cup final, which they won, was after start of Dewar Shield.

Date		Opponents		Score	Crowd	Scorers
1923-24						
08-09-26	SF	Falkirk	h	0-1	3,000	-
1924-25						
17-08-27	SF	Falkirk	h	0-1	4,000	-
1935-36						
02-10-35	SF	Aberdeen	h	2-3	3,800	Robertson; Reid
1938-39						
17-08-38	SF	Aberdeen	h	1-0	7,500	Coats

1944-45 No competition.

1945-46 Dundee unable to participate since Forfarshire Cup final, which they won, was after start of Dewar Shield.

Date		Opponents		Score	Crowd	Scorers
1946-47						
30-04-47	SF	St Johnstone	a	2-1	5,500	Pattillo; Juliussen
07-05-47	SF2	St Johnstone	h	4-2 (6-3)	5,400	Gunn 2; Smith; Ewen
07-04-48	F1	Falkirk	a	0-1	4,000	-
12-04-48	F2	Falkirk	h	4-0 (4-1)	12,500	Boyd; Stewart 3

1947-48* (*Dundee, who eventually lost in FCSF, were entered since F/Cup not yet decided)

Date		Opponents		Score	Crowd	Scorers
21-04-48	SF1	Alloa	h	3-0	4,500	Stewart; Pattillo; Ewen
28-04-48	SF2	Alloa	a	4-2 (7-2)	n/a	Gunn 2; Boyd; Stewart
25-08-48	F1	St Johnstone	a	4-2	n/a	Gunn; Stott 3
08-09-48	F2	St Johnstone	h	9-2(13-4)	11,000	Pattillo 4; Stott 3; Ewen; Andrews

John McPhail - centre-half netted double in final against Keith in 1976.

1948-49
18-04-49	SF1	Aberdeen	a	0-1	12,000	-
04-05-49	SF2	Aberdeen	h	2-1	6,000	Stott; Ewen
04-10-49	SFR	Aberdeen	h	3-2	14,000	Fraser 2; Pattillo
18-02-50	F1	St Johnstone	h	1-1	8,000	Fraser
10-04-50	F2	St Johnstone	a	5-2 (6-3)	7,000	Gerrie 2; Pattillo; Andrews; Gunn

1949-50 Dundee won 1949-50 Forfarshire Cup but, since final was after start of Dewar Shield, Dundee United played in Dewar Shield.

1950-51 Similarly, in 1950-51, Dundee United won FCF, but Dundee were entered in Dewar Shield.
03-05-51	SF1	St Johnstone	h	4-0	1,700	Copland 3; Innes o.g.
05-05-51	SF2	St Johnstone	a	4-2 (8-2)	1,000	Copland 3; Steel

Due to play Aberdeen in the final but this was never played.

1955-56
08-10-56	SF	St Johnstone	a	2-1	1,500	Watt 2
12-01-57	F	Stirling Alb.	a	0-6^	n/a	-

^ Dundee 'A' team

1956-57
02-05-58	F*	Fraserburgh	a	3-2	n/a	McGrory; Stewart; Sneddon

1957-58
14-10-57	SF	St Johnstone	a	6-3	3,000	Cousin 3; Sneddon; Henderson; Warren
03-05-58	F	Buckie Thistle	a	1-1	2,000	Cox

(Dundee win trophy on toss of a coin)

1960-61
02-11-60	SF	Keith	h	9-0	1,000	Gilzean 5; Curlett 2; Robertson 2
24-10-61	F	St Johnstone	h	4-2	3,000	Cousin 2; Smith; Penman (pen)

1965-66
03-10-66	F*	Deveronvale	h	7-0	2,000	J. McLean 4; Murray; Kinninmonth; Houston

1966-67
12-11-69	SF	Falkirk	h	2-2	1,100	Gilroy; Scott
26-11-69	SFR	Falkirk	a	2-5	1,500	Georgeson 2

1967-68
11-10-71	SF	St Johnstone	a	1-0	3,300	Wallace
24-04-72	F	Falkirk	h	3-1	1,000	J. Scott 3

1971-72
31-07-76	F*	Keith	a	6-0	600	McPhail 2; Pirie 2; Hoggan; Robinson

* semi-finalists unknown

Dens scoring aces - Syd Gerrie and Johnny Pattillo.

New York Tourney 1962

Section 1
	P	W	D	L	F A	PTS
America (Brazil)	5	3	2	0	11-8	8
Reutlingen (W. Ger)	5	3	1	1	6-4	7
Guadaljara (Mexico)	5	1	2	2	7-7	4
Palermo (Italy)	5	1	2	2	7-8	4
Dundee	**5**	**1**	**2**	**2**	**9-11**	**4**
Hajduk (Yugoslavia)	5	1	1	3	8-10	3

Summer Cup

Season 1963-64 (p 137)
	P	W	D	L	F A	PTS
Aberdeen	6	4	0	2	14- 8	8
Dundee Utd	6	3	2	1	9- 9	8
Dundee	**6**	**2**	**3**	**1**	**12- 9**	**7**
St Johnstone	6	0	1	5	5-14	1

Summer Cup

Season 1964-65 (p137)
	P	W	D	L	F A	PTS
Dundee Utd	6	6	0	0	21-6	12
Aberdeen	6	3	0	3	8-9	6
Dundee	**6**	**2**	**0**	**4**	**10-15**	**4**
St Johnstone	6	1	0	5	7-16	2

Hardy souls - a view of the Dundee v. Celtic game from the south side of Dens Park in March 1958, two years before the enclosure was built. Driving rain and sleet restricted the crowd to 5,000 spectators, most of whom were in the stand and stand enclosure.

DC Thomson

CENTENARY SEASON TO FORGET

The 1993 close season brought little comfort for fans of the Dens Park club. The Dark Blues were fined £5,000 for their poor disciplinary record and it was mid-July before Dens chairman Ron Dixon returned to Dundee after a six month absence. He maintained that Simon Stainrod - twice sacked by the Dundee-based directors - would continue as manager, but many were unconvinced over the final outcome.

Then came news of the sudden death of former Dundee and Scotland right-back, Alex Hamilton, at the age of 55. "Hammy" had been one of the most flamboyant characters ever to pull on a Dark Blue jersey and, along with former full-back partner Bobby Cox, he had been a popular matchday figure in the Dens Park Executive Lounge. His exuberance would be sorely missed.

Former Scotland international keeper Jim Leighton joined Hibernian for a nominal fee. Andy Kiwomya, Ivo Den Biemen, Steve Campbell and Lionel David were added to those previously released, although the Frenchman made a surprise return following a trial period with Sheffield United.

Under-21 international midfielder Andy Dow signed a new contract for Dundee but a Dens Park administrative error saw him sign for Chelsea on freedom of contract. Despite Dundee's £1 million valuation, a fee of £275,000 was accepted with Chelsea agreeing to take just 25% - as opposed to the 50% previously agreed - of any future transfer fee should Billy Dodds be sold by Dundee. Since the end of last term, ten players had left Dens, leaving Dundee with a first-team squad of 20 players but this was boosted by the arrival of Arbroath striker Paul Tosh for a fee of £100,000.

Pre-season performances were disappointing. Following a 1-0 home win over Second Division champions Clyde, the Dark Blues travelled to play English non-league sides Lancaster City (0-0), who Tayport Juniors later thrashed 6-1, and Netherfield (6-2). And when Dundee fell 4-1 to last season's Premier strugglers Airdrie at Broomfield, prospects for the new campaign looked far from bright.

This was confirmed when a sluggish performance at Rugby Park saw Dundee fortunate to depart with only a 1-0 defeat from newly promoted Killie. And, although there was an improvement against Motherwell the following week, the return of a ponderous Simon Stainrod did little for the morale of the 4,356 Dens crowd, a 2-1 reverse leaving them bottom of the Premier League.

Dundee had been short of experience for their opening games with Duffy (4 games) and Dodds (1 game) suspended, and Dinnie and Bain both out with long-term knee injuries. Nevertheless, Ron Dixon and Simon Stainrod remained confident the club would finish in the top six by the end of the season.

However, the Dark Blues had also laboured in the League Cup, only beating lowly Meadowbank 3-1 after extra-time and penalties. Spirits were flagging but on August 18th Dundee made headline news when they signed Polish international midfielders Dariusz Adamczuk (23) and Piotr Czachowski (27). According to chairman Ron Dixon, each had cost £500,000, "We have seen that we are not going to get anywhere unless we really go for it and have decided to roll the dice and see what happens."

Adamczuk, who had been signed from Eintracht Frankfurt, had gained 5 caps, while the more experienced Czachowski, from Legia Warsaw, had made 45 appearances for his country. Czachowski was ineligible until Home Office clearance was received along with one of the three remaining Scottish League permits for non-EEC players but Adamczuk, who also held a German passport, made his debut in the 1-1 draw with Aberdeen at Dens

Their arrival came as a tremendous boost to all associated with the club and Billy Dodds was quick to withdraw his transfer request. And, despite a disappointing attendance of 7,655, the Wieghorst-inspired Dark Blues gained a deserved point when Dodds bundled in an equaliser soon after half-time. The hard-running Tosh had ensured an uncomfortable afternoon for Dons veteran Alex McLeish and, although Adamczuk had not played for two months after a dispute with Eintracht, he too had displayed great commitment as well as flashes of pace and skill.

Heads you lose - Gary McKeown beats team-mate Paul Tosh to head for goal only for Motherwell keeper Sieb Dykstra to accidentally punch the ball into his own net.   DC Thomson

Under Pressure - Steve Pittman, Jamie McGowan, Paul Tosh, Dusan Vrto, Jim Duffy and Ray Farningham watch anxiously as the ball bounces just wide of the Dundee goal in a match with Dundee United at Tannadice. DC Thomson

The new-found optimism was quickly shattered when an unchanged side lost 2-1 to Hibs in the third round of the League Cup at Easter Road. The team had been a pale shadow of that which had matched Aberdeen, with only a late consolation goal by Danish trialist Henrik Neilson - released soon afterwards due to his poor fitness level - as consolation.

Dundee had failed to win any of their opening five games and, within 48 hours Jim Duffy replaced Simon Stainrod as manager. Stainrod (34) was given the newly created post of Director of Football Operations with responsibility for the buying and selling of players as well as developing a comprehensive youth policy and scouting system. But, by November, the flamboyant Yorkshireman had become the forgotten man of Dens and it was little surprise when he quit, later returning to management with First Division Ayr United.

There was no dream start for Jim Duffy whose first game in charge coincided with his playing return in a 2-0 league defeat by Hibs at Easter Road. Former Dundee and Dunfermline boss Jocky Scott was on the bench but speculation that he might become Duffy's assistant proved unfounded with another Dens "old boy", reserve coach John McCormack, later given that role.

In September, Partick Thistle's Ray Farningham (32) was signed on freedom of contract with the fee later set at £28,500 by the transfer tribunal. The Dundonian made his debut in the 1-1 draw with Rangers at Dens but centre-half Garry Paterson was the standout, cracking home the opener then blotting out the formidable striking partnership of Mark Hateley and Duncan Ferguson.

However, with three teams from 12 to be relegated that season it was soon clear that Dundee faced a bitter battle for Premier survival. By the end of the month, defeats by Dundee United (a) 0-1, Raith Rovers (h) 0-1 and St Johnstone (a) 1-2 left them bottom, three points behind Raith and Partick and six behind St Johnstone, having failed to win any of their opening 10 games.

A groin operation meant the loss of the influential Morten Wieghorst for six weeks, but on October 2nd Dundee finally recorded their first win of the season. A Paterson header and a spectacular 45 yard chip by Croatian trialist Dragutin Ristic earned a 2-0 success over Hearts at Dens. Ristic, (28), previously with Italian Fifth Division side Benevento, was signed and with Piotr Czachowski settling nicely into central midfield, a draw with Partick Thistle (2-2) and home wins against Kilmarnock (1-0) and Hibs (3-2) took Dundee to the nine point mark by November 6th.

The hard-tackling Dariusz Adamczuk had regained his fitness and now looked every inch an international player, particularly in a holding role in central midfield. The Pole netted the winner against Killie before impressing at left-back following an injury to Steve Pittman, but, near the end of another great performance against Hibs, he was red-carded for a retaliatory tackle on Darren Jackson. That was his eighth appearance for the Dark Blues but, with his wife finding it hard to settle, his spell at Dens was to prove short-lived and a few days later he joined Udinese for a fee then reported as £800,000.

The popular Pole was soon forgotten as goals by Ritchie and Czachowski brought a splendid 2-1 win over Hearts at Tynecastle to take Dundee within two points of Raith and St Johnstone and five below fourth-bottom Partick Thistle. And, with the next three fixtures against their three main rivals, it was hoped they would soon pull clear of the bottom position. However, all three

Dariusz Adamczuk - Polish star made just eight appearances for Dundee.

No chance - Gerry Britton thunders home his penalty kick in the Scottish Cup tie against St Mirren at Dens as John McQuillan and two Paisley defenders look on.

DC Thomson

three matches ended in defeat as did the Dens derby against Dundee United and it was now obvious that the Dark Blues had major problems.

An attempt was made to sign Tommy Coyne from Tranmere Rovers but the former Dens striking ace preferred to join strong-going Motherwell. Nevertheless, experience did arrive in the rugged form of centre-half Noel Blake (32), who signed from Bradford City for £15,000. His debut coincided with a 1-1 draw with Celtic at Dens but, by early in the New Year, defeats by Motherwell (h) 1-3, Kilmarnock (a) 0-1 and Hibs (a) 0-2 left few in any doubt that Dundee were bound for the First Division.

Just 24 hours after losing at Easter Road came the shock news that Billy Dodds had joined Tayside relegation rivals St Johnstone along with £60,000 rated midfielder Grant McMartin in a deal worth £420,000. The initial fury of the fans was somewhat dampened by the £250,000 double signing of Partick Thistle forwards George Shaw (24) and Gerry Britton (23) and there was only muted criticism during the 1-0 defeat by Aberdeen at Dens. Nevertheless, the fans were highly critical that their star striker had been allowed to join a nearby club and a representative group of supporters and sponsors were invited to meet manager Jim Duffy and the Dundee-based board.

"It was my decision and mine alone", said Duffy. "The league position dictated that changes were necessary and, with no cash to spend, Dodds was made available. St Johnstone were the only club interested and, although Billy could have stayed, I was somewhat surprised when he chose to join another struggling club."

"I agree that Dodds is a good player but he publicly stated that he would not again play for Dundee in the First Division. In my opinion, he never really formed a telling partnership with any of the strikers - Keith Wright included - who played alongside him and if we waited until he was out of contract at the end of the season we would have had to accept a lesser fee."

Under the Taylor Report, Dundee had until 1997 to make their ground all-seated. However, the Football Trust had exhausted their funds and were currently unable to pay their 50% share of the proposed £3.4 million south stand, while local councils were unwilling to provide £1m towards the ice sports and conference centre. Over the festive period there had been concern over reports that Dundee had discussed sharing Tannadice with Dundee United but rumours that the Dark Blues were about to fold were strenuously denied by vice-chairman Malcolm Reid.

Dundee had managed just a solitary point from their previous nine games but, by February 12th, the enthusiasm generated by Shaw and Britton contributed towards four successive draws with Rangers (h) 1-1, Raith Rovers (h) 2-2, Dundee United (a) 1-1 and St Johnstone (a) 1-1. Wieghorst had given Dundee a deserved first-half lead against Rangers but the Ibrox table-toppers pounded the home defence after half-time, and, despite the heroics of Paul Mathers, Gordon Durie equalised near the end.

Gerry Britton had replaced the skilful but somewhat one-paced "Ricky" Ristic, who nevertheless had earlier shown his finishing ability with five goals. However, the clever Croatian made a dramatic reappearance as substitute when he grabbed a late equaliser against Dundee United at Tannadice. Working a glorious 1-2 with Wieghorst he clipped the ball past Dutch goalkeeper Van de Kamp, who earlier had saved a George Shaw penalty .

Four days later, the Dark Blues beat Clydebank 2-1 in a Scottish Cup third round replay at Stirling Albion's Forthbank Stadium. Dundee had struggled for long periods in the first tie at Kilbowie and only a spectacular 25 yarder by substitute Paul Tosh, six minutes from time, had maintained their interest in the cup.

Around 50 Dundee fans came on to the pitch to celebrate, but things turned ugly when a few got involved in a fracas with Bankies keeper Alan Monaghan. The referee ordered both teams to the dressing rooms but order was quickly restored and the match completed despite

Clydebank's demands that it should be abandoned due to the dazed state of their keeper.

All associated with Dundee expressed their condemnation but fears that the club might be expelled from the Cup proved groundless. The S.F.A executive committee were highly critical of the pitch invasion and also of Clydebank's failure to provide adequate policing. However, they decided that the fans had not intentionally stopped the match and ordered that the Dens replay be switched to a neutral venue with both clubs later given a severe censure.

The cash-strapped Dark Blues had anticipated a 3,000 plus attendance at Dens and, although Forthbank had a 2,500 capacity, just 700 tickets were allocated to each club. Those were only available from official supporters clubs who were compelled to forward fans' details to the S.F.A. and in the event only 856 turned up. Goals by Britton and Shaw gave Dundee a two goal lead, but the sending off of young Neil McCann for retaliation just on half-time ensured a second half struggle. A late Sweeney goal put them under severe pressure and only a timely goal-line clearance by Steve Pittman saved the day.

Dundee United were also at home in the fourth round and Dundee's tie against First Division St Mirren was switched to Sunday, February 20th. The Paisley side opened brightly and Lavety put them ahead after 16 minutes. Eight minutes later, Gerry Britton levelled with a penalty and, with Wieghorst and Farningham finally stamping their authority in midfield, Shaw got a second after 56 minutes. It was a game full of flowing football and it was not until three minutes from time that Britton raced through to clinch matters with a third for Dundee.

Jim Duffy had used the Dodds cash wisely. As well as signing Shaw and Britton, he had fixed up promising youngsters Neil McCann (19), Craig Tully (18) and Gordon Tannock (19) on new two and a half year deals. He had also raided the Highland League, spending £15,000 on Elgin City midfielder Mike Teasdale (24) and another £5,000 on Keith striker Jim Hamilton (18).

Now the Dark Blues further strengthened their squad by adding French goalkeeper Michel Pageaud from Valenciennes for £70,000 with Falkirk's Neil Duffy arriving in exchange for Jamie McGowan and Dragutin Ristic. In addition, Falkirk received £150,000 with Bairns keeper Ian Westwater - valued at £60,000 - also moving to Dens in a deal valued at £170,000 in total.

The Duffy move was controversial. Hearts had recently had a £210,000 bid refused but now the high-scoring midfielder appeared to be valued at just £110,000! Duffy's previous club, Dundee United, were due 25% of any subsequent transfer fee less the £35,000 they had already received. Now they stood to get nothing and their suspicions were further fuelled when Westwater joined Dunfermline for £15,000 a few weeks later, without ever making a first-team appearance for Dundee.

However, while travelling to complete the signings, Jim Duffy was involved in a serious car crash, and with the manager badly shaken it was necessary for John McCormack to finalise the deals. It was the second near miss for a Dundee player that season. In August, Lionel David had swallowed his tongue after sustaining a fractured skull during a training match and only the prompt action of physio Jim Crosby saved his life.

There was no doubting the seriousness of Dundee's league position but they appeared to have a reasonable chance of reaching the Scottish Cup semi-finals when they were paired with Kilmarnock at Rugby Park on March 12th. In a game played at a frantic pace, there was little between the sides, and, when the flying McCann was bundled off the ball following an inch-perfect pass by Wieghorst, the resultant spot kick gave Dundee a golden opportunity to edge in front.

Gerry Britton took the kick, only to see his shot saved by former Dundee keeper Bobby Geddes who also parried his follow-up effort. That miss proved costly, for, minutes later, Killie's Tom Brown beat the recalled Paul Mathers with a brave diving header for the only goal of the game.

Dundee then began to get their fair share of league points but the other strugglers did likewise and, in late March, financial circumstances dictated the £150,000 transfer of Stevie Frail to Hearts. That same month, Bob Paterson resigned as a director while Isobel Sneddon, a familiar figure on the admin side at Dens since 1952, was another to depart.

On April 23rd, a 2-0 home defeat by Celtic finally condemned Dundee to the First Division but they were to finish the season in style. A Neil Duffy goal earned a 1-1 draw with third-placed Aberdeen at Pittodrie, there was a sparkling display in a 4-0 home win over Hibs and a 0-0 draw against six-in-a-row League Champions, Rangers, meant a dignified Premier League exit at Ibrox.

But, although almost inevitable since January, relegation for the second time in four years came as a severe blow and plans for ground reconstruction would go on indefinite hold. Yet although a massive 11 points had separated Dundee from safety, no fewer than 14 of their 23 defeats had been by a single goal. They got off to a bad start when experienced men like Duffy and Dinnie were badly missed, and never really recovered.

Eyes down - Dundee midfielder Neil Duffy shrugs off a challenge from Peter Hetherston of Raith Rovers.   DC Thomson

Dundee's Foreign Legion - Dariusz Adamczuk, Piotr Czachowski, Dusan Vrto and Dragutin Ristic grimace as a free-kick thunders past their heads. At one stage, Dundee had players of seven non British nationalities at Dens. DC Thomson

The delayed decision over who would manage the side was crucial with neither Stainrod or Duffy able to implement any close season planning. Although there were a number of injuries, those were no more than expected in the frantic Premier League, but the increasing number of suspensions due to indiscipline - Britton, Frail, Dinnie and McQuillan were all suspended - did little to help the cause. Much of the damage had been caused by a shaky rearguard, where the confidence of Mathers - such an impressive performer the previous season, suffered from the defensive inconsistency in front.

The erratic Paterson was not the answer at centre-half and, although Jim Duffy (35) still had plenty to offer, he was at the stage where he required reliable men around him. Dinnie was just that sort of player but, after just 12 games in the previous 14 months, a recurrence of his knee ligament trouble saw him make only a further 10 appearances. Frail, McQuillan and Pittman all excelled going forward but the first two were prone to lapses of concentration in defence and although Pittman was the better defender he was liable to some rash challenges.

Dribbling ace - 16-year-old Ian Anderson looked an excellent prospect on his showing against Hibs. DC Thomson

However, if Pageaud and Blake been in place from the start of the season, and had Adamczuk remained to team up with Neil Duffy, Shaw and Britton, the outcome may well have been very different.

Nevertheless, there had been a marked improvement since mid-January with only six defeats from 22 games. Jim Duffy had completely reshaped the playing staff, bringing in 12 players - Tosh, Adamczuk, Czachowski, Farningham, Mobilio, Blake, Duffy, Shaw, Britton, Pageaud, Teasdale, Hamilton and moving on 11 - Adamczuk, Dodds, Frail, McMartin, Ristic, McGowan Westwater, Mobilio, Armstrong, Christie and David (the last three were released during the season, while Canadian striker Dom Mobilio departed after just a couple of months). But, most importantly for a club of Dundee's stature, some very promising youngsters had emerged.

Neil McCann had all the skills of the traditional winger - electrifying pace and the ability to beat his full-back and deliver a telling ball. Already he had made a name for himself in the Premier League and had also been an outstanding success for the Scotland Under-21's, particularly at the close-season Toulon Tournament where a number of top clubs had expressed their interest.

Left-back Craig Tully was given his debut against Celtic while another 18-year old, striker Jim Hamilton, and right-winger Ian Anderson (16) had done well after coming off the bench against Hibs. And when Anderson coolly sent a penalty kick past Scotland keeper Jim Leighton, he became the youngest player ever to score in a Premier League game.

Fledgling Dundee boss was a strong advocate of a youth policy claiming, "It might not be something Dundee have been associated with in the past but the importance of a successful youth policy simply cannot be overestimated. For clubs like ourself it is vital because attracting and working with good youngsters is the only way to ensure a constant supply of new talent."

It had been a difficult season but the Dens directors had been impressed by Duffy's dedication and vision. They were convinced that he was the right man to secure the club's long term future and after he had been persuaded to sign a three year contract, one of his first steps was to get Neil McCann to extend his contract until 1997.

SO NEAR, YET SO FAR

Towards the end of the 1993-94 season came news that would save Dundee around £60,000 per annum on interest charges. Ron Dixon had repaid the £570,000 owed to the Bank of Scotland and, although the club were now due him that amount, it would be in the form of an interest-free debenture. However, almost a year after the death of Alex. Hamilton came the sad news that another of Dundee's 1961-62 League Championship winning squad, Andy Penman (51), had died after a long term illness.

The sale of Steve Frail had left Dundee with an operating profit of £66,000 but, although there were no departures, Gary McKeown, Alan Dinnie and the transfer-seeking Steve Pittman failed to agree terms and began the season on monthly contracts. Scotland Under-21 international defender Kevin Bain, who had started just a handful of games after undergoing two knee operations, was transfer listed along with Paul Ritchie and Garry Paterson.

Paterson joined Ayr United for £25,000, of which £1,875 went to his old junior club, Lochore Welfare. Piotr Czachowski, whose last appearance had been in early January, was no longer part of the plans and he returned to Poland while his agent tried to find him another club. Charlie Nicholas was offered the post of player-coach but, despite getting a better offer from Dundee, he chose to remain with Celtic for another year,

Dundee prepared for the new season with a 3-2 win over Albion Rovers at Cliftonhill, then undertook a short tour of North West England and Northern Ireland before losing 4-1 to Endsleigh Division One side Wolves at Dens. Jim Duffy was content to take a low key approach to Dundee's prospects. "It will be a highly competitive league but I see the relegated sides, Raith Rovers and St Johnstone - who had signed Dunfermline's Northern Ireland international striker George O'Boyle after selling Billy Dodds to Aberdeen for £800,000, Dunfermline and Airdrie fighting it out with ourselves for the automatic promotion place."

"Last term, we used 35 players but I have a nucleus of eight or nine men around whom I intend to build the side. These guys can compete with the best in the division and I am hopeful youngsters like Jim Hamilton and Ian Anderson will push themselves into contention. We certainly have better players than some other clubs but that in itself is no guarantee of success because the best players don't always win."

Dundee's promotion challenge got off to an excellent start and three wins over St Mirren (h) 2-0, Stranraer (h) 3-1 and St Johnstone (a) 1-0 and a draw against Airdrie (h) 1-1 left them in pole position, two points clear of Dunfermline. The triumph over promotion favourites St Johnstone was a major boost to morale but Dundee might well have run riot against the over-robust Stranraer who had five players booked and should have had two

Quick off the mark - right-back John McQuillan provided Dundee with attacking options.   DC Thomson

players sent off had the referee taken firmer action.

In the League Cup, two second half goals by Paul Tosh earned a 3-0 home win over the newly formed Caledonian Thistle, thus ensuring a plum second round tie against Celtic at Dens on August 31st. The Dark Blues were undaunted by their Premier opponents and despite John Collins firing Celtic into a ninth minute lead, Ray Farningham headed the equaliser soon afterwards. In 67 minutes, Dundee skipper Dusan Vrto - recently capped for Slovakia - was ordered off for a professional foul on Paul McStay. The Celtic captain was also given his marching orders for retaliation but it was the visitors who emerged victorious, with Andy Walker netting the winner.

Alan Dinnie and Steve Pittman were prominent in Dundee's opening games, but following serious breaches of club discipline the pair were suspended for the game with Stranraer. Seven days later, Dinnie (31) was transferred to Partick Thistle for £30,000 with Pittman (27) - scorer in the 1-0 win over St Johnstone - joining him at Firhill on freedom of contract. Although Dundee wanted £75,000 for U.S.A. international Pittman, his fee was later fixed at £27,500, twice the figure Thistle had offered.

Over the next few weeks, Jim Duffy strengthened his squad by signing Meadowbank left-back Mark Hutchinson (19) for £9,000 and former Dundee United midfielder Andy Cargill (19) on a free transfer. However, doubts over the wisdom of selling two experienced defenders were heightened when defeats at Clydebank (2-5) and Ayr (2-3) left Dundee four points behind new league leaders, Dunfermline.

Gerry Britton had given Dundee a first minute lead at Kilbowie, but the promptings of the wily Davie Cooper

Heat of battle - Dundee striker Gerry Britton is tackled by Airdrie defender Graham Hay in the B&Q Cup Final. DC Thomson

soon had their defence in complete disarray. It was a similar story at Ayr where Simon Stainrod ensured that the Dundee goal came under a barrage of corners and long throws, and once again the Dens men had failed the test.

Dundee then entertained Dunfermline in an amazing roller-coaster of a game. The free-flowing Pars deservedly went ahead only for Shaw (38, 57 minutes) to put Dundee 2-1 up. Within a minute Smith equalised for Dunfermline, then Tosh volleyed home Dundee's third and Britton made it 4-2 with five minutes remaining. But, with victory in sight, Dundee conceded a penalty after a fatal lapse of concentration in defence. French scored from the spot and 60 seconds later McCathie rose amidst a crowded six-yard box to head a dramatic equaliser.

Nevertheless, the Dark Blues progressed to the semi-final of the B&Q Cup by defeating Arbroath (h) 5-0, Caley Thistle (a) 1-1 (after extra-time and penalties) and Morton (h) 2-1 with injuries, suspensions and loss of form allowing transfer-listed Kevin Bain to make his return at Inverness. That gave the defender the opportunity to re-establish himself and the Fifer was a key man in the floodlit semi-final clash at Dunfermline on October 18th.

Once again, the old rivals served up a thriller and, with Bain and the recalled Jim Duffy outstanding in the face of intense early pressure, the Dundee defence held firm. Bain put them ahead with a penalty, Neil McCann netted a second after a Westwater blunder and, despite a late goal by Tod, the Dark Blues were through to meet Airdrie in the final at McDiarmid Park.

The Dens defence had tightened up after their earlier shaky spell, and league wins over Hamilton (h) 2-0, St Mirren (a) 2-1, St Johnstone (h) 1-0 and a 1-1 draw away to Raith Rovers - young Ian Anderson equalising with a last-ditch free-kick - left them joint second with Airdrie, just two points behind the leaders, Dunfermline.

Jim Duffy's decision to rebuild his side some months earlier had been vindicated. That term, the striking partnership of George Shaw and Gerry Britton had paid dividends - Shaw had found the net six times, while Britton had already scored 13 goals, four of them in a B&Q Cup match against Arbroath at Dens.

So, by the afternoon of the B&Q Cup Final on Sunday, November 6th, there was great enthusiasm with some 7,000 of the 8,844 fans backing the Dark Blues - a figure that might have been exceeded had more tickets been available. Dundee fielded: Pageaud; McQuillan, J. Duffy, Bain, Vrto; Tosh, Farningham, Wieghorst, McCann; Shaw, Britton. Subs. Blake, Hamilton, Thompson (gk). Airdrie: Martin; Stewart, Sandison, Hay; Boyle, Harvey, Davies, Black, Jack; Cooper, Lawrence. Subs. A.Smith, T. Smith, McCulloch (gk).

Dundee started well but soon got bogged down in a tough midfield struggle. In 28 minutes, slack defending at a throw-in allowed Harvey to put the Diamonds in front but Dundee levelled just before the interval when Hay conceded an own goal after pressure by Britton.

In 62 minutes, a rash Tosh tackle allowed Boyle to put Airdrie ahead from the spot but, 14 minutes later, Gerry Britton thundered home a fierce cutback from George Shaw to make it 2-2. After an indifferent start to the season due to intense speculation that he was to join Celtic, Neil McCann was back to his electrifying best and it was Dundee who looked the likelier winners in extra-time.

But with only nine minutes remaining and a penalty shoot-out on the cards, Michel Pageaud could only parry a harmless looking shot by Harvey and Airdrie substitute Andy Smith crashed home the winner. The result was a big disappointment for all connected with Dundee. Farningham, McCann and Wieghorst had been best but, in the crucial midfield area the uncompromising Black had ensured the Danish international was given minimal space in which to operate and the elusive Harvey emerged as the key man for Airdrie.

Dundee recovered with a 2-0 home win over Clydebank before again falling to Airdrie (1-2) at Cumbernauld's Broadwood Stadium. In both games, Dundee had lost control for long spells and it was clear that the height and defensive strengths of Neil Duffy were being missed in midfield. However, an eight game unbeaten run against Stranraer (a) 2-0, Ayr United (h) 1-1, Dunfermline (a) 1-0, Raith Rovers (h) 2-1, Hamilton (a) 1-0, St Mirren (h) 4-0, Stranraer (h) 2-0 and St Johnstone (a) 2-2 put them back on the rails and by early 1995, they had established a six point lead over nearest rivals Airdrie with Dunfermline and Raith Rovers two points further behind.

On December 3rd, a hard fought game at Dunfermline ended in glory when Paul Ritchie - who had earlier turned down a £20,000 move to Montrose - netted the winner after fellow substitute Ian Anderson's shot rebounded from the post. That set up an intriguing home clash with Raith Rovers who had sensationally defeated Celtic in the League Cup Final after extra-time and penalties.

Dalziel put an impressive Raith ahead with a 62nd minute penalty after Bain was red-carded for fisting a net-bound shot over the bar. Dundee fought back strongly and Jim Hamilton levelled from the penalty spot. Urged on by the home support, the Dark Blues went all-out for the

Wee Blue devil - George Shaw in full flight against Kilmarnock at Dens in 1994. Over the past two seasons, the popular striker has been Dundee's top scorer, netting a total of 28 goals. Striking partner Gerry Britton (left), who arrived from Partick Thistle at the same time, also contributed to the Dens Park cause with another 22 goals.
DC Thomson

Dundee F.C. 1994-95 (BACK, left to right) Jim Hamilton, Paul Ritchie, Michel Pageaud, Noel Blake, Neil Duffy, Barry Thomson, Morten Wieghorst, Kevin Bain. MIDDLE - Mike Teasdale, Alan Dinnie, Gerry Britton, Craig Tully, Paul Mathers, Paul Tosh, George Shaw, Ray Farningham, Gordon Tannock. FRONT - Jim Duffy (player-manager), Jim Crosby (physio), Steve Pittman, Gary McKeown, John McQuillan, Dusan Vrto (captain), Marcus Dailly, Neil McCann, Ian Anderson and John McCormack (coach).
DC Thomson

Match programme from a Dundee v. Rangers game in 1965.
Apart from an early version which showed the main stand,
this front page format was unchanged from 1947 until 1966.

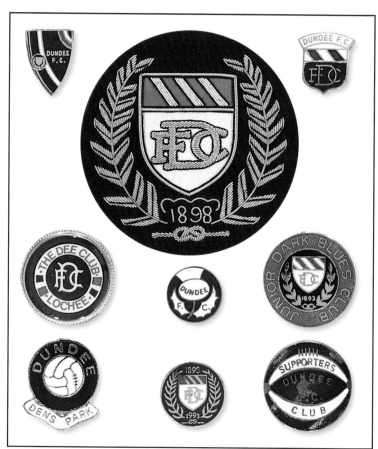

Official Dundee F.C. blazer badge and enamel supporters' club badges down
the years. TOP (left to right) - 1980's and 1970's. MIDDLE - 1970's, 1960's and
1980's. BOTTOM - 1970's, 1990's, 1940's through 1950's

Stephen Borland

Dundee F.C. European Cup semi-finalists 1962-63. (BACK, left to right) Alex. Hamilton, Bobby Seith, Ian Ure, Bert Slater, Bobby Wishart,
Bobby Cox (captain). FRONT - Sammy Kean (coach), Gordon Smith, Andy Penman, Alan Cousin, Alan Gilzean, Hugh Robertson and Bob
Shankly (manager).

DC Thomson

Sky high - ace marksman Alan Gilzean, who later headed the winner, soars above Gordon Banks in Scotland's 1-0 Hampden triumph over England in 1964. Denis Law and Davie Wilson of Scotland and England's Maurice Norman and Jimmy Armfield look on. "Gillie" made 22 appearances in the Dark Blue of Scotland, five as a Dundee player and 17 while at Tottenham Hotspur.
Stephen Borland

Dundee F.C. 1971-72. (BACK, left to right) Manager John Prentice, Davie Swan, Mike Hewitt, Dave Soutar, Jim Easton, Ron Selway, John Duncan, Ally Donaldson, George Stewart, Maurice Friel (coach). FRONT - Bobby Wilson, Alex. Kinninmonth, Joe Gilroy, Alex. Bryce, Gordon Wallace, Jocky Scott, Jimmy Wilson, Jim Steele and Doug Houston.
Stephen Borland

They Wore The Dark Blue

Morten Wieghorst - Danish international midfielder with great skill and attacking flair. An exciting player to watch and difficult to stop once in full flight.

DC Thomson

Kevin Bain - captained the Scottish Under-16 team which reached the World Youth final in 1989. The Under-21 international defender turned in some brilliant displays last term.

DC Thomson

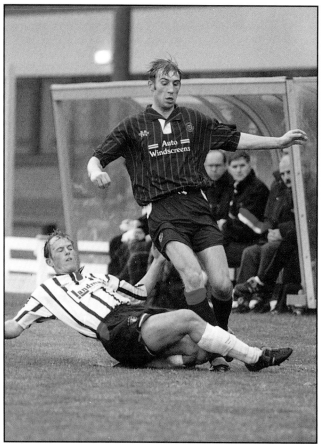

Jim Hamilton - the 19-year old striker has come on leaps and bounds since arriving at Dens. Was recently rewarded with a Scottish Under-21 cap against Brazil.

DC Thomson

Neil McCann - a left-winger with electrifying pace, he likes to take on defenders and create scoring opportunities. Has a bundle of Under-21 international caps.

DC Thomson

Rocket shot - Dundee's Under-21 international defender Kevin Bain crashes the ball past Clydebank keeper Gary Matthews to set the Dark Blues on the way to a 2-0 win at Dens. The Dundee players in the background are Andy Cargill, Morten Wieghorst, Dusan Vrto and Jim Hamilton.

DC Thomson

winner and it duly came when Morten Wieghorst weaved his way forward before cracking home a fierce low shot.

That left Raith 11 points behind the Dens men and on Wednesday, January 11th, Dundee salvaged an important point from Tayside promotion rivals St Johnstone. Dundee started well but Saints recovered to take a 2-1 lead with 10 minutes remaining. But with the game deep into injury time Vrto took yet another long throw. Home keeper Alan Main fumbled the ball and when Noel Blake hitch-kicked back across goal, Dens substitute Gerry ·Britton was there to head home.

Then Dundee lost a great chance of opening a 10 point gap over Airdrie when they lost 1-0 to the second placed Broadwood side at Dens, a result which cost them their unbeaten home record. However, a 3-0 win at gale-swept Clydebank again put them six points clear and, on January 29th, they met Premier League strugglers Partick Thistle in the third round of the Scottish Cup at Dens.

Thistle included Alan Dinnie, Steve Pittman, Albert Craig and Derek McWilliams but the Dens "Old Boys" were shocked in 12 minutes when Shaw dived to head home an inch perfect cross by McCann. On the half hour, Foster netted after the ball rebounded from the woodwork but the "goal" was disallowed for offside with Pageaud beyond the striker and only one defender, Vrto, between Foster and the goal. However, the visitors were on top and soon after half-time Craig fired home the equaliser. Thistle continued to press strongly but with two minutes remaining, Jim Hamilton connected with a John McQuillan cross to send a looping header past keeper Nicky Walker for the winner.

The wiry Hamilton was strong in the air and had excellent ball control and passing ability. After a good spell in October, the teenager returned to the bench but later replaced the suspended Britton, retaining his place when the Glaswegian resumed. In January, he was named as Bell's Whisky's "Young Player of the Month" and with his tally of six goals in eight games attracting the attention of a number of top clubs, he was given a two year extension to his contract.

By this stage, all the promotion hopefuls had gone through a bad spell but, although recently threatening to take a commanding lead, Dundee's results in February were to have a devastating effect on their Premier aspirations. On February 4th, they fell 3-2 to second placed Dunfermline at Dens and a chance of opening up a nine point gap over the Pars had gone.

Pageaud was unlucky to be sent off after diving at the feet of the onrushing Petrie with the striker appearing to run into the keeper after flicking the ball to the side. Mathers came on as substitute keeper in place of Wieghorst but his first action was to pick the ball out of the net from the resultant penalty. Twice 10-man Dundee levelled through Tosh and Britton, but, with 18 minute remaining, Fleming's inswinging corner deceived Mathers and the ball sailed high into the net.

Dundee had played well without getting the breaks but next Saturday they lost 1-0 at Ayr, where an abysmal display prompted an angry Jim Duffy to fine his players. Now Raith Rovers, who had recorded eight straight wins since losing at Dens in December, shared top spot and it was the Fifers who would provide the opposition in the fourth round of the Scottish Cup at Dens.

Farningham and Neil Duffy returned after injury and, with the elusive Cameron and Crawford well shackled, Dundee deservedly led 1-0 at the interval. Soon afterwards, Blake retired with a hamstring injury, but when Tosh substituted, Farningham dropped back into defence and Raith were handed the initiative. In 71 minutes, Dundee's luck finally ran out when Graham equalised and nine minutes later Rowbotham scored the winner when his speculative 35-yard ball bounced past through a clutch of players and past the unsighted Pageaud.

A week later the sides met again, this time in a vital top of the table league clash at Stark's Park. Despite the absence of Blake and Jim Duffy, Dundee's three-man central defence of Farningham, Bain and Vrto helped weather the early home pressure. And with the industrious Andy Cargill a standout in midfield, Dundee had their chances

Hotshot - George Shaw blasts in a shot in the 2-1 win over Raith Rovers at Dens, a result which put Dundee 11 points above the Kirkcaldy side in mid December. Looking on are Dundee's Neil Duffy and Ronnie Coyle of Raith.

DC Thomson

They Wore The Dark Blue

Dens disaster - Michel Pageaud dives desperately but can't stop Barry Wilson's opener for Raith Rovers in the vital promotion clash at Dens in April. Micky Cameron (Raith), Noel Blake, Jim Duffy and Gordon Dalziel (Raith) look on.   DC Thomson

to win, although, in the end, they were not unhappy with the 0-0 outcome.

Meanwhile, Piotr Czachowski had returned to Dundee to pursue a claim regarding part of his signing-on fee, but the matter was dropped when the Polish international was transferred to Polish club LKS Ptak for £150,000. That was £80,000 less than the £230,000 Dundee had paid, although the Dark Blues stood to get another £50,000 should he move on again.

Encouraged by their display at Kirkcaldy, the Dark Blues maintained their momentum with home wins over Hamilton (2-0) and Clydebank (3-2) before travelling to Broadwood to meet Scottish Cup semi-finalists Airdrie on March 25th. This time Dundee were well prepared for a physical contest and Farningham, Neil Duffy and a fired-up Wieghorst showed great tenacity in turning the midfield battle their way. Up front, the bustling Paul Ritchie caused Airdrie all sorts of problems and, soon after half-time, Farningham headed the opener. As Airdrie pushed forward, Dundee looked increasingly menacing on the break and it was no surprise when a late Shaw double completed a good day's work for the Dark Blues.

Dundee were back on top, two points clear of Dunfermline and five points ahead of Raith Rovers. Now only seven games remained and there were around 2,500 Dundee fans amongst the 8,500 crowd at East End Park for the big showdown with Dunfermline. Backed by a strong wind, the Pars dominated much of the first half but with the interval fast approaching, a 35-yard cross from Shaw out near the touchline flew high into the net past an astounded Van De Kamp!

Although the Fifers exerted the bulk of the pressure in the second period and Pageaud was forced into some heroic saves, Dundee missed some good chances on the counter attack. But, just when it seemed they were to escape with maximum points, Ivo Den Biemen popped up to head the equaliser, seven minutes from time. Dundee remained two points ahead of the Pars but, although they had done well to get four points from two hazardous away

games, Raith went joint top after winning their postponed game at Clydebank three days later.

The Dark Blues next hurdle was against relegation-threatened Ayr United at Dens. But with Simon Stainrod's side again intent on a spoiling game, it was 34 minutes before Neil Duffy headed the opener from a Hutchison cross. Just on the interval, Ayr keeper Duncan, who had persistently wasted time at goal kicks, was sent off for handling outside his area and, in an effort to utilise their extra man, Dundee brought on McCann for Farningham.

However, it was Ayr who moved up a gear, scoring a 60th minute penalty when Jim Duffy was harshly penalised after an overhead kick struck his arm. Later Britton was ordered off for a bad challenge on an Ayr defender but, with only seconds remaining, Wieghorst was sent crashing in the box. George Shaw, who had previously failed from the spot against Dundee United and Caley Thistle, stepped up to take the penalty, but to the dismay of his team-mates and the fans, his shot was saved by substitute keeper McIntosh.

Now Raith were two points clear and Dunfermline were also ahead of Dundee on goal-difference. To add to Dundee's misery, Britton, who had been sent off twice and booked eight times that season, was suspended and like the injured Kevin Bain (ribs) and Dusan Vrto (foot) he would miss the four remaining games. Hamilton was drafted in alongside Shaw and with Tosh and McCann out wide, it was an ultra-attacking Dundee side that lined up against Hamilton Accies at Firhill on April 15th.

A penetrating run and cross by McCann set up Shaw for a sixth minute opener and a superb hat-trick by Hamilton put Dundee 4-0 up by half-time. Peter Duffield got a consolation goal for Accies as Dundee took their foot off the accelerator but it was a delighted Dens support that departed from Glasgow after the game. Raith had lost 1-0 at home to Airdrie, Dunfermline had drawn 1-1 with St Johnstone at Perth and once again, Dundee were top of the First Division. Just four games remained and with the title race at boiling point, there was a tremendous build up

Ice cool - Jim Hamilton sends St Johnstone's Alan Main the wrong way from the penalty spot to keep Dundee in the promotion hunt. Right - French keeper Michel Pageaud became a cult figure with the fans with a string of brilliant performances. DC Thomson

for Dundee's stiffest test of the campaign against strong-going Raith Rovers before a near 8,000 crowd at Dens.

Following a nervy opening spell, Dundee had Raith pinned back for the last 20 minutes of the first half, but, thanks largely to the inspiration of Jimmy Nicol in midfield, the Kirkcaldy men held on. After the break, Raith were again forced back, but the visitors drew first blood with a lightning counter-attack in 68 minutes. Cameron failed to connect with Wilson's speculative low cross, but Pageaud had anticipated him getting a touch and dived too late to prevent the ball bouncing in at the far corner.

Nine minutes later, Tosh replaced Blake, but, like the Hutchison substitution against Ayr a fortnight earlier, the defensive balance was fatally upset. This time, the ubiquitous Barry Wilson, whose father Bobby Wilson had been a big favourite at Dens, attacked down the left, and when the ball came over Crawford made it 2-0 for Raith.

There was no way back for the Dark Blues and the larger than usual home support went home bitterly disappointed, as they had done previously that term on other important occasions like the B&Q Cup Final, the Scottish Cup tie

against Raith and the home games against Dunfermline. Three games remained but there was another upset when Neil McCann was ruled out of the game against St Mirren at Love Street after contracting a virus while with the Scotland Under-21's in San Marino.

Paul Tosh, whose powerful running down the right had been so effective at Firhill a fortnight earlier, was his replacement but he looked uncomfortable in his new left-wing role. Another tactical ploy saw Farningham at right-back with McQuillan taking his place at right midfield but it was relegation threatened St Mirren who looked the promotion challengers in a scrappy first-half. In 55 minutes, Hewitt cracked in a fine goal for the Buddies and only then, once Tosh and McQuillan switched positions, did Dundee get their act together.

Surging forward, a series of chances were created but scorned, notably when Neil Duffy blasted a close-range effort off the the the bar. The big push had come too late and, with veteran keeper Campbell Money in unbeatable form, there was no way through for the Dark Blues, whose promotion hopes now hung by a thread. Raith had beaten St Johnstone 2-1 at McDiarmid, and although Dunfermline had only drawn 0-0 at home with Airdrie, Dundee had to win their last two games and hope for slip-ups elsewhere.

As expected, St Johnstone provided stern opposition in the penultimate game at Dens. The nervy looking Dark Blues could make little impression in a first half stalemate but the introduction of the tricky Ian Anderson in 55 minutes proved decisive. After yet another attacking run, the youngster sent a well-timed pass to Farningham and when the midfielder was tripped in the box, Hamilton beat Main from the penalty spot. The game raged from end to end but when Boyle equalised with a penalty in 80 minutes, Saints looked the likelier to win. However, in a stirring finale, a fine cross by McQuillan was headed across goal by Blake and George Shaw bundled the ball into the net.

Meanwhile, Dunfermline and Raith Rovers had fought out a 0-0 draw at Kirkcaldy, leaving Dundee level but behind the Pars on goal difference and three points behind Raith. The Dark Blues had to win their final game at Stranraer and hope for a Raith defeat at Hamilton, which would give Dundee the title on goal difference and with it, automatic promotion. Alternately, a Dunfermline slip-up at home to Clydebank would allow Dundee to pip them for the play-off position although a Pars win meant Dundee having to win by at least six goals at Stranraer.

On a bright, sunny day, the Dark Blues had around 1,200 vociferous fans at far off Stair Park. In nine minutes, Anderson was obstructed in the box and Hamilton converted the penalty. However, the Dark Blues were unable to press home their advantage and it was not until the 62nd minute that Wieghorst got a second after a tremendous run from the halfway line.

Great gaps then appeared in the home defence and, after Wieghorst made it 3-0 in 80 minutes, only the heroics of keeper Barney Duffy prevented Dundee from running riot. Shaw and Tosh added to the tally, and at the end of an emotionally charged afternoon, Dens fans staged a pitch invasion to cheer their heroes from the field.

By then, it was known that Raith had drawn 0-0 and Dunfermline had won 2-1, results which condemned the Dark Blues to another term in the First Division. Sadly, one more point would have guaranteed Dundee the title and Premier League football, while another two goals would have ensured a play-off with Aberdeen, who had finished second bottom of the Premier League.

A second goal in the first period at Stair Park might well have opened the floodgates and it could be argued that the pace and power of Tosh from the start might have worn down Stranraer, with the the tricky Anderson held back for later. However, the damage had been done earlier, for, although the Dark Blues had won more games and scored more goals than any other First Division side, they had too often failed when it really mattered. They had won only three of the 12 games against their three main promotion rivals and had managed just two points out of a possible 12 from the relegated Ayr United.

Experienced players are essential for any side seeking promotion. The loss of battle-hardened defenders like Alan Dinnie and Steve Pittman for just £57,500 may well have been a contributory factor in Dundee's failure espe-

Sunny Stranraer - Neil McCann takes on a home defender but the day was to end in disappointment.   DC Thomson

cially since Bain and Vrto missed the crucial run-in through injury while Farningham, Vrto and Blake all sat out games through suspension. Nevertheless, player-boss Jim Duffy (36) set a fine example in central defence but although his heading and timing in the tackle remained second to none, there were times when defensive adjustments left him fatally exposed.

Thus, for the third successive year, it was a worrying close season for Dundee supporters. Would another term in the First Division mean the club selling their best players or perhaps even reverting to part-time football for the first time since 1947? Of the 15 most prominent full-time clubs, only Dundee and Dunfermline had not initiated any significant ground improvements. Most fans appreciate that promotion failure has delayed any reconstruction plans but with new stands springing up all over Scotland, many may ask why, with crowds at some other dog tracks on the wane, reportedly the best part of £1m was risked in bringing greyhound racing to Dens?

In the event, the commencement of dog racing in Autumn 1994 does not appear to have benefitted the football club. There was understandable uproar when the Billy Steel Lounge was renamed "Trap Seven" while the depopulation of the stand enclosure (now the racing concourse), the most visible part of Dens when T.V. cameras are present, gives the impression that the ground is almost totally deserted.

However, it was an equally difficult summer for the Dens Park board, who, in the continued absence of chairman Ron Dixon - apparently there have been only brief telephone conversations with the chairman since February - have been operating under severe cash restraints.

Prospects looked good when the Canadian took over in late 1991 with around £1m spent on 18 players, first to secure promotion then to keep the Dark Blues in the Premier League. At the start of season 1993-94, nearly £500,000 - not £1m as quoted, but still a large amount for Dundee - was spent on Adamczuk and Czachowski, although

Danish delight - Morten Wieghorst leaves Raith Rovers former Dens star, Ian Redford trailing in his wake as he heads for goal.   DC Thomson

They Wore The Dark Blue

Good move - Dundee directors Nigel Squire and John Black watch as manager Jim Duffy signs a three year contract in 1994.
DC Thomson

Adamczuk was sold soon afterwards and not replaced. £15,000 was made available for Noel Blake but it is understood that Jim Duffy then had to sell Billy Dodds to generate cash for further new players and, subsequently, he was also compelled to sell Frail, Dinnie and Pittman.

Around the time that Simon Stainrod moved "upstairs", it would appear that Ron Dixon decided to make no further investment in the playing staff. This view is perhaps reinforced by the 1994 sale of the former Bowbridge Works site on Dens Road, previously earmarked as a carpark for the proposed Ice-Rink and Conference centre at Dens, although the chairman did provide an interest-free loan to clear the bank debt that same year. Perhaps, initially, Mr Dixon - who knew little about football far less Dundee F.C. - relished the challenge of restoring the Dark Blues to the forefront of Scottish football, only later to realise that a long term committment was required.

However, with huge sums required to bring stadia up to the standards of the Taylor Report, the 10-team Premier League has become a footballing version of Russian Roulette and relegated full-time sides face the prospect of financial ruin in the First Division. With the risks so high, potential investors are less inclined to put their money into football and there is little doubt that the quality of play has suffered accordingly with players under enormous pressure to get results.

The chairmen of most full-time clubs and many knowledgeable football observers such as Derek Johnstone, Gordon Smith and Joe Harper believe that the Premier League should be expanded to 16 clubs, a view shared by UEFA, who indicated that countries could soon face a reduction in their UEFA Cup place allocation unless they change to a league of at least 16 teams.

Nevertheless, Jim Duffy is determined to bring the good times back to Dens although he is much too shrewd to make any grand claims. "Since Dundee's last trophy win in 1973, the supporters have had nothing but empty promises, false dawns and crushed expectations. I think there are three ways I can give them back a successful club; one is money, two is time and three is luck. I have have never had any of the first and it remains to be seen whether I will get, or have any of, the other two."

The likelihood is that the manager, who has done well on limited resources, will get the time. Recent comments seem to indicate that the highly respected Duffy, whose 205 League and Cup games puts him amongst the 40 players with the most appearances for Dundee, will now direct operations from the touchline. And with Noel Blake - reputedly the highest earner at Dens - released along with Paul Ritchie, and John McQuillan joining St Johnstone on freedom of contract, it will be a new-look defence at Dens next season.

Significantly, two of the newcomers - ex-Falkirk, St Mirren and Instant Dict (Hong Kong) centre-half Roddy Manley (30) and ex-Aberdeen and Falkirk left-back Tommy McQueen (32), were defenders. Both were obtained on free transfers while small fees were paid for midfielders Andy Matheson (Forres Mechanics) and Marino Keith (Fraserburgh).

However, despite the lack of major signings, there is the makings of a good side at Dens and Dundee should again be among the prime contenders for promotion. The skillful Morten Wieghorst and Dusan Vrto are both full internationalists while the impressive trio of Kevin Bain, Neil McCann and Jim Hamilton all have Scottish Under-21 caps.

Last term, burly French goalkeeper Michel Pageaud turned in some outstanding performances and his popularity was reflected when he was voted Dundee F.C. Supporters Clubs' "Player of the Year". After earlier looking likely to accompany his unsettled family back to France, it came as a major boost when he declared his intention to honour the remaining year of his contract.

With Vrto, along with Bain and Wieghorst, starting the new season on monthly contracts, Neil Duffy assumed the captaincy and, in a pre-season game against English Premiership side Bolton Wanderers at Dens (2-2), he looked highly impressive alongside Manley in central defence with Bain and Vrto making up a solid back four. Up front, Dundee are well off with Shaw, top scorer for the past two seasons, Britton, Hamilton and Tosh all proven finishers. And with players of the calibre of McCann, Wieghorst, Anderson and the dynamic Cargill, there is an abundance of skill and craft in midfield.

The manager has built up a tremendous team spirit and there is also plenty of competition for places. The transfer-seeking Mathers is again looking sharp while Teasdale, McQueen, Hutchison, Tully, McKeown, the versatile Farningham, who also does an excellent job coaching Dundee's youth players, and perhaps Matheson and Keith, will press strongly for first-team places.

It is hoped that the £87,500 awarded by the Transfer tribunal for John McQuillan will be used to secure Bain, Vrto and Wieghorst, with any future fee for Dariusz Adamczuk - again a Dundee player after Udinese failed to pay Dundee the balance of £200,000 and currently looking for another club - used to clear the club's debt. With the unexpected relegation of Dundee United, there will be fierce rivalry between the two Dundee clubs, Dunfermline, Airdrie, St Johnstone and possibly St Mirren for promotion. It promises to be a thrilling campaign and with the Tannadice outfit labelled favourites, there will will be an even stronger Dens resolve to rise to the challenge. Go to it, Dundee!